Lecture Notes in Computer Science 2728

Edited by G. Goos, J. Hartmanis, and J. van Leeuwen

Springer
Berlin
Heidelberg
New York
Hong Kong
London
Milan
Paris
Tokyo

Erwin M. Bakker   Thomas S. Huang
Michael S. Lew   Nicu Sebe
Xiang (Sean) Zhou (Eds.)

Image and Video Retrieval

Second International Conference, CIVR 2003
Urbana-Champaign, IL, USA, July 24-25, 2003
Proceedings

 Springer

Series Editors

Gerhard Goos, Karlsruhe University, Germany
Juris Hartmanis, Cornell University, NY, USA
Jan van Leeuwen, Utrecht University, The Netherlands

Volume Editors

Erwin M. Bakker, Michael S. Lew
Leiden University, LIACS Media Lab
Niels Bohrweg 1, 2333 CA, Leiden, The Netherlands
E-mail: {erwin,mlew}@liacs.nl

Thomas S. Huang
Beckman Institute for Advanced Science and Technology
University of Illinois at Urbana-Champaign
405 N. Mathews Avenue, Urbana, IL 61801, USA
E-mail: huang@ifp.uiuc.edu

Nicu Sebe
University of Amsterdam
Kruislaan 403, 1098 SJ, Amsterdam, The Netherlands
E-mail: nicu@science.uva.nl

Xiang (Sean) Zhou
Siemens Corporate Research
755 College Road East, Princeton, NJ 08540, USA
E-mail: xiang.zhou@scr.siemens.com

Cataloging-in-Publication Data applied for

A catalog record for this book is available from the Library of Congress.

Bibliographic information published by Die Deutsche Bibliothek
Die Deutsche Bibliothek lists this publication in the Deutsche Nationalbibliografie;
detailed bibliographic data is available in the Internet at <http://dnb.ddb.de>.

CR Subject Classification (1998): H.3, H.2, H.4, H.5.1, H.5.4-5, I.4

ISSN 0302-9743
ISBN 3-540-40634-4 Springer-Verlag Berlin Heidelberg New York

Springer-Verlag Berlin Heidelberg New York
a member of BertelsmannSpringer Science+Business Media GmbH

http://www.springer.de

© Springer-Verlag Berlin Heidelberg 2003
Printed in Germany

Typesetting: Camera-ready by author, data conversion by DA-TeX Gerd Blumenstein
Printed on acid-free paper   SPIN: 10929056   06/3142   5 4 3 2 1 0

Preface

Welcome to the 2nd International Conference on Image and Video Retrieval, CIVR 2003. The goal of CIVR is to illuminate the state of the art in visual information retrieval and to stimulate collaboration between researchers and practitioners. This year we received 110 submissions from 26 countries. Based upon the reviews of at least 3 members of the program committee, 43 papers were accepted for the research track of the conference.

First, we would like to thank all of the members of the Program Committee and the additional referees listed below. Their reviews of the submissions played a pivotal role in the quality of the conference. Moreover, we are grateful to Nicu Sebe and Xiang Zhou for helping to organize the review process; Shih-Fu Chang and Alberto del Bimbo for setting up the practitioner track; and Erwin Bakker for editing the proceedings and designing the conference poster.

Special thanks go to our keynote and plenary speakers, Nevenka Dimitrova from Philips Research, Ramesh Jain from Georgia Tech, Chris Porter from Getty Images, and Alan Smeaton from Dublin City University. Furthermore, we wish to acknowledge our sponsors, the Beckman Institute at the University of Illinois at Urbana-Champaign, TsingHua University, the Institution of Electrical Engineers (IEE), Philips Research, and the Leiden Institute of Advanced Computer Science at Leiden University.

Finally, we would like to express our thanks to several people who performed important work related to the organization of the conference: Jennifer Quirk and Catherine Zech for the local organization at the Beckman Institute; Richard Harvey for his help with promotional activity and sponsorship for CIVR 2003; and to the organizing committee of the first CIVR for setting up the international mission and structure of the conference.

May 21, 2003   Thomas S. Huang and Michael S. Lew

International Conference on Image and Video Retrieval 2003 Organization

Organizing Committee

General Co-chairs:	Thomas S. Huang
	(Univ. of Illinois at Urbana-Champaign, USA)
	Michael S. Lew
	(LIACS Media Lab & Leiden University,
	The Netherlands)
Program Co-chairs:	Nicu Sebe
	(University of Amsterdam, The Netherlands)
	Xiang (Sean) Zhou (Siemens Research, USA)
Practitioner Co-chairs:	Shih-Fu Chang (Columbia University, USA)
	Alberto Del Bimbo (University of Florence, Italy)
Publications Chair:	Erwin M. Bakker
	(LIACS Media Lab & Leiden University,
	The Netherlands)

Program Committee

Kiyo Aizawa	University of Tokyo
Erwin M. Bakker	Leiden University
Alberto Del Bimbo	University of Florence
Shih-Fu Chang	Columbia University
Tsuhan Chen	Carnegie Mellon University
Qiang Cheng	Wayne State University
John Eakins	University of Northumbria
Peter Enser	University of Brighton
Graham Finlayson	University of East Anglia
David Forsyth	Univ. of California at Berkeley
Theo Gevers	University of Amsterdam
Alan Hanjalic	Delft University of Technology
Richard Harvey	University of East Anglia
Thomas S. Huang	Univ. of Illinois at Urbana-Champaign
Horace Ip	City University of Hong Kong
Jean-Michel Jolion	INSA Lyon
Avi Kak	Purdue University
Josef Kittler	University of Surrey
Suh-Yin Lee	National Chiao Tung University
Clement Leung	University of Melbourne
Michael S. Lew	Leiden University

Paul Lewis	University of Southampton
Jiri (George) Matas	CVUT Prague
Jan Nesvadba	Philips Research
Eric Pauwels	CWI
Maria Petrou	University of Surrey
Yong Rul	Microsoft Research
Stan Sclaroff	Boston University
Nicu Sebe	University of Amsterdam
Ibrahim Sezan	Sharp Labs of America
Behzad Shahraray	ATT Research
Linda Shapiro	University of Washington
Alan Smeaton	Dublin City University
Arnold Smeulders	University of Amsterdam
Sanghoon Sull	Korea University
Tienlu Tan	Chinese Academy of Sciences
Qi Tian	University of Texas at San Antonio
Guangyou Xu	TsingHua University
HongJiang Zhang	Microsoft Research Asia
Xiang (Sean) Zhou	Siemens Research

Additional Reviewers

Joni Alon	Boston University
Vassills Athitsos	Boston University
Ana B. Benitez	Columbia University
Paul Browne	Dublin City University
Joe Carthy	University College Dublin
Terrence Chen	Univ. of Illinois at Urbana-Champaign
Yunqlang Chen	Siemens Research
Jie Cheng	Siemens Research
K. Cheung	City University of Hong Kong
Seung Soo Chun	Korea University
Csaba Czirjek	Dublin City University
Charlie Dagli	Univ. of Illinois at Urbana-Champaign
Guilherme DeSouza	Purdue University
Orla Duffner	Dublin City University
Shahram Ebadollahi	Columbia University
Jonathan Edwards	University of Northumbria
Murat Erdem	Boston University
Stuart Gibson	University of East Anglia
Xiaodong Gu	Microsoft Research Asia
Richard den Hollander	Delft University of Technology
Winston Hsu	Columbia University
Xiasheng Hua	Microsoft Research Asia
Louis Huang	Columbia University
Mark Hulskes	CWI

Feng Jing	Microsoft Research Asia
Jung-Rim Kim	Korea University
Yeon-Ho Kim	Purdue University
Mingjing Li	Microsoft Research Asia
Rui Li	Boston University
Huitao Luo	Hewlett-Packard Research Lab
Yufei Ma	Microsoft Research Asia
Sean Marlow	Dublin City University
Kieran McDonald	Dublin City University
Masaki Miura	Columbia University
Munehiro Nakazato	University of Illinois at Urbana-Champaign
Jung-Hwan Oh	University of Texas at Arlington
Sangwook Oh	Korea University
Hao Pan	Sharp Labs of America
Jae Park	Purdue University
Christina Pavlopoulou	Purdue University
David Sadlier	Dublin City University
Thomas Sodring	Dublin City University
Nicola Stokes	University College Dublin
Xinghua Sun	TsingHua University
Kentaro Toyama	Microsoft Research
Matthias Voigt	Siemens Research
Khanh Vu	Oklahoma State University
Yong Wang	Columbia University
Christian Wolf	INSA Lyon
H.S. Wong	City University of Hong Kong
Yi Wu	Univ. of California at Santa Barbara
Lexing Xie	Columbia University
Hangjun Ye	TsingHua University
Aamin Ye	Dublin City University
Youngrock Yoon	Purdue University
Dongqing Zhang	Columbia University
Tong Zhang	Hewlett-Packard Research Lab

Sponsors

The Beckman Institute, TsingHua University Philips Research
The Institution of Electrical Engineers (IEE)
The Leiden Institute of Advanced Computer Science, Leiden University
Univ. of Illinois at Urbana-Champaign

Table of Contents

Feature Based Retrieval (Poster)

Semantics/Learning I (Poster)

Video Retrieval I (Oral)

User Studies (Oral)

Applications (Oral)

Semantics/Learning II (Poster)

Video Retrieval II (Poster)

Video Summarization & Analysis (Poster)

Performance (Poster)

The State of the Art
in Image and Video Retrieval

Nicu Sebe[1], Michael S. Lew[2], Xiang Zhou[3],
Thomas S. Huang[4], and Erwin M. Bakker[2]

[1] University of Amsterdam, The Netherlands
nicu@science.uva.nl
[2] Leiden University, The Netherlands
{mlew,erwin}@liacs.nl
[3] Siemens Corporate Research, USA
xiang.zhou@scr.siemens.com
[4] University of Illinois at Urbana-Champaign, USA
huang@ifp.uiuc.edu

Image and video retrieval continues to be one of the most exciting and fastest-growing research areas in the field of multimedia technology. What are the main challenges in image and video retrieval? Despite the sustained efforts in the last years, we think that the paramount challenge remains bridging the semantic gap. By this we mean that low level features are easily measured and computed, but the starting point of the retrieval process is typically the high level query from a human. Translating or converting the question posed by a human to the low level features seen by the computer illustrates the problem in bridging the semantic gap. However, the semantic gap is not merely translating high level features to low level features. The essence of a semantic query is understanding the meaning behind the query. This can involve understanding both the intellectual and emotional sides of the human, not merely the distilled logical portion of the query but also the personal preferences and emotional subtones of the query and the preferential form of the results.

Another important aspect is that digital cameras are becoming widely available. The combined capacity to generate bits of these devices is not easy to express in ordinary numbers. And, at the same time, the growth in computer speed, disk capacity, and most of all the rapid expansion of the web will export these bits to wider and wider circles. The immediate question is what to do with all the information. One could store the digital information on tapes, CD-ROMs, DVDs or any such device but the level of access would be less than the well-known shoe boxes filled with tapes, old photographs, and letters. What is needed is that the techniques for organizing images and video stay in tune with the amounts of information. Therefore, there is an urgent need for a semantic understanding of image and video.

Creating access to still images is still hard problem. It requires hard work, precise modeling, the inclusion of considerable amounts of a priori knowledge and solid experimentation to analyze the contents of a photograph. Luckily, it can be argued that the access to video is somehow a simpler problem than access to still images. Video comes as a sequence, so what moves together most likely

E. M. Bakker et al. (Eds.): CIVR 2003, LNCS 2728, pp. 1–8, 2003.

forms an entity in real life, so segmentation of video is intrinsically simpler than a still image, at the expense of only more data to handle. So the potential to make progress on video in a semantic understanding is there.

Moving from images to video adds several orders of complexity to the retrieval problem due to indexing, analysis, and browsing over the inherently temporal aspect of video. For example, the user can pose a similarity based query of "find a video scene similar to this one." Responding to such a query requires representations of the image and temporal aspects of the video scene. Furthermore, higher level representations which reflect the structure of the constituent video shots or semantic temporal information such as gestures could also aid in retrieving the right video scene.

Several new paradigms have emerged along the themes of image and video understanding. Examples include semantic image video retrieval models, interactive retrieval paradigms, affective and emotional interaction, image and video retrieval based on human perception, human computer interaction issues in image and video retrieval, learning and relevance feedback strategies, and intelligent summaries.

In the proceedings, several papers touch upon the semantic problem and give valuable insights into the current state of the art. Dimitrova [8] summarizes the main research topics in automatic methods for high-level description and annotation. Enser and Sandom [10] present a comprehensive survey of the semantic gap issues in visual information retrieval. Their goal is to provide a better informed view on the nature of semantic information needed and on the representation and recovery of semantic content across the broad spectrum of image retrieval activity. Naphade and Smith [27] argue that semantic understanding of multimedia content necessitates models for semantic concepts, context, and structure. In this context, they propose a hybrid framework that can combine discriminant and generative models for structure and context. Another framework for video content understanding using context and multimedia ontologies is proposed by Jaimes et al [16]. They present an expert system that uses a rule-based engine, domain knowledge, visual detectors, and metadata. Detecting semantic concepts from video using temporal gradients and audio classification is proposed by Rautiainen et al [35]. Sanchez et al [38] analyze different ways of coupling the information from multiple visual features in the representation of visual contents using temporal models based on Markov chains. Similarly, Yan et al [47] present an algorithm for video retrieval that fuses the decisions of multiple retrieval agents in both text and image modalities. An integrated image content and metadata search and retrieval across multiple databases is presented by Addis et al [1]. Audio-assisted video scene segmentation for semantic story browsing is investigated by Cao et al [5].

Application-specific issues are discussed in several papers. Liu and Kender [21] present a new approach for content-analysis and semantic summarization of instructional videos, while Miura et al [24] investigate cooking videos application. Domain-specific information is also used by Lay and Guan [20] for the retrieval of artworks by color artistry concepts. The documentary video application is covered by Velivelli et al [45]. They observed that the amount of information from the visual component alone was not enough to convey a semantic context but the audio-video fusion conveyed a much better semantic context. Audio-visual synchrony is also used by Nock et al [28] for speaker localization. The news video application is discussed by Pickering et al [33]. They describe their system which captures television news with accompanying subtitles and identifies and extracts news stories from the video. Lexical chain analysis is used then to provide a summary of each story and the important entities are highlighted in the text. The area of sports video is covered by Barcelo et al [4], Miyamori [25], and Baillie and Jose [3].

An important segment of papers discusses the human computer interaction issues in visual information retrieval. Cohen et al [7] present an evaluation of facial expression recognition techniques. They focus on the design of the classifiers used for emotion recognition in two types of settings: static and dynamic classification. Video retrieval of human interactions using model-based motion tracking and multilayer finite stare automata is discussed by Park et al [31]. User studies are performed by Goodrum et al [11] and Hughes et al [15]. Goodrum et al [11] study the search moves made by the users as they transition from one search state to another. Their goal is to identify patterns of search state transition used and the overall frequency of specific state transitions. Hughes et al [15] present an eyetracking study on how people view digital video surrogates. Their subjects were eyetracked to determine where, when, and how long they looked at text and image surrogates. The subjects looked at and fixated on titles and descriptions more than on the images. Also, most people used the text as an anchor from which to make judgments about the search results and used the images as confirmatory evidence for their selection. Sawahata and Aizawa [39] discuss the problems related to the indexing of personal video captured by a wearable imaging system. Accessing and organizing home videos present technical challenges due to their unrestricted content and lack of story line. In this context, Odobez et al [29] propose a spectral method to group video shots into scenes based on their visual similarity and temporal relations. Similarly, Mulhem and Lim [26] propose the use of temporal events for organizing and representing home photos using a structured document formalism and hence a new way to retrieve photos of an event using both image content and temporal context.

An important challenge in visual information retrieval comes from the dynamic interpretation of images under different circumstances. In other words, the perceptual similarity depends upon the application, the person, and the context of usage. Therefore, the machine not only needs to learn the associations, but also has to learn them on-line with a user in the loop. Several papers address learning and relevance feedback issues in image and video retrieval. Relevance feedback with multilevel relevance judgment is discussed by Wu et al [46]. They consider relevance feedback as an ordinal regression and present a relevance feedback scheme based on a support vector learning algorithm for ordinal regression. Similarly, a constructive learning algorithm-based RBF neural network for relevance feedback is proposed by Qian et al [34]. Several effective learning algorithms using global image representations are used for region-based image retrieval by Jing et al [17]. Howe [14] has a closer look at boosting for image retrieval and classification. The author, performs a comparative evaluation of several top algorithms combined in two different ways with boosting. Learning optimal representation for image retrieval application is investigated by Liu et al [22]. The authors use a Markov chain Monte Carlo stochastic gradient for finding representations with optimal retrieval performance on given datasets. The selection of the best representative feature and membership assignment for content-based image retrieval is discussed in [44].

An overview of challenges for content-based navigation of digital video is presented by Smeaton and Over [43]. The authors present a summary of the activities in the TREC Video track in 2002 where 17 teams from across the world took part. A fast video retrieval technique under sparse training data is proposed by Liu and Kender [23]. Observing that the moving objects' trajectories play an important role in content-based retrieval in video databases, Shim and Chang [42] present an efficient similar trajectory-based retrieval algorithm for moving objects in video databases. A robust content-based video copy identification scheme dedicated to TV broadcast is presented in [18]. The recognition of similar videos is based upon local features extracted at interest points. Similarly, Shao et al [41] extract local invariant descriptors for fast object/scene recognition based on local appearance. Video similarity detection issues are also discussed in [13].

In addition, new techniques are presented for a wide range of retrieval problems, including object matching [19], shape-based retrieval [2], searching in large-scale image databases [48], hierarchical clustering in multidimensional index structures [6], k-d trees for database indexing [40], image retrieval based on fractal codes [32], as well as applications in areas of historical watermarks [36], trademarks [9], and web image retrieval [30].

In order for image and video retrieval to mature, we will need to understand how to evaluate and benchmark features, methods, and systems. An efficiency comparison of two content-based retrieval systems is presented in [37]. Similarly, a performance comparison between different similarity models for CBIR with relevance feedback is presented by Heesch et al [12].

References

[1] M. Addis, M. Boniface, S. Goodall, P. Grimwood, S. Kim, P. Lewis, K. Martinez, and A. Stevenson. Integrated image content and metadata search and retrieval across multiple databases. In *International Conference on Image and Video Retrieval*, pages 88–97. Lecture Notes in Computer Science, vol. 2728, Springer, 2003. 2

[2] N. Arica and F. Yarman-Vural. A compact shape descriptor based on the beam angle statistics. In *International Conference on Image and Video Retrieval*, pages 148–157. Lecture Notes in Computer Science, vol. 2728, Springer, 2003. 4

[3] M. Baillie and J.M. Jose. Audio-based event detection for sports video. In *International Conference on Image and Video Retrieval*, pages 288–297. Lecture Notes in Computer Science, vol. 2728, Springer, 2003. 3

[4] L. Barcelo, X. Oriols, and X. Binefa. Spatio-temporal decomposition of sport events for video indexing. In *International Conference on Image and Video Retrieval*, pages 418–427. Lecture Notes in Computer Science, vol. 2728, Springer, 2003. 3

[5] Y. Cao, W. Tavanapong, and K. Kim. Audio-assisted scene segmentation for story browsing. In *International Conference on Image and Video Retrieval*, pages 428–437. Lecture Notes in Computer Science, vol. 2728, Springer, 2003. 2

[6] Z. Chen, J. Ding, M. Zhang, and W. Tavanapong. Hierarchical clustering-merging in multidimensional index structures. In *International Conference on Image and Video Retrieval*, pages 78–87. Lecture Notes in Computer Science, vol. 2728, Springer, 2003. 4

[7] I. Cohen, N. Sebe, Y. Sun, M.S. Lew, and T.S. Huang. Evaluation of expression recognition techniques. In *International Conference on Image and Video Retrieval*, pages 178–187. Lecture Notes in Computer Science, vol. 2728, Springer, 2003. 3

[8] N. Dimitrova. Multimedia content analysis: The next wave. In *International Conference on Image and Video Retrieval*, pages 8–17. Lecture Notes in Computer Science, vol. 2728, Springer, 2003. 2

[9] J.P. Eakins, K. Jonathan Riley, and J.D. Edwards. Shape feature matching for trademark image retrieval. In *International Conference on Image and Video Retrieval*, pages 28–37. Lecture Notes in Computer Science, vol. 2728, Springer, 2003. 4

[10] P.G.B. Enser and C.J. Sandom. Towards a comprehensive survey of the semantic gap in visual image retrieval. In *International Conference on Image and Video Retrieval*, pages 279–287. Lecture Notes in Computer Science, vol. 2728, Springer, 2003. 2

[11] A.A. Goodrum, M.M. Bejune, and A.C. Siochi. A state transition analysis of image search patterns on the web. In *International Conference on Image and Video Retrieval*, pages 269–278. Lecture Notes in Computer Science, vol. 2728, Springer, 2003. 3

[12] D. Heesch, A. Yavlinski, and S. Rüger. Performance comparison of different similarity models for CBIR with relevance feedback. In *International Conference on Image and Video Retrieval*, pages 438–447. Lecture Notes in Computer Science, vol. 2728, Springer, 2003. 4

[13] C-H. Hoi, W. Wang, and M. Lyu. A novel scheme for video similarity detection. In *International Conference on Image and Video Retrieval*, pages 358–367. Lecture Notes in Computer Science, vol. 2728, Springer, 2003. 4

[14] N.R. Howe. A closer look at boosted image retrieval. In *International Conference on Image and Video Retrieval*, pages 58–67. Lecture Notes in Computer Science, vol. 2728, Springer, 2003. 4

[15] A. Hughes, T. Wilkens, B.M. Wildemuth, and G. Marchionini. Text or pictures? An eyetracking study of how people view digital video surrogates. In *International Conference on Image and Video Retrieval*, pages 259–268. Lecture Notes in Computer Science, vol. 2728, Springer, 2003. 3

[16] A. Jaimes, B.L. Tseng, and J.R. Smith. Modal keywords, ontologies, and reasoning for video understanding. In *International Conference on Image and Video Retrieval*, pages 239–248. Lecture Notes in Computer Science, vol. 2728, Springer, 2003. 2

[17] F. Jing, M. Li, L. Zhang, H-J. Zhang, and B. Zhang. Learning in region-based image retrieval. In *International Conference on Image and Video Retrieval*, pages 198–207. Lecture Notes in Computer Science, vol. 2728, Springer, 2003. 4

[18] A. Joly, C. Frelicot, and O. Buisson. Robust content-based video copy identification in a large reference database. In *International Conference on Image and Video Retrieval*, pages 398–407. Lecture Notes in Computer Science, vol. 2728, Springer, 2003. 4

[19] S. Kim, S. Park, and M. Kim. Central object extraction for object-based image retrieval. In *International Conference on Image and Video Retrieval*, pages 38–47. Lecture Notes in Computer Science, vol. 2728, Springer, 2003. 4

[20] J. Lay and L. Guan. Concept-based retrieval of art documents. In *International Conference on Image and Video Retrieval*, pages 368–377. Lecture Notes in Computer Science, vol. 2728, Springer, 2003. 2

[21] T. Liu and J.R. Kender. Spatial-temporal semantic grouping of instructional video content. In *International Conference on Image and Video Retrieval*, pages 348–357. Lecture Notes in Computer Science, vol. 2728, Springer, 2003. 2

[22] X. Liu, A. Srivastva, and D. Sun. Learning optimal representations for image retrieval applications. In *International Conference on Image and Video Retrieval*, pages 48–57. Lecture Notes in Computer Science, vol. 2728, Springer, 2003. 4

[23] Y. Liu and J.R. Kender. Fast video retrieval under sparse training data. In *International Conference on Image and Video Retrieval*, pages 388–397. Lecture Notes in Computer Science, vol. 2728, Springer, 2003. 4

[24] K. Miura, R. Hamada, I. Ide, S. Sakai, and H. Tanaka. Associating cooking video segments with preparation steps. In *International Conference on Image and Video Retrieval*, pages 168–177. Lecture Notes in Computer Science, vol. 2728, Springer, 2003. 2

[25] H. Miyamori. Automatic annotation of tennis action for content-based retrieval by integrated audio and visual information. In *International Conference on Image and Video Retrieval*, pages 318–327. Lecture Notes in Computer Science, vol. 2728, Springer, 2003. 3

[26] P. Mulhem and J-H. Lim. Home photo retrieval: Time matters. In *International Conference on Image and Video Retrieval*, pages 308–317. Lecture Notes in Computer Science, vol. 2728, Springer, 2003. 3

[27] M. Naphade and J.R. Smith. A hybrid framework for detecting the semantics of concepts and context. In *International Conference on Image and Video Retrieval*, pages 188–197. Lecture Notes in Computer Science, vol. 2728, Springer, 2003. 2

[28] H.J. Nock, G. Iyengar, and C. Neti. Speaker localisation using audio-visual synchrony: An empirical study. In *International Conference on Image and Video Retrieval*, pages 468–477. Lecture Notes in Computer Science, vol. 2728, Springer, 2003. 3

[29] J-M. Odobez, D. Gatica-Perez, and M. Guillemot. Spectral structuring of home videos. In *International Conference on Image and Video Retrieval*, pages 298–307. Lecture Notes in Computer Science, vol. 2728, Springer, 2003. 3

[30] G. Park, Y. Baek, and H-K. Lee. Majority based ranking approach in web image retrieval. In *International Conference on Image and Video Retrieval*, pages 108–117. Lecture Notes in Computer Science, vol. 2728, Springer, 2003. 4

[31] S. Park, J. Park, and J.K. Aggarwal. Video retrieval of human interactions using model-based motion tracking and multi-layer finite state automata. In *International Conference on Image and Video Retrieval*, pages 378–387. Lecture Notes in Computer Science, vol. 2728, Springer, 2003. 3

[32] M.H. Pi, C.S. Tong, and A. Basu. Improving fractal codes-based image retrieval using histogram of collage errors. In *International Conference on Image and Video Retrieval*, pages 118–127. Lecture Notes in Computer Science, vol. 2728, Springer, 2003. 4

[33] M.J. Pickering, L. Wong, and S.M. Rüger. ANSES: Summarisation of news video. In *International Conference on Image and Video Retrieval*, pages 408–417. Lecture Notes in Computer Science, vol. 2728, Springer, 2003. 3

[34] F. Qian, B. Zhang, and F. Lin. Constructive learning algorithm-based RBF network for relevance feedback in image retrieval. In *International Conference on Image and Video Retrieval*, pages 338–347. Lecture Notes in Computer Science, vol. 2728, Springer, 2003. 3

[35] M. Rautianen, T. Seppanen, J. Pentilla, and J. Peltola. Detecting semantic concepts from video using temporal gradients and audio classification. In *International Conference on Image and Video Retrieval*, pages 249–258. Lecture Notes in Computer Science, vol. 2728, Springer, 2003. 2

[36] K. Jonathan Riley, J.D. Edwards, and J.P. Eakins. Content-based retrieval of historical watermark images: II - electron radiographs. In *International Conference on Image and Video Retrieval*, pages 128–137. Lecture Notes in Computer Science, vol. 2728, Springer, 2003. 4

[37] M. Rummukainen, J. Laaksonen, and M. Koskela. An efficiency comparison of two content-based image retrieval systems, GIFT and PicSOM. In *International Conference on Image and Video Retrieval*, pages 478–487. Lecture Notes in Computer Science, vol. 2728, Springer, 2003. 4

[38] J.M. Sanchez, X. Binefa, and J.R. Kender. Combining multiple features in temporal models for the representation of visual contents in video. In *International Conference on Image and Video Retrieval*, pages 208–217. Lecture Notes in Computer Science, vol. 2728, Springer, 2003. 2

[39] Y. Sawahata and K. Aizawa. Indexing of personal video captured by a wearable imaging system. In *International Conference on Image and Video Retrieval*, pages 328–337. Lecture Notes in Computer Science, vol. 2728, Springer, 2003. 3

[40] G.J. Scott and C-R. Shyu. EBS k-d tree: An entropy balanced statistical k-d tree for image databases with ground-truth labels. In *International Conference on Image and Video Retrieval*, pages 448–457. Lecture Notes in Computer Science, vol. 2728, Springer, 2003. 4

[41] H. Shao, T. Svoboda, T. Tuytelaars, and L. van Gool. HPAT indexing for fast object/scene recognition based on local appearance. In *International Conference on Image and Video Retrieval*, pages 68–77. Lecture Notes in Computer Science, vol. 2728, Springer, 2003. 4

[42] C-B. Shim and J-W. Chang. Efficient similar trajectory-based retrieval for moving objects in video databases. In *International Conference on Image and Video Retrieval*, pages 158–167. Lecture Notes in Computer Science, vol. 2728, Springer, 2003. 4

[43] A. Smeaton and P. Over. TRECVID: Benchmarking the effectiveness of information retrieval tasks in video. In *International Conference on Image and Video Retrieval*, pages 18–27. Lecture Notes in Computer Science, vol. 2728, Springer, 2003. 4

[44] M. Uysal and F. Yarman-Vural. Selection of the best representative feature and membership assignment for content-based fuzzy image database. In *International Conference on Image and Video Retrieval*, pages 138–147. Lecture Notes in Computer Science, vol. 2728, Springer, 2003. 4

[45] A. Velivelli, C-W. Ngo, and T.S. Huang. Detection of documentary scene changes by audio-visual fusion. In *International Conference on Image and Video Retrieval*, pages 218–228. Lecture Notes in Computer Science, vol. 2728, Springer, 2003. 3

[46] H. Wu, H. Lu, and S. Ma. Multilevel relevance judgment, loss function, and performance measure in image retrieval. In *International Conference on Image and Video Retrieval*, pages 98–107. Lecture Notes in Computer Science, vol. 2728, Springer, 2003. 3

[47] R. Yan, A. Hauptmann, and R. Jin. Multimedia search with pseudo-relevance feedback. In *International Conference on Image and Video Retrieval*, pages 229–238. Lecture Notes in Computer Science, vol. 2728, Springer, 2003. 2

[48] H. Ye and G. Xu. Fast search in large-scale image database using vector quantization. In *International Conference on Image and Video Retrieval*, pages 458–467. Lecture Notes in Computer Science, vol. 2728, Springer, 2003. 4

Multimedia Content Analysis: The Next Wave

Nevenka Dimitrova

Philips Research, 345 Scarborough Rd.,
Briarcliff Manor, NY 10510, USA
Nevenka.Dimitrova@Philips.com

Abstract. We have witnessed a decade of exploding research interest in multimedia content analysis. The goal of content analysis has been to derive automatic methods for high-level description and annotation. In this paper we will summarize the main research topics in this area and state some assumptions that we have been using all along. We will also postulate the main future trends including usage of long term memory, context, dynamic processing, evolvable generalized detectors and user aspects.

1   Introduction

After a decade of exploding interest in the multimedia content analysis and retrieval [1,6,8,15], there has been enough research momentum generated that we can finally reflect on the overall progress. The goal has been to develop automatic analysis techniques for deriving high level descriptions and annotations, as well as coming up with realistic applications in pursuit of the killer application. Meanwhile the MPEG-7 has standardized the description of metadata – data describing information in the content at various levels. Applications range from home media library organization that contains volumes of personal video, audio and images, multimedia lectures archive, content navigation for broadcast TV and video on demand content. The tools have emerged from traditional image processing and computer vision, audio analysis and processing, and information retrieval.

In this paper we will first present an overview of the active research areas in video content analysis in Section 2. Next, we will make high level observations about the current practices in Section 3. Section 4 will attempt to provide future directions. Section 5 will conclude the paper.

2   Active Research Areas

In Figure 1 we show a conceptual pyramid where the sides represent visual, audio, auxiliary (e.g. data provided by content creator) data and textual processing. The features computed range from low level – closer to the base of the pyramid to the high level semantics – closer to the top. Although there is variability in terminology,

E. M. Bakker et al. (Eds.): CIVR 2003, LNCS 2728, pp. 9-18, 2003.

we have seen that the algorithms can be largely categorized in "detectors," intermediate descriptors such as genre, structure, event, and affective descriptors and high level "abstractors." Detectors in turn can be very basic, for example face detection, videotext detection as well as complex: for example anchor detector based on face detector and shot classifier. The high level abstractors reveal the essence of the underlying content. For example, a summary will contain the essential content elements in a condensed form with less data. Examples of these features will be given in the following subsections.

2.1   Object Detection Algorithms

These detectors bring important semantic information in the video content analysis and indexing. Basic object detectors in video include videotext detection and face detection. At the generic level both have to first delineate the desired object from the "background" via simple image processing operators such as color, edge, and shape extractors and then apply area filters in order to focus on finding the desired shape.

Textual information brings important semantic clues in video content analysis such as name plates, beginning and ending credits, reporter names, etc. We investigated a method for detection and representation of text in video segments. The method consists of seven steps: Channel Separation, Image Enhancement, Edge Detection, Edge Filtering, Character Detection, Text Box Detection, and Text Line Detection [1]. Our results show that this method can be applied to English as well as non-English text (such as Korean) with precision and recall of 85%.

2.2   Computing Scenes: Micro vs. Macro Boundaries

Temporal boundary detection was initially a very active area of research [9]. The temporal segmentation referred to shot boundary detection. However, boundaries are also detected at the scene level as well as the program structure level. We can think of these boundaries as: micro (e.g. shots), macro (e.g. scene) and mega (program structure) boundaries.

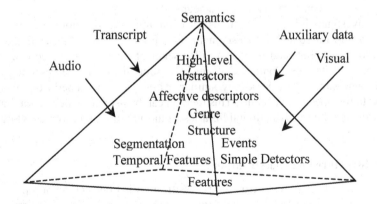

Fig. 1. The video research pyramid

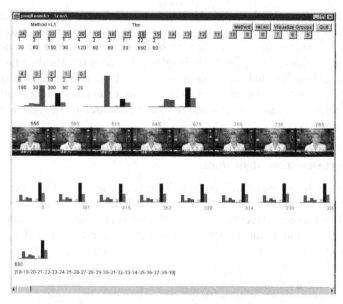

Fig. 2. Superhistogram representation of a news video program

Micro boundaries are associated to the smallest video units -- video microunits -- for which a given attribute is constant or slowly varying. The attribute can be any feature in the visual, audio, or text domain. Macro boundaries delineate collections of video micro segments that are clearly identifiable, organic part of an event defining a structural (action) or thematic (story) unit. Mega boundaries delineate collections of macro segments which exhibit a structural and feature (e.g. audio-visual) consistency.

Note that although in the literature it is well accepted that scenes comprise of one or more shots, there are complete movies or long sections of movies that defy this rule. Instead, a single shot consists of multiple scenes. Complete movies such as Hitchcock's "Rope" and consumer home video comprise of seemingly a single shot. Each scene boundary within the movie would represent a micro-segment – while multiple scenes can comprise a macro-segment.

We investigated different methods for computing super–histograms for color representation of micro and macro segments (see Figure 2). We build cumulative histograms for video shots and scenes. A video segment can be represented with the color histograms of its most dominant scenes. The superhistograms representing episodes of the same sitcom look strikingly similar, while TV news superhistograms are not similar to the ones from sitcoms. This method can be used for video classification and retrieval in studio archival, digital libraries, authoring tools, and web crawling.

2.3   Structure and Classification

The first notable step in structure and classification is to detect the non-program segments such as commercials and future program announcements. Furthermore, after the commercial segments have been isolated, the inner structure of the program can be recovered. Video programs such as news, talk shows, game shows, sports programs have an internal structure and detectable well-defined format. This provides transparency of the program content and gives users direct overview and access to meaningful modules of the program. To this end, we developed a multimodal analysis system, called Video Scout, for processing video, extracting and analyzing transcript, audio and visual aspects, determining the boundaries of program segments and commercial breaks and extracting a program summary from a complete broadcast [12].

2.4   Genre Detection

In absence of electronic program guide or metadata describing the video content, we need to use automatic methods for genre detection. Video content classification is a necessary tool in the current merging of entertainment and information media. Systems that help in content management have to discern between different categories of video in order to provide for fast retrieval. We developed a method for video classification based on face and text trajectories [10] based on the observation that in different TV categories there are different face and text trajectory patterns. Face and text tracking is applied to arbitrary video clips to extract faces and text trajectories. We used Hidden Markov Models (HMM) to classify a given video clip into predefined categories, e.g., commercial, news, sitcom and soap. Our results show classification accuracy of over 80% for HMM method on short video clips.

2.5   Multimedia Summary

Video summarization is the process of condensing the content into a shorter descriptive form of the original content. There is a variety of flavors that have been considered under the topic of summarization: video skimming, highlights, and various types of multimedia summaries. Next, we distinguish between local summaries for part of a program (e.g. for a scene), global summaries for the entire program, and meta-level summaries of a collection of programs.

Video skim is a temporally condensed form of the video stream that preferably preserves the most important information. A method for generating visual skims based on scene analysis and using the grammar of film language is presented in [17]. Ma et al. proposed an attention model that includes visual, audio, and text modalities for summarization of videos [13].

Video highlights is a form of summary that aims at including the most important events in the video. Various methods have been introduced for extracting highlights from specific subgenre of sports programs: goals in soccer video [7], hits in tennis video, touch down in baseball, important events in car racing video [13] and others.

Multimedia video summary is a collection of audio, visual, and text segments that preserve the essence and the structure of the underlying video (e.g. pictorial summary, story boards, surface summary). Uchihashi et al., present methods for automatically creating pictorial summaries of videos [18] using image and audio analysis to find relative importance of segments. The output consists of static images linked to the video and the users can interact with it. Surface level summarization takes into account the structure of the video. For example, Agnihotri et al. present a surface summarization method for talk shows that includes representative elements for the host portion and each of the guests [2]. The system consists of: transcript extractor, program type classifier, cue extractor, knowledge database, temporal database, and inference engine. Aner et al. introduce mosaic-based scene representation for clustering of scenes into physical settings [5].

Meta-level summaries provide an overview of a whole cluster of related videos. For example, meta summary of all available news items from Web and TV sources is provided by the MyInfo system [11] (see Figure 3). Summary of the news items is extracted by the reportage analysis and presented according to a personal profile.

Fig. 3. Summary of Web and TV news items in MyInfo

3   Current Practices and Assumptions

We rarely pause to reflect on the well accepted practices and assumptions that we use in multimedia content analysis. Here we will make observations based on our own work and the papers in the recent literature.

3.1   Short Memory

Short" of course is a relative term. In audio processing usually 20ms window is used in order to make local assessments which are further used for audio segmentation and classification. In video, for cut detection usually the window is two frames, for soft scene transitions (fade, dissolve) the window can be half a minute. In all these cases the length of the temporal window is dictated by the detection task. Information about the wider scope of the signal is usually not used.

This kind of short-term memory that we are using for specialized tasks is reminiscent of a special type of medical condition. The main hero in the movie "Memento," Leonard, is suffering from a condition called anterograde amnesia, which means that he cannot create new long-term memories. His attention span is about 15 minutes and the current memories cannot be permanently implanted in his brain. He operates by using notes, Polaroid snapshots and tattoos (externalized substitute for long term memory). How does this analogy translate to multimedia processing? Short-term buffers are used and most of the information that could be deemed useful in the long term is thrown away. However, we think that the short term memory processing has two consequences: a) loss of accuracy and b) brittleness. In the face detection example: the experience shows that the changing lighting conditions usually mean that we get false negatives although the face is consistently present in the whole shot.

3.2   Focused Processing

Currently in content analysis the processing is specifically directed to find an object, behavior, or event. As an example, in face detection the algorithm starts with skin-tone detection, followed by shape filtering, and in some cases, post-analysis that tries to reduce the number of false alarms and missed faces. In the process, the algorithm would miss what is "obvious" to us due to variations in color, position and occlusion. The focus of the algorithms is on the features that describe the face and not on the anatomical features or the physical laws – since the face does not appear and disappear within a split second.

In image face detection there is usually limited additional information. However, in video face detection the motion information is also available and this can be exploited as well. Instead of focused processing on a few frames, the algorithms can take into account the physical laws and the cinematographic practices.

3.3   Utilizing Available Features

Visual, auditory and text features have been used to extract content descriptors. In most cases, the assumption has been that we can use color, motion, shape, and text features to define objects and events of interest. In this past decade we did not question whether these features are the most representative of the underlying content for the task at hand. Features that were available were used and re-used in order to generate more detectors. Feature selection has only recently come to be the focus of attention.

3.4   Inherent Production Syntax

Produced video such as TV programs and movies follow cinematographic principles. The language syntax is present in the final produced movie or TV program. In movie production, the main syntactic elements include camera angles, continuity, cutting (multiple perspectives of the current and introduction of new scenes), close-ups, and composition. Content analysis area devises methods for recognition of structure, where structure represents the syntactic level composition of the video content. In specific domains, high-level syntactic structures may correspond well to distinctive semantic events. For example, we rely on the video news to have anchor shots and reportage shots in order to convey the full background of the story and on-the-scene information. We also rely on the production syntax being consistent without frequent changes.

Another assumption is linear progressive passage of time – which is the common sense model from our own experience in the real world. However, while this is true of many TV programs, in movie making, flashbacks are also used in order to fill in gaps in the present story. In the movie "Memento" if we assign letters to the backward color scenes and numbers to the monochrome scenes, then what the director Christopher Nolan presents is the following sequence of scenes: opening credits, 1, V, 2, U, 3, T, 4, S, 5, R, 6, Q ... all the way to 20, C, 21, B, and, finally, a scene Klein calls 22/A [4]. A skimming method can operate by making assumptions of the forward and backward passage of time. However, if this assumption is not verified, we might cut off the last portion of the shot – which in the backward case means the most important part of the shot.

4   Next Wave

The new trends are to get down to earth with the recognized assumptions and develop beyond the areas from which we originated and learned.

4.1   Memory

Memory is important aiding factor in content analysis with long-term goals. In this respect our methods are designed to just keep very localized information about the current computations. However, in multimedia processing we need to keep more information for longer periods of time, such as full programs, episodes and genres. Here we refer to long-term behavior of features in not only a single shot/scene but the whole (TV) program or even the whole series or genre. A director chooses to use a particular editing style, color scheme, that is consistent throughout the movie (e.g. in sitcoms: limited number of background sets, regular cast, and theme). The "long term" behavior of features can be thought of as "priors" in probabilistic terms and used for both high level processing and improving results of the low level detectors [12].

4.2   Multimedia Context

Context is the larger environmental knowledge that includes the laws of biology, physics and common sense. In philosophical terms, we have been using what can be termed the "Hume" model of signal processing where the only things that exist in the present frame are real, and we should transcend to the "Kant" model where there is a representation which accounts for contextual knowledge and assumptions about the "apriory models" - expected behavior of the entities that are sought for.

4.3   Dynamic Processing for the Evolving Production Process

As observed earlier, multimedia content analysis can rely on the inherent syntactic structure in order to devise methods for structure analysis of video. However, the main issue is that an ever evolving media – both TV programs and films strive to break the old rules and introduce novelty. In film it is the introduction of novel camera techniques, in news it is the Web page–like appearance showing simultaneously multiple sources of information that are orthogonal to the main news story (e.g. weather, stock information, breaking news highlights at the bottom of the screen). This issue presents great challenge in the long term, because most of our methods for content analysis require training and assume that the production rules are not going to change fast.

4.4   Domain Specific Processing: Specific vs. General Detectors

We need to be able to generate new detectors and methods in order to learn new concepts that are evolving all the time. Repetitiveness is one of the most important aspects of the objects and events in both spatial and temporal domain and reason for applying learning methods and statistical pattern recognition [16,19].

We have made domain (genre) specific methods which have targeted focus. We have impressive results especially in news analysis and retrieval, sports highlights detection. The question is which of these methods can be generalized with little effort to the other domains and which ones would perform better on a certain domain – better than any general detector.

4.5   User Input and Feedback

We explore research topics under the assumption that people are going to need the results. However, user needs analysis studies are necessary to see what are the important algorithms, topics and their relevance. Also, testing the final results and surveying the usefulness of the system aspects will provide insights into applications that can eventually have impact in our everyday life.

5   Conclusions

In creating video databases we travel the round trip: from brains to bits and back. In film production we started with an idea expressed in a script, and then followed by production and capture of this idea into bits. Accessing this information in a video database requires enabling to travel from the bits back to consumption and playback. The applications are in enabling to travel this path from bits back to brains in the enterprise, home environment and accessing public information. We should look at the generators of the content, not only the 3500 movies that Hollywood and its equivalents around the world produce every year, but also all the camera devices in surveillance, mobile communication, live event streaming, conferencing and personal home video archives.

In this paper we summarized the global trends of multimedia content processing and we presented a view outlining the future research directions. In this endeavor I believe that we have to expand our algorithms and theory to include context, memory, dynamic processing, general evolvable detectors and user aspects in order to tackle the wide array of applications.

References

[1] Lalitha Agnihotri and Nevenka Dimitrova, Text Detection in Video Segments, IEEE Workshop on Content Based Access to Image and Video Libraries, June 1999.

[2] Lalitha Agnihotri, Kavitha Devara, Thomas McGee, and Nevenka Dimitrova, "Summarization of Video Programs Based on Closed Captioning", SPIE Conf. on Storage and Retrieval in Media Databases, San Jose, CA, January 2001, pp. 599-607.

[3] Aigrain P., Zhang H.J., Petkovic D., "Content-based Representation and Retrieval of Visual Media: A State-of-the-Art Review", International Journal of Multimedia Tools and Applications, Kluwer Academic Publishers, Vol.3, No.3, 1996.

[4] A. Klein, Everything you wanted to know about "Memento", Salon.com, 6/28/2001. http://archive.salon.com/ent/movies/feature/2001/06/28 /memento_analysis/ index.html

[5] A. Aner and J. R. Kender, "Video Summaries through Mosaic-Based Shot and Scene Clustering", In Proc. European Conf. on Computer Vision, Denmark, May 2002.

[6] Shih-Fu Chang, What is the Holy Grail of Content-Based Media Analysis?, IEEE Multimedia, Spring 2002.

[7] S. Dagtas, T. McGee, and M. Abdel-Mottaleb, "Smart Watch: An automated video event finder", ACM Multimedia'2000, LA California, October 2000.

[8] Dimitrova N., Sethi I., Rui Y., "Media Content Management", in Design and Management of Multimedia Information Systems: Opportunities and Challenges, edited by Mahbubur Rahman Syed, Idea Publishing Group, 2000.

[9] Dimitrova, N., Agnihotri, L., and Jainschi, R., Temporal Video Boundaries, in Video Mining, A. Rosenfeld, D. Doermann, D. Dementhon eds., Kluwer, 2003, pp. 63-92.

[10] N. Dimitrova, L. Agnihotri, and G. Wei, Video Classification based on HMM using Text and Faces, EUSIPCO 2000.

[11] N. Haas, R. Bolle, N. Dimitrova, A. Janevski, and J. Zimmerman, Personalized News Through Content Augmentation and Profiling, IEEE ICIP, September 22-25, 2002.

[12] R.S. Jasinschi, N. Dimitrova, T. McGee, L. Agnihotri, J. Zimmerman, D. Li, "Integrated Multimedia Processing for Topic Segmentation and Classification", In the Proceedings of IEEE Intl. Conf. on Image Processing (ICIP), Greece, 2001.

[13] Yu-Fei Ma; Lie Lu; Hong-Jiang Zhang; Mingjing Li, "A User Attention Model for Video Summarization," ACM Multimedia 2002, Juan Les Pin, December 1-5, 2002.

[14] M. Petkovic, V. Mihajlovic, W. Jonker, "Multi-Modal Extraction of Highlights from TV Formula 1 Programs", IEEE Conf. on Multimedia and Expo, Lausanne, 2002.

[15] Smeulders A.W.M., Worring M., Santini S., Gupta A., and Jain R. Content-Based Image Retrieval at the End of the Early Years. *IEEE Transactions on Pattern Analysis and Machine Intelligence*, 22(12):1349–1380, December 2000.

[16] J. R. Smith, C-Y. Lin, M. Naphade, A. Natsev and B Tseng, Statistical Techniques for Video Analysis and Searching, in Video Mining, A. Rosenfeld, D. Doermann, D. Dementhon eds., Kluwer Academic Publishers, 2003, 259-284.

[17] H. Sundaram; L. Xie; S-F Chang, A Utility Framework for the Automatic Generation of Audio-Visual Skims , ACM Multimedia 2002, Juan Les Pin, December 1-5, 2002.

[18] S. Uchihashi, J. Foote, A. Girgensohn and J. Boreczky, Video Manga: Generating semantically meaningful video summaries, ACM Multimedia 1999, pp 383-392.

[19] L. Xie, S-F Chang, A. Divakaran, H. Sun, Mining Statistical Video Structures, Video Mining, A. Rosenfeld, D. Doermann, D. Dementhon eds, Kluwer 2003, 285- 324.

TRECVID: Benchmarking the Effectiveness of Information Retrieval Tasks on Digital Video

Alan F. Smeaton[1] and Paul Over[2]

[1] Centre for Digital Video Processing,
Dublin City University, Glasnevin, Dublin, 9, IRELAND
Alan.Smeaton@dcu.ie
[2] Retrieval Group, Information Access Division
National Institute of Standards and Technology
Gaithersburg, MD 20899-8940, USA
Over@nist.gov

Abstract. Many research groups worldwide are now investigating techniques which can support information retrieval on archives of digital video and as groups move on to implement these techniques they inevitably try to evaluate the performance of their techniques in practical situations. The difficulty with doing this is that there is no test collection or any environment in which the effectiveness of video IR or video IR sub-tasks, can be evaluated and compared. The annual series of TREC exercises has, for over a decade, been benchmarking the effectiveness of systems in carrying out various information retrieval tasks on text and audio and has contributed to a huge improvement in many of these. Two years ago, a track was introduced which covers shot boundary detection, feature extraction and searching through archives of digital video. In this paper we present a summary of the activities in the TREC Video track in 2002 where 17 teams from across the world took part.

1   Introduction

TREC is an annual exercise which has been running for 11 years and benchmarks the effectiveness of systems on various information retrieval tasks. TREC has world-wide participation and in the 2002 running, 93 groups took part in a variety of specialist "tracks" or activities. The TREC philosophy has always been to facilitate open, metrics-based evaluation and over the last few years TREC has run tracks on searching web documents, cross-lingual information retrieval, retrieval from spoken documents, retrieval from text documents in languages besides English such as Spanish and Chinese, question-answering, retrieval from text documents which have been corrupted by an OCR process, and others.

TREC is coordinated by the National Institute for Standards and Technology (NIST) in Gaithersburg, Md., USA, though groups taking part in TREC are funded

E. M. Bakker et al. (Eds.): CIVR 2003, LNCS 2728, pp. 19–27, 2003.
© Springer-Verlag Berlin Heidelberg 2003

from other sources or are self-funded. The *modus operandi* for TREC is that NIST will gather and distribute data (web pages, text documents, spoken radio news broadcasts, etc.) to participants who have signed up for a TREC track. Participants then install this data on their own IR system – depending on what the track is about – and on a given date, NIST will distribute a set of perhaps 50 topics or descriptions of an information need. Each group will then run each topic on the data using their own system and will send back the top-ranked X documents, where X could be as large as 1000, depending on the task. NIST then pools the top-ranked N (e.g. 100 or 200) documents from each submitted result from across all participating groups for each of the topics and then this pool of "documents" is manually evaluated for relevance to the topic in question. This establishes a ground truth of relevant documents for each topic and once this ground truth is available, the performance of each group' submitted results can be measured against this ground truth using measures such as precision and recall. The ground truth produced by pooling for the TREC text document collections has also been demonstrated to be useful for evaluating systems which did not contribute to the pool.

In 2001 a track on video information retrieval was introduced into TREC, covering three tasks, namely shot boundary detection, high-level feature detection, and searching. The goal of the track was to promote research in content-based retrieval from digital video by beginning the development of a laboratory-style evaluation using tasks which, although abstracted to make them manageable, modeled realworld tasks. In 2002 this track had 17 participating teams, up from 12 in the previous year, and used 73 hours of video material, up from 11 hours the previous year.

Acquiring realistically useful video data for research purposes is a notoriously difficult task because of copyright considerations and in TREC 2002 we used video data mainly from the Internet Archive Movie [1]. This consisted of advertising, educational, industrial and amateur films from 1930 to 1970 which was produced by corporations, non-profit organisations, trade groups, etc. This data is not ideal in that it is noisy and some of the 170+ videos have a sepia tint, but it does represent real archive data which people do want to search among. The 73.3 hours of data used was partitioned into 4.85 hours used for the shot boundary test, 23.26 hours used for training of feature detectors, 5.07 hours of feature testing and 40.12 hours used for the search testing. For TREC 2002 the test collections for feature extraction and search were segmented into shots by one of the participating groups (CLIPS-IMAG) and results for these two tasks were reported in terms of this common set of shot definitions.

In this paper we give a brief review of the achievements of the TREC2002 video track and for each of the three tasks we describe the task, the data used, a summary of the approaches taken by participants and the results obtained by those participants. Each of these three tasks is addressed in each of the following sections.

2   The Shot Boundary Detection Task

Work on algorithms for automatically recognizing and characterizing shot boundaries has been going on for some time with good results for many sorts of data and especially for abrupt transitions between shots. The shot boundary test collection for the 2002 TREC task comprised 18 videos totaling 4 hours and 51 minutes. The total size of the collection is 2.88 gigabytes and the videos contained a total of 545,068 frames and 2,090 shot transitions.

Reference data corresponding to the shot transitions was created by a student at NIST whose task was to identify all transitions and assign each to one of the following categories:

- 1466 hard cuts (70.1%) or no transitions, i.e., last frame of one shot followed immediately by the first frame of the next shot, with no fade or other combination;
- 511 dissolves (24.4%) where the shot transition takes place as the first shot fades out while the second shot fades in;
- 63 fades out/in to black and back (3.0%) where the shot transition takes place as the first shot fades out and then the second fades in;
- 50 other (2.4%) i.e. everything not in the previous categories e.g., diagonal wipes.

Gradual transitions are generally harder to recognize than abrupt ones and the proportion of gradual transitions to hard cuts in this collection is about twice that reported in [2] or [3]. Participating groups in this task were allowed up to 10 submissions each and these were compared automatically to the shot boundary reference data created manually at NIST. Detection performance for cuts and for gradual transitions was measured by precision and recall and results are shown in Figures 1 and 2. Some systems (e.g., CLIPS) demonstrate good control of the precision/recall tradeoff.

As illustrated, performance on gradual transitions lags, as expected, behind that on abrupt transitions and the numbers in parentheses give the number of runs submitted by each group. It can be seen that some groups (e.g., CLIPS and RMIT) seem to have good control of precision-recall tradeoff. Almost all of the groups who took part in this task used some form of frame-frame comparison but different groups varied how frames to be compared were selected. Further details of the approaches taken can be seen in the papers submitted by each group to the TREC proceedings [4]. The shot boundary detection task is included in the evaluation in part as an introductory problem, the output of which is needed for higher-level tasks such as search. Groups can participate for the first time in this task, develop their infrastructure, and move on to more complicated tasks the next year.

3   The Feature Extraction Task

The automatic extraction of high-level features from video is itself an interesting task but if it serves to help in video navigation and searching then its importance increases. The objective of the feature extraction task was to begin work on benchmarking feature extraction effectiveness and to allow the exchange of feature detection output among participants. The task is as follows: given a small dataset of just over 5 hours of video (1,848 shots) with common shot bounds, locate up to 1,000 shots which contain each of 10 binary features where the frequency of these features varied from rare (e.g. monologue) to everywhere (e.g. speech or instrumental sound) in the dataset. The feature set chosen was suggested in on-line discussions by track participants and was deliberately kept small so as to be manageable in this first iteration of the task.

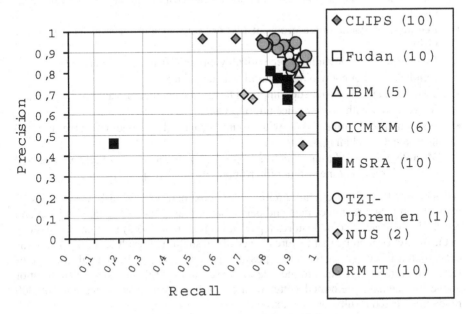

Fig. 1. Precision and Recall for Hard Cuts

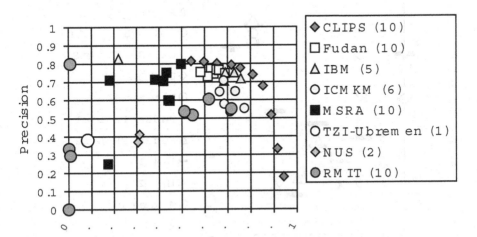

Fig. 2. Precision and Recall for Gradual Transitions

The ten features and their definitions are:

- **Outdoors**, a shot containing a recognizably outdoor location;
- **Indoors**, a shot containing an indoor location;
- **Face,** a shot containing at least one human face with nose, mouth and both eyes visible;
- **People,** shot containing a group of two or more humans, each at least partially visible;
- **Cityscape,** shot containing a recognizably city or urban or suburban setting;
- **Landscape,** shot containing a natural inland setting;
- **Text Overlay,** shot with superimposed text, large enough to read;
- **Speech,** shot with human voice uttering words;
- **Instrumental Sound,** shot with sound produced by one or more musical instruments, including percussion;
- **Monologue,** shot during which a single person is at least partially visible and speaker for a long time without interruption by another speaker;

All submitted results from all groups who took part in this task were assessed manually to create reference data and performance was measured using precision and recall. In the case of some features (speech, instrumental sound) the number of shots in the dataset containing that feature exceeded the submitted result set (1,000) and this created an artificial upper bound on possible precision scores. In general, the size of test set was small in relation to the size of the result set. Still, almost all systems at or above the median, preformed better than a baseline created by evaluating 100,000 randomly created results for each feature.

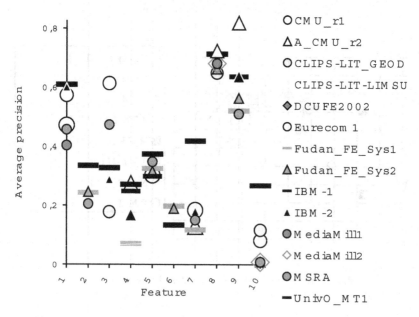

Fig. 3. Average Precision by Feature for All Runs at the Median or Above

The results of group submissions are presented in Figure 3. These results show average precision for each of the 10 features, for each group which achieved the median result or above and these results vary enormously in their dispersion among features, as well as in their mean. In general, though, some of the results are disappointingly poor. For some like instrumental sound and speech, performance is reasonable but for others such as detection of cityscape or landscape, people, indoors, text overlay or monologue the performance is poor. This could be attributed to insufficient effort made by groups, operational errors or the difficulty of the task itself. The most likely explanation is that groups who did take part in this task underestimated the complexity of the task and the resources necessary to achieve good performance.

For the dozen or so groups which did this task, most hand-labeled some part of the training data and used a machine learning approach, such as a support vector machine on either the video or the audio track. It is to be expected that for whichever of these features are run again in a future TREC Video track, performance will be much improved.

4   The Search Task

The third and final task in the 2002 TREC Video track was the search task, and this took two forms. The very difficult task of fully automatic topic-to-query translation was set aside for a future TREC video track and so two more modest forms of searching were supported. In the "manual" search task, a human, expert in the search system interface, was allowed to interpret each topic and to create one optimal query which was run once, and the results submitted to NIST for assessment. In the "interactive" search task, groups were allowed much more flexibility in using real users to formulate queries, search, browse, re-formulate and re-query, etc., for as long as was necessary.

The data to be searched in the search task consisted of 176 videos with 14,524 shots and was chosen because it represented an established archive of publicly available material that one could imagine being searched. The topics in the both of the search tasks were designed as multimedia descriptions of an information need, such as somebody searching a large archive of video might have in the course of collecting material to include in a larger video. Twenty-five topics were created by NIST and each contained a text description of the information need plus some examples in other media such as video clips or images. Of the 25 topics, 22 had video examples (average 2.7), 8 had images (average 1.9) and others had audio. The topics requested either specific or generic people (George Washington or football players), specific or generic things (golden gate bridge or sailboats), locations (overhead views of cities), activities (rocket taking off) or combinations (people spending leisure time at the beach).

The task in both search tasks was to return up to 100 shots from the collection (of over 14,000 shots) which might be relevant to the topic, using pre-defined and agreed shot boundaries. To help groups develop more sophisticated video retrieval systems, several groups (CLIPS, DCU, IBM, MediaMill, LIMSI and MS Research Asia) ran their detectors or speech recognition systems on this search data set and made their outputs available to other groups, marked up in MPEG-7. This contributed enormously to making the track a more integrated and cooperative effort.

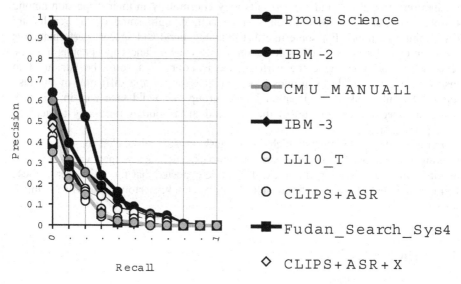

Fig. 4. Mean Average Precision for Top Ten Runs for the Manual Search Task

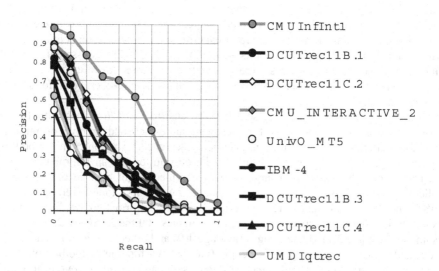

Fig. 5. Mean Average Precision for Top Ten Runs for the Interactive Search Task

Results submitted from each group had their top 50 shots pooled and then manually judged for relevance by assessors from NIST;subsequent judgment of the remaining shots in each result set found few additional relevant shots except for topics which already had many.. As with other TREC tasks, once the assessments had been made and this reference data available, evaluation of the performance in terms of precision and recall was possible. Results in terms of mean average precision for the top ten manual runs are presented in Figure 4 (for manual runs) and in Figure 5 (for interactive search runs. Beneath the averages across the 25 topics there was a large amount of variability by topic. Groups who submitted runs in the interactive search task also logged the time spent by their users on each topic and the mean average precision versus mean elapsed time spent searching, showed no correlation between search time, and performance. Time spent in interactive searching varied from an average of about 1 minute per topic for one group, up to almost 30 minutes per topic for another group.

The performance of interactive searching is, as expected, better on average than the performance of manual searching. In absolute terms, the performance of the search systems is quite good but could, of course, be improved. For a first real iteration of the search task on a sizeable data set, some groups have performed quite well and the spread of performances across different groups is quite good.

Of the dozen or so groups who took part in the search task, a true kaleidoscope of approaches was represented. Some groups used interactive video browsing systems with sets of real users carrying out searches under controlled environments; many groups used the automatic speech recognised transcript as a fundamental part of their search system; one group used an image retrieval system on video keyframes, in an interactive framework. Further details of the approaches taken can be seen in the papers submitted by each group to the TREC proceedings [4]. The jury is still out on two important search issues. The reliable usefulness of features in search generally or in specific situations has yet to be demonstrated. Similarly, the proper role and usefulness of non-text elements in the topic is not yet clear. Matching the text of the topic against text derived automatically from the video's audio track usually delivered better overall results than searches based on just the visual elements or a combination of the text and the visual elements in a topic. But for topics requesting a particular camera motion (e.g. locomotive approaching the viewer) text from ASR would be unlikely to help. It is too early to draw convincing conclusions about these two issues.

5   Conclusions

Evaluation of the effectiveness of different approaches to information retrieval from digital video archives is something that is rapidly becoming or crucial importance as the more and more techniques are developed and are being tested. It is crucial to have common testbeds and evaluation metrics in order to allow comparisons across systems and this is the primary motivation behind the TREC Video track. A similar approach to evaluation of image retrieval and image browsing can be found in the Viper project at the University of Geneva [5].

While there may be some disappointments associated with the TREC Video Track activity in 2002 in terms of the overall quality of the results for feature extraction especially, the track has been very successful in demonstrating a collaborative, shared, and effective evaluation of shot boundary detection, feature extraction, and video searching on a common dataset and using common and agreed metrics. This can be regarded as a real achievement by the track and the success of the collaborative aspect of the track in terms of open exchange of derived features in MPEG-7 format has shown that really effective video navigation depends on having a range of features which can be accurately extracted from video and automatic feature extraction will form an important part of future TREC video track activities. In terms of open questions, there are many, such as how the limitations of the dataset influence the conclusions that we can reach and what can be said about the balance between precision and recall ? Details of the types of errors that are being made by different feature classifiers and by different approaches to search will appear in the follow-up analysis of the different groups which will be reported by those groups elsewhere, but at this early stage of the TREC video track evaluation, it is too early to draw any really meaningful conclusions.

In terms of future activities, the TREC Video track will become an independent 1-2 day workshop (TRECVID 2003) taking place at NIST just before the main TREC conference. It will continue with a larger dataset and more groups participating. For 2003 we will have 120 hours of 1998 news video and more of the same in 2004. It is expected that the three basic tasks of segmentation, feature extraction, and searching, will also continue, probably with some more features and with 50 topics instead of 25 The guidelines for 2003 are currently being developed. Data from the previous video tracks is available to researchers. The latest information about the TREC video retrieval evaluation effort is available from the website: http://www-nlpir.nist.gov/projects/trecvid/.

Authors' note: An extended version of this paper containing a more detailed analysis of the results and brief descriptions of the approaches taken by the participating groups, appeared in the proceedings of the TREC 2002 Conference.

References

[1] The Internet Archive Movie Archive. http://www.archive.org/movies
[2] Boreczky, J.S., and Rowe, L.A. (1996) Comparison of video shot boundary detection techniques. In I.K. Sethe and R.C. Jain (Eds.) Storage and Retrieval for Still Image and Video databases IV, Proc. SPIE 2670, pp.170-179., San Jose, Calif. USA.
[3] Ford, R.M. (1999). A quantitative Comparison of Shot Boundary Detection Metrics. In: M.M. Yueng, B.-L. Yeo and C.A. Bouman (Eds.) .) Storage and Retrieval for Still Image and Video databases IV, Proc. SPIE 3656, pp.666-676, San Jose, Calif. USA.
[4] The TREC 2002 Proceedings:
http://trec.nist.gov/pubs/trec11/t11_proceedings.html.
[5] Müller, W., Marchand-Maillet, S., Müller, H. and Pun, T. Towards a fair benchmark for image browsers, In SPIE Photonics East, Voice, Video, and Data Communications, Boston, MA, USA, November 5-8 2000.

Shape Feature Matching
for Trademark Image Retrieval

John P. Eakins, K. Jonathan Riley, and Jonathan D. Edwards

School of Informatics
University of Northumbria
Newcastle NE1 8ST, UK
{john.eakins,jon.riley,jonathan.edwards}@unn.ac.uk

Abstract. Shape retrieval from image databases is a complex problem. This paper reports an investigation on the comparative effectiveness of a number of different shape features (including those included in the recent MPEG-7 standard) and matching techniques in the retrieval of multi-component trademark images. Experiments were conducted within the framework of the ARTISAN shape retrieval system, and retrieval effectiveness assessed on a database of over 10 000 images, using 24 queries and associated ground truth supplied by the UK Patent Office. Our results show clearly that multi-component matching can give better results than whole-image matching. However, only minor differences in retrieval effectiveness were found between different shape features or distance measures, suggesting that a wide variety of shape feature combinations and matching techniques can provide adequate discriminating power for effective retrieval.

1 Introduction

1.1 Background

Content-based image retrieval (CBIR) remains a highly active area of research, with a number of potentially important applications, including fingerprint identification, trademark registration, and design archive management. However, the capabilities of current technology still fall short of most users' requirements [1]. This is particularly true of shape retrieval. No satisfactory general-purpose shape-matching technique has yet been developed, due in large part to the difficulty of devising shape similarity measures that accurately model human visual perception [2].

The research reported here is part of an ongoing investigation into ways of representing shape to a retrieval system in a perceptually significant manner. The aim of our current study is to validate a number of hypotheses on which our ARTISAN trademark image retrieval system [3] has been based, in order to provide a basis for further work. This paper reports a comparison of the effectiveness of several different types of shape measure and matching technique for trademark similarity matching.

E. M. Bakker et al. (Eds.): CIVR 2003, LNCS 2728, pp. 28-38, 2003.

1.2   Techniques for Measuring Shape Similarity

Many techniques for shape similarity matching have been proposed over the last twenty years. Some, such as boundary deformation [4], are based on direct matching of shape boundaries. However, these tend to be computationally expensive, so most techniques are based on the comparison of shape features extracted from the image under consideration. These include simple features such as aspect ratio, circularity, and transparency [5], "natural" measures of triangularity, ellipticity and rectangularity [6], Fourier descriptors [7], moment invariants [8], and Zernike moments [9]. Two types of feature are of particular significance though their incorporation in the new MPEG-7 standard (http://www.cselt.it/mpeg/public/mpeg–7_visual_xm.zip) - the angular radial transform (ART), and curvature scale-space coefficients [10].

2   Trademark Image Retrieval

2.1   Previous Work

Trademark registration is an activity of considerable importance. Trademark registries around the world have a duty to ensure that all new trademarks submitted for registration are sufficiently distinct from existing marks to avoid any risk of confusion. Analysing trademark image similarity is a complex process. Wu et al [11] have identified three components of similarity - shape, structure and semantics. Traditionally, trade mark registries have relied on manually-assigned codes from schemes such as the Vienna classification [12], which mixes all three elements to some extent. By contrast, most automatic systems have concentrated on shape.

Two main CBIR approaches to trademark retrieval have been reported in the literature. The first, following Kato's TRADEMARK [13] system, aimed to extract and match features from whole images. Kato used *GF-vectors* computed from normalized images for matching. Later workers have used a variety of measures, including a combination of edge direction histograms and moment invariants [14], Zernike moments [15], and histograms of local curvature and phase computed from Gaussian derivatives of image intensity [16].

The second approach regards trademark images as multi-component objects, capable of being matched at more than one level. Examples include Wu et al's STAR system [11], which uses Fourier descriptors and moment invariants extracted from human-segmented trademark images, and Peng and Chen's method [17] of approximating each image component as a set of (possibly overlapping) closed contours, and representing each contour as a list of angle. It is currently not possible to assess the relative effectiveness of these two approaches, since no comparative evaluation studies have yet been reported.

2.2   The ARTISAN Project

The ARTISAN system [3], developed at the University of Northumbria in collaboration with the UK Patent Office, is based on similar principles to STAR. The first prototype used a combination of simple global features calculated both from individual image components and from families of components derived automatically using principles derived from Gestalt psychology [18]. Evaluation of retrieval effectiveness yielded encouraging results, though performance proved not to be consistent enough for operational use.

Version 2 of ARTISAN [20] incorporated a number of important changes, including the use of multiresolution analysis to remove texture and improve the system's robustness to noise, new ways of grouping low-level components into higher-level regions, and a wider range of shape and structural features. Boundary creation within version 2 is performed by segmenting a multi-resolution representation of the trademark following the method of Burt and Adelson [21]. A set of decision rules is used to select the most appropriate resolution(s) for boundary extraction (for details see [20]). Region boundaries are identified using a smoothed histogram trough detection algorithm similar to the method of Pauwels et al [22].

The current version of our system (now known as TRIFFID) incorporates a variety of shape measures calculated both at whole-image and component level. It provides considerable flexibility when searching, allowing users to select from a wide range of alternative shape features and matching techniques, including selective matching on individual image components.

3   The Current Investigation

3.1   Aims and Objectives

Our prototype ARTISAN system provides users with a wide range of choice - between whole-image and component-based matching, between a range of alternative shape features to use for matching, and between a range of alternative matching paradigms. This allows us to test a number of hypotheses about the nature of shape representation and matching for multi-component images, including the following:

(a) Component-based matching of trademark images using boundary-based shape measures is more effective than whole-image matching using region-based measures.
(b) Some types of distance measure are more effective than others in modelling human relevance judgements.
(c) Some types of shape feature are more effective than others in modelling human relevance judgements.

While it is unlikely that any single investigation can provide *conclusive* proof of any of these hypotheses, it is our belief that the experiments reported here are capable of generating strong evidence either in support or refutation.

3.2   Methodology

3.2.1   Shape Features Used

The retrieval system used to test these hypotheses was ARTISAN version 2.1, based on the version described in [20], but enhanced with a number of additional types of shape feature and matching paradigm as described below. This computes and stores the following "whole-image" features for every image in the database:

(a) The 7 normal moment invariants φ_n defined by Hu [10];

(b) The 4 affine moment invariants defined by Flusser and Suk [24];

(c) The 36 angular radial transform (ART) coefficients defined in the draft MPEG-7 standard [25];

(d) In addition, it stores the following features for each individual *component* of every image added to the database (see [20] for definitions of these features);

(e) "simple" shape descriptors: aspect ratio, circularity, and convexity (ratio of the region's area to that of its convex hull);

(f) 3 "natural" shape descriptors proposed by Rosin [6]: triangularity, rectangularity and ellipticity;

(g) 8 normalized Fourier descriptors;

(h) A set of curvature scale space peaks, computed as specified in the draft MPEG-7 standard [25].

Finally, a number of additional parameters are computed, including *relative size* (the ratio of the area of each component to the area of the largest component in the image) and *centroid distance*, the normalized distance between the centroids of the component and the whole image. These allow matching by structure as well as shape.

3.2.2 Matching Techniques

The system provides several alternative means of matching a query shape. For this study, two are of particular interest:

Whole-image matching, where similarity scores between query and stored images are computed from feature vectors based on user-selected shape measures using user-selected distance measures.

All-component matching, where overall similarity scores are computed from component feature vectors (again based on user-selected shape measures) in both query and stored images, using the *asymmetric simple* method shown in previous trials of ARTISAN [19] to give the highest retrieval effectiveness.

In each case, a distance measure is calculated between the query image and each image in the database. The top-ranking *n* stored images (which can be the entire database) are then sorted into distance order and displayed to the user.

3.2.3 Evaluation Methods Used

The process of evaluating retrieval effectiveness is far from straightforward [23]. The approach adopted in this paper follows the methodology developed for our evaluation of the original version of ARTISAN [19]. A set of 24 query trademarks selected by staff at the UK Trade Marks Registry for evaluation of the first version of ARTISAN was run against the 10 745 image database of abstract geometric trademarks also supplied by the Registry. Results were compared with relevance judgements already generated by human trademark examiners, which formed our "ground truth". This approach ensured that the performance of each set of features was compared against the same benchmark - though it is still open to the criticism that the human judgements forming our ground truth were based on overall assessments of image similarity (potentially based in shape, structure and semantics), not necessarily judgements based purely on shape.

Several different experiments were performed, testing the effect of different combinations of shape feature, distance measure and matching paradigm, as described in the next section. In every case, all 24 queries were run against all 10 745 images, and the entire database sorted into order of similarity to the query. Retrieval effectiveness was measured using normalized precision P_n, normalized recall R_n, and last-place ranking L_n, as in the original ARTISAN evaluation [19]. Each of these measures gives an estimate of retrieval effectiveness in the range 0-1 (1 representing perfection), but emphasizes different aspects of system performance. Last-place ranking L_n, which indicates the system's ability to retrieve *all* relevant images, is a particularly important measure in the context of trademark image retrieval.

4   Results

4.1   Whole-Image vs. Component-Based Matching

For these experiments, the 24-image query set was run against the database using three different whole-image feature sets:

(a) The 36 ART coefficients defined in the MPEG-7 standard;
(b) The 7 normal moment invariants defined by Hu;
(c) The 4 affine moment invariants defined by Flusser and Suk;

and one component-based feature set:

(d) three simple descriptors (SD), three Rosin descriptors (RD), eight Fourier descriptors (FD), and relative size - the feature combination found to work best in previous evaluation experiments [20].

In each case, image distances were calculated using the city-block or L_1 distance measure (see below).

Table 1. Comparative effectiveness of whole-image and component-based features for retrieval. All results are expressed as mean ± standard error over 24 test queries

Features used for matching:	P_n	R_n	L_n
Whole-image features:			
Angular Radial Transform	0.53 ± 0.05	0.82 ± 0.03	0.40 ± 0.06
7 normal moment invariants	0.32 ± 0.04	0.65 ± 0.04	0.23 ± 0.05
4 affine moment invariants	0.28 ± 0.03	0.65 ± 0.03	0.22 ± 0.04
Component-Based Features:			
3SD + 3RD + 8 FD + size	0.70 ± 0.04	0.94 ± 0.02	0.72 ± 0.06

Results are shown in table 1. It can clearly be seen that ART is significantly ($P <$ 0.001, Wilcoxon matched-pairs, signed-rank test) more effective than either of the other two whole-image features, whichever measure of retrieval performance is used. Combining ART with the other whole-image features (detailed results not reported here) consistently lowered retrieval effectiveness. However, component-based matching using the combination of simple, Fourier and Rosin descriptors proved significantly ($P <$ 0.01 or better, depending on retrieval effectiveness measure used) more effective than any of the whole-image measures. These results provide strong support for hypothesis (a) - that component-based matching is more effective than whole-image matching.

4.2   Effectiveness of Different Distance Measures

For these experiments, the 24-image query set was run against the database using ART (the best-performing whole-image measure) and 3SD+3RD+8FD+size (the best-performing component-based combination), using five different distance measures:

(a) The city-block metric

$$L_1 = \frac{1}{n}\sum_{i=1}^{n}\left|q_i - s_i\right|$$

(b) Euclidean distance

$$L_2 = \frac{1}{n}\sum_{i=1}^{n}\sqrt{(q_i - s_i)^2}$$

(c) Matusita distance

$$M = \sqrt{\sum_{i=1}^{n}\left(\sqrt{q_i} - \sqrt{s_i}\right)^2}$$

(d) Modified Bhattacharya distance

$$B_{mod} = -\ln\left(\frac{\sum_{i=1}^{n}\sqrt{q_i \times s_i}}{\sqrt{\sum_{i=1}^{n}q_i} \times \sqrt{\sum_{i=1}^{n}s_i}}\right)$$

(e) Divergence

$$D = \sum_{i=1}^{n}\left[(q_i - s_i)\ln\frac{q_i}{s_i}\right]$$

Results are shown in table 2. Differences between the different distance measures are all negligible, with the possible exception of the L_n scores for whole-image features, where the Bhattacharya distance appears to perform slightly better than the other distance measures. Even here, the only difference to approach statistical significance ($P < 0.02$, Wilcoxon matched-pairs, signed-rank test) was that between Bhattacharya and Euclidean distance. For component-based matching, there are no significant differences at all. Overall, these results provide no compelling evidence to support hypothesis (b) - the null hypothesis that there are no significant differences between distance measures cannot be rejected.

Table 2. Comparative effectiveness of different distance measures. All results are expressed as mean ± standard error over 24 test queries

Distance measure:	Image-based feature (ART)			Component-based features (3SD+3RD+3FD+size)		
	P_n	R_n	L_n	P_n	R_n	L_n
City-block	0.53 ± 0.05	0.82 ± 0.03	0.40 ± 0.06	0.70 ± 0.04	0.94 ± 0.02	0.72 ± 0.06
Euclidean	0.52 ± 0.05	0.80 ± 0.03	0.35 ± 0.06	0.68 ± 0.04	0.92 ± 0.02	0.67 ± 0.06
Matusita	0.53 ± 0.04	0.83 ± 0.03	0.47 ± 0.05	0.69 ± 0.04	0.93 ± 0.02	0.69 ± 0.07
Bhattacharya	0.54 ± 0.04	0.83 ± 0.03	0.51 ± 0.05	0.68 ± 0.04	0.92 ± 0.02	0.66 ± 0.07
Divergence	0.53 ± 0.04	0.82 ± 0.03	0.47 ± 0.05	0.68 ± 0.04	0.93 ± 0.02	0.66 ± 0.06

4.3   Effectiveness of Different Shape Features

For these experiments, the 24-image query set was run against the database in component-matching mode, making no use of size or layout parameters, and using the following sets of features:

(a) The three "simple" features described above (3SD);
(b) The three Rosin descriptors described above (3RD);
(c) Eight Fourier descriptors (8FD);
(d) Curvature-scale-space peaks (CSS), both as a single measure and in combination with aspect ratio and circularity, as recommended in the MPEG-7 standard;
(e) various combinations of these features.

Our implementation of CSS matching differed in one respect from the method specified in the MPEG-7 standard - no pre-screening was used to reject images whose components differed in aspect ratio or circularity by more than a set threshold. Preliminary investigations showed that this rejected a significant number of relevant images, which could not therefore be included in the ranking process.

Results are shown in table 3. Both CSS and Rosin descriptors *on their own* perform significantly less well than the best combinations of features ($P < 0.01$, Wilcoxon matched-pairs signed-rank test, whichever effectiveness measure is used). Combining CSS matching with aspect ratio and circularity, as recommended in the MPEG-7 standard, significantly improves its effectiveness ($P < 0.01$), though it still performs significantly less well ($P < 0.01$) than feature combinations such as Rosin plus Fourier descriptors, which appear to be particularly effective. Adding simple descriptors and/or CSS matching to this combination resulted in no significant increase in performance. Our results thus provide some evidence to support hypothesis (c) - though only in the case of individual feature sets. Most of the combinations tested gave virtually identical results in our trials.

Table 3. Comparative effectiveness of different shape features. All results are expressed as mean ± standard error over 24 test queries

Shape feature(s) used:	P_n	R_n	L_n
CSS alone	0.46 ± 0.05	0.81 ± 0.03	0.45 ± 0.05
3 Rosin descriptors	0.51 ± 0.04	0.85 ± 0.02	0.51 ± 0.05
CSS, aspect ratio and circularity	0.58 ± 0.05	0.89 ± 0.02	0.63 ± 0.06
3 simple descriptors	0.61 ± 0.04	0.91 ± 0.02	0.66 ± 0.05
8 Fourier descriptors	0.63 ± 0.05	0.91 ± 0.02	0.67 ± 0.06
CSS + 3SD	0.63 ± 0.04	0.91 ± 0.02	0.67 ± 0.05
CSS + 8FD	0.65 ± 0.05	0.92 ± 0.02	0.69 ± 0.06
3RD + 8FD	0.67 ± 0.04	0.93 ± 0.02	0.72 ± 0.05
3SD + 3RD + 8FD	0.68 ± 0.04	0.93 ± 0.02	0.72 ± 0.05
All four sets of features	0.68 ± 0.04	0.93 ± 0.01	0.72 ± 0.05

4.4   Individual Shape Matching Results

However, average results for a whole set of queries tell only part of the story. Individual query results can prove equally illuminating. For example, table 4 shows some examples of the ranks at which individual target images were retrieved in response to a given query images, using the different shape measures defined above:

Analysis of these results is still under way. It is already clear, however, that some target images are proving uniformly easy to retrieve, and some uniformly difficult. Nearly every type of shape feature scores well on some images, but badly on others. It is not always true that combining shape features gives better results than using them on their own!

Table 4. Retrieval rankings (out of possible 10745) for given target image (column 2) against given query (column 1), using different shape features as specified above.

Query image	Target image	Shape features used					
		Simple	Rosin	Fourier	CSS	All shape	Shape and size
▽	▽	1	6	10	2	2	1
▽	⬟	45	2	186	75	14	12
▽	△	36	1013	272	160	100	6
▽	⟁	1498	64	1667	1716	933	20
✻	◉	8	7	14	12	9	9
✻	◉	16	25	6	18	6	6
✻	◉	163	1815	612	53	259	156
✻	◉	21	239	36	31	18	12

5   Conclusions and Further Work

Our results show clearly that for the test collection with which we have been working (abstract geometric images from the UK Trade Marks Registry), matching on the basis of boundary features extracted from individual image components is significantly more effective than matching on whole images using region-based features. Whether the segmentation and region grouping techniques currently used for ARTISAN are optimal - or even significantly better than simple segmentation - is an issue we are currently researching. Our investigations into human segmentation behaviour [26] suggest that there is considerable scope for improvement in this area.

Our results in other areas are less clear-cut. We found no significant differences between the different distance measures used to compute image similarity, suggesting that the best metric to use is L_1, because of its lower computational overhead. We found some differences in effectiveness between different shape features, but these were mostly marginal. The only really striking difference noted was that for whole-image matching, the angular radial transform is markedly superior than either normal or affine moment invariants. This would appear to be consistent with the findings of the MPEG-7 evaluation panel, who selected ART as one of the shape descriptors to include in their standard.

Few statistically-significant differences in the relative effectiveness of different boundary-based shape descriptors were found, and it is debatable whether any of these would ever be operationally significant. We have been unable to confirm the findings of the MPEG-7 evaluation panel who selected curvature-scale space matching as the boundary-based descriptor of choice. CSS matching appears to have no clear advantage over other techniques in trademark retrieval - indeed in our trials it appeared slightly but significantly *less* effective than feature sets such as a combination of Rosin and Fourier descriptors.

It is quite possible that other comparative experiments, based on different sets of queries, test collections, and ground truth could reach different conclusions from this study. Given the degree of user subjectivity present even in apparently clear-cut applications such as trademark retrieval, no one study can definitively establish the relative effectiveness of different matching techniques. Our findings emphasize the importance of replicating all results with other test collections in the hope that consensus will eventually emerge. In this respect, the Benchathlon initiative (http://www.benchathlon.net/), which aims to promote comparative trials of different systems on comparable data sets in the same way as the TREC text retrieval experiments, is much to be welcomed.

Further work planned for this area includes an investigation of the effectiveness of using selected regions of query images for database matching, the usefulness of relevance feedback in improving system performance, and - most importantly - the development of improved methods of modelling subjective image appearance as foreshadowed in [26]. We also hope to be able to validate our findings on additional test collections - though the difficulty of obtaining reliable ground truth in the form of human relevance judgements from large test collections should not be underestimated.

Acknowledgements

The assistance of Patrick Warnat and Ravishankar Aithala in developing parts of the software and carrying out retrieval experiments is gratefully acknowledged.

References

[1]   Eakins, J P and Graham, M E: Content-based image retrieval JISC Technology Applications Programme Report 39 (1999)

[2]   Scassellati, B et al: Retrieving images by 2-D shape: a comparison of computation methods with human perceptual judgements. In: Storage and Retrieval for Image and Video Databases II, Proc SPIE 2185 (1994) 2-14

[3]   Eakins, J P, Boardman, J M and Graham, M E: Similarity retrieval of trademark images. IEEE Multimedia 5(2) (1998) 53-63

[4]   Jain, A K et al: Object matching using deformable templates. IEEE Transactions on Pattern Analysis and Machine Intelligence 18(3) (1996) 267-277

[5]   Levine, M D: Vision in man and machine, ch 10. McGraw-Hill, N Y (1985)

[6]   Rosin, P L: Measuring shape: ellipticity, rectangularity and triangularity. In: Proceedings of 15th International Conference on Pattern Recognition, Barcelona, 1 (2000) 952-955

[7]   Zahn, C T and Roskies C Z: Fourier descriptor for plane closed curves. IEEE Transactions on Computers C-21 (1972) 269-281

[8]   Hu, M K: Visual pattern recognition by moment invariants. IRE Transactions on Information Theory IT-8 (1962) 179-187

[9]   Teh, C H and Chin, R T: Image analysis by methods of moments. IEEE Transactions on Pattern Analysis and Machine Intelligence 10(4) (1988) 496-513

[10]   Mokhtarian, F S et al: Efficient and Robust Retrieval by Shape Content through Curvature Scale Space. In: Proceedings of International Workshop on Image DataBases and MultiMedia Search, Amsterdam (1996) 35-42

[11]   Wu, J K et al: Content-based retrieval for trademark registration. Multimedia Tools and Applications 3 (1996) 245-267

[12]   International Classification of the Figurative Elements of Marks (Vienna Classification), Fourth Edition. ISBN 92-805-0728-1. WIPO, Geneva (1998)

[13]   Kato, T: Database architecture for content-based image retrieval. In: Image Storage and Retrieval Systems, Proc SPIE 2185 (1992) 112-123

[14]   Jain, A K and Vailaya, A: Shape-based retrieval: a case study with trademark image databases. Pattern Recognition 31(9) (1998) 1369-1390

[15]   Kim, Y S and Kim, W Y: Content-based trademark retrieval system using a visually salient feature. Image and Vision Computing 16 (1998) 931-939

[16]   Ravela, S and Manmatha, R: Multi-modal retrieval of trademark images using global similarity. Internal Report, University of Massachusetts at Amherst (1999)

[17]   Peng, H L and Chen, S Y: Trademark shape recognition using closed contours. Pattern Recognition Letters 18 (1997) 791-803

[18]   Wertheimer, M: Untersuchungen zur Lehre von der Gestalt. Psychologische Forschung 4 (1923) 301-350,. Translated as: Laws of organization in perceptual forms in: A Sourcebook of Gestalt Psychology, (Ellis, W D, ed). Humanities Press, New York (1950)

[19]   Eakins, J P et al Evaluation of a trademark retrieval system, in 19th BCS IRSG Research Colloquium on Information Retrieval, Robert Gordon University, Aberdeen (1997)

[20]   Eakins, J P et al: A comparison of the effectiveness of alternative feature sets in shape retrieval of multi-component images. In: Storage and Retrieval for Media Databases 2001, Proc SPIE 4315 (2001) 196-207

[21]   Burt P J and Adelson E H: The Laplacian pyramid as a compact image code. IEEE Transactions on Computers 31(4) (1983) 532-540

[22]   Pauwels, E J and Frederix, G: Content-based image retrieval as a tool for image understanding. In: Multimedia Storage and Archiving Systems IV, Proc SPIE 3846 (1999) 316-327

[23]   Müller H et al: The truth about Corel - evaluation in image retrieval in: Proceedings of CIVR2002, London, July 2002. Lecture Notes in Computer Science 2383 (2002) 28-49

[24]   Flusser J and Suk T: Pattern recognition by affine moment invariants. Pattern Recognition 26(1) (1993)167-174

[25]   Jeannin S et al: MPEG-7 visual part of eXperimetation Model V 7.0. ISO N3521, Beijing (2000)

[26] Ren, M, Eakins, J P and Briggs, P: Human perception of trademark images: implications for retrieval system design. Journal of Electronic Imaging 9(4) (2000) 564-575

Central Object Extraction
for Object-Based Image Retrieval

Sungyoung Kim[1], Soyoun Park[2], and Minhwan Kim[2]

[1] Dept. of Multimedia, Changwon College, Changwon, Korea
`sykim@changwon-c.ac.kr`
[2] Dept. of Computer Engineering, Pusan National Univ., Pusan, Korea
{`yescandoit, mhkim`}`@pusan.ac.kr`

Abstract. An important step in content-based image retrieval is finding an interesting object within an image. We propose a method for extracting an interesting object from a complex background. Interesting objects are generally located near the center of the image and contain regions with significant color distribution. The significant color is the more frequently co-occurred color near the center of the image than at the background of the image. A core object region is selected as a region a lot of pixels of which have the significant color, and then it is grown by iteratively merging its neighbor regions and ignoring background regions. The final merging result called a central object may include different color-characterized regions and/or two or more connected objects of interest. The central objects automatically extracted with our method matched well with significant objects chosen manually.

1   Introduction

The goal of content-based image retrieval (CBIR) is to find all images in a given database depicting scenes or objects of some specified type by users. The images are searched and matched usually based on image features such as color, texture, shape, and spatial layout. However, we know that there is obvious semantic gap between what user-queries represent based on the low-level image features and what the users think. Thus many researchers have investigated techniques that retain some degree of human intervention either during input or search thereby utilizing human semantics, knowledge, and recognition ability effectively for semantic retrieval. These techniques called relevance feedbacks are capable of continuous learning through run-time interaction with end-users. Semantic feature finding approaches have been also studied, which tried to extract semantic information directly from images. Automatic classification of scenes (into general types such as indoor/outdoor or city/landscape) [1] and automatic object recognition are examples of such efforts. Eakins [2] reviewed related works to semantic information finding and argued the importance of artificial intelligence techniques in further advances of the semantic retrieval field.

E. M. Bakker et al. (Eds.): CIVR 2003, LNCS 2728, pp. 39–49, 2003.

However, he also pointed out that a complete understanding of image contents at the semantic level was not an essential prerequisite for successful image retrieval.

On the one hand, many researchers believe that the key to effective CBIR performance lies in the ability to access images at the level of objects because users generally want to search for the images containing particular object(s) of interest. Several region-based retrieval methods [3-5] are proposed, because regions are correlated well with objects in an image. Kam *et al.* [4] tried to cluster regions into classes each of which might be a group of separated regions, while Carson *et al.* [3] represented and accessed each region separately. Especially, Wang *et al.* [5] tried to represent content and context of regions based on color-texture classification to provide a way for semantic retrieval.

There are some methods that automatically discriminate *region(s) of interest* from the other less useful regions in an image. Osberger and Maeder [6] tried to determine the perceptual importance of different regions in a gray-scale image, which was computed based on human visual attention and eye movement characteristics. Wang *et al.* [5] used some influence factors of visual attention [6] to represent saliency of semantic categories. Lu and Guo [7] tried to identify and remove big background regions that could hamper the retrieving results. Huang *et al.* [8] automatically segmented an image into foreground and background regions. Their algorithm is suitable for images that have the foreground regions away from image corners and a smooth and slightly textured background. So it is hard to anticipate good results in complex scenes. Serra and Subirana [9] extracted saliency areas of attention by finding texture frame curves that were defined as the virtual image curves lying along the center of texture boundaries. They defined a feature inertia surface by simulating the VI-cortex of human brain and tried to determine the frame curves by using their adaptive non-Cartesian networks. Even though the proposed method suffers from computational burden to extract accurate frame curves, the extracted regions of attention are meaningful because the pre-attentive texture discriminatory system of the human visual system is simulated.

We believe that *object(s) of interest* in an image provides higher-level information than *region(s) of interest* in the image does. However, detecting the object(s) of interest is an unresolved issue [9]. First, there is not a clear definition of the object of interest. For example, is a nose an object of interest in a human face image? Second, it is often ambiguous to define an object of interest. What is the object of interest in an image where a butterfly on a flower is? Third, it is very difficult to separate complete objects, such as a car or a person, from arbitrary and complex natural scenes. Fourth, one object is usually divided into several regions since conventional segmentation methods divide an image based on similarity of low-level features [10]. On the one hand, fortunately, a single dominant object tends to be at center of an image, which may represent content of the image very well. For example, a giraffe may be the dominant object in the image where it eats some leaves in a grassy plain in Africa.

In this paper, we describe a method that automatically extracts central objects even though they show various color and texture characteristics in a complex background. We assume that all our images in the database have one or more objects of interest. A central object in an image is defined as a set of characteristic regions located near the center of the image. These regions are characterized as having significant color distribution compared with surrounding regions. A central object may contain more than two regions with different color characteristics from each other. More than two objects of interest may be also considered as a central object if they lie near together at center of an image. First of all, significant pixels in color and texture are determined by using the difference between the correlogram [11] for the center area of an image and one for the surrounding region. Then two types of core regions are determined to characterize the foreground and the background in the image. One is the core object region that has a lot of significant pixels; the other is the core background region that is adjacent to the corners or borders of the image. The core object region is extended through merging its unlabeled neighbor regions, if they have similar color distribution to it but are very dissimilar to the core background region in color distribution. The final merging result, a set of regions connected to each other, is the central object. Although sometimes the extracted central objects are not complete, we expect that they are very useful for object-based image retrieval and help users to effectively retrieve relevant images.

2   Localization of Central Objects

2.1   Definition of Central Objects and a Default Attention Window

A central object in a color image is defined as the region that satisfies the following conditions.

(1) It is located near the center of the image,
(2) It has significant color and texture characteristics against its surrounding area,
(3) Its size is relatively big, and
(4) Its boundary pixels have relatively strong edginess.

It makes sense that the center area of an image is treated more importantly than the border area of the image. Some of center regions are expected to more effectively represent contents of the image than the border regions to do, because people tend to locate the most interesting object at the center of the frame when they take a picture. The center of an image is defined as the region in the center 25% of the image [5,6]. A central object should be significant at least in color and texture characteristics against its surrounding area. We cannot guess or use its shape information. However, we can confine the minimum size of a central object to be 5% of the total image size, because people taking pictures tend to have the most interesting object occupy a large extent of the picture. The condition of strong edginess can be also accepted reasonably.

Usefulness of the condition of the center area was tested by evaluating the location and size of the minimum bounding rectangles (MBRs) for the manually extracted central objects in various types of test images. Fig. 1(a) shows the distribution of occurrence of the central objects in the normalized image, where a brighter pixel represents higher occurrence. Average values for the width, height, left boundary position, and upper one of the 1000 MBRs were 0.46, 0.43, 0.26, and 0.29, respectively (Fig. 1(b)). We see that center area of an image is very useful for finding central objects. Fig. 1(c) shows a rectangle whose width and height are determined by a half of those of a given image, respectively. This rectangle is called a default attention window (DAW) in this paper.

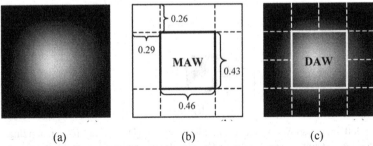

(a)   (b)   (c)

Fig. 1. The left image shows distribution of occurrence of manually extracted central objects in various types of test images. The center image shows the manually attention window (MAW) whose average size and position are determined by evaluating the minimum bounding rectangles for the manually extracted central objects in 1000 test images. The right image shows a default attention window (DAW) that is defined in this paper as the region in the center 25% of the image

2.2   Significant Features in the Default Attention Window

Color correlations [11] can characterize color distribution and basic color texture well in a region. In this paper, significant color correlations are first searched from the DAW to localize the location of a central object in an image. A significantly correlated color (SCC) is defined as the color pair (c_i, c_j) that satisfies Eq. (1), where $C_{DAW}(c_i, c_j)$ and $C_{SR}(c_i, c_j)$ are the count of (c_i, c_j) in the correlogram C_{DAW} for the DAW and one in C_{SR} for the surrounding region (Fig. 2(a)), respectively. The correlograms are computed by using the dynamic programming algorithm [11] with the distance set $D = \{1\}$.

$$\frac{C_{DAW}(c_i, c_j) - C_{SR}(c_i, c_j)}{C_{DAW}(c_i, c_j)} \geq 0.1 \tag{1}$$

Fig. 2(a) shows the DAW and the surrounding region in a leopard image. Fig. 2(b) shows the back-projected significant pixels to a binary image plane. The significant pixels are defined as the adjacent pixels one of which has the color c_i and the other one the color c_j from a SCC (c_i, c_j). We can see in Fig. 2(b) that the SCCs are able to represent dominant colors and textures in the leopard.

2.3   Central Object Localization

The size and location of the DAW need to be adjusted for the central object to be localized more compactly and effectively. After the morphological closing operation followed by the opening one is applied to the back-projected binary image, a MBR for the biggest connected component of significant pixels is selected. Then the MBR is contracted so that more than 70% of the contracted MBR is filled with the significant pixels. The center of the contracted MBR is selected as average point of the significant pixels in the connected component and its aspect ratio is kept the same as that of the MBR. The contracted MBR is called an adjusted attention window (AAW) in this paper. We can see that the AAW in Fig. 2(c) includes the central object (leopard) more effectively than the DAW in Fig. 2(a) does. The set of significant features needs to be updated because the DAW is replaced with the AAW.

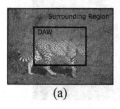 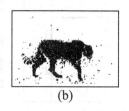 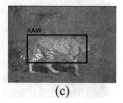

(a)   (b)   (c)

Fig. 2. The left image shows a default attention window (DAW) and its surrounding region. The center image shows the back-projected significant pixels. The right image shows an adjusted attention window (AAW) that surrounds the leopard more compactly and effectively

3   Extraction of Central Objects

3.1   Core Object Regions

A set of connected significant regions among the segmented regions by the *JSEG* segmentation algorithm [12] is selected so that it is suitable for representing core of the central object in an image. A significant region is the region that satisfies the following conditions:

(1) The ratio of the number of significant pixels to the size of the region is high.
(2) More than half of the region lies in the AAW.
(3) The size of the portion of the region in the AAW is relatively large.

These conditions are merged and represented in the Eq. (2). The RS_i is ratio of the number of significant pixels in the i-th region to its size TS_i. The IS_i is the number of pixels in the i-th region which are also in the AAW. The LRS is the largest value among all IS's. The weight α and the threshold t_{PC} for PC are both 0.5 by default.

$$PC_i = \alpha(RS_i) + (1-\alpha)(\frac{IS_i}{LRS} \times \frac{IS_i}{TS_i}) \geq t_{PC} \ and \ \frac{IS_i}{TS_i} \geq 0.5 \tag{2}$$

If the significant regions are separated, a set of the connected significant regions of maximum size is selected as a core object region (COR). The COR may include two or more different color-characterized significant regions. Fig. 3(a) shows the COR in the leopard image.

3.2   Background Analysis

Information of the background in an image is very useful for removing the background [7] and discriminating the foreground from the background [8]. It is also useful for improving the extraction accuracy of central objects in this paper by prohibiting the core object region from being over-extended.

The background is determined in this paper by collecting the following background regions (BRs):

(1) Corner regions in an image.
(2) The region that is adjacent to two or more boundaries of the image.
(3) The region a large portion of whose boundary is adjacent to a boundary of the image.
(4) The region that is adjacent to a relatively horizontal line extracted by the Hough transformation, but less than half of the region lies in the AAW and the ratio of the number of significant pixels to the size of the region is less than 0.3.
(5) The region that is adjacent to and similar in color distribution to any one of the regions in (1)-(4), which is called a extended background region.
(6) The region that is adjacent to and similar in color distribution to an extended background region.

Fig. 3(b) shows the background at the leopard image. We can see that there still remain unlabeled regions between the COR and the background.

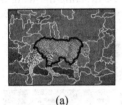 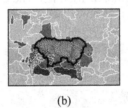 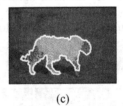

      (a)   (b)   (c)

Fig. 3. The left image shows the core object region in a leopard image, which represents significant features of the leopard well. The center image represents the extended background regions. The right image shows the central object (leopard) that is extracted by growing the core object region against the extended background regions

3.3   Growing of the Core Object Region

An unlabeled region that is adjacent to any significant region of the COR is merged to the COR based on its background dissimilarity and an extension cost. The background dissimilarity is defined as the color dissimilarity of the unlabeled region R to the background, $1-max_i\{S(R,BR_i)\}$. The BR_i indicates the i-th background region and the $S(R,BR_i)$ represents the color similarity between the region R and the region BR_i. The extension cost C is defined as in Eq. (3), where RS is ratio of the number of significant pixels in the region R to its size and CBS represents the common boundary strength between the region R and the adjacent significant regions $\{SR_i's\}$ of the COR. Common boundary strength is defined as ratio of the numbers of strong edge pixels to the number of pixels in the common boundary. Edge strength of each common boundary pixel is computed based on the dissimilarity of local color distribution in [13] and the strong edge pixels are defined as the pixels whose edge strength is greater than the $(0.8 \times$ the maximum edge strength).

$$C =1-[0.4\,max_i\{S(R, SR_i)\}+0.3\,RS +0.3\,(1-CBS)] \tag{3}$$

The unlabeled region R is merged to the COR if its background dissimilarity and its extension cost, C, are greater than 0.8 and 0.5, respectively. A newly merged region is considered as a significant region and such growing process is repeated until there are no more unlabeled regions that can be merged. Fig. 3(c) shows the final merging result that is accepted as the central object in the leopard image.

4   Experimental Results and Discussions

The proposed method is evaluated on various test images selected from the Corel photo-CD, which are classified into five classes such as animal, butterfly, car, fish, and flower. There are 100 test images in each class. Fig. 4 shows some examples of the central objects that are extracted by the proposed method. Fig 4 (a) and (b) show central objects that are extracted from simple and complex backgrounds, respectively. We can see that multiple colored central objects are well extracted. Fig. 4(c) shows that multiple objects of interest can be also extracted well if they are neighbored with each other in the image space. On the one hand, Fig. 4(d) shows some of wrong results. The under-extracted lion occurred because of the wrong AAW and similarity of the body to the background in color distribution. The error in extracting the wing of the butterfly happened because of separated wings and the bear was over-extracted because of the similarly colored neighbor regions.

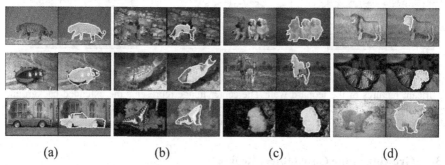

(a)   (b)   (c)   (d)

Fig. 4. Examples of central objects; (a)-(c) relatively well-extracted ones, (d) under- or over-extracted ones

Fig. 5(a) shows the sorted accuracies of the extracted central objects. The accuracy A of an extracted central object by the proposed method is defined as in Eq. (4). The S_M, S_U, and S_O represent the cardinality of M, $M-(M\cap E)$, and $E-(M\cap E)$, respectively, where E represents the set of pixels in the extracted central object and M one in the manually extracted central object. The average accuracies for the animal, butterfly, car, fish, and butterfly class images are 0.7, 0.68, 0.56, 0.74 and 0.86, respectively.

$$A = \frac{\max\{S_M - (S_U + S_O), 0\}}{S_M} \tag{4}$$

Fig. 5(b) shows color similarities between the extracted central objects (animals and cars) by the proposed method and the manually extracted ones. The color similarity is computed by using an extended color histogram intersection (ECHI) method that is defined as in Eq. (5), because 64 adaptively quantized colors are used to represent each test image. The adaptively quantized color distribution of the extracted central object by the proposed method is represented as $P = \{(\mathbf{p}_1,w_{p1}), (\mathbf{p}_2,w_{p2}),\ldots, (\mathbf{p}_m,w_{pm})\}$, where $\mathbf{p}_i$ is the representative color of a i-cluster and w_{pi} is the normalized weight of $\mathbf{p}_i$, that is, $\Sigma w_{pi} = 1$. The $Q = \{(\mathbf{q}_1,w_{q1}), (\mathbf{q}_2,w_{q2}),\ldots, (\mathbf{q}_n,w_{qn})\}$ represents one of the manually extracted central objects. The parameter α and β in the color similarity function $S_{ECHI}(d)$ are set to 0.0376 and 0.3. The $d_{L2}(\mathbf{p},\mathbf{q})$ represents the Euclidean distance between two color vectors, $\mathbf{p}$ and $\mathbf{q}$.

$$ECHI(P,Q) = \sum_{i=1}^{n} \min(f_{total}(i), w_{qi})$$

$$f_{total}(i) = \sum_{k=1}^{m} S_{ECHI}(d_{L2}(\mathbf{p}_k,\mathbf{q}_i)) \min(w_{pk}, w_{qi}), \quad S_{ECHI}(d) = \frac{\max\{e^{-\alpha d} - \beta, 0\}}{1 - \beta} \qquad (5)$$

We can see in Fig. 5(b) that even the central objects with low accuracy show relatively high color similarity. This means that the extracted central objects with low accuracy can represent color characteristics of the real central objects. Thus the extracted central objects can be effectively used in object-based image retrieval.

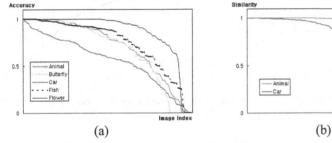

(a)   (b)

Fig. 5. The left image shows extraction accuracy curves for five classes of test images. The right image shows color similarities between the extracted central objects (animals and cars) by the proposed method and the manually extracted ones

The inaccuracy (1-A) can be represented by $\min\{(S_U /S_M) + (S_O /S_M), 1\}$. The (S_U /S_M) and the (S_O /S_M) represent inaccuracy of under-extraction and of over-extraction, respectively. Fig. 6(a) shows the inaccuracy curve and the under-extraction inaccuracy for 30 animal images with low accuracy, while Fig. 6(b) for the 30 car images. Each small rectangle on the horizontal axis shows that wrong significant regions are included in the core object region. We can see that the inaccuracy in the animal images is caused by the under-extraction or over-extension of wrong significant regions, while one in the car images depends greatly on only the under-extraction inaccuracy.

Fig. 7 shows that the accuracy of the extracted central object is higher than one of the core object region in most cases. Thus it is turned out that the growing process through background analysis is useful in extracting central objects with high accuracy.

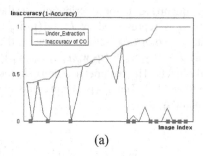
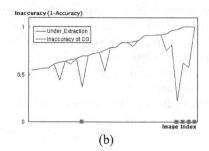

Fig. 6. This figure shows distributions on inaccuracy of central object and one of under-extraction: (a) for 30 animal images with low accuracy in Fig. 5(a), (b) for 30 car images

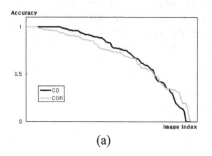
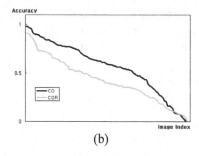

(a)   (b)

Fig. 7. Accuracy comparison between core object regions and central objects: (a) for animal images, (b) for car images

Fig. 8. Leftmost two images show ambiguous cases of determining the central object. Rightmost two images show the extracted central objects by the proposed method in this paper

Fig. 9. Examples of little useful results for the image without any object of interest

It is ambiguous to define central objects in the left two images of Fig. 8. Our method extracts the butterfly and the flower together in the first image and only the fish near center in the second image. However, someone may be interested in only the butterfly or both the fishes.

While the proposed method showed good results for the images with object(s) of interest, its results for the images without any objects of interest were of little use

(Fig. 9). Thus the method cannot be used in determining whether an image includes object(s) of interest.

5   Conclusions

We presented a novel method for extracting central objects. Experimental results showed that the proposed method could extract meaningful central objects well even from complex background images without any prior-knowledge. The extracted central objects expect to be effectively used in object-based image retrieval because they can represent the color-characteristics of real central objects well.

Acknowledgement

This work was supported by grant No.R01-2000-00275 from the Basic Research Program of the Korea Science & Engineering Foundation and partially by Pusan National University Research Grant.

References

[1]   Vailaya, A., Figueiredo, M.A.T., Jain, A.K., and Zhang, H.J.: Image Classification for Content-Based Indexing. IEEE Trans. on Image Processing. **10(1)** (2001) 117-130

[2]   Eakins, J.P.: Towards Intelligent Image Retrieval. Pattern Recognition. **35** (2002) 3-14

[3]   Carson, C., Thomas, M., Belongie, S., Hellerstein, J.M., and Malik, J.: Blobworld: A System for Region-Based Image Indexing and Retrieval. VISUAL'99. Amsterdam, Netherlands, (1999) 509-516

[4]   Kam, A.H., Ng, T.T., Kingsbury, N.G., and Fitzgerald, W.J.: Content Based Image Retrieval through Object Extraction and Querying. IEEE Workshop on Content-based Access of Image and Video Libraries. (2000) 91-95

[5]   Wang, W., Song, Y., and Zhang, A.: Semantics Retrieval by Region Saliency. Int'l Conf. on Image and Video Retrieval. (2002) 29-37

[6]   Osberger, W. and Maeder, A.J.: Automatic Identification of Perceptually Important Regions in an Image. IEEE Int'l Conf. on Pattern Recognition. (1998) 701-704

[7]   Lu, Y. and Guo H.: Background Removal in Image Indexing and Retrieval. Int'l Conf. on Image Analysis and Processing. (1999) 933-938

[8]   Huang, Q., Dom, B., Steels, D., Ashely, J., and Niblack, W.: Foreground/Background Segmentation of Color Images by Integration of Multiple Cues. Int'l Conf. on Image Processing. **1** (1995) 246-249

[9]   Serra, J.R. and Subirana, J.B.: Texture Frame Curves and Regions of Attention Using Adaptive Non-cartesian Networks. Pattern Recognition. **32** (1999) 503-515

[10]   Tamaki, T., Yamamura, T., and Ohnishi, N.: Image Segmentation and Object Extraction Based on Geometric Features of Regions. SPIE Conf. on VCIP'99, 3653 (1999) 937-945

[11] Huang, J., Kumar, S.R., Mitra, M., Zhu, W.J., and Zabih, R.: Image Indexing Using Color Correlograms. Proc. Computer Vision and Pattern Recognition. (1997) 762-768

[12] Deng, Y., Manjunath, B.S., and Shin, H.: Color Image Segmentation. IEEE Conf. on Computer Vision and Pattern Recognition. 2 (1999) 446-451

[13] Park, C., Kim, S., Kim, J., and Kim, M.: Color Image Segmentation for Content Based Image Retrieval Using a Modified Color Histogram Intersection Technique. Int'l Conf. on Multimedia Technology and Its Applications. (2003) 146-151

Learning Optimal Representations
for Image Retrieval Applications

Xiuwen Liu[1], Anuj Srivastava[2], and Donghu Sun[1]

[1] Department of Computer Science, Florida State University
Tallahassee, FL 32306
Phone: (850) 644-0050 **Fax:** (850) 644-0058
`liux@cs.fsu.edu`
[2] Department of Statistics, Florida State University
Tallahassee, 32306

Abstract. This paper presents an MCMC stochastic gradient algorithm for finding representations with optimal retrieval performance on given image datasets. For linear subspaces in the image space and the spectral space, the problem is formulated as that of optimization on a Grassmann manifold. By exploiting the underlying geometry of the manifold, a computationally effective algorithm is developed. The feasibility and effectiveness of the proposed algorithm are demonstrated through extensive experimental results.

1   Introduction

With the advances in imaging and video sensor technology, digital images and video data are available at an increasing speed. Content-based image and video retrieval has attracted great attention in many applications. Despite significant advances in recent years, the performance of image retrieval algorithms is still not satisfactory as the users are interested in semantically meaningful images, which, unfortunately, is computationally very difficult to capture. This problem is known as the semantic gap [13, 14].

In this paper, we present an algorithm that can be used to improve retrieval performance by explicitly finding optimal representations for retrieval applications. While it does not solve the semantic gap problem, it offers a method to reduce the semantic gap through labeled training images. The key to the proposed algorithm is to formulate the problem on Grassmann manifold and to utilize an effective optimization algorithm on the manifold. The experimental results demonstrate the feasibility and effectiveness of the proposed method.

The paper is organized as follows. In Section 2 we formulate the problem and present an MCMC stochastic solution. Section 3 shows extensive experimental results to demonstrate the feasibility and effectiveness of the proposed algorithm. Section 4 concludes the paper.

E. M. Bakker et al. (Eds.): CIVR 2003, LNCS 2728, pp. 50–60, 2003.

2   Optimal Linear Subspace for Retrieval

In this paper, we adopt an example-based learning methodology to compute representations that provide optimal retrieval performance. This assumption can be generally satisfied for image retrieval applications, as labeled images can be generated or collected interactively using some existing retrieval systems.

2.1   Image and Spectral Spaces

Before we introduce the main algorithm for finding optimal linear subspaces, we briefly describe two spaces that are used in this paper, namely the image space and the spectral space. In first case, each image is viewed as one point in a high dimensional vector space. This framework has been widely used in recognition, where principal component analysis and Fisher discriminant analysis are derived based on this formulation. It is easy to see that in this representation all the images need to have the same length in order to perform dimension reduction using subspace methods.

The other representation used in this paper is called the *spectral* space [10], where each image is represented by a vector formed by concatenating histograms of filtered images obtained using a set of filters. The filters can be designed based on some mathematical criteria or can be learned from images [7]. This representation has been shown to be effective for texture classification as well as face and object recognition. Recently, it has been shown systematically through sampling [7] that it is sufficient to synthesize faces and objects. See [10] and references therein for details on the spectral representation.

2.2   Problem Formulation

We start with a formulation of the problem for finding optimal linear representations [9, 8], where the performance can be estimated. Mathematically, let $U \in \mathbb{R}^{n \times d}$ be an orthonormal basis of an d-dimensional subspace of $\mathbb{R}^n$, where n is the size of an image (or the length of the spectral representation) and d is the required dimension of the optimal subspace ($n >> d$). For an image I (or its spectral representation), considered as a column vector of size n, the vector of coefficients is given by $a(I, U) = U^T I \in \mathbb{R}^d$. In case of spectral representation, $a(I, U) = U^T H(I)$, where $H(I)$ represents the histograms of filtered images. Let $\mathcal{G}_{n,d}$ be the set of all d-dimensional subspaces of $\mathbb{R}^n$; it is called a Grassmann manifold [2]. Let U be an orthonormal basis in $\mathbb{R}^{n \times d}$ such that $span(U)$ is the given subspace and let $F(U)$ be a retrieval performance measure associated with a system that uses U as the linear representation. That is, $F : \mathcal{G}_{n,d} \mapsto \mathbb{R}_+$ is the performance function and we want to search for the optimal subspace defined as:

$$\hat{U} = \underset{U \in \mathcal{G}_{n,d}}{\operatorname{argmax}} F(U) \tag{1}$$

We perform the search in a probabilistic framework by defining a probability density function

$$f(X) = \frac{1}{Z(T)} \exp(F(X)/T) \tag{2}$$

where $T \in \mathbb{R}$ plays the role of temperature and f is a density with respect to the Haar measure on the set $\mathcal{G}_{n,d}$.

2.3   Optimization via Simulated Annealing

We have chosen a Monte Carlo version of simulated annealing process to estimate the optimal subspace $\hat{U}$. Since the Grassmann manifold $\mathcal{G}_{n,d}$ is a curved space, the gradient process has to account for its intrinsic geometry. We first describe a deterministic gradient process (of F) on $\mathcal{G}_{n,d}$ and then generalize it to a Markov chain Monte Carlo (MCMC) type simulated annealing process.

The performance function F can be viewed as a scalar-field on $\mathcal{G}_{n,d}$. A necessary condition for $\hat{U}$ to be a maximum is that for any tangent vector at $\hat{U}$, the directional derivative of F, in the direction of that vector, should be zero. The directional derivatives on $\mathcal{G}_{n,d}$ are defined as follows. Let E_{ij} be an $n \times n$ skew-symmetric matrix such that: for $1 \leq i \leq d$ and $d < j \leq n$,

$$E_{ij}(k,l) = \begin{cases} 1 & \text{if } k = i,\ l = j \\ -1 & \text{if } k = j,\ l = i \\ 0 & \text{otherwise} \end{cases} \tag{3}$$

There are $d(n-d)$ such matrices and they form an orthogonal basis of the vector space tangent to $\mathcal{G}_{n,d}$ at identity. The gradient vector of F at any point U is defined to be a skew-symmetric matrix given by:

$$A(U) = (\sum_{i=1}^{d} \sum_{j=d+1}^{n} \alpha_{ij}(U)E_{ij}) \in \mathbb{R}^{n \times n},$$
$$\text{where } \alpha_{ij} = \frac{F(Q_t^T e^{\epsilon E_{ij}} \tilde{I}_d) - F(U)}{\epsilon}. \tag{4}$$

where α_{ij} is the finite approximation of the directional derivative of F in the direction given by E_{ij}, $e^{\epsilon E_{ij}}$ is an $n \times n$ rotation matrix, and $Q_t \in \mathbb{R}^{n \times n}$ is any orthogonal matrix such that $Q_t U = \begin{bmatrix} I_d \\ 0 \end{bmatrix} \equiv \tilde{I}_d \in \mathbb{R}^{n \times d}$. For numerical implementation, given a step size $\Delta > 0$, we will denote the discrete gradient process by X_t. Then, a discrete updating along the gradient direction is given by:

$$X_{t+1} = Q_t^T \exp(\Delta A_t) Q X_t$$
$$\text{where } A_t = \sum_{i=1}^{d} \sum_{j=d+1}^{n} \alpha_{ij}(X_t)E_{ij} \tag{5}$$

The gradient process X_t given by Eqn. 5 can be stuck in a local maximum. To alleviate the local maximum problem, a stochastic component is often added to the gradient process to form a diffusion [4]. Both simulated annealing and stochastic gradients have [12] frequently been used to seek global optimizers [3].

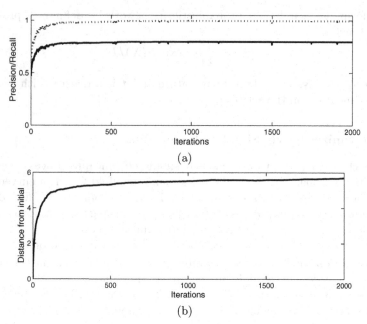

Fig. 1. Temporal evolution of the optimization algorithm. Here $d = 20$, $R = 10$, $k_{db} = 8$, and $k_{query} = 2$. (a) Plots of retrieval precision (solid line) and the corresponding recall (dotted line). (b) Distance of X_t from X_0

To obtain stochastic gradients, we add a random component to Eqn. 4 according to

$$\tilde{A}(X_t)\varDelta = A(X_t)\varDelta + \sqrt{2\varDelta T}\sum_{i=1}^{d}\sum_{j=d+1}^{n} w_{ij}(t)E_{ij}, \qquad (6)$$

where $w_{ij}(t)$'s are $i.i.d$ standard normals. Under this setting, the discrete time update of the stochastic process becomes the following:

$$X_{t+1} = Q_t^T \exp(\tilde{A}(X(t))\varDelta)\tilde{I}_d,$$
$$Q_{t+1} = \exp(-\varDelta \, dX_t)Q_t \qquad (7)$$

In case of MCMC simulated annealing, we use this stochastic gradient process to generate a candidate for the next point along the process but accept it only with a certain probability. That is, the right side of the second equation in Eqn. 7 becomes a candidate Y that may or may not be selected as the next point X_{t+1}.

Algorithm 1 MCMC Simulated Annealing: Let $X(0) = U_0 \in \mathcal{G}_{n,d}$ be any initial condition. Set $t = 0$.

1. Calculate the gradient matrix $A(X_t)$ according to Eqn. 4.
2. Generate $d(n - d)$ independent realizations, w_{ij}'s, from standard normal density. With X_t, calculate the candidate value Y as X_{t+1} according to Eqns. 6 and 7.
3. Compute $F(Y)$, $F(X_t)$, and set $dF = F(Y) - F(X_t)$.
4. Set $X_{t+1} = Y$ with probability $\min\{\exp(dF/T_t), 1\}$, else set $X_{t+1} = X_t$.
5. Modify T, set $t = t + 1$, and go to Step 1.

The resulting process X_t forms a Markov chain. This algorithm is a particularization of Algorithm A.20 (p. 200) in the book by Robert and Casella [12]. Please consult that text for the convergence properties of X_t.

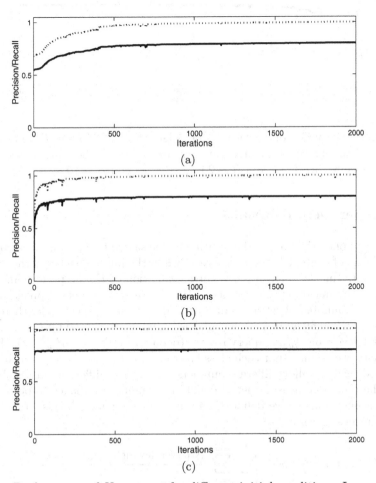

Fig. 2. Performance of X_t versus t for different initial conditions. In each plot, the solid line represents the precision measure and the dashed line corresponding recall measure. (a) $X_0 = U_{PCA}$. (b) $X_0 = U_{ICA}$. (c) $X_0 = U_{FDA}$

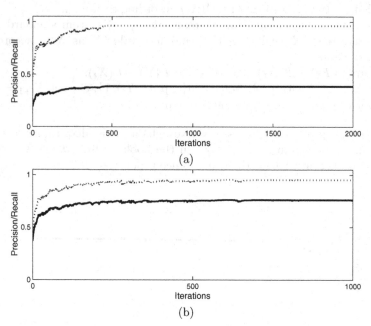

Fig. 3. Performance of X_t versus t for different values of d and R. In each plot, the solid line represents the precision measure and the dashed line corresponding recall measure. (a) $d = 5$ and $R = 20$. (b) $d = 10$ and $R = 10$

3 Experimental Results

We have applied the proposed algorithm to the search for optimal linear bases in the context of content-based image retrieval in the image space and the spectral space. Note that the algorithm requires evaluation of F (the performance measure) for any linear representation U. Here we use the retrieval precision as F with a fixed number of retrieved images [11]. To be more specific, let there are C classes in an image dataset; each class has k_{db} images (denoted by $I_{c,1}, \ldots, I_{c,k_{db}}$) to be retrieved and k_{query} query images (denoted by $I'_{c,1}, \ldots, I'_{c,k_{query}}$). Here for simplicity, we assume that each class has the same k_{db} and k_{query}, which can be modified easily to allow different numbers of images in different classes. To evaluate the precision measure, let R denote the number of images to be retrieved for each query image, we define F as the average retrieval precision for all the query images, given by

$$F(U) = \frac{1}{Ck_{query}} \sum_{c=1}^{C} \sum_{i=1}^{k_{query}} \frac{\text{No. of relevant images retrieved}}{R}. \tag{8}$$

Because the total number of relevant images is known in this setting, for each $F(U)$, the corresponding average *recall* measure is given by $F(U) * R/k_{db}$. Note that the optimal performance of $F(U)$ is given by $\min\{1, k_{db}/R\}$.

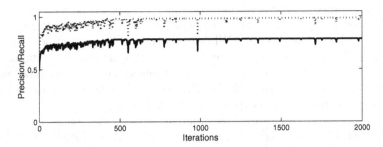

Fig. 4. Temporal evolution of X_t on the ORL dataset in the spectral space. Here $d = 20$, $R = 10$, $k_{db} = 8$, and $k_{query} = 2$. Here solid line shows the retrieval precision and dotted line the corresponding recall

Before we proceed further, we briefly describe the two image datasets that have been used in our experiments: the ORL face recognition dataset[1] and a Brodatz texture dataset[2]. The ORL dataset consists of faces of 40 different subjects with 10 images each. The texture dataset consists of textures of 40 textures with 16 images in each class. We are currently applying this algorithm to commonly used image retrieval datasets.

Figures 1 - 4 show the results on the ORL database with different initial conditions in both the image space and the spectral space. Figure 1 shows a case with a random initial condition. Fig. 1(b) (the distance plot) highlights the fact that the algorithm moves effectively on the Grassmann manifold going large distances along the chain. Together with Fig. 1(a), it shows multiple subspaces that lead to perfect performance.

Figure 2 shows three cases when X_0 is set to U_{PCA}, U_{ICA}, or U_{FDA}. FDA was calculated using a procedure given in [1] and ICA was calculated using a FastICA algorithm proposed by Hyvärinen [6]. In these experiments, $d = 20$, $R = 10$, $k_{db} = 8$, and $k_{query} = 2$. While these commonly used linear bases provide a variety of performances, the proposed algorithm converges to subspaces with the best retrieval precision performance regardless of the initial condition. While U_{FDA} in this particular case gives a performance close to the optimal one, however the optimality of U_{FDA} depends on the assumptions that the underlying distributions are Gaussian and linear discriminant function is used [9]. Therefore, theoretically, U_{FDA} produces only suboptimal performance (see [9] for examples). Similar to the earlier result, these results also point to the effectiveness of this optimization approach. In fact, for any chosen initial condition, the search process converges to a perfect solution (in that it gives the best achievable performance) and moves effectively along the Grassmann manifold. Also these solutions are quite different from each other, allowing additional constraints to be imposed.

---

[1] http://www.uk.research.att.com/facedatabase.html

[2] http://www-dbv.cs.uni-bonn.de/image/texture.tar.gz

We have studied the variation of optimal performance versus the subspace rank denoted by d and the number of images retrieved denoted by R. Fig. 3 shows two cases with $d = 5$ and $d = 10$. While the optimal solution does not achieve the best achievable performance, it is very close to that as shown by the precision and recall curves. In some image retrieval applications, the computation time may be more important than the performance. The algorithm can be used to find the best compromise between accuracy and computation.

The previous three figures show different cases in the image space. As face images used here are roughly aligned, the linear representations in the image space work well on the ORL dataset. Fig. 4 shows a case in the spectral space on the ORL dataset. It shows that the performance using spectral representation is comparable with that in the image space. The significance of the result is that it shows the spectral representation is sufficient to characterize different faces. In addition, it can be used to characterize textures, making it a good representation for image retrieval applications where images are not confined to particular types in general.

Figures 5 and 6 show the results on the texture dataset. Fig. 5 shows a typical case in the image space, where Fig. 5(a) shows the performance and Fig. 5(b) the corresponding distance from X_0. As Fig. 5(b) shows, the MCMC algorithm moves effectively in the image space as the distance is constantly increasing. However, the performance, (shown in Fig. 5(a)), while improved significantly compared to the initial performance (the precision is improved from 0.139 to 0.544), is still not satisfactory. The main reason is that texture models must be translation invariant while the subspaces of the image space are not. In contrast, the subspaces in the spectral space are very effective. Fig. 6 shows two typical cases. The algorithm converges quickly to representations that give the optimal achievable performance. Note that while the performance does not change, the representations are constantly evolving, which shows there are multiple solutions that have the perfect performance.

These results underscore two important points about Algorithm 1: (i) the algorithm is consistently successful in seeking optimal linear basis from a variety of initial conditions, and (ii) the algorithm moves effectively on the manifold $\mathcal{G}_{n,d}$ with the final solution being far from the initial condition. We have also compared empirically the performances of these optimal subspaces with the frequently used subspaces, namely U_{PCA}, U_{ICA}, and U_{FDA}. Fig. 7 shows the precision/recall performance for the ORL dataset in the image space. The plots are obtained by varying R, the number of retrieved images. This comparison confirms the effectiveness of the optimal representation and shows a potential significant performance improvement.

4   Conclusion

In this paper, we have proposed a simulated annealing algorithm on Grassmann manifolds to find the optimal linear subspaces in the image space and the spectral space for image retrieval applications. The experimental results demonstrate that

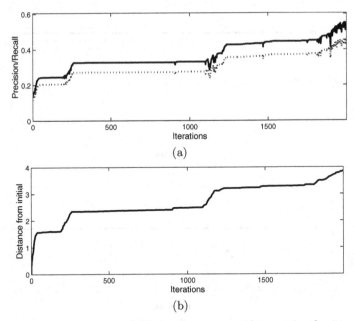

Fig. 5. Temporal evolution of X_t on the texture dataset in the image space. Here $d = 20$, $R = 10$, $k_{db} = 12$, and $k_{query} = 4$. (a) Plots of retrieval precision (solid line) and the corresponding recall (dotted line). (b) Distance of X_t from X_0

the algorithm provides an effective tool to improve retrieval performances. The algorithm also makes it possible to improve any performance measure that can be evaluate numerically. For example, it can be used to incorporate the feedbacks from users by defining a performance measure that depends on the feedbacks.

Obviously, developing an effective content-based image retrieval system, involves many factors, some theoretical and some implementational. To the authors' best knowledge, this algorithm is the first attempt to systematically find optimal representations for image retrieval applications. While the datasets used are not very large compared to typical image retrieval datasets, they consist of representative natural images and therefore the experimental results are convincing and significant. We believe that our algorithm provides an effective tool that can be used to improve performance significantly.

Acknowledgments

We thank the producers of the ORL and texture datasets for making them available to the public. This research has been supported in part by the grants NSF DMS-0101429, ARO DAAD19-99-1-0267, and NMA 201-01-2010.

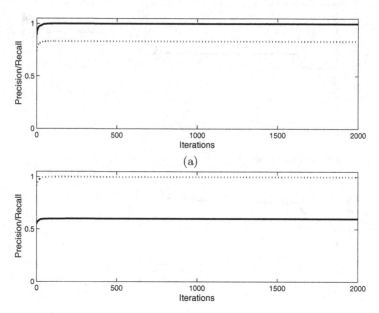

Fig. 6. Performance of X_t versus t for the texture dataset with different values of R in the spectral space. the solid line represents the precision measure and the dashed line corresponding recall measure. Here $d = 20$, $k_{db} = 12$, $k_{query} = 4$. (a) $R = 10$. (b) $R = 20$

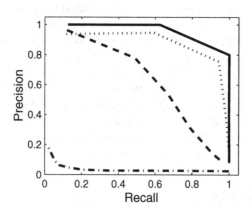

Fig. 7. The precision/recall performance of different linear subspaces on the ORL dataset. Here solid line is the optimal basis from the gradient search process, dotted line FDA, dashed line PCA, and dash-dotted line ICA. The results are obtained by varying the number of images retrieved (R)

References

[1] P. N. Belhumeur, J. P. Hepanha, and D. J. Kriegman, "Eigenfaces vs. fisherfaces: Recognition using class specific linear projection," *IEEE Transactions on Pattern Analysis and Machine Intelligence*, vol. 19(7), pp. 711–720, 1997. 56

[2] W. M. Boothby, *An Introduction to Differential Manifolds and Riemannian Geometry*, Academic Press, 2003. 51

[3] S. Geman and C.-R. Hwang, "Diffusions for global optimization," *SIAM J. Control and Optimization*, vol. 24(24), pp. 1031–1043, 1987. 52

[4] U. Grenander and M. I. Miller, "Representations of knowledge in complex systems," *Journal of the Royal Statistical Society*, vol. 56(3), pp. 549–603, 1994. 52

[5] U. Helmke and J. B. Moore, *Optimization and Dynamical Systmes*, Springer, 1996.

[6] A. Hyvarinen, "Fast and robust fixed-point algorithm for independent component analysis," *IEEE Transactions on Neural Networks*, vol. 10, pp. 626–634, 1999. 56

[7] X. Liu and L. Cheng, "Independent spectral representations of images for recognition," *Journal of the Optical Society of America A*, in press, 2003. 51

[8] X. Liu and A. Srivastava, "Stochastic search for optimal linear representations of images on spaces with orthogonality constraints," in *Proceedings of the International Workshop on Energy Minimization Methods in Computer Vision and Pattern Recognition*, 2003. 51

[9] X. Liu, A. Srivastava, and Kyle Gallivan, "Optimal linear representations of images for object recognition," *IEEE Transactions on Pattern Recognition and Machine Intelligence*, under review, 2003 (Available at http://www.stat.fsu.eud/~anuj). 51, 56

[10] X. Liu and D. L. Wang, "A spectral histogram model for texton modeling and texture discrimination," *Vision Research*, vol. 42, no. 23, pp. 2617–2634, 2002. 51

[11] H. Muller, W. Muller, D. M. Squire, S. Marchand-Maillet, and T. Pun, "Performance evaluation in content-based image retrieval: overview and proposals," *Pattern Recognition Letters*, vol. 22, pp. 593–601, 2001. 55

[12] C. P. Robert and G. Casella, *Monte Carlo Statistical Methods*, Springer, 1999. 52, 54

[13] Y. Rui, T. S. Huang, "Image retrieval: Current techniques, promising directions and open issues," *Journal of Visual Communication and Image Representation*, vol. 10, pp. 39–62, 1999. 50

[14] A. W. M. Smeulders, M. Worring, S. Santini, A. Gupta, and R. Jain, "Content-based image retrieval at the end of the early years," *IEEE Transactions on Pattern Analysis and Machine Intelligence*, vol. 22, pp. 1–32, 2000. 50

A Closer Look at Boosted Image Retrieval

Nicholas R. Howe

Smith College
Northampton, Massachusetts

Abstract. Margin-maximizing techniques such as boosting have been
generating excitement in machine learning circles for several years now.
Although these techniques offer significant improvements over previous
methods on classification tasks, little research has examined the application of techniques such as boosting to the problem of retrieval from
image and video databases. This paper looks at boosting for image retrieval and classification, with a comparative evaluation of several top
algorithms combined in two different ways with boosting. The results
show that boosting improves retrieval precision and recall (as expected),
but that variations in the way boosting is applied can significantly affect
the degree of improvement observed. An analysis suggests guidelines for
the best way to apply boosting for retrieval with a given image representation.

1 Introduction

The fields of machine learning and visual information retrieval have independently each seen gratifying research progress of late. Boosting [4], support vector machines [1] and other so-called *large-margin techniques* consistently demonstrate improved performance when applied on top of older, more established
classification methods from machine learning. Simultaneously, researchers in the
field of image and video retrieval have devised new representations that allow
quick comparisons between images based upon multiple cues – color and texture
distributions, for example. Retrieval techniques using automatically extracted
feature vectors, such as color correlograms [8], redundant banks of texture filters [3], and others [7] have shown measurable improvements over earlier, more
simplistic methods such as color histograms [11]. These two bodies of research
combined have the potential to generate powerful image classification and retrieval algorithms, and video retrieval algorithms by extension. Unfortunately,
with a few exceptions [12, 2], very little current research appeals to both fields
by incorporating the best elements of each. The combination of the newer image
analysis techniques with the concurrent advances in machine learning turns out
to contain subtle complexities that have not been adequately addressed to date.

Incorporating boosting into retrieval algorithms necessarily implies moving
away from the single-image query typical of many works on information retrieval [3, 7, 8, 11], since boosting requires a *set* of positive and negative examples to work. Fortunately, there is a movement afoot in the field as a whole in

E. M. Bakker et al. (Eds.): CIVR 2003, LNCS 2728, pp. 61–70, 2003.
© Springer-Verlag Berlin Heidelberg 2003

this direction, toward approaches that might automatically compare images in a collection with a library of different models for classification and subsequent retrieval via keywords. A boosted classifier provides a promising candidate model for such a library. If single-image queries are desirable or necessary for some applications, then boosting may still prove useful, employing the top set of retrieved images (hand-classified online by the user) as the training set. In this mode, boosting represents a way to move from simply retrieving a few images related to the query, toward locating the entire set of images of a target class that are available in the database.

While this paper does not attempt to address all these possibilities at once, it does examine the fundamentals of combining boosting with a range of promising image comparison methods. It examines several candidate approaches (as detailed in Section 2), since the best way to incorporate boosting using these techniques has not yet been established. In particular, a novel approach is developed herein using conic decision boundaries that allows boosting to be combined with any of the leading image representations. Section 3 gives the experimental procedure, and a summary of the findings appears in Section 4. The experimental results show the conic-boundary method to work better with the high-dimensional image representations that are becoming more common today.

2   The Problem

Several characteristics of image comparison techniques make the straightforward application of boosting difficult. Image representations typically exhibit a high number of linearly nonseparable dimensions. This makes the use of machine learning mainstays such as C4.5 [9] both slower and less effective than they are in the sorts of problems typically looked at by the learning community. The comparison metrics developed for image retrieval, on the other hand, also form an incomplete foundation for boosting. Oriented towards retrieval rather than classification, they do not address the issue of establishing a classification threshold. More significantly, these techniques are designed to measure image similarities given a *single* target image; they do not necessarily handle a set of target images, possibly with weights indicating their importance. For boosting, incorporating such a weighted set of targets is essential.

The naïve approach to expanding from a single-target technique to a multiple-target technique would be to use some linear combination of the representations of the multiple targets, such as the mean. Unfortunately, this method does not work: typically the combined representation is significantly *worse* at picking out members of the class than many of the individual training examples alone [6]. This reflects the complexity of image classes: they tend to be only diffusely clustered in any given image representation, interspersed with non-members of the class, and rife with outliers. Linear combinations of positive feature vectors typically lie closer to negative examples than to the positive examples they are drawn from, and therefore serve as a poorer basis for classification.

2.1   Boosting in Context

Boosting began as a technique for combining differently-trained classifiers with unique sets of strengths and weaknesses. Properly done, a weighted vote of each classifiers' predictions can reinforce the strengths and cancel out the weaknesses [10]. Thus a classification algorithm that displays marginal success (accuracy slightly better than chance) can be "boosted" into an algorithm with much higher accuracy. AdaBoost [4] first provided a widely known algorithmic approach to boosting. Since then, many variants have appeared that seek to address some of its shortcomings, such as intolerance to errors in the training data [5], but AdaBoost continues to be widely used.

AdaBoost and boosting algorithms in general require a base learning algorithm, often referred to as a *weak learner*, that can classify any set of weighted instances with better than 50% accuracy. With a two-class system, such weak learners are not hard to develop: nearly any division of the space of possible instances will do. Although the theoretical results place only weak requirements on the base algorithm, empirical experience suggests that more powerful base classifiers tend to work better when boosted [4]. The base classifier is trained in successive rounds on different subsets or weightings of the initial training data, producing the required set of differently-trained classifiers that can be combined to produce a final, more reliable classification. Those interested in retrieval applications should note that the algorithm actually produces a numeric score for each instance that when thresholded yields a classification, but which might as easily be used to rank the images for retrieval.

Boosting has been shown to exhibit a number of desirable properties, particularly a resistance to overfitting the training data. Yet in spite of the success of boosting in other areas, little work has been done to date in applying it to images. Tieu and Viola [12] use a feature-selection algorithm equivalent to simple boosting, but the focus of their work is elsewhere. Perhaps one reason that so little attention has been devoted to the topic is that researchers working with images have focused mainly on retrieval rather than classification. Only recently have algorithms developed that offer reasonable classification performance on any but the simplest of image categories.

2.2   Two Approaches

In order to apply boosting to most extant image representations designed for retrieval, one must first decide how to adapt a representation designed for pairwise determination of similarity so as to produce a class decision boundary. In doing so, one may decide to adopt an approach that has more of the flavor found in traditional machine learning, or one may opt instead for an approach that retains more of the flavor of the original image retrieval technique. This paper looks at representatives of both of these paths. The first approach uses simple single-dimension thresholded decision boundaries. Intuitively, it looks for dimensions (a.k.a. *features*) demonstrating exceptional values that happen to be highly correlated with membership in the class. The second approach uses the entire vector for comparison. It achieves this by using a thresholded cosine metric (measuring the angle between two normalized vectors) to yield classifiers whose decision surfaces are hypercones. Intuitively, it looks for images that are similar enough to the exemplar image according to the cosine metric. One might expect either or both of these approaches to work better, depending upon the underlying image representation chosen.

Regardless of the method, any simple classifier used for boosting must conform to a few simple assumptions. As input it receives two collections of vectors, V_p and V_n, containing respectively the representations of positive and negative training examples of the class to be learned. In addition it receives a collection of weights on these vectors, W_p and W_n, indicating the importance placed upon learning to classify the corresponding training example. From these inputs, the classifier should generate a rule that classifies any image representation $\mathbf{v}$ as either a class member or not; this may be thought of as a function from the space of possible representations $\mathcal{V}$ onto $\{0, 1\}$. Section 3.1 describes several common image feature spaces $\mathcal{V}$ used in this paper.

Two features of most image representations make them somewhat different from many of the types of data typically used with boosting. They tend to be of very high dimension, with some schemes using tens of thousands of dimensions [6, 12]. The correlations between individual dimensions tend to be unknown and presumably highly complicated. Furthermore, any single individual dimension typically has low correlation with any interesting image class: there are few "smoking guns". These considerations have led to the development of the two techniques described in detail below, one which concentrates on individual features, and one which looks at the vector representation as a whole.

Feature-Based Boosting The first method, denoted hereafter as *feature-based boosting*, or *FBoost* for brevity, creates a simple classifier as follows. For each dimension in $\mathcal{V}$, it sorts the values found in V_p and V_n, removing duplicates, to determine a complete set of candidate decision thresholds. It then scores each of these decision thresholds in terms of the weighted error rate it would generate if used as a classifier on the training set. The best threshold is computed for each individual dimension, and the best of these becomes the rule used to classify unknown instances.

Feature-based boosting represents a fairly traditional way to apply boosting. Tieu and Viola [12] adopt this approach in their work. From a machine-learning viewpoint, FBoost is equivalent to using decision trees with a single branch (also called *decision stumps*) as the base classifier. Friedman, Hastie, & Tibshirani [5] present evidence that the simplicity of the decision stumps as compared to full decision trees is unimportant, as it may be counteracted by performing a sufficient number of boosting steps.

Vector-Based Boosting The second method, denoted hereafter as *vector-based boosting*, or *VBoost* for brevity, represents a non-traditional application of boosting concepts with no close analogues known to the author. Hypercones form the decision surface of the base classifier. Class membership may be quickly determined by thresholding the dot product of the normalized candidate feature vector with the unit vector along the axis of the hypercone. (Although this is equivalent to selecting a single feature under some arbitrary basis transformation, the transformation changes with each round of boosting.)

Implementing boosting effectively with this type of classifier turns out to require some creativity. If only the positive training instances are used as cone axes in creating the weak classifiers, then the resulting set of decision boundaries lacks enough variety for effective boosting. (The algorithm quickly reaches a point where none of the available decision boundaries are of high quality.) On the other hand, allowing any axis at all leaves an infinite number of possible decision boundaries to check, with no guide towards finding the best one. A compromise heuristic is therefore used, with reasonable results produced in practice. The algorithm described below consistently generates individual classifiers with greater than 50% accuracy even after many successive rounds of boosting.

Let $\mathbf{v}_p$ and $\mathbf{v}_n$ be the sum of the vectors in V_p and V_n respectively, as weighted by the weights in W_p and W_n. Consider the hyperplane that bisects the angle between $\mathbf{v}_p$ and $\mathbf{v}_n$. Experience shows that the majority of the weight of positive examples will tend to lie on one side of the hyperplane, while the majority of the weight of negative examples will tend to lie on the other side. (Usually the positive examples are clustered on the $\mathbf{v}_p$ side, but if this is not the case the algorithm simply exchanges the classification labels for that round of boosting.) The dot product with a vector orthogonal to the bisecting hyperplane therefore proves useful in discriminating between positive and negative examples (see Figure 1). The heuristic algorithm calculates the orthogonal vector $\mathbf{v}_\perp$ according to Equation 1 and then computes its dot product with all the training vectors.

$$\mathbf{v}_\perp = \mathbf{v}_p - \frac{\mathbf{v}_n \cdot (\mathbf{v}_p + \mathbf{v}_n)}{\|\mathbf{v}_p + \mathbf{v}_n\|} \tag{1}$$

As was the case for the previous classifier, the range of dot products between $\mathbf{v}_\perp$ and the elements of the training set offers a finite choice of decision thresholds. The best can be chosen simply by computing the weighted training error for each possibility. VBoost runs relatively faster as the number of dimensions rises, because threshold selection happens only once, as opposed to once per dimension for FBoost.

3   Experimental Procedure

The experimental procedure described below has three axes of variation: the image representation used, the type of base classfier used for boosting, and the image category used. Of these, the comparisons between image representations and between base classifiers are most interesting. All experiments are performed on the same set, comprising 20,100 images from the Corel photo library. Corel images have been used in many works on image retrieval, and more details on

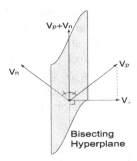

Fig. 1. Schematic illustration of $\mathbf{v}_\perp$

this set of images are available elsewhere [6]. The Corel collection exhibits strong correlations in image composition within many image categories.

All experiments use 5×2-fold cross-validation: For each of five replications, the image set is split in half, with half of the positive instances in each fold. Each fold is used to train a classifier, and its performance is tested on the opposite fold. Comparing results across the five replications provides an estimate of the deviation.

3.1   Image Representation

Three image representations (correlograms, Stairs, T-V) come from relatively recent work on ways of describing images that preserve multiple primitive image cues: color, texture, relative location, etc. Correlograms [8] assemble statistical information about color co-occurrences on the pixel level. Correlogram features are of the form "the probability that a pixel B at distance x from pixel A has the same color as A." Stairs [7] explicitly records the patches of color and texture found in different locations within the image. Thus each feature in Stairs represents the presence or absence of a patch with one discrete combination of color, texture, and location. An unnamed technique introduced by Tieu and Viola [12], henceforth referred to as T-V, registers the output of banks of layered color and texture filters. A feature in this representation corresponds to the output of a set of three successively applied filters summed over the entire image. Finally, color histograms [11] are a well-established representation, included here as a control. Each feature in a color histogram represents the percentage of the image that is of a particular discrete color.

The T-V representation is altered somewhat here in order to achieve a practical algorithm. The original representation stores about 50,000 numbers per image. With a collection of 20,100 images, therefore, the entire data set occupies roughly 8 GB of memory. While this may easily fit on a disk, it will not fit into memory for efficient processing. An approximation yields the necessary reduction in required memory: the values are normalized by subtracting the mean for each feature and dividing by the standard deviation, after which values differing from the mean by fewer than 2.5 standard deviations are set to zero. This allows the data to be stored as a sparse matrix with about 10^7 elements. Tieu and Viola hypothesize that the success of their method stems from extreme feature values in the range of 4 or more standard deviations, so we posit that this approximation should not unduly affect performance. On the other hand, it is problematic for the images that show no features at all with values more than 2.5 standard deviations from the mean (roughly one third of the test collection). Tieu and Viola do not address the memory issue since they run tests with only 3000 images.

3.2 Boosting Application

Strictly speaking, only one boosting algorithm, AdaBoost [4], is used in all experiments. Rather, the variations presented come from changing the base classifier used, as described in the previous section. Although the base classifier used for boosting makes no difference in theory, common wisdom holds that some bases make for better boosting than others. Because the two methods used here work quite differently, any disparity in their performance should be instructive. As a control, the experiment includes a third, unboosted classifier. In order to give a more meaningful comparison to the boosted algorithms, this is not simply a single application of the base classifier (which does quite poorly). Rather, the control is a nearest-neighbor classifier using the best exemplars of the class as selected by a greedy additive approach [6], a method which outperforms retrieval using any single exemplar image.

3.3 Image Categories

Five hand-defined categories reflect a moderate range of difficulty and subject category: *Sun* (226 images of sunrises and sunsets), *Wolf* (110 images of wolves), *Church* (101 images of churches), *Tiger* (100 images of tigers), and *Car* (100 images of Formula 1 race cars). Although the number of categories is small, the choices include both natural and manufactured objects, full scenes and specific entities within scenes, and wide variation in ease of retrieval.

4 Results

Table 1 shows the mean area under a recall-precision curve computed for each of the 60 ($4 \times 3 \times 5$) experimental conditions, as a percent of total possible area. The data are grouped by image category, since the most interesting variations in performance show up when the category is held constant. The deviations shown come from the variation observed between the five folds of the experiment.

The results display some interesting trends. First of all, boosting improves recall and precision over the corresponding control in nearly all cases (36 out of 40 comparisons). This result is not automatic, since the control case is not a (straw-man) single application of the boosted classifier, but an effective nearest-neighbor classifier using the best exemplars of the class. A single application of the unboosted base classifier in fact does little better than chance (Table 2).

Table 1. Percent area under the recall-precision curve for two boosting methods and an unboosted control. The best method in each group of three is boldface, as are methods with overlapping standard deviations. The best method in each group of twelve is underlined, as are methods with overlapping standard deviations

Method	Hist	Corr	Stairs	T-V	
Control	5.0 ± 0.7	19.3 ± 1.7	17.8 ± 1.9	0.7 ± 0.1	Sun
VBoost	27.2 ± 4.0	**57.2 ± 4.1**	26.4 ± 1.8	**19.8 ± 2.3**	
FBoost	**39.3 ± 4.8**	41.4 ± 8.9	**31.4 ± 2.2**	**21.6 ± 3.2**	
Control	1.7 ± 0.3	2.0 ± 0.6	1.4 ± 0.1	0.5 ± 0.0	Church
VBoost	**2.4 ± 0.5**	<u>**5.9 ± 3.0**</u>	<u>**3.7 ± 1.4**</u>	**1.8 ± 0.5**	
FBoost	**2.5 ± 0.4**	<u>**4.7 ± 1.3**</u>	<u>**6.0 ± 1.3**</u>	**1.8 ± 0.5**	
Control	37.2 ± 3.0	12.9 ± 3.9	2.7 ± 0.2	0.4 ± 0.0	Car
VBoost	14.6 ± 1.5	50.0 ± 3.8	**52.9 ± 4.4**	2.3 ± 0.4	
FBoost	**56.3 ± 5.4**	**61.1 ± 5.0**	**49.8 ± 3.6**	2.0 ± 0.6	
Control	43.2 ± 3.8	30.1 ± 3.3	2.5 ± 0.2	0.4 ± 0.0	Tiger
VBoost	11.8 ± 0.7	35.9 ± 3.0	13.7 ± 2.2	**0.8 ± 0.2**	
FBoost	**49.6 ± 5.8**	**46.7 ± 4.8**	**22.9 ± 3.6**	0.6 ± 0.1	
Control	9.2 ± 1.5	12.3 ± 3.1	4.1 ± 0.6	0.5 ± 0.0	Wolf
VBoost	6.6 ± 0.9	**13.5 ± 1.9**	**14.4 ± 3.9**	1.6 ± 0.3	
FBoost	**9.8 ± 1.6**	10.5 ± 1.1	**16.8 ± 4.8**	2.2 ± 0.7	

4.1 Comparing Boosting Types

Comparisons between the two types of boosting reveal trends according to the underlying image representation. For the histograms, feature-based boosting consistently performs better, achieving significantly higher performance on four of the five image classes. (Bold face type indicates the best boosting method in each category, along with any other method whose range of standard deviation overlaps with that of the best.) Correlograms give mixed results, with each boosting method doing better on two categories, and the fifth a statistical toss-up. For the Stairs and T-V, most of the results are statistically close, although FBoost does distinguishably better on two of the categories with Stairs.

Interestingly, the two methods appear most similar when the number of dimensions in the feature space grows large. The representations are listed in the table from left to right in order of increasing vector length: histograms (128 dimensions), correlograms (512), Stairs (19,200) and T-V (46,875). The last two columns show the largest number of statistical ties, and use the largest feature spaces. This result is interesting in that VBoost is much faster than FBoost for large dimensions, suggesting that it may be a better choice in these cases. (Another possibility is that some other factor may unite the two right-hand columns, such as a higher intercorrelation of the individual dimensions.)

Table 2. Percent area under the recall-precision curve for a single iteration of the base classifier. Without boosting, results are scarcely better than chance

Method	Hist	Corr	Stairs	T-V	Chance	Category
base VBoost	1.1 ± 0.1	19.7 ± 3.7	3.8 ± 1.1	1.7 ± 0.7	1.1	Sun
base FBoost	2.0 ± 0.9	5.9 ± 3.5	4.5 ± 1.3	7.3 ± 1.7		Sun
base VBoost	0.5 ± 0.1	0.5 ± 0.1	1.4 ± 1.0	0.5 ± 0.0	0.5	Chu.
base FBoost	0.5 ± 0.1	0.5 ± 0.1	0.6 ± 0.1	0.5 ± 0.1		Chu.
base VBoost	0.6 ± 0.1	7.8 ± 2.1	0.5 ± 0.0	0.5 ± 0.0	0.5	Car
base FBoost	0.7 ± 0.3	0.5 ± 0.0	0.8 ± 0.4	0.5 ± 0.1		Car
base VBoost	0.5 ± 0.1	1.2 ± 0.5	0.5 ± 0.0	0.5 ± 0.1	0.5	Tig.
base FBoost	0.5 ± 0.1	0.5 ± 0.1	0.8 ± 0.5	0.5 ± 0.0		Tig.
base VBoost	0.6 ± 0.1	1.1 ± 0.5	2.2 ± 0.6	0.6 ± 0.1	0.5	Wolf
base FBoost	0.6 ± 0.0	0.6 ± 0.1	2.6 ± 1.4	0.6 ± 0.1		Wolf

4.2 Comparing Image Representations

Several other trends reveal themselves in Table 1. First, although the T-V representation improves considerably under boosting, the ultimate performance using it does not match that of the other three representations. This may be in part because of the representational restrictions imposed, as described in Section 3.1. However, without some such approximation, it is difficult to see how to apply the technique to larger data sets.

Of the other three representations, histograms display the best overall score on one category (*Tiger*), correlograms on two (*Sun* and *Car*), and Stairs on two (*Church* and *Wolf*). The latter two categories proved hardest overall, implying that boosted Stairs may do well on more difficult visual concepts. However, at least one of the boosted correlogram results was statistically close to the best on every image category, so this may be the best method of those surveyed to choose when little is known about the target concept.

5 Conclusion

Boosting becomes relevant for image retrieval in two contexts: in systems where the user can provide a set of positive and negative exemplars (perhaps hand-labeled from the results of an initial retrieval attempt), and in systems designed to automatically annotate large collections with class tags according to previously learned concepts, for subsequent keyword retrieval. The results presented here may be viewed as indications of the potential of such systems, as well as (from a machine-learning perspective) raw classification ability. As expected, boosting improves the retrieval of image classes virtually across the board. The two different methods described herein for constructing boostable classifiers from a base image representation both yield better results than a competitive unboosted control. Of these, the method based upon individual features shows better results when the number of dimensions in the image representation is small, but runs slowly when the number of dimensions becomes large. For large feature spaces, the method based upon the entire vector runs more quickly while showing comparable performance. The former represents traditional applications of boosting, while the latter uses a novel type of decision boundary for the base classifier. This work shows that choices must be made about how to combine advanced image representations with boosting, and that the best approach may vary depending upon the image representation chosen and the classes to be learned.

References

[1] C. J. C. Burges. A tutorial on support vector machines for pattern recognition. *Data Mining and Knowledge Discovery*, 2(2):121–167, 1998. 61

[2] O. Chapelle, P. Haffner, and V. Vapnik. Support vector machines for histogram-based image classification. *IEEE Neural Networks*, 10(5):1055–1064, 1999. 61

[3] J. S. De Bonet and P. Viola. Structure driven image database retrieval. *Advances in Neural Information Processing*, 10, 1997. 61

[4] Y. Freund and R. E. Schapire. Experiments with a new boosting algorithm. In *Proceedings of the Thirteenth International Conference on Machine Learning*, pages 148–156, 1996. 61, 63, 67

[5] J. Friedman, T. Hastie, and R. Tibshirani. Additive logistic regression: a statistical view of boosting. Technical report, Dept. of Statistics, Stanford University, 1998. 63, 64

[6] N. R. Howe. *Analysis and Representations for Automatic Comparison, Classification and Retrieval of Digital Images*. PhD thesis, Cornell University, May 2001. 62, 64, 66, 67

[7] N. R. Howe and D. P. Huttenlocher. Integrating color, texture, and geometry for image retrieval. In *Proceedings of the IEEE Computer Society Conference on Computer Vision and Pattern Recognition*, pages "II:239–246", Los Alamitos, CA, 2000. IEEE Computer Society. 61, 66

[8] J. Huang, S. Ravi Kumar, M. Mitra, W. J. Zhu, and R. Zabih. Image indexing using color correlograms. In *Proceedings of the IEEE Computer Society Conference on Computer Vision and Pattern Recognition*, pages 762–768, Los Alamitos, CA, 1997. IEEE Computer Society. 61, 66

[9] J. R. Quinlan. *Programs for Machine Learning*. Morgan Kaufmann, San Mateo, CA, 1993. 62

[10] R. E. Schapire. The strength of weak learnability. *Machine Learning*, 5(2):197–227, 1990. 63

[11] M. Swain and D. Ballard. Color indexing. *International Journal of Computer Vision*, 7(1):11–32, 1991. 61, 66

[12] K. Tieu and P. Viola. Boosting image retrieval. In *Proceedings of the IEEE Computer Society Conference on Computer Vision and Pattern Recognition*, volume I, pages 228–235, 2000. 61, 63, 64, 66

HPAT Indexing for Fast Object/Scene Recognition Based on Local Appearance

Hao Shao[1], Tomáš Svoboda[1], Tinne Tuytelaars[2], and Luc Van Gool[1,2]

[1] Computer Vision Lab
Swiss Federal Institute of Technology
Zürich, Switzerland
{haoshao,svoboda,vangool}@vision.ee.ethz.ch
[2] ESAT, PSI
Katholieke Universiteit Leuven
Leuven, Belgium
{tinne.tuytelaars,luc.vangool}@esat.kuleuven.ac.be

Abstract. The paper describes a fast system for appearance based image recognition . It uses local invariant descriptors and efficient nearest neighbor search. First, local affine invariant regions are found nested at multiscale intensity extremas. These regions are characterized by nine generalized color moment invariants. An efficient novel method called HPAT (hyper-polyhedron with adaptive threshold) is introduced for efficient localization of the nearest neighbor in feature space.

The invariants make the method robust against changing illumination and viewpoint. The locality helps to resolve occlusions. The proposed indexing method overcomes the drawbacks of most binary tree-like indexing techniques, namely the high complexity in high dimensional data sets and the boundary problem. The database representation is very compact and the retrieval close to realtime on a standard PC. The performance of the proposed method is demonstrated on a public database containing 1005 images of urban scenes. Experiments with an image database containing objects are also presented.

1   Introduction

Most content-based image retrieval systems focus on the overall, qualitative similarity of scenes. Hence, global aspects like color gamuts and coarse spatial layout are among the features most often used. This paper deals with a somewhat different kind of retrieval, in the sense that images are sought that contain the same, prominent objects as the query image. One could e.g. look for images on the Internet with the same statue as contained in the query image, or the system could recognize one's location, by taking an image and looking for the most similar image in a large database of images taken all over a city. The latter type of application is given as an example further in the paper.

For the rather stringent type of similarity search propounded here, global and qualitative features no longer suffice. Hence, we propose the use of local

E. M. Bakker et al. (Eds.): CIVR 2003, LNCS 2728, pp. 71–80, 2003.

color patches as features, which are compared rather precisely. In particular, we propose to extract so-called invariant regions, which have become popular recently [1, 5, 2, 7]. Here, we use the intensity-based regions proposed by Tuytelaars and Van Gool [7]. Invariant regions correspond to small image patches, constructed around special seed points (here intensity extrema). These regions are special in that they automatically adapt their shapes in the image to the viewpoint of the camera. The crux of the matter is that this adaptation takes place without any knowledge about the viewpoint and without any comparison with other images in which the same regions are visible. Thus, in principle, the same physical parts are extracted from two images of the same scene, even if these have been taken from different viewpoints (and possibly under different illumination as well). In section 2.1, we introduce a multiscale approach that improves the repeatability of these regions. Once such regions have been extracted, the color pattern that they enclose is described on the basis of invariant features. The feature vectors make it possible to match invariant regions very efficiently, using hashing techniques. Such matching lies at the heart of our approach, since the similarity between images is quantified as the number of matching features.

However, since one image is represented by a large set of local invariant regions, the amount of data in the feature space is much higher than for global methods. As a result, feature matching becomes more complex and is usually performed in a high-dimensional space. Under these conditions, finding the nearest neighbor can become quite time consuming. Nene and Nayar proposed an efficient method to overcome this problem [4]. We contribute to this method by proposing a hyper-polyhedron instead of a hyper-cube as a better approximation of the hyper-sphere. The hyper-polyhedron approximation reduces the number of feature vectors to be searched for the nearest neighbor, thus saving computation time.

The structure of the paper is as follows. Section 2 describes the overall system, with special attention to the way in which more stable invariant regions are extracted using a multiscale approach. Section 3 discusses the indexing structure based on the HPAT idea. Finally, section 4 demonstrates experiments on several public databases. Section 5 concludes the paper.

2 Retrieving Images

2.1 A More Stable Invariant Region Extractor

In [7], Tuytelaars and Van Gool describe a practical method to extract local invariant features. More precisely, they extract elliptical regions constructed around intensity extrema. Here, we present a slight modification to this method, which from our experiments seems to significantly improve the stability or repeatability of the method. More precisely, we select the intensity extrema used as seed points in a more stable way. To this end, we apply a Gaussian scale space. This can be constructed very efficiently thanks to the separability of the Gaussian kernel. We use five different scale level representations (the original image, plus four smoothed versions with a scale factor of $1.2, 1.4, 1.8$ and 2.2).

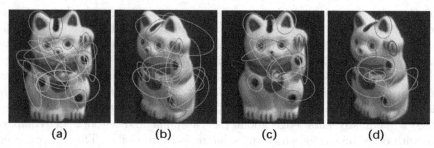

(a)   (b)   (c)   (d)

Fig. 1. Two different views of the same object, with some invariant regions overlayed (red: regions that have been extracted in both images, yellow: regions that have been extracted in only one image). Note how the red regions cover the same physical parts of the scene. **(a, b)** regions extracted with the method of [7], **(c,d)** regions extracted with more stable intensity extrema

Then, a non-maximum suppression algorithm finds the local intensity extrema at each scale level, as in the original method. However, only those local extrema which are repeated at different scales are considered as stable and are used to extract invariant regions. Fig. 1 shows an example of the regions extracted with the proposed method as well as those extracted with the original method. In total, the improved method extracts 20 and 16 regions on the two views, with 8 of them being repeated, while the original method extracts 26 and 21 regions, with the same number of repeated regions. The repeatability has clearly improved, which not only saves computation time during the retrieval process but also may improve the recognition accuracy.

One could argue that the extracted intensity extrema are not really invariant under affine transformations, due to the isotropic Gaussian smoothing. However, intensity extrema that are found over several scales will also be found after an affine transformation with anisotropic scaling smaller or comparable to the scale change between the scale levels. Moreover, the method does not strictly rely on the affine-invariance of the seed points, as the next step of the region extraction method is robust to their inaccurate localization[7].

2.2 Matching Invariant Regions

Finding correspondences between two views is then performed by means of a nearest region classification scheme, based on feature vectors of invariants computed over the affine invariant image regions. As in the region extraction step, we consider invariance both under affine geometric changes and linear photometric changes, with different offsets and different scale factors for each of the three color bands. More precisely, each region is described by a set of nine generalized color moment invariants, as described in [3].

The Mahalanobis distance is a good measure to compare such feature vectors, as it correctly takes into account the different variability of the elements of the feature vector as well as their correlation. During the offline construction of the database, the original space is rotated based on the covariance matrix, such that Mahalanobis distance is reduced to Euclidean distance.

2.3   Retrieving Images

The actual recognition of objects or scenes then goes as follows. First, we build a database with representative images for all the known objects or scenes (with possibly more than one image per object or scene). Then, in the offline pre-processing, we extract invariant regions and invariant feature vectors for all the images in the database, compute the covariance matrix, and store the rotated feature vectors in the database as well, with pointers to the corresponding image. Then, during the online recognition phase, a query image is processed in exactly the same way (extraction of invariant regions, computation of feature vectors, and rotation according to the covariance matrix). For each feature vector, we look for the nearest neighbor in the database, using fast indexing methods as explained in section 3, and add a vote to the corresponding image. This way, images in the database showing the same object or scene as the query image will get a high number of votes. Simply ranking the database images based on the number of matches finishes the retrieval.

3   Indexing Based on a Hyper-polyhedron Approximation of the Hypersphere and with an Adaptive Threshold

Nene and Nayar [4] proposed an efficient algorithm for nearest neighbor search. It uses a hyper-cube as an approximation of the hyper-sphere. The algorithm begins with selecting the points that are in between a pair of parallel planes $X1$ and $X3$ perpendicular to the first coordinate axis (see Fig. 2) and adds them to a list, called the candidate list. Next, it trims the candidate list by discarding points that are not in between another pair of parallel planes $X2$ and $X4$, corresponding to the second dimension. This procedure is repeated for each dimension to end up with a hypercube of size $2r$ centered around the query point. Once we have this trimmed candidate list, the closest point is found using an exhaustive search. The method can be implemented very efficiently. However, the hyper-cube approximation of the hyper-sphere deteriorates very quickly with increasing dimensions. For instance, in case of 9 dimensions, the volume of the hyper-sphere is only 0.7% of the hyper-cube volume. This results in unnecessary computation during the exhaustive search phase. Here, we propose a more accurate approximation of the hyper-sphere based on a hyper-polyhedron.

3.1   Hyper-polyhedron

We explain the proposed hyper-polyhedron approximation in 2D space, although the ideas hold for higher dimensional spaces as well. As can be seen in Fig. 2, left, the point P_c is not within the circle even though it falls inside the square. For higher dimensions, there will be many more such points. As a result, using

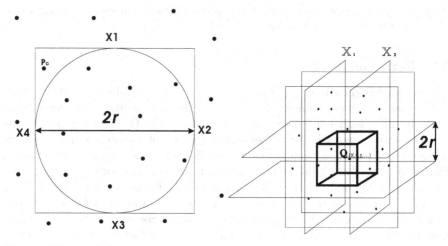

Fig. 2. Two and three dimensions case of Hypercube. The corner points like p_c fall within the hyper-cube but not within the hyper-sphere

the hyper-cube method, the candidate list includes many useless corner points such as P_c. Instead of using two pairs of parallel planes, we propose to use four, see Fig. 3. The additional four planes are perpendicular to two new *lifted* coordinates x_{12} and x_{21}. These lifted coordinates are projections of the x_1, x_2 coordinates onto a rotated coordinate axes frame:

$$x_{12} = (x_1 + x_2)/\sqrt{2}, \text{ and } x_{21} = (x_1 - x_2)/\sqrt{2}. \tag{1}$$

In general, for the n-dimensional case we need $n(n-1)$ auxiliary dimensions. The lifted coordinates are used only for trimming the space, i.e., to construct the hyperpolyhedron. This phase is very efficient. Only the "true" n coordinates are used during the (time-consuming) exhaustive search.

It is clear that the hyper-polyhedron is a much better approximation of the hypersphere than the hypercube. The volume of the hypercube is given by

$$V_{hc} = (2r)^n \tag{2}$$

with r the radius of the inscribed hypershere, while the volume of the hyper-polyhedron is given by (see the appendix for a derivation of this formula)

$$V_{hp} = (2r)^n (\sqrt{2} - 1)^n \left[1 + \sum_{k=1}^{n} \binom{n}{k} 2^{1-k/2} \right] \tag{3}$$

The volume of the hyperpolyhedron grows much slower with increasing number of dimensions than the hypercube, which grows exponentially. The volume of the hypersphere, on the other hand, remains more or less constant and even decreases for high dimensional spaces. For the 9-dimensional case, the hyper-polyhedron takes only 8.8% of the hypercube volume. Of course, constructing the

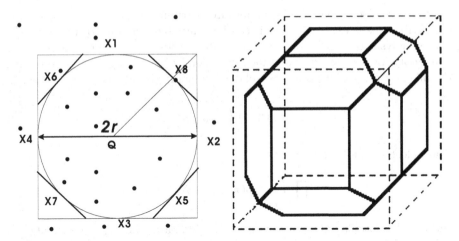

Fig. 3. Reduction the volume by using more planes in two dimensions and the illustration of three dimensions

hyper-polyhedron has its price: it needs $n(n-1)$ more candidate list trimmings (scalar comparisons) than the original hyper-cube method. In return, we save $(1 - \frac{V_{hp}}{V_{hc}}) * m$ distance computations, with m the average number of feature vectors inside the hypercube after trimming. Approximately, our method is more efficient if

$$n(n-1) < \frac{m(1 - \frac{V_{hp}}{V_{hc}})\mathcal{O}_d(n)}{2\mathcal{O}_c} . \qquad (4)$$

with $\mathcal{O}_d(n)$ the computational complexity of the distance computation and $\mathcal{O}_c$ complexity of the scalar comparisons. The ratio $\mathcal{O}_d(n)/\mathcal{O}_c$ varies on different computer platforms. Our experiments on PC showed that $\mathcal{O}_d(n)/\mathcal{O}_c \approx 150$ for $n = 9$. On a PDA, without a floating point unit, this number will be even higher and our method even more desirable.

3.2   Ranking the Dimensions

The order of the dimensions in the trimming procedure may be arbitrary. We always end up with the same hyper-polyhedron. However, proper ranking may save some computation time. We use the ranking suggested by Nene and Nayar [4]. More precisely, we start slicing in the dimension that discards the highest number of points from the trimmed list.

3.3   Adaptive Threshold

It is apparent that the cost of the proposed algorithm depends critically on the radius r. Setting r too high results in a huge increase in cost, while setting r too small may result in an empty candidate list [4]. Nene and Nayar proposed a solution for two special cases — normal and uniform distribution of the point sets.

Here, we propose a general solution for any distribution $p(x_i)$. The computation of distributions is expensive, but it can be computed beforehand. Based on the above analysis, our goal is to find the smallest r for which the candidate list is non-empty. Let us assume a specific query point $Q(x_1, x_2, x_3, ..., x_n)$. Assuming the different dimensions are uncorrelated, the joint probability is defined as

$$p(\mathbf{x}) = \prod_{i=1}^{n} p(x_i) \,. \tag{5}$$

If we select r such that

$$\prod_{i=1}^{n} \int_{x_i-r}^{x_i+r} p(x_i) dx_i \times N \geq 1 \,, \tag{6}$$

with N the total number of points in the database, the expected number of points inside the hyperpolyhedron ≥ 1. We can approximate the integral for a small neighborhood around Q by a rectangle which yields

$$\prod_{i=1}^{n} 2rp(x_i) \times N \geq 1 \,. \tag{7}$$

To overcome the problem of hypercube corner point mentioned in [4], we use $r/\sqrt{2}$ to replace r and do exhaustive search in the hyper-polyhedron illustrated in the Fig. 3 right. To ensure the hyper-polyhedron is not empty, a safe factor k is introduced into Eq. 7. The desired function which selects the right r is

$$r \geq \sqrt[n]{\frac{k\sqrt{2}}{2N \times \prod_{i=1}^{n} p(x_i)}} \,. \tag{8}$$

4   Experiments

We experimented with our system on several databases. First, we use the often used coil-100 object database. For each object, 5 views(view 0, 100, 215, 270, 325) were included in our database, and another 3 views (view 25, 250, 255) were used as query images. The recognition rate is about 59.5%. The main reason for such a poor performance is that some objects are too simple to extract enough affine regions. If the simple objects for which less than four regions can be extracted are not included, the recognition rate goes up to 77.3%. We designed the proposed method with respect to real world conditions. It is robust to affine transforms, partial occlusions, background changes and (to some extent) illumination changes.

We are mainly motivated by a virtual tourist guide application. We created a rather representative database containing 201 buildings in Zürich [6]. Each of the buildings has been photographed from five different viewpoint. These 1005 images have been captured in different seasons and different weather. The images are subsampled to the resolution 320 × 240. In total, 57095 affine regions

Fig. 4. Retrieval results on ZuBuD database. First one is query image, others are returned images with descending order of matches. Top row: Best match is the correct one. Mid row: Correct image is not at top fist position but second. Bottom row: Failure. The query image which is highly occluded by a tree

have been located in the database images. The 115 query images are not included in the database. They have been captured with a different camera and under different photometric conditions. Our method returns the correct match for 99 images. For an additional 10 images, it gives the correct match within the top five. Only 6 images have not been recognized among the first five and are considered as failures. The complete recognition process needs about 1.5 - 1.7 seconds for one query image on PIII at 1GHz. Most of the time is spent on the invariant region extraction. It should be noted that our code is not yet well optimized, so there is still room for improvement. The top row in Fig.4 shows one recognition example in which the query image was occluded by a tram. The mid row illustrates one retrieval result in which the correct result is not at the top first position but at the second. The bottom row demonstrates a failure because of significant occlusions in the query image.

5   Conclusions

In this contribution, a method to retrieve images from a database based on local features was proposed. It makes it possible to search in a database for images containing the same object or scene as shown in a query image, even in case of large changes in viewpoint, occlusions, partial visibility, changes in the illumination conditions, etc. The use of invariance together with efficient indexing allow close to realtime performance. By approximating a hypersphere by a hyperpolyhedron and including an adaptive threshold, the amount of expensive distance computations can be reduced, at the cost of extra scalar comparisons. This is particulary useful in the foreseen application on PDA which typically has no floating point unit. The effective indexing technology provides acceptable searching speed for most applications. It is suitable for two types of queries: range search and k-nearest-neighbor search. When the database becomes bigger, correct recognition rates decline because too many similar regions are found in other images, especially since most buildings have similar colors and features. Adding a re-ranking procedure as a postprocessing step that would include more expensive operations like epipolar geometry verification or cross-correlation could probably further improve the retrieval accuracy.

Acknowledgement

This work is supported by Polyproject-Wearable computing of Swiss Federal Institute at Zurich and the National Fund for Scientific Research Flanders (Belgium).

References

[1] A. Baumberg. Reliable feature matching across widely separated views. In *Computer Vision and Pattern Recognition*, pages 774–781, 2000 72

[2] Krystian Mikolajczyk and Cordelia Schmid. An affune invariant interest points detector. In *European Conference on Computer Vision*, pages 128–142, 2002 72

[3] F. Mindru, T. Moons, and L. Van Gool. Recognizing color patterns irrespective of viewpoint and illumination. In *Computer Vision and Pattern Recognition*, pages 368–373, 1999 73

[4] Sameer A. Nene and Shree K. Nayar. A simple algorithm for nearest neighbor search in high dimensions. *IEEE Transactions on Pattern Analysis and Machine Intelligence*, 19, 1997 72, 74, 76, 77

[5] J. Matas O. Chum, M. Urban and T. Pajdla. Robust wide baseline stereo from maximally stable extremal regions. In *British Machine Vision Conference*, 2002 72

[6] Hao Shao, Tomáš Svoboda, and Luc Van Gool. ZuBuD — Zürich buildings database for image based recognition. Technical Report 260, Computer Vision Laboratory, Swiss Federal Institute of Technology, March 2003. Database downloadable from http://www.vision.ee.ethz.ch/showroom/ 77

[7] T. Tuytelaars and Van Gool. Wide baseline stero based on local affinely invariant regions. In *British Machine Vision Conference*, 2000 72, 73

A   Volume of the Hyperpolyhedron

To find the total volume of the n-dimensional hyperpolyhedron, we subdivide the n-dimensional hypercube into a set of rectangular boxes as illustrated in figure 5 for the two-dimensional case, and compute for each of these boxes how much of its volume is occupied by the hyperpolyhedron. More precisely, the hypercube is divided by intersecting it with $2n$ hyperplanes Π_i given by the equation

$$x_i = \pm a/2, i = 1..n \,,$$
$$a = 2(\sqrt{2} - 1)r \,,$$
$$b = \sqrt{2}(\sqrt{2} - 1)r \,.$$

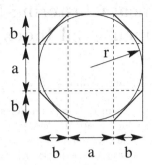

Fig. 5. Two-dimensional hyperpolehydron

This way, the volume of the n-dimensional hyperpolyhedron can be written as

$$V_n(r) = \sum_{k=0}^{n} N_k v_k a^{n-k} b^k$$

with N_k the number of boxes with dimensions $a^{n-k}b^k$ and v_k the percentage of the subvolume occupied by the hyperpolyhedron. Indeed, due to symmetry reasons all the subvolumes with the same dimensions will have similar positions relative to the hyperpolyhedron and hence will have a similar percentage of their volume occupied by the hyperpolyhedron.

The number N_k of boxes with dimensions $a^{n-k}b^k$ is given by

$$N_k = \binom{n}{k} 2^k, k = 1..n$$

with $\binom{n}{k} = \frac{n!}{(n-k)!k!}$ the number of combinations of k out of n.

The percentage of each subvolume occupied by the hyperpolyhedron v_k can be shown to be

$$v_0 = 1 \,,$$
$$v_k = (1/2)^{k-1}, k = 1..n \,.$$

Combining all these equations, the volume of a n-dimensional hyperpolyhedron can be written as

$$V_n(r) = a^n + \sum_{k=1}^{n} \binom{n}{k} 2 a^{n-k} b^k$$

$$= 2^n r^n (\sqrt{2} - 1)^n \left[1 + \sum_{k=1}^{n} \binom{n}{k} 2^{1-k/2} \right] \,.$$

Hierarchical Clustering-Merging
for Multidimensional Index Structures

Zhan Chen, Jing Ding, Mu Zhang, Wallapak Tavanapong, and Johnny S. Wong

Department of Computer Science
Iowa State University
Ames, IA 50011, U.S.A.
{zchen,jding,zhangmu,tavanapo,wong}@cs.iastate.edu

Abstract. The R-tree family index structures are among the most common index structures used in multidimensional databases. To improve the search performance it is very important to reduce the overlap between bounding regions in the R-tree. However the arbitrary insertion order in the tree construction procedure might result in tree structures inefficient in the search operations. In this paper we propose a new technique called Hierarchical Clustering-Merging (HCM) to improve the tree construction procedure of the R-tree family index structures. With this technique we can take advantage of the data distribution information in the data set to achieve an optimized tree structure and improve the search performance.

1   Introduction

Digital images and videos have become an important part of many applications that affect various aspects of our daily lives, such as distance learning, electronic commerce, and disease diagnoses. These applications rely on effective content-based retrieval of images and videos that satisfy users' queries. Since an image or a key-frame in one shot of a video can be represented by a multidimensional feature vector, many multidimensional indexing techniques have been proposed to provide efficient access to multimedia databases. Among the most commonly known indexing techniques are the R-tree [1] family index structures. In the R-tree and its variants [2, 3, 4], the data set is partitioned and a hierarchy of nested bounding regions is built. The bounding region of a high level node contains the bounding regions of nodes at lower levels, and the bounding region of a leaf contains the actual data objects.

In the search operations of the R-tree family index structures, one starts from the root and traverses down subtrees whose bounding regions intersect the query region. When a leaf is reached, the regions of data objects in the leaf are tested against the query region. It has been pointed out by previous research [4] that the overlap between bounding regions degrades the search performance. This is because all the subtrees whose bounding region intersects the query region need to be searched. When the dimensionality of data objects increases, the overlap becomes more serious. Hence, it is crucial to maintain optimal tree structures

E. M. Bakker et al. (Eds.): CIVR 2003, LNCS 2728, pp. 81–90, 2003.

with minimum overlap in order to improve the search performance. However, this requirement cannot be guaranteed by the traditional tree construction procedure, which is simply a random sequence of insertion operations. To insert a data object, the tree is traversed from the root down to a leaf. At each level, the node whose bounding region needs the least enlargement is chosen and its bounding region is updated to enclose the new data object. When the data objects are inserted in arbitrary order, the resulting tree structure is prone to have serious overlap [10]. So it is very important to collect some data distribution information of the data set and find out a better insertion sequence before tree construction.

On the other hand, the traditional tree construction procedure is also not time-efficient. When the tree gets larger, it takes more time to traverse from the root to a leaf. As the initialization of a database usually involves a huge number of data object insertions, it will be more reasonable if we treat the tree construction procedure differently than just a sequence of repeated insertion operations.

We propose a new technique called **Hierarchical Clustering-Merging (HCM)** to improve the tree construction procedure of the R-tree family index structures. Following are some highlights of our scheme:

1. We use a hierarchical clustering algorithm to preprocess the data set. This algorithm takes advantage of the data distribution information of the data set to optimize the tree structure. Our experiments on both uniform data sets and real data sets demonstrate that the HCM-enhanced R-tree outperforms both the original R-tree [12] and the SR-tree [13] in nearest neighbor search.
2. We develop a merging algorithm to build the tree from data clusters. This algorithm optimizes the tree structure and is very effective in reducing the time cost of building the tree. Our performance study shows that even if we take into account of the time spent on data preprocessing, the total tree construction time cost is still comparable to that of the original R-tree and the SR-tree.
3. HCM technique is highly flexible and scalable. It can be applied to different variants in the R-tree family index structures and all original features of these index structures are maintained. Parameters in HCM can be configured to adapt to different data sets. We also provide the method of computing optimal parameters to achieve best search performance.

The remainder of this paper is as follows. In Section 2, we discuss some related work. In Section 3, we describe the proposed Hierarchical Clustering-Merging technique, using the R-tree as an example. In Section 4, we present the results and analysis of the performance study. The last section provides our conclusions.

2   Related Work

The R-tree can be used not only in spatial databases but also in image databases where each data object is regarded as a data point, since each image can be abstracted as a multidimensional feature vector. The R-tree is based on a hierarchy of nested MBRs (minimum bounding rectangle). Each tree node, including the internal nodes and the leaf nodes, has a corresponding MBR. The MBR of an internal node is the minimum bounding rectangle that encloses all the MBRs of its children, while the MBR of a leaf node is the minimum bounding rectangle that encloses all the data points inside the leaf. Each node contains between m and M entries unless it is the root.

The SR-tree [2] is one of the most successful variants of the R-tree by integrating bounding spheres and bounding rectangles. A bounding region in the SR-tree is the intersection of a bounding sphere and a bounding rectangle. The SR-tree can improve the performance in the search operations because overlap between bounding regions is reduced.

Several packing schemes [5, 6, 7] are proposed to improve the tree construction procedure of the R-tree. The basic idea is to partition the data set into groups of equal size and fill each leaf with one group of data points, then repeatedly pack the nodes at one level into the nodes at a higher level until the root of the tree is reached. As these schemes intend to build a complete tree and the resulting tree structure is less flexible for later updates, they are usually more suitable for static databases.

3   Proposed Scheme

3.1   Clustering-Merging

As we mentioned earlier, the search performance of the R-tree highly depends on the tree structure. Less overlap between MBRs leads to better performance. For a given data set, different insertion orders in tree construction might result in different tree structures. So it is very important to collect some information on the distribution of the data set and find out a better way to construct the R-tree.

An intuition for an ideal insertion order is that the new data point to be inserted should be as close to some existing data points in the tree as possible. When we insert a new data point, we start from the root and search downward. At each level we always choose a node whose MBR needs the least enlargement. Therefore, if the new data point is close to some data points in the tree, the enlargement of MBRs along the search path can be reduced. Thus the probability of overlap between MBRs can also be reduced, which is critical to improve the search performance.

Based on this observation, our first step is to group data points that are close to each other together. We use clustering technique to achieve this purpose. Clustering [8, 9] is widely used to group data items together according to some similarity measures. Here Euclidean distance is used as the similarity measure between data points. We partition the data set into a number of clusters so that data points close to each other are grouped together. If the data points in the same cluster are inserted into the R-tree in a consecutive order, the resulting tree structure should have less overlap than the case when insertions are in an arbitrary order.

To build the R-tree from the clusters, a simple way is sequential insertion. We first insert data points from cluster 1 into the tree, then data points from cluster 2, and so on. But this method has two disadvantages. First, when we begin to insert data points from a new cluster into the tree, these new data points are prone to be scattered inside the tree, thus data points from different clusters will get mixed up, which contradicts the goal of clustering. The second problem is that it has no improvement on the tree construction time cost. Each time we insert a new data point, we still need to traverse from the root of the whole tree down to a leaf.

Here we propose a merging algorithm to build the tree. The idea is to build a small R-tree from each cluster and merge all the small R-trees together into one large R-tree. During the procedure data points from different clusters are not mixed up, so overlap can be minimized. We will show in the performance study the merging algorithm costs less time than sequential insertion.

3.2   Hierarchical Clustering-Merging

Before considering what specific clustering algorithm to use, a more important issue is how to determine the number of clusters. If this number is very small, there will be too many data points in one cluster and the within-cluster scatter will be too large. On the other hand, if we partition the data set into many clusters, although data points within one cluster are closer to each other, but when we merge two clusters, they might be too far away from each other. In either case, the resulting tree structure might still have serious overlap. Moreover, if the number of clusters is very large, the average number of data points in one cluster will be very small. This leads to very low space utilization.

So if there is only one level of clusters, the performance improvement is limited regardless of the number of clusters created. Further improvement can be achieved by using hierarchical clusters. We first partition the data set into k clusters, then we recursively partition each cluster into k sub-clusters. After h partitions, the result is a cluster tree of degree k and height h. There are k^h leaves in the tree and each leaf is a cluster. Then we build the R-tree from the cluster tree. Clusters at the same level in the a subtree are merged together, which guarantees data points close to each other are always merged first, thus overlap can be reduced to minimum. In following sections we will discuss how to determine the optimal values of k and h.

3.3   Algorithm Details

k-Means Clustering. k-means clustering algorithm [11] is used in our scheme to partition the data set. It creates k clusters with minimum within-cluster scatter, so data points close to each other are grouped together, which is the feature we desire. k-means algorithm is also simple to implement and the computation cost is relatively low. It can be applied to a wide range of data sets, so there is no specific restrictions to the data sets.

Merging. The most important operation in the merging procedure is to merge two R-trees together. As the original R-tree does not provide such an operation, we develop a new operation *MergeTree* which merges two R-trees $RT1$ and $RT2$ into one. Without loss of generality, here we assume the height of $RT1$ is no less than the height of $RT2$. The algorithm of *MergeTree* is as follows:

1. If the height of $RT1$ is larger than that of $RT2$, and the number of entries in the root of $RT2$ is larger than or equal to m, we insert $RT2$ into $RT1$ using the operation *InsertSubtree*.
2. If the heights of $RT1$ and $RT2$ are the same, or the number of entries in the root of $RT2$ is smaller than m (which is possible for the root), we need to deal with each entry individually. If the root of $RT2$ is a leaf, then each entry of the root points to a data point. We insert all the data points into $RT1$ using the original insertion operation of the R-tree. If the root of $RT2$ is not a leaf, then each entry of the root points to a child node. In this case, we insert the subtrees rooted at each child node into $RT1$ using *InsertSubtree*.

Following is the pseudocode of *MergeTree*.

```
MergeTree(RT1, RT2) {
    if ((RT1->height > RT2->height) &&
        (RT2->root->entry_no >= m))
        InsertSubtree(RT1, RT2->root);
    else if (RT2->root->height == 0)
            for each entry i in RT2->root
                InsertPoint(RT1, RT2->root->entry[i])
        else
            for each entry i in RT2->root
                InsertSubtree(RT1, RT2->root->entry[i])
}
```

The operation *InsertSubtree* inserts a subtree rooted at node n into RT. The algorithm is as follows:

1. Starting from the root of RT, choose a child whose MBR needs least enlargement to enclose the MBR of n.
2. Repeat until a node m is reached whose height is $n \rightarrow height + 1$.
3. Insert n as a child of m.

InsertSubtree works in a similar way to the original *InsertPoint* operation of the R-tree. Both algorithms start from the root and traverse down the tree by selecting a child node whose MBR needs the least enlargement. However, *InsertPoint* traverses down the tree until a leaf is reached while *InsertSubtree* stops at a node whose height is one more than the height of node n. The split operation on the R-tree will be invoked after an insertion operation if necessary. All the original R-tree features are still maintained. The same idea can be applied to other R-tree family index structures. Fig. 1 shows an example of merging two trees.

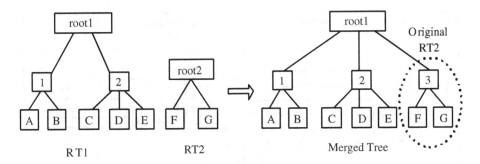

Fig. 1. A merging example

4   Performance Study

We implemented HCM based on the R-tree source code from [12] and the clustering algorithm source code from [11]. Here we compare the performance of the HCM-enhanced R-tree with the original R-tree and the SR-tree [13]. Both uniform data sets and real data sets are used in our experiments. The uniform data sets have a dimensionality of 10, and the data value on each dimension is uniformly distributed between $[0, 1)$. The data set size ranges from 20,000 to 100,000 data points. The real data sets consist of color image histogram vectors with the dimensionality of 27. The data set size ranges from 5,000 to 15,000 images. Nearest neighbor search is performed to evaluate the search performance. We search 20 nearest neighbor data points in each test and compute the average execution time in 1,000 tests. The execution time includes both CPU time and disk I/O time in order to reflect the overall performance. The page size is set to 4,096 bytes. The minimum utilization of each page (m/M) is set to 40%. All experiments are done on a PC with Pentium 4 1.8GHZ CPU, 256MB memory, and Red Hat 7.3 operating system.

4.1   Optimal Parameters

As we mentioned earlier, two parameters are very important to the performance of HCM: k and h. k is the number of clusters to create in each partition and h is the number of times partitioning is executed. In the cluster tree, k is the degree of the tree and h is the height of the tree. The total number of clusters created is k^h.

Let us first evaluate the effect of h and fix k. Intuitively, if we increase the value of h, we have more levels of clusters. Hence, clustering should be more accurate and the resulting R-tree should have less overlap. The problem is when the partitioning should stop. We notice that the lowest level of MBRs is the MBR of a leaf, and the MBR of a leaf can not be further reduced by clustering data points within the leaf. So if the number of data points in one cluster is equal to the maximum number of data points that can be stored in one leaf, further

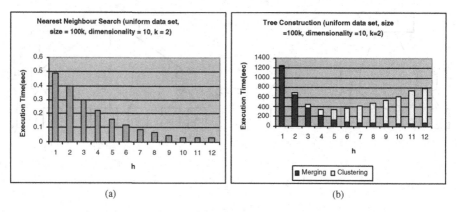

Fig. 2. Effect of h on the performance of HCM

partitioning is not necessary. If the data set size is S, the average number of data points in one cluster is $M = S/k^h$. If the page size is p bytes, the dimensionality is d and the size of the data value on each dimension is v bytes, the storage space for each data point is $2dv$ bytes. Here both lower bound and upper bound on each dimension need to be stored, although they are the same for a data point. The maximum number of data points that can be stored in one leaf is $N = p/(2dv)$. When $M = N$, h can be computed by $h = \log_k(2dvS/p)$. For data sets with different distribution patterns, dimensions, data value sizes etc., the optimal value of h might vary, but $h = \log_k(2dvS/p)$ can be regarded as an upper bound.

The experiment results also verify our calculation. Fig. 2 (a) shows the search performance on a uniform data set of 100,000 data points with a dimensionality of 10. The value of k is set to 2, which represents the simplest partitioning scheme. As the page size is 4096 bytes, the dimensionality is 10 and data type is 4-byte float, using the above formula the optimal value of h should be 10 or 11. We can see from the graph when h increases, the execution time in nearest neighbor search decreases. When h reaches 10, there is little further improvement, which fits our calculation result very well. We also found that the execution time in nearest neighbor search when $h = 10$ is only about 7% of the time when $h = 1$. The search performance improvement is dramatic, which demonstrates the importance of data preprocessing.

Another concern is whether the tree construction time cost will become too large when h increase, since the total number of clusters increases very quickly. In Fig. 2 (b) we can see when h increases, more time is needed for clustering, but the time spent on merging keeps decreasing. The overall tree construction time cost eventually increases gradually but is well under control when the optimal value of h is reached. It can be seen our merging algorithm is very effective in reducing the tree construction time cost.

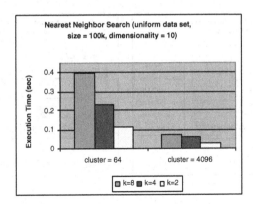

Fig. 3. Performance comparison of differnt h and k combinations

Given the total number of clusters k^h, there are different combinations of h and k. We prefer a larger value of h and a smaller value of k instead of a smaller h and a larger k. From the analysis in Section 3, a larger h reduces overlap, but a larger k does not necessarily have the same effect. When the number of clusters created in one partition increases, although the within-cluster scatter is reduced, the distance between some clusters might increase. When clusters far from each other are merged, more overlap will occur. So reducing h to increase k is not advised.

The experiment results also verify this estimation. Two representative examples are shown in Fig. 3. When $k^h = 64$, the combinations of k and h can be $k = 2$, $h = 6$ or $k = 4$, $h = 3$ or $k = 8$, $h = 2$. When $k^h = 4,096$, the combinations can be $k = 2$, $h = 12$ or $k = 4$, $h = 6$ or $k = 8$, $h = 4$. In both cases, the smaller values of k perform better. In following evaluations we always set the value of k to 2 to get the best performance.

4.2   Nearest Neighbor Search

Fig. 4 (a) shows the search performance of the HCM-enhanced R-tree (referred to as HCM in following discussion), the original R-tree and the SR-tree in uniform data sets. The value of h is increased from 1 to 3 and then to 6. In all cases, HCM performs better than the original R-tree. It begins to outperform the SR-tree when $h = 6$ and the performance is further improved when $h = 9$. Fig. 4 (b) shows the results in real data sets. As the dimensionality is larger, The performance of the SR-tree degrades seriously. The advantage of HCM now becomes more significant. It outperforms both the R-tree and the SR-tree even in the case $h = 1$. When $h = 3$ and $h = 6$ the performance is further improved. In both types of data sets, the performance improvement also becomes more obvious when the size of the data set increases.

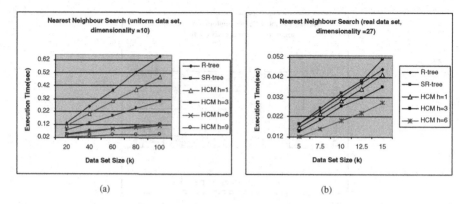

Fig. 4. The search performance comparison

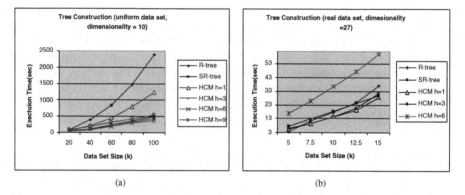

Fig. 5. The tree construction cost comparison

4.3 Tree Construction

Fig. 5 shows the tree construction time cost of HCM, the original R-tree and the SR-tree. In most cases, the total time cost of HCM is close to that of the original R-tree and the SR-tree. In real data sets, the time cost is higher when $h = 6$ because more time is needed for clustering when the dimensionality increases. But this one-time cost only happens during the initialization of the database and $h = 6$ is already close to the optimal value. Considering the time cost reduction in the search operations it is still acceptable.

5   Conclusions

From the performance study we can see HCM improves the search performance of the R-tree significantly. This shows the importance of data distribution information of the data set to the tree structure. We also propose the method to calculate the optimal parameter values to achieve the best search performance. Although the data preprocessing procedure costs extra time, due to the time reduction in our merging algorithm, the total tree construction time cost is still reasonable.

References

[1] O. Guttman, "R-tree: A Dynamic Index Structure for Spatial Searching", in Proc. ACM SIGMOD, pp.47-57, 1984

[2] N. Katayama and S. Satoh, "The SR-tree: An Index Structure for High-Dimensional Nearest Neighbor Queries", In Proc. of the ACM SIGMOD, pp. 369-380, 1997

[3] N. Beckmann, H. P. Kriegel, R. Schneider, B. Seeger, "The R*-tree: An Efficient and Robust Access Method for Points and Rectangles", In Proc. of ACM SIGMOD International Conference on Management of Data, pp. 322-331, May 1990

[4] T. Sellis, N. Roussopoulos, and C. Faloutsos, "The R+-tree: A dynamic index for multi-dimensional objects," in Proc. of 13th Conf. Very Large Databases, Brighton, U. K., pp. 507-518, Sept. 1987

[5] I. Kamel, C. Faloutsos, "On Packing R-trees", in Proc. of the 2nd International Conference on Information and Knowledge Management, pp. 490-499, Arlington, VA, November 1993

[6] Roussopoulos, D. Leifker, "Direct Spatial Search on Pictorial Databases Using Packed R-trees", in Proc. of ACM SIGMOD International Conference on Management of Data, pp. 17-31, 1985

[7] Scott T. Leutenegger et al, "STR: A Simple and Efficient Algorithm for R-tree Packing", in Proc. of the 13rd IEEE International Conference on Data Engineering, pp. 497-506, Birmingham U. K., 1997

[8] Ng and J. Han, "Efficient and Effective Clustering Method for Spatial Data Mining", VLDB'94, pp. 144-155, Santiago, Chile, Sept. 1994

[9] A.K. Jian, M. N. Murty, and P. J. Flynn, "Data clustering: A review", ACM Computing Sur-veys, vol. 31, no. 3, September 1999

[10] G. Lu, "Techniques and data structures for efficient multimedia retrieval based on similarity", pp. 372 -384, IEEE Transactions on Multimedia, Vol. 4, No. 3, Sept. 2002

[11] Open Source Clustering Software: http://bonsai.ims.u-tokyo.ac.jp/~mdehoon/software/cluster/index.html

[12] Source code of multi-dimensional indexing techniques: http://dias.cti.gr/~ytheod/research/indexing/

[13] The SR-tree: http://research.nii.ac.jp/~katayama/homepage/research/srtree/English.html

Integrated Image Content and Metadata Search and Retrieval across Multiple Databases

Matthew Addis[1], Mike Boniface[1], S. Goodall[2], Paul Grimwood[1], Sanghee Kim[2],
Paul Lewis[2], Kirk Martinez[2], and Alison Stevenson[1]

[1] IT Innovation
University of Southampton
SO16 7NP, UK.
{mja,mjb,pg,as}@it-innovation.soton.ac.uk
[2] Department of Electronics and Computer Science
University of Southampton
SO17 1BJ, UK.
{sg02r,sk,phl,km}@ecs.soton.ac.uk

Abstract. This paper presents an updated technical overview of an integrated content and metadata-based image retrieval system used by several major art galleries in Europe including the Louvre in Paris, the Victoria and Albert Museum in London, the Uffizi Gallery in Florence and the National Gallery in London. In our approach, the subjects of a query (e.g. images, textual metadata attributes), the operators used in a query (e.g. SimilarTo, Contains, Equals) and the rules that constrain the query (e.g. SimilarTo can only be applied to Images) are all explicitly defined and published for each gallery collection. In this way, cross-collection queries are dynamically constructed and executed in a way that is automatically constrained to the capabilities of the particular image collections being searched. The application of existing, standards based, technology to integrate metadata and content based queries underpins an open standards approach to extending interoperability across multiple image databases.

1   Introduction

Museums and galleries often have several digital collections ranging from public access images to specialized scientific images used for conservation purposes. Cross-collection access is recognised as important, for example to compare the treatments and conditions of Europe's paintings, which form a core part of our cultural heritage. The ARTISTE project [1], partly funded by the European Union under the fifth framework, has developed a system for the automatic indexing and cross-collection search and retrieval of high-resolution art images. Four major European galleries are involved in the project: the Uffizi in Florence, the National Gallery and the Victoria and Albert Museum in London, and the Centre de Recherche et de Restauration des

E. M. Bakker et al. (Eds.): CIVR 2003, LNCS 2728, pp. 91–100, 2003.

Musées de France (C2RMF) which is the Louvre related restoration centre. The ARTISTE system currently holds over 160,000 images and 5,000,000 textual metadata items from four separate collections owned by these partners.

2   Overview

Images of the art objects in a museum or gallery collection are held in an Object Relational Database Management System (ORDBMS) from NCR. Images are stored as Binary Large Objects (BLOBS). ARTISTE uses a wide variety of image processing algorithms [2][3][4][5] as the basis of content-based retrieval. Each algorithm is applied to the images in the collection to generate a set of image content descriptors called 'feature vectors'. The feature vectors are then integrated and stored with the text metadata for each image in the database.

When a content-based search needs to be made, the required algorithm is run on the query image to create a query feature vector. For example, the user might have a query image of a particular object that they wish to locate in a collection. Alternatively, the user might have a query image containing a particular range of colours and wish to find images with similar colours in the image collection. The query feature vector is then compared with all the corresponding feature vectors for the images in the collection. The comparison of feature vectors results in a measure of distance between the query image and each image in the collection. The images in the collection are then returned to the user as a series of thumbnails in order of increasing distance.

The use of a multi-tier architecture allows physical distribution of the system components so that cross-collection searching can be performed when the image collections are physically located at each of the gallery sites. This is achieved by having a local image database and ARTISTE server at each site that owns an image collection. The use of open standards such as OAI [6] and SRW [7] provides the basis of interoperability between systems installed at different galleries and allows other software systems, for example digital libraries, to work with ARTISTE.

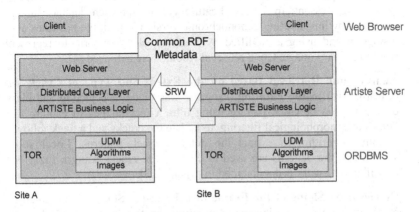

Fig 1. ARTISTE system architecture

3   Image Content Based Analysis

One of the aims of the ARTISTE project was not only to apply some standard algorithms for content based image retrieval in a gallery context [19][24], but also, through consultation with the end users, to address requirements for new or modified content based approaches meeting their specific needs. Standard algorithms for colour similarity matching included colour and grey scale histograms and an implementation of the colour coherence histogram [15] which incorporates spatial information. A colour picker applet allows users to retrieve images containing particular colours. These can be selected from a colour patch, or by mixing colours in HSB, RGB, or Lab space. Texture matching was based on energy coefficients in the pyramid wavelet transform [17] using Daubechies wavelets [18]. Other wavelet decompositions and basis functions were implemented and compared along with Gabor filter banks but the incorporated approach was chosen as the best compromise between retrieval accuracy and computational efficiency [20]. Some of the specific requirements for non standard content analysis from the galleries, which were addressed in the project, are summarised below. Our collaborators included groups interested in restoration and some of the requirements were more concerned with, for example, the restoration framework than the art work itself.

- **An Ability to Retrieve Images Based on a Sub-image Query i.e. where the Query is only a Part of the Database Image**. This was addressed by introducing multi-scale variants of some of the standard algorithms. Each database image was divided into 64 by 64 pixel patches, feature vectors were calculated for each patch, the resolution was reduced by a factor of 2 on each axis and the process repeated recursively until the image was represented as nearly as possible by a single patch. Retrieval involved finding the best matching patch across all searched images and gave approximate location information for the matching sub-image. See [5] for further details.

- **An Ability to Handle Retrieval Using Low Quality Query Images Such as Faxed Images of Postcards of Art Works.** The problem here was that the query images were essentially binary. Feature vectors for each database image were generated by thresholding a monochrome version at multiple positions across the histogram and using a modified pyramid wavelet transform to represent each resulting binary image. Good retrieval results were achieved [4].

- **Analysis and Retrieval Based on the Extent and Type of Crack Patterns (Craquelure) in the Painting.** Progress was made in detecting and classifying different types of crack pattern using ultra violet images to capture the basic crack data, morphological filtering to isolate the cracks and a track following and thinning algorithm to extract the detailed crack patterns. Local and global statistics of the patterns are used to classify the cracks using a fuzzy K-means classifier. The work is documented in [3] and [23].

- **Retrieval by Shape of the Frame of a Painting.** Some of the galleries had a requirement to retrieve images of paintings by the shape of their border and a border location algorithm was implemented using a snake to close in on the object within an image. The border so obtained was classified using a neural net algorithm to allocate the shape to one of a number of frame shape classes such as rectangular, oval, triptych.

- **Characterisation of UV Reflectance of Paintings (as an Indicator of the Extent of Previous Restoration Work).** Dark regions of a UV image may be indicative of previous restoration work and retrieval and quantification of such areas was a particular goal. It was initially expected that we would be able to automatically threshold the UV image at an appropriate level and extract an appropriate estimate of the proportion of dark spots under UV lighting. However, inconsistencies in UV spot images made automation difficult and a stand-alone tool was developed for the partners to allow them to manipulate the UV images interactively – thereby helping to make their prognosis faster and easier.

Most of the retrieval algorithms used nearest neighbour matching in some multidimensional feature space in order to find good matches to a query. However, since multiple content based retrieval algorithms were to be used in a single search, for example to find the best match in terms of both colour coherence and texture, and also results were to be aggregated when querying across multiple collections, it was necessary to find a way of combining similarity measures. A normalisation procedure was introduced for each class of feature vector which transformed distance measures in that feature space to a probability of finding a better match than the one returned. This was achieved by generating an approximation to the cumulative probability distribution for distances in that feature space by comparing all combinations of a large sample of the images in the collections and fitting the distribution with a polynomial function which could be used to normalise the distances for that feature space. The normalisation was built into the feature matching modules so that when a distance is calculated it is returned as a probability, with zero indicating a perfect match and 1 indicating the worst possible match. Although several assumptions are implicit in this process, it provided a good mechanism for combining content based retrieval processes from the different algorithms and returned a more meaningful estimate of the similarity based on the characteristics of the collections in the system.

4   Integrated Metadata and Image Content-Based Analysis

Current digital library query representations and protocols, such as z39.50 [12], deal entirely with textual metadata. This is not sufficient for multimedia digital libraries such as ARTISTE, where searches can be made on image content as well as textual metadata. In particular, current protocols have the following restrictions.

- There are no methods for specifying image content as a metadata item;
- There are no operators defined relating to image content;
- There are no methods for carrying out searches that result in the execution of image processing algorithms.

ARTISTE has addressed each of these issues by using RDF and RDFS [13] to define a query ontology [16] which defines and describes the objects, methods and operators required to build a query based on either image content, textual metadata or a combination of the two. All items that can be queried are described by a 'Query Item' hierarchy. A Query Item can be an image, properties of an image (such as colour or shape), or attributes associated with an image (conventional metadata such as textual and numeric items). The operations that can be performed on Query Items are also explicitly defined as Query Operators. Current Query Operators include exact operators (such as equals, less than, etc.) and fuzzy operators (such as similar to). RDF is also used to define the syntax and semantics for standard metadata terms. Each collection provides a mapping that relates these standard metadata terms to individual database table and column values. Thus queries specified using the RDF contain no concrete mappings to actual database fields. Therefore they can be passed without alteration to multiple gallery sites. At each site it will be translated to SQL and in particular the Dublin Core [8] Title is translated to the appropriate table and column name for the local metadata schema. In this way the ARTISTE system provides the ability to execute queries across multiple, distributed collections without requiring each collection to conform to a standard schema. Benefits of this RDF approach include:

- The use of RDF mapping provides a flexible solution to cross-collection searching;
- Mapping to a common schema allows common semantics to be supported without needing changes to local metadata and schemas;
- Users can be dynamically constrained in their querying through use of a 'Query Context' so that they only request queries that are within the common capabilities of a set of collections;
- Multilingual translation of metadata attribute names allows the user to use their native language when specifying which attributes to search over for multiple collections;
- Free text translation is a possible solution to multilingual searching of metadata content.

5   Extending Interoperability

The extensive use of RDF in ARTISTE provides a way to establish common semantics between heterogeneous digital libraries containing image collections. These common semantics include how to perform content-based analysis as well as textual metadata searching. This goes a long way towards interoperability between multiple digital libraries. In fact, this is sufficient to enable cross-collection search and retrieval between ARTISTE systems. However, common semantics are not enough to provide interoperability with third-party systems. To achieve this requires adoption of standards for the process of search and retrieval itself, i.e. use of standard protocols.

As stated above, existing information retrieval standards have been traditionally concerned with text based searching. Therefore ARTISTE is participating in an initiative [7] to redesign the primary open standard for interoperability between digital libraries, z39.50, using web technologies such as XML and SOAP. The initiative has proposed a Search and Retrieve Web Service (SRW) based on the z39.50 protocol for searching databases that contain metadata and objects [7]. ARTISTE is one of the early implementers of SRW and has extended the capabilities of SRW to enable image content and metadata based searches over multiple collections. ARTISTE has been working with the z39.50 community to incorporate the ability to deal with content-based searching of images and thus expand international standards of information retrieval.

The Common Query Language (CQL) [25] proposed by the SRW specification supports metadata based querying but makes no provision for content based queries. For example there is no provision to specify image analysers in combination with image operators and the search term is always assumed to be a text string. The limitations of the language were addressed by extending the protocol in those areas where it does not cover image content based querying and by maintaining close contact with the z39.50 community developing the SRW specifications.

The ARTISTE CAQL [14][10] expands CQL to provide support for image content queries by adding image operator (img-op), image analyser (img-analyser) and an image expression (img-exp) to the language.

```
primary ::=result-set-expression | [index-name rel-op]
adj-expr |  index-name img-op img-analyser img-exp
```

The SRW CQL specification of result-set-expression and index-name remains unchanged in the ARTISTE CAQL. The ARTISTE CAQL further specifies elements necessary to an image content query

```
img-op ::= "SimilarTo" | "PartOf"

img-analyser ::= identifier

img-expr ::= url
```

It can be seen from the definition of img-expr above that query images are specified as URLs. The same approach is used for query result images. Some examples of CAQL queries are given below.

```
dc.Creator contains Vinci and
artisteCore.VisibleLightImage SimilarTo CCV
http://artiste.it-
innovation.soton.ac.uk/test_images/test.jpg
```

This query combines a Dublin Core 'Creator' metadata search with an image content-based query that uses the 'CCV' algorithm to find images that are 'SimilarTo' the referenced query image 'test.jpg'.

```
dc.Subject = TEXTILE and artisteCore.VisibleLightImage
PartOf MCCV http://artiste.it-
innovation.soton.ac.uk/test_images/test.jpg and
dc.Creator contains Morris "and" William
```

This query combines a textual metadata search involving the Dublin Core attributes 'Subject' and 'Creator' with an image content-based query that uses the 'MCCV' algorithm to find images that have the referenced query image as 'part of' them, i.e. as a sub-image.

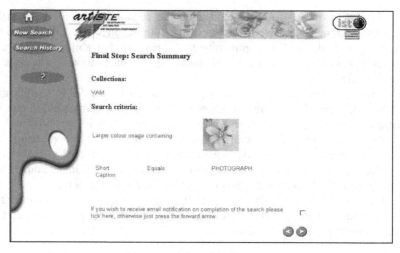

Fig. 2. Sample ARTISTE query

6   Results

The ARTISTE system provides seamless access to multiple distributed image collections, enabling dynamic searching of high resolution art by image content and metadata [22]. The example query (Figure 2) shows a query combining image content and metadata searching across the Victoria and Albert Museum collection. The query uses the Multi-scalar Colour Coherence algorithm to find larger images containing the specified sub image where those larger images have been marked up as 'Photograph'. The results (Figure 3) show the system finds the photograph containing the query image as well as other photographs containing similar shapes and colours.

Fig. 3. Sample ARTISTE query results

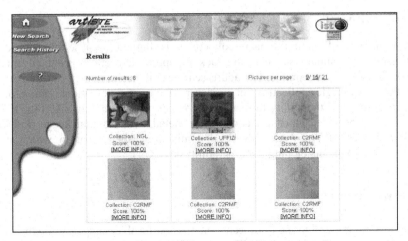

Fig. 4. Sample ARTISTE cross collection query results

The results of a second query are shown in Figure 4. The query was executed across three collections located variously at the National Gallery, the Uffizi Gallery and C2RMF and the metadata search term 'Dublin Core Creator' was selected from an automatically generated list of only those terms available which can be mapped to fields in each and every one of the selected collections. The results show images returned from each of the collections.

A demonstration system is available for interested users [9] to test [11] and ARTISTE has also released a standalone client which provides access to the demonstration collection via the SRW interface [26].

7   Observations and Future Work

Digital library support for multimedia content-based search and retrieval is in its infancy and is not accommodated by current standards. We believe the full benefit of multimedia search and retrieval can only be realised through seamless integration of content-based analysis techniques. This requires modification to existing standards as well as a review of the use of semantics in achieving digital library interoperability. In particular, machine understandable descriptions of the semantics of textual metadata, multimedia content, and content-based analysis can provide a foundation for a new generation of flexible and dynamic digital library tools and services. In essence, this is the application of Semantic Web [21] techniques to digital library interoperability. ARTISTE has begun this work and it will continue in the SCULPTEUR project [27]. SCULPTEUR aims to extend digital image library technology to support more diverse multimedia objects as well as use evolving semantic web technologies such as OWL to generate, structure and link together metadata in museum collections. Among the challenges the project will face are the storage and retrieval of 3D multimedia objects, the development of algorithms for content-based analysis of 3D objects, and the development of new protocols for interoperability between digital libraries.

8   Conclusions

The exploitation of cultural image collections is limited because of a lack of conformance to common schema, and lack of appropriate and convenient access methods. The ARTISTE project has addressed these issues not simply by providing access through a single application but by incorporating into international standards of information retrieval the ability to deal with content based searching. ARTISTE has both used and provided input to standards for metadata and digital image libraries. The significance of the work will be determined by the extent to which it is incorporated into the developing interoperability standards.

Acknowledgements

The authors are grateful to the European Commission for their support through grants IST-1999-11978 and IST-2001-35372 and to their collaborators on the ARTISTE project (NCR (Dk), Giunti Interactive Labs (I), Uffizi Gallery (I), The National Gallery (UK), C2RMF (FR), and the Victoria & Albert Museum (UK)) for image data and useful conversations.

References

[1]   ARTISTE http://www.artisteweb.org
[2]   Addis, M., Lewis, P., Martinez, K. "ARTISTE image retrieval system puts European galleries in the picture", Cultivate Interactive http://www.cultivate-int.org/issue7/artiste/
[3]   F. S. Abas and K. Martinez (2002) Craquelure Analysis for Content-Based Retrieval. IEEE DSP 2002 conference. July 2002
[4]   M.F.A.Fauzi and P.H.Lewis Query by Fax for Content Based Image Retrieval CIVR, Lecture Notes in Computer Science, vol2383, 91-99,2002 Springer Verlag
[5]   S Chan, K Martinez , P Lewis, C. Lahanier & J. Stevenson Handling Sub-Image Queries in Content-Based Retrieval of High Resolution Art Images. International Cultural Heritage Informatics Meeting p.157-163. September 2001
[6]   Open Archives Initiative http://www.openarchives.org/
[7]   ZING Search and Retrieve Web service
       http://www.loc.gov/z3950/agency/zing/srw/
[8]   DublinCore metadata initiative http://www.dublincore.org/
[9]   Artiste User Interest Group. Contact: M. Cecil-Wright
       mcw@it-innovation.soton.ac.uk
[10]   "D6.2 Impact on World-Wide Metadata Standards"
       http://www.it-innovation.soton.ac.uk/artiste/documentation/ D6.2.final.pdf
[11]   ARTISTE public dissemination system http://artiste.it-innovation.soton.ac.uk/
[12]   z39.50 http://lcweb.loc.gov/z3950/agency/
[13]   Resource Description Framework http://www.w3.org/RDF/

[14] "D6.1 Distributed Query Layer and Metadata Report" http://www.it-innovation.soton.ac.uk/artiste/documentation/D6.1final.pdf

[15] G Pass, R Zabih, & J Miller. Comparing Images Using Color Coherence Vectors. MultiMedia, p65-73. ACM, 1996

[16] Artiste Core schema http://artiste.it-innovation. soton.ac.uk/rdf/ArtisteCore.rdf

[17] S.G.Mallat, A theory for multiresolution signal decomposition: The Wavelet Representation, IEEE Transactions on Pattern Analysis and Machine Intelligence, 11, 674--693, July 1989

[18] Daubechies, "The wavelet transform t-frequency localisation and signal analysis",IEEE Transactions on Information Theory, vol36,pp. 961-1005,1990

[19] J. Cupitt & K. Martinez, "VIPS: an image processing system for large images", Proc. SPIE conference on Imaging Science and Technology, San Jose, Vol. 2663, 1996, pp 19-28

[20] M.F.A.Fauzi, "Texture Based Image Retrieval using Multiscale sub-image Matching", Image and Video Communications and Processing 2003 (to be published)

[21] The Semantic Web http://www.semanticweb.org/

[22] P. Allen, M. Boniface, P. Lewis, K. Martinez "Interoperability between Multimedia Collections for Content & Metadata-Based Searching", 11th WWW Conference, Hawaii. 7-11 May 2002 http://www2002.org/CDROM/alternate/196/index.html

[23] F. Salleh Abas and K. Martinez, "Classification of Painting Cracks for Content-Based Analysis", Machine Vision Applications in Industrial Inspection XI, 2003 (to be published)

[24] W. M. Smeulders, M. Worring, S. Santini, A. Gupta, & R. Jain. Content-Based Image Retrieval at the End of the Early Years. In Transactions On Pattern Analysis And Machine Intelligence, volume 22 of 12, pages 1349-1380. IEEE, December 2000

[25] ZING CQL specification
http://www.loc.gov/z3950/agency/zing/cql/cql-syntax.html

[26] ARTISTE SRW Service demonstration
http://artiste.it-innovation.soton.ac.uk/srw

[27] SCULPTEUR EC IST project number 35372 http://www.sculpteurweb.org

Multilevel Relevance Judgment, Loss Function, and Performance Measure in Image Retrieval

Hong Wu, Hanqing Lu, and Songde Ma

National Laboratory of Pattern Recognition
Institute of Automation, Chinese Academy of Sciences
P.O.Box 2728, Beijing 100080, China
{hwu,luhq,masd}@nlpr.ia.ac.cn

Abstract. Most learning algorithms for image retrieval are based on dichotomy relevance judgement (relevance and non-relevance),though this measurement of relevance is too coarse. To better identify the user needs and preference, a good retrieval system should be able to handle multilevel relevance judgement. In this paper, we focus on relevance feedback with multilevel relevance judgment. We consider relevance feedback as an ordinal regression problem, and discuss its properties and loss function. Since traditional performance measures such as precision and recall are based on dichotomy relevance judgment, we adopt a performance measure that is based on the preference of one image to another one. Furthermore, we develop a new relevance feedback scheme based on a support vector learning algorithm for ordinal regression. Our solution is tested on real image database, and promising results are achieved.

1 Introduction

In the past few years, relevance feedback has been used as a key component in content-based image retrieval, and a lot of algorithms are proposed. Most current relevance feedback (RF) algorithms [1, 2, 3] only use dichotomy relevance judgment, relevance or non-relevance. But this dichotomy measurement of relevance is too coarse. To better identify the user needs and preferences, the degree of relevance should be accounted for. As stated in [4], an ideal system should allow the user to specify how good an example is for his needs. Based on the notion of user preference, Yao [6] justifies the measurement of user judgments with an ordinal scale.

When using dichotomy relevance judgement, some RF algorithms (e.g. experiments in [5]) only use labelled relevant examples, and relevance feedback in such cases is intrinsically a density estimation problem. Other algorithms [1, 2, 3] use both the labelled relevant and irrelevant examples, and relevance feedback is treated as a two-class classification problem . When using multilevel relevance judgment, some works [4, 5] use the goodness scores to weight relevant examples in their learning algorithms. But this has two drawbacks, one is that if the user is not aware of the implication of the multivalued relevance scale, it may be misused [6]; the other is irrelevant examples are not used in their learning algorithms. We

E. M. Bakker et al. (Eds.): CIVR 2003, LNCS 2728, pp. 101–110, 2003.
© Springer-Verlag Berlin Heidelberg 2003

think that relevance feedback can be treated as ordinal regression, as in information retrieval [7, 11]. And due to the properties of ordinal regression, its loss function can be formed based on the information about the relative order induced by the relevance values. For dichotomy relevance judgment, precision and recall are widely used as the performance measure, and normalized precision and recall are also proposed to better account for the ranking effect [10]. For multilevel relevance judgment, some proposed measures using the absolute relevance value are questionable [6]. Here we suggest to use the normalized distance-based performance measure (ndpm) [6] as the performance measure, which is based on the preference of one document to another. Furthermore, we develop a new relevance feedback scheme based on a support vector learning algorithm for ordinal regression[7, 8, 9]. Our solution for relevance feedback is tested on real image dataset, and compared with some other methods in the literature. In this paper, some conclusions are borrowed from information retrieval, since we think image retrieval share the same properties with information retrieval on the aspects we care. And the term document and image are used interchangeably.

The article is organized as follow. In section 2, we state why relevance feedback can be considered as ordinal regression and introduce its loss function. The performance measure based on the notion of user preference is presented in section 3. In section 4, we present the support vector learning algorithm for ordinal regression. Experimental setup and results is presented in section 5, followed by conclusions and future works.

2   Relevance Feedback as Ordinal Regression

2.1   Learning Relevance Scale as Ordinal Regression

Relevance feedback is an interactive learning technique. In the retrieval process, the user is asked to give judgement on the current outputs of the system, and the system dynamically learns and refines the query to capture the user's information requirement. In the past few years, it has attracted much attention and various methods have been proposed. But most current RF algorithms only use dichotomy relevance judgment, relevance or non-relevance. It is obvious that not all the relevant images share the same degree of relevance, as is stated in [4] that the ideal system should allow the user to specify how good an example is for his needs. This suggests the use of multilevel relevance judgment. Based on the notion of user preference, it is stated in [6] that, if a user preference relation on documents obeys two basic axioms, asymmetry and negative transitivity, the measurement of user judgments can be measured with an ordinal scale, e.g. predefined multivalued relevance scale. The asymmetry axiom requires that a user cannot prefer d to d' and at the same time prefer d' to d. The negative transitivity axiom states that if a user does not prefer d to d', nor d' to d'', the user should not prefer d to d''. Here, we assume the asymmetry and negative transitivity as the principles that a user must follow when giving the judgment. Although, in practice, how to design such an ordinal scale is an important issue, it is beyond the scope of this paper.

Given a training set of objects and their associated target, machine learning focuses on finding dependencies between objects and target values. Formally speaking, given an i.i.d sample $S = \{(x_i, y_i)\}_{i=1}^{l} \sim P_{XY}^{l}$ and a set H of mapping h from X to Y, a learning procedure selects one mapping such that the risk functional is minimized. In relevance feedback, after user labelled images with relevance values (number or verbal), the learning algorithm is trying to select a optimal mapping, and predict the relevance values of the unlabelled images. The problem of predicting variables of ordinal scales is called ordinal regression. It shares properties with classification and metric regression, and also has its own ones. Like in classification Y is a finite set, and like in metric regression there exists an ordering among the element of Y, but in contrast to regression estimation Y is a non-metric space. Ordinal regression was studied in information retrieval [7, 11], but not yet investigated in image retrieval.

2.2   A Risk Formulation for Ordinal Regression

Due to the properties of ordinal regression, there are some problem in defining an appropriate loss function. Different from regression, there exists no metric in the space Y; different from classification the simple 0-1 loss function does not reflect the ordering in Y. Since no loss function $l(y, \hat{y})$ can be found that acts on true ranks y and predicted ranks $\hat{y}$, it is suggested in [8] to exploit the ordinal nature of the elements of Y by considering the order on the space X induce by each mapping $h : X \rightarrow Y$. The proposed loss function $l_{pref}(\hat{y}_1, \hat{y}_2, y_1, y_2)$ acts on pairs of true ranks (y_1, y_2) and predicted ranks $(\hat{y}_1, \hat{y}_2)$.

Consider an input space $X \subset R^n$ with objects being represented by feature vectors $\mathbf{x} = (x_1, ..., x_n)^T \in R^n$ where n denotes the number of features. Furthermore, let us assume that there is an outcome space $Y = \{r_1, ..., r_m\}$ with ordered ranks $r_m \succ_Y r_{m-1} \succ_Y ... \succ_Y r_1$. The symbol $\succ_Y$ denotes the ordering between different ranks and can be interpreted as "is preferred to ". Suppose that an i.i.d. sample $S = \{(x_i, y_i)\}_{i=1}^{l} \subset X \times Y$ is given. Let us consider a model space $H = \{h(\cdot) : X \mapsto Y\}$ of mappings from objects to ranks. Moreover, each such function h induces an ordering $\succ_X$ on the elements of the input space by the following rule

$$\mathbf{x}_i \succ_X \mathbf{x}_j \Leftrightarrow h(\mathbf{x}_i) \succ_Y h(\mathbf{x}_j). \tag{1}$$

A distribution independent model of ordinal regression has to single out the function h_{pref}^* which induces the ordering of the space X that incurs the smallest number of inversions on pairs $(\mathbf{x}_1, \mathbf{x}_2)$ of objects. Given a pair $(\mathbf{x}_1, y_1)$ and $(\mathbf{x}_2, y_2)$ of objects we have to distinguish between two different outcomes: $y_1 \succ_Y y_2$ and $y_2 \succ_Y y_1$. Thus, the probability of incurred inversion is given by the following risk functional,

$$R_{pref}(h) = E[l_{pref}(h(\mathbf{x}_1), h(\mathbf{x}_2), y_1, y_2)], \tag{2}$$

with

$$l_{pref}(\hat{y}_1, \hat{y}_2, y_1, y_2) = \begin{cases} 1 & \begin{array}{l} if \quad y_1 \succ_Y y_2 \\ and \ \neg(\hat{y}_1 \succ_Y \hat{y}_2) \end{array} \\ 1 & \begin{array}{l} if \quad y_2 \succ_Y y_1 \\ and \ \neg(\hat{y}_2 \succ_Y \hat{y}_1) \end{array} \\ 0 & else \end{cases} \tag{3}$$

The ERM principle recommends taking the mapping which minimizes the empirical risk $R_{emp}(h; S)$,

$$R_{emp}(h; S) = \frac{1}{l^2} \sum_{i=1}^{l} \sum_{j=1}^{l} l_{pref}(h(\mathbf{x}_i), h(\mathbf{x}_j), y_i, y_j) \tag{4}$$

which can be effectively represented based on a new training set whose elements are pairs of objects. Using the shorthand notation $\mathbf{x}^{(1)}$ and $\mathbf{x}^{(2)}$ to denote the first and second object of a pair, the new training set $S' : X \times X \times \{-1, +1\}$ can be derived from S if we use all 2-sets $\{(\mathbf{x}_i^{(1)}, y_i^{(1)}), (\mathbf{x}_i^{(2)}, y_i^{(2)})\}$ from S where either $y_i^{(1)} \succ_Y y_i^{(2)}$ or $y_i^{(2)} \succ_Y y_i^{(1)}$, i.e.

$$S' = \{((\mathbf{x}_i^{(1)}, \mathbf{x}_i^{(2)}), \Omega(y_i^{(1)}, y_i^{(2)}))\}_{i=1}^{t} \tag{5}$$

$$\Omega(y_1, y_2) = sign(y_1 \ominus y_2) \tag{6}$$

where $\ominus$ is the rank difference and t is the cardinality of S'.

In [7, 8, 9], the authors also give an important theoretical conclusion. Assume a training set S of size l drawn i.i.d. according to an unknown probability measure P_{XY} on $X \times Y$, then for each $h : X \mapsto Y$ the following equality holds true

$$\frac{l^2}{t} R_{emp}(h; S) = R_{emp}^{0-1}(h; S') = \frac{1}{t} \sum_{i=1}^{t} l_{0-1}(\Omega(h(\mathbf{x}_i^{(1)}), h(\mathbf{x}_i^{(2)})), \Omega(y_i^{(1)}, y_i^{(2)})) \tag{7}$$

Taking into account that each function $h \in H$ defines a function $p : X \times X \mapsto \{-1, 0, +1\}$ by

$$p(\mathbf{x}_1, \mathbf{x}_2) = \Omega(h(\mathbf{x}_1), h(\mathbf{x}_2)), \tag{8}$$

equation (7) shows that the empirical risk of a certain mapping h on a sample S is equivalent to the empirical risk based on the l_{0-1} loss of the related mapping p on the sample S' up to a constant factor t/l^2 which depends neither on h nor on p. Thus, the problem of ordinal regression can be reduced to a classification problem on pairs of objects. This problem is also called the problem of preference learning.

3 Performance Measure for Image Retrieval

For dichotomy relevance, precision and recall [10] are widely used as performance measures. Normalized precision and recall [10] are also proposed to account for the ranking effect of output of the retrieval system. For multilevel relevance judgement, some modified measurements were proposed, such as Keen's revised precision and recall measures. But the use of the absolute values for performance measure may not necessarily be meaningful, as they are not invariant to strictly monotonic increasing transformations of the absolute values [6]. A different way is using the information about the relative order induced by the relevance values. Some measures based on the preference of one document to another have been proposed in information retrieval. Here we adopt ndpm [6] as performance measure for image retrieval.

Let us introduce the notion of preference relation. A relation R is called a preference relation, which is a subset of the Cartesian product $D \times D$: $R = \{(d, d') | d$ is preferred to or more relevant than $d'\}$. Assuming the user preference obeys asymmetry and negative transitivity, the user preference relation is also called a user ranking. A measurement of effectiveness of retrieval system may be defined by examining the agreement or disagreement between the user and the system ranking. The distance between two ranking R_1 and R_2 on the set of documents D can be calculated by:

$$\beta(R_1, R_2) = \sum_{d,d'} \delta_{R_1, R_2}(d, d') \tag{9}$$

where the summation is over all unordered document pairs. Let $\delta_{R_1, R_2}(d, d')$ count 0 if R_1 and R_2 agree on d and d', Let $\delta_{R_1, R_2}(d, d')$ count 1 if R_1 and R_2 are compatible on d and d', and Let $\delta_{R_1, R_2}(d, d')$ count 2 if R_1 and R_2 contradict on d and d'.

By adopting an acceptable ranking criterion, the system performance can be evaluated independent of how the system ranks the documents in the same equivalence class of user preference (relevance scale). Such an acceptable ranking can be derived by arbitrarily rearranging the documents in the same equivalence class. Let $\Gamma_u(D)$ denote the set of all acceptable rankings of the user ranking R_u. The following distance-based performance measure (dpm) is suggested:

$$dpm(R_u, R_s) = \min_{R \in \Gamma_u(D)} \beta(R, R_s) \tag{10}$$

To evaluate the performance of every query equally, a normalized distance-based performance measure (ndpm) can be defined in terms of distance relative to the maximum distance, namely,

$$ndpm(R_u, R_s) = \frac{dpm(R_u, R_s)}{\max_{R \in \Gamma(D)} dpm(R_u, R)} \tag{11}$$

where $\max_{R \in \Gamma(D)} dpm(R_u, R)$ is the maximum distance between R_u and all rankings. And ndpm can be computed by:

$$ndpm(R_u, R_s) = \frac{2C^- + C^u}{2C} \tag{12}$$

where C^- is the number of contradictory pairs, C is the number of all pairs in user ranking R_u, C^u is the number of pairs which are considered as indifference by the system ranking, but not by the user ranking. In real retrieval situation, the system ranking is a linear order, so C^u is 0. This performance measure is defined for a single query. For a set of queries, the mean normalized measure can be computed.

4   Support Vector Machine for Ordinal Regression

Although there may exist some other solutions for ordinal regression, here we use the support vector learning algorithm proposed in [7, 8, 9]. This algorithm is similar to Support Vector Machines [12] and enforces large margin rank boundaries. And it is easily extended to non-linear utility functions using the "kernel trick".

The ordinal value can be considered as a coarsely measured latent continuous variable $U(\mathbf{x})$, thus we can model ranks as disjunctive intervals on the real line

$$y = r_i \Leftrightarrow U(\mathbf{x}) \in [\theta(r_{i-1}), \theta(r_i)] \tag{13}$$

where the function U (latent utility) and $\theta = (\theta(r_0), ..., \theta(r_m))^T$ are to be determined from the training data. Let us consider a linear utility function $U : X \rightarrow R$

$$U(\mathbf{x}) = \mathbf{w}^T \mathbf{x} \tag{14}$$

which is related to a mapping h from objects to ranks by (13). We assume that $\theta(r_0) = -\infty$ and $\theta(r_m) = +\infty$. We know that $U(\mathbf{x})$ incurs no error for the i-th example in the training set S' iff

$$z_i \mathbf{w}^T \mathbf{x}_i^{(1)} > z_i \mathbf{w}^T \mathbf{x}_i^{(2)} \Leftrightarrow z_i \mathbf{w}^T (\mathbf{x}_i^{(1)} - \mathbf{x}_i^{(2)}) > 0 \tag{15}$$

where $z_i = \Omega(y_i^{(1)}, y_i^{(2)})$ was used. Note that the preference relation is expressed in term of the difference of feature vectors $\mathbf{x}_i^{(1)} - \mathbf{x}_i^{(2)}$, which can be thought of as the combined feature vector of the pair of objects. By assuming a finite margin between the n-dimensional feature vectors $\mathbf{x}_i^{(1)} - \mathbf{x}_i^{(2)}$ of classes $z_i = +1$ and $z_i = -1$, we define parallel hyperplanes passing through each pair $(\mathbf{x}_i^{(1)}, \mathbf{x}_i^{(2)})$ by

$$z_i[\mathbf{w}^T (\mathbf{x}_i^{(1)} - \mathbf{x}_i^{(2)})] \geq 1 - \xi_i, \ i = 1, \dots, t \tag{16}$$

where the non-negative ξ_i measure the degree of violation of the i-th constraint. The weight vector $\mathbf{w}^l$ that maximizes the margin can now be determined by minimizing the squared norm $\|\mathbf{w}\|^2 + C \sum_{i=1}^{t} \xi_i$ under the constraint (16). This approach is closely related to the idea of canonical hyperplanes used in Support Vector classification. In [8], the author gave the theoretical justification for the applicability of SRM. Introducing Lagrangian multipliers and performing unconstrained optimization with respect to $\mathbf{w}$ lead to the dual problem of finding α^l such that it maximizes

$$\alpha^l = \max_{\substack{0 \le \alpha \le C1 \\ \alpha^T z = 0}} \left[1^T \alpha - \frac{1}{2} \alpha^T \mathbf{Z}^T \mathbf{QZ}\alpha \right] \tag{17}$$

with $\mathbf{z} = (z_1, ..., z_t)^T$, $\mathbf{Z} = diag(\mathbf{z})$, and $Q_{ij} = (x_i^{(1)} - x_i^{(2)})^T(x_j^{(1)} - x_j^{(2)})$. This is a standard QP-problem and can efficiently be solved using techniques from mathematical programming. Given the optimal vector α^l as solution to (17), the optimal weight vector $\mathbf{w}^l$ can be written as a linear combination of differences of feature vectors from the training set (Kuhn-Tucker conditions):

$$\mathbf{w}^l = \sum_{i=1}^{t} \alpha_i^l z_i (\mathbf{x}_i^{(1)} - \mathbf{x}_i^{(2)}) \tag{18}$$

To estimate the rank boundaries we note that due to Equations (16) the difference in utility is greater or equal to one for all training examples with $\xi_i = 0$ (or equivalently $\alpha_i < C$). Thus if $\Theta(k) \subset S'$ is the fraction of objects from the training set with $\xi_i = 0$ and rank difference of exactly one starting from rank r_k, then the estimation of $\theta(r_k)$ is given by

$$\theta(r_k) = \frac{U(\mathbf{x}_1) + U(\mathbf{x}_2)}{2} \tag{19}$$

where $(\mathbf{x}_1, \mathbf{x}_2) = \arg\min_{(x_i, x_j) \in \Theta(k)} [U(\mathbf{x}_i; \mathbf{w}^l) - U(\mathbf{x}_j; \mathbf{w}^l)]$. In other words, the optimal threshold $\theta(r_k)$ for rank r_k lies in the middle of the utilities of the closet (in the sense of their utility) objects of r_k and r_{k+1}. After the estimation of the rank boundaries, a new object is classified according to Equation (13). We should point out, that as a learning algorithm for relevance feedback, we need not compute ranks for all images, just use the utilities of all images to rank them.

The extension to non-linear utility functions follows the same reasoning as with non-linear SVM [12]. Let us introduce a mapping $\Phi(\mathbf{x}) : X \mapsto Z$ of X into the so called "feature space" Z, and we have a non-linear utility

$$U(\mathbf{x}) = \mathbf{w}^T \Phi(\mathbf{x}), \tag{20}$$

Assume the feature space Z is a reproducing kernel hilbert space, then it is uniquely determined by the kernel function $K : \mathbf{X} \times \mathbf{X} \to R$, which has the property $K(\mathbf{x}_i, \mathbf{x}_j) = \Phi(\mathbf{x}_i)^T \Phi(\mathbf{x}_j)$. Then Q_{ij} is simplified to

$$Q_{ij} = K(x_i^{(1)}, x_j^{(1)}) - K(x_i^{(1)}, x_j^{(2)}) - K(x_i^{(2)}, x_j^{(1)}) + K(x_i^{(2)}, x_j^{(2)}) \tag{21}$$

which avoids explicit computation of the mapping $\mathbf{x} \mapsto \Phi(\mathbf{x})$. And the utility function can be computed as

$$U(\mathbf{x}) = \mathbf{w}^T \Phi(\mathbf{x}) = \sum_{i=1}^{l} \alpha_i^l z_i (K(\mathbf{x}_i^{(1)}, \mathbf{x}) - K(\mathbf{x}_i^{(2)}, \mathbf{x})) \tag{22}$$

5   Experimental Results

In this experiment we compare our approach which using a support vector learning algorithm for ordinal regression (SVOR) with the relevance feedback algorithm (WT) in [4, 5] and multi-class SVM (SVM-MC) using one-against-all strategy. Test was conducted on real-world images. We use a heterogeneous image database, which consists of 1,200 images from the Corel dataset. It has 12 classes each with 100 images. These are elephants, tigers, flowers, eagles, people, clouds, beach, architecture, balloon, plane, autumn, and texture. Virtual features used in our system are color histogram, color moments, wavelet-based texture and directionality. Color histogram is taken in HSV color space with quantization into 8x4=32 colors. The first three moments from each of the three color channels are used for color moments. 24 dimension PWT wavelet features and 8 directionality features are also used to construct totally 73-dimension feature vector. "Gaussian Normalization" is used to make the value of each feature component be in the range of [-1,1].

For simplicity, we use three relevance levels in our experiments: relevance, partial relevance, and non-relevance. 40 query images are randomly selected, 10 from tigers class, 10 from clouds class, 10 from people class, and the others from beach class. The grandtruth is constructed as follows. For the queries from tiger class, all images from other classes are considered as non-relevance, and the images in tiger class are further divided into relevance and partial relevance by a user. The grandtruth for the queries from clouds, people and beach class are constructed in the same way. We designed an automatic process to perform relevance feedback. For each query, the system uses Euclidean distance metric to rank images at the first round; after that, three iterations of relevance feedback are performed. At each iteration, the system automatically labels relevance, partial relevance or non-relevance for the returned first 20 images according to the grandtruth.

For SVOR and SVM-MC, we use the Gaussian kernel $K(\mathbf{x}, \mathbf{y}) = e^{-\gamma \|\mathbf{x}-y\|^2}$ with $\gamma = 0.1$ and a trade-off parameter C=1000. The algorithm is coded in C, and the quadratic programming is solved using Platt's SMO [13]. For WT, we use regularization terms to keep the covariance matrix from singularity.

To evaluate the performance, the mean ndpm for all 40 queries is calculated. Note that the smaller value of ndpm means the better performance of the system. We also give hit rates in the first 100 outputs for relevant and partially relevant images respectively. We think they are more intuitive. The results of the three iterations of relevance feedback are presented in Table 1, 2 and Figure 1. From the

Table 1. Relevance and partial relevance hit rates at different iterations

	iter0	iter1	iter2	iter3
WT	9.6/21.8	11.8/25.6	13.1/28.1	14.6/31.6
SVOR	9.6/21.8	15.6/27.3	18.9/35.5	21.3/42.3
SVM-MC	9.6/21.8	14.1/24	17.1/30.6	19.4/41.1

Table 2. ndpm at different iterations

	iter0	iter1	iter2	iter3
WT	0.2	0.219	0.196	0.172
SVOR	0.2	0.16	0.098	0.065
SVM-MC	0.2	0.184	0.128	0.073

results, we can see SVOR outperform WT and multi-class SVM. This indicate that SVOR can use the ordering information implied in Y more effectively.

6   Conclusion and Future Works

In this paper, we focus on multilevel relevance judgment for image retrieval, which is an extension and complementary to dichotomy relevance judgment. We propose that relevance feedback can be regarded as ordinal regression, and state its properties and loss function. For image retrieval with multilevel relevance judgment, we also introduce a performance measure, which is based on the preference of one document on another one. Furthermore, we develop a relevance feedback scheme using a support vector learning algorithm for ordinal regression. Experimental results illustrate the effectiveness of our solution.

For ordinal regression, the pairs of objects are used for training, so the training samples are increasing very fast when relevance feedback goes on. Hence other solutions and fast algorithms for ordinal regression should be developed to make the solution more practical.

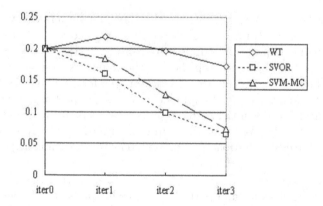

Fig. 1. ndpm at different iterations

References

[1] Meilhac, C., and Nastar, C.: Relevance feedback and category search in image databases. In IEEE International Conference on Multimedia Computing and Systems, Florence, Italy (1999)

[2] Wu, Y., Tian, Q., Huang, T. S.: Disciminant EM algorithm with Application to Image Retrieval. Proc. IEEE Conf. Computer Vision and Pattern Recognition, Hilton Head Island, SC (2000)

[3] Zhang, L., Lin, F. and Zhang, B.: Support vector machine for image retrieval. IEEE Int'l Conf. on Image Processing. Thessaloniki, Greece (2001)

[4] Ishikawa, Y., Subramanya, R. and Faloutsos, C.: MindReader: Query databases through multiple examples. in Proc. Of the 24th VLDB Conf. NY (1998)

[5] Rui, Y. and Huang, T. S.: Optimizing Learning In Image Retrieval. Proc. of IEEE Int Conf on Computer Vision and Pattern Recognition (CVPR), Hilton Head, SC (2000)

[6] Yao, Y. Y.: Measuring retrieval effectiveness based on user preference of documents. Journal of the American Society for Information Science, 46(2) (1995) 133–145

[7] Herbrich, R., Graepel, T., Bollmann-Sdorra, P. and Ober-mayer K.: Learning a preference relation for information retrieval. In Proceedings of the AAAI Workshop Text Categorization and Machine Learning, Madison,USA (1998)

[8] Herbrich, R., Graepel, T. and Ober-mayer, K.: Regression models for ordinal data: A machine learning approach. Technical report, TU Berlin. TR-99/03 (1999)

[9] Herbrich, R., Graepel, T., and Obermayer, K.: Support Vector Learning for Ordinal Regression. In Proceedings of the Ninth International Conference on Articial Neural Networks (1999) 97–102

[10] Van Rijsbergen, D. J. Information retrieval. London: Butter-worths. (1979)

[11] Wong, S. K. M., Yao, Y. Y., & Bollmann, P.: Linear structure in information retrieval. In proceedings of the 11th Annual International ACM SIGIR Conference on Research and Development in Information Retrieval (1998) 219–232

[12] Vapnik, V. Statistical Learning Theory. New York: John Wiley and Sons. (1998)

[13] Platt, J. C.: Fast training of support vector machines using sequential minimal optimization. in Advances in Kernel Methods: Support Vector Machines, B. Scholkopf, C. Burges, and A. Smola, Eds. Cambridge, MA:MIT Press (1998)

Majority Based Ranking Approach in Web Image Retrieval

Gunhan Park, Yunju Baek, and Heung-Kyu Lee

Division of Computer Science
Department of Electrical Engineering & Computer Science
Korea Advanced Institute of Science and Technology
373-1 Kusung-Dong Yusong-Gu Taejon, 305-701, Republic of Korea
{gunhan,yunju,hklee}@rtlab.kaist.ac.kr

Abstract. In this paper, we address a ranking problem in web image retrieval. Due to the growing availability of web images, comprehensive retrieval of web images has been expected. Conventional systems for web image retrieval are based on keyword- based retrieval. However, we often find undesirable retrieval results from the keyword based web image retrieval system since the system uses the limited and inaccurate text information of web images ; a typical system uses text information such as surrounding texts and/or image filenames, etc. To alleviate this situation, we propose a new ranking approach which is the integration of results of text and image content via analyzing the retrieved results. We define four ranking methods based on the image contents analysis of the retrieved images; (1) majority-first method, (2) centroid-of-all method, (3) centroid-of-top K method, and (4) centroid-of-largest-cluster method. We evaluate the retrieval performance of our methods and conventional one using precision and recall graphs. The experimental results show that the proposed methods are more effective than conventional keyword-based retrieval methods.

1   Introduction

The rapid growing of web environment, and advances of technology have led us to access and manage huge images easily in various areas. The comprehensive retrieval of the image collections on the web become the important research and industrial issue.

The web image retrieval has different characteristics from typical content-based image retrieval(CBIR) systems. In general, web images have the related text annotations which could be obtained from the web pages where images are contained. So conventional web image retrieval systems utilize the text information of the images, and work as text(keyword) retrieval systems. Some systems use the texts and simple image information(e.g. image size, image format, graph/non-graph, etc.), and other systems provide the user input interface for relevance feedback.

Existing web image search systems allow users to search for images via keywords interface and/or via query by image example. Generally, the system

E. M. Bakker et al. (Eds.): CIVR 2003, LNCS 2728, pp. 111–120, 2003.

presents pages of representative thumbnail images to the user. The user then marks one or more images as relevant to the query. The visual image features for these images are then used in defining a visual query. However, it is often observed that there are many wrong results in high rank from the keyword-based image retrieval. Moreover, it is difficult to guarantee that there will be even one expected image shown in the initial page. Sclaroff called this the page zero problem[8].

To alleviate such a problem, we propose a new ranking approach that provides the better retrieval performance using image contents of retrieved results. Our approach is basically based on a integration of results of text and image contents via analyzing the retrieved results. The proposed approach determines the candidates using keyword first, and then automatically re-ranks images using visual features of retrieved results. We define four ranking methods based on the cluster analysis and majority of retrieved images. In experiments, we show that the proposed ranking approach improves retrieval performance of web image retrieval as compared to conventional one.

The paper is organized as follows. In Section 2, we briefly summarize the related work on web image retrieval. Our approach is described in Section 3. In Section 4, we present experimental results and discussions. Conclusions will be given in the last section.

2   Related Work

In recent years, there has been a number of research about CBIR systems. Most of the research has concentrated on feature extraction of an image, e.g., QBIC[2], VisualSeek[3], SIMPLicity[5], Netra[4], and Blobworld[6]. None of these systems provides a web search method; these systems are not based on textual cues. However, several systems have been developed for web image retrieval. These web image retrieval methods utilize different attributes; textual cues. PictoSeek[9] indexes images collected from the web. First, the system uses pure visual information, then it uses text information to classify the images. A similar system, Webseek[3] performs user helped classification. The system makes categories, and searches images within category, and provides category browsing and a search by example. Webseer[10] retrieves images using keywords, and additional image information that express the size of image, format of image, and simple classification information(e.g., graph, portrait, computer generated graphic, close-up, number of faces etc.). ImageRover[8] system allows the user to specify the image via keywords, an example image and relevance feedback. The ImageRover approach is most similar in spirit to that of WebSeer; however, ImageRover differs in that it allows searches of Web images based directly on image contents. ImageRover also proposed a method combining textual and visual cues using LSI(latent Semantic Indexing).

Generally, we can summarize the mechanism of conventional web image retrieval as follows : 1) the system retrieves the images using keywords or simple information about an image(not image contents such as color, texture, and shape). 2) the system provides the interface to select relevant images from the first retrieved results(relevance feedback mechanism). 3) the system retrieves the images using selected images or/and keywords. 4) the system refines the results in repeating step 2 and step 3.

As shown in the previous systems keywords may help guide the search, and also become the important evidence in web image retrieval. Unfortunately, keywords may not accurately or completely describe image contents. Information about image contents directly from the image must also be added to retrieval processing. So in this paper, we propose a new approach that improve the retrieval performance using image contents analysis. Our approach will be described in detail in next section.

3 Majority-Based Ranking Approach

In this section, we describe a new ranking approach using image contents analysis. We also define four ranking methods based on the cluster analysis and majority of retrieved images. The difference from previous scheme with a relevance feedback mechanism is that we re-rank the results without assistance from the user(i.e. our approach is automatic). We will explain image features and clustering methods at first, and then we will explain the our approach using these features and the clustering methods.

3.1 Image Features and Clustering Methods

Various image features such as color, shape and texture have been developed in the literature. In a typical image retrieval model, image features are represented as a vector in a n-dimensional vector space. Color is an important attribute for describing the contents of image. Color histogram, that represents the proportion of specific colors in images, has been widely used among color representation methods. It has been known that color histogram in the CBIR provides reasonable retrieval performance when we use the HSV(Hue, Saturation, Value) color space, 128 quantization level, and the histogram intersection as a similarity function. The HSV color model is most frequently used for CBIR because it presents human perception well. The histogram intersection is calculated as follows; $H(I, I') = \sum_{i=1}^{n} min(f_i, f_i')/(\sum_{i=1}^{n} f_i')$. If the size of an image is same, histogram intersection is equivalent to the use of the sum of absolute differences or city-block metric[1]. In this paper, we use the city- block metric for similarity computation. City-block distance is defined as follows :

$$D_{city-block}(I, I') = \sum_{i=1}^{n} |f_i - f_i'| \tag{1}$$

Many clustering techniques for improving retrieval effectiveness have been proposed in the information retrieval literature, and also proposed in CBIR[11][12]. We use clustering methods to group the images and to select the representative image features for our approach.

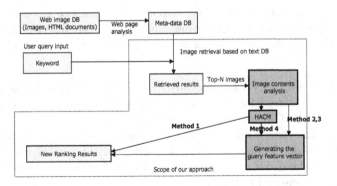

Fig. 1. Overview of the proposed approach

The hierarchical agglomerative clustering methods(HACM) are known to be effective in information retrieval applications. There are several methods to make a tree structure (it is usually called as a dendrogram[7]) for the HACM. We use group average link, and Ward's method among the clustering methods. The advantages of each method are well compared in the literature[13][14]. There are three approaches to the implementation of the general HACM. Among them, we use the stored matrix approach. We first calculate a N by N matrix containing all pairwise dissimilarity values using an association of measure function, and the Lance-Williams update formula makes it possible to re-calculate the dissimilarity between cluster centers using only the stored values. Eq. (2) shows the update formula, and Table 1 shows its parameters[7].

$$d_{C_{i,j}C_k} = \alpha_i d_{C_i C_k} + \alpha_j d_{C_j C_k} + \beta d_{C_i C_j} + \gamma |d_{C_i C_k} - d_{C_j C_k}| \qquad (2)$$

3.2   Proposed Ranking Methods

In our web image retrieval, we utilize the retrieved results from keyword-based retrieval which is commonly used as web image retrieval systems; then the results are re-ranked with the proposed ranking approach. Fig 1 shows the architecture and the scope of our approach.

The brief explanation of proposed ranking approach is as follows; we analyze the top-N retrieval results, and re-ranks images according to the majority-based

Table 1. Lance-Williams parameters

HACM	α	β	γ
Group average link	$m_i/(m_i + m_j)$	0	0
Ward's method	$(m_i + m_k)/(m_i + m_j + m_k)$	$-m_k/(m_i + m_j + m_k)$	0

algorithms that we propose. Our basic hypothesis is that the more popular images have the higher probability to be desirable images. Based on this hypothesis, we propose the four methods that represent image contents for ranking as follows.

- **Method 1 (majority-first method)** : This method is using the majority property of retrieved images. For this method, we partition the retrieved images using HACM, and then we order the clusters according to the size of clusters. In other words, the largest cluster ranks first, and the sequence of clusters is determined as decreasing order of the size of cluster. After determining the order of clusters, we ranks the images within a cluster by distance to a centroid of the cluster.
- **Method 2 (centroid-of-all method)** : This method uses the centroid of the whole images of the retrieved results. Thus the centroid is represented as the average of retrieved images. Using this centroid as a query vector(a feature vector of a query image), the system is turned into conventional CBIR; the system ranks the images using a similarity function to this feature vector.
- **Method 3 (centroid-of-top-K method)** : This method uses the centroid of the K top-ranked images. Since there are many undesirable images in retrieved results, we only select some of top ranked images. We use 20 for K in the experiments. Like method 2, the centroid is used as a query vector for the CBIR system to re-rank the results.
- **Method 4 (centroid-of-largest-cluster method)** : In the fourth method, we use the centroid of the largest cluster as a query vector for image searching. In this method, we use the effect of the clustering to select a query vector. We assume the original rank is not important in this method as different from method 2 and 3.

In our methods, we define the centroid $C(A_I)$ of image set A_I as follows.

$$C(A_I) = \frac{\sum_{v \in A_I} v}{|A_I|} \qquad (3)$$

where $|A_I|$ is a size of A_I and v is a feature vector of an image.

Using the four ranking methods and the two clustering methods, we evaluate the proposed approach in the next section.

4   Experimental Results

4.1   Experimental Environments: Test Collections

We conducted experiments using retrieved images from Naver[1], and Google[2] for some keywords : tiger, car, sea, etc. We gathered the top-200 images from results

---

[1] http://www.naver.com is one of the most popular search engines in Korea. This search engine retrieve the relevant image among over 10 million ones on the web.

[2] see http://www.google.com

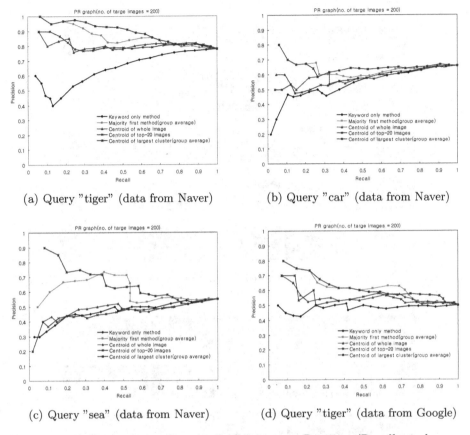

(a) Query "tiger" (data from Naver)   (b) Query "car" (data from Naver)

(c) Query "sea" (data from Naver)   (d) Query "tiger" (data from Google)

Fig. 2. Comparison of retrieval effectiveness: Precision/Recall graphs

of a search engine for experiments, and evaluate the effectiveness in comparing the precision and recall value. Precision and recall are calculated as follows : precision = number of relevant retrieved images/total number of retrieved images, recall = number of relevant retrieved images/number of all relevant images. For the evaluation, we marked relevant images and irrelevant images manually about top-200 images. Naver basically use text annotations for image retrieval in web image album service, and Google use image filenames and frequency of user selection. Acquired images for our experiments are subject to change, but tendency of results is similar to our experimental data.

4.2   Results

The goal of the experiment is to evaluate the retrieval effectiveness of the proposed methods. The results of experiments are shown in Fig 2. The results show precision/recall graphs about initial method(keyword only retrieval) and our four

Rerieved Results(from naver.com image search)

(a) the retrieved results from Naver

Rerieved Results(Re-ranking by clustering : group average)

(b) the retrieved results using the proposed method(centroid-of-largest-cluster)

Fig. 3. The retrieval example using "tiger" (data from Naver)

methods : majority-first method, centroid-of-largest-cluster method, centroid-of-all method, and centroid-of-top-20 method. In the case of two methods based on HACM, the results are reported only for the method(group average link) with the better effectiveness.

The results in Fig. 2 show that the centroid-of-largest-cluster and majority-first methods have better effectiveness among four proposed methods. We think

Rerieved Results(from google.com image search)

(a) the retrieved results from Google

Rerieved Results(Re-ranking by clustering : group average)

(b) the retrieved results using the proposed method(centroid-of-largest-cluster)

Fig. 4. The retrieval example using "tiger" (data from Google)

that the reason is because other methods contain the more wrong images in calculating the centroid, and the clustering methods reflect characteristics of images well.

The retrieval examples of the initial method and our methods are shown in Fig. 3, and Fig. 4. We used a centroid-of-largest-cluster method and group average link clustering for these examples. It is clear that relevant images to the keyword query are ranked higher in the proposed methods than in the initial method.

It should be noticed that the effectiveness of the proposed method has improved significantly compared to the initial method. As shown in the results of experiments, in which case many relevant images are contained in the top-200 results the effectiveness of retrieval has improved significantly(Fig. 2(a)), while in the case of a few relevant images in the results the effectiveness has improved a little(Fig. 2(d)) relatively.

The overhead of this algorithm is that it has additional computation time for constructing the clusters. However, the algorithm has little added computational time(0.08 second for clustering, 0.02 second for ordering) since it performs on small number(200) of the images. We performed the experiments using Red Hat Linux 7.2 and a Pentium III 800 MHz system.

5   Conclusions

In this paper, we have proposed a new ranking approach which is the integration of results of text and image contents : majority based ranking approach. It has an advantage that it can use the contents of image in determining the rank of web images. We compared a keyword-based retrieval method and four proposed methods in our experiments. Experimental results show that the majority based approach, especially with the centroid-of-largest-cluster method, has better effectiveness than the initial method using only text evidence. Since our approach can use additional information of retrieved images, we believe that the majority based ranking approach will be a good effectiveness enhancement method compared to a general keyword-based retrieval method. In future work, we plan to apply other methods using various image features to our approach.

References

[1] M. J. Swain, and D. H. Ballad, "Color Indexing," International Journal of Computer Vision, Vol. 7, No. 1, pp. 11-32, 1991. 113
[2] C. Faloutsos, R. Barber, M. Flickner, J. Hafner, W Niblack, D. Petkovic, and W. Equitz, "Efficient and Effective Querying by Image Content," Journal of Intelligent Information Systems, Vol. 3, No. 3/4, pp. 231-262, 1994. 112
[3] J. R. Smith, "Integrated Spatial and Feature Image Systems : Retrieval, Analysis and Compression," Doctoral Dissertations, Columbia University, 1997. 112
[4] W. Y. Ma and B. S. Manjunath, "NeTra: a toolbox for navigating large image databases", Multimedia Systems, Vol. 7, No. 3, pp. 184-198, 1999. 112
[5] J. Z. Wang, J. Li, and G. Wiederhold, "SIMPLIcity: Semantics-sensitive Integrated Matching for Picture Libraries,'" IEEE Transactions on Pattern Analysis and Machine Intelligence, Vol. 23, No. 9, pp. 947-963, 2001. 112
[6] C. Carson, S. Belongie, H. Greenspan, and J. Malik, "Blobworld: Image Segmentation Using Expectation-Maximization and Its Application to Image Querying," IEEE Transactions on Pattern Analysis and Machine Intelligence, Vol. 24, No. 8, pp. 1026-1038, 2002. 112

[7] W. B. Frakes, and R. Baeza-Yates, "Information Retrieval : Data Structures & Algorithms," Prentice Hall, 1992. 114

[8] S. sclaroff, M. la Cascia, S. Sethi, and L. Taycher, "Unifying Textual and Visual Cues for Content-Based Image Retrieval on the World Wide Web," Computer Vision and Image Understanding, Vol. 75, No.1/2, pp. 86-98, 1999. 112

[9] T. Gevers and A. W. M. Smeulders, "Pictoseek: A content-based image search engine for the WWW," Proceedings of International Conf. On Visual Information Systems, pp. 93-100, 1997. 112

[10] C. Frankel, M. J. Swain, and V. Athitsos, "WebSeer : An Image Search Engine for the World Wide Web," University of Chicago Technical Report TR-96-14, 1996. 112

[11] A. Tombros, R. Villa, R., and C. J. Van Rijsbergen, "The effectiveness of query-specific hierarchic clustering in information retrieval," Information Processing & Management, Vol. 38, No. 4, pp. 559-582, 2002. 113

[12] G. Park, Y Baek, and H. K. Lee, "A Ranking Algorithm Using Dynamic Clustering for Content-Based Image Retrieval,", the Challenge of Image and Video Retrieval(CIVR2002): International Conference on Image and Video Retrieval, pp. 316-324, 2002. 113

[13] E. M. Voorhees, "The cluster hypothesis revisited," Proceedings of 8th ACM SI-GIR International Conference on Research and Development in Information Retrieval, pp. 188-196, 1985. 114

[14] P. Willett, "Recent trends in hierarchic document clustering : A critical review," Information Processing & Management, Vol. 24, No. 5, pp. 577-587, 1988. 114

Improving Fractal Codes Based Image Retrieval Using Histogram of Collage Errors

Ming Hong Pi[1], Chong Sze Tong[1] and Anup Basu[2]

[1]Dept. of Mathematics, Hong Kong Baptist University, Kowloon Tong, Hong Kong
minghong@cs.ualberta.ca and cstong@hkbu.edu.hk
[2]Dept. of Computing Science, University of Alberta, Edmonton AB, T6G 2V4, Canada
anup@cs.ualberta.ca

Abstract: Collage error is a quantitative measure of the similarity between range block and "best-matching" domain block. It is relatively robust compared with the fractal encoding parameters which can be quite sensitive to changes in the domain block pool. However, up to now, fractal-based image indexing techniques are developed based on the fractal encoding parameters while collage error is overlooked. In the paper, we propose three composite statistical indices by combining histogram of fractal parameters with the histogram of collage errors to improve fractal codes based indexing technique. Experimental results on a database of 416 texture images show that the proposed indices not only reduce computational complexities, but also enhance the retrieval rate, compared to existing fractal-based retrieval methods.

1 Introduction

Since Jacquin presented a block-based fractal compression scheme by partition iterated function system, which is popularly known as fractal block coding [1], fractal coding has brought a great deal of attention [1-3] as a new promising image compression techniques. Based on the fractal codes, a few indexing techniques have been proposed recently.

Zhang *et al.* [4] proposed a fractal indexing technique where the fractal codes are directly used as the image index (referred to as the FC technique). However, the FC technique is based on direct match between the fractal codes of query image and of candidate images, and hence, retrieval is very slow. In addition, the corresponding fractal codes cannot be used to reconstruct the retrieved image.

Schouten *et al.* [5] extended the histogram-based technique to fractal domain. The authors proposed to employ histogram of contrast scaling parameters as an image index (referred to as the HWQCS technique). The indexing technique is very fast, however, its retrieval rate is not high enough.

Pi *et al.* [6] further proposed to employ the 2-D joint histogram of range block means and contrast scaling parameters as an image index (referred to as the HNFP technique). Compared to other fractal codes-based image retrieval technique, the HNFP technique greatly improved the retrieval rate. However, its computational complexity needs to be reduced.

E. M. Bakker et al. (Eds.): CIVR 2003, LNCS 2728, pp. 121-130, 2003.

Up to now, all the attention to fractal-based indexing technique is concentrated on the fractal codes, while the importance of collage error has been ignored. However, the range block collage error measures the similarity between the range block and "best-matching" domain block and is a more meaningful and robust measure of the self-similarity characteristic of the image. By contrast, the fractal transform parameters can be quite sensitive to the change in domain block pool.

It has been demonstrated that histograms of fractal parameters capture statistical characteristic of texture images efficiently [5, 6]. Thus while we propose to exploit the histogram of collage errors as an image index, we further propose three composite statistical indices by combining histogram of collage errors and histogram of fractal parameters to enhance retrieval rate and reduce computational complexity. Experimental results indicate that the proposed techniques not only reduce computational complexities significantly, but also enhance retrieval rate.

The remainder of the paper is organized as follows. Section 2 present fractal block coding with range block mean and contrast scaling and collage error. Section 3 describes the proposed indices. Experimental results are reported in Section 4, which is followed by the conclusions.

2 Review of Fractal Coding and Indexing

In the section, we first present fractal block coding with range block mean and contrast scaling parameter [3] and collage error, then introduce fractal indexing technique.

2.1 Fractal Coding

For each range block R, fractal block coding seeks to minimize the following distortion

$$E(R,D) = \left\| R - \bar{r}_i U - s_j (D - \bar{d} U) \right\|^2 \tag{1}$$

over $D \in \Omega$ (domain block pool) with respect to a set of the pre-quantized fractal parameters $\{\bar{r}_i\}_{i=1}^{I}$ and $\{s_j\}_{j=1}^{J}$ (I and J is quantization level for $\bar{r}$ and s, respectively). Note that in Eq. (1), U is a matrix whose elements are all ones and $\|\|$ is the 2-norm, and $\bar{d}$ is the mean of the pre-contractive domain blocks. The fractal code of range block R is

$$(s, \bar{r}, x_D, y_D) = \arg \min_{D \in \Omega} E(R, D)$$

where (x_D, y_D) is top-left corner coordinate of the "best-matching" domain block. The collage error of R is calculated as

$$\hat{E}(R) = \min_{D \in \Omega} \sqrt{E(R,D)/B \times B}$$

At the decoder, the reconstructed image is generated by recursive iterations starting with the range-averaged image [7] using the following iteration [8]

$$R^{(n)} = \bar{r}\,U + s\;(D^{(n-1)} - \bar{d}^{\,(n-1)}U)$$

2.2   Fractal Indexing

It has been demonstrated in the literature that image histogram (of pixel values) provides a good indexing performance, while being computationally inexpensive [9]. Schouten *et al.* [5] extended this technique to fractal domain and proposed HWQCS technique where the histogram of weighted quad-tree contrast scaling parameter s is used as the image index. For single level fractal coding, the index degrades into histogram of s expressed as:

$$p_s(s_j) \quad (j = 1,2,\cdots,J)$$

Pi *et al.* [6] further extended the HWQCS technique, proposed the HNFP technique where histogram of $\bar{r}$ and the joint histogram of $\bar{r}$ and s as statistical indices, which are expressed as:

$$p_{\bar{r}}(\bar{r}_i) \;\; (i = 1,\cdots,I) \;\; \text{and} \;\; \{q(\bar{r}_i, s_j)\} \;\; (i = 1,\cdots,I;\, j = 1,\cdots,J)$$

The HNFP indexing technique greatly improve retrieval rate, compared with existing fractal-based retrieval methods, however, the computational complexity need be reduced.

3   The Proposed Statistical Indices

Collage error measures the similarity between the range block and "best-matching" domain block and provides a quantitative description of the self-similarity of the image. Hence, collage error is an important component in fractal indexing techniques. We first propose histogram of collage errors as a statistical index. To further enhance retrieval rate, we propose three composite indices by combining histogram of collage errors and histogram of fractal parameters. These indices are described in detail below.

3.1   Index-1

Histogram of collage errors efficiently capture the statistical characteristic of texture images, hence it is expected to provide a high retrieval rate.

Collage error is real-valued and its distribution has a relatively short tail. Hence, before we count histogram of collage errors, collage errors are rounded into the closest integer if collage errors are smaller than $T-1$, or are clipped into $T-1$ if collage errors exceed $T-1$ (T is a user-specified clipping threshold). Histogram of collage errors is referred as Index-1 and is expressed as:

$$p_e(k) \quad (k = 0,1,2,\cdots,T-1)$$

In order to enhance the retrieval rate, it is necessary to combine the statistical information from both collage error and fractal parameters. Using tensor product and weight averaging, we construct three composite indices.

3.2   Index-2

In consideration of both retrieval rate and computational complexity, we first combine histogram of s with Index-1 by tensor product. This composite index is referred as Index-2 and is expressed as follows:

$$\{p_s(s_j)\}_{j=1}^{J} \otimes \{p_e(k)\}_{k=0}^{T-1} = \{p_s(s_j)^* p_e(k)\}_{k=0,j=1}^{T-1,J} \qquad (2)$$

Index-2 is regarded as the approximation of 2D joint histogram of contrast scaling parameters and collage errors. Although, in theory, 2D joint histogram or tensor product is expected to capture statistical characteristic of texture image, the dimension is greatly magnified.

3.3   Index-3

To avoid rapid growth in dimension, we construct composite indices by weighting histogram of collage errors and histogram of s. The composite index is referred as Index-3 and is expressed as follows:

$$w_1\{p_e(k)\}_{k=0}^{T-1} + (1-w_1)\{p_s(s_j)\}_{j=1}^{J} \qquad (3)$$

where w_1 and $(1-w_1)$ are the weights of the histograms of collage errors and histogram of s, respectively.

3.4   Index-4

The fractal transform from the range block to its "best-matching" domain block is determined by s, $\bar{r}$ and collage error. Hence, the 3-D joint histogram of $\bar{r}$, s and collage error precisely captures the statistical characteristic between range block and "best- matching" domain block. However, the dimension of the 3-D joint histogram is $T \times J \times I$, which even exceeds the total number of range blocks. As a result, most bins are empty and redundant. In addition, because the dimension is very high, the 3-D joint histogram is unable to be employed as an image index in real-time retrieval system. To reduce the redundancy, we construct a composite index by weighting index-3 and histogram of $\bar{r}$, which is referred as Index-4 and expressed as follow.

$$w_2[w_1\{p_e(k)\}_{k=0}^{T-1} + (1-w_1)\{p_s(s_j)\}_{j=1}^{J}] + (1-w_2)\{p_{\bar{r}}(\bar{r}_i)\}_{i=1}^{I} \qquad (4)$$

where $w_1 w_2$, $(1-w_1)w_2$ and $(1-w_2)$ are the weights of the histograms of collage errors, histogram of s, and histogram of $\bar{r}$, respectively.

Weight averaging is better combination than tensor product as far as computational complexity is concerned. Index-3 is $T+J$ and Index-4 is $T+J+I$ in length, while Index-2 is $T \times J$ in length. Our experimental results demonstrate weight averaging efficiently exploits individual histograms to achieve high retrieval rate.

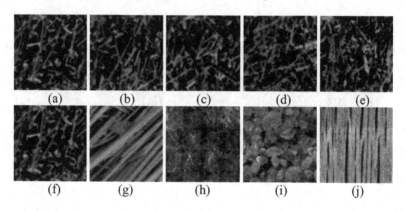

(a)   (b)   (c)   (d)   (e)

(f)   (g)   (h)   (i)   (j)

Fig. 1. Examples of 128x128 texture images. (a)-(e) Five similar images; (f)-(j) Five different texture images; (a) and (f) is the same image.

3.5   Similar Measurement

To measure the similarity between the query image and the candidate images, we adopt L_1-norm as the distance metric between the proposed indices. If $f_Q(\cdot)$ and $f_C(\cdot)$ are the histograms of the query image and candidate image, respectively, and V is index length, the distance between the two images is calculated as follows.

$$d_{L_1}(Q,C) = \frac{1}{V}\left\|f_Q(\cdot) - f_C(\cdot)\right\|_{L_1}$$

Fig. 1 shows five similar and five different texture images. Histogram of collage errors (i.e. Index-1), histogram of contrast scaling parameters, and tensor product of histogram of s and of collage errors (i.e. Index-2) corresponding to these images are plotted in Fig 2. In most cases, the corresponding indices are close for similar texture images, and different for the dissimilar texture images. Fig. 3 further demonstrates L_1 distance between the proposed indices. The first image in Fig. 1 is regarded as a query image, and other four images are regarded as candidate images. It is observed from Fig. 3 that the distances between similar images are far smaller than those between dissimilar images.

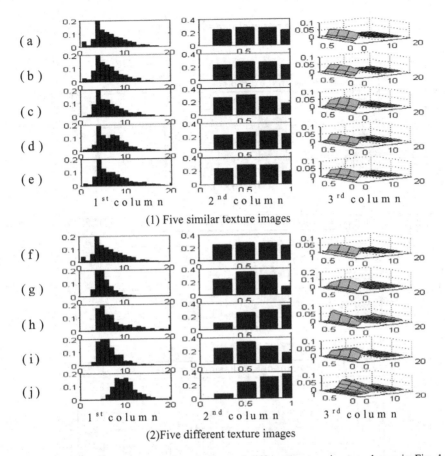

Fig. 2. Histogram corresponding to five similar and different texture images shown in Fig. 1, the 1st column shows Index-1, the 2nd column shows histogram of contrast scaling parameters, the 3rd column shows Index-3. $J = 4$ and $T = 20$.

4 Performance Evaluation

In this section, we present the performance of the proposed techniques and compare them with other retrieval methods.

We use twenty-six 512x512 gray-scale Brodatz texture images [8]. Each image is divided into sixteen 128x128 non-overlapping subimages to create a test database of Z=416 texture images. Each subimage is fractal encoded using adaptive search [3]. $\bar{r}$ is quantized to 6 bits, and s is quantized to 2 bits. Let F be the number of subimages (in this case F=16), and m_z be the number of correctly retrieved images at z-th test, the average retrieval rate is then calculated as

$$\text{Average retrieval rate} = \sum_{z=1}^{Z} m_z \Big/ (FxZ)$$

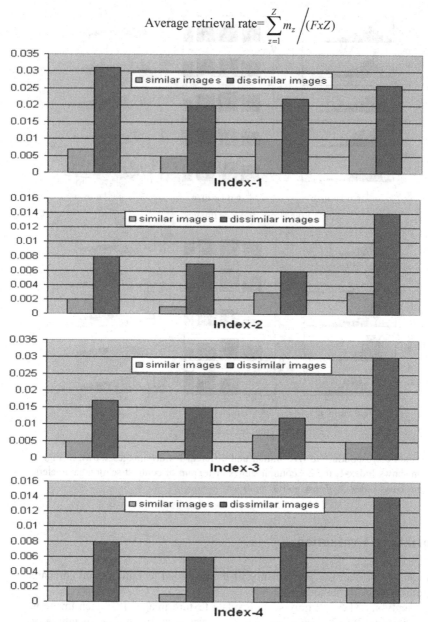

Fig. 3. L_1 distance between similar images and L_1 distance between dissimilar images

It is observed from Fig. 4 that the retrieval rate using Index-1 rapidly increases as clipping threshold T goes up. However, after T reaches a *gateway* value (in this case, $T = 13$), the retrieval rate almost remains constant. This is expected because 95% collage errors are smaller than the gateway value. As a result, even if T increases, no change happens to Index-1.

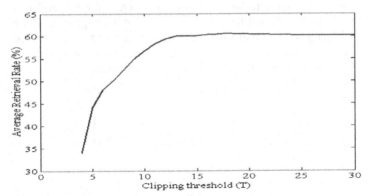

Fig. 4. Average retrieval rate vs. clipping threshold T .

In order to enhance the retrieval rate, we construct Index-2, Index-3 and Index-4 by combining histogram of fractal parameters with Index-1. It is observed from Table 1 that all composite indices provide a performance superior to Index-1. This is expected because the composite indices exploit the statistical information from both collage error and fractal parameters.

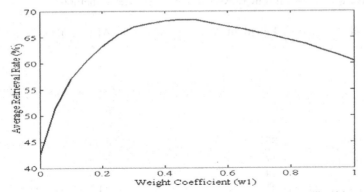

Fig. 5. Average retrieval rate vs. the weight w_1 ($T = 20$).

Index-2 is an approximation to 2D joint histogram of contrast scaling parameters and collage errors. Hence, the retrieval rate using Index-2 is very close to that using 2D joint histogram. Fig. 4 shows retrieval rates vs. the weight w_1 using Index-3. It is observed the retrieval rate peaks around $w_1 = 0.5$. The retrieval rate corresponding to $w_1 = 0.5$ is the same as that using 2D joint histogram.

Fig 6 demonstrates the retrieval rates vs. the weight w_2 using Index-4 when $w_1 = 0.5$. It is observed that the retrieval rate peaks around $w_1 = w_2 = 0.5$. The corresponding retrieval rate is 75%.

We compare the proposed indices with existing fractal indexing techniques: the HWQCS [5] and HNFP techniques [6]. Under the same computational complexity, the retrieval rate using the HWQCS technique is 44.5%, whereas the retrieval rate using Index-1 is 52.6% (see Fig. 4) and increase 8%. Note that if clipping threshold T is very small, the clipping histogram distorts the true distribution of collage errors, and hence the retrieval rate is very low. For example, the retrieval rate using Index-1 is 33.8% when $T = 4$, while the retrieval rate of the HWQCS technique is 42.6%.

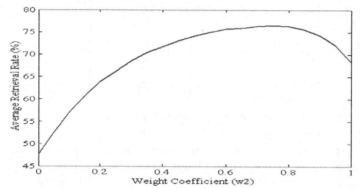

Fig. 6 Average retrieval rate vs. the weight w_2 ($T = 20$, $w_1 = 0.5$).

Table 1. Average Retrieval Rate (ARR) of different retrieval methods.

Retrieval Method	Length of the feature vector	ARR (%)
HWQCS [5] (L=1)	4	42.6
	8	44.5
HNFP [6]	256	71
Index-1	13	60
	20	60.4
Index-2	52	67.4
	80	67.5
Index-3 ($w_1 = 0.5$)	17	67.4
	24	68.3
Index-4 ($w_1 = w_2 = 0.5$)	81	74.2
	88	75
2-D histogram	52	66.7
	80	66.9
3-D histogram	3328	80
	5120	79.7
GGD-KLD [10]	18	69.9

Considering both retrieval rate and computational complexity, the three composite indices improve the retrieval rate using the HNFP technique. Index-3 and the HNFP provide almost same retrieval rate, however, the length of Index-3 is 17, whereas, the length used by the HNFP technique is 256. Compared to the HNFP technique, Index-4 increase the retrieval rate by 4%, but the length of Index-4 equals 88, reducing to one third of that of the HNFP technique (see Table 1).

It is observed from table 1 that 3D joint histogram indeed improves the retrieval rate at the expense of computational complexity. However, as we point out, because of the much higher computational complexity, the 3-D joint histogram is unable to be employed as an image index in real-time retrieval system. Index-4 provides optimal approximation to 3D histogram in term of both retrieval rate and computational complexity.

It is observed from Table 1 that Index-3 provides the performance comparable to the GGD-KLD technique that employs wavelet-based statistical indices [10] in both retrieval rate and computational complexity.

5 Conclusions

In this paper, we have proposed four statistical indices based on collage error and fractal parameters. The proposed indices further improve the retrieval rate, and significantly reduce the computational complexity, compared to existing retrieval methods. Although our discussion is focused on the single level fractal block coding, we can extend the proposed indexing technique into multilevel fractal block coding by multilevel histogram indexing.

References

1. A. E. Jacquin, "Fractal image coding: A review", *Proc. IEEE*, vol. 81, no.10, pp. 1451-1465, 1993.
2. E. W. Jacobs, Y. Fisher, and R. D. Boss, "Image Compression: A Study of Iterated Transform Method," *Signal Processing*, vol. 29, pp. 251-263, Dec. 1992.
3. C. Tong and M. Pi, "Fast Fractal Image compression using Adaptive Search," *IEEE Trans. on IP*, vol.10, pp.1269-1277, Sep. 2001.
4. A. Zhang, B. Cheng and R. Acharya, "An Approach to Query-by-texture in Image Database System," *Proceedings of the SPIE Conference on Digital Image Storage and Archiving Systems*, Philadelphia, October, 1995.
5. B. Schouten and P. Zeeuw, "Image Databases, Scale and Fractal Transforms", *Proceedings of ICIP*, vol. 2, pp. 534 –537, 2000.
6. M. Pi, M. Mandal, and A.Basu, "Image retrieval based on Histogram of New Fractal Parameters," *Proceedings of ICASSP*, Hong Kong, April 2003.
7. Y. H. Moon, H. S. Kim, and J. H. Kim, "A Fast Fractal Decoding Algorithm Based on the Selection of an Initial Image," *IEEE Trans. on IP*, vol.9, no.5, pp.941-945, May 2000.
8. M. Pi, A. Baus, and M. Mandal, "A new decoding algorithm based on range block mean and contrast scaling," *Proceedings of ICIP*, Barcelona, Spain, September 2003.
9. M. J. Swain and D. H. Ballard, "Color Indexing," *International Journal of Computer Vision*, vol. 7, no. 1, pp. 11-32, 1991.
10. M. N. Do and M. Vetterli, "Wavelet-based Texture Retrieval Using Generalized Gaussian Density and Kullback-Leibler Distance," *IEEE Trans. on IP*, vol. 11, no.2, pp.146-158, Feb. 2002.
11. http://www.cipr.rpi.edu/resource/stills/brodatz.html.

Content-Based Retrieval
of Historical Watermark Images:
II - Electron Radiographs

K. Jonathan Riley, Jonathan D. Edwards, and John P. Eakins

School of Informatics, University of Northumbria
Newcastle NE1 8ST, UK
{jon.riley,jonathan.edwards,john.eakins}@unn.ac.uk

Abstract. Providing content-based access to archives of historical watermarks involves a number of problems. This paper describes the further development and evaluation of SHREW, a shape-matching system for watermark images based on techniques developed for the ARTISAN trademark retrieval system. It also compares the effectiveness of different image preprocessing techniques required to enable the system to cope with electron radiographs of watermark images. Finally, it reports comparative studies of the relative effectiveness of different approaches to watermark image matching.

1   Introduction

1.1   Background

Watermarks have been used in Western papermaking since the late thirteenth century. Each watermark provides an indication of the origin and authenticity of the sheets of paper bearing that mark. It is introduced into the paper during sheet formation, via the attachment of a wire design sewn to the surface of the perforated papermakers' mould. Each sheet of paper taken from the same mould is identical. Since the papermaker's mould has historically been hand-made, watermark analysis provides historians, criminologists and others with an opportunity to identify and date paper samples.

Capturing the watermark images from the original papers can be problematic since many can be obscured by various types of media on top of the paper or secondary supports underneath it. A number of reproduction methods are in use, including tracings, rubbings, transmitted light photography, and radiographic techniques. Tracings are relatively easy to produce, but are subjective and often lack accuracy. Rubbings are also cheap and quick to produce, though do not give such good images as radiography. Transmitted light photography can produce a clear image, but details of the watermark are often obscured by the media layer. Radiographic techniques can overcome many of the problems inherent in other methods, although they risk introducing additional noise into the recorded images.

E. M. Bakker et al. (Eds.): CIVR 2003, LNCS 2728, pp. 131-140, 2003.
© Springer-Verlag Berlin Heidelberg 2003

1.2   Watermark Matching and Identification

Currently, matching an unknown watermark to known ones is a difficult and time consuming task. Researchers must work manually and painstakingly through thousands of drawings of marks and their supporting text - often having to use reference sources available for consultation only in specialist libraries. A number of manual classification codes have been devised to assist scholars in this task, such as the Briquet classification [1] and the more recent IPH (International Association of Paper Historians) code [2].

The availability of digitized watermark images on the Web, searchable by CBIR techniques, would clearly be a boon to many researchers in the field. However, only two such systems have yet been reported in the literature[1]: the SWIC (Search Watermark Images by Content) system of Rauber et al [3] and our own Northumbria Watermarks Archive [4]. Rauber's system can retrieve images using either manually-assigned codes such as Briquet's, or automatically extracted features such as the number, shape and relative locations of image regions. Our own system, still under development, has used retrieval techniques adapted from our ARTISAN trademark retrieval system [5] to provide automatic shape similarity matching.

1.3   The Northumbria Watermarks Archive

The Northumbria Watermarks Archive is intended to provide a freely accessible research tool for art and paper historians, forensic scientists and paper conservators. It is intended to draw together and cross-reference existing records in addition to being the starting point for a progressive and interactive collation of new and related information. In addition to the provision of identification information for watermarks and paper, the archive is intended to include extensive data on paper technology, paper history, artists' materials and preservation/conservation issues. A pilot version of the collection, catalogued in accordance with the IPH standard, and searchable by shape similarity, should soon be available on the World-Wide Web.

A previous paper [6] described our investigations into techniques for shape matching of watermark images in the form of tracings. A CBIR system known as SHREW was developed, providing both whole-image and component-based shape matching of watermark images, and retrieval effectiveness evaluated on a set of digitized tracings from the Churchill watermarks collection [7]. Overall, the most effective retrieval was provided using whole-image matching based on the angular radial transform (ART), part of the MPEG-7 standard for multimedia content description [8]. Component matching was generally less successful unless considerable pre-processing was undertaken to reduce noise in stored images.

---

[1] Care should be taken to distinguish our work on images of historical watermarks on paper from the much bigger field of digital watermarking, as exemplified by papers such as [9] and [10]. Digital watermarks are (normally invisible) bit strings, designed to be resistant to tampering, inserted into digital images to protect their owners' intellectual property rights. Many techniques have been proposed for designing, embedding and detecting such bit strings. However, none of these appear relevant to the current problem.

1.4   Aims of Current Investigation

The aim of our current investigation is to extend our work on matching watermark tracings to the much more challenging area of electron radiographs, which are much more susceptible to image noise of the kind shown in Fig. 1. As before, we are interested primarily in the extent to which the retrieval techniques developed for our ARTISAN trademark image retrieval system [5] can prove effective with such images, and the image pre-processing necessary to achieve acceptable performance. Additional project objectives include comparing the effectiveness of different techniques for noise reduction in watermark images, and comparing the retrieval effectiveness of different approaches to matching of watermark images. We then aim to draw general conclusions about the effectiveness of our approach.

2   Methodology

2.1   Electron Radiography of Watermark Images

The technique of watermark detection through electron (emission) radiography was developed at the Deutsche Staatsbibliothek and Technische Universität in Berlin [11]. It has been used successfully to record watermarks at the Koninklijke Bibliotheek, den Haag, the Netherlands [12]. The technique uses an X-ray beam, aimed at a heavy metal material (usually lead), to produce electrons. These are transmitted through the paper containing the watermark to photographic film. The technique is normally capable of producing a faithful copy of the watermark even where the surface of the paper is covered with other media.

As with any recording technique, some noise inevitably creeps into the resultant images (see Fig 1), including:

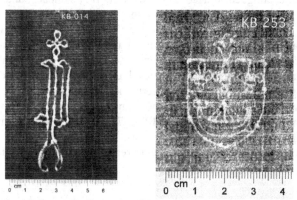

Fig. 1. Examples of electron-radiographs with low (left) and high (right) amounts of noise

- The paper background - in addition to identifying the watermark other paper density changes are also identified. These include the paper flocking, and a faint image of the rectangular grid used to hold the paper fibres together during manufacture. This shows up as a series of widely-spaced vertical *chain lines* and closely-spaced horizontal *laid lines.*

- Surface noise - depending on the type of inks used, traces of the material printed or inscribed on the surface noise can appear in the recorded image.
- Uneven backgrounds - it can be difficult to maintain uniform background pixel intensity throughout the image, and some images show evidence of considerable local intensity fluctuations.
- Blurring - where watermarks have to be extracted from thick paper, or from books where it is impossible to place the page evenly on a flat photographic plate, some blurring of the recorded image is inevitable.

2.2   Watermark Image Preprocessing

The raw materials for our study were 1000 digitised electron-radiographs kindly donated by the Koninklijke Bibliotheek. All images were first normalized to fit within a 512×512 bounding box, to facilitate the use of segmentation algorithms developed for ARTISAN. For different experiments they were then subjected to one or more of the following procedures:

- None (feature extraction was performed directly on grey-scale images).
- Thresholding to convert the grey-scale to bilevel images, by replacing the intensity $I(x,y)$ of each pixel with the value 255 where $I(x,y) > T_l$, and 0 otherwise. After considerable experimentation, the lower quartile of pixel intensity was chosen as the threshold T_l.
- Noise reduction. Several different filters were applied so that their effectiveness in smoothing out random noise could be investigated. After preliminary tests, an edge-preserving 5×5 Kuwahara filter [13] was selected for our main trials.
- Bandpass filtering. Laid lines are normally regularly spaced, close to the horizontal, with a frequency around 50Hz, while chain lines are approximately vertical, with a frequency around 2 Hz. To remove these lines and emphasize the watermark shape itself, images were transformed to the frequency domain with a standard fast Fourier transform, subjected to either a 50Hz low-pass filter or a vertical bandstop filter tuned to remove the lowest-frequency peaks on the y-axis (around 40-60Hz for most images), and transformed back into the spatial domain.

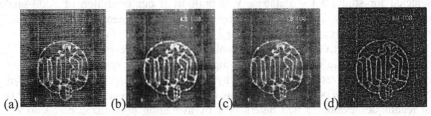

Fig. 2. Effects of different types of image preprocessing: (a) original image; (b) 50 Hz low-pass filter; (c) 40-60 Hz vertical bandstop filter; (d) vertical bandstop filter and deconstruction

- Deconstruction. To reduce the effect of local fluctuations in image intensity, a deconstructed image $I'(x,y) = I(x,y) - B(x,y)$ was generated, where $B(x,y)$ is a background image created by the repeated application of a 5×5 median filter (15 applications of the filter appeared to give the best results).

- Morphological operations. The morphological *close* operator ($\mathbf{X} = \mathbf{X} \bullet \mathbf{B}$, where $\mathbf{B}$ is a structuring element - for our experiments, a discrete circular kernel of radius r pixels was used) was applied in some experiments to strengthen the thin line elements present in many of the tracings, in an attempt to prevent these lines from being lost in subsequent processing.

2.3   Feature Extraction

Two separate sets of features were extracted for our experiments:

Three sets of *whole-image features* were computed, both directly from raw images and from images subjected to noise reduction as indicated above. The features extracted were ART as defined in the MPEG-7 standard [8], the 7 normal moment invariants defined by Hu [14], and the 4 affine moment invariants defined by Flusser and Suk [15].

Three sets of *component-based features* were computed from images subjected to various combinations of the noise reduction techniques described above, and then segmented as indicated in [16], generating a set of regions defined by closed boundaries for each image. For some studies (see below) an extra cleanup stage was applied to remove two types of small insignificant boundaries - noise at the edges of the image (distance from image centroid/area > 2.5) and remaining fragments of laid lines (aspect ratio > 5 and angle to horizontal $\leq 6°$). From the boundary of each of these regions, the following shape descriptors were then extracted:

(i)   aspect ratio, circularity, and convexity as defined in [16];

(ii)   triangularity, ellipticity and rectangularity as defined by Rosin [17]

(iii)   8 normalized Fourier descriptors as defined in [18].

2.4   Shape Matching and Evaluation of Effectiveness

For each combination of image preprocessing and feature extraction techniques selected for study, a test database was built from our collection of 1000 electron radiograph images. This was then searched by our experimental SHREW system, as described in our previous paper [6]. Fig 3 shows the results of a typical search.

The overall effectiveness of each combination of image enhancement and shape matching technique was evaluated, using a set of 19 test query images and sets of expected search results, assembled by colleagues in the Conservation Unit at Northumbria University. As in previous trials, the effectiveness of each combination of techniques evaluated was determined by averaging normalized precision P_n and normalized recall R_n scores [19] over each of the 19 queries.

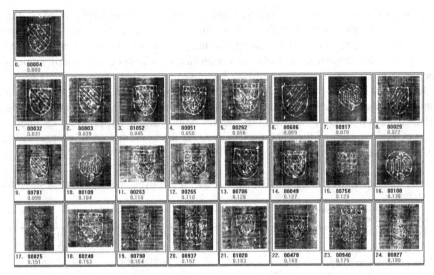

Fig. 3. Typical retrieval results from SHREW, showing the query image (top line) and the first 24 retrieved images in order of similarity

3   Retrieval Results

The first set of experiments investigated the effectiveness of matching on features computed from whole images. Four databases were built, deriving features respectively from the original grey-scale images, low-pass filtered images, deconstructed images, and images segmented into regions as specified in [16]. Each of the 19 queries was then run against each database, using each of the three whole-image features defined above. Table 1 shows the results of these experiments:

Table 1. Effectiveness of whole-image features for retrieval. All results are expressed as mean ± standard error over 19 test queries

Image preprocessing carried out	Shape features used for comparison					
	Angular Radial Transform		Normal moment invariants		Affine moment invariants	
	P_n	R_n	P_n	R_n	P_n	R_n
None	0.30 ± 0.03	0.62 ± 0.03	0.28 ± 0.02	0.61 ± 0.03	0.27 ± 0.02	0.58 ± 0.03
Low-pass filtering	0.30 ± 0.03	0.62 ± 0.03	0.30 ± 0.02	0.62 ± 0.03	0.24 ± 0.02	0.55 ± 0.02
Vertical bandstop (vbs) filtering	0.30 ± 0.03	0.61 ± 0.03	0.30 ± 0.03	0.61 ± 0.03	0.24 ± 0.02	0.55 ± 0.02
Deconstruction	0.31 ± 0.03	0.64 ± 0.04	0.27 ± 0.03	0.57 ± 0.03	0.21 ± 0.02	0.50 ± 0.02
Deconstruction & vbs filtering	0.33 ± 0.03	0.63 ± 0.04	0.28 ± 0.03	0.56 ± 0.03	0.23 ± 0.02	0.51 ± 0.02
Deconstruction & thresholding	0.28 ± 0.02	0.61 ± 0.03	0.28 ± 0.02	0.60 ± 0.03	0.28 ± 0.02	0.60 ± 0.02

In contrast to our previous study [6], no significant differences in effectiveness could be observed between different whole-image features, with the exception that when deconstruction and vbs filtering was used, the angular radial transform proved slightly but significantly more effective than affine moment invariants ($P < 0.01$, Wilcoxon matched-pairs, signed-ranks test). Disappointingly, none of the image enhancement techniques tested appeared to make any significant difference to overall retrieval effectiveness.

The second set of experiments was designed to measure the effectiveness of component-based matching using various combinations of Kuwahara filtering, vertical bandstop filtering, and deconstruction before segmentation. The 19 queries were run against each of the databases built using the combination of preprocessing steps under study, with results as shown in Table 2.

Table 2. Effectiveness of component-based features for retrieval, and the effect of different noise filters

Noise filter used	P_n	R_n
None	0.26 ± 0.03	0.50 ± 0.03
5×5 Kuwahara filter	0.29 ± 0.02	0.57 ± 0.03
Vertical bandstop filter	0.31 ± 0.03	0.57 ± 0.03
Vertical bandstop plus Kuwahara filter	0.25 ± 0.02	0.51 ± 0.03
Deconstruction plus Kuwahara filter	0.38 ± 0.05	0.62 ± 0.05
Deconstruction, vertical bandstop & Kuwahara filter	0.37 ± 0.04	0.63 ± 0.04

As we found with watermark tracings, the combinations of noise-reduction and component-based matching technique tested here appeared to have no compelling advantages over the whole-image based methods listed in Table 1. Noise removal using Kuwahara filtering, vertical bandstop filtering, and deconstruction all appeared to have a positive effect on retrieval performance, though combinations of these techniques had less predictable effects. However, none of the differences observed were statistically significant (Wilcoxon matched-pairs, signed-ranks test).

In our previous study [6], morphological operations on extracted boundaries were shown to have a beneficial effect. Hence a further set of experiments was performed, to investigate the effects of applying the morphological *closure* operator, both alone and in combination with insignificant boundary removal as outlined above. The results of these experiments are shown in Table 3.

Table 3. Effectiveness of component-based matching using the *closure* operator with or without insignificant boundary removal. All images were preprocessed by deconstruction and Kuwahara filtering as indicated above

Insignificant boundary removal	Radius of structuring kernel	P_n	R_n
Not applied	0 (no closure)	0.38 ± 0.05	0.62 ± 0.04
	2 pixels	0.36 ± 0.05	0.59 ± 0.04
	4 pixels	0.33 ± 0.02	0.62 ± 0.03
	6 pixels	0.28 ± 0.03	0.58 ± 0.03
Applied	0 (no closure)	0.38 ± 0.05	0.62 ± 0.04
	2 pixels	0.42 ± 0.05	0.64 ± 0.04
	4 pixels	0.42 ± 0.03	0.69 ± 0.04
	6 pixels	0.36 ± 0.03	0.63 ± 0.03

From these results it can be seen that while neither closure nor insignificant line removal has any beneficial effect when applied singly, they do appear to improve retrieval effectiveness when applied together, though the differences observed were not statistically significant). However, the combination of Kuwahara filtering, deconstruction, insignificant boundary removal and closure did generate a significant improvement in retrieval effectiveness when compared to no preprocessing at all ($P < 0.01$, Wilcoxon matched-pairs signed-ranks test).

4   Conclusions and Further Work

The results presented here reinforce our previous conclusion [6] that techniques developed for trademark image retrieval can provide effective retrieval of historical watermarks. However, the highest level of retrieval effectiveness achieved with electron radiographs (P_n 0.42 ± 0.03; R_n 0.69 ± 0.04) compares unfavourably with the best figures achieved with tracings (P_n 0.67 ± 0.05; R_n 0.89 ± 0.02). This is not surprising, given the much higher levels of noise in electron radiographs, but suggests that more work is needed before our system can provide a level of performance adequate to meet user needs.

In contrast to our previous study, we could find no significant differences between the three whole-image shape features - though ART still emerged as marginally the most effective measure, and is probably the shape feature of choice when whole-image region-based matching is required. Again in contrast to our previous study, component-based matching appeared slightly more effective than whole-image matching, though none of the observed difference in effectiveness were statistically significant. If the standard of image segmentation could be improved (not an unreasonable expectation), we suspect that component-based matching would prove to be significantly more effective than whole-image matching, as it is for trademark image matching [20]. As observed previously, some form of component-based matching is essential where a user wishes to query a database to identify all watermarks which match a specified component of an image.

Two aspects of our study proved disappointing. Firstly, noise reduction by filtering of frequency-domain images proved much less effective than had been hoped. Although bandstop filtering produced what looked like relatively noise-free images, it had little or no effect on eventual retrieval performance. On this occasion the improvement in visual appearance proved deceptive. Secondly, the combination of filters and matching techniques that proved most effective for retrieval of tracings of watermark images bore no resemblance to the most effective combination for electron radiographs. This implies that different preprocessing and search techniques may be needed for each type of image - and maybe for each collection. Hence the task of preparing a large and heterogeneous collection of watermark images for public searching on the Web is likely to be very time-consuming.

Future work on this project will aim at identifying improved and if possible widely-applicable noise-reduction segmentation techniques, based on findings on human perceptual segmentation [21]. A particularly promising technique for identifying shape boundaries from perceptually salient edges which we intend to investigate is that of Mahamud et al [22]. We will also examine to extent to which different combinations of features (both whole-image and component-based) can be combined to provide more effective retrieval. Finally, we aim to develop techniques for partial shape matching, allowing users faced with an arbitrary fragment of a watermark to identify images containing that fragment.

Acknowledgements

We would like to express our sincere appreciation to Jean Brown and Richard Mulholland of the Conservation Unit, University of Northumbria, for providing advice and assistance throughout the project. Thanks are also due to Gerard van Thienen, Curator of Incunabula, Koninklijke Bibliotheek, den Haag, the Netherlands, for providing access to their collection of watermarks. The financial support of the UK Arts and Humanities Research Board is also gratefully acknowledged.

References

[1]   Briquet, C M: Les Filigranes. Karl Hiesermann, Leipzig (1907)

[2]   International Standard for the Registration of Paper with or without Watermarks, International Association of Paper Historians (IPH), English Version 2.0, 1997

[3]   Rauber, C, Pun, T and Tschudin, P: Retrieval of images from a library of watermarks for ancient paper identification. In: Proceedings of EVA 97, Elektronische Bildverarbeitung und Kunst, Kultur, Historie, Berlin (1997)

[4]   Brown, J E et al: When images work faster than words - the integration of CBIR with the Northumbria Watermarks Archive. To be presented at ICOM-CC 13th triennial meeting, Rio de Janeiro, Sept 2002

[5]   Eakins, J P, Boardman, J M and Graham, M E: Similarity retrieval of trademark images. IEEE Multimedia 5(2) (1998) 53-63

[6]   Riley, K J & Eakins, J P: Content-based retrieval of historical watermark images. I- tracings. In: Proceedings of CIVR2002, London, July 2002. Lecture Notes in Computer Science 2383 (2002) 253-261

[7]   Churchill, W A. Watermarks in Paper in Holland, England, France etc. in the XVII and XVIII Centuries and their Interconnection, Menno Hertzberger & Co. Amsterdam, 1935

[8]   Available on the Web at
       http://www.cselt.it/mpeg/public/mpeg–7_visual_xm.zip

[9]   Zeng, W J and Liu, B: A statistical watermark detection technique without using original images for resolving rightful ownership of digital images. IEEE Transactions on Image Processing 8(11) (1999) 1534-1548

[10]   Tang, C W and Hang, H M: A feature-based robust digital image watermarking scheme. IEEE Transactions on Signal Processing 51(4) (2003) 950-959

[11]   Schnitger, D, Ziesche, E and Mundry, E: Elektronenradiographie als Hilfsmittel für die Identifizierung schwer oder nicht erkennbarer Wasserzeichen. pp 49-67 in: Gutenberg Jahrbuch 58, Mainz (1983)

[12] van Thienen, G: Watermarks in incunabula printed in the Low Countries. Available on the Web at http://watermark.kb.nl/

[13] Kuwahara, M et al: Digital Processing of Biomedical Images. Plenum Press, New York (1976) 187-203

[14] Hu, M K: Visual pattern recognition by moment invariants. IRE Transactions on Information Theory IT-8 (1962) 179-187

[15] Flusser, J and Suk, T: Pattern recognition by affine moment invariants. Pattern Recognition 26(1) (1993) 167-174

[16] Eakins, J P et al: A comparison of the effectiveness of alternative feature sets in shape retrieval of multi-component images. In: Storage and Retrieval for Media Databases 2001, Proc SPIE 4315 (2001) 196-207

[17] Rosin, P L: Measuring shape: ellipticity, rectangularity and triangularity. In: Proceedings of 15th International Conference on Pattern Recognition, Barcelona (2000) vol 1, 952-955

[18] Zahn, C T and Roskies, C Z: Fourier descriptor for plane closed curves. IEEE Transactions on Computers C-21 (1972) 269-281

[19] Salton, G: The SMART retrieval system - experiments in automatic document processing. Prentice-Hall, Englewood Cliffs, New Jersey (1971)

[20] Eakins, J P et al: Shape feature matching for trademark image retrieval. Presented at CIVR2003, and published in this volume

[21] Ren, M, Eakins, J P and Briggs, P: Human perception of trademark images: implications for retrieval system design. Journal of Electronic Imaging 9(4) (2000) 564-575

[22] Mahamud, S et al: Segmentation of multiple salient closed contours from real images. IEEE Transactions on Pattern Analysis and Machine Intelligence (2003), in press

Selection of the Best Representative Feature and Membership Assignment for Content-Based Fuzzy Image Database

Mutlu Uysal and Fatoş T. Yarman-Vural

Middle-East Technical University, Ankara
{uysal,vural}@ceng.metu.edu.tr

Abstract. A major design issue in content-based image retrieval system is the selection of the feature set. This study attacks the problem of finding a discriminative feature for each class, which is optimal in some sense. The class-dependent feature is, then, used to calculate the membership value of each object class for content-based fuzzy image retrieval systems. The Best Representative Feature (BRF) for each class is identified in a training stage. Then, using the BRF of each object class, the segment groups in the images are labeled by the membership values of each object class. The segment groups are obtained in a greedy algorithm by minimizing the distance between each training object and the segment groups, using the BRF. This minimum distance is taken as the membership value of the training object for that particular segment group. Finally, the query object is matched to each segment group in a fuzzy database using the membership values of segment groups. The BRF is selected among the MPEG-7 descriptors. The proposed scheme yields substantially better retrieval rates compared to the available fixed feature content-based image retrieval systems.

1 Introduction

Content-based image retrieval (CBIR) systems become an attractive research area due to the demand created by the increasing size of the image and video resources. Instead of manually annotating the text-based keywords, images are indexed by their own visual content, such as color, texture, and shape. In Image processing literature, there is a wide range of descriptors for CBIR systems. Some of these descriptors have been standardized by the Moving Picture Experts Group (MPEG) [1].

Although MPEG-7 provides a variety of descriptors, selection of a set of descriptors for an image data is an open research issue in content-based image retrieval systems. For example, given an image, composed of a house and sky in the background, the house is best described by shape features, whereas the description of the sky, requires color and texture features [2].

E. M. Bakker et al. (Eds.): CIVR 2003, LNCS 2728, pp. 141-151, 2003.
© Springer-Verlag Berlin Heidelberg 2003

In most of the image retrieval systems, the images in the database are compared to the query image with a common set of features, which represents all the objects and/or classes in the database. As the size of the database increases, the degree of separation of the image collection with the same set of features decreases. Recently, several authors attack this problem by using relevance feedback approach [3]. However, the performance of this approach heavily depends on the user. Also, as the number and the diversity of images in the database increase, these methods fail to give satisfactory results compared to the fixed-feature set databases [4].

Applying fuzzy processing techniques to CBIR has been extensively studied in the literature. In [5], fuzzy logic is developed to interpret the overall color information of images. Nine colors that match human perceptual categories are chosen as features. In [6], a color histogram approach is proposed. A class of similarity distances is defined based on fuzzy logic operations. In [7], a fuzzy logic approach for region-based image retrieval is proposed. In the retrieval system, an image is represented by a set of segmented regions, each of which is characterized by a fuzzy feature set reflecting color, texture and shape properties. The resemblance of two images is then defined as the overall similarity between two families of fuzzy features.

In this study, we propose to use different feature for each object class. A robust approach identifies Best Representative Feature (BRF) for each object class, which maximizes the correct match in a training set. The groups of segments in the pre-segmented image collection is then labeled by a set of membership values according to the distance to each training object class by using the BRF for that class. Therefore, the system learns how to search an object and find the answer to the queries according to the labels of the segment groups in the database.

In the fuzzy database querying, the system asks the questions like "Is this almost a bird?" or "Find me objects which consists of some tigers or some horses". The queries are defined using the membership values.

2   Rationale behind the Approach

Consider, a 2-class classification problem, with n and m images in each class, respectively. As a total, we have '$n+m$' images. Assume that n is close to m. Let the images in class-1 be very similar to each other according to color features, but not similar according to shape features; whereas the images in class-2 be very similar to each other according to shape and dissimilar according to color features. In an image retrieval system, if only color feature is used for comparison, a performance of nearly 50% is obtained. Color features give satisfactory results for the objects in class-1 and poor results for the objects in class-2. In order to improve the performance, the system should query images in class-1 with color features and images in class-2 with shape features. This is the main motivation behind the proposed retrieval system, where the best representative feature is identified for each object class by using a training stage.

3   The System

The proposed system consists of four major modules:

1.   Segmentation Module,
2.   Training Module,
3.   Segment Grouping and Membership Assignment Module,
4.   Fuzzy Database Query Module.

In the following these modules are summarized.

1.   Segmentation Module: The images are segmented into regions using the N-cut segmentation algorithm of [8]. It is well known that this algorithm performs over-segmentation, which mostly yields objects or parts of the objects. The images in the database are stored as the output of this segmentation module for the further processing steps.

2.   Training Module: The major goal of the training module is to select the BRF for each object class among a set of MPEG-7 descriptors [1]. A training set is formed by entering the objects from each pre-defined class. The objects are selected by the user as sub-images with rectangular areas. The top-left and bottom-right coordinates of the objects are entered by the mouse and these points are stored in the database. Then, for each class of objects in the training set, the images in that class are queried by a different feature selected from MPEG-7 descriptors. The most similar objects to the query image, is returned to the user by each feature. The winner feature, which retrieves the highest number of objects belonging to that class is identified as the *best representative feature* of that class.

Mathematically speaking, let $F = \{f_1, f_2, \ldots, f_N\}$ be the feature set and $T = \{t_1, t_2, \ldots, t_k\}$ be the class of training objects, where there are "i" objects in each class and t_{ki} denotes the ith object in the kth class, then the following algorithm summarizes the training module:

Training Algorithm :

Step 1: *For each training object class t_k, repeat (if all training objects are processed go to step 7)*

Step 2: *For each feature f_n in F, repeat (if all features are processed go to step 6)*

Step 3: *For each object t_{ki} in training class t_k, repeat (if all objects are processed go to step 5)*

Step 4: *Retrieve the most similar "i" objects to the object t_{ki}, according to the feature f_n and find the number of objects also in class t_k among the retrieved "i" similar objects. Call this number d_{ki}. Go to step 3.*

Step 5: *Calculate the average of all d_{ki} to obtain the retrieval performance of f_n for the training class t_k. Call this average distance for feature f_n for class t_k as $av(f_{kn})$ Go to step 2.*

Step 6: *Find the best representative feature for training class t_k by finding the greatest $av(f_{kn})$'s. Go to step 1.*

Step 7: *Stop.*

In this study, only one feature is selected as the winner feature, but it is trivial to extend the BRF to k-best representative features by including a large set of MPEG-7 descriptors and finding the best k-representative feature among them. In this case it is possible to mix the features by using some weights obtained from a Neural Network architecture, in the training module.

3.   Segment Grouping and Membership Assignment Module: The output of the N-cut segmentation algorithm is a set of regions (Figure-1), which represent a single object or part of an object. Therefore, in most cases, the regions should be combined to form an object. For this purpose, the objects in the training set and their BRF's are used. Group of segments are compared to the objects in the training set with respect to the BRF. The distance between the segment group and the training object is minimized. The minimum distance between the segment group and the training object is assigned as the membership value of the segment group for that particular object class.

Tracing all combination of segments is an N-P complete problem. To decrease the search space size, a greedy-based search algorithm is developed as given below:

Segment Grouping and Labeling Algorithm:

Step 1: For each training object class t_i, repeat (if all training objects are processed go to step 13)

Step 2: For each image (i_j) in the image collection (N-Cut segmented images) repeat (if all images are processed go to step 12)

Step 3: For each segment in the selected image repeat (if all segments are processed go to step 7)

Step 4: Calculate the distance of the selected segment to the trained object $t_{i,}$, using the best representative feature for that object.

Step 5: Find the segment, which has the smallest distance and call it s_k

Step 6: Go to Step 3

(Until this step, we found the most similar segment to the trained object. From now on, we will try to decrease the distance by combining the neighboring segments)

Step 7: For each neighboring segment of the segment s_k repeat (if all neighboring segments are processed and the error does not decrease any more, go to step 11)

Step 8: Combine the selected neighbor segment and the segment s_k and calculate the distance

Step 9: If the distance is smaller than the recent minimum distance, call this new combined region as s_k, else discard the combination.

Step 10: Go to step 7

Step 11: Segment s_k is the most similar segment (which consists of a group of segments of the N-cut algorithm) to the trained object class t_i in the image i_j. Call its distance as d_k. Go to Step 2.

Step 12: Normalize the distances d_k for the segments s_k with Formula-1 given below, and label the membership value of the training object class t_i for image i_j as the calculated normalized distance. Go to Step 1.

Step 13: Stop

During the calculation of the membership values, a normalization process is necessary to compare different distances obtained by different features. This is basically because of the incompatible measures for different MPEG-7 descriptors between the training objects and segment groups. In order to eliminate this incompatibility, the maximum and minimum distances to the query image are used to normalize the distances.

Let the distance of the most dissimilar object be D_{max}, the distance of the most similar object be D_{min}, and the calculated distance be D_{cal}, then the normalized distance can be obtained by:

$$\text{Normalized Distance} = D_{max} - D_{cal} / (D_{max} - D_{min}). \qquad (1)$$

4. Fuzzy Database Querying: Suppose in the training phase, the system learned a set of objects and their BRF's. If we have a large image database, which is automatically segmented by N-Cut algorithm, it is not possible to obtain reliable results by using crisp parameters to search for an object among these segments. Fuzziness is needed in such a search, because descriptions of image contents usually involve inexact and subjective concepts and also users can identify their queries better with linguistic variables rather than numbers.

The output of the segment grouping algorithm provides us a very convenient infrastructure to construct a fuzzy database. The proposed system uses fuzzy object-oriented database modeling FOOD proposed in [9]. For each fuzzy attribute, a fuzzy domain and a similarity matrix are defined. Similarity matrices represent the relation within the fuzzy attributes. Fuzziness may occur at three different levels in this fuzzy object-oriented database model, the attribute level, the object/class level and the class/super class level. In this study, we are specifically interested in the fuzziness at attribute and object/class level. For each of the query segment group, the inclusion degree of this segment group to the training classes is calculated by using membership values. The segment is identified as the class whose inclusion degree is greatest.

Let us explain the fuzzy query with an example. Suppose the system trained 3 objects, which are "plane", "horse" and "leopard", and the N-Cut segmented images in Figure-1 will be searched for these objects. The following fuzzy linguistic variables are proposed: Almost = [0.85, 1.0], Some = [0.7, 0.85], A little = [0.55, 0.7], Few = [0.40, 0.55]. After applying greedy-based segment grouping algorithm, the membership values are computed as shown in Table 1.

Table 1. Images and Corresponding Membership Values

	PLANE MEMBERSHIP	HORSE MEMBERSHIP	LEOPARD MEMBERSHIP
Image 1	0.923769	0.412534	0.635566
Image 2	0.856751	0.589010	0.706071
Image 3	0.845345	0.742654	0.947400
Image 4	0.839860	0.742057	0.935919
Image 5	0.814194	0.900858	0.846719
Image 6	0.678255	0.892642	0.787659

By using "Images and Corresponding Membership Values" Table, and fuzzy linguistic variables, almost, some, a little, and few, we obtain Table 2, which is called Image Fuzzy Linguistic Variable Table.

Table 2. Image Fuzzy Linguistic Variable Table

	PLANE MEMBERSHIP	HORSE MEMBERSHIP	LEOPAR MEMBERSHIP
Image 1	AlmostPlane(AP)	FewHorse (FH)	AlittleLeopar (LL)
Image 2	AlmostPlane (AP)	AlittleHorse (LH)	SomeLeopar (SL)
Image 3	SomePlane (SP)	SomeHorse (SH)	AlmostLeopar (AL)
Image 4	SomePlane (SP)	SomeHorse SH)	AlmostLeopar (AL)
Image 5	SomePlane (SP)	AlmostHorse(AH)	SomeLeopar (SL)
Image 6	AlittlePlane (LP)	AlmostHorse (AH)	SomeLeopar (SL)

For "almost" and "some" fuzzy linguistic variables, fuzzy representations of the images in the database become:

Fuzzy Rep. of Image 1 = {AlmostPlane} = {AP}
Fuzzy Rep. of Image 2 = {AlmostPlane,SomeLeopar} = {AP,SL}
Fuzzy Rep. of Image 3 = {SomePlane,SomeHorse,AlmostLeopar} = {SP,SH,AL}
Fuzzy Rep. of Image 4 = { SomePlane,SomeHorse,AlmostLeopar } = {SP,SH,AL}
Fuzzy Rep. of Image 5 = { SomePlane,AlmostHorse,SomeLeopar } = {SP,AH,SL}
Fuzzy Rep. of Image 6 = { AlmostHorse,SomeLeopar } = {AH,SL}

In this particular example, there are 3 object classes and 4 linguistic variables for each query object class. As a result, a 12x12 similarity matrix is constructed by considering the similarities of the objects and the linguistic variables. This matrix is given in Table 3. The user can change the similarity degrees, according to the application domain.

Table 3. Similarity Matrix

μ_s	AP	SP	LP	FP	AH	SH	LH	FH	AL	SL	LL	FL
AP	1	0.85	0.70	0.55	0.3	0.25	0.20	0.15	0.30	0.25	0.20	0.15
SP	0.85	1	0.85	0.55	0.25	0.3	0.25	0.20	0.25	0.3	0.25	0.20
LP	0.70	0.85	1	0.85	0.20	0.25	0.3	0.25	0.20	0.25	0.3	0.25
FP	0.55	0.70	0.85	1	0.15	0.20	0.25	0.3	0.15	0.20	0.25	0.30
AH	0.3	0.25	0.20	0.15	1	0.85	0.70	0.55	0.50	0.45	0.40	0.35
SH	0.25	0.3	0.25	0.20	0.85	1	0.85	0.55	0.45	0.50	0.45	0.40
LH	0.20	0.25	0.3	0.25	0.70	0.85	1	0.85	0.40	0.45	0.50	0.45
FH	0.15	0.20	0.25	0.3	0.55	0.70	0.85	1	0.35	0.40	0.45	0.50
AL	0.3	0.25	0.20	0.15	0.50	0.45	0.40	0.35	1	0.85	0.70	0.55
SL	0.25	0.3	0.25	0.20	0.45	0.50	0.45	0.40	0.85	1	0.85	0.55
LL	0.20	0.25	0.3	0.25	0.40	0.45	0.50	0.45	0.70	0.85	1	0.9
FL	0.15	0.20	0.25	0.30	0.35	0.40	0.45	0.50	0.55	0.70	0.85	1

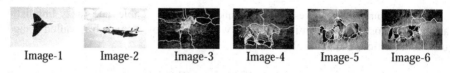

| Image-1 | Image-2 | Image-3 | Image-4 | Image-5 | Image-6 |

Fig. 1. N-Cut segmented images used in fuzzy querying

For a query "Find me objects which are almost horse," firstly, Image Fuzzy Linguistic Variable Table and Similarity Matrix in Table 3 are constructed. Then, the following inclusion formula in FOOD modeling [4] calculates the inclusion (INC) degree of each image:

$$INCLUSION = Avg[Max(\mu s(x_{ij}, y_k))] ,\qquad(2)$$

where μs denote the similarity values in Table 3, x_{ij} denote the jth fuzzy representation of the ith image in the database and y_k denote the kth fuzzy representation of the query. Inclusion degrees of each image for the "almost horse" query are calculated as:

INC(Image 1) = Avg(Max(μs(AP,AH))) = Avg(0.3) = 0.3

INC(Image 2) = Avg(Max(μs(AP,AH), μs(SL,AH))) = Avg(Max(0.3,0.45)) = 0.45

INC(Image 3) = Avg(Max(0.25,0.85,0.50)) = 0.85

INC(Image 4) = Avg(Max(0.25,0.85,0.50)) = 0.85

INC(Image 5) = Avg(Max(0.25,1.00,0.45)) = 1.00

INC(Image 6) = Avg(Max(1.00,0.45)) = 1.00

The final step for the query processing is to sort the inclusion values for matching the objects and output the ones that are greater than a threshold value. If the threshold is chosen as 0.85, Image-5 and Image-6 of Fig. 1. are retrieved.

Figure-2 shows the segments found by Segment Grouping and Membership Assignment Algorithm and their corresponding inclusion values for the query "Find me objects, which are almost horse."

4   Experimental Results

The proposed content-based fuzzy image retrieval system is developed in C++ Builder and tested over a subset of Corel Draw image database. 10 object classes: *Antelope, Bird, Cotton Texture, Fish, Flag, Horse, Leopard, Plane, Polar Bear and Sun Set* are selected from the images of Corel Draw. In order to form the training set, for each class, 10 images are selected. Test set for the queries are formed by randomly selecting additional 5 images from the Corel Draw for each class. Total of 150 images in the training and test sets are segmented using the N-cut segmentation algorithm, yielding unlabelled regions.

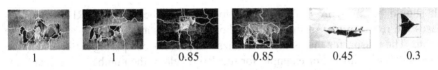

| 1 | 1 | 0.85 | 0.85 | 0.45 | 0.3 |

Fig. 2. Segment groups and corresponding inclusion degrees

In the first set of experiments, 100 training images are used to find the best representative feature (BRF) for each object class. For this purpose, the objects in each class are retrieved, by using five different features from MPEG-7 descriptors, namely *dominant color, color structure, scalable color, edge histogram and region based shape*. The descriptor, which results in the highest retrieval rate, is labeled as the BRF for that particular object class. Table-4 shows the BRF for each of the classes obtained in the training module. Note that region based shape never wins against the other features to become the BRF, whereas, the color structure becomes BRF for 7 object classes. The dominant color is selected as the BRF for bird and fish classes. Scalable color is the BRF for cotton texture classes and the edge histogram is the BRF for the flag and plane classes. During the queries, the proposed system uses the BRF for each object class.

Second set of experiments tests the performance of the BRF for each class, compared to using a fixed feature. For this purpose, the queries are done, by fixing a feature for all the classes and measuring the correct retrieval rates in the training set. The queries are also done, by using the BRF for each object class. The first five columns of Table-5 indicate the correct retrieval rates, when one of the five MPEG-7 features is fixed for all the object classes. The last column indicates the correct retrieval rates when the BRF is used for each object class in the query. In the table, 'DC' stands for dominant color, "CS" for color structure, "SC" for scalable color, "EH" for edge histogram, "RS" for region-based shape and "BRF" for the best representative feature obtained in the training module. During the experiments, for each image in the training set, 5 relevant images were shown to the user for each of the MPEG-7 descriptors. Since there are 10 images in each training class, 50 images were shown to the user for each of the MPEG-7 descriptors for each class. Therefore, the numbers in Table-5 are the numbers of relevant images out of 50. An analysis of Table-5 indicates that when a fixed descriptor is used during the queries, color structure gives the highest retrieval rate, which is 75.6%. However, if the BRF is used for each object class, then the correct retrieval rate reaches to 80.2%, which significantly outperforms the fixed feature method even for the best overall feature.

Table 4. Best representative feature and their corresponding image classes

BRF	OBJECT CLASSES
Dominant Color (DC)	Bird, Fish
Color Structure (CS)	Antelope, Horse, Leopard, Polar Bear, Sun Set
Scalable Color (SC)	Cotton, Texture
Edge Histogram (EH)	Flag, Plane
Region-based Shape(RS)	-

It should be noted from Table-5 that for some of the classes, BRF method increases the retrieval rate of the fixed methods, but for some others, it may decrease the rate. The reason for this is the normalization process comparing different feature values with each other. For example for the "Bird" class, the number of relevant images is 40 for DC fixed method, and 31 for the BRF method. 9 of the correct results are eliminated from the set. But for the class "Leopard", the number of relevant images is 47 for CS fixed method and 50 for the BRF method. 3 of the correct results are added to the set. Note that, the overall performance of the BRF method is better than the fixed feature methods as seen from Table-5.

Table 5. Performance of the best representative feature vs. fixed feature methods

OBJECTS	DC	CS	SC	EH	RS	BRF
Antelope	32	**38**	29	25	24	38
Bird	**40**	30	25	22	21	31
Cotton Texture	27	25	**43**	32	23	23
Fish	**34**	30	23	21	20	26
Flag	31	37	37	**50**	22	48
Horse	49	50	44	37	26	50
Leopard	35	47	36	35	20	**50**
Plane	25	37	17	44	21	**46**
Polar Bear	34	39	23	35	18	**41**
Sun Set	29	45	8	16	26	**48**
TOTAL	336	378	285	317	221	**401**
PERCENTAGE	67,2	**75,6**	57	63,4	44,2	**80,2**

In the third set of experiments, the performance of the BRF approach with segment grouping algorithm over N-Cut segmented images is tested. 5 images per each image class are randomly selected among Corel Draw image database. These images are different from the ones used in training phase. The segment searching and membership assignment algorithm is applied to each of the image in the test set. The membership values for each of the images are calculated. In these experiments, firstly the membership values are sorted. Then, the number of correctly labeled images in the first 5 images, whose membership values are the greatest, are counted. The results are given in Table-6.

After the labeling process for each of the images, fuzzy queries like "Show me pictures, which contain almost Leopard objects" are performed. Figure-4 shows a sample query results and membership values. The inclusion value, for all of the 5 query results are calculated as 1.

o_1: 0.978520 o_2: 0.975756 o_3: 0.975655 o_4: 0.973467 o_5: 0.972190

Fig. 3. A Sample query results and membership values for the query "almost leopard"

Table 6. Performance of the BRF approach and segment grouping algorithm

CLASS	# of Correctly Labeled images out of 5 images	CLASS	# of Correctly Labeled images out of 5 images
Antelope	3	Horse	3
Bird	2	Leopard	5
Cotton Texture	2	Plane	4
Fish	4	Polar Bear	4
Flag	3	Sun Set	4
TOTAL	34	PERCENTAGE	68

The groups that have been found by segment grouping algorithm are signed by yellow rectangles in Figure-3. It should be noted that, for some of the objects, only a part of the object is labeled. This result is due to the greedy logic used in the grouping algorithm.

5   Conclusions and Future Works

In this study, an object-based image retrieval system is developed by using a different feature for each class. This system finds the Best Representative Feature (BRF) for each object in the database and indexes the object by that feature. The query object is compared with the objects in the database, based on the BRFs, which are identified in the training phase.

The BRF approach avoids the unnecessary comparisons, improves the speed and correct retrieval rates of the queries. Unrelated features are not taken into consideration and redundancies in using similar features are eliminated.

The BRF approach, also, solves the dimensional curse problem. In other words, if the number of dimensions exceeds a certain threshold value, the indexing structures begin to perform worse than the sequential scan.

In this study, only one feature is used as the BRF. In the later stages of this study, more than one feature will be identified as the k-best representative feature set, and the system will find the weights of each feature in training phase. In querying phase, the calculated weights for each feature will be used to find the most similar images to the query image.

In our study, the objects are identified by grouping the N-Cut Segmented images. This process is performed automatically without using any annotation. For finding the best segment groups, which represent an object, a greedy algorithm is used. This heuristic can be improved to obtain better results.

Finally, in the proposed system, the user can query the database by using fuzzy linguistic variables. The extensions to improve the membership assignment and efficiency of fuzzy similarity matching are an ongoing research topic.

Acknowledgements

The authors are grateful to Prof. Adnan Yazıcı for his suggestions and comments during the preparation of this study.

References

[1] L. Cieplinski, W. Kim, J.-R. Ohm, M. Pickering, and A.Yamada, MPEG-7 Visual part of eXperimentation Model Version 12.0,12/06/2001

[2] Zoran Stejic,Eduardo M. Iyoda,Yasufumi Takama,Kaoru Hirota.Content-based Image Retrieval Through Local Similarity Patterns Defined by Interactive Genetic Algorithm. GECCO-2001, San Francisco, USA, pp. 390-397,July 2001

[3] Ilaria Bartolini, Paolo Ciaccia, Florian Waas, FeedbackBypass: A New Approach to Interactive Similarity Query Processing, The VLDB Journal,2001

[4] S. Berchtold,C. Bohm,D. Keim, and H. Kriegel. A cost Model for nearest neighbor search in high-dimensional data space. In Proc. ACM Symp. On Principles of Database Systems,pages 78-86, Tuscon, Arizona,1997

[5] S. Kulkami, B. Verma, P. Sharma, and H. Selvaraj, Content-Based Image Retrieval Using a Neuro-Fuzzy Technique, Proc. IEEE Int. Conf. Neural Networks, pp. 846-850,1999

[6] C. Vertan and N. Boujemaa, Embedding Fuzzy Logic in Content-Based Image Retrieval, NAFIPS '00, pp. 85-89, July 2000

[7] Y. Chen, J. Z. Wang, A Region-based Fuzzy Feature Matching Approach to Content-Based Image Retrieval, IEEE Transactions and Pattern Analysis and Machine Intelligence, Vol. 24, No. 9 September 2002

[8] Jianbo Shi, Jitendra Malik, Normalized Cuts and Image Segmentation, IEEE Transactions and Pattern Analysis and Machine Intelligence,1997

[9] Yazici and R. George, Fuzzy Database Modeling. Physica-Verlag, 1999

A Compact Shape Descriptor
Based on the Beam Angle Statistics

Nafiz Arica and Fatoş T. Yarman-Vural

Computer Engineering Department
Middle East Technical University
06531 Ankara / Turkey
{nafiz,vural}@ceng.metu.edu.tr

Abstract. In this study, we propose a compact shape descriptor, which represents the 2-D shape information by 1-D functions. For this purpose a two-step method is proposed. In the first step, the 2-D shape information is mapped into 1-D moment functions without using a predefined resolution. The mapping is based on the beams, which are originated from a boundary point, connecting that point with the rest of the points on the boundary. At each point, the angle between a pair of beams is taken as a random variable to define the statistics of the topological structure of the boundary. The second order statistics of all the beam angles is used to construct 1-D Beam Angle Statistics (BAS) functions. In the second step, the 1-D functions are further compressed by using Discrete Fourier Transforms applied on the BAS functions of the shape boundary. BAS function is invariant to translation, rotation and scale. It is insensitive to distortions. Experiments are done on the dataset of MPEG 7 Core Experiments Shape-1. It is observed that proposed shape descriptor outperforms the popular MPEG 7 shape descriptors.

1   Introduction

Shape descriptors are important tools in content-based image retrieval systems, which allow searching and browsing images in a database with respect to the shape information. The goal of the shape descriptors is to uniquely characterize the object shape, in a large image database with large within-class-variances and small between-class-variances. A vigorous shape descriptor should be invariant under affine transform and insensitive to noise. It should contain sufficient information to resolve distinct images and compact enough to ignore the redundancies in the shapes. Additionally, it should give results consistent to human visual system.

The shape description methods can be divided into three main categories; contour based [11], [8], [4], image based [7] and skeleton based descriptors [9]. In the Core Experiment CE-Shape-1 for the MPEG-7 standard, the performance of above referenced shape descriptors are evaluated. Among them, the descriptors proposed in [11]

E. M. Bakker et al. (Eds.): CIVR 2003, LNCS 2728, pp. 152-162, 2003.

and [8] outperform the others in most of the experiments. In [11], the scale space approach is applied to shape boundary. The simplified contours are obtained by the scale-space curve evolution, based on contour smoothing with a Gauss function. The scale space image of the curvature function is then used as hierarchical shape descriptor. In [8], the scale of shapes are reduced by a process of curve evolution and represented in tangent space. To compute the similarity measure, the best possible correspondence of visual parts is established. Unfortunately, the techniques mentioned above rely on the threshold values corresponding to the resolution of the shape representation, which depends on the level of the smoothness of the images in the database. The methods have, also, limited performance under noise.

The motivation of this paper is to find a compact representation of the two-dimensional shape information without a predefined resolution scale. For this purpose a two-step method is proposed. In the first step, a mapping, which transforms the 2-D shape information into a set of 1-D functions, is formed. This mapping is consistent with the human visual system, preserving all the convexities and concavities of the shape. In the second step the 1-D function is further compressed by using Discrete Fourier Transforms.

The proposed descriptor is based on the beams, which are the lines connecting a point with the rest of the points on the boundary. The characteristics of each boundary point can be extracted by using the beams. The angle between each pair of beams is taken as the random variable at each point on the boundary. Then, the moment theorem provides the statistical information, which is used to obtain the desired 1-D Beam Angle Statistics (BAS) functions, where the valleys and hills of the first moment correspond to concavities and convexities of the object shape. After the representation of 2-D shape boundary as a set of 1-D BAS functions, further compression is realized by using the Spectral Coefficients of the functions.

The main contribution of this study is to eliminate the use of a heuristic rule or empirical threshold value in representation of shape boundaries in a predefined resolution scale. The proposed method also gives globally discriminative features to each boundary point by using all other boundary points. Another advantage of this representation is its consistency with human perception through preserving the concave and convex parts of the shapes. It provides a compact representation of shapes, which is insensitive to noise and affine transform. It is invariant to size, orientation and position of the object.

2   Mapping 2-D Shape Information into a Set of 1-D Functions

Curvature function is a popular 1-D representation of 2-D shape information and has been an inspiration of many studies related to shape analysis [10], [5]. The curvature function can be computed as the derivative of the contour's slope function. In a discrete grid, this can be performed by K-slope method. K-slope at a boundary point is defined as the slope of a line connecting that point with its Kth right neighbor. Then, the K-curvature at a boundary point is defined as the difference between the K-slope at that pixel and the K-slope of its Kth left neighbor.

The K-curvature function may be exploited to form an appropriate shape descrip-tor, if one could identify an optimal value for the parameter K, which extracts the concavities and convexities of the shape at a predefined scale settled by K. At this point, we need a rigorous technique to identify the scale parameter K, which dis-criminates a wide range of shapes in large image databases. In [1], the curvature function is obtained by using a fixed K value and then it is filtered in order to stress the main features. Another study [12] uses an adaptive K value by changing it ac-cording to the distance between relevant points. However, choosing a single K value cannot capture the exact curvature information for all varieties of shapes in a large database.

Figure 1 b, c and d indicate the plot of K-curvature function for a sample shape with various K values. Note that the plots for small K capture fine details. By in-creasing K, it is possible to plot fine to curse representation of a closed boundary as a one-dimensional function. Examining these figures shows that each peak and valley of the curvature function plot corresponds to a convexity, and a concavity of the shape. For this particular example, the shape information is preserved in the peaks corresponding to the head, tail and fins. The remaining peaks and valleys of the cur-vature plot are rather redundant details that result from the noise in the shape, leading mismatches in the image database. Therefore, one needs to select an appropriate K to avoid this redundant information. Selection of K defines the amount of smoothing of the shape and highly depends on the context of the image. If K smoothes the ripples corresponding to some context information, this will result in important information loss. On the other hand, if the ripples correspond to noise, keeping them will increase the number of convexities and concavities, which may carry superfluous shape in-formation. As a result, the problem of selecting a generic K, which resolves the nec-essary and sufficient information for all the images, has practically no solution, due to the diversity of the shape context in large databases.

The above discussion leads us to somehow find a representation, which employs the information in K-curvature function for all values of K. Superposition of the plots of K-curvature function for all K, yields impractically large data with no formal way of representation, as indicated in figure 1.e.

In this study, we attack this problem by modeling the shape as the outcomes of a stochastic process, which is generated by the same source at different scales. In this model, Figure 1.e shows the possible outcomes of the shape curvature plot, which generates the fish shape. At a given boundary point $p(i)$, the value of K-curvature function is assumed to be a function of a random variable K and may take one of the 1-D function indicated in the figure, depending on the values of K. Therefore, K-curvature function for each K, can be considered as the output of a stochastic process.

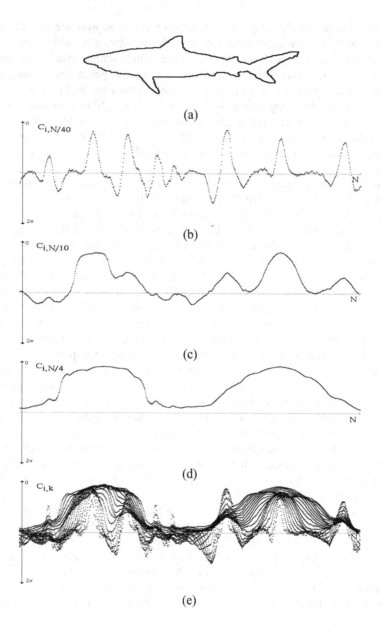

Fig. 1. a) A sample shape boundary and K-Curvatures for b) K=N/40, c) N/10, d) N/4 and e) $C_{i,k}$ Plots for N/40...N/4 from Top to Bottom Respectively.

Mathematically speaking, let the shape boundary $B = \{\, p(1),...,p(N) \,\}$ is represented by a connected sequence of points,

$$p\ (i) = \big(x(i)\,,\, y\ (i)\big) \qquad i = 1,...N \quad , \tag{1}$$

where N is the number of boundary points and p(i) = p(i+N). For each point p(i), the **beams** of *p(i)* is defined as the set of vectors;

$$L\left[p(i)\right]=\left\{V_{i+j}, V_{i-j}\right\} \qquad (2)$$

where V_{i+j} and V_{i-j} are the forward and backward vectors connecting p(i) with the points, p(i+j) and p(i-j) in the boundary, for j=1,...N/2 .Figure 2 indicates the beams and beam angle at point p(i), respectively.

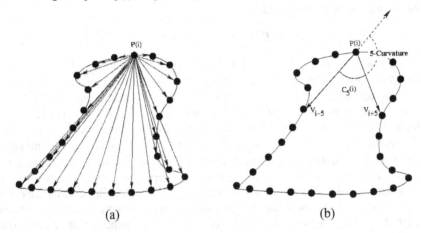

Fig. 2. a) The beams of point p(i), b) The 5-Curvature and the beam angle for K=5 at the boundary point *p(i)*

The slope of each beam , V_{i+K} is then calculated as,

$$\theta_{V_{i+l}} = tan^{-l} \frac{\Delta y_{i+l}}{\Delta x_{i+l}}, \qquad l = \pm K. \qquad (3)$$

For the point *p(i)* and for a fixed K, the beam angle between the forward and backward beam vectors, is then computed as (see figure 2.b).

$$C_K(i) = \left(\theta_{V_{i-K}} - \theta_{V_{i+K}}\right). \qquad (4)$$

Note that, beam angle for a fixed K is nothing but the K-curvature function (which takes values between 0 and 2π).

Now, for each boundary point *p(i)* of the curve Γ, the beam angle $C_K(i)$ can be taken as a *random variable* with the probability density function $P_K(C_K(i))$ and $C_K(i)$ vs. *i* plot for each K becomes an outcome of the stochastic process which generates the shape at different scales. Therefore, Beam Angle Statistics (BAS), may provide a stochastic representation for a shape descriptor. For this purpose, m[th] moment of the random variable $C_K(i)$ is defined as follows:

$$E\left[C^m(i)\right] = \sum_K C_K^m P_K(C_K(i)) \qquad m = 0,1,2,3,... \qquad (5)$$

In the above formula E indicates the expected value operator and $P_K(C_K(i))$ is the probability density function of $C_K(i)$. Note that the maximum value of K is N/2, where N represents the total number of boundary points. Note also that, the value of $C_K(i)$ approaches to 0 as K approaches to N/2. During the implementations, $P_K(C_K(i))$ is approximated by the histogram of $C_K(i)$ at each point $p(i)$.

The moments describe the statistical behavior of the beam angle at the boundary point $p(i)$. Each boundary point is, then, represented by a vector whose components are the moments of *the beam angles:*

$$\Gamma(i) = \left[E[C^1(i)], \ E[C^2(i)],... \right] = \left[\Gamma^1(i), \Gamma^2(i),... \right] . \qquad (6)$$

The shape boundary is finally represented by plotting the moments of $C_K(i)$'s for all the boundary points. In the proposed representation, the first moment $\Gamma^1(i)$ preserves the most significant information of the object. Figure 3, indicates the first three moments of boundary points for the sample shape of figure 1.a. For this particular example, it should be noted that the first moment suffice to represent the convexities and concavities of the shape. The second moment $\Gamma^2(i)$ increases the discriminative power of the representation. The third moment $\Gamma^3(i)$ on the other hand, does not bring any additional significant information to the representation. The order of the statistics naturally depends on the characteristics of the probability density function, $P_K(C_K(i))$. Central limit theorem provides us a strong theoretical basis to assume Gaussian distribution for each point $p(i)$ for large N. This implies that second order statistics is sufficient for representing most of the shape information provided that we have enough samples on shape boundary.

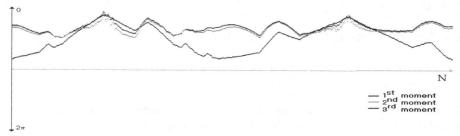

Fig. 3. Third order statistics of Beam Angle for the shape in figure 1.a.

The details of BAS function, explained above, can be found in [2].

3   Compression of BAS Functions

After mapping 2-D shape information into the 1-D BAS functions, the next step is to construct a compact feature vector, which retains the information in the BAS functions. For this purpose, two different approaches are proposed. In the first approach, Fourier descriptors are used as the entries of feature vector. The second approach identifies the Nyquist rate for the overall image database in frequency domain and performs sampling on 1-D BAS functions in the space domain.

3.1   Fourier Descriptors

Fourier Descriptors (FD) are commonly used technique for characterizing the shape boundary. Basic advantages of FD method in addition to the well-established theory of Fourier Transformations, include the ability to characterize a shape boundary with a small size descriptors. Besides, FDs are easy to derive and achieve good representation.

For a given m^{th} moment BAS function $\Gamma^m(i)$, the spectral coefficients is calculated by

$$a_n^{(m)} = \frac{1}{N} \sum_{i=0}^{N-1} \Gamma^m(i) \, exp(-j2\pi i / N) \qquad m = 1,...,M \qquad (7)$$

In order to achieve invariance in starting point of boundary extraction, phase information is ignored and only the magnitudes $| a^{(m)}_n |$ are used. The coefficients are also normalized by dividing the magnitudes with the DC component, $| a^{(m)}_0 |$. Then, the T lowest frequency Fourier coefficients are used to construct the feature vector. T is taken as a variable in the experiments and used to identify the Nyquist rate. Finally, the feature vector for a given BAS function is formed as follows:

$$F^{(m)} = \left[\frac{|a_1^{(m)}|}{|a_0^{(m)}|}, \frac{|a_2^{(m)}|}{|a_0^{(m)}{}_0|}, ..., \frac{|a_T^{(m)}|}{|a_0^{(m)}|} \right] \qquad m = 1,...,M \qquad (8)$$

The shape boundary is then represented by concatenating $F^{(m)}$'s for each BAS functions, $\Gamma^1(i)$ and $\Gamma^2(i)$. The similarity between two shapes is measured by Euclidean distance between features $[F^{(1)},..., F^{(M)}]$ extracted from the BAS moment functions.

3.2   Sampling by Fourier Transformation

The easiest method for feature extraction from BAS functions is to perform sampling with equal distance. However, there is a trade off between the sampling rate and the accuracy of the representation. As the sampling rate decreases, the method loses information about the visual parts (convexities and concavities). In order to find an optimal sampling rate, Fourier analysis is utilized in this study.

The feature extraction is performed in two steps. In the first step, the Fourier Transform of the BAS functions $\Gamma^m(i)$, are calculated. In the second step, Inverse Fourier transformation of the first T coefficients is calculated. In other words, low-pass filter on the frequency domain is performed. T is taken as variable during the experiments to find the optimal rate for the images in the database.

The similarity between the features is measured by Optimal Correspondent Subsequence (OCS) algorithm [13]. The objective in similarity measurement is to minimize the distance between two vectors by allowing deformations. This is achieved by first solving the correspondence problem between items in feature vectors and then computing the distance as a sum of matching errors between corresponding items. Dynamic programming technique is employed for minimizing the total distance between corresponding items by building a minimum distance table, which accumulates the information of correspondence.

4   Experiments

The performance of the BAS descriptor is tested in the data set of MPEG 7 Core Experiments Shape-1 Part B, which is the main part of the Core Experiments. The total number of images in the database is 1400. There are 70 classes of various shapes, with 20 images in each class. Each image is used as query and the number of similar images, which belong to the same class, was counted in the top 40 matches. Since the maximum number of correct matches for a single query image is 20, the total number of correct matches is 28000.

In the first set of experiments the BAS descriptor is compared with the popular descriptors of MPEG7. For this purpose, the boundaries of objects are mapped into mean and variance BAS functions. Then, 100 points from each BAS function with equal distances are used as the feature vector. C_i values between 0 and 2π for the boundary points are taken as it is. Then, elastic matching algorithm is employed for similarity measurement. The proposed descriptor correctly matches 81.4% of the images. In Table 1, the comparison of the BAS function with the recently reported results of [3] (Shape Context), [8] (Tangent Space), [11] (Curvature Scale Space), [7] (Zernika Moments), [4] (Wavelet) and [9] (Directed Acyclic Graph) is provided. As it is seen from the table, the proposed descriptor performs better then the best-performance descriptors available in the literature, for the data set of MPEG CE Shape-1 part B.

Table 1. Best Performances on MPEG 7 CE Shape-1 Part B

	Shape Context	Tangent Space	CSS	Zernika Moment	Wavelet	DAG	**BAS**
Similarity Results (%)	76.51	76.45	75.44	70.22	67.76	60	**81.4**

Using the row BAS functions as the shape descriptor is computationally expensive because of the dimension of the feature space and the complexity of the elastic matching algorithm. The first step is to further compress the size of feature vector to a "reasonable" dimension. At this point, Fourier theorems provide us convenient tools to represent the BAS functions in a more compact form. In the second set of experiments, the Fourier transform of BAS functions are used to find an optimal sampling rate. In the transform domain the Fourier spectrum is truncated after the T coefficients. The descriptor is, then, defined by using the T components of the inverse transform. It is observed that, for $T > 64$, no further improvement is achieved. The reason for this, is depicted in figure 4, where the power spectrum of BAS mean function extracted from a sample image is plotted. The plot shows the rapid decay of the spectral coefficients which becomes zero after $n=60$. Table 2 indicates the results of using inverse Fourier transform as a shape descriptor for various T values. Note that even for $T = 32$ the descriptor yields better results than the other MPEG-7 descriptors reported in the literature.

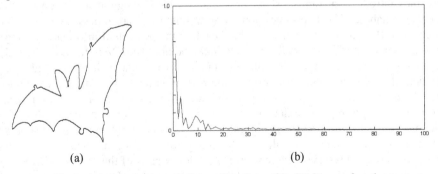

(a)   (b)

Fig 4. a) A Sample shape b) Power Spectrum of its BAS mean function

Finally, in order to avoid the complexity of elastic matching algorithm, the Fourier descriptors of BAS function are used and the similarity is simply measured by the Euclidean distance. This approach is indeed very fast and simple with the consider-able tradeoff in the retrieval rate as indicated in Table 3. The decrease in the retrieval rates is expected due to the loss of the phase information. However, when compared to the available FD methods, it is observed that the BAS function FD's outperforms the centroid distance function FD`s, which is reported as the best FD method in [6]. Note that the BAS FD`s give considerably better results even only the first order BAS is used.

Table 2. Comparison of row BAS Function and its inverse Fourier Transform with various T values

Dimension	Similarity Results (%)	
	Sampling with Equal Distance	Sampling By Fourier Transfrom
$T=8$	55.2	64.3
$T=16$	69	72.8
$T=32$	77.7	80.4
$T=64$	81.3	81.3

Table 3. Comparison of Fourier Descriptors on BAS Function and Centroid Distance Function with various T values

Dimension	Similarity Results (%)		
	Centroid Dis-tance Function FD's	BAS FD's	
		1st moment	1st + 2nd Moment
$T=8$	65.46	67.51	70.66
$T=16$	66.61	68.91	72.05
$T=32$	66.72	69.12	72.21
$T=64$	66.73	69.13	72.23

5   Conclusion

This study introduces a compact shape descriptor for identifying the similar objects in an image database. The two-dimensional object silhouettes are represented by one-dimensional BAS moment functions, which capture the perceptual information using the statistics of the beam angles of individual points. The BAS functions avoid smoothing and preserve the available information in the shape. It also avoids the selection of a threshold value to represent the resolution of the boundary, thus elimi-nates the context-dependency of the representation to the data set. Therefore, rather than using a single representation of the boundary, at a predefined scale, the BAS functions gather the information at all scales. It gives globally discriminative features to each boundary point by using all other boundary points. It is consistent with human perception through preserving the concave and convex parts of the shapes. The com-putational cost of BAS fuction is reduced by using the Discrete Fourier Transforms.

References

[1]   Agam, G., Dinstein, I., Geometric Separation Of Partially Overlapping Nonrigid Objects Applied to Automatic Choromosome Classification. IEEE Trans. PAMI, 19, (1997) 1212-1222

[2]   Arica, N., Yarman-Vural F. T, BAS: A Perceptual Shape Descriptor Based On The Beam Angle Statistics, Pattern Recognition Letters, vol: 24/9-10, (2003) 1627-1639

[3]   Belongie, S., Malik, J., Puzicha, J., Shape Matching and Object Recognition Using Shape Contexts. IEEE Trans. PAMI, 24, 4, (2002) 509-522

[4]   Chuang, G., Kuo, C. –C., Wavelet Descriptor of Planar Curves: Theory and Applications. IEEE Trans. Image Processing, 5, (1996) 56-70

[5]   Cohen, F. S., Huang, Z., Yang, Z., Invariant Matching and Identification of Curves Using B-Splines Curve Representation. IEEE Trans. Image Processing, 4, (1995) 1-10

[6]   Zhang, D., Lu, G., A Comparative Study Of Fourier Descriptors for Shape Rep-resentation and Retrieval. ACCV2002, Asian Conference on Computer Vision, (2002) 646-651

[7]   Khotanzad, A., Hong, Y. H., Invariant Image Recognition By Zernike Mo-ments. IEEE Trans. PAMI, 12, (1990) 489-497

[8]   Latecki, L. J., Lakamper, R., Shape Similarity Measure Based on Correspon-dence of Visual Parts. IEEE Trans. PAMI, 22, 10, (2000) 1185-1190

[9]   Lin, L. –J., Kung, S. Y.,. Coding and Comparison of Dags as a Novel Neural Structure With Application To Online Handwritten Recognition. IEEE Trans. Signal Processing, (1996)

[10]   Loncaric, S., A survey of Shape Analysis Techniques. Pattern Recognition, 31, (1998) 983-1001

[11]   Mokhtarian, F., Abbasi, S., Kittler, J., Efficient and Robust Retrieval By Shape Content Through Curvature Scale Space. Image Databases and Multimedia Search, A. W. M. smeulders and R. Jain ed., 51-58 World Scientific Publication (1997)

12] Urdiales, C., Bandera, A., Sandoval, F., Non-parametric Planar Shape Representation Based on Adaptive Curvature Functions. Pattern Recognition, 35, (2002) 43-53
13] Wang Y. P., Pavlidis T., Optimal Correspondence of String Subsequences. IEEE Trans. PAMI, 12, (1990) 1080-1087

Efficient Similar Trajectory-Based Retrieval
for Moving Objects in Video Databases

Choon-Bo Shim and Jae-Woo Chang

Dept. of Computer Engineering,
Research Center of Industrial Technology, Engineering Research Institute
Chonbuk National University, Jeonju, Jeonbuk 561-756, South Korea
{cbsim,jwchang}@dblab.chonbuk.ac.kr

Abstract. Moving objects' trajectories play an important role in doing content-based retrieval in video databases. In this paper, we propose a new k-warping distance algorithm which modifies the existing time warping distance algorithm by permitting up to k replications for an arbitrary motion of a query trajectory to measure the similarity between two trajectories. Based on our k-warping distance algorithm, we also propose a new similar sub-trajectory retrieval scheme for efficient retrieval on moving objects' trajectories in video databases. Our scheme can support multiple properties including direction, distance, and time and can provide the approximate matching that is superior to the exact matching. As its application, we implement the Content-based Soccer Video Retrieval (CSVR) system. Finally, we show from our experiment that our scheme outperforms Li's scheme (no-warping) and Shan's scheme (infinite-warping) in terms of precision and recall measures.

1   Introduction

Due to the wide spreading of mobile communication facilities such as PCS, PDA, and CNS (Car Navigation System) as well as the rapid increment of sport video data such as soccer, hockey, and basketball, it is required to deal with them. Recently, a lot of researches have been done on efficient management and storing for the various information of moving objects, especially being an important research topic in the field of video analysis and video database applications [1, 2]. Meanwhile, the trajectory of moving objects can be represented as a spatio-temporal relationship combining its spatial and temporal property, which plays an important role in doing video analysis & retrieval in video databases [3, 4]. A typical trajectory-based user query on the spatio-temporal relationship is as follows: *"Finds all objects whose motion trajectory is similar to the trajectory shown in a user interface window"*. A moving object is defined as a salient object that is continuously changing at its spatial location over the time. The trajectory of a moving object is defined as a collection of consecutive motions, each being represented as a spatio-temporal relationship. The moving objects' trajectories are the subject of concern by a user in video databases.

E. M. Bakker et al. (Eds.): CIVR 2003, LNCS 2728, pp. 163-173, 2003.

Similar sub-trajectory retrieval means searching for sub-trajectories in data trajectories which are similar to a given query trajectory.

In this paper, we first propose a new k-warping algorithm which calculates a k-warping distance between a given query trajectory and a data trajectory by permitting up to k replications for an arbitrary motion of a query trajectory to measure the similarity between two trajectories. Based on our k-warping algorithm, we also propose a new similar sub-trajectory retrieval scheme for efficient retrieval on moving objects' trajectories in video databases. Our scheme can support multiple properties including direction, distance, and time as well as a single property of direction, which is mainly used for modeling moving objects' trajectories. In addition, our schemes can provide the approximate matching which is superior to the exact matching.

This paper is organized as follows. In Section 2, we introduce related researches on similar sub-trajectory retrieval. In Section 3, we propose a new k-warping distance algorithm and describes new similar sub-trajectory retrieval scheme based on our k-warping algorithm. In Section 4, we implement the Content-based Soccer Video Retrieval (CSVR) system as its applications and provide the performance analysis of our schemes. Finally, we draw our conclusions and suggest future work in Section 5.

2   Related Work

There have been two main researches on retrieval based on similar sub-trajectory by measuring the similarity between a given query trajectory and data trajectories, i.e., Li's scheme and Shan's scheme. First, Li et al. [3, 4] represented the trajectory of a moving object as eight directions, such as North(NT), Northwest(NW), Northeast(NE), West(WT), Southwest(SW), East(ET), Southeast(SE), and Southwest(SW). They represented as (S_i, d_i, I_i) the trajectory of a moving object A over a given time interval I_i where S_i is the displacement of A and d_i is a direction. For a set of time interval $<I_1, I_2, ..., I_n>$, the trajectories of A can be represented as a list of motions, like $<(S_1, d_1, I_1), (S_2, d_2, I_2), . . . , (S_n, d_n, I_n)>$. Based on the representation for moving objects' trajectories, they present a similarity measures to computes the similarity of spatio-temporal relationships between two moving object. Let $\{M_1, M_2, ..., M_m\}$ $(m \geq 1)$ be the trajectory of moving object A, $\{N_1, N_2, ..., N_n\}$ be the trajectory of moving object B, and $m \leq n$. The similarity measure between the trajectory of object A and that of object B, TrajSim(A, B), is computed by using the similarity distances of directional relations as follows. Here, minDiff(A, B) and maxDiff(A, B) are the smallest distance between A and B and the largest distance, respectively.

$$TrajSim(A, B) = \frac{\max Diff(A, B) - \min Diff(A, B)}{\max Diff(A, B)} \qquad (\forall j, 0 \leq j \leq n - m)$$

Secondly, Shan and Lee [5] represented the trajectory of a moving object as a sequence of segments, each being expressed as the slope with real angle ranging from 0 to 360 degree for content-based retrieval. They also proposed two similarity measure algorithms, OCM (Optimal Consecutive Mapping) and OCMR (Optimal Consecutive Mapping with Replication), which can measure similarity between query trajectory $Q=(q_1, q_2, ..., q_M)$ and data trajectory $V=(v_1, v_2, ..., v_N)$. The OCM algorithm that supports exact matching measures the similarity for one-to-one segment mapping between query trajectory and data trajectory. Meanwhile, The OCMR algorithm supports approximation matching. In order to measure the similarity, each motion of query trajectory can be permitted to map with more than one motions of data trajectory. Figure 1 shows the relation of OCMR.

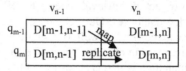

Fig. 1. Relation of OCMR between D[m, n] and D[i, j]

Here, $d(q_i, v_j)$ means distance function which computes distance between q_i and v_j and D[M, N] is minimum cost table which used to measure the minimum distance with replication between query trajectory and data trajectory. There are two possible relations between D[m, n] and D[i, j] for some combinations of smaller i-th and j-th. That is, map means that the motion v_n is mapped with the motion q_m, D[m,n] = D[m-1,n-1]+$d(q_m, v_n)$ and replication means that the motion v_n is replicated to mapped with the motion q_m, D[m, n]=D[m-1,n]+$d(q_m,v_n)$.

3   Similarity Measure Algorithm

We first present three considerations for supporting efficient similar sub-trajectory retrieval on moving objects and effective approximation matching in video databases.

Consideration 1: The time warping transformation used for a similar sub-sequence matching in sequence databases can allow the infinitive replication of a data sequence as well as a query sequence. However, for similar sub-trajectory retrieval in video databases, it should allow the replication of only a query trajectory.

Consideration 2: The time warping transformation for a similar sub-sequence matching can allow the infinitive replication of an arbitrary motion. However, for the similar sub-trajectory retrieval, it should allow the replication of up to the fixed number (k) of motions, so called k-warping distance.

Consideration 3: For modeling motions being composed of the trajectory of a moving object, it should support multiple properties including direction(angle), distance, and time as well as the single property of direction.

The consideration 1 is generally needed for supporting an approximation matching from similar sub-trajectory retrieval and the considerations 2 and 3 are needed for improving the effectiveness of the approximation matching. In addition, the considerations 2 and 3 are very sensitive according to application areas, such as soccer and hockey. The similar subsequence matching approach which is used for the existing time warping transformation does not satisfy all of the above three considerations. The reason is why the characteristic of data used in sequence database is different from that of trajectory data of moving objects in video databases.

Generally, the sequence data has a detailed and elaborate feature and the number of elements consisting of a sequence reaches scores or hundreds. On the other hand, the trajectory data of moving objects in video databases are composed of motions over a time interval and the number of motions consisting of a trajectory is less than scores. In addition, the Shan's OCMR scheme can satisfy the considerations 1, but it does not satisfy the considerations 2 and 3.

Therefore, we propose a new k-warping distance algorithm which can support an approximation matching and satisfy the above three considerations as its similarity measure algorithm. Our k-warping distance algorithm applies the concept of time warping transformation [6,7,8] used in time series databases to the trajectory data of moving objects. In order to satisfy the consideration 3, we can generally define the trajectory of moving objects as a collection of consecutive motions consisting of n-dimensional properties. However, for our k-warping distance algorithm, we define the trajectory of moving objects as a set of motions which consist of two-dimensional properties.

[Definition 1] The trajectory of moving object S is defined as a set of consecutive motions, S= (s[1], s[2], ..., s[|S|]), where each motion s[k] is composed of two-dimensional properties, that is, angle property(A_i) and distance property(D_i), s[i]=(A_i, D_i).

For the similarity between one of motions of a given query trajectory q[i] and that of data trajectory s[j], we define a distance function as d_{df}(q[i], s[j]).

[Definition 2] A distance function, d_{df}(q[i], s[j]), to measure the similarity between the arbitrary motion s[i] of a data trajectory S and the arbitrary motion q[j] of a query trajectory Q is defined as follows. Here d_{ang} is a distance function for the angle property for all the motions of a trajectory and d_{dis} is a distance function for the distance property. s[i, 1] and s[i, 2] are the angle and the distance value of the i-th motion in a trajectory S, respectively. α and β mean the weight of the angle and the distance, respectively, when $\alpha+\beta=1.0$.

$d_{dis} = |$ s[i, 2] - q[j, 2] $|$

if $|$ s[i, 1] - q[j, 1] $| > 180$
    then d_{ang}(s[i, 1], q[j, 1]) = (360 - $|$ s[i, 1] - q[j, 1] $|$)
    else d_{ang}(s[i, 1], q[j, 1]) = $|$ s[i, 1] - q[j, 1] $|$

$d_{df} = ((d_{ang} / 180) * \alpha) + (d_{dis}/100) * \beta)$

For efficient similar sub-trajectory retrieval, we define a new k-warping distance which modifies the time warping distance.

[Definition 3] Given two trajectory of moving objects S and Q, the k-warping distance D_{kw} is defined recursively as follows:

$D_{kw}(0, 0) = 0, D_{kw}(S, 0) = D_{kw}(0, Q) = \infty$

$D_{kw}(S, Q) = D_{base}(S[1], Q[1])+min(\{D_{kw}((S[2+i:-], Q), 0 \le i \le k), D_{kw}(S[2:-],$
    $Q[2:-])\})$

$D_{base}(a, b) = d_{df}(a, b)$

```
int k-warping_distance(S, Q, k)
{
   Input:
           S[]: Data Trajectory;
           Q[]: Query Trajectory;
           k: the number of warping(replication);
   Output:
           kw_dist:minimum distance acquired using k-
warping;

kwTbl[MAXSIZE];    // k-warping table;
for i=0 to |S|-1 do
for j=0 to |Q|-1 do
           kwTbl[j+i*|Q|] = 999.0f;

for i=0 to |S|-|Q| do {       // make k-warping table
for n=0 to |Q|-1 do {
y_p = i+n; x_p = n;
kwTbl[x_p+(y_p*|Q|)] = d_df(S[y_p],Q[x_p]);
} // end for n
for j=0 to |Q|-1 do {
for m=0 to k-1 do {
for n=0 to |Q|-1 do {
  y_p = 1 + I + (j*k) + m + n;
  x_p = n;
  if((y_p>=|S|)||(y_p>x_p+(|S|-|Q|))) break;
  if(j == n)
     kwTbl[x_p+(y_p*|Q|)]=kwTbl[x_p+((y_p-1)*|Q|)] +
d_df(S[y_p],Q[x_p]);
            else
  kwTbl[x_p+(y_p*|Q|)]=d_df(S[y_p],Q[x_p])+
min(kwTbl[x_p+((y_p-1)*|Q|)],
kwTbl[(x_p-1)+((y_p-1)*|Q|)]);
} // end for n
       } // end for m
} // end for j
 } // end for I
kw_dist = 999.0f;   // initializes
for i=0 to |S|-1 do { // find the minimum k-warping
dist.
if(kw_dist > twTbl[(|Q|-1)+(i*|Q|)]) {
kw_dist = twTbl[(|Q|-1)+(i*|Q|)];
y = i; x = |Q|;
}
 }
return kw_dist;
}
```

Fig. 2. k-warping distance algorithm

Our k-warping distance algorithm is shown in Figure 2. It calculates a k-warping distance between a given query trajectory Q and a data trajectory S by permitting up to k replications for an arbitrary motion of a query trajectory Q. When the motions of a data trajectory and a query trajectory are represented by rows and columns in the cumulative table respectively, our a k-warping distance algorithm finds a minimum distance starting from the first column of the first row within the last column of the last row by replicating an arbitrary motion of a query trajectory up to k times. In addition, since a motion of a trajectory is modeled as both angle property and distance property, our algorithm measures a similarity between a data trajectory S and a query trajectory Q by considering both properties.

For example, by using our k-warping distance algorithm based on both angle and distance property of moving objects' trajectories, a similarity distance among all motions between a data trajectory S={(45,10), (0,10), (355,10), (345,10), (4,40), (325,45)} and a query trajectory Q={(45,10), (0,10), (325,10)} can be calculated in Figure 3(a). Its k-warping table is created as shown in Figure 3(b). The value of the last column of the last row means the minimum distance 0.30 by permitting the infinitive replications of the query trajectory Q as shown in trajectory S_1. Truly, the similarity value is 0.7(=1-0.3) by infinitive replications in Shan's scheme. On the other hand, in the case of k-warping distance, the motion of q[0] in the query trajectory Q corresponds to the s[0] in the data trajectory S, the motion of q[1] to the s[1], the motion of q[1] to the s[2], and the motion of q[2] to the s[3] respectively as shown in trajectory S_2. Finally, we can find a path starting from the first column of the first row within the last column of the last row, thus obtaining the minimum distance by permitting up to k(=2) replications. We can summarize the differences of distance between each motion of the query and the data trajectory on the path, that is, |q[0]-s[0]|+|q[1]-s[1]|+|q[1]-s[2]|+|q[2]-s[3]|= 0.00 + 0.00 + 0.02 + 0.07 = 0.09. This value is the minimum distance between the two trajectories when using our k-warping distance algorithm, namely, the maximum similarity value, 0.91(=1-0.09).

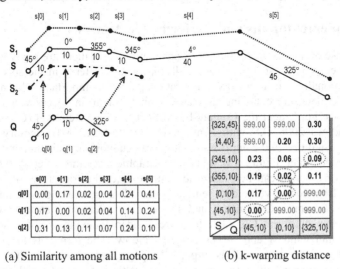

(a) Similarity among all motions   (b) k-warping distance

Fig. 3. Example of our k-warping distance algorithm (k=2)

In addition, we propose a new similar sub-trajectory retrieval scheme based on our k-warping algorithm. Our scheme can accept the replications of up to a fixed k number for all the motions of a moving object's trajectory. By using our scheme, we can obtain a higher recall than the performance in an initial query trajectory. The fixed replication number k depends on the characteristic of data domain in application areas. For example, in case of similar sub-trajectory retrieval for a salient object like football or hockey puck, a small fixed replication number k can improve retrieval effectiveness because the number of motions of a trajectory is below 10 in general. In case of an application area for the tracking of a mobile terminal like PCS or PDA, a large fixed replication number k improves retrieval effectiveness because the number of motions is large in general.

Fig. 4. GUI for soccer video indexing in CSVR system

4   Implementations and Performance Analysis

We make use of soccer video data as its application since there are many trajectories data of salient objects such as soccer ball, player, and referee in the soccer ground field. Additionally, the trajectory information plays an important role in indexing soccer video data and detecting the scene with 'goal in' in soccer video database. Therefore, we implement the Content-based Soccer Video Retrieval (CSVR) system under Windows 2000 O.S with Pentium III-800 and 512 MB memory by using Microsoft Visual C++ 6.0 compiler so that we can support the indexing and searching on soccer video data. Figure 4 first shows a Graphic User Interface(GUI) for soccer video indexing which can help users to easily extract the trajectory information of soccer ball from soccer video data semi-automatically, e.g. moving direction, moving distance, # of frame, player name, and so on. We implement it so as to work well under Window platform. Our GUI for soccer video indexing is composed of two windows: main window and soccer ground window. The former is to browse raw soccer video data formatted as mpeg (*.mpeg) and to extract the trajectory information of soccer ball and main player. The latter is to transform the location of soccer ball on raw video through the main window data into an absolute location on the coordinate of soccer ground field. For this, we make use of 'affine transformation algorithm' which is mainly used in computer vision or image processing fields [9].

Figure 5 depicts a GUI for soccer video retrieval which can help users to retrieve the results acquired in soccer video databases. We implemented it by JAVA application in order to work well independently without regard to system platform. We can provide three types of user query, that is, trajectory-based query, semantic-based query, and actor-based query as shown in the left part of Figure 5. The trajectory-based query is based on the trajectory of moving objects such as soccer ball and player as the following query: *"Finds all video shots whose trajectory is similar to the trajectory sketched by a user on soccer video retrieval interface"*. The semantic-based query is based on important semantics such as 'penalty kick', 'corner kick' and 'goal in' in soccer video databases: *"Finds all video shots including a scene 'goal in'.* Finally, the actor-based query is based on the interested player name such as 'Ronaldo', 'Rivaldo' and 'Zidane' in soccer video databases: *"Finds all video shots including a scene 'goal in' by planer name 'Ronaldo'.* The retrieved results on a user query are provided in the form of trajectory images with the similar trajectory as shown in the right part of Figure 5. We can browse them in the order of the degree of relevance to a user query. The real soccer video shot corresponding to the trajectory image retrieved can be shown by clicking its trajectory image with the mouse button.

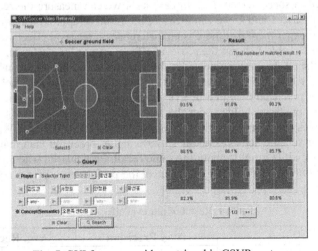

Fig. 5. GUI for soccer video retrieval in CSVR system

In order to verify the usefulness of our similar sub-trajectory retrieval scheme based on our k-warping distance algorithm, we do the performance analysis by using real soccer video data. Since the soccer video data has many trajectories of soccer balls (user-interesting salient objects), we extract the trajectories of moving objects from the soccer ball. Most of video data used in our experiment which are formatted as MPEG file (*.mpeg) include a shot of 'getting a goal'. We extract the trajectories of a soccer ball by manually tracing the ball in a ground field. For our experiment, we make forty query trajectories consisting of twenty in 'the right field' and twenty in 'the left field' from the half line of the ground field. Our experimental data used for our performance analysis as follows: the number of data is 350, the average motion number of data trajectory is 8, and the number of query is 40.

For our performance analysis, we compare our scheme with the Li's and Shan's ones in terms of retrieval effectiveness, that is, average precision and recall measures [10]. Let RD (Relevant data in Database) be the number of video data relevant to a given query which are selected from the database, RQ (Retrieved data by Query) be the total number of data retrieved by a given query, and RR (Relevant data that are Retrieved) be the number of relevant data retrieved by a given query. In order to obtain RD, we make a test panel which selects relevant data manually from the database. The test panel is composed of 10 graduate school students from our computer engineering department. The precision measure is defined as the proportion of retrieved data being relevant, that is, RR/RQ and the recall measure is defined as the proportion of relevant data being retrieved, that is, RR/RD.

For our performance comparison, we adopt the 11-point measure [10] which is most widely used for measuring the precision and recall. We consider the weight of angle (W_a) and the weight of distance (W_d) since we use both angle and distance for modeling the trajectory of moving objects. We also take into account the number of replications (k) since k is a very important parameter for an application area. Here we do our experiment when k=0, 1, and 2 owing to the characteristics of the trajectory of the soccer ball in soccer video data. In case k=0, we can measure the result of exact matching. In case k=1 and 2, we can measure the result of approximate matching. We show from our experiment that there is no difference on retrieval effectiveness when k is greater than 2. Table 1 shows the retrieval effectiveness of our scheme, Li's scheme, and Shan's scheme. In case we consider the importance of the angle and that of the distance equally (W_a=0.5 and W_d=0.5), it is shown that our scheme achieves about 10-15% higher precision than that of Li's and Shan's schemes while it acquires about 10-15% higher precision holds about the same recall. In case we consider the angle about two times more importantly than the distance (W_a =0.7 and W_d=0.3), it is shown that our scheme achieves about 15-20% higher precision than that of Li's and Shan's schemes while it holds about the same recall. Particularly, when the weight of angle is over two times than that of distance, the performance of our scheme is the best.

Table 1. Result of retrieval effectivness

		Avg. Precision			Avg. Recall		
	# of warping	k = 0	k = 1	k = 2	k = 1	k = 1	k = 2
W_a:W_d= 0.7:0.3	Li's Scheme	0.25			0.45		
	Shan's Scheme	0.30			0.44		
	Our Scheme	0.39	0.44	0.45	0.50	0.46	0.47
W_a:W_d= 0.5:0.5	Li's Scheme	0.25			0.45		
	Shan's Scheme	0.30			0.44		
	Our Scheme	0.33	0.34	0.38	0.51	0.50	0.51

In terms of the number of replications (k), we show that the performance of our scheme when k=1 is better than the performance when k=0. Also, The performance when k=2 is better than the one of when k=1. That is, approximate matching is efficient than exact matching for similar sub-trajectory retrieval based on moving objects.

5   Conclusions and Future Work

In this paper, we first proposed a new k-warping distance algorithm which modified the existing time distance algorithm by permitting up to k replications for an arbitrary motion of a query trajectory to calculate the similarity between two trajectories. Based on our k-warping distance algorithm, we also proposed a new similar sub-trajectory retrieval scheme for efficient retrieval on moving objects' trajectories in video databases. Our scheme can replicate all the motions of a trajectory's motions with a fixed number. Our scheme can support multiple properties including angle, distance, and time as well as can provide the approximate matching which is able to obtain more good result than the exact matching. Finally, we show from our experiment that our scheme outperforms Li's scheme (no-warping) and Shan's scheme (infinite-warping) in terms of precision and recall measures. In case the weight of angle is over two times than that of distance, the performance of our scheme is the best and achieves about 15-20% performance improvement against Li's and Shan's schemes. In terms of the number of replications (k), we show that the performance of our scheme when k=2 is better than the performance when k=1. As future work, it is required to study on indexing methods when the amount of trajectory data of moving objects is very large so that we can support good retrieval efficiency on a user query.

References

[1]   L. Forlizzi, R. H. Guting, E. Nardelli, and M. Schneider, "A Data Model and Data Structures for Moving Objects Databases", Proc. of ACM SIGMOD Conf, pp. 319-330, 2000.

[2]   R. H. Guting, et al., "A Foundation for Representing and Querying Moving Objects", ACM Transaction on Database Systems, Vol. 25, No. 1, pp. 1-42, 2000.

[3]   J. Z. Li, M. T. Ozsu, and D. Szafron, "Modeling Video Temporal Relationships in an Object Database Management System," in Proceedings of Multimedia Computing and Networking(MMCN97), pp. 80-91, 1997.

[4]   J. Z. Li, M. T. Ozsu, and D. Szafron, "Modeling of Video Spatial Relationships in an Objectbase Management System," in Proceedings of International Workshop on Multimedia DBMS, pp. 124-133, 1996.

[5]   M. K. Shan and S. Y. Lee, "Content-based Video Retrieval via Motion Trajectories," in Proceedings of SPIE Electronic Imaging and Multimedia System II, Vol. 3561, pp. 52-61, 1998.

[6]   B. K. Yi, H. V. Lagadish, and C. Faloutsos, "Efficient Retrieval of Similar Time Sequences Under Time Warping," In Proc. Int'l. Conf. on Data Engineering, IEEE, pp. 201-208, 1998.

[7]   S. H. Park, et al.,"Efficient Searches for Simialr Subsequence of Difference Lengths in Sequence Databases," In Proc. Int'l. Conf. on Data Engineering. IEEE, pp. 23-32, 2000.

[8]   S. W. Kim, S. H. Park, and W. W. Chu, "An Index-Based Approach for Similarity Search Supporting Time Warping in Large Sequence Databases," In Proc. Int'l. Conf. on Data Engineering. IEEE, pp. 607-614, 2001.

[9]   H.S. Yoon, J. Soh, B.W. Min, and Y.K. Yang, "Soccer image sequences mosaicing using reverse affine transform," In Proc. of International Technical Conference on Circuits/Systems, Computers and Communications, pp. 877-880, 2000.

[10] G. Salton and M. McGill, An introduction to Modern Information Retrieval, McGraw-Hill, 1993.

Associating Cooking Video Segments with Preparation Steps

Koichi Miura[1], Reiko Hamada[1], Ichiro Ide[2],
Shuichi Sakai[1], and Hidehiko Tanaka[1]

[1] The University of Tokyo
7-3-1 Hongo, Bunkyo-ku, Tokyo, 113-0033, Japan
{miura,reiko,sakai,tanaka}@mtl.t.u-tokyo.ac.jp
[2] National Institute of Informatics
2-1-2 Hitotsubashi, Chiyoda-ku, Tokyo 101-8430, Japan
ide@nii.ac.jp

Abstract. We are trying to integrate television cooking videos with corresponding cookbooks. The cookbook has the advantage of the capability to easily browse through a cooking procedure, but understanding of actual cooking operations through written explanation is difficult. On the other hand, a video contains visual information that text cannot express sufficiently, but it lacks the ease to randomly browse through the procedures. We expect that their integration in the form of linking preparation steps (text) in a cookbook and video segments should result in complementing the drawbacks in each media. In this work, we propose a method to associate video segments with preparation steps in a supplementary cookbook by combining video structure analysis and text-based keyword matching. The result of an experiment showed high accuracy in association per video segments, i.e. annotating the video.

1 Introduction

1.1 Background

Following the advance in telecommunication technology, large amount of multimedia data has become available from broadcast video. Multimedia data analysis is becoming important to store and retrieve them efficiently. Generally, multimedia data consist of image, audio and text. Individual research on analysis of each media has been made, but thorough understanding of multimedia data through single-media processing has shown limitation. To overcome this limitation, integrated processing that mutually supplements the incompleteness of information derived from each media could be a solution. Many attempts have been made to index video by means of multimedia integration, but sufficient accuracy for practical use has not necessarily been achieved since their subjects were too general.

We are trying to integrate television cooking videos with corresponding cookbooks. Such limitation of the target domain should lead to realistic integration

E. M. Bakker et al. (Eds.): CIVR 2003, LNCS 2728, pp. 174–183, 2003.

accuracy for practical use using relatively simple technologies. Cooking program is a kind of an instruction video, and in most cases, a supplementary cookbook describing the same recipe is provided. The cookbook has the advantage of the capability to easily browse through a cooking procedure, but understanding of actual cooking operations through written explanation is difficult. On the other hand, a video contains visual information that text cannot express sufficiently, but it lacks the ease to randomly browse through the procedures. We expect that their integration in the form of linking preparation steps (text) in a cookbook and video segments should result in complementing the drawbacks in each media. Moreover, various applications, such as indexing and extracting knowledge, should be possible using the result of the integration.

In this paper, we propose a method to associate video segments and preparation steps in supplementary cookbooks.

1.2   Related Works

Many attempts have been made on integrative multimedia processing for video indexing. In the Informedia project[1], they analyzed mainly news and documentary videos using advanced single media analysis techniques. It achieved significant results, but study on associating videos with external documents is not considered.

As an example of an attempt to associate videos with external documents, there is a work on aligning articles in television news programs and newspapers[2]. They refer to nouns that co-occur in open-captions of news videos and newspaper articles, but contents of the video other than open-caption texts (image and speech transcripts, or closed-captions) are not analyzed.

Another work on synchronization between video and drama scripts[3] also refers to external documents. They extract patterns from each media and synchronize them by DP matching to analyze semantic structures of a video from corresponding documents. The order of scenes in the video is basically synchronous to that in drama scripts, differ between the video and the document. whereas in cooking programs, the order of steps often differ between videos and cookbooks. Moreover, a step may consist of several separate video segments. There may also be omitted steps in the video, or extra video segments. These characteristics make it difficult to employ DP matching for our purpose, thus we have to gather hints from each media and integrate them appropriately.

1.3   System Overview

The outline of the proposed method is shown in Fig. 1. First, the video and the preparation steps in a supplementary cookbook are analyzed. The video is structured by image analysis as described in Section 3, and the preparation steps are analyzed as described in Section 4. Next, the structured video and preparation steps are associated as described in Section 5.

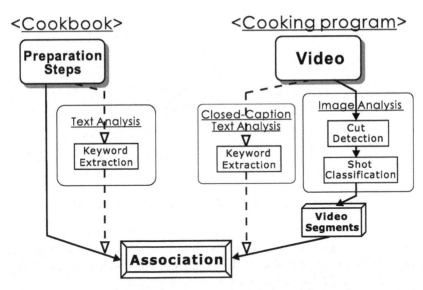

Fig. 1. System overview of associating cooking video with supplementary cookbook

2   Structural Analysis of Cooking Video

2.1   Image Analysis

Definition of Video Segment First, cut detection is performed to a video stream. Many cooking programs are taken in a studio under good lighting condition, so cut detection is easier than in general video. In this work, we adopt a method that uses DCT clustering[4].

After cut detection, shots are classified. As shown in Fig. 2, shots in cooking videos could be categorized into (a)face shot and (b)hand shot. (a)Face shots are furthermore categorized into (a1)full shot and (a2)bust shot.

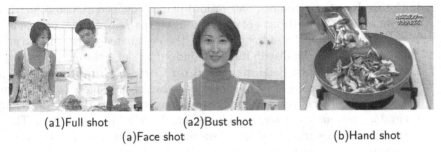

(a1)Full shot   (a2)Bust shot   (b)Hand shot
                (a)Face shot

Fig. 2. Shot classes in cooking video

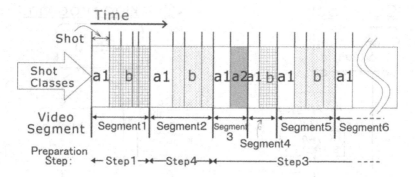

Fig. 3. Example of a shot structure in a cooking video

An example of a shot structure of a cooking video is shown in Fig. 3. Here, we observed that over 90% of the head shots of video segments corresponding to beginnings of preparation steps were full shots (a1).

Following this observation, we define a "video segment", which is the minimal unit for the association. Thus, a "video segment" is a sequence of shots that begins with a full shot and ends with a shot before the next full shot, as shown in Fig. 3.

Face Shot Detection Detection of face shots is particularly important since they become clues to detect full shots in order to segment the video. Face shots contain significantly large human faces in the images, so they are detected by detecting face regions.

Although various advanced methods to extract face regions exist, in our method, we employ a simple and robust method as follows, since only their existence, locations, and sizes are needed in this work.

1. **Detect Skin Colored Regions:**
   The modified HSV color system[5] is used to detect skin colored regions. V(Value) is used only for excluding dark regions. A certain rectangular region in the H(Hue)-Sm (Modified Saturation) plane is defined as skin color. The distribution of sampled skin-colored regions on the H-Sm plane is shown in Fig. 4. Pixels whose H and Sm drop in the designated rectangular region that circumscribes the distribution, are judged as skin-colored.
2. **Determine the Face Regions Based on Certain Conditions:**
   The detected skin-colored regions may contain not only faces but also similarly colored objects such as hand, wooden spatula, and table. To exclude them, face regions are determined based on the following conditions. These conditions were defined considering specific features of cooking videos.
   - Exclude over-sized or under-sized regions.
   - Exclude regions that touch the frame boundary.

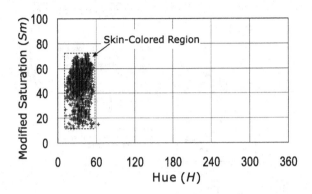

Fig. 4. Skin-colored region on the H-Sm plane[6]

- Assume that the sizes of regions are similar when more than one region
  exist.
- Assume that at least a part of the region is located in the upper-half of
  the image.

We classified the (a)face shot into (a1)full shot and (a2)bust shot based on
the size and the number of face regions.

2.2 Closed-Caption Text Analysis

The contents of audio speech is an important hint for the association. In our
method, we use "closed-caption text" that is provided from broadcasting sta-
tions as a transcript of speech, instead of performing speech recognition. In case
of programs lacking closed-caption texts, speech recognition will be needed in
order to obtain transcripts, but sufficient performance will not be expected to
be achieved in this case.

Morphological analysis of closed-caption texts is performed in order to extract
nouns and verbs. Next, keywords, such as ingredients and verbs, are extracted.
Details on keyword extraction are described in section 3 with cookbook analysis.

3   Text Analysis of Cookbook

A recipe in a cookbook consists of a "list of ingredients" and a "preparation
steps" part as shown in Fig. 5. "Preparation steps" give explanation on how to
cook the "list of ingredients".

The following procedure is taken to extract keywords from both preparation
steps and closed-caption texts.

- Perform morphological analysis.

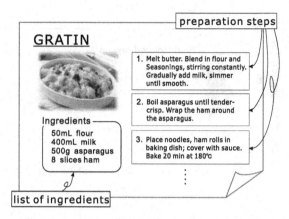

Fig. 5. Example of cooking textbook

- Extract ingredient nouns that appear in the "list of ingredients" and all the verbs as keywords.
- Ingredient nouns and all the verbs in a single sentence are regarded as related keywords.

When a step to be analyzed refers to a preceding step as shown in the following example, it is supplemented with all ingredient nouns in the step referred to.

step 1:	Tomato and tuna are cut in square by 2cm, and are mixed in a bowl.
step 2:	Add some olive oil, salt and soy sauce to $[1]_{(step\#)}$, and marinate.

Considering verbs, in order to cope with the difference of notations between preparation steps and closed-caption texts, a conceptual dictionary is created and employed. An example of this dictionary is shown in Tab. 1.

Table 1. Example of the conceptual dictionary

words	corresponding cooking motion
slice mince ...	cut
put in pour in ...	add

4   Association Method

The aim of this work is to associate "video segments" with "preparation steps". In cooking programs, the order of steps are not always synchronous between a video and a cookbook. Moreover, a single step often corresponds to several video segments. On the other hand, there may be omitted steps in the video, or extra video segments.

Considering such irregularities, the following procedure based on the extracted keywords is taken to associate "video segments" with "preparation steps". An example of the association is shown in Fig. 6. The score of a keyword that takes in account of the rareness of the keywords is defined as follows:

$$\frac{1}{M} \times \frac{1}{N} \left(\begin{array}{l} M : \text{Number of steps containing the keyword} \\ N : \text{Number of video segments containing the} \\ \quad \text{keyword in the closed-caption texts} \end{array} \right)$$

1. All keywords in a video segment are compared to the keywords in each preparation step.
2. When both ingredient nouns and related verbs in a segment match those in a preparation step,
   Match with a single step: Associate the video segment with the step.
   Match with several steps: The video segment could belong to several steps. The association is determined referring to the steps that preceding and succeeding video segments are associated to.
3. When no steps match, add the score of the keywords to the steps which has a keyword in common. The video segment is associated with the step with the highest score. If several steps have the highest score, the steps that preceding and succeeding video segments are associated to are referred to.
4. When a video segment could not be associated since the preceding and succeeding video segments are not associated, and thus could not be referred to yet, it will be associated later. The procedure repeats until no more associations could be made.

5   Experiment

5.1   Face Shot Detection

We detected face shots from the first frames of 600 shots (approximately 100 minutes) taken from a Japanese cooking program. The result of face shot detection is shown in Tab. 2. In this experiment, cut detection was manually done to evaluate face shot detection individually, although the result of cut detection applying the DCT clustering method[4] showed over 95% accuracy in a preliminary experiment.

The result of face shot and face region detection is shown in Tab. 2. The number of correctly detected shots is N_C, misdetected shots is N_M, and oversighted shots is N_O. Recall is $N_C/(N_C + N_O)$, and precision is $N_C/(N_C + N_M)$.

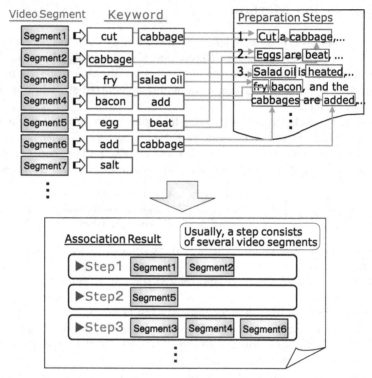

Fig. 6. Example of the association process

The misdetections were mainly due to detecting similarly colored regions such as chicken, meat or wall. The oversights were mainly due to the size of face regions depending on face directions. Although many oversights of face regions are observed in (a1)full shot as shown in Tab. 2, the recall of face shot detection is not much affected, since usually more than two persons exist in a (a1)full shot. Thus, relatively high shot detection rates were achieved despite low recall in face region detection. We consider the result sufficient for actual application to video structuring within the proposed method.

Table 2. Result of face shot detection

Shot class	Correct N_C	Misdetection N_M	Oversight N_O	Recall	Precision
(a1)Full shot	169	24	25	87%	88%
(a2)Bust shot	68	18	20	77%	79%

5.2   Associating Video Segments with Preparation Steps

Finally, we made an evaluation experiment that associates video segments with preparation steps. In this experiment, the target cooking videos consist of 20 recipes, with the length of approximately 150 minutes in total, taken from a Japanese cooking program and its supplementary cookbook. Note that shot classification was manually done to evaluate the association individually. The result of the association is shown in Tab. 3.

"*Video Segment → Step*" in Tab. 3 shows the association ability per video segment, where a video segment associated with a correct step is regarded as correct. On the other hand, "*Video Segment ← Step*" shows the association ability per preparation step, where a step without lack of associated video segments is regarded as correct. Finally, in "*Video Segment ↔ Step*", a step that has neither much nor little video segments is regarded as correct. Note that when a video segment is associated to two steps, each association is counted as 0.5. *Other* are blocks that were not associated to any step. *Accuracy* is calculated by *Correct/Total*.

As shown in the result of "*Video Segment → Step*" in Tab. 3, over 80% of video segments were correctly associated with preparation steps. Since the primary aim of the association method is to annotate video segments with preparation steps, this result indicates that the proposed method is effective.

Since the method does not consider temporal order, the association succeeded in most cases when the order of video and preparation steps were different, and also when a step consisted of several separate video segments.

6   Conclusions

This paper proposed and examined a method to associate cooking videos with preparation steps in a supplementary cookbook. A method to associate video segments with preparation steps was proposed, based on a structured cooking video. The experiment showed high accuracy in association per video segments, i.e. indexing the video. This high accuracy should be considered as the result of using domain specific knowledge.

In the future, closed-caption texts and preparation steps in supplementary cookbooks should be analyzed more precisely in order to improve the association accuracy. Furthermore, we will investigate on a more precise video structure analysis and association method to give videos corresponding to sentences. Various

Table 3.   Result of the association

Evaluation	Total	Correct	Miss	Other	Accuracy
Video Segment → Step	242	203.5	29.5	9	84.1%
Video Segment ← Step	94	74	20	–	79%
Video Segment ↔ Step	94	59	35	–	62%

applications, such as indexing, extracting knowledge and constructing a database of cooking operations, should be possible using the result of this work.

Although, some modifications, such as redefining the conceptual dictionary, should be required, the proposed association method may be applied to other educational videos with clear video structures and corresponding textbooks.

Acknowledgments

The sample cooking video images are taken from the "Video Media Database for Evaluation of Video Processing" [7].

References

[1] Wactlar, H. D., Hauptmann, A. G., Christel, M. G., Houghton, R. A., Olligschlaeger, A. M.: Complementary video and audio analysis for broadcast news archives. Comm. ACM **45** (2000) 42–47 175

[2] Watanabe, Y., Okada, Y., Tsunoda, T., Nagao, M.: Aligning articles in TV newscasts and newspapers (in Japanese). Journal of JSAI **12** (1997) 921–927 175

[3] Yaginuma, Y., Sakauchi, M.: Content-based retrieval and decomposition of TV drama based on intermedia synchronization. In: First Intl. Conf. on Visual Information Systems. (1996) 165–170 175

[4] Ariki, Y., Saito, Y.: Extraction of TV news articles based on scene cut detection using DCT clustering. In: Proc. Intl. Conf. on Image Processing. (1996) 847–850 176, 180

[5] Matsuhashi, S., Nakamura, O., Minami, T.: Human-face extraction using modified HSV color system and personal identification through facial image based on isodensity maps. In: IEEE Canadian Conf. on Electrical and Computer Engineering '95. (1995) 909–912 177

[6] Ide, I., Yamamoto, K., Tanaka, H.: Automatic video indexing based on shot classification. In: First Intl. Conf. on Advanced Multimedia Content Processing (AMCP '98). (1998) 99–114 178

[7] Babaguchi, N., Etoh, M., Satoh, S., Adachi, J., Akutsu, A., Ariki, Y., Echigo, T., Shibata, M., Zen, H., Nakamura, Y., Minoh, M., Matsuyama, T.: Video database for evaluating video processing (in Japanese). Tech. Report of IEICE, PRMU2002-30 **102** (2002) 69–74 183

Evaluation of Expression Recognition Techniques

Ira Cohen[1], Nicu Sebe[2,3], Yafei Sun[2], Michael S. Lew[3], and Thomas S. Huang[1]

[1] Beckman Institute
University of Illinois at Urbana-Champaign, USA
[2] Faculty of Science
University of Amsterdam
The Netherlands
[3] Leiden Institute of Advanced Computer Science
Leiden University
The Netherlands

Abstract. The most expressive way humans display emotions is through facial expressions. In this work we report on several advances we have made in building a system for classification of facial expressions from continuous video input. We introduce and test different Bayesian network classifiers for classifying expressions from video. In particular we use Naive-Bayes classifiers and to learn the dependencies among different facial motion features we use Tree-Augmented Naive Bayes (TAN) classifiers. We also investigate a neural network approach. Further, we propose an architecture of hidden Markov models (HMMs) for automatically segmenting and recognizing human facial expression from video sequences. We explore both person-dependent and person-independent recognition of expressions and compare the different methods.

1 Introduction

It is argued that to truly achieve effective human-computer intelligent interaction (HCII), there is a need for the computer to be able to interact naturally with the user, similar to the way human-human interaction takes place. Humans interact with each other mainly through speech, but also through body gestures, to emphasize a certain part of the speech and display of emotions. One of the important way humans display emotions is through facial expressions.

Ekman and Friesen [5] developed the Facial Action Coding System to code facial expressions where movements on the face are described by a set of action units (AUs). Ekman's work inspired many researchers to analyze facial expressions by means of image and video processing. By tracking facial features and measuring the amount of facial movement, they attempt to categorize different facial expressions. Recent work on facial expression analysis and recognition [18, 10, 16, 6, 12, 4, 11] has used these "basic expressions" or a subset of them. In [14], Pantic and Rothkrantz provide an in depth review of many of the research done in automatic facial expression recognition in recent years. These methods are similar in that they first extract features, then these features are

E. M. Bakker et al. (Eds.): CIVR 2003, LNCS 2728, pp. 184–195, 2003.
© Springer-Verlag Berlin Heidelberg 2003

used as inputs into a classification system, and the outcome is one of the prese-
lected emotion categories. They differ mainly in the features extracted from the
videos and in the classifiers used to distinguish between the different emotions.

Our work focuses on the design of the classifiers used for performing the
recognition following extraction of features using our real time face tracking
system. We describe classification schemes in two types of settings: dynamic and
'static' classification.

The 'static' classifiers use feature vectors related to a single frame to perform
classification (e.g., Neural networks, Bayesian networks). More specifically, we
use two types of Bayesian network classifiers: Naive Bayes, in which the features
are assumed independent given the class, and the Tree-Augmented Naive Bayes
classifier (TAN). While Naive-Bayes classifiers are often successful in practice,
they use the very strict and often unrealistic independence assumption. To account for this, we use the TAN classifiers which have the advantage of modeling
dependencies between the features without much added complexity compared
to the Naive-Bayes classifiers. We were also interested in using a neural network approach. Dynamic classifiers take into account the temporal pattern in
displaying facial expression. We propose a multi-level HMM classifier, combining
the temporal information which allows not only to perform the classification of
a video segment to the corresponding facial expression, as in the previous works
on HMM based classifiers [12, 11], but also to automatically segment an arbitrary long video sequence to the different expressions segments without resorting
to heuristic methods of segmentation.

An important aspect is that while the 'static' classifiers are easier to train
and implement, the dynamic classifiers require more training samples and many
more parameters to learn.

2   Face Tracking and Feature Extraction

The face tracking we use in our system is based on a system developed by Tao and
Huang [17] called the Piecewise Bézier Volume Deformation tracker. This face
tracker uses a model-based approach where an explicit 3D wireframe model of
the face is constructed. In the first frame of the image sequence, landmark facial
features such as the eye corners and mouth corners are selected interactively.
The generic face model is then warped to fit the selected facial features. The face
model consists of 16 surface patches embedded in Bézier volumes. The surface
patches defined in this way are guaranteed to be continuous and smooth. The
shape of the mesh can be changed by changing the locations of the control points
in the Bézier volume.

Once the model is constructed and fitted, head motion and local deformations of the facial features such as the eyebrows, eyelids, and mouth can be
tracked. First the 2D image motions are measured using template matching between frames at different resolutions. Image templates from the previous frame
and from the very first frame are both used for more robust tracking. The measured 2D image motions are modeled as projections of the true 3D motions onto

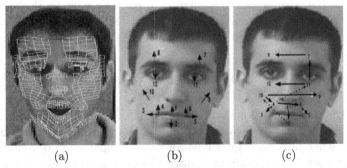

(a)   (b)   (c)

Fig. 1. (a) The wireframe model, (b) The facial motion measurements, (c) The learned TAN structure for the facial features. Dashed lines represent links that are relatively weaker than the others

the image plane. From the 2D motions of many points on the mesh, the 3D motion can be estimated by solving an overdetermined system of equations of the projective motions in the least squared sense. Figure 1(a) shows an example from one frame of the wireframe model overlayed on a face being tracked.

The recovered motions are represented in terms of magnitudes of some predefined motion of various facial features. Each feature motion corresponds to a simple deformation on the face, defined in terms of the Bézier volume control parameters. We refer to these motions vectors as Motion-Units (MU's). Note that they are similar but not equivalent to Ekman's AU's and are numeric in nature, representing not only the activation of a facial region, but also the direction and intensity of the motion. The 12 MU's used in the face tracker are shown in Figure 1(b). They are used as the basic features for the classification scheme described in the next sections.

3   The Static Approach

We use Bayesian network classifiers and a neural network for recognizing facial expressions given the tracking results provided by the face tracking algorithm. Our classifiers are 'static' in the sense that their features are tracking results at each point in time.

3.1   Bayesian Networks for Expression Recognition

A Naive-Bayes classifier is a probabilistic classifier in which the features are assumed independent given the class. Although the Naive-Bayes model does not reflect in many cases the true underlying model generating the data, it is still observed to be successful as a classifier in practice. The reason for the Naive-Bayes model's success as a classifier is attributed to the small number of parameters needed to be estimated, thus offsetting the large modeling bias with a small estimation variance [7].

Given a Bayesian network classifier with parameter set Θ, the optimal classification rule under the maximum likelihood (ML) framework to classify an observed feature vector of n dimensions, $X \in R^n$, to one of $|C|$ class labels, $c \in \{1, ..., |C|\}$, is given as:

$$\hat{c} = argmax_c \ P(X|c; \Theta) \tag{1}$$

Based on the observation that the strong independence assumption may seem unreasonable for our application (the facial motion measurements are highly correlated when humans display emotions), we decided to go beyond the Naive-Bayes assumption. Therefore, we wanted to find a way to search for a structure that captures the dependencies among the features. Of course, to attempt to find all the dependencies is an NP-complete problem. So, we restricted ourselves to a smaller class of structures called the Tree-Augmented-Naive Bayes (TAN) classifiers [8]. The joint probability distribution is factored to a collection of conditional probability distributions of each node in the graph.

In the TAN classifier structure the class node has no parents and each feature has as parents the class node and at most one other feature, such that the result is a tree structure for the features. Friedman et al. [8] proposed using the TAN model as a classifier, to enhance the performance over the simple Naive-Bayes classifier. The existence of an efficient algorithm to compute the best TAN model makes it a good candidate in the search for a better structure over the simple NB. This method is using the modified Chow-Liu algorithm [1] for constructing tree augmented Bayesian networks [8]. The algorithm finds the tree structure among the features that maximizes the likelihood of the data by computation of the pairwise class conditional mutual information among the features and building a maximum weighted spanning tree (MWST) using the pairwise mutual information as the weights of the arcs in the tree.

For facial expression recognition, the learned TAN structure can provide additional insight on the interaction between facial features in determining facial expressions. Figure 1(c) shows a learned tree structure of the features (our Motion Units) learned using our database of subjects displaying different facial expressions (more details on the experiments are in Section 5). The arrows are from parents to children MUs. From the tree structure we see that the TAN learning algorithm produced a structure in which the bottom half of the face is almost disjoint from the top portion, except for a weak link between MU 4 and MU 11.

We have recently showed that using NB or TAN classifiers can achieve good results for facial expression recognition, where the choice between each structure depends mainly on the size of the training set [3].

3.2   Neural Network Approach

In a neural network based classification approach, a facial expression is classified according to the categorization process the network learned during the training phase. In our implementation, we used the approach proposed by Padgett and Cottrell [13]. For classification of the tracking results provided by the face tracking algorithm into one of 6 basic categories (happiness, sadness, anger, fear, surprise, and disgust) plus Neutral emotion category, we use a back-propagation neural network. The input to the network consists of the 12 MU extracted by the face tracking algorithm. The hidden layer of the NN contains 10 nodes and employs a nonlinear Sigmoid activation function [13]. The output layer of the NN contains 7 units, each of which corresponds to one emotion category.

For training and the testing of the neural network we use the same training and testing data as in the case of Bayesian Networks. See Section 5 for more details.

4   The Dynamic Approach

The dynamic approach employs classifiers that can use temporal information to discriminate between different expressions. The logic behind using the temporal information is that expressions have a unique temporal pattern. When recognizing expressions from video, the use of temporal information can lead to more robust and accurate classification results compared to methods that are 'static'.

4.1   Expression Recognition Using Multi-level HMM

The method we propose automatically segments the video to the different facial expression sequences, using a multi-level HMM structure. To solve the segmentation problem and enhance the discrimination between the classes we propose the achitecture shown in Figure 2. This architecture performes automatic segmentation and recognition of the displayed expression at each time instance. The motion features are continuously used as input to the six emotion-specific HMMs. The state sequence of each of the HMMs is decoded and used as the observation vector for the high-level Markov model. This model consists of seven states, one for each of the six emotions and one for Neutral. The Neutral state is necessary as for the large portion of time, there is no display of emotion on a person's face. In this implementation of the system, the transitions between emotions are imposed to pass through the Neutral state since our training data consists of facial expression sequences that always go through the Neutral state.

The recognition of the expression is done by decoding the state that the high-level Markov model is in at each point in time since the state represents the displayed emotion. The training procedure of the system is as follows:

- Train the emotion-specific HMMs using a hand segmented sequence.
- Feed all six HMMs with the continuous (labeled) facial expression sequence. Each expression sequence contains several instances of each facial expression with *neutral* instances separating the emotions.
- Obtain the state sequence of each HMM to form the six-dimensional observation vector of the higher-level Markov model, i.e., $O_t^h = [q_t^{(1)},...,q_t^{(6)}]^T$,

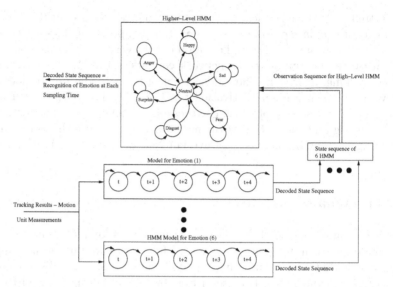

Fig. 2. Multi-level HMM architecture for automatic segmentation and recognition of emotion

where $q_t^{(i)}$ is the state of the ith emotion-specific HMM. The decoding of the state sequence is done using the Viterbi algorithm [15].

- Learn the probability observation matrix for each state of the high-level Markov model using $P(q_j^{(i)}|S_k) = \{$expected frequency of model i being in state j given that the true state was $k\}$, and

$$B^{(h)} = \{b_k(O_t^h)\} = \left\{\prod_{i=1}^{6}(P(q_j^{(i)}|S_k)\right\} \qquad (2)$$

where $j \in (1, Number\ of\ States\ for\ Lower\ Level\ HMM)$.

- Compute the transition probability $A = \{a_{kl}\}$ of the high-level HMM using the frequency of transiting from each of the six emotion classes to the *neutral* state in the training sequences and from the *neutral* state to the other emotion states. For notation, the *neutral* state is numbered 7 and the other states are numbered as in the previous section. All the transition probabilities could also be set using expert knowledge.

- Set the initial probability of the high-level Markov model to be 1 for the *neutral* state and 0 for all other states. This forces the model to always start at the *neutral* state and assumes that a person will display a *neutral* expression in the beginning of any video sequence. This assumption is made just for simplicity of the testing.

The steps followed during the testing phase are very similar to the ones followed during training. The face tracking sequence is used as input into the lower-level HMMs and a decoded state sequence is obtained using the Viterbi algorithm.

The decoded lower-level state sequence O_t^h is used as input to the higher-level HMM and the observation probabilities are computed using Eq. (2). Note that in this way of computing the probability, it is assumed that the state sequences of the lower-level HMMs are independent given the true labeling of the sequence. This assumption is reasonable since the HMMs are trained independently and on different training sequences. In addition, without this assumption, the size of B will be enormous, since it will have to account for all possible combinations of states of the six lower-level HMMs, and it would require a huge amount of training data.

Using the Viterbi algorithm again for the high-level Markov model, a most likely state sequence is produced. The state that the HMM was in at time t corresponds to the expressed emotion in the video sequence at time t. To make the classification result robust to undesired fast changes, a smoothing of the state sequence is done by preserving the actual classification result if the HMM did not stay in a particular state for more than T times, where T can vary between 1 and 15 samples (assuming a 30Hz sampling rate). The introduction of the smoothing factor T will cause a delay in the decision of the system, but of no more than T sample times.

5   Experiments

We use two different databases, a database collected by us and the Cohn-Kanade database [9]. The first is a database of subjects that were instructed to display facial expressions corresponding to the six types of emotions. All the tests of the algorithms are performed on a set of five people, each one displaying six sequences of each one of the six emotions, starting and ending at the Neutral expression. Each video sequence was used as the input to the face tracking algorithm. The sampling rate was 30Hz, and a typical emotion sequence is about 70 samples long (~2s).

We use our database in two types of experiments. First we performed person dependent experiments, in which part of the data for each subject was used as training data, and another part as test data. Second, we performed person independent experiments, in which we used the data of all but one person as training data, and tested on the person that was left out.

The Cohn-Kanade database [9] consists of expression sequences of subjects, starting from a Neutral expression and ending in the peak of the facial expression. There are 104 subjects in the database. Because for some of the subjects, not all of the six facial expressions sequences were available to us, we used a subset of 53 subjects, for which at least four of the sequences were available. For each person there are on average 8 frames for each expression, which makes insufficient data to perform person dependent tests. Also, the fact that each sequence ends in the peak of the facial expression makes the use of our dynamic multi-level HMM classifier impractical since in this case each sequence counts for an incomplete temporal pattern.

Table 1. Person-dependent facial expression recognition rates

Subject	NB	TAN	NN	HMM
1	81.69%	85.94%	82.37%	80.05%
2	84.54%	89.39%	85.23%	85.71%
3	83.05%	86.58%	81.17%	80.56%
4	79.25%	82.84%	80.05%	88.89%
5	71.74%	71.78%	75.23%	77.14%
Average	80.05%	83.31%	80.81%	82.46%

For the frame based methods, we measure the accuracy with respect to the classification result of each frame, where each frame in the video sequence was manually labeled to one of the expressions (including Neutral). The accuracy for the temporal based methods is measured with respect to the misclassification rate of an expression sequence, not with respect to each frame.

5.1 Results Using Our Database

A person-dependent test is first tried. Tables 1 shows the recognition rate of each subject and the average recognition rate of the classifiers.

The fact that subject 5 was poorly classified can be attributed to the inaccurate tracking result and lack of sufficient variability in displaying the emotions.

It is also important to observe that taking into account the dependencies in the features (the TAN model) gives significantly improved results. Also, the neural network approach gives comparable results to all the other methods.

The confusion matrix for the TAN classifier is presented in Table 2. The analysis of the confusion between different emotions shows that most of the confusion of the classes is with the Neutral class. This can be attributed to the arbitrary labeling of each frame in the expression sequence. The first and last few frames of each sequence are very close to the Neutral expression and thus are more prone to become confused with it. We also see that most expression do not confuse with Happy.

Table 2. Person-dependent confusion matrix using the TAN classifier

Emotion	Neutral	Happy	Anger	Disgust	Fear	Sad	Surprise
Neutral	79.58	1.21	3.88	2.71	3.68	5.61	3.29
Happy	1.06	87.55	0.71	3.99	2.21	1.71	2.74
Anger	5.18	0	85.92	4.14	3.27	1.17	0.30
Disgust	2.48	0.19	1.50	83.23	3.68	7.13	1.77
Fear	4.66	0	4.21	2.28	83.68	2.13	3.00
Sad	13.61	0.23	1.85	2.61	0.70	80.97	0
Surprise	5.17	0.80	0.52	2.45	7.73	1.08	82.22

Table 3. Recognition rate for person-independent test

Classifier	NB	TAN	NN	Multilevel HMM
Recognition rate	64.77%	66.53%	66.44%	58.63%

The confusion matrices for the HMM based classifiers (described in details in [2]) show similar results, with Happy achieving near 100%, and Surprise approximately 90%.

We saw that a good recognition rate was achieved when the training sequences were taken from the same subject as the test sequences. A more challenging application is to create a system which is person-independent. For this test all of the sequences of one subject are used as the test sequences and the sequences of the remaining four subjects are used as training sequences. This test is repeated five times, each time leaving a different person out (leave-one-out cross-validation). Table 3 shows the recognition rate of the test for all classifiers. In this case, the recognition rates are lower compared with the person-dependent results. This means that the confusions between subjects are larger than those within the same subject.

The TAN classifier provides the best results. One of the reasons for the misclassifications is the fact that the subjects are very different from each other (three females, two males, and different ethnic backgrounds); hence, they display their emotion differently. Although it appears to contradict the universality of the facial expressions as studied by Ekman and Friesen [5], the results show that for practical automatic emotion recognition, consideration of gender and race play a role in the training of the system.

Table 4 shows the confusion matrix for the TAN classifier. We see that Happy, Fear, and Surprise are detected with high accuracy, and other expressions are greatly confused mostly with Neutral. Here the differences in the intensity of the expressions among the different subjects played a significant role in the confusion among the different expressions.

Table 4. Person-independent average confusion matrix using the TAN classifier

Emotion	Neutral	Happy	Anger	Disgust	Fear	Sad	Surprise
Neutral	76.95	0.46	3.39	3.78	7.35	6.53	1.50
Happy	3.21	77.34	2.77	9.94	0	2.75	3.97
Anger	14.33	0.89	62.98	10.60	1.51	9.51	0.14
Disgust	6.63	8.99	7.44	52.48	2.20	10.90	11.32
Fear	10.06	0	3.53	0.52	73.67	3.41	8.77
Sad	13.98	7.93	5.47	10.66	13.98	41.26	6.69
Surprise	4.97	6.83	0.32	7.41	3.95	5.38	71.11

Table 5. Recognition rates for Cohn-Kanade database

Classifier	NB	TAN	NN
Recognition rate	68.14%	73.22%	73.81%

5.2   Results Using the Cohn-Kanade Database

For this test we first divided our database in 5 sets which contain the sequences corresponding to 10 or 11 subjects (three sets with 11 subjects, two sets with 10 subjects). We used the sequences from a set as test sequences and the remaining sequences were used as training sequences. This test was repeated five times, each time leaving a different set out (leave-one-out cross-validation). Table 5 shows the recognition rate of the test for all classifiers. Note that the results obtained with this database are much better than the ones obtained with our database. This is because in this case we have more training data. For training we had available the data from more than 40 different persons. Therefore, the learned model is more accurate and can achieve better classification rates when using the test data.

In average the best results were obtained using the NN followed by TAN and NB. The confusion matrix for the NN classifier is presented in Table 6. In this case, Surprise was detected with over 91% accuracy and Happy with over 77% accuracy. The other expressions are greatly confused with each other.

6   Summary and Discussion

In this work, we presented several methods for expression recognition from video. Our intention was to perform an extensive evaluation of our methods using static and dynamic classification.

In the case of 'static' classifiers the idea was to classify each frame of a video to one of the facial expressions categories based on the tracking results of that frame. The classification in this case was done using Bayesian networks classifiers and neural networks. A legitimate question is, "Is it always possible to learn the TAN structure from the data and use it in classification?" Provided that there

Table 6. Person-independent average confusion matrix using the NN classifier

Emotion	Neutral	Happy	Anger	Disgust	Fear	Sad	Surprise
Neutral	77.27	0.21	2.89	9.09	2.27	5.37	2.89
Happy	0	77.87	10.66	0.82	10.66	0	0
Anger	2.04	1.36	74.83	20.41	0	1.36	0
Disgust	1.14	3.41	7.95	73.86	1.14	11.36	1.14
Fear	2.86	27.62	0.95	3.81	63.81	0.95	0
Sad	4.20	7.94	6.15	18.32	4.35	57.14	11.90
Surprise	0	0	0	0	1.01	7.07	91.92

is sufficient training data, the TAN structure indeed can be extracted and used in classification. However, when the data is insufficient the learned structure is unreliable and the use of the Naive-Bayes classifier is recommended. Also, it is important to observe that the neural network approach provided similar results compared to the Bayesian Networks approach.

In the case of dynamic classifiers the temporal information was used to discriminate different expressions. The idea is that expressions have a unique temporal pattern and recognizing these patterns can lead to improved classification results. This was done using the multi-level HMM architecture which does not rely on any pre-segmentation of the video stream.

When one should use a dynamic classifier versus a 'static' classifier? This is a difficult question to ask. It seems, both from intuition and from our results, that dynamic classifiers are more suited for systems that are person dependent due to their higher sensitivity not only to changes in appearance of expressions among different individuals, but also to the differences in temporal patterns. 'Static' classifiers are easier to train and implement, but when used on a continuous video sequence, they can be unreliable especially for frames that are not at the peak of an expression. Another important aspect is that the dynamic classifiers are more complex, therefore they require more training samples and many more parameters to learn compared with the static approach. A hybrid of classifiers using expression dynamics and static classification is the topic of our future research.

References

[1] C.K. Chow and C.N. Liu. Approximating discrete probability distribution with dependence trees. *IEEE Transactions on Information Theory*, 14:462–467, 1968. 187

[2] I. Cohen. Automatic facial expression recognition from video sequences using temporal information. In *MS Thesis*, University of Illinois at Urbana-Champaign, Dept. of Electrical Engineering, 2000. 192

[3] I. Cohen, N. Sebe, L. Chen, and T.S. Huang. Facial expression recognition from video sequences: Temporal and static modeling. *to appear in Computer Vision and Image Understanding*, 2003. 187

[4] G. Donato, M.S. Bartlett, J.C. Hager, P. Ekman, and T.J. Sejnowski. Classifying facial actions. *IEEE Transactions on Pattern Analysis and Machine Intelligence*, 21(10):974–989, 1999. 184

[5] P. Ekman and W.V. Friesen. *Facial Action Coding System: Investigator's Guide.* Consulting Psychologists Press, Palo Alto, CA, 1978. 184, 192

[6] I.A. Essa and A.P. Pentland. Coding, analysis, interpretation, and recognition of facial expressions. *IEEE Transactions on Pattern Analysis and Machine Intelligence*, 19(7):757–763, July 1997. 184

[7] J.H. Friedman. On bias, variance, 0/1-loss, and the curse-of-dimensionality. *Data Mining and Knowledge Discovery*, 1(1):55–77, 1997. 186

[8] N. Friedman, D. Geiger, and M. Goldszmidt. Bayesian network classifiers. *Machine Learning*, 29(2):131–163, 1997. 187

[9] T. Kanade, J. Cohn, and Y. Tian. Comprehensive database for facial expression analysis, 2000. 190

[10] A. Lanitis, C.J. Taylor, and T.F. Cootes. A unified approach to coding and interpreting face images. In *Proc. 5th International Conference on Computer Vision (ICCV'95)*, pages 368–373, 1995. 184

[11] N. Oliver, A. Pentland, and F. Bérard. LAFTER: A real-time face and lips tracker with facial expression recognition. *Pattern Recognition*, 33:1369–1382, 2000. 184, 185

[12] T. Otsuka and J. Ohya. Recognizing multiple persons' facial expressions using HMM based on automatic extraction of significant frames from image sequences. In *Proc. Int. Conf. on Image Processing (ICIP'97)*, pages 546–549, 1997. 184, 185

[13] C. Padgett and G.W. Cottrell. Representing face images for emotion classification. In *Conf. Advances in Neural Information Processing Systems*, pages 894–900, 1996. 188

[14] M. Pantic and L.J.M. Rothkrantz. Automatic analysis of facial expressions: The state of the art. *IEEE Transactions on Pattern Analysis and Machine Intelligence*, 22(12):1424–1445, 2000. 184

[15] L.R. Rabiner. A tutorial on hidden Markov models and selected applications in speech processing. *Proceedings of IEEE*, 77(2):257–286, 1989. 189

[16] M. Rosenblum, Y. Yacoob, and L.S. Davis. Human expression recognition from motion using a radial basis function network architecture. *IEEE Transactions on Neural Network*, 7(5):1121–1138, September 1996. 184

[17] H. Tao and T.S. Huang. Connected vibrations: A modal analysis approach to non-rigid motion tracking. In *Proc. IEEE Conference on Computer Vision and Pattern Recognition (CVPR'98)*, pages 735–740, 1998. 185

[18] N. Ueki, S. Morishima, H. Yamada, and H. Harashima. Expression analysis/synthesis system based on emotion space constructed by multilayered neural network. *Systems and Computers in Japan*, 25(13):95–103, Nov. 1994. 184

A Hybrid Framework for Detecting the Semantics of Concepts and Context

Milind R. Naphade and John R. Smith

IBM Thomas J. Watson Research Center
Pervasive Media Management Group
Hawthorne, NY 10532
{naphade,jsmith}@us.ibm.com

Abstract. Semantic understanding of multimedia content necessitates models for the semantics of concepts, context and structure. We propose a hybrid framework that can combine discriminant or generative models for concepts with generative models for structure and context. Using the TREC Video 2002 benchmark corpus we show that robust models can be built for several diverse visual semantic concepts. We use a novel factor graphical framework to model inter-conceptual context for 12 semantic concepts of the corpus. Using the sum-product algorithm [1] for approximate or exact inference in these factor graph multinets, we attempt to correct errors made during isolated concept detection by forcing high-level constraints. This results in a significant improvement in the overall detection performance. Enforcement of this probabilistic context model enhances the detection performance further to 22 % using the global multinet, whereas its factored approximation also leads to improvement by 18 % over the baseline concept detection. This improvement is achieved without using any additional training data or separate annotations.

1   Introduction

With the increasing focus on semantic cues for video retrieval, automatic trainable techniques for learning models of the desired semantics are needed. The primary difficulty lies in the gap between low-level media features and high-level semantics. Early attempts to address this include detection of audio-visual events like explosion [2] and semantic visual templates [3]. To support retrieval based on high-level queries like '*Cityscape* or *Transportation*', etc. we need models for the event explosion and site beach. To support semantic concept detection, we proposed a probabilistic multimedia object (*multiject*) [2], which models the presence or absence of a semantic concept in terms of computational multimedia features. A *Multiject* can belong to any of the three categories: objects (*car, man, helicopter*), sites (*outdoor, beach*), or events (*explosion, man-walking*). There is however a limit on the detection performance that we may be able to achieve if the models are built without the use of domain knowledge or context.

E. M. Bakker et al. (Eds.): CIVR 2003, LNCS 2728, pp. 196–205, 2003.
© Springer-Verlag Berlin Heidelberg 2003

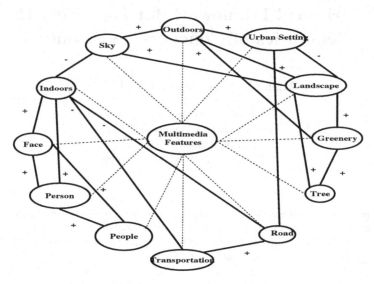

Fig. 1. A conceptual multinet showing relations between 12 visual concepts

Intuitively it is clear that the presence of certain semantic concepts suggests a high possibility of detecting certain other multijects. Similarly some multijects are less likely to occur in the presence of others. The detection of *sky* and *greenery* boosts the chances of detecting a *Landscape*, and reduces the chances of detecting *Indoors*. It might also be possible to detect some concepts and infer more complex concepts based on their relation with the detected ones. Detection of human speech in the audio stream and a face in the video stream may lead to the inference of *human talking*. To integrate all the multijects and model their interaction, we proposed the network of multijects which we termed as a multinet [4]. A conceptual figure of a multinet is shown in Figure 1 with positive (negative) signs indicating positive (negative) interaction.

In this paper we present the implementation of a hybrid framework for modeling concepts and context. Discriminant training has shown to improve detection performance of the multijects [5]. On the other hand the graphical multinet that we proposed [4] for a small number of concepts demonstrated performance improvement over generatively trained multijects. In this paper we combine multiject models built using discriminant training along with a graphical multinet that models joint probability mass functions of semantic concepts. We use the multijects to map the high level concepts to low-level audio-visual features. We also use a probabilistic factor graph framework, which models the interaction between concepts within each video shot as well as across the video shots within each video clip. Factor graphs provide an elegant framework to represent the stochastic relationship between concepts, while the sum-product algorithm provides an efficient tool to perform learning and inference in factor graphs. Using exact as well as approximate inference (through loopy probability propagation) we show that there is significant improvement in the detection performance.

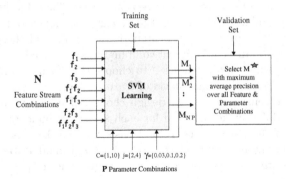

Fig. 2. SVM Learning: Optimizing over Multiple Possible Feature Combinations and Model Paramaters

2   Modeling Concepts: Support Vector Machines for Multiject Models

The generic framework for modeling semantic concepts from multimedia features [2, 6] includes an annotation interface, a learning framework for building models and a detection module for ranking unseen content based on detection confidence for the models (which can be interpreted as keywords). Suitable learning models include generative models [7] as well as discriminant techniques [5]. Positive examples for interesting semantic concepts are usually rare. In this situation it turns out that discriminant classification using support vector machines [8] performs better. The support vector machines project the original feature dimension using nonlinear kernel functions and attempt to find that linear separating hyperplane in the higher dimensional space, which maximizes generalization capability. For details see Vapnik [8]. For annotating video content so as to train models, a lexicon is needed. An annotation tool that allows the user to associate the object-labels with an individual region in a key-frame image or with the entire image was used[1]. to create a labeled training set. For experiments reported here the models were built using features extracted from key-frames. Figure 2 shows the feature and parameter selection process incorporated in the learning framework for optimal model selection and is described below.

2.1   Design Choices

Assuming that we extract features for color, texture, shape, structure etc., it is important to fuse information from across these feature types. One way is to build models for each feature type including color, structure, texture and shape. We also experiment with early feature fusion by combining multiple feature

---

[1] Available at http://www.alphaworks.ibm.com/tech/videoannex.

types at an early stage to construct a single model across different features. This approach is suitable for concepts that have sufficiently large number of training set exemplars and feature types, that are believed to be correlated and dependent. We can simply concatenate one or more of these feature types (appropriately normalized). Different combinations can then be used to construct models and the validation set is used to choose the optimal combination. This is feature selection at the coarse level of feature types.

To minimize sensitivity to the design choices of model parameters, we experiment with different kernels and for each kernel we build models for several combinations of the parameters. Radial basis function kernels usually perform better than other kernels. In our experiments we built models for different values of the RBF parameter γ (variance), relative significance of positive vs. negative examples j (necessitated also by the imbalance in the number of positive vs. negative training samples) and trade-off between training error and margin c. While a coarse to fine search is ideal, we tried 3 values of γ, 2 values of j and 2 of c. Using the validation set we then performed a grid search for the combination that resulted in highest average precision.

3 Modeling Context: A Graphical Multinet Model for Learning and Enforcing Context

To model the interaction between multijects in a multinet, we proposed a *factor graph* [1, 4] framework. Factor graphs subsume graphical models like Bayesian nets and Markov random fields and have been successfully applied in the area of channel error correction coding [1] and specifically, iterative decoding. Let $\mathbf{x} = \{x_1, x_2, \ldots, x_n\}$ be a vector of variables. A *factor graph* visualizes the factorization of a global function $f(\mathbf{x})$. Let $f(\mathbf{x})$ factor as

$$f(\mathbf{x}) = \prod_{i=1} f_i(\mathbf{x}^{(i)}) \tag{1}$$

where $\mathbf{x}^{(i)}$ is the set of variables of the function f_i. A factor graph for f is defined as the bipartite graph with two vertex classes V_f and V_v of sizes m and n respectively such that the ith node in V_f is connected to the jth node in V_v iff f_i is a function of x_j. For details please see [1]. **We will use rectangular blocks to represent function nodes and circular nodes to represent variable nodes.**

Many signal processing and learning problems are formulated as optimizing a global function $f(\mathbf{x})$ marginalized for a subset of its arguments. The **sum-product algorithm** allows us to perform this efficiently, though in most cases only approximately. It works by computing messages at the nodes using a simple rule and then passing the messages between nodes according to a reasonable schedule. A message from a function node to a variable node is the product of all messages incoming to the function node with the function itself, marginalized for the variable associated with the variable node. A message from a variable node to a function node is simply the product of all messages incoming to the

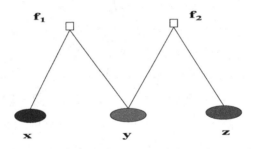

Fig. 3. An example of function factorization. $f(x, y, z) = f_1(x, y) \star f_2(y, z)$

variable node from other functions connected to it. If the factor graph is a tree, exact inference is possible using a single set of forward and backward passage of messages. For all other cases inference is approximate and the message passing is iterative [1] leading to loopy probability propagation. Because relations between semantic concepts are complicated and in general contain numerous cycles (e.g., see Figure 1) this provides the ideal framework for modeling context.

3.1   Relating Semantic Concepts in a Factor Graph

We now describe a shot-level factor graph to model the probabilistic relations between various frame-level semantic features F_i obtained by using the distance of the test set examples from the separating hyperplane as a measure of confidence. To capture the co-occurrence relationship between the twelve semantic concepts at the frame-level, we define a function node which is connected to the twelve variable nodes representing the concepts as shown in Figure 4[2]. This function node depicted by the rectangular box at the top represents the joint mass function $P(F_1, F_2, F_3, .., F_N)$. The function nodes below the variable nodes provide the individual SVM-based multiject's confidences i.e. $(P(F_i = 1|X), P(F_i = 0|X))$, where F_i is the th concept and X is the observation (features). These are then propagated to the function node. At the function node the messages are multiplied by the joint mass function estimated from the training set. The function node then sends back messages summarized for each variable. This modifies the soft decisions at the variable nodes according to the high-level relationship between the twelve concepts.

In general, the distribution at the function node in Figure 4 is exponential in the number of concepts (N) and the computational cost may increase quickly. To alleviate this we can enforce a factorization of the function in Figure 4 as a product of a set of local functions where each local function accounts for co-occurrence of two variables only. This modification is shown in Figure 5.

---

[2] Since we will present results using 12 concepts, the multinets in this paper depict 12 variable nodes.

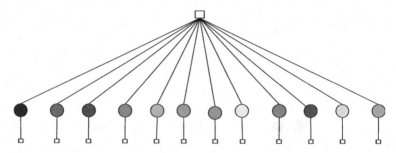

Fig. 4. A simple factor graph multinet using a single global function

Each function at the top in Figure 5 represents the joint probability mass of those two variables that are its arguments (and there are C_2^N such functions) thus reducing the complexity from exponential to polynomial in the number of concepts. For 12 concepts, there are 66 such local functions and the global function is approximated as a product of these 66 local functions. The factor graph is no longer a tree and exact inference becomes hard as the number of loops grows. We then apply iterative techniques based on the sum-product algorithm to overcome this.

4   Experimental Setup and Results

4.1   TREC Video 2002 Corpus: Training & Validation

The National Institute for Standards and Technology (NIST) has constituted a benchmark for evaluating the state of the art in semantic video detection and retrieval. For this Video TREC 2002 Concept Detection Benchmark NIST

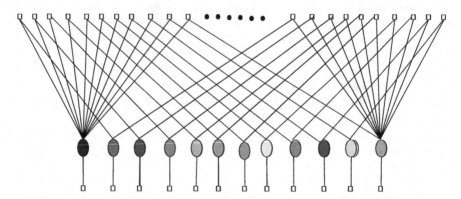

Fig. 5. An efficient implementation by a loopy approximation. Replacing the global function in 4 by a product of C_2^N local functions, where N is the number of variable nodes for concepts. For $N = 12$, there are 66 local functions

provided a data set of 24 hours of MPEG video for the concept development and later tested the detectors using a 5 hour test set (See [9], [10] for details of the corpus). We partitioned the NIST development set into a 19 hour training set and a 5 hours validation set. NIST defined non-interpolated average precision over a fixed number of retrieved shots as a measure of retrieval effectiveness. Let R be the number of true relevant documents in a set of size S; L the ranked list of documents returned. At any given index i let R_i be the number of relevant documents in the top i documents. Let $I_j = 1$ if the jth document is relevant and 0 otherwise. Assuming $R < S$, the non-interpolated average precision (**AP**) is then defined as

$$\frac{1}{R} \sum_{i=1}^{S} \frac{R_j}{j} * I_j \tag{2}$$

4.2   Lexicon

We created a lexicon with more than hundred semantic concepts for describing events, sites, and objects [2]. For experiments reported in this paper, we will confine to 12 concepts that had a support of 300 or more examples in the training set. These 12 concepts are

- Scenes: Outdoors, Indoors, Landscape, Cityscape, Sky, Greenery
- Objects: Face, Person, People, Road, Transportation Vehicle, Tree

4.3   Feature Extraction

After performing shot boundary detection and key-frame extraction [11] each keyframe was analyzed to detect the 5 largest regions described by their bounding boxes. The system then extracts the following low level visual features at the frame-level or global level as well as the region level for the entire frame as well as each of the regions in the keyframes.
Color Histogram (72): 72-bin YCbCr color space ($8 \times 3 \times 3$).
Color Correlogram (72): Single-banded auto-correlogram coefficients extracted for 8 radii depths in a 72-bin YCbCr color space.
Edge Orientation Histogram (32): Using a Sobel filtered image and quantized to 8 angles and 4 magnitudes.
Co-occurrence Texture (48): Based on entropy, energy, contrast, and homogeneity features extracted from gray-level co-occurrence matrices at 24 orientations [4].
Moment Invariants (6): Based on Dudani's moment invariants [4] for shape description
Normalized Bounding Box Shape (2): The width and the height of the bounding box normalized by that of the image.

Table 1. Concept Detection Performance Measure listed in the decreasing order of number of positive examples in a training set of 9603 keyframes

Semantic Concept	SVM baseline	Global Multinet	Factored Multinet
Outdoors	0.653	0.692	0.681
Person	0.235	0.295	0.285
People	0.417	0.407	0.415
Sky	0.506	0.59	0.562
Indoors	0.476	0.483	0.477
Face	0.282	0.442	0.445
Cityscape	0.174	0.241	0.204
Greenery	0.208	0.229	0.207
Transportation	0.294	0.38	0.38
Tree	0.146	0.16	0.166
Road	0.209	0.334	0.33
Landscape	0.497	0.537	0.499

4.4 Results

Having trained the 12 multiject models using SVM classifiers we then evaluate their performance on the validation set. This is used as the baseline for comparison with the context enforced detection. Details of the baseline detection are presented elsewhere (see [6]). The detection confidence is then modified using the multinet to enforce context. We evaluate performance of the globally connected multinet of Figure 4 model as well as the factored model of Figure 5. The comparison using the average precision measure (Equation 2) is shown in Table 1.

The mean improvement in average precision using the global unfactored multinet is 22 %. The approximation of the global multinet using the factored version also improves the average precision by 18 %. This improvement is thus very comparable to the improvement using the global multinet. Importantly, this improvement is achieved without using any additional training data or annotation. Also it is worth noticing that across all concepts the maximum improvement is as much as 58 % with the factored approximation (60 % for the unfactored global function), with almost no concept suffering any deterioration in performance. The Precision Recall curves (not presented here due to lack of space) also show consistently better performance using the multinet models.

5   Concluding Remarks

In this paper we present a hybrid framework that can combine discriminant or generative models for concepts with generative models for structure and context. Using the TREC Video 2002 benchmark corpus and 12 semantic concepts from this corpus we show that robust models can be built for several diverse visual semantic concepts. We use a novel factor graphical framework to model inter-conceptual context. Using the sum-product algorithm [1] for approximate or exact inference in these factor graph multinets, we attempt to correct errors made during isolated concept detection by forcing high-level constraints. This results in a significant improvement in the overall detection performance. Enforcement of this probabilistic context model enhances the detection performance further to 22 % using the global multinet, whereas its factored approximation also leads to improvement by 18 % over the baseline concept detection. This improvement is achieved without using any additional training data or annotation. Also it is worth noticing that across all concepts the maximum improvement is as much as 58 %, with almost no concept suffering any deterioration in performance. Future research included incorporating temporal smoothing using hidden Markov chains to enforce temporal context as in [12], [4].

Acknowledgement

The IBM TREC team for annotation, shot detection, classifier averaging, feature extraction.

References

[1] F. Kschischang, B. Frey, and H. Loeliger, "Factor graphs and the sum-product algorithm," *IEEE Transactions on Information Theory*, vol. 47, no. 2, pp. 498–519, 2001. 196, 199, 200, 204

[2] M. Naphade, T. Kristjansson, B. Frey, and T. S. Huang, "Probabilistic multimedia objects (multijects): A novel approach to indexing and retrieval in multimedia systems," in *Proceedings of IEEE International Conference on Image Processing*, Chicago, IL, Oct. 1998, vol. 3, pp. 536–540. 196, 198, 202

[3] S. F. Chang, W. Chen, and H. Sundaram, "Semantic visual templates - linking features to semantics," in *Proceedings of IEEE International Conference on Image Processing*, Chicago, IL, Oct. 1998, vol. 3, pp. 531–535. 196

[4] Milind R. Naphade, Igor Kozintsev, and Thomas S. Huang, "A factor graph framework for semantic video indexing," *IEEE Transactions on Circuits and Systems for Video Technology*, vol. 12, no. 1, pp. 40–52, Jan 2002. 197, 199, 202, 204

[5] M. Naphade and J.Smith, "The role of classifiers in multimedia content management," in *SPIE Storage and Retrieval for Media Databases*, San Jose, CA, Jan 2003, vol. 5021. 197, 198

[6] M. Naphade, C. Lin, A. Natsev, B. Tseng, and J. Smith, "A framework for moderate vocabulary visual semantic concept detection," submitted to IEEE ICME 2003. 198, 203

[7] M. Naphade, S. Basu, J. Smith, C. Lin, and B. Tseng, "Modeling semnatic concepts to support query by keywords in video," in *IEEE International Confernce on Image Processing*, Rochester, NY, Sep 2002. 198

[8] Vladimir Vapnik, *The Nature of Statistical Learning Theory*, Springer, New York, 1995. 198

[9] "TREC Video Retrieval," 2002, National Institute of Standards and Technology, http://www-nlpir.nist.gov/projects/trecvid/. 202

[10] W. H. Adams, A. Amir, C. Dorai, S. Ghoshal, G. Iyengar, A. Jaimes, C. Lang, C. Y. Lin, M. R. Naphade, A. Natsev, C. Neti, H. J. Nock, H. Permutter, R. Singh, S. Srinivasan, J. R. Smith, B. L. Tseng, A. T. Varadaraju, and D. Zhang, "IBM research TREC-2002 video retrieval system," in *Proc. Text Retrieval Conference (TREC)*, Gaithersburg, MD, Nov 2002. 202

[11] S. Srinivasan, D. Ponceleon, A. Amir, and D. Petkovic, "What is that video anyway? In search of better browsing," in *Proceedings of IEEE International Conference on Multimedia and Expo*, New York, July 2000, pp. 388–392. 202

[12] M. R. Naphade, R. Wang, and T. S. Huang, "Classifying motion picture soundtrack for video indexing," in *IEEE International Conference on Multimedia and Expo*, Tokyo, Japan, AUgust 2001. 204

Learning in Region-Based Image Retrieval

Feng Jing[1], Mingjing Li[2], Lei Zhang[2], Hong-Jiang Zhang[2], and Bo Zhang[3]

[1] State Key Lab of Intelligent Technology and Systems
Beijing 100084, China
jingfeng00@mails.tsinghua.edu.cn
[2] Microsoft Research Asia
49 Zhichun Road, Beijing 100080, China
{mjli,i-lzhang,hjzhang}@microsoft.com
[3] State Key Lab of Intelligent Technology and Systems
Beijing 100084, China
dcszb@mail.tsinghua.edu.cn

Abstract. In this paper, several effective learning algorithms using global image representations are adjusted and introduced to region-based image retrieval (RBIR). First, the query point movement technique is considered. By assembling all the segmented regions of positive examples together and resizing the regions to emphasize the latest positive examples, a composite image is formed as the new query. Second, the application of support vector machines (SVM) in relevance feedback for RBIR is investigated. Both the one class SVM as a class distribution estimator and two classes SVM as a classifier are taken into account. For the latter, two representative display strategies are studied. Last, a region re-weighting algorithm is proposed inspired by those feature re-weighting ones. Experimental results on a database of 10,000 general-purpose images demonstrate the effectiveness of the proposed learning algorithms.

1 Introduction

Most of the early researches on content-based image retrieval (CBIR) have been focused on developing effective global features [6][14][18]. While these researches establish the basis of CBIR, the retrieval performance is still far from users' expectations. The main reason is acknowledged to be the gap between low-level features and high-level concepts. To narrow down this semantic gap, two techniques have been widely used: region-based features to represent the focus of the user's perceptions of image content [1][8][16] and learning techniques, e.g. relevance feedback (RF), to learn the user's intentions [4][7][10][12][15][17].

Many early CBIR systems perform retrieval based primarily on global features. It is not unusual that users accessing a CBIR system look for objects, but the aforementioned systems are likely to fail, since a single signature computed for the entire im-

E. M. Bakker et al. (Eds.): CIVR 2003, LNCS 2728, pp. 206–215, 2003.
© Springer-Verlag Berlin Heidelberg 2003

age cannot sufficiently capture the important properties of individual objects. Region-based image retrieval (RBIR) systems [1][16] attempt to overcome the drawback of global features by representing images at object-level, which is intended to be close to the perception of human visual system [16].

One of the interactive learning techniques is relevance feedback (RF) initially developed in text retrieval [13]. RF was introduced into CBIR during mid 1990's and has been shown to provide dramatic performance boost in retrieval systems [7][12][15][17]. The main idea of it is to let users guide the system. During retrieval process, the user interacts with the system and rates the relevance of the retrieved images, according to his/her subjective judgment. With this additional information, the system dynamically learns the user's intention, and gradually presents better results.

Although RF has shown its great potential in image retrieval systems that use global representations, it has seldom been introduced to RBIR systems. Minka and Picard performed a pioneering work in this area by proposing the FourEyes system [10]. FourEyes contains three stages: grouping generation, grouping weighting and grouping collection.

The main purpose of this paper is to integrate region-based representations and learning techniques and allows them to benefit from each other. To do that, on the one hand, two RF methods are proposed. One is the query point movement (QPM) algorithm with speedup techniques. The other is introducing three SVM schemes based on a new kernel. On the other hand, a novel region re-weighting scheme based on users' feedback information is proposed. The region weights that coincide with human perception improve the accuracy of both initial query and the following relevance feedback. Furthermore, the region weights could not only be used in a query session, but be also memorized and accumulated for future queries.

The organization of the paper is as follows: Section 2 describes the basic elements of a RBIR system including: image segmentation, image representation and image similarity measure. The RF strategies using QPM and SVM are described in Section 3 and Section 4 respectively. The region re-weighting scheme is presented in Section 5. In Section 6, we provide experimental results that evaluate all aspects of the learning schemes. Finally, we conclude in Section 7.

2   Region-Based Image Retrieval

2.1   Image Segmentation

The segmentation method we utilized is proposed in [9]. First, a criterion for homogeneity of a certain pattern is proposed. Applying the criterion to local windows in the original image results in the H-image. The high and low values of the H-image correspond to possible region boundaries and region interiors respectively. Then, a region growing method is used to segment the image based on the H-image. Finally, visually similar regions are merged together to avoid over-segmentation.

2.2   Image Representation

Currently, the spatial relationship of regions is not considered, and an image is represented by a set of its regions. To describe a region, we use two properties: the features of the region and its importance weight. Two features are adopted. One is the color moment [14] and the other is the banded auto-correlogram [6]. For the former, we extract the first two moments from each channel of CIE-LUV color space. For the latter, the HSV color space with inhomogenous quantization into 36 colors [18] is adopted. Considering that the size of the regions may be small, we use $b = d = 2$ in the current computation [6]. Therefore, the resulting 36 dimensional feature suggests the local structure of colors. Since color moments measure the global information of colors, the two features are complementary to each other and the combination enables them benefit from each other. The area percentage of regions is used as its importance weight in Section 2, 3, 4 temporarily. More satisfactory weighting methods are discussed in Section 5. The only requirement is that the sum of importance weights of an image should be equal to 1.

2.3   Image Similarity Measure

Based on the image representation, the distance between two images is measured using the Earth Mover's Distance (EMD) [11]. EMD is based on the minimal cost that must be paid to transform one distribution into another. Considering that EMD matches perceptual similarity well and can operate on variable-length representations of the distributions, it is suitable for region-based image similarity measure.

   In this special case, a signature is an image with all the regions corresponding to clusters, and the ground distance is the L_1 distance between the features of two regions. EMD incorporates the properties of all the segmented regions so that information about an image can be fully utilized. By allowing many-to-many relationship of the regions to be valid, EMD is robust to inaccurate segmentation.

3   Query Point Movement

3.1   The Optimal Query

Inspired by the query-point movement (QPM) method [12], a novel relevance feedback approach to region-based image retrieval is proposed [8]. The basic assumption is that every region could be helpful in retrieval. Based on this assumption, all the regions of both initial query and positive examples are assembled into a pseudo image, which is used as the optimal query at next iteration of retrieval and feedback process. The importance of the regions of optimal query is normalized such that the sum of them is equal to 1. During the normalization, regions of those newly added positive examples, which reflect the user's latest query refinement more precisely, are emphasized by given more importance. As more positive examples are available, the number of regions in the optimal query increases rapidly. Since the time required calculating image similarity is proportional to the number of regions in the query, the retrieval speed will slow down gradually. To avoid this, regions similar in the feature space are merged into larger ones together via clustering. This process is similar to region merging in an over-segmented image.

3.2   RF Using QPM

The RF process using QPM technique is summarized as follows.

The initial query is regarded as a positive example for the sake of simplicity. At the first iteration of feedback, all regions of positive examples are assembled into a composite image, in which similar regions are grouped into clusters by k-means algorithm. Regions within a cluster are merged into a new region. The feature of the new region is equal to the average feature of individual regions, while the importance of it is set to the sum of individual region importance divided by the number of positive examples. This composite image is used as the optimal query example.

In the following iterations, only the optimal query is treated as a positive example with all other prior examples being ignored. That is, there is exactly one prior positive example, which is treated equally as newly added positive examples. This implies that the importance of the prior positive examples gradually decays in the optimal query, and the importance of the newly added ones is emphasized accordingly.

4   SVM-Based RF

As a core machine learning technology, SVM has not only strong theoretical foundations but also excellent empirical successes [5]. SVM has also been introduced into CBIR as a powerful RF tool, and performs fairly well in the systems that use global representations [3][15][17].

Given the RF information, generally two kinds of learning could be done in order to boost the performance. One is to estimate the distribution of the target images, while the other is to learn a boundary that separates the target images from the rest. For the former, the so-called one-class SVM was adopted [4]. A kernel based one-class SVM as density estimator for positive examples was shown in [4] to outperform the whitening transform based linear/quadratic method. For the latter, the typical form of SVM as a binary classifier is appropriate [15][17]. A SVM captures the query concept by separating the relevant images from the irrelevant images with a hyperplane in a projected space.

When SVM is used as a classifier in RF, there are two display strategies. One strategy is to display the most-positive (MP) images and use them as the training samples [17]. The MP images are chosen as the ones farthest from the boundary on the positive side, plus those nearest from the boundary on the negative side if necessary. The underlying assumption is that the users are greedy and impatient and thus expects the best possible retrieval results after each feedback. It is also the strategy adopted by most early relevance feedback schemes. However, if we assume the users are cooperative, another strategy is more appropriate. In this strategy, both the MP images and the most-informative (MI) images are displayed. Additional user feedbacks, if any, will only be performed on those MI images, while the MP images are shown as the final results. Tong and Chang [15] proposed an active learning algorithm to select the samples to maximally reduce the size of the version space. Following the principle of maximal disagreement, the best strategy is to halve the version space each time. By taking advantage of the duality between the feature space and the parameter space, they showed that the points near the boundary can approximately achieve this goal. Therefore, the points near the boundary are used to approximate the MI points.

4.1   EMD-Based Kernel

Unlike the global feature, the region-based representations of images are of variable length, which means both the inner product and the L_p norm are not applicable. As a result, the common kernels, such as the polynomial kernel and Gaussian kernel are inappropriate in this situation.

To resolve the issue, a generalization of Gaussian kernel is introduced:

$$k_{GGaussian}(x, y) = \exp(-d(x, y)/2\sigma^2) \tag{1}$$

where d is a distance measure in the input space.

Since the distance measure here is EMD, a particular form of the generalized Gaussian kernel with d being EMD is considered. More specific, the proposed kernel is:

$$k_{GEMD}(x, y) = \exp(-EMD(x, y)/2\sigma^2) \tag{2}$$

5   Region Re-weighting

Enlightened by the idea of feature re-weighting [12] and the *TF*IDF* (Term Frequency * Inverse Document Frequency) weighting in text retrieval, we designed a *RF*IIF* (Region Frequency * Inverse Image Frequency) weighting scheme. It uses users' feedback information to estimate the region importance of all positive images. The basic assumption is that important regions should appear more times in the positive images and fewer times in all the images of the database.

Before we go into details, we first introduce some notations and definitions that will be used to illustrate the region importance.

Two regions are deemed as similar, if the L_1 distance between their feature vectors is less than a predefined threshold.

A region R and an image I is defined to be similar if at least one region of I is similar to R. We use $s(R, I)$ to denote this relationship: $s(R, I) = 1$ if R is similar to I, while $s(R, I) = 0$ otherwise.

Assume that there are totally N images in the database, which are represented by $\{I_1, ..., I_N\}$. Also assume that we are calculating the region importance of I that consists of regions $\{R_1, R_2, ..., R_n\}$. I is actually one of the positive examples identified by a user in feedback. Note that the original query image is also considered to be a positive example. Let all the positive examples be $\{I_1^+, ..., I_k^+\}$

For each region R_i, we define a measure of region frequency (*RF*), which reflects the extent to which it is consistent with other positive examples in the feature space. Intuitively, the larger the region frequency value, the more important this region is in representing the user's intention. The region frequency is defined in the following way.

$$RF(R_i) = \sum_{j=1}^{k} s(R_i, I_j^+)$$ (3)

On the other hand, a region becomes less important if it is similar to many images in the database. To reflect the distinguishing ability of a region, we define a measure of inverse image frequency (*IIF*) for region R_i :

$$IIF(R_i) = \log(N \Big/ \sum_{j=1}^{N} s(R_i, I_j))$$ (4)

which is analogous to the *IDF* (inverse document frequency) in text retrieval.
Based on the above preparations, we now come to the definition of the region importance:

$$RI(R_i) = \frac{RF(R_i) * IIF(R_i)}{\sum_{j=1}^{n}(RF(R_j) * IIF(R_j))}$$ (5)

Basically, the importance of a region is its region frequency weighted by the inverse image frequency, and normalized over all regions in an image such that the sum of all region importance weights is equal to 1.

Since to "common" users the region importance is similar, it can be cumulated for future use. More specific, given a region R_i, its cumulate region importance (*CRI*) after l ($l > 0$) updates is defined as:

$$CRI(R_i, l) = \frac{(l-1) * CRI(R_i, l-1) + RI(R_i)}{l}$$ (6)

where $RI(R_i)$ is the latest *RI* of R_i calculated from formula (3) and $CRI(R_i, 0)$ is initialized to be the area percentage (*AP*) of R_i. Note that once the *RI* of a region is learned, its *CRI* will have nothing to do with its *AP*.

6   Experimental Results

The algorithm was evaluated with a general-purpose image database of about 10,000 images from COREL. 1,000 images were randomly chosen from totally 79 categories as the query set. All the experimental results are averages of the 1,000 queries. The implementation of SVM was based on the source code of LibSVM [2].

We simulated users' feedback as follows. For a query image, 5 iterations of user-and-system interactions were carried out. At each iteration, the system examined the top 20 images, excluding those positive examples labeled in previous iterations. Images from the same (different) category as the initial query image were used as new positive (negative) examples. At next iteration, all positive and negative images were placed in top and bottom ranks respectively, while others were ranked according to a certain criteria.

Considering that it is difficult to design a fair comparison with existing RBIR systems that use RF, such as the FourEyes [10] system whose purpose is annotation, we compared our QPM-based RF method with the one proposed by Rui Yong in [12] which uses both QPM and feature re-weighting. Since [12] requires global features, the auto-correlogram is adopted. As in [6], we consider the RGB color space with quantization into 64 colors. The distance set D = {1, 3, 5, 7} is used for computing, which results in a feature vector of 256 dimensions. The results are shown in Figure 1. The accuracy in this and also other figures of this paper means the average precision within top 30 images, i.e. average P(30). As shown in the figure, before any feedback, the accuracy of region-based representation is higher than that of auto-correlogram by 4%., which suggests the advantage of region based representation. Furthermore, our method consistently yields better performance after one iteration and its accuracy after 5 interactions is higher than that of [12] by 12%.

The SVM-based RF methods using region representation and kernel k_{GEMD} is evaluated by comparing with those using global representation and Laplacian kernel. All the three strategies mentioned in Section 4 are considered: one class SVM (SVM(OC)), two classes SVM displaying MP images (SVM(MP)), and two classes SVM displaying MI images (SVM(MI)). The Laplacian kernel is chosen because of its superiority over other kernels, e.g. Gaussian kernel, in histogram-based applications [3]. Figure 2, 3, 4 show the comparison results. No matter what strategy is used, region-based algorithm consistently performs better than global-based one. Let us use Figure 3 as an example, where SVM(MP) strategy is adopted. After five iterations of feedback, the region-based algorithm boosts its accuracy (56%) more than global-based one(52%) using auto-correlogram by 4%.

The proposed RF methods are also compared with each other. The results are shown in Figure 5. Three conclusions could be drawn from the figure. First, two classes SVM performs better than both SVM(OC) and QPM. In this experiment, the accuracy of SVM(MP) is higher than that of QPM by 20% after five iterations of feedback. The results suggest that negative examples are helpful if appropriately used. Second, SVM(OC) performs almost the same as QPM. Last, there is neglectable difference between SVM(MP) and SVM(MI).

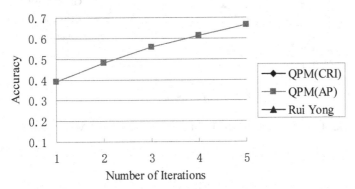

Fig. 1. Accuracy comparison of Rui Yong's method and QPM

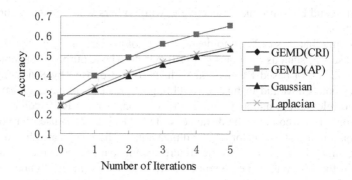

Fig. 2. Accuracy comparison of different kernels for SVM(OC) strategy

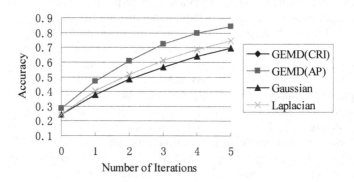

Fig. 3. Accuracy comparison of different kernels for SVM(MI) strategy

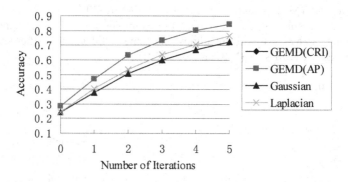

Fig. 4. Accuracy comparison of different kernels for SVM(MP) strategy

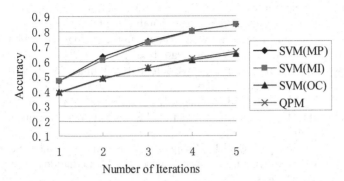

Fig. 5. Accuracy comparison of different learning algorithms using CRI for RBIR

To evaluate the region re-weighting scheme, 5,000 random query and feedback sessions were carried out, during which the *CRI*s were cumulated and memorized. The feedback process was performed by using SVM as a binary classifier and displaying the MP images, which is the best learning strategy of all the proposed ones. The influence of *CRI* on the proposed RF algorithms is shown in Figure 1-4. For example, in Figure 3, before any feedback, the one using *CRI* is better than that using AP by 8%. After five iterations of feedback, the method using *CRI* boosts its accuracy (35%) more than that using AP (25%) by %. The results show that *CRI* enables those region-based RF techniques starting from a higher level and boosts the retrieval performance in a faster way.

7   Conclusion

In this paper, three learning schemes for RBIR are proposed with the first one using QPM and speedup techniques, the second one enabling both one class and two classes SVMs by introducing a new kernel, and the third one borrowing ideas of feature re-weighting to achieve region re-weighting. Experimental comparisons with the corresponding global representation-based algorithms on large scale database show the effectiveness of the proposed schemes. Integrating other kernel-based learning algorithms, e.g. BiasMap [7], into RBIR is our ongoing research.

References

[1]   Carson, C., et al, "Blobworld: a system for region-based image indexing and retrieval," Third Int. Conf. On Visual Information Systems, 1999.

[2]   Chang, C.-C., and Lin, C.-J., "Training nu-support vector classifiers: theory and algorithms." Neural Computation, 13 (9), 2119-2147.

[3]   Chapelle, O., Haffner, P., Vapnik, V. N., "Support vector machines for histogram-based image classification," IEEE Transactions on Neural Networks, 10(5):1055-1064, Sept. 1999.

[4]   Chen, Y., et al, "One-class SVM for Learning in Image Retrieval," IEEE Intl Conf. on Image Proc. (ICIP'2001), Thessaloniki, Greece, October 7-10, 2001

[5]   Cristianini, N., Shawe-Taylor, J., "An Introduction to Support Vector Machines." Cambridge University Press, Cambridge, UK, 2000.

[6]   Huang, J., et al, "Image indexing using color correlograms". In Proc. IEEE Comp. Soc. Conf. Comp. Vis. and Patt. Rec., pages 762--768, 1997.

[7]   Huang, T.S., et al, "Learning in Content-Based Image Retrieval". The 2nd International Conference on Development and Learning , 2002

[8]   Jing, F., Li, M., Zhang, H.J., Zhang, B., "Region-based relevance feedback in image retrieval", Proc. IEEE International Symposium on Circuits and Systems (ISCAS), 2002.

[9]   Jing, F., Li, M., Zhang, H.J., Zhang, B., "Unsupervised Image Segmentation Using Local Homogeneity Analysis", Proc. IEEE International Symposium on Circuits and Systems, 2003.

[10]   Minka, T.P., Picard, R.W., "Interactive Learning Using A Society Of Models", Pattern Recognition, vol. 30, no. 4, pp. 565-581, April 1997.

[11]   Rubner, Y., et al, "A Metric for Distributions with Applications to Image Databases." Proceedings of the 1998 IEEE International Conference on Computer Vision, January 1998.

[12]   Rui, Y., and Huang, T.S., "Optimizing Learning in Image Retrieval", Proceeding of IEEE int. Conf. On Computer Vision and Pattern Recognition, Jun. 2000.

[13]   Salton, G., "Automatic text processing", Addison-Wesley, 1989.

[14]   Stricker, M. and Orengo, M., "Similarity of Color Images", in Storage and Retrieval for Image and Video Databases, Proc. SPIE 2420, pp 381-392, 1995.

[15]   Tong, S. and Chang, E. "Support vector machine active leaning for image retrieval," ACM Multimedia 2001, Ottawa, Canada.

[16]   Wang, J. Z., Li, J., Wiederhold, G., "SIMPLIcity: Semantics-sensitive Integrated Matching for Picture Libraries", PAMI, vol. 23, 2001.

[17]   Zhang, L., Lin, F.Z., Zhang, B. "Support Vector Machine Learning for Image Retrieval", IEEE International Conference on Image Processing, October, 2001.

[18]   Zhang, L., Lin, F.Z., Zhang, B. "A CBIR method based on color-spatial feature". IEEE Region 10 Annual International Conference 1999:166-169

Multiple Features in Temporal Models for the Representation of Visual Contents in Video*

Juan M. Sánchez[1], Xavier Binefa[1], and John R. Kender[2]

[1] Dept. d'Informàtica, U. Autònoma de Barcelona
08193, Bellaterra, Barcelona, Spain
juanma@cvc.uab.es,Xavier.Binefa@uab.es
[2] Dept. of Computer Science, Columbia University
New York, NY 10027
jrk@cs.columbia.edu

Abstract. This paper analyzes different ways of coupling the information from multiple visual features in the representation of visual contents using temporal models based on Markov chains. We assume that the optimal combination is given by the Cartesian product of all feature state spaces. Simpler model structures are obtained by assuming independencies between random variables in the probabilistic structure. The relative entropy provides a measure of the information loss of a simplified structure with respect to a more complex one. The loss of information is then compared to the loss of accuracy in the representation of visual contents in video sequences, which is measured in terms of shot retrieval performance. We reach three main conclusions: (1) the full-coupled model structure is an accurate approximation to the Cartesian product structure, (2) the largest loss of information is found when direct temporal dependencies are removed, and (3) there is a direct relationship between loss of information and loss of representation accuracy.

1 Introduction

Many descriptions of visual contents based on low-level features have been developed so far. The MPEG-7 standard for content description considers some of them in its definition [1]. However, most concepts are usually better described by multiple features. The problem is how to merge information from several visual cues in one single representation. Their combination is not easy, and usually leads to the definition of *ad hoc* similarity measures or to a complex interaction between the user and the system. For example, many retrieval systems require the specification of weights for each feature in the definition of the query [2].

In this paper, we analyze ways of coupling information from different features in the framework of temporal models based on Markov chains that was

---

* Work supported by CICYT grant TEL99-1206-C02-02. Partial funding from Visual Century Research.

E. M. Bakker et al. (Eds.): CIVR 2003, LNCS 2728, pp. 216–226, 2003.

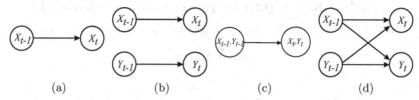

Fig. 1. Graphical representation of the model structures discussed in the text: (a) Single MC, (b) Independent MC's, (c) Cartesian-product MC, and (d) Coupled MC's

used in [3] for representing visual contents and in [4] for object localization in video. The main advantage of this framework is that the different levels of coupling between features are given by assumptions of dependency between random variables. Also, a widely used low-level description like feature histogramming is considered as a particular case where no dependencies exist, and thus can be directly compared. The more independency assumptions we make, the less information to describe the data will be available. Therefore, the model will have less cost in time and space, but its description of visual contents will be less accurate. Through all the paper, we assume that the best way of combining features is to consider a Cartesian product state space. This does not mean that the results that can be obtained using this assumption are going to be the best for the user, but it provides the case where the most information about the relationship between features is considered. In some scenarios, we might not be interested on such a tight coupling of the features, or even on considering temporal information. The probabilistic framework will naturally lead us to the relative entropy as a measure of the loss of information of a simplified model structure with respect to the true structure. Relative entropy is a measure of the distance between distributions that has been used for structure learning in Bayesian networks [5]. For practical purposes, it is important to know if there is a relationship between the loss of information caused by the use of simplified model structures and their accuracy to represent data. We show experimental results on content-based retrieval tests that provide significant conclusions about this relationship.

2 Description of Temporal Behavior

One of the simplest ways to describe a single-feature temporal process is a single first-order discrete Markov chain:

$$P(X) = P(X_1) \prod_{t=2}^{m} P(X_t|X_{t-1}) \tag{1}$$

A graphical representation of this PDF is shown in fig. 1(a). The likelihood of a realization $x = \{x_1, \ldots, x_m\}$, $x_i \in S$, of a MC with respect to a parameterization of a MC model can be expressed as follows:

$$P(x) = P(x_1) \exp \left[\sum_{(i,j) \in S^2} C_{ij|x} \log T_{ij} \right] \qquad (2)$$

where $T_{ij} = P(X_t = j | X_{t-1} = i)$ and $C_{ij|x}$ is the number of times that state j follows state i in x, i.e. the temporal cooccurrence of states i and j. Note that the likelihood tends to 0 when the length of the chain grows. This fact causes an obvious computational problem for long chains, but also implies that the likelihoods of chains with different lengths cannot be directly compared. However, we can consider the number of times that each different transition probability appears in the summation in eq. (2) and normalize their frequency in the product. Given the cooccurrences C_{ij} of states i and j in consecutive time steps in the chain, eq. (2) can be expressed in terms of a normalized cooccurrence matrix $\bar{C}$, whose elements are:

$$\bar{C}_{ij|x} = \frac{C_{ij|x}}{\sum_{(i,j) \in S^2} C_{ij|x}}, \quad \forall (i,j) \in S^2 \qquad (3)$$

The likelihood of a length-normalized realization of a MC is then given by:

$$P(x) = \exp \left[\sum_{(i,j) \in S^2} \bar{C}_{ij|x} \log T_{ij} \right] \qquad (4)$$

Given that our probabilistic model is defined as a fully-observed directed graphical model (i.e., there are no hidden variables), the maximum likelihood transition probabilities are directly obtained from an observation x as normalized frequencies:

$$T_{ij} = \frac{C_{ij|x}}{\sum_{j \in S} C_{ij|x}}, \quad \forall i \in S \qquad (5)$$

The most straightforward way to extend the MC framework in order to integrate information provided by different features is to consider a set of independent MC's, one for each feature. Given a set of f features, we consider a set of chains $X = \{X^1, \ldots, X^f\}$, one for each feature, with different state spaces S^i, $\forall i \in [1, f]$. The PDF of the new model that includes information from all the features is:

$$P(X) = P(X^1, \ldots, X^f) = \prod_{i \in F} P(X^i) \qquad (6)$$

where X^i is the sequence of random variables associated to feature i, and $P(X^i)$ is given by eq. (1) for each feature. This is the most computationally efficient extension to multiple features. However, the assumption of independence between features is not always true. A more realistic approach must consider dependencies and interactions that may exist between them.

If we consider a full dependency between variables at every time instant, while they also depend on the value of the variables at the previous time, we are considering the model shown in fig. 1(c). This model is a single MC with a new Cartesian product state space $S^* = S^1 \times \ldots \times S^f$. All the features are tightly coupled, thus it can be considered the optimal way of representing dependencies between them. The main drawback here is that the number of parameters grows exponentially with the number of features as n^{2f} (assuming that all the features have the same number of states).

However, we can use this model as a starting point and make assumptions on it, so that the model is simplified and the cost is reduced. First, we can assume independence between the features at the same time instant, while they still depend on all the features at the previous time. This assumption is expressed by the following factorization of the transition probabilities:

$$P(X_t^{1..f}|X_{t-1}^{1..f}) = \prod_{i \in F} P(X_t^i|X_{t-1}^{1..f}) \tag{7}$$

where $X_j^{1..f} = (X_j^1, \ldots, X_j^f)$. The joint PDF is then given by:

$$P(X) = P(X_1^{1..f}) \prod_{t=2}^{m} P(X_t^{1..f}|X_{t-1}^{1..f}) \tag{8}$$

$$= \prod_{i \in F} P(X_1^i) \prod_{t=2}^{m} P(X_t^i|X_{t-1}^{1..f}) \tag{9}$$

This new model, depicted in fig. 1(d), is called coupled Markov chains (CMC) model. The complexity of this model is still $\mathcal{O}(n^{f+1})$, which is lower than in the Cartesian-product case, but still grows exponentially with the number of features. Its graphical representation allows us to easily represent other independencies by removing links from its structure. Independencies between features can be determined either by an expert or automatically using the method presented in the next section. Note that we can obtain a model of independent chains by removing all the crossed links, and even a model of simple independent histograms of the features by removing all the links. Every independency assumption turns into a reduction of the cost in time and space of the model. Table 1 shows the cost of the model structures discussed here.

3 Structure Learning

The problem of structure learning consists of finding the optimal configuration of a model with respect to some criteria. In our case, the structure of the model is given by the dependencies between the random variables involved. These dependencies are represented by directed links in a graph where the nodes are the variables. Our problem is how to decide what links can be removed, that is, what variables are independent from each other.

Table 1. Cost of different model structures with 2 features

Structure	Size	$n = 16$	$n = 8$	$n = 4$
Cartesian (CP)	n^4	65536	4096	256
Full coupled (FC)	$2n^3$	8192	1024	128
Partial coupled (PC)	$n^3 + n^2$	4352	576	80
Independent (I)	$2n^2$	512	128	32
Partial temporal (PT)	$n^2 + n$	272	72	20
Histograms (H)	$2n$	32	16	8

The single MC is the simplest model with dependencies between variables. Given this model structure, the likelihood of a length-normalized observation is given by eq. (4). Noting that the normalized cooccurrence matrix of a realization x is actually a joint distribution $\bar{C}_{ij|x} = P(X_t = j, X_{t-1} = i | X = x)$, the log-likelihood can be rewritten as follows[1]:

$$\mathcal{L}\{P(x)\} = \sum_{(i,j)\in S^2} P(j, i|x) \log P(j|i) \tag{10}$$

When the observation x is the same that we used to estimate the parameters of the model, eq. (10) is minus the conditional entropy of X_t given X_{t-1}, $H[P(X_t|X_{t-1})]$. We will omit the conditioning on x of $P(j, i|x)$, as we will assume this fact from now on unless it may lead to confusion. Let us consider a second probability distribution $P'(X_t|X_{t-1}) = P(X_t)$, i.e. X_t does not depend on X_{t-1}. The log-likelihood for this new distribution is[2]:

$$\mathcal{L}\{P'(x)\} = \sum_{(i,j)\in S^2} P(j, i) \log P'(j|i) = \sum_{j\in S} P(j) \log P(j) \tag{11}$$

$P(X_t)$ may contain less information about the random variable X_t due to the lack of knowledge about a second random variable (X_{t-1}) that may be important. This loss of information is given by the relative entropy (also known as cross entropy or Kullback Leibler distance) between the two distributions:

$$D(P||P') = \sum_{(i,j)\in S^2} P(j, i) \log \frac{P(j|i)}{P(j)} \tag{12}$$

If the loss of information of $P'(X)$ with respect to $P(X)$ is close to zero, then the two distributions are very similar and there was no real dependency of X_t on X_{t-1}. In that case, considering the temporal dependencies is not necessary, which can be graphically expressed as the removal of the link from X_{t-1} to X_t. Equation (12) is the loss of information when we represent a sequence using a simple histogram, instead of considering a first-order temporal dependency. This way of measuring the loss of information between distributions has two

---

[1] Notation: $P(j, i) = P(X_t = j, X_{t-1} = i)$ and $P(j|i) = P(X_t = j|X_{t-1} = i)$.
[2] Notation: $P(j) = P(X_t = j)$.

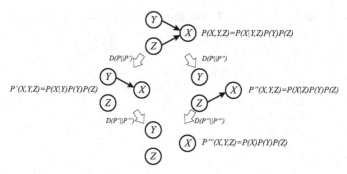

Fig. 2. Example of the process of removing dependencies between variables (links) from the structure

important properties. Consider the distributions graphically represented in fig. 2. It is easy to show that the following holds:

$$D(P||P''') = D(P||P') + D(P'||P''') \tag{13}$$
$$= D(P||P'') + D(P''||P''') \tag{14}$$

That is, the length of the path from P to P''' is the sum of the partial paths, and does not depend on what link is removed first.

Also, given that our structures are always defined by directed acyclic graphs (DAG's), the relative entropies between them can be computed locally. Consider the CMC and the independent MC's models from fig. 1(d and b), with their respective probability distributions P_C and P_I. The relative entropy between them is[3]:

$$D(P_C||P_I) = \sum_{i,j,k,l} P(i,j,k,l) \log \frac{P(i|k,l)P(j|k,l)}{P(i|k)P(j|l)}$$
$$= \sum_{i,k,l} P(i,k,l) \log \frac{P(i|k,l)}{P(i|k)} + \sum_{j,k,l} P(j,k,l) \log \frac{P(j|k,l)}{P(j|l)} \tag{15}$$

That is, the total relative entropy is the sum of local relative entropies. Considering these two properties we can build a space of feasible structures like in fig. 3, and attach costs to the links between structures and the structures themselves. Different criteria can be used to decide when a reduced structure is the optimal with respect to the true one. We can specify an acceptance threshold on the relative entropy, that will determine the loss of information that we want to afford. Note from eq. (13) that the loss of information increases monotonically with the length of the path in the space of structures. Once the threshold is exceeded, the rest of the path can be automatically discarded.

---

[3] Notation: $P(i,j,k,l) = P(X_t = i, Y_t = j, X_{t-1} = k, Y_{t-1} = l)$.

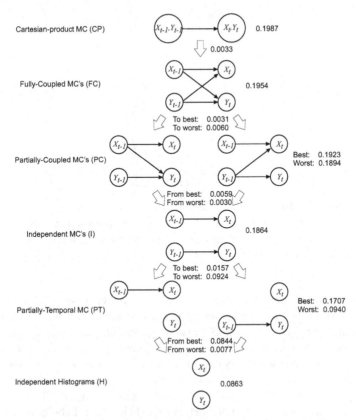

Fig. 3. Space of feasible model structures considering two features, and the paths between them defined by successive independency assumptions. Costs correspond to the Friends test sequence (see section 4)

4   Experiments

The goal of our experiments is to analyze the effect of the loss of information caused by the use of a simplified model structure on their accuracy to represent visual data. For this purpose, we have performed retrieval experiments using three test sequences of different domains: News (121 shots), Soccer (232 shots) and Friends (205 shots). We will describe the shots using one color and one motion feature, like we did in our previous works (see [3] and [4] for specific details about the representation of visual contents in video). We have considered the Cartesian product structure as the optimal way of representing the possible causal dependencies between color and motion that may exist. From there, we will analyze the behavior of the structures in the space shown in fig. 3. In the case of partial models (either in the coupled or in the temporal sense) we will differentiate between the best and the worst partial structure. The best structure

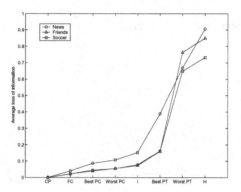

Fig. 4. Loss of information of different model structures with respect to the Cartesian-product structure given by relative entropies. Results are averages over all the shots of our test sequences. Model structure identifiers are the same as in fig. 3

is the one with the lowest loss of information, and vice versa. Note that being the best or the worst partial structure is decided for each different shot.

From our test data, fig. 4 shows the average loss of information of the different model structures over all the shots of the different domains. The three domains of video contents that we are working on are shown, in order to perceive possible differences in the behavior of the structures. In general, we observe that the most important loss of information appears when temporal links within the same feature are removed. Particularly, in the Friends and the Soccer sequences the temporal information of one of the features (color in some shots, motion in some others) is even more relevant than the temporal information of the other. In the News sequence, the temporal information of both features appears to be equally relevant. In any case, the information provided by the crossed links is less relevant than the temporal information within the same features. However, a significant loss of information can be noticed, especially in the News sequence. Particularly, this happens when the shot contains objects with different color and motion features than the rest of the scene, like the wavy flag shown in fig. 5. In this case, information about the relationship between the white and blue colors in the flag and its wavy motion is contained in the crossed links. It is also important to note that the loss of information of the fully coupled structure with respect to the Cartesian is very small despite the large reduction in storage size.

Our measure of quality of the retrieval is based on the classical precision, defined as the total number of correct clips ($N_{correct}$) over the total number of clips retrieved ($N_{retrieved}$). Correct shots are determined by the retrieval results obtained using the Cartesian product structure. When $N_{retrieved}$ is relatively large with respect to the total number of shots in the database (N_{total}), the precision is not meaningful by itself. Even a random selection of shots in the

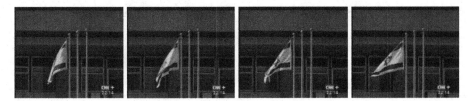

Fig. 5. Images from a shot where the crossed links between color and motion features are very significant for representing their relationship in the scene

database would have a high precision. It is more meaningful to measure the improvement of the precision over the precision of a random selection. This measure is given by Cohen's κ statistic:

$$\kappa = \frac{Precision - Precision_{random}}{1 - Precision_{random}} \tag{16}$$

where $Precision_{random}$ is the expected value of precision when the results are selected randomly.

Figure 6 shows the κ statistic of the precision for different values of $N_{retrieved}$ in the three videos used in our experiments. The results are averages using the leave-one-out method for all the shots in the database. The results obtained are consistent with the previously computed loss of information. That is, the higher loss of information of the structure, the less accurate retrieval results are obtained. Particularly, results show that the fully coupled structure is a very good approximation of the ideal Cartesian product structure (over 90% of correct clips retrieved in all cases). Also, the performance of the simple histograms is very low, which means that the temporal evolution of features is relevant for describing visual contents that may have dynamic behaviors. Therefore, accumulating static image descriptors through several images in a sequence is not an appropriate approach to represent temporal sequences.

It is important to observe that the loss of performance of simplified model structures is directly related to their loss of information about the original data. For instance, note the large difference of performance in the Friends sequence between the partial temporal structure and the histograms in fig. 6(top-left), which is related to the large loss of information between those structures shown in fig. 4. This similarity between the relative differences in performance and the loss of information can also be noticed in the News and the Soccer sequence. We cannot establish a numerical or analytical relationship, but there is an obvious qualitative dependency between them.

5   Conclusions

After the experiments shown in this paper, we have reached the following conclusions:

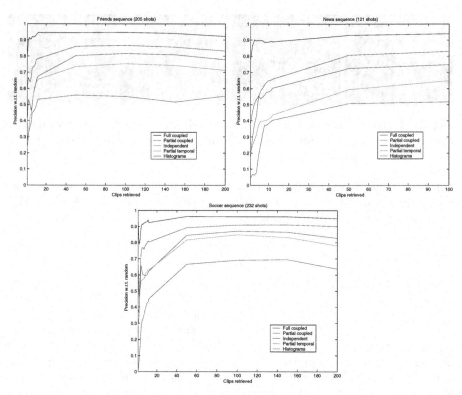

Fig. 6. Evaluation of retrieval using different model structures with our three test videos. Clips retrieved using the Cartesian product model structure are taken as ground-truth. Results are given as the improvement of precision over a random selection of shots. Measures were taken for $N_{retrieved} = \{1..12, 50, 100, 150, 200\}$

- The fully coupled model structure is an accurate approximation to the Cartesian product structure, and its cost is enormously reduced.
- The largest loss of information occurs when the temporal dependency within the same feature is removed. Therefore, it is not a good approach to represent visual contents with dynamic behaviors by accumulating static image descriptions of the images in the sequence.
- The crossed links between features are important when there are elements in the scene with a clear dependency between them, like in our example of the wavy flag.
- For content-based video retrieval, the higher loss of information of the model structure we are using, the less accurate retrieval results are obtained.
- The loss of performance of simplified model structures is directly related to their loss of information about the data we are representing.

References

[1] Manjunath, B. S., Salembier, P., Sikora, T., eds.: Introduction to MPEG 7: Multimedia Content Description Language. John Wiley & Sons (2002) 216
[2] Naphade, M. R., Huang, T. S.: Extracting semantics from audiovisual content: the final frontier in multimedia retrieval. IEEE Transactions on Neural Networks **13** (2002) 793–810 216
[3] Sánchez, J. M., Binefa, X., Kender, J. R.: Coupled Markov chains for video contents characterization. In: Proc. International Conference on Pattern Recognition, Quebec, Canada (2002) 217, 222
[4] Sánchez, J. M., Binefa, X., Kender, J. R.: Multiple feature temporal models for object detection in video. In: Proc. IEEE International Conference on Multimedia and Expo, Lausanne, Switzerland (2002) 217, 222
[5] Jensen, F. V.: An introduction to Bayesian Networks. UCL Press (1996) 217

Detection of Documentary Scene Changes
by Audio-Visual Fusion

Atulya Velivelli[1], Chong-Wah Ngo[2], and Thomas S. Huang[1]

[1] Beckman Institute for Advanced Science and Technology, Urbana
{velivell,huang}@ifp.uiuc.edu
[2] City University of Hong Kong, Hong Kong
cwngo@cs.cityu.edu.hk

Abstract. The concept of a documentary scene was inferred from the audio-visual characteristics of certain documentary videos. It was observed that the amount of information from the visual component alone was not enough to convey a semantic context to most portions of these videos, but a joint observation of the visual component and the audio component conveyed a better semantic context. From the observations that we made on the video data, we generated an audio score and a visual score. We later generated a weighted audio-visual score within an interval and adaptively expanded or shrunk this interval until we found a local maximum score value. The video ultimately will be divided into a set of intervals that correspond to the documentary scenes in the video. After we obtained a set of documentary scenes, we made a check for any redundant detections.

1 Introduction

A rapid increase in digital video data over the past few years has given rise to importance for video data indexing. The first step towards alleviating this problem is organizing a video into semantically tractable units called *scenes*. A scene is defined as a collection of shots that occur at the same location or that are temporally unified. A *shot* is defined as an unbroken sequence of frames taken from one camera. In [1, 2], scene change is detected by extracting visual features such as chromatic edit detection feature and color feature from the video (image sequence). Recently there has been interest in using both audio and visual information for scene change detection. In [3], different audio classes are detected sequentially, and this information is later combined with the probability value for a visual cut detection. In [4], scene breaks are detected as audio-visual breaks, where each break is based on dissimilarity index values calculated for audio, color and motion features. Even in this case there is no specific audio-visual fusion strategy.

In [5], they first obtain a set of audio scenes and a set of video (visual) scenes by using different criteria for audio scene break and video (visual) scene break. These breaks are then merged to obtain audio-visual scene breaks.

E. M. Bakker et al. (Eds.): CIVR 2003, LNCS 2728, pp. 227–238, 2003.

We introduce the concept of a documentary scene and use an audio-visual score value (which is a weighted combination of an audio score and a video score) to divide the video into a set of documentary scenes. The audio score and the visual score are generated by procedures evolved out of the observations that we make on the video data. The video data that we used for making observations and for experimenting is from the NIST Special Database 26.

The rest of paper is organized as follows. Section 2 introduces the concept of documentary scene and then outlines the major steps of our approach. Section 3 describes the generation of visual label patterns while Section 4 presents a maximum-likelihood based method to generate audio class labels. Section 5 describes our audio-visual fusion strategy. Section 6 proposes an adaptive scheme and redundancy check to detect documentary scene changes. Finally, Section 7 presents the experimental results and Section 8 concludes this paper.

2   Overview of Our Approach

In this section we define the concept of a documentary scene, which was inferred by analyzing the video data. Critical observations made on the data will also be stated. The proposed approach in this paper is then presented based on these observations.

2.1   Concept of a Documentary Scene

The NIST videos show contiguous shots with little visual similarity while the topic or the semantic context described by the audio remains same. Hence we conclude that a documentary video can be modelled as a union of several semantically tractable topic level units known as *documentary scenes*, where there is a semantic correlation between the audio component and the visual component of videos. The common observations from documentary videos include:

1. Within a documentary scene, similar video frames occur either contiguously or with a temporal separation of some dissimilar frames; hence, the total number of similar frames within an interval is a measure for a documentary scene.
2. In most cases, the audio class label at the beginning of a documentary scene is same as the audio class label at the end of a documentary scene.
3. In some cases the audio component has less information to contribute, while visually there is a strong semantic correlation in the background image of the video frames. For example as shown in Figure 1, the semantic context is the discussion on a new project. The selected frames in Figure 1 show the machine drawings associated with the project in background.
4. In most cases the visual pattern has a counterpart audio pattern. An audio-visual sequence shown below explains this observation.

$$\text{audio class :} \quad \text{speech} \leftarrow \text{speech+siren} \leftarrow \quad \text{speech}$$
$$\text{visual sequence :} \text{aircraft} \leftarrow \quad \text{hanger fire} \quad \leftarrow \text{officer speaking}$$

Fig. 1. A few frames with a similar visual background

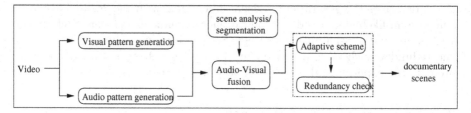

Fig. 2. Proposed approach for detecting documentary scenes

2.2 Proposed Approach

Based on the above observations, we propose a scheme, as illustrated in Figure 2, for detecting documentary scenes. Given a video, the proposed approach first generates a visual pattern (observation 1) and an audio pattern (observations 2, 4) respectively based on similarity measures. Scene analysis (observation 3) will be conducted for foreground and background segmentation[1]. The collected data from visual, audio and scene analysis will be integrated for audio-visual fusion. The scene change detector is composed of two main steps: adaptive scheme and redundancy check.

3 Generating Visual Label

In this section, we present the method for generating a visual label pattern. We first perform shot boundary detection and then select the keyframes. Using the auto-correlogram method described in [6], we label the keyframes extracted from the video.

3.1 Selection and Labelling of Keyframes

To label the video keyframes, we first detect the shot boundaries using the technique in [7]. Each shot is composed of several temporal units. We extract a video frame at the middle of a temporal unit (30 frames) as a keyframe. The video frame rate is 30 frames/s. The similarity measure for labelling the

---

[1] In this paper, we will not present the details of scene analysis, interested readers can refer the details of our approach in [9, 10].

keyframes is based on the color auto-correlogram [6] of keyframes. A critical part of this algorithm is the appropriate selection of similarity threshold η'. In our approach, we employ Neyman-Pearson hypothesis to determine η', which will be elaborated later.

To label a keyframe $\mathcal{I}^{(i)}$, we find $\beta_i = \text{argmin}_{1 \leq j < i} \left| \mathcal{I}^{(i)} - \mathcal{I}^{(j)} \right|$. If $\left| \mathcal{I}^{(i)} - \mathcal{I}^{(\beta_i)} \right| < \eta'$, we label it with index β_i ($\mathcal{I}^{(i)}$ is considered similar to $\mathcal{I}^{(\beta_i)}$), else with i ($\mathcal{I}^{(i)}$ is considered dissimilar to preceding frames). Where $\left| \mathcal{I}^1 - \mathcal{I}^2 \right|$ denotes the auto-correlogram distance measure between $\mathcal{I}^1$ and $\mathcal{I}^2$. The example below shows the original keyframe index and the resulting keyframe labels after applying the algorithm:

$$Keyframe\ index \leftarrow 1\ 2\ 3\ 4\ 5\ 6\ 7\ 8\ 9\ 10\ 11$$
$$Keyframe\ label \leftarrow 1\ 2\ 2\ 4\ 5\ 6\ 2\ 4\ 9\ 9\ \ 5$$

The above labelling pattern indicates that the keyframe with index 2 is similar to the keyframe with index 3; hence the keyframe with index 3 also gets a label 2, while the keyframe with index 4 is not similar to any of the 3 preceding keyframes and hence gets a label 4.

3.2   Threshold Selection

We use the Neyman-Pearson hypothesis testing, which is explained in detail in [8], to determine the value of threshold η'. We first calculate the distances between all combinations of the N images and we assume that the distances can be modelled as two Gaussian distributions, corresponding to the similar and the dissimilar images . The value of threshold η' is

$$\eta' = \sigma\ \phi^{-1}(\alpha) + \mu \tag{1}$$

where, σ^2, μ are the variance and mean of the Gaussian distribution with a larger variance. We assume that the larger variance Gaussian corresponds to the dissimilar images.

$$\phi(x) = \frac{1}{\sqrt{2\pi}} \int_{-\infty}^{x} e^{\frac{-t^2}{2}}\ dt \tag{2}$$

α is the false alarm tolerance and $\phi^{-1}(x)$ denotes the inverse of $\phi(x)$.

In our case we have decided a false alarm tolerance of 5%, as it is a good trade off between false alarm and the detection over a wide range of data; hence, $\alpha = 0.05$. Substituting $\alpha = 0.05$ in Equation (1), we obtain a corresponding value for η'.

4   Generating Audio Label

In this section we describe the generation of an audio class label pattern. We select 3 videos from the total of 8 in the NIST database for training purposes. The audio training data is annotated into 6 audio classes.

4.1   Audio Data Models

We manually segment the training data containing 3 different audio files that are extracted as the audio stream of the video files, and then label each segment as belonging to one of 6 different classes: speech, speech + music, music, speech + noise, noise, and silence. We employ a Gaussian mixture model [11] for audio class identification. For each of these six audio classes, we first calculate a 30-dimensional audio feature vector. The audio feature vector consists of 13 mel frequency cepstrum coefficients. Another 13 components correspond to the first derivative of the original 13 coefficients. Then we have the short time energy, the short time zero crossing rate, and their first derivatives. We extract this feature vector over all the audio files meant for training. Then we estimate a Gaussian mixture model M_i for the audio class i which is defined by the parameter set $P_i(\mu_i, \Sigma_i, w_i)$, consisting of the mean vectors μ_i, covariance matrices Σ_i, and mixture weight vectors w_i.

4.2   Class Label Identification

The goal of audio class label identification is to find the model M_i that best explains each frame of the test data represented by a sequence of N audio frames $\{f_n\}_{n=1,..,N}$. The audio frame rate is 100 frames/s. Maximum-likelihood criterion is used for classification. The class label c_n for frame f_n is $c_n = \arg\max_i \log p_i(f_n|\mu_i, \Sigma_i, w_i)$, where p_i is the probability of a frame belonging to the Gaussian mixture model $P_i(\mu_i, \Sigma_i, w_i)$.

Similar to the visual data labelling explained in the previous section, we also generate a counterpart audio class label pattern for N frames $\{f_n\}_{n=1,..,N}$, as $\{c_n\}_{n=1,..,N}$.

5   Audio-Visual Fusion

In this section, we first define some terms that will be used for audio-visual fusion with respect to the interval $[s \quad t]$, where s and t denote the indices of video keyframes. In the case of audio definitions we map the index to corresponding audio frame. Appropriate weights are then statistically selected to linearly combine audio and visual information for detecting documentary scene changes.

Visual Similarity Count: We denote the set of similar keyframes as $VS = \{V_i|V_i = V_j, j \neq i\}$, the normalized visual similarity count $vsc(s,t)$ is

$$vsc(s,t) = \frac{|VS|}{(t - s + 1)} \tag{3}$$

where $|.|$ denotes the size of a set.

Audio Similarity Count: AC_m is the number of audio frames $\in$ class m, the normalized audio similarity count $asc(s,t)$ is

$$asc(s,t) = \frac{\max_{1 \leq m \leq K} AC_m}{Number\ of\ audio\ frames\ in\ this\ interval} \tag{4}$$

where K is the total number of audio classes.

Audio Delta Function: This function returns 1 if the audio class of the frames in the begining of the interval is same as those in the end. S_i is the log-likelihood of the audio class of the initial r audio frames, denoted as $A_s = \{a_n\}_{n=s,...,s+r-1}$ belonging to the ith audio class model. We have

$$S_i = \log p_i(A_s|\mu_i, \Sigma_i, w_i) = \sum_{n=s}^{s+r-1} \log p_i(a_n|\mu_i, \Sigma_i, w_i). \tag{5}$$

Furthermore, let T_i denotes the log-likelihood of the audio class of the ending r frames, denoted as $A_t = \{a_n\}_{n=t-r+1,...,t}$ belonging to the ith audio class model. We have

$$T_i = \log p_i(A_t|\mu_i, \Sigma_i, w_i) = \sum_{n=t-r+1}^{t} \log p_i(a_n|\mu_i, \Sigma_i, w_i). \tag{6}$$

Finally, the audio delta function $\delta_a(s,t)$ is defined as

$$\delta_a(s,t) = \delta(L_s - L_t). \tag{7}$$

where $L_s = \arg\max_i S_i$ is the label corresponding to the initial r frames, and $L_t = \arg\max_i T_i$ is the label corresponding to the ending r frames.

Visual Delta Function: This function $\delta_v(s,t)$ returns 1 if the video frames between the keyframes within the index interval $[s\ \ t]$ have a similar background. Figure 3 shows the detailed algorithm of this function. Each common background scene is represented as $back_i$, and x_i is used to represent the start of $back_i$, while y_i represents its end. The details for finding the common background scenes can be found in [9].

5.1   Audio-Visual Score

The audio score $S_a(s,t)$ is the sum of the audio similarity count, and the audio delta function :

$$S_a(s,t) = asc(s,t) + \delta_a(s,t). \tag{8}$$

The visual score $S_v(s,t)$ also is the sum of the visual similarity count, and the visual delta function :

$$S_v(s,t) = vsc(s,t) + \delta_v(s,t). \tag{9}$$

> **Input:** $\{back_i\}_{i=1,...,N}$ the set of common background scenes, interval
> $[s \quad t]$, tolerance value ϵ
> **Output:** $\delta_v(s,t)$
> 1. **for** $i = 1, \ldots, N$ **do:**
>   1.1   **Initialize:** $\delta_v(s,t) \leftarrow 0$
>   1.2   **if** $|x_i - s| < \epsilon$ and $|y_i - t| < \epsilon$
>   1.3   **then** $\delta_v(s,t) \leftarrow 1$

Fig. 3. Algorithm for visual delta function

The audio-visual score [12], $S_{av}(s,t)$ is a weighted combination of the audio and visual score.

$$S_{av}(s,t) = w_a \, S_a(s,t) + w_v \, S_v(s,t). \tag{10}$$

where w_a is the audio weight, w_v is the visual weight, and $w_a + w_v = 1$.

5.2   Selection of Mixture Weights

Since w_a and w_v can affect the result of audio-visual score, we apply a statistical method to approximate their optimal values. We learn the optimal value of the mixture weight ω denoted as ω^{opt} from the training data by minimizing a cost function $C(\omega)$ which is the smoothed recognition error rate [13]:

> **Input:** $L + 1$, Δ, *entries.*
>   - $L + 1$: The initial size of the interval $[s \ t]$, which will be
>   either expanded or shrunk
>   - Δ: The step size by which the interval is each time
>   expanded or shrunk as shown in Figure 5
>   - *entries*: The index of the last keyframe in the video
>   as shown in Figure 5
> **Output:** $\{documentary_i\}_{i=1,...,N}$ a set of documentary scenes
>
> 1. Initializing the begining and end of the interval and its index:
> $s \leftarrow 1, \, t \leftarrow L + 1$ and $i \leftarrow 1$
>
> 2. **while** $t <$ *entries,* perform the below steps:
>   2.1   **if** $S_{av}(s,t) > \{S_{av}(s,t+\Delta)$ and $S_{av}(s,t-\Delta)\}$ (indicates a local maximum)
>   2.2 $documentary_i \leftarrow [s \ t]$ (indicates the detection of documentary scene)
>   2.3 $i \leftarrow i + 1$ (counting each detected documentary scene)
>   2.4   we re-initialize the interval: $s \leftarrow t + 1, t \leftarrow s + L - 1$
>   2.5   **else if** $S_{av}(s,t+\Delta) > S_{av}(s,t-\Delta)$
>   2.6   we expand the interval by Δ: $t \leftarrow t + \Delta$
>   2.7   **else** we shrink the interval by Δ: $t \leftarrow t - \Delta$

Fig. 4. Algorithm for adaptive scheme

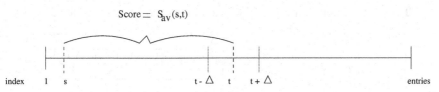

Fig. 5. The audio-visual score $S_{av}(s, t)$ evaluated over the interval $[s\ t]$ is compared with the score evaluated over $[s, t + \Delta]$ and $[s, t - \Delta]$

$$C(\omega) = \frac{1}{R} \sum_{i=1}^{R} \frac{1}{1 + e^{\{-\xi S_{av}^i(\omega)\}}} , \xi > 0 \tag{11}$$

where

$$S_{av}^i(\omega) = \omega\, S_a^i + (1 - \omega)\, S_v^i. \tag{12}$$

S_a^i is the audio score for the ith training clip, and S_v^i is the visual score for the ith training clip. This cost function is evaluated by selecting R clips from the training videos such that they do not correspond to a documentary scene. Minimizing the cost function $C(\omega)$ with respect to ω, while substituting a positive value for ξ results in $\omega^{opt} = 0.7$. Hence, the optimal value of audio weight $\omega_a = 0.7$ and the optimal value of the visual weight $\omega_v = 0.3$.

6   Detecting Documentary Scene Change

6.1   Adaptive Scheme

In the adaptive scheme, the audio-visual score within an interval is first evaluated. This interval will be adaptively expanded or shrunk until a local maximum is found. The detailed algorithm can be found in Figure 4.

6.2   Redundancy Check

The visual delta function and the audio delta function tend to be the cause of some redundant detections. In fact, certain redundant detections can be eliminated by the careful investigation of neighbouring documentary scenes. To cope with this problem, we merge neighbouring documentary scenes on the basis of a new score. The audio-visual merging score $S_{av}^M(s, t)$ is a weighted combination of the audio similarity count and the visual similarity count:

$$S_{av}^M(s, t) = \omega^{opt}\, asc(s, t) + (1 - \omega^{opt})\, vsc(s, t) \tag{13}$$

The details of algorithm for redundancy check can be found in Figure 6.

Table 1. Results at the end of the adaptive scheme stage for $\Delta=3$

video	$\Delta = 3$			
	Duration	Human Detections	Machine Detections	Number of hits
1	489 s	29	27	21
2	382 s	13	22	6
3	523 s	11	14	8
4	743 s	22	40	9
5	493 s	14	28	5

Table 2. Results at the end of check for redundancy stage for $\Delta=3$

video	$\Delta = 3$			
	Duration	Human Detections	Machine Detections	Number of hits
1	489 s	29	27	21
2	382 s	13	12	10
3	523 s	11	14	8
4	743 s	22	22	17
5	493 s	14	16	9

7   Experimental Results

The experimental data used is from NIST Special Database 26. Out of the eight videos, three were used for training while the remaining five were used for testing. We use Figure 7 to depict a detected documentary scene. In Figure 7, the top row, from left to right, shows the award, a performer, and an instrument. The bottom row shows President Clinton, the audience, and the award being handed over with an industrial lab in the background. This documentary scene is a description of the Malcolm Baldrige Quality Award. Although there are many visual changes throughout this documentary scene, the underlying semantic context remains the same.

Input: Result of the adaptive scheme $\{documentary_i\}_{i=1,..,N}$
Output: The merged output set $\{documentary_i\}_{i=1,..,N}$

1. **while** $i < N$, **do:**
    1.1   **if** $S_{av}^M(s_i, t_{i+1}) > \{S_{av}(s_i, t_i)$ and $S_{av}(s_{i+1}, t_{i+1})\}$
    1.2   **merge** $[s_i\ t_i]$ and $[s_{i+1}\ t_{i+1}]$: $documentary_i \leftarrow [s_i\ t_{i+1}]$
    1.3   **adjust** the index and length: $i \leftarrow i - 1, N \leftarrow N - 1$
    1.4   **else** go to the next documentary scene: $i \leftarrow i + 1$

Fig. 6. Algorithm for redundancy check

Fig. 7. A documentary scene from test video 2

We adopt recall and precision for the performance evaluation:

$$recall = \frac{Number\ of\ hits}{Human\ Detections} \qquad (14)$$

$$precision = \frac{Number\ of\ hits}{Machine\ Detections} \qquad (15)$$

where, hit is defined as the detection by both human subjects and machine. Tables 1 and 2 show the experimental results, by the adaptive scheme and redundancy check, for $\Delta=3$. As indicated in Tables 1 and 2, number of hits in videos 2, 4 and 5 are increased after the redundancy check. The number of hits remain the same for videos 1 and 3 before and after applying the redundancy check. The recall and precision of the proposed approach on the five tested videos can be found in Table 3.

We further investigate the effectiveness of the approach by varying the parameter Δ. The recall-precision values for $\Delta = 3$ are constantly better than the values for $\Delta = 4$ or 5, as indicated in Table 3.

Table 3. A comparison of recall - precision values for $\Delta = 3, 4, 5$ after making a check for redundancy

video	$\Delta = 3$		$\Delta = 4$		$\Delta = 5$	
	recall	precision	recall	precision	recall	precision
1	.72	.78	.59	.71	.45	.57
2	.77	.83	.54	.64	.62	.80
3	.73	.57	.55	.40	.45	.36
4	.77	.77	.45	.56	.41	.45
5	.64	.56	.50	.54	.43	.46

8 Conclusion

We have presented a scheme out of certain observations that we made on the audio-visual characteristics of documentary videos. This scheme is basically a two stage process. In the first stage, we find a set of documentary scenes by a weighted fusion of the audio score and the video score. In the second stage, we make a check for any redundant detections, and, if any, we merge those documentary scenes. It is observed through experiments that in the cases where the end of the adaptive scheme itself gives optimal number of hits, even after making a check for redundancy they remain unchanged. However, in the cases where there is actually a redundancy in detection, merging neighbouring documentary scenes actually increases the number of hits. This scheme has been successful in detecting documentary scene changes, with each of them having a common underlying semantic context. Future work would focus on how to identify this semantic context probably by classifying them into few learnt categories.

References

[1] A. Hampapur, R. Jain , and T. Weymouth, "Digital video segmentation," in *Proceedings of ACM Multimedia* , San Francisco CA, October 1994, pp. 357-364. 227

[2] J. R. Kender and B. L. Yeo, "Video scene segmentation via continuous video coherence," in *CVPR* , Santa Barbara CA, June 1998. 227

[3] C. Saraceno and R. Leonardi, "Audio as support to scene change detection and characterization of video sequences," in *Proceedings of ICASSP,* vol 4, 1997, pp. 2597-2600. 227

[4] J. Huang, Z. Liu, and Y. Wang, "Integration of audio and visual information for content-based video segmentation," in *ICIP*, Chicago, 1998. 227

[5] H. Sundaram and S.-F. Chang, "Video scene segmentation using audio and video features," in *ICME,* New York, July 28-Aug 2, 2000. 227

[6] J. Huang, "Color-spatial image indexing and applications," Ph.D. dissertation, Cornell University, 1998. 229, 230

[7] 229
C. W. Ngo, T. C. Pong, and R. T. Chin, "Video partitioning by temporal slice coherency," *IEEE Transactions on Circuits and Systems for Video Technology,* vol. 11, Aug 2001, pp. 941-953.

[8] H. V. Poor, *An Introduction to Signal Detection and Estimation.* New York: Springer, 2nd ed., 1994. 230

[9] 229, 232
C. W. Ngo, T. C. Pong and H. J. Zhang, "Motion-based video representation for scene change detection," *International Journal of Computer Vision,* vol. 50, No. 2, Nov, 2002.

[10] 229
C. W. Ngo, "Motion Analysis and Segmentation through Spatio-temporal Slices Processing," *IEEE Trans. on Image Processing,* Feb, 2003.

[11] D. A. Reynolds and R. C. Rose, "Robust text-independent speaker identification using Gaussian mixture speaker models," *IEEE Transactions on Speech and Audio Processing,* vol. 3, no. 1, pp. 72-83, Jan 1995. 231

[12] B. Maison, C. Neti, and A. Senior, "Audio-visual speaker recognition for video broadcast news: some fusion techniques," in *IEEE Multimedia Signal Processing Conference (MMSP99)*, Denmark, Sept 1999. 233

[13] L. Rabiner and B. H Juang, *Fundamentals of speech recognition*. New Jersey: Prentice Hall International Inc, 1993. 233

Multimedia Search with Pseudo-relevance Feedback

Rong Yan, Alexander Hauptmann, and Rong Jin

School of Computer Science
Carnegie Mellon University
Pittsburgh, PA, USA
{yanrong,alex,rong}@cs.cmu.edu

Abstract. We present an algorithm for video retrieval that fuses the decisions of multiple retrieval agents in both text and image modalities. While the normalization and combination of evidence is novel, this paper emphasizes the successful use of negative pseudo-relevance feedback to improve image retrieval performance. Although we have not solved all problems in video information retrieval, the results are encouraging, indicating that pseudo-relevance feedback shows great promise for multimedia retrieval with very varied and errorful data.

1   Video Retrieval from Mixed Text and Image Queries

In this paper, we present an algorithm for the task of video retrieval. A query, consisting of a text description plus images or video is posed against a video collection, and relevant shots are to be retrieved. Our system accomplishes this by fusing the retrieval results of multiple retrieval agents. The overall system can be decomposed into several agents, including a text-oriented retrieval agent, which is responsible for finding the text in the speech transcripts [4] and Video OCR [3], a video-information oriented agent which is responsible for searching the 'manually' provided movie abstracts and titles) and a basic nearest neighbor image matching agent which can be combined with classification-based pseudo-relevance feedback (PRF). The motivation of the classifier based PRF approach is to improve the image retrieval performance by feeding back relevance estimates based on the initial search results into a classifier and then refining the retrieval result using the classification output. This approach will be described in more detail in the next section. To address the issue of comparability between retrieval scores produced by different types of agents, the retrieval scores of these agents are converted into posterior probabilities in an attempt to create normalized output scores. The posterior probabilities are then linearly combined to generate the final ranking decisions.

E. M. Bakker et al. (Eds.): CIVR 2003, LNCS 2728, pp. 238-247, 2003.
© Springer-Verlag Berlin Heidelberg 2003

2   Image Retrieval
with Classification Pseudo-relevance Feedback

2.1   Traditional Image Retrieval Framework

Content-based image retrieval (CBIR) [1, 5] has been studied for many years. The task requires the image search engine to find a set of images from a given image collection that is similar to the given query image. Traditional methods for CBIR are based on a vector space model [14]. These methods represent an image as a set of features and the difference between two images is measured through a similarity function between their feature vectors. While there have been no large-scale, standardized evaluations of image retrieval systems, most image retrieval systems are based on features representing color [6], texture, and shape that are extracted from the image pixels [12].

'Nearest neighbor' search is the most straightforward approach to find matching images. It contains the implicit assumption that for each feature the class posterior probabilities (distributions) are approximately constant [16] for matching and non-matching images. However nearest neighbor search suffers from two major drawbacks. First, the nearest neighbor might assign equal weight to both the relevant features and irrelevant features. Thus, if a large number of the features of an image are irrelevant to the query, the retrieval accuracy will suffer dramatically, since many images similar with respect to the irrelevant features will be preferred. It is therefore reasonable to select a subset of features or re-weight the features before the nearest neighbor search. However, most feature selection techniques require either large amounts of labeled data or knowledge of the way the classes are distributed with respect to each feature. Applying feature selection to the retrieval problem becomes rather difficult since usually only a small number of (image) query examples are given. Relevance feedback [15] is one effective way to gather information about the class distribution through iterative interaction with users. Through either feature re-weighting or query refinement, relevance feedback has been shown to be a powerful tool for providing more accurate retrieval results [15]. However, it is not possible to obtain user judgments in automatic retrieval tasks. The second drawback to nearest neighbor search is the fixed similarity metric. Since an appropriate similarity measure can vary with different datasets and different queries, any fixed similarity metric is unlikely to work well over all possible queries and data collections. To address this, Hastie et al. [16] have proposed an adaptive nearest neighbor algorithm in which the similarity metric can be locally adapted to the features relevant for each query point and globally optimized using dimensionality reduction. In a similar spirit, we observe that that some learning algorithms can model the data distributions even with very few training data points, so therefore we postulate that they are also feasible candidates to remedy the drawbacks of the nearest neighbor search.

2.2   A Classification-Based Pseudo-relevance Feedback Approach

As noted before, nearest neighbor search suffers from a lack of adaptability. Recent studies have shown that some well-established classification algorithms [21] can yield better generalization performance than nearest neighbor type algorithms. Following this direction, we propose a classification-based pseudo-relevance feedback approach outlined below in an attempt to apply SVM ensembles to refine the initial retrieval result in content-based video retrieval.

2.2.1 Retrieval as Classification with Additional Training Examples from PRF

Quite naturally, information retrieval can be treated as a binary classification problem, where the positive data are the relevant examples in the collection and the negative data are irrelevant ones. However, information retrieval and classification have inherent differences. Typically, a retrieval algorithm might only obtain a small amount of training 'data' from the images that form the query, and even more crucially, there is no negative training data at all. To apply a classification algorithm to the retrieval problem, we have to provide more training data for the classifiers. One possibility is to identify the potential positive and negative class labels of unlabeled image examples in the collection with aid of the hints from initial search results. This is what we call pseudo-relevance feedback (PRF) in our work.

Therefore, the basic idea for our approach is to augment the retrieval performance by incorporating classification algorithms via PRF, with the choice of training examples based on the initial retrieval results. Standard PRF methods, which originated from the filed of text information retrieval [17], view the top-ranked documents as positive examples. Most text-based PRF methods update the feature weights based on the word frequency in the top ranked documents. However, due to the limited accuracy of current video retrieval systems, even the very top-ranked results are not always the relevant, correct answers that meet the users' information need, so they cannot be used as reliable positive examples for relevance feedback.

However, we discovered that it is quite appropriate to make use of the *lowest* ranked documents in the collection, because these documents are very likely to be negative examples. Therefore, after the initial search, we can construct a classifier to produce a more reliable retrieval score, where the positive data are the query image examples and the negative data are sampled from the least relevant image examples. The classification confidence is then merged with the initial retrieval scores as the final score.

From the viewpoint of machine learning, the approach presented here can be thought of as positive example based learning or partially supervised learning [18, 19]. It has been proved [18] that accurate classifiers can be built with sufficient positive and unlabeled data without any negative data. These results provide a sound theoretical justification for our approach. However, the goal of these learning algorithms differs from our approach, because they mostly aim at assigning examples into one of the given categories, instead of producing a ranked list of the examples. Another line of research related to this work is learning with a small set of labeled data. Transductive learning is one of the most popular paradigms to handle small numbers of labeled data. Transductive learning has recently been successfully applied in the area of image retrieval [20]. However, that work is also different from ours because we do not have any certain negative labels at all.

2.2.2 SVM Ensembles

In our experiments, support vector machines (SVMs) [21] serve as our base classifier, since SVMs are known to yield good generalization performance compared to other classification algorithms. The decision function is of the form

$$y = sign\left(\sum_{i=1}^{N} y_i \alpha_i K(x, x_i) + b\right)$$

where x is the d-dimensional feature vector of a test example, $y \in \{-1,1\}$ is a class label, x_i is the vector for the ith training example, N is the number of training examples, $K(x, x_i)$ is a kernel function, $\alpha = \{\alpha_1, ..., \alpha_N\}$ and b are the parameters of the model. These α_i's can be learned by solving following quadratic programming (QP) problem,

$$\text{min}\quad Q(\alpha) = -\sum_{i=1}^{N} \alpha_i + \frac{1}{2}\sum_{i=1}^{N}\sum_{j=1}^{N} \alpha_i \alpha_j y_i y_j K(x_i, x_j)$$

subject to $\sum_{i=1}^{N} \alpha_i y_i = 0$ and $0 \le \alpha_i \le C \forall i$

However in our case, since the number of negative data examples is often much larger than the positive data set, it might be a bad idea for SVMs to train on all of the positive and negative data at one time. This asymmetric data distribution often leads to a trivial SVM classifier that produces negative output for all possible input data. Recent years have seen several attempts at addressing the rare class problem using different techniques such as up sampling, down sampling [22], boosting [23] and biased discriminant analysis [25].

Along this direction, Yan et al. [24] have proposed a hierarchical classification solution by using SVM ensembles to tackle the imbalanced data set problem. To generate training sets with balanced distributions without either removing any training data or significantly increasing the training time, they first decompose the negative data into several partitions, and combine all the positive examples with each partition of negative examples to be an individual subset. A set of constituent SVMs is trained independently on every subset of the training set. Finally, all constituent SVMs will be combined by various strategies, including majority voting, sum of the posterior probability, and meta-classifiers (stacking). In this work, we adopt a similar framework, with the modification that a logistic regression algorithm is used to combine the output of the constituent SVMs.

2.2.3 Algorithm Details

The overall procedure of our image retrieval algorithm can be summarized as follows:

1. Generate the initial classification results by nearest neighbor search for *color* features of all the images in the collection.
2. Generate the initial classification results by nearest neighbor search for *texture* features of all the images in the collection.

3. Utilize all the query images as positive data. Let m be the number of query images.
4. Construct a negative sub-collection based on the initial retrieval results. In our implementation, the 10% least relevant images from the collection are chosen as the negative sub-collection. We sample k groups of negative data from the negative sub-collection, where each group contains m query images. Each group of negative data is combined with the positive data as a training set.
5. Build a classifier from each training set to produce new relevance score $f_i(x)(1 \leq i \leq k)$ for any images x, where i is the index of training set. $f_i(x)$ is set to 1 for positive prediction and 0 for negative prediction.
6. Combine the outputs of all the classifiers in the form of a logistic regression, which is

$$P_{PRF}(y=1|x) = \frac{\exp(\beta_0 + \sum_{i=1}^{k}\beta_i f_i(x))}{1 + \exp(\beta_0 + \sum_{i=1}^{k}\beta_i f_i(x))}$$

In our system, we simply set β_0 as 0, $\beta_i(1 \leq i \leq k)$ as equal values.

Our approach, as presented here, utilizes the collection distribution knowledge to refine the retrieval result. Due to the good generalizability of the SVM algorithm, the more relevant features are automatically more likely to be highly weighted. Also the approach yields a better similarity metric than the fixed one based on finding the largest margin between the positive and negative data examples for the current query.

3   Combination of Multiple Agents

Ultimately, the scores from multimodal agents have to be fused together to produce a final rank list for each query. The first step to integrate different types of relevance scores is to convert all the relevance scores into posterior probabilities. The conversion of PRF approach is described in section 2.2.3. For nearest neighbor type approached, the rank of each video shot is scaled to the range of [0, 1] by linear transformation. This normalized rank can be viewed as the posterior probability, which is, $P(y=1|x) = 1 - R/R_{max}$ where R_{max} is the maximum rank.

All these posterior probabilities are simply linear combined to be the final score,

$$Score_I = b_c P_{color}(y=1|x) + b_t P_{texture}(y=1|x) + b_{PRF} P_{PRF}(y=1|x)$$
$$Score = a_I Score_I + a_T P_{text}(y=1|x) + a_m P_{movie}(y=1|x)$$

where a_I, a_T, a_m is the weight for image agent, text agent, video-information agent respectively. In our current implementation, a_I, a_T, a_m are set to be 1, 1, 0.2. b_c, b_t, b_{PRF} are the weights for the three image retrieval agents: Nearest Neighbor on color, Nearest Neighbor on texture and classification PRF, which are either set to be 0 or 1 in our contrastive experiments reported below.

4   Experimental Results

The video data came from the video collection provided by the TREC Video Retrieval Track. The definitive information about this collection can be found at the NIST TREC Video Track web site: http://www-nlpir.nist.gov/projects/trecvid/. The Text REtrieval Conference evaluations are sponsored by the National Institute of Standards and Technology (NIST) with additional support from other U.S. government agencies. Their goal is to encourage research in information retrieval from large amounts of text by providing a large test collection, uniform scoring procedures, and a forum for organizations interested in comparing their results. The first Video Retrieval Track evaluation was performed in 2001. Its purpose was the investigation of content-based retrieval from digital video. The retrieval evaluation centered around the shot as the unit of information retrieval rather than the scene or story/segment as the video document to be retrieved.

The 2002 Video Collection for the Video TREC retrieval task consisted of ~40 hours of MPEG-1 video in the search test collection. The content came from the Internet Archive and Open Video websites, consisting mostly of documentary television from the 50's and 60's. This translated to 1160 segments as processed by Carnegie Mellon University's Informedia system [10, 11] or 14,524 shots where the boundaries were provided as the common shot reference of the Video TREC evaluation effort. We extracted a total of 292,000 I-frames directly from the MPEG-1 compressed video files to represent the video's visual information.

The actual 25 queries of the 2002 Video Retrieval track had an average of 2.7 video examples each, as well as an average of 1.9 image examples. The queries can be categorized into four general types:

- **Specific Item or Person**
  Eddie Rickenbacker, James Chandler, Abraham Lincoln, George Washington, The Golden Gate Bridge, The Price Tower in Bartlesville, Oklahoma, etc.

- **Specific 'Facts'**
  The Arch in Washington Square Park in New York City, an image of a map of the continental United States, etc.

- **Instances of a Category**
  Football players, overhead views of cities, one or more women standing in long dresses, etc.

- **Instances of Events/Activities**
  People spending leisure time at the beach, one or more musicians with audible music, crowd walking in an urban environment, a locomotive approaching the viewer.

A sample query for images of George Washington, was represented in XML as:

```
<!DOCTYPE videoTopic SYSTEM "videoTopics.dtd">

<videoTopic num="077">

<textDescription text="Find pictures of George
Washington" />

<imageExample src= "http: //www.cia.gov/csi/
monograph/firstln/955pres2.gif" desc="face" />

videoExample src="01681.mpg"  start="09m25.938s"
stop="09m29.308s" desc="face" />
```

The above query example contains both a still image as well as a short video clip of about 3.5 seconds depicting an image of a portrait of George Washington. A sample image from the collection video is shown at right.

4.1   Image Features

Two kinds of low-level image features are used by our system: color features [6] and texture features. We generate both types of features for each subblock of a 3*3 image tessellation. The color feature is comprised of the central and second-order color moments for each separate color channel, where the three channels come from the HSV (Hue-Saturation-Value) color space [26]. We use 16 bins for hue and 6 bins for both saturation and value. The texture features are obtained from the convolution of the subblock with various Gabor Filters. In our implementation, 6 angles are used and each filter output is quantized into 16 bins. We compute a histogram for each filter and again generate their central and second-order moments as the texture feature. In total, we obtained 18 features for each subblock and concatenate them into a longer vector of 144 features for every image. In a preprocessing step, each element of the feature vectors is scaled by the covariance of its dimension.   We adopted the Euclidean distance as the similarity measure between two images.

4.2   Speech Recognition

The audio processing component of our video retrieval system splits the audio track from the MPEG-1 encoded video file, and decodes the audio and down samples it to 16kHz, 16bit samples. These samples are then passed to a speech recognizer. The speech recognition system we used for these experiments is a state-of-the-art large vocabulary, speaker independent speech recognizer. For the purposes of this evaluation, a 64000-word language model derived from a large corpus of broadcast news transcripts was used. Previous experiments had shown the word error rate on this type of mixed documentary-style data with frequent overlap of music and speech to be 35 – 40% [11].

4.3   Text Retrieval

All retrieval of textual material was done using the OKAPI formula [2]. The exact formula for the Okapi method is shown in Equation (1)

$$Sim(Q,D) = \sum_{qw \in Q} \left\{ \frac{tf(qw,D)\log(\frac{N - df(qw) + 0.5}{df(qw) + 0.5})}{0.5 + 1.5\frac{|D|}{avg\_dl} + tf(qw,D)} \right\} \quad (1)$$

where $tf(qw,D)$ is the term frequency of word qw in document D, $df(qw)$ is the document frequency for the word qw and avg_dl is the average document length for all the documents in the collection. No relevance feedback at the text level was used.

As noted before, video information agent uses externally provided video information as another source to improve retrieval performance. For each query, the score of a video shot is set to 1 if any keyword of the query can be found in the video titles/abstracts for the corresponding movie, otherwise the score is set to 0.

4.4   Results

We report our results in terms of mean average precision in this section, as shown in Table 1. Four different combinations of the retrieval agents are compared in this table, including the combination of text agent (Text), video information agent for externally supplied movie titles and abstracts (VI), nearest neighbor on color (Color), nearest neighbor on texture (Texture) and classification-based PRF (PRF). The results show an increase in retrieval quality using the classification-based PRF technique. While the text information from the speech transcript accounts for the largest proportion of the mean average precision (0.0658), only a minimal gain was observed in the mean average precision when the 'movie title' and abstract were searched (0.0724) in addition to the speech transcripts. The image retrieval component provided further improvements in the scores to a mean average precision of 0.1046. Finally, the PRF technique managed to boost the mean average precision to the final mean average precision score of 0.1124. Further experiments are needed to investigate how the various parameter settings and combination strategies affect the performance of PRF approach.

Table 1. Video retrieval results on the 25 queries of the 2003 TREC video track evaluation

Approach	Precision	Recall	Mean Average Precision
Text only (Speech Recognition)	0.0348	0.1445	0.0658
Text + Video Information (VI)	0.0348	0.1445	0.0724
Text + VI + Color + Texture	0.0892	0.220	0.1046
Text + VI + Color + Texture + PRF	0.0924	0.216	0.1124

5   Conclusions

We present an algorithm for video retrieval by fusing the decisions of multiple retrieval agents in both text and image modalities. While the normalization and combination of evidence is novel, this paper emphasizes the successful use of negative pseudo-relevance feedback to improve image retrieval performance. While the results are still far from satisfactory, PRF shows great promise for multimedia retrieval in very noisy data. One of the future directions of this approach is to study the effect of different classification algorithms and explore better combination strategies than a simple linear combination of the individual agents.

Acknowledgements

This work was partially supported by National Science Foundation under Cooperative Agreement No. IRI-9817496, and by the Advanced Research and Development Activity (ARDA) under contract number MDA908-00-C-0037.

References

[1]   Hafner, J. Sawhney, H.S. Equitz, W. Flickner, M. and Niblack, W. "Efficient Color Histogram Indexing for Quadratic Form Distance," IEEE Trans. Pattern Analysis and Machine Intelligence, 17(7), pp. 729-736, July, 1995

[2]   Robertson S.E., et al.. Okapi at TREC-4. In The Fourth Text Retrieval Conference (TREC-4). 1993

[3]   Sato, T., Kanade, T., Hughes, E., and Smith, M. Video OCR for Digital News Archive. In Proc. Workshop on Content-Based Access of Image and Video Databases. (Los Alamitos, CA, Jan 1998), 52-60

[4]   Singh, R., Seltzer, M.L., Raj, B., and Stern, R.M. "Speech in Noisy Environments: Robust Automatic Segmentation, Feature Extraction, and Hypothesis Combination," IEEE Conference on Acoustics, Speech and Signal Processing, Salt Lake City, UT, May, 2001

[5]   A.W.M. Smeulders, M. Worring, S. Santini, A. Gupta and R. Jain, "Content-Based Image Retrieval at the End of the Early Years," IEEE Trans. Pattern Analysis and Machine Intelligence, 22(12), pp. 1349-1380, December, 2000

[6]   Swain M.J. and Ballard, B.H. "Color Indexing," Int'l J. Computer Vision, vol. 7, no. 1, pp. 11-32, 1991

[7]   Tague-Sutcliffe, J.M., "The Pragmatics of Information Retrieval Experimenta-tion, revised," Information Processing and Management, 28, 467-490, 1992

[8]   TREC 2002 National Institute of Standards and Technology, Text REtrieval Conference web page, http://www.trec.nist.gov/, 2002

[9]   TREC Video Retrieval Track, http://www-nlpir.nist.gov/ projects/trecvid/

[10]   Wactlar, H.D., Christel, M.G., Gong, Y., and Hauptmann, A.G. "Lessons Learned from the Creation and Deployment of a Terabyte Digital Video Library", IEEE Computer 32(2): 66-73

[11] Informedia Digital Video Library Project Web Site. Carnegie Mellon University, Pittsburgh, PA, USA. URL http://www.informedia.cs.cmu.edu

[12] Del Bimbo " Visual Information Retrieval", Morgan Kaufmann Ed., San Francisco, USA, 1999

[13] Mojsilovic, J. Kovacevic, J. Hu, R.J. Safranek, and S.K. Ganapathy, "Matching and Retrieval Based on the Vocabulary and Grammar of Color Patterns," IEEE Trans. Image Processing, 9(1), pp. 38-54, 2000

[14] Gong, Y. Intelligent Image Databases: Toward Advanced Image Retrieval. Kluwer Academic Publishers: Hingham, MA

[15] Y. Rui, T. S. Huang, and S. Mehrotra, "Content-based image retrieval with relevance feed-back in Mars," in Proc. IEEE Conf. Image Processing, 1997, pp. 815-818

[16] T. Hastie and R. Tibshirani. Discriminant adaptive nearest neighbor classification and regression. In David S. Touretzky, Michael C. Mozer, and Michael E. Hasselmo, editors, Advances in Neural Information Processing Systems, volume 8, pages 409--415. The MIT Press, 1996

[17] Carbonell, J., Y. Yang, R. Frederking and R.D. Brown, "Translingual Information Retrieval: A Comparative Evaluation," Proceedings of IJCAI, 1997

[18] Liu, B., Lee, W.S., Yu, P.S. and Li, X., Partially Supervised Classification of Text Documents, Proc. 19th Intl. Conf. on Machine Learning, Sydney, Australia, July 2002, 387-394

[19] F. Denis. PAC learning from positive statistical queries. In ALT 98, 9th International Conference on Algorithmic Learning Theory, volume 1501 of Lecture Notes in Artificial Intelligence, pages 112-126. Springer-Verlag, 1998

[20] Y. Wu, Q. Tian, and T. Huang. Discriminant-em algorithm with application to image retrieval. In Proceedings to the IEEE Conference on Computer Vision and Pattern Recognition, volume 1, pages 222--227, June 2000. 12

[21] V.N. Vapnik (1995). The Nature of Statistical Learning Theory. Springer

[22] Foster Provost, "Machine Learning from Imbalanced Data Sets 101/1", AAAI Workshop on Learning from Imbalanced Data Sets, AAAI Press, Menlo Park, CA, 64-68

[23] M.V. Joshi, R.C. Agarwal, V. Kumar, "Predicting Rare Classes: Can Boosting Make Any Weak Learner Strong? ", the Eighth ACM SIGKDD International Conference on Knowledge Discovery and Data Mining, Edmonton, Canada, July 2003

[24] R. Yan, Y. Liu, R. Jin, A. G Hauptmann, "On Predicting Rare Class with SVM Ensemble in Scene Classification", To Appear in International Conference on Acoustics, Speech, and Signal Processing 2003, Hong Kong, China, April, 2003

[25] X. S. Zhou, T. S. Huang, "Small Sample Learning during Multimedia Retrieval using BiasMap", in Proc. IEEE Conf. Computer Vision and Pattern Recognition, Hawaii, Dec. 2001

[26] O. Chapelle, P. Haffner and V. Vapnik, "SVMs for histogram-based image classification ", IEEE Transaction on Neural Networks, 9, 1999

Modal Keywords, Ontologies, and Reasoning for Video Understanding

Alejandro Jaimes, Belle L. Tseng, and John R. Smith

Pervasive Media Management
IBM T.J. Watson Research Center
Hawthorne, NY 10532 USA
ajaimes@ee.columbia.edu
{belle,jsmith}@us.ibm.com

Abstract. We proposed a novel framework for video content under-standing that uses rules constructed from knowledge bases and multi-media ontologies. Our framework consists of an expert system that uses a rule-based engine, domain knowledge, visual detectors (for objects and scenes), and metadata (text from automatic speech recognition, re-lated text, etc.). We introduce the idea of *modal keywords,* which are keywords that represent *perceptual concepts* in the following catego-ries: *visual* (e.g., sky), *aural* (e.g., scream), *olfactory* (e.g., vanilla), *tactile* (e.g., feather), and *taste* (e.g., candy). A method is presented to automatically classify keywords from speech recognition, queries, or related text into these categories using WordNet and TGM I. For video understanding, the following operations are performed automatically: scene cut detection, automatic speech recognition, feature extraction, and visual detection (e.g., sky, face, indoor). These operation results are used in our system by a rule-based engine that uses context information (e.g., text from speech) to enhance visual detection results. We discuss semi-automatic construction of multimedia ontologies and present ex-periments in which visual detector outputs are modified by simple rules that use context information available with the video.

1   Introduction

In the last few years many techniques have been developed to automatically analyze and index multimedia. Much of the work has focused on developing *visual detectors* that are either highly constrained within a specific domain or that use generic tech-niques that are often applied without domain-specific constraints. Typically objects (e.g., face, sky, etc.) or scenes (e.g., indoor, outdoor, etc.) are detected automatically.

In this paper, we investigate the use of context and domain knowledge within a reasoning framework for video understanding. First we define *video understanding* and propose a model that defines *context* specifically for automatic video analysis. Then we propose a novel framework for video understanding based on three main

E. M. Bakker et al. (Eds.): CIVR 2003, LNCS 2728, pp. 248-259, 2003.

components as illustrated in Figure 1: (1) inputs, (2) modal keywords and knowledge bases, and (3) reasoning engine.

An input video is first segmented into shots and aligned with speech from Automatic Speech Recognition (ASR) to obtain *Video Content Alignment (AVA)* units 0. Different visual detectors (e.g., sky, face, etc.) are applied to the video, and the text available with the video (e.g., metadata, ASR) is processed. From the related text we obtain *modal keywords* (using WordNet 0 and TGM I 0), which are keywords that represent perceptual concepts in a given modality. *Visual* keywords, for example, represent entities that can be visualized (e.g., visual: sky, car, face; non-visual: think, feel, etc.). Modal keywords can be used to filter (i.e., select only modal keywords) or expand any text (e.g., expand only modal keywords with synonyms). We explore how the processed text can be used to aid in the construction of ontologies (to build domain knowledge bases) or directly by the reasoning engine. The reasoning engine consists of a set of manually constructed rules. The rules modify the visual detector output confidence scores according to a set of context rules that determine, for the particular video shot being processed, how likely it is for the given objects (or scenes) to appear in the video. The context is given by the inputs (metadata, ASR, detector outputs) and domain-specific knowledge encoded in the rules.

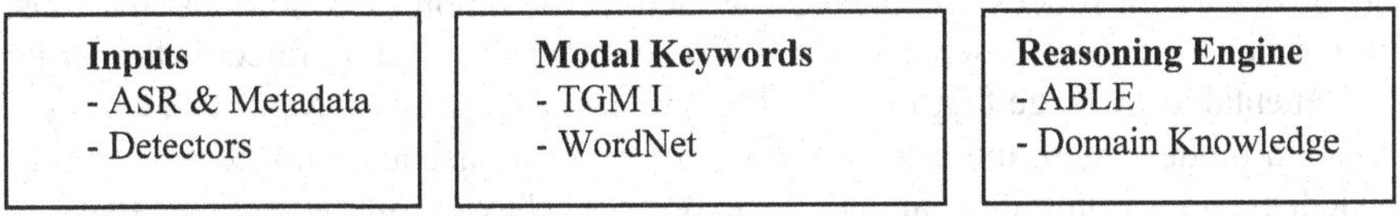

Inputs	**Modal Keywords**	**Reasoning Engine**
- ASR & Metadata	- TGM I	- ABLE
- Detectors	- WordNet	- Domain Knowledge

Figure 1. System overview of video understanding framework.

1.1 Related Work

Our concept of modal keywords is new, but some related research includes the following. In 0 keywords are obtained from documents and assigned to media (images, video, audio) according to several criteria such as distance from the keywords in the document to the media. In 0 a lexicon contains concepts and distances between concepts to determine the semantic distance between queries and documents in a database. In 0 the pronoun in a text query is detected and classified into various types. Pronouns are then interpreted based on nouns found in the query and a new query is generated using the nouns. In Symbol Grounding research 0 the goal is to assign non-symbolic representations to symbolic ones. In language grounding, for example, language is connected to referents in the language user's environment. In 0 textual descriptions of visual scenes are automatically learned and generated: words are assigned to visual elements. WordNet has been used widely in information retrieval for query and database expansion 0, and in the retrieval of images using caption information 00 among others.

Ontologies have been used for photo annotation 0, audio structuring and retrieval 0, and image organization, browsing and retrieval 00, among others. Construction is often entirely automatic 0, or entirely manual 0. Context has been used in fields such as psychology and robotics 0, in applications of aerial imagery 0, and in Information

Retrieval 0. It has also been treated for context sensitive perception with a focus on analogies between perceptual concepts 0, and in a probabilistic frameworks 0.

In the Informedia Project 0 audio, metadata, and video are combined in automatic video indexing, but there is no reasoning component. Other approaches 00, focus on automatically discovering relationships between text and visual features (or between concepts and visual attributes), but do not use domain-specific knowledge bases.

1.2   Outline

In section 2 we describe context, video understanding, and introduce modal keywords. In section 3 we describe our approach to construct multimedia ontologies. In section 4 we describe our reasoning engine and knowledge sources. In section 5 we present experimental results and we conclude in section 6.

2   Meaning and Context

Context, broadly defined, is the set of interrelated conditions in which something exists or occurs. In robotics, context is defined as the union of conditions that must hold in order for a step to be executed 0. Context has also been defined as the larger environmental knowledge that includes the laws of biology and physics and common sense— a model where there is a representation which accounts for common sense knowledge and assumptions about the expected behavior of the entities that are sought for 0. For purposes of automatic video indexing of visual content, we define context as follows 0.

- Context is the set of interrelated conditions in which visual entities (e.g., object, scenes) exist.

Contextual information can be provided at many levels by many different sources. Depending on the specific video, several types of information may be available (e.g., short summary, keywords, closed captions, text from automatic speech recognition, description in a program guide, etc.).

In our framework, the goal is to use any information available with the video to define a context for the visual entities that may appear (e.g., if the speech in a video mentions the word track, it is more likely for a train go appear in the scene).

2.1   Modal Keywords

In 00 a distinction was made between visual and non-visual concepts. We expand this idea by defining different categories of keywords to represent different types of *perceptual concepts*. The goal of such classification is to automatically select or expand only text that is directly related to the modality of interest. We argue that these distinctions will have a broad impact not only in automatic processing of multimedia documents, but also in future affective computing applications[1]. We classify concepts represented by keywords into the following *modal keyword* categories.

- *Visual:* visible entities or events (e.g., car, sky, house)
- *Aural:* audible entities or events (e.g., scream, yell, crash)
- *Tactile:* entities or events that can be touched (e.g., fabric, silk, water)
- *Olfactory:* entities or events that can be smelled (e.g., incense, perfume, vanilla)
- *Taste:* entities or events that can be tasted (e.g., candy, fruit, ice cream)

As the examples suggest, the categories are not mutually exclusive. Many objects can fall into several or all of the categories. The keyword apple represents a visual entity (the fruit) that can be touched, smelled, and tasted. An apple by itself cannot be heard, but we can hear an apple as it is being eaten, for example.

In order to automatically select keywords in the different categories, we use the WordNet lexical database 0. We exploit our knowledge of different types of entities and use the following WordNet synset categories, among others.

- *Visual keywords:* person, physical object, natural phenomenon, animal.
- Aural keywords: ear.
- *Tactile keywords:* touch, sensation, tactual sensation, tactile sensation, feeling.
- *Olfactory keywords:* smell, odor, odour, olfactory sensation, olfactory perception.
- *Taste keywords:* flavorer, flavourer, flavoring, flavouring, seasoner, seasoning.

We use WordNet to automatically filter text from ASR and from metadata descriptions to select only words in the desired category: only words whose WordNet "–hypernym" categories fall into the classes above are selected. WordNet is also used to expand textual documents (metadata, ASR and queries) with synonym words within the categories. It is possible to combine this approach to detect modal keywords with additional knowledge sources such as TGM I 0, a thesaurus of terms constructed to be used specifically for describing visual materials. From our input text (ASR, metadata) we select *only* those terms that are in TGM I and process those terms using WordNet as just described (not all natural phenomenon are visible, but those that are visible are included in TGM I).

Although filtering, expansion, and contraction approaches have been used in the past, these do not focus specifically on *modal keywords*. In retrieval of multi-modal documents, however, users are primarily interested in the non-textual content of such documents (e.g., sound, visual entities). The selection of modal keywords, therefore, has a significant advantage over existing techniques since it specifically extracts/expands the text that directly relates to the modal concepts of interest to users (e.g., objects, etc.).

Modal keywords can be used to build multimedia ontologies and to determine context. It is desirable, for example, to select from ASR text only those words (e.g., visual keywords) that relate directly to what is depicted in the video and to modify the confidence scores of visual detectors based on ASR text.

---

[1] Tactile, olfactory, and taste keywords relate strongly to future affective computing multimedia applications.

3   Multimedia Ontologies

An *ontology* is a formal, explicit specification of a domain. Typically, an ontology consists of *concepts*, concept *properties*, and *relationships* between concepts. In an ontology, concepts are represented by terms. In a *multimedia ontology* concepts, properties, and relationships might be represented by multimedia entities (images, graphics, video, audio 0) or terms.

Ontologies have applications in many areas including natural language translation, medicine, standardization of product knowledge, electronic commerce, and geographic information systems, among others 0. *Multimedia* ontology application areas include the following.

- *Content visualization:* table of contents and browsing.
- *Content indexing:* to improve indexing consistency in manual annotation systems 0 (e.g., *apartment* instead of *flat*), or in the propagation of labels in automatic indexing systems (e.g., *face* implies *person*).
- *Knowledge sharing:* annotated multimedia collections can be more easily shared if they use a common conceptual representation.
- *Machine Learning:* annotation consistency is necessary in approaches based on learning techniques that use training sets.
- *Reasoning:* information not explicit in the data may be obtained automatically with the use of ontologies.

In the data-driven approach described in 0, we semi-automatically construct a multimedia ontology using a video collection **V**. The ontology includes concepts **C**, their properties, and their relationships. For each of the videos we apply the following steps: (1) automatic scene cut detection, (2) automatic speech recognition, (3) parsing of metadata, and (4) automatic content analysis 0. Pre-processing consists of steps one through three, after which the ontology can be constructed based on textual content alone. Step four forms the basis for manually adding multimedia components to the ontology.

3.1   Pre-processing

Automatic scene cut detection is performed to break up the video into shots. For automatic speech recognition (ASR) we use the system described in 0, which yields a time stamped list of recognized words and silence tags. Alignment is then performed to assign text to specific video shots, which results in Audio Visual Alignment (AVA) units (a video is divided into coherent shots with corresponding speech transcripts). In addition, we parse metadata, if available with the videos, to extract the relevant information (e.g., movie titles).

3.2   Textual Content

We process the text (ASR, annotations, metadata) using standard text mining techniques implemented in KAON 00, a tool for semi-automatically building ontologies.

KAON was chosen because it integrates text mining techniques with an ontology management module. First, stop words are eliminated (e.g., *a, the, in, etc.*). Then, word stemming is performed (e.g., *going* replaced with *go*) to obtain *terms* and *compound terms* (e.g., social worker). For each term or compound term, the *frequency*, *TFIDF* (term frequency weighted by inverse document frequency), and *entropy* (logarithmic term frequency weighted by entropy of terms over the documents) scores are computed. Using this data we manually select relevant concepts. Terms with high TFIDF score, for example, might represent important ontology *concepts*. Once relevant concepts have been selected, relationships between them are discovered using KAON, which uses an algorithm for discovering generalized association rules. Relevant relationships are then manually selected for inclusion in the ontology. For example, relationships may be *hierarchical* (concept x is related to concept y) or of *property* (concept x is a property of concept y).

Modal keywords can be used to process the text automatically to facilitate the construction of multimedia ontologies of different modalities: visual, aural, olfactory, tactile, and taste. These ontologies can then be used for multimedia understanding using modality-specific knowledge.

3.3   Visual Content

As part of TREC 2002 00 we built a system that includes search on metadata, ASR, and annotations, as well as content-based search and clustering based on *syntax* (e.g., color, texture, etc.), and *semantics* (e.g., face, indoor, sky, music, monologue, etc.). We use this system to support the construction of multimedia ontologies (similar to 0). We start with the text tools described *and* using the TREC retrieval tool (unlike 00) we assign visual entities to textual *concepts*, *relationships*, or *properties* in the ontology and select visual entities as *concepts*, *relationships*, or *properties* in the ontology.

4   Reasoning About Knowledge

The Audio Visual Alignment (AVA) units, obtained from Automatic Speech Recognition, are passed along with visual detector outputs and any other information available with the video to the *Reasoning Module (RM)*, which consists of a set of rules, domain-specific knowledge bases, a working memory, and an inference engine.

In our current implementation domain knowledge consists mainly of context rules (e.g., to determine the types of visual information that can be expected from a certain type of video), where the confidence scores of visual detectors are changed depending on the video context. Although in our current implementation the components are not fully integrated yet, our main knowledge sources include WordNet, TGM I, and the ontologies we construct semi-automatically.

5   Experimental Results

We used 24 hours of video from *TREC 2002* 00. The videos consist of color and black and white educational films from the 1940s-1960s 0. Each of the videos was manually annotated[2] shot by shot using *VideoAnnex* 0, which allows users to label regions and scenes. For each of the videos we have the following data.

- *Annotations:* we generated a total of 22,815 annotations from 189 unique terms representing objects (face, people, etc.), scenes (indoors, outdoors, etc.), audio (music, speech, etc.), and audio-visual objects (e.g., monologue). These annotations applied to the entire key-frame associated with the shot (e.g., indoors), or to individual regions within the key-frame.
- *ASR:* speech recognition produced 391,945 terms for the videos in the collection, out of which only 11,234 were unique terms.
- *Metadata:* a short description for each film with fields such as producer, and title, and a short summary (e.g., *dramatization of important military events*). We obtained approximately 5,000 metadata terms.
- *Detectors:* features were extracted from each of the annotated examples and detectors were learned using machine learning algorithms (see 0).

We performed three different experiments using this dataset. First, we constructed ontologies using ASR, metadata, and annotations 0. Then we experimented with a simple rule that modifies visual detector outputs using ASR terms and their frequencies 0. Finally, we experimented with manually selected context-keywords to modify the confidence scores of visual detectors.

To create ontologies we manually selected relevant concepts by first examining frequent terms, and terms with the highest TFIDF score. Table 1 shows the TFIDF scores separately for each collection. In the ASR the most frequent words are people, time, way, day and life. For the metadata they are world, film, war, organization, and industry. For annotations they are person, people, sky, face, and building. In this experiment we found that although the individual scores are indicators of a particular term's importance, the selection cannot be made based on the scores alone and general knowledge is necessary in making the selection. The same results were obtained with the relationships, which are discovered using KAON 0.

Table 1. Terms with highest TFIDF score (T)

ASR	T	Metadata	T	Annotations	T
Prodigy	110	*Safety*	2.21	*Chicken*	6.37
Social worker	90	*Health*	2.0	*Bicycle*	6.37
Bike	77	*War*	1.8	*Cannon*	6.37
Golden Gate	73	*Industry*	1.7	*People dancing*	6.37
Cigarette	58	*Agriculture*	1.6	*Factory setting*	6.37

---

[2] The IBM TREC 2002 team implemented the IBM TREC system and annotated the content.

For the second set of experiments we tested a simple rule that adds the scores of visual detectors and detectors built using only text from ASR (using term frequencies). As described in 0, we were able to obtain improvements on the classification tasks (Figure 2).

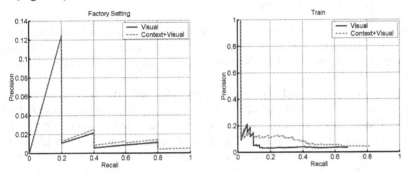

Fig. 2. Performance improvements of two visual detectors using a simple combination rule.

In a separate experiment we used context information from ASR text to enhance the performance of individual detectors. In particular, we compared the performance of individual visual detectors (animals, farm fields, sports events, and trains) constructed using only visual information against visual detectors whose confidence scores are modified by domain-specific rules that use the ASR text associated with each Audiovisual Alignment Units (section 4).

Individual detectors were built using a training set as described earlier (see also 0). For the visual+context detectors we modified the confidence scores of each visual detector as follows: (1) scores of visual detectors were rank-normalized; (2) a list of "context-keywords" was manually constructed for each detector using WordNet as a knowledge-source; (3) a rule was constructed for each detector which modifies the detector's confidence score if *context-keywords* appear in the ASR that corresponds to the specific AVA unit.

For the concept *train*, for example, some of these context-keywords include *railroad, train, rail, track,* and *freight.* The context-keywords were manually selected using WordNet as a knowledge base. The word train has several senses (e.g., the verb to train, train as in train of thought, etc.) which make a fully automatic process difficult. Currently, therefore, we combine the WordNet knowledge-base as a source of information and domain-specific knowledge input manually (i.e., the selection of the relevant context-keywords from the WordNet list of words related to the concept). Given a concept C, therefore, we construct a set of relevant context-keywords $CK=\{k_1, k_2, .., k_n\}$. For a given AVA unit we have an associated detection confidence score for a concept C, an associated text from ASR, and the set of context-keywords CK for the concept C. The score S(C) of the detector for concept C is modified using a window-based approach based on the ASR text as follows: let S'(C,U) reflect the modified confidence score using the context information for concept C and AVA unit U. First, we initialize these scores as: S'(C,U) = S(C,U). Then, we perform the following loops.

256   Alejandro Jaimes et al.

For each AVA unit u in U
  For each context-keyword k_i in CK=$\{k_1, k_2, .., k_n\}$
   For each ASR transcript t in the AVA unit u
    If (transcript t = context-keyword c_i) then
      S'(C,U-1) += 0.05; S'(C,U) += 0.3; S'(C,U+1) += 0.05;

Where 0.05 represents a 5% rank normalized score enhancement and 0.3 represents a 30% rank normalized score enhancement. These weights are determined heuristically and can be adopted to reflect the rare presence of the concept in the test collection (Figure 3).

The results in figures 2 and 3 are preliminary in the sense that only a few concepts were used, the rules are simple, and the ontologies constructed are not integrated with the rules. These results, however, suggest that the integration of knowledge sources (e.g., WordNet), domain-knowledge (i.e., manual selection) and context (ASR) can lead to visual detection improvements. Although the modal keywords were not explicitly used in these experiments, the context-keywords are all visual keywords, so a visual keyword filter could have been used.

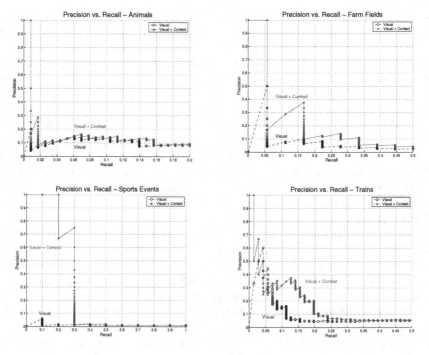

Fig. 3. Performance using visual detectors and visual+context detectors.

6   Conclusions and Future Work

We proposed a novel framework for video content understanding that uses rules constructed from knowledge bases and ontologies. Our framework consists of an expert system that uses a rule-based engine, domain knowledge, visual detectors (for objects and scenes), and metadata (text from automatic speech recognition, related text, etc.). We introduced *modal keywords,* which are keywords that represent *perceptual concepts* in the following categories: *visual* (e.g., sky), *aural* (e.g., scream), *olfactory* (e.g., vanilla), *tactile* (e.g., feather), and *taste* (e.g., candy). A method is presented to automatically classify keywords from speech recognition, queries, or related text into these categories using WordNet. For content understanding our system receives as input a video and the following operations are performed automatically: scene cut detection, automatic speech recognition, feature extraction, and visual detection (e.g., sky, face, indoor). These operation results are used in by a rule-based engine that uses context information (e.g., text from speech) to enhance visual detection results. We explored the construction of multimedia ontologies to be used in a reasoning framework and presented experiments in improving the output of visual detectors using context information.

Our future work includes more experiments to explore different detector combination strategies within our framework using ABLE [250] and domain-specific knowledge sources (ABLE is a reasoning environment that includes several inference engines and a language for the construction of rules); research into the systematic construction of domain-specific rules from training data; experiments involving modal keywords; and further integration of the components we have described.

The authors would like to thank the IBM TREC 2002 team for their valuable contributions.

References

[1]   Y.A. Aslandogan, et al. "Using semantic contents and WordNet in image retrieval," *ACM SIGIR Conference on Research and Development in Information Retrieval,* Philadelphia, 1997

[2]   Baldonado, M., Chang, C.-C.K., Gravano, L., Paepcke, A., "The Stanford Digital Library Metadata Architecture," *Int. J. Digit. Libraries 1,* pp. 108–121, 1997

[3]   B. Adams, A. Amir, C. Dorai, S. Ghoshal, G. Iyengar, A. Jaimes, C. Lang, C. Lin, A. Natsev, M. Naphade, C. Neti, H. Permuter, R. Singh, J. Smith, S. Srinivasan, B. Tseng, T. Ashwin, D. Zhang, "IBM Research TREC 2002 Video Retrieval System," in *proceedings NIST TREC 2002,* Nov., 2002

[4]   K. Barnard and D.A. Forsyth, "Learning the semantics of words and pictures", in*Proc. IEEE International Conference on Computer Vision,* pp. 408-415, July, 2001

[5]   A.B. Benitez, J.R. Smith, and S.-F. Chang, "MediaNet: A Multimedia Information Network for Knowledge Representation," IS&T/SPIE-2000, Vol. 4210, Boston, MA, Nov. 2000

[6]   B. Benitez and S.-F. "Chang, Semantic Knowledge Construction from Annotated Image Collections," *Proc. IEEE ICME-2002*, Lausanne, Switzerland, Aug 26-29, 2002

[7]   Bhandari, et al. "Computer program product and method for using natural language for the description, search, and retrieval of multi-media objects," U.S.Pat. 5,895,464, April 1999

[8]   Bosco et al. "Context and Multimedia Corpora," *Context '01, 3rd International and Interdisciplinary Conference on Modeling and Using Context*, Dundee, Scotland, July 2001

[9]   M. Dastani et al., "Modeling Context Effect in Perceptual Domains," *3rd International and Interdisciplinary Conference on Modeling and Using Context*, Dundee, Scotland, July 2001

[10] M.J. Denber, "Computer program product for retrieving multi-media objects using natural language having a pronoun," U.S. Patent 6,233,547, May 2001

[11] N. Dimitrova, *Expert Panel Statement*, in Borko Furht and Oge Marques eds *Handbook of Video Databases*, CRC Press, March 2003 (to appear)

[12] J. Durkin, *Expert Systems: Design and Development*, Prentice Hall, Englewood Cliffs, NJ, 1994

[13] E.j. Guglielmo, et al., ``Natural-language retrieval of images based on descriptive captions," *ACM Transactions on Information Systems* 14 (3), pp. 237 – 267, July 1996

[14] N. Guarino, "Formal Ontology and Information Systems," in *proc. FOIS '98*, Trento, Italy, July 1998

[15] S. Harnad, "The Symbol Grounding Problem," Physica D 42: 335-346, 1990

[16] Jaimes and J.R.Smith, "Semi-automatic, Data-Driven Construction of Multimedia Ontologies," ICME 2003, Baltimore, MD, 2003

[17] Jaimes. Conceptual Structures and Techniques for Indexing and Organization of Visual Information. Ph.D. thesis, Electrical Engineering Department, Columbia U., February 2003

[18] Jaimes, M. Naphade, H. Nock, J.R. Smith, and B.L. Tseng, "Context Enhanced Video Understanding," *SPIE Storage and Media Databases 2003*, Santa Clara, CA, January 2003

[19] IBM Alphaworks (Video Annex and ABLE: *http://www.alphaworks.ibm.com*)

[20] Informedia project (http://www.informedia.cs.cmu.edu)

[21] Internet Movie Archive (http://www.moviearchive.org)

[22] L. Khan and D. McLeod, "Audio Structuring and Personalzied Retrieval Using Ontologies," in *proc. IEEE Advances in Digital Libraries (ADL 2000)*, Washington, DC, May 2000

[23] Library of Congress Thesaurus for Graphic Materials I (TGM I), 1995. (*http://www.loc.gov/rr/print/tgm1/*)

[24] Maedche, et al., "Seal- tying up information integration and web site management by ontologies," *IEEE Data Engineering Bulletin*, Vol. 25, March 2002

[25] Miller, George A. ``WordNet: a lexical database for English." In: *Communications of the ACM* 38 (11), November 1995, pp. 39 – 41

[26] S. Mukherjea et al. "Method and Aparathus for assigning keywords to objects," U.S. Patent 6,317,740, Nov., 2001

[27] E.d.S. Moreira , "Embedded Video Content and Context Awareness," Proceedings of the CHI 2000 Workshop on "The What, Who, Where, When, Why and How of Context-Awareness," The Hague, Netherlands, 2000

[28] M. McKeown, et al., "Ruled-based interpretation of aerial imagery," *IEEE Transactions on Pattern Analysis and Machine Intelligence*, Vol. 7, No.5, pp. 570--585, 1985

[29] M. Naphade, I.V. Kozintsev, and T.S. Huang, "Factor graph framework for semantic video indexing, " *IEEE Transactions on Circuits and Systems for Video Technology,* Vol. 12 No. 1, pp. 40 -52, Jan. 2002

[30] Natsev, M. Naphade, and J.R. Smith, "Exploring Semantic Dependencies for Scalable Concept Detection," *IEEE ICIP 2003*, Barcelona, Spain, October 2003

[31] N.C. Rowe, "Marie-4: A High-Recall, Self-Improving Web Crawler That Finds Images Using Captions," *IEEE Intelligent Systems*, July/August, 2002

[32] D.K. Roy, "Learning Visually-Grounded Words and Syntax for a Scene Description Task," *submitted to Computer Speech and Language*, 2002

[33] A.F. Smeaton, and I. Quigley, ``Experiments on using semantic distances between words in image caption retrieval," In *Proceedings of the 19th Annual International Conference on Research and Development in Information Retrieval*, pp. 174 – 180, Zürich, 1996

[34] A.Th. Schreiber, et al., "Ontology-Based Photo Annotation," *IEEE Intelligent Systems*, May-June 2001

[35] http://www.semanticweb.org

[36] N. Shiotani and S. Miyamoto, "Image Retrieval System Using an Iconic Thesaurus," in Proc. *IEEE Int. Conf. On Intelligent Processing Systems*, Oct. 1997

[37] S. Russell and P. Norvig, *Artificial Intelligence: A Modern Approach*, Prentice Hall, Englewood Cliffs, N.J., 1995

[38] G. Salton and M. J. McGill. *Introduction to Modern Information Retrieval*, McGraw Hill Computer Science Series, New York, 1983

[39] R. Tansley, "The Multimedia Thesaurus: An Aid for Multimedia Retrieval and Navigation," Master Thesis, Computer Science, University of Southhampton, UK, 1998

[40] TREC Video Retrieval Track (http://www-nlpir.nist.gov/projects/trecvid/)

[41] B.L. Tseng, C. Lin, M. Naphade, A. Natsev, J.R. Smith, "Normalized Classifier Fusion for Semantic Visual Detection," IEEE International Conference on Image Processing, 2003

[42] J. Yang, et al., "Thesaurus-Aided Approach for Image Browsing and Retreival," in *proc. IEEE ICME 2001*, pp. 313-316, Tokyo, Japan, Aug. 2001

[43] Weissman., et al. "Meaning-based information organization and retrieval," United States Patent 6,453,315, Sept. 2002

Detecting Semantic Concepts from Video Using Temporal Gradients and Audio Classification

Mika Rautiainen[1], Tapio Seppänen[1], Jani Penttilä[2], and Johannes Peltola[2]

[1] MediaTeam Oulu,
P.O.BOX 4500, FIN-90014 University of Oulu, Finland
{firstname.lastname@ee.oulu.fi}
http://www.mediateam.oulu.fi
[2] VTT Technical Research Centre of Finland,
P.O. Box 1100, Kaitoväylä 1, FIN-90571 Oulu, Finland
{firstname.lastname@vtt.fi}

Abstract. In this paper we describe new methods to detect semantic concepts from digital video based on audible and visual content. Temporal Gradient Correlogram captures temporal correlations of gradient edge directions from sampled shot frames. Power-related physical features are extracted from short audio samples in video shots. Video shots containing people, cityscape, landscape, speech or instrumental sound are detected with trained self-organized maps and kNN classification results of audio samples. Test runs and evaluations in TREC 2002 Video Track show consistent performance for Temporal Gradient Correlogram and state-of-the-art precision in audio-based instrumental sound detection.

1 Introduction

In the last decade, content-based indexing methods for multimedia documents have been studied widely to obtain new tools for access and retrieval. Research work is motivated by a growing amount of digital multimedia content, most notably the distributed content in the Internet. Prototype retrieval systems have been developed around the world, and even commercialized. [1][2][3][4][5]

The tools for semantic retrieval are mainly relying on lexical information extracted from the video. The most successful search systems are based on automatic speech recognition transcripts (ASR), video optical character recognition (video-OCR) and manually annotated meta-information. However, visual and audible data conveys a lot of adjunct information that could also be utilized in the search, if the algorithms were competent enough. The detection and recognition of every visual and audible object would give profound settings for searching. It is, however, very complicated to construct generally applicable object detection for video retrieval; it would be more reasonable to start with detection of simpler conceptual objects. For example, detecting the presence or absence of people, or scene settings, such as indoor/outdoor locations,

E. M. Bakker et al. (Eds.): CIVR 2003, LNCS 2728, pp. 260-270, 2003.

would provide value-added content-based attributes for the query definition. Semantic concept vocabulary could expand classic content-based example queries that are traditionally based solely on computations of low-level feature similarities.

Naphade *et al.* [6] have proposed a framework of probabilistic multimedia objects for modeling audiovisual semantics and demonstrated it with *sky, water, forest, rocks* and *snow* concepts [7]. Chang *et al.* [8] presented semantic visual templates using examples of *sunsets* and *high-jumpers* concepts. Del Bimbo [9] has introduced detection scheme of four semiotic classes: *practical, playful, utopic* and *critical,* measuring expressiveness of commercial videos and utilized them in retrieval of advertisement videos. IBM has developed statistical models for over ten concepts [10] for their Video TREC retrieval system. Their models are categorized into events (*launch* etc.), scenes (*greenery* etc.) and objects (*vehicle* etc.).

In this paper we present our simple, yet powerful approaches to detect audio and visual semantics from video data. We evaluated the performance of our approaches in TREC-2002 Video Track semantic feature detection task, where we tested our methods with a subset from ten semantic features that video systems from around the world endeavoured to detect [11]. The concepts that we tested our approaches with were *people, cityscape, landscape, speech* and *instrumental sound..* Section 2 describes the methodologies. Section 3 describes the experiments in TREC-2002 evaluation. Finally, Section 4 summarizes the results with conclusions.

2   Detecting Semantic Concept Features

In this section we introduce two methods to train detection of semantic concepts from video shots. The motivation for this work arose from the earlier research we have made in the fields of audio and video analysis [16][20]. Derived from the previous work, our two approaches diverge based on the modality containing the principal semantic information of the concept in question. The two approaches for video and audio based detection are respectively: 1) self-organizing maps with a feature capturing video shot's temporal correlations of gradient edges and 2) kNN-based audio sample classification scheme.

2.1   Detecting People, Cityscape and Landscape

We have developed a straightforward way to utilize visual features in detection of people, cityscape and landscape concepts from video shots. Our method is based on video frame edge properties and pre-trained self-organizing maps (SOMs). It operates by creating confidence values for video shots based on their organization in SOM. The greatest challenge in semantics detection is robustness over varying video quality. Heterogeneous video data from multiple sources has ranging color and illumination, which will often degenerate detection output. A well-known approach to classify city and landscape images is to use edge direction features [12]. They are based on discrimination between natural and non-natural structures using either the coherency of edge directions (Edge Direction Coherence Vectors) or statistical edge probabilities (edge direction histograms). For example, objects such as buildings cumulate edge histograms in horizontal and vertical orientations whereas natural views may have a more evenly distributed histogram of different orientations.

The use of gradients adopts functionality of the human visual system (HVS), in which antagonist retinal receptive fields excite impulses to achromatic neural channels from stimuli caused by spatial lightness contrasts, such as object edges or texture patterns. The opponent neurons with center-surround receptive fields in HVS are also assumed to gather information about chromaticity contrasts of opponent colors [18]. This would indicate that chromaticity edge histograms could also be meaningful in recognition and detection. However, a recent study [19] in color texture classification shows that the discriminatory power of color information degrades greatly in differing illumination conditions. Mäenpää et al. found that even with the chromatic normalization, luminance information was still found to be more discriminative than color under varying illumination (e.g. having changing color or geometry). This condition is very likely to occur in heterogeneous video databases with mixed data quality. Therefore it would be more justifiable to prefer other than chromatic properties in semantic concept detection from largely varying video data. Edge direction histograms are based on relative instead of absolute luminance differences and are therefore less affected by overall changes in illumination levels. While color cannot heuristically be considered as a significant cue for categorizing landscape and cityscape scenes, it could be a factor in detection of people. The use of gradient-based concept detector is intuitive for tasks where semantics are profoundly in the gestalt of the global visual structure, therefore usable in detecting images about cityscapes, landscapes and large people groups, for example.

Temporal Gradient Correlogram. Temporal Gradient Correlogram (TGC) is computed from local correlations of specific edge orientations as an autocorrelogram, whose elements correspond to probabilities of fixed edge directions to occur at particular spatial distances during a video frame sequence. The feature is computed from 20 video frames sampled evenly over the duration of a video shot. Temporality has been argued to contain important properties for content-based retrieval [20]. Due to temporal sampling, TGC autocorrelogram, denoted as TGC, is able to capture also temporal probabilities in spatial edge orientations. From each sample frame, the edge orientations are quantized into four segments depending on their orientation being horizontal, vertical or either of the diagonal directions. The TGC feature is thus computing higher-order texture statistics similar to a well-known Gray Level Cooccurrence Matrix [21]. However, TGC is less dependent on overall luminance levels since the correlation is computed from gradient edge directions instead of the quantized luminance values as Haralick et al. have proposed.

First, the gradient image frames are extracted from the sampled video shot using Prewitt edge detection kernels [22]. Prior to computation of an autocorrelogram the gradients of each pixel with an average magnitude exceeding a pre-defined threshold T are used to compute quantized direction image D. Empirically, T is set 12 in our experiments. Each $D(x,y)$ contains integer values from 0 to 4. Value 0 indicates that the gradients do not exceed the threshold T. Values 1 to 4 represent orientations of horizontal, vertical and two diagonal lines with steps of $\pi/4$.

Finally, the TGC is computed for each shot from every obtained direction image. Let N be the number of sample frames D^n taken from a shot S. In our experiments,

N is set to 20. The value of n varies from 1 to N providing an index in the sample frame sequence. The temporal gradient correlogram is computed as

$$\overline{\gamma}_{c_i,c_j}^{(d)}(S) \equiv \Pr_{p_1 \in D_{c_i}^n, p_2 \in D^n} \left[p_2 \in D_{c_j}^n \middle| |p_1 - p_2| = d \right] \tag{1}$$

which gives the probability that given any pixel p_1 of direction value c_i, a pixel p_2 at a distance d from the given pixel p_1 is of direction c_j among the shot's sample frames D^n. Following the experiments with color correlograms [20], we have defined $i=j$ with spatial pixel distances $d=\{1,3,5,7\}$ measured with L_∞ norm. To measure the differences between different TGC vectors, we have used Minkowski norm L_1, which has been used successfully in content-based retrieval with color correlograms [20,23].

Skin Descriptor. In an attempt to make the feature vector more discriminative to detect people, we detected skin-colored local regions and generated a four-valued vector describing the relative size and structure of consistent skin areas in a video shot frame. The structure of our descriptor adopted some interesting properties of Motion Activity Descriptor from MPEG-7 standard [24], such as the ability to indirectly express the number, size, and shape of active regions in the frame.

To detect skin-colored regions, we trained a self-organizing map based on localized HSV color histogram feature, named HSV Sector Histogram. This histogram is localized on regions that appear in images containing skin. The HSV color space is first quantized into 540 bins: 30 for H, 6 for S and 3 for V channel. The starting offset for the bins in H channel is rotated $-2\pi/60$ degrees to fit color hues better into uniform clusters. 60-bin sector histogram is empirically constructed from representative skin colors with the following ranges of hue, saturation and value

$$h > H_{max} - \frac{H_{max}}{60}$$

$$h \le \frac{6 * H_{max}}{30} - \frac{H_{max}}{60}$$

$$\frac{S_{max}}{6} < s \le S_{max} \tag{2}$$

$$\frac{V_{max}}{3} < v \le V_{max}$$

where   h,s and v   are values of hue, saturation and value
H_{max}, S_{max} and V_{max} are maximum values for hue, saturation and value

A hexagonal SOM with 30x27 nodes was initialized and trained with sample HSV Sector Histograms extracted from 10x10 image regions of 82 images containing people in different environments. After training, the map nodes were labeled using manually marked skin areas from 40 key frames that were selected from sample video shots. The labeling procedure marked 'skin' nodes by finding the best matching nodes for the sample histograms of manually marked skin blocks. The trained and labeled map was then used to detect 10x10 skin regions from every shot's key frame in the database. The detected 10x10 regions were used to create the final four-parameter feature vector.

Skin descriptor vector was constructed of four values that were extracted from detected skin blocks in a shot key frame. The first value was *relative amount* of skin, which was a simple discrete value between 1 and 5 describing the ratio of skin-colored blocks to the total number of blocks. Next values indicated the number of *long*, *medium* and *short zero runs* (adjacent non-skin blocks) between skin-colored local regions measuring the uniformity of skin structured areas.

The relative amount was determined using the following rules:

$$R = \begin{cases} 1 & , if\ s < 0.08 \\ 2 & , if\ 0.08 \le s < 0.16 \\ 3 & , if\ 0.16 \le s < 0.24 \\ 4 & , if\ 0.24 \le s < 0.32 \\ 5 & , if\ s \ge 0.32 \end{cases} \tag{3}$$

where R is the quantized relative amount of skin,
              s is the proportional amount of skin blocks in a key frame

The number of long, medium and short zero runs were determined by the number of adjacent non-skin blocks in the rows of raster-scanned image. If the length of a consistent run exceeded 2/3 of the total width of the frame, it was recognized as a long run, and if the size was between 1/3 and 2/3, it was counted as a medium run. Finally, runs less than 1/3 of frame width were considered to be short runs.

Due to the degraded quality of color information in the test videos, the prognosis for the success of the skin detector was initially set low. However, an optimistic assumption was made that the detected skin regions would assist the edge features at least in the detection of people. Therefore the feature values were concatenated with the TGC feature vector in our secondary test run.

Training by Propagating Small Example Sets. To find the shots containing a certain semantic concept, we selected sets of example shots from the collection of videos that were separated from the test data for training purposes. A total of 13 example shots were selected for people ($K=13$), and 10 for both cityscape and landscape ($K=10$). The TGC and TGC+SKIN feature vectors were computed from the example shots and used in retrieval of shots in the Feature Test Collection. Our test system consisted of two SOMs that were generated using TGC and concatenated TGC+SKIN features. To find the shots with the largest confidence for a concept, we used all the selected example shots to locate sets of best matching units from SOM. Therefore the procedure of detecting concepts was practically a propagation of concept labels to the closest neighbor nodes and samples within. From these nodes, the closest shots for each example were selected using the shortest L_1 distances. All distance values in result set R_k were scaled with the greatest distance in the set. After this, the sets of results ($R_1,...,R_K$) were combined with fuzzy Boolean *OR* operation to form the final ranked result set with 600 result shots. Ranking of the final result set based on minimum of $1...K$ distance values assigned for each S. The following formulas describe the combination procedure:

$$S_n = min(\frac{D_1}{D_{1max}},...,\frac{D_K}{D_{Kmax}})$$ (4)

$$R_{combined} = \{S_1,...,S_{600}\}$$ (5)

where S_n =   minimum distance of a result shot to the examples $1...K$

D_k =   distance to the query example k, ∞ if S is not contained in a result set R_k

D_{kmax} =   maximum distance to the query example k in its result set R_k

$R_{combined}$ =   Combined and ranked final set of results

2.2   Detecting Speech and Instumental Sound

The classification of audio signal between speech and music is a widely studied problem [13][14][15]. Our approach is based on kNN classification as described by Penttilä *et al.* in [16].

The classification between speech and music was computationally very inexpensive using only four power-related features. A 3-second window of the signal was divided into 50 ms frames overlapping by 10 ms, and the power inside every frame was computed. The four features used were the variance of the frame-by-frame power, and the variance of the first and the second order differentials of the power, and finally, low energy ratio [17], which was computed as the proportion of 50ms frames with RMS power less than a fixed threshold of the mean RMS power. Other speech related features, such as spectral pitch and harmonic content, were omitted for efficiency reasons. A 20% threshold for low energy ratio gave the best results with independent training material, and the spread of the four features was increased by log transformations. In training, the features were normalized to zero-average and unit standard deviation. The translation and scaling parameters for each feature were used in classification to normalize the test signal.

The classification of samples was performed using kNN with k set to 3. The final classification results of 3-second segments were presented as low-pass filtered time series. Low-pass filtering reduced the effect of single classification errors and smoothed the transition points between longer segments of speech and music. In addition, mixed signals (containing both speech and music) that would produce a fluctuating series of classification results with a traditional binary decision classifier are now presented as 'gray' areas that belong to both classes. The new trail of annotation labels shows the degree of certainty of belonging to either class for each three-second audio segment at a time. The numerical results were scaled between 0 and 1, and the weighted mean of the classifications inside each shot was used as the confidence measure for instrumental sound detection. The confidence for speech detection was determined as such that the sum of these values was always 1.

The training database was assembled from a vast assortment of CD's and digitally recorded speech samples from Finnish radio broadcasts. The sample format was 22050 Hz mono with 15-second sample length. The database contained conversations and single speaker sections using several speakers from both sexes. Also music from various styles and genres was included. The database contained about 20 min of speech and 40 min of music.

The confidence value for a shot to contain speech or music was derived from the weighted average of speech/music classification results of 3-second segments. 1000 most confident shots were evaluated in the experiments. The performance was measured using precision computed from the result set.

3   Experiments in TREC 2002 Video Track

TREC 2002 Video Track, organized by the National Institute of Standards and Technology, was the second organized video benchmark focusing on content-based video retrieval using open, metrics-based evaluation [11]. TREC 2002 Video Track evaluated systems in shot boundary detection, semantic feature (concept) detection, manual search and interactive search tasks. Our full participation in the event is reported in [25], the experiments with semantic feature detection are described in detail here.

3.1   Experimental Setup

The video database contained 68.5 hours of rather old video material from Open Video Project [26] and Internet Archive [27]. The videos were from the 1930's to 1960's with large variations in audio and color quality. The video data was split into Search Test (40.12 hrs), Feature Development (23.26 hrs) and Feature Test Collections (5.07 hrs).

The task of detecting semantic features was to give a list of at most 1000 video shots ranked according to the highest possibility of detecting the presence of the feature. A standard set of shot boundaries and a list of semantic feature definitions were given to the participants. Each feature was assumed to be binary, i.e. it is either present or absent in the video shot. Feature Development Collection provided videos to train the detection systems, whereas the actual test runs were committed in Feature Test Collection. The categories we experimented were *People*, *Cityscape*, *Landscape*, *Speech* and *Instrumental Sound*. [11]

3.2   Results

In the evaluation, NIST used pooling of submitted results that simplifies the process with minor effects on results [27]. Feature Test Collection was used in the experiments. NIST provided the segmentation of video shots: over 1800 shots for the Feature Test and over 7800 for the Feature Development Collection.

TREC 2002 Video Track evaluation uses average precision and precision in standard recall points as a performance measure [27]. Average precision is a single-valued measure reflecting the performance over all relevant documents. It is the average of the precisions after each relevant document is retrieved. A relevant document that is not in the result set is assumed to have a precision of 0.

Table 1. Average precisions of TGC, TGC+SKIN and AUDIO for semantic concept runs. Best, worst and median results of all participating runs are shown for each category

Categ.	max	median	min	TGC	TGC+SKIN	AUDIO
People	0.274	0.071	0.008	0.248	0.168	-
Cityscape	0.374	0.299	0.036	0.299	0.197	-
Landscape	0.198	0.190	0.128	0.193	0.128	-
Speech	0.721	0.649	0.570	-	-	0.645
Instr.sound	0.637	0.475	0.057	-	-	0.637

The average precisions are shown in Table 1. Also the best, median and worst results of all participating systems are presented.

The results show that TGC was most efficient in detecting cityscapes, which may be a result of structured edges dominant in typical cityscape scenes. The poorly performing skin feature was degrading the results even in the people category, unveiling the futility of color in low-saturated videos. Overall, the TGC-based concept detection had consistent median or above-median performance among all participating systems in TREC 2002 Video Track. The detection of speech and instrumental sound from audio signal had a mean precision of 0.641, being higher than the mean precision of 0.246 in people, city and landscape categories. The detection of instrumental sound was state-of-the-art. Table 2 shows the amount of shots with overlapping concepts in TREC experiment ground truth data. Diagonal cells show the total of shots containing a certain feature. Table indicates that nearly half of the people shots were located in urban setting. 39 shots were considered to have both city and landscape view, which was caused either by slow camera transitions between urban and natural areas or by failure to detect a shot boundary between sequential camera runs. The amount of overlap is even larger with audio concepts.

Table 2. Number of shots in the ground truth data with one or two concepts. Visual and audio.

Concept	People	Cityscape	Landscape	Concept	Speech	Music
People	486	223	33	Speech	1382	977
Cityscape	223	521	39	Music	977	1221
Landscape	33	39	127			

4   Summary and Conclusions

Temporal Gradient Correlogram captures the structural properties of video shot segments in a way that is appropriate for varying color and illumination quality. A simple training of semantic concepts using self-organizing maps was presented and its efficiency was demonstrated in a five-hour test video collection. The performance was consistently above or equal to median in TREC 2002 Video Track evaluation. TGC had problems with shots resulting from the failed shot change detection. Such shots consisted of two or more separate camera runs having very different contexts, which confused the computation of gradient correlations over the time sequence. The shots with large motion resulted in blurred image samples, which affected the computation of gradients. However, if the image edge details were visible in at least one sample, TGC algorithm was able to successfully capture the correlations of gradient directions from that single instance. This interesting fact should be investigated further in future research together with comprehensive testing of TGC against other state-of-the-art visual features [29].

Speech and instrumental sound detection was based on classification of short temporal sound samples using power-related features. It proved to be effective among videos with only adequate sound quality. Based on TREC 2002 Video Track evaluation, the performance was state-of-the-art in detection of shots with instrumental sound.

The semantic concept detection was tested with video data having remarkably heterogeneous content and quality. The early developments of video technology during the 20th century was clearly visible in the data and provided the most challenging environment for video content algorithms; the results indicate this aspect clearly.

Acknowledgement

We like to thank the National Technology Agency of Finland (Tekes) and the Academy of Finland for supporting this research.

References

[1]   IBM CueVideo Toolkit. http://www.almaden.ibm.com/projects/cuevideo.shtml (27.2.2003)
[2]   Informedia. http://www.informedia.cs.cmu.edu/ (27.2.2003)
[3]   Flickner, M., Sawhney, H., Niblack, W., Ashley, J., Huang, Q., Dom, B., Gorkani, M., Hafner, J., Lee, D., Petkovic D., Steele, D., and, Yanker, P.: Query by image and video content: The QBIC system. In IEEE Computer Magazine 28, (1995) 23-32
[4]   Smeaton, A: Browsing digital video in the Físchlár system. Keynote presentation at Infotech Oulu International Workshop on Information Retrieval, Oulu, Finland (2001)
[5]   Virage, Inc. http://www.virage.com/ (27.2.2003)
[6]   Naphade, M.R., Kristjansson, T., Frey, B., Huang, T.S.: Probabilistic multimedia objects (multijects): a novel approach to video indexing and retrieval in multimedia systems. In proceedings of International Conference on Image Processing, vol. 3. (1998) 536 -540
[7]   Naphade, M.R., Huang, T.S.: Semantic video indexing using a probabilistic framework. In proceedings of 15th International Conference on Pattern Recognition, Vol. 3. (2000) 79 -84
[8]   Chang S.F., Chen W., Sundaram H.: Semantic visual templates – linking features to semantics. In Proceedings of IEEE International Conference on Image Processing, vol. 3. (1998) 531-535

[9]   Del Bimbo, A.: Expressive semantics for automatic annotation and retrieval of video streams. IEEE International Conference on Multimedia and Expo, Vol.2. (2000) 671 -674

[10] Naphade, M.R., Basu, S., Smith, J.R., Ching-Yung Lin, Tseng, B.: A statistical modeling approach to content based video retrieval. Proceedings of 16th International Conference on Pattern Recognition, Vol.2. (2002) 953 -956

[11] TREC Video Retrieval Evaluation. http://www-nlpir.nist.gov/projects/trecvid/ (27.2.2003)

[12] Vailaya, A., Jain, A., Hong Jiang Zhang: On image classification: city vs. landscape. Proceedings of IEEE Workshop on Content-Based Access of Image and Video Libraries. (1998) 3-8

[13] Carey M., Parris E., Lloyd-Thomas H.: A comparison of features for speech, music discrimination. Proc. ICASSP (1999)

[14] Hoyt J. & Wechsler H.: Detection of human speech in structured noise. Proc. ICASSP (1994)

[15] Saunders J.: Real-time discrimination of broadcast speech/music. Proc. ICASSP (1996)

[16] Penttilä J., Peltola J., Seppänen T.: A speech/music discriminator-based audio browser with a degree of certainty measure. Proceedings of Infotech Oulu International Workshop on Information Retrieval, Oulu, Finland, (2001) 125-131

[17] Scheirer E., Slaney M.: Construction and evaluation of a robust multifeature speech/music discriminator. Proc. ICASSP (1997)

[18] DeValois, R.L., DeValois K.K.: Neural coding of color. In E.C.Carterette and M.P.Friedman (eds.) Handbook of perception, vol. 5. New YorK: Academic press (1975) 117-166

[19] Mäenpää T., Pietikäinen M. & Viertola J.: Separating color and pattern information for color texture discrimination. Proceedings of 16th International Conference on Pattern Recognition, vol. 1. Quebec City, Canada (2002) 668-671

[20] Rautiainen M., Doermann D.: Temporal color correlograms for video retrieval. Proceedings of 16th International Conference on Pattern Recognition, Quebec City, Canada (2002)

[21] Haralick, R., Shanmugam, K., Dinstein, I.: Textural features for image classification, IEEE Transactions on Systems, Man and Cybernetics, vol. 3. (1973) 610-621

[22] Prewitt, J.M.S.: Object enhancement and extraction. In B.S.Lipkin and A. Rosenfeld, (eds) Picture Processing and Psychopictorics, Academic Press, New York (1970)

[23] Huang, J., Kumar, S.R., Mitra, M., Zhu W.J.: Image indexing using color correlograms. Proceedings of IEEE Computer Society Conference on Computer Vision and Pattern Recognition, San Juan, Puerto Rico (1997) 762-768

[24] Manjunath, B.S., Salembier, P., Sikora, T.: Introduction to MPEG-7: Multimedia Content Description Language. Wiley, John & Sons, Inc. (2002)

[25] Rautiainen, M., Penttilä, J., Vorobiev, D., Noponen, K., Väyrynen, P., Hosio, M., Matinmikko, E., Mäkelä, S.M., Peltola, J., Ojala, T., Seppänen, T.: TREC 2002 Video Track experiments at MediaTeam Oulu and VTT. Text Retrieval Conference TREC 2002 Video Track, Gaithersburg, MD (2002)

[26] Open Video Project. http://www.open-video.org/ (27.2.2003)
[27] Internet Archive Home Page. http://webdev.archive.org/movies/movies.php (27.2.2003)
[28] Voorhees, E.M.: Overview of TREC 2001. Proceedings of the Tenth Text REtrieval Conference TREC-10 (2001)
[29] Smeulders, A.W.M., Worring, M., Santini, S., Gupta, A., Jain, R.: Content-based image retrieval at the end of the early years. IEEE Transactions on Pattern Analysis and Machine Intelligence, Vol. 22., Issue 12 (2000) 1349 -1380

Text or Pictures? An Eyetracking Study
of How People View Digital Video Surrogates

Anthony Hughes, Todd Wilkens, Barbara M. Wildemuth, and Gary Marchionini

Interaction Design Lab, School of Information and Library Science
University of North Carolina at Chapel Hill
Chapel Hill, NC 27599-3360
Phone: (919)962-8366; Fax: (919)962-8071
ahughes@unc.edu, tpodd@email.unc.edu,
{wildem,march}@ils.unc.edu

Abstract. One important user-oriented facet of digital video retrieval research involves how to abstract and display digital video surrogates. This study reports on an investigation of digital video results pages that use textual and visual surrogates. Twelve subjects selected relevant video records from results lists containing titles, descriptions, and three keyframes for ten different search tasks. All subjects were eye-tracked to determine where, when, and how long they looked at text and image surrogates. Participants looked at and fixated on titles and descriptions statistically reliably more than on the images. Most people used the text as an anchor from which to make judgments about the search results and the images as confirmatory evidence for their selections. No differences were found whether the layout presented text or images in left to right order.

1 Introduction

Digital video is an active research area on many fronts, ranging from storage and transfer challenges to psychological studies of multichannel information processes. The Open Video Project (www.open-video.org) currently has more than 1800 video segments with a variety of automatically and manually generated metadata elements. The repository is used as a testbed for creating and testing highly interactive user interfaces for digital video (See [1] for an overview of the project and [2] for details regarding one of the previous user studies). These interfaces are crucially dependent on surrogates (metadata that 'stands for' the full object) that provide context and clarity during the retrieval process. These surrogates are displayed via a search results page containing objects that have been retrieved in response to a query. Before downloading a video, users rely on the system's representation of those videos to make relevance judgments. While textual surrogates are often revealing, because they must be read and decoded, they are often unable to characterize the rich amounts and types of data that can be transferred through visual media. It is assumed that

E. M. Bakker et al. (Eds.): CIVR 2003, LNCS 2728, pp. 271–280, 2003.

utilizing visual surrogates will help users develop a more thorough understanding of the videos retrieved. In order to develop the most useful mix of textual and pictorial representations of video objects, this study used eye tracking methods to explore the ways in which people interact with these media within the context of a video retrieval system interface.

2   Background

Eye tracking has been used to study people's processing of textual and pictorial information in a variety of contexts. Since the late 1880's there has been scientific interest in human eye movements and their ability to reveal cognitive strategies [3]. Of the many different patterns of eye movement, the saccade and point of fixation are most pertinent to a study of human computer interaction [4].   A saccade is a quick movement of the eye for the purposes of redefining the immediate visual field. During a saccadic interval, the eye doesn't collect information but is simply moving from one place to another [5]. A point of fixation is the period between saccades, typically ranging from 200-600ms[1], in which a stable visual point is held and information can be viewed [4,5,6]. An analysis of saccades and fixations can capture the wide range of visual perceptions and, presumably, cognitive processes people undergo when accessing information from a computer generated visual display [4,7].

A review of the literature provides few examples of research regarding people's eye movements as they integrated both textual and visual elements in an information seeking context. As noted by Rayner et al. [8], this may be due to the fact that the bulk of this research has probably been conducted by advertising agencies and the majority of it is not made readily available to the scientific community.

Faraday and Sutcliffe [9] studied the contact points between textual and pictorial elements. They suggested that a contact point "or co-reference between an image and a text" [9, pg. 29] should be carefully crafted to ensure that the maximum amount of encoded information is passed along to the viewer. Their findings revealed that, participants sought to link textual descriptions to visual depictions in a simple manner and if the link wasn't clear, participants often became confused as to how the two channels could be synthesized into a coherent whole. This work was based upon earlier research conducted by Hegarty [10,11]. As her participants viewed instructional diagrams comprised of both visual and textual directions, they constructed representations of the instructional material that were mainly text based. Across analyses, imagery was found to supplement an initial and lasting impression that was decoded from the textual material.

The remaining research was generated by investigations of people's interactions with advertising materials. This work is mainly interested in what pieces of an advertisement are most likely to capture a user's interest. Work by Fox et. al. [12] and Lohse [13] are representative examples. A final study of particular interest was con-

---

1 Due to the fact the fixation points are under voluntary control, fixation time can last as long as two or three seconds, depending on level of interest, but they generally fall within the 200-600 ms range.

ducted by Rayner et. al. [8]. That work used magazine advertisements as source material for participants conducting searching related tasks. Participants were directed to, for example, "decide which skin lotion and body wash to buy", from a series of advertisements that contained both pictorial and textual elements. Results indicated that participants spent a majority of their time looking at the textual portions of the advertisement. While this was true, it was hypothesized that participants spent more time on the text due to the fact that images are more quickly and easily decoded than words. Their work also pointed to the fact that eye movement patterns are heavily affected by task. The current study is intended to address the interplay between text and images.

3   Study Methods

Twelve undergraduate students each completed ten search problems. As they browsed the results page for each search, their eye movements were tracked. They also completed a learning preference questionnaire and were debriefed at the completion of the study. The study methods are described in detail in this section.

The 12 subjects who participated in this study were all undergraduate students from UNC-CH. They came from a variety of departments, included 9 females and 3 males, and had a mean age of 20 (ranging from 18 to 24). All of the participants reported using computers on a daily basis and 4 of the 12 reported watching videos or films on a daily basis while the remainder (8) watched weekly. Half the participants reported searching for videos or films on a daily or weekly basis with the other half searching only occasionally or never. Each subject spent about two hours in the study and received $20 for participation.

3.1   Learning Preference, Layout Design and Lookzones

Because this study was asking users to view both pictures and text, it was hypothesized that verbal or visual learning preferences might affect results. Kirby, Moore and Schofield's [14] Verbalizer Visualizer Questionnaire (VVQ) was used to assess these preferences. The VVQ contains three sections of ten questions each dealing with, respectively, verbal themes, visual themes and questions regarding dreams. The questions regarding dreams were dropped due to their lack of relevance to this study. Scores on the verbal and visual scales were analyzed directly and were also used to categorize participants as verbal, visual or balanced. Participants were categorized with verbal or visual preference if the difference between their verbal and visual scores were more than or equal to three. If their scores were less than or equal to two, they were categorized as balanced.

Because this study intended to assess how users interacted with a search results page that included text and pictures, it became clear that the placement of either text or picture on the page might play a large part in how the participant used them. It was hypothesized that, due to the left-to-right reading habits of Western culture, whatever information was placed on the left hand side might be used first. To account for this possibility, two versions of the search results page were designed, one with the textual metadata on the left and the visual metadata on the right and one in which the placement was reversed. As users interacted with the search results pages, they were given either design one or design two depending on the protocol.

Because this study was also interested in how participants employed either visual or textual metadata, zones were defined for each instantiation of a search page, that delineated three areas-text, pictures and other. Areas that had titles and descriptions were assigned to the text zone, areas that had poster frames were assigned to the picture zone, and areas that included neither textual nor pictorial metadata (i.e. scrollbar, etc.) were defined as an "other" zone.

3.2   Study Procedures

The OpenVideo eye tracking study was conducted in the Interaction Design Lab at UNC-CH using an ASL 504 eye tracker and Flock of Birds head tracker. A separate piece of software called GazeTracker was used to correlate eye tracking data with data from the user workstation. A combination of the two was used as the basis for analysis and discussion of results. Based on a review of the literature [3,4,5,6,7], a threshold of 200 ms. was used to define fixations.

Each session included ten trials and in each trial the subjects were given a search stimulus and one search results page. Each page contained between 20-25 video segments. For example, while viewing the appropriate search results page, the participant was asked to find a video "That discusses the destruction earthquakes can do to buildings." The first eight stimuli were topical and the remaining two asked subjects to select a video they might like. Each participant interacted with both page designs and search tasks that were counterbalanced to control for order effects.

After completing the ten searches, participants were debriefed with such questions as: Which of the two designs did you prefer and why? Name two or three strengths of the design you prefer. Name two or three weaknesses. Did the text give you different information than the pictures? If so, could you describe the difference?

In analyzing the data, we first asked how participants utilized text, pictures or other zones as they browsed the results pages. In addition, the effects of the layout, the search task, and the participants' learning preferences were investigated. These results were analyzed with a variety of tools (e.g., GazeTracker, SAS, MS Excel) and methods, including analysis of variance and contingency tables.

Table 1. Summary of performance for all participants over all search tasks

	Text		Pictures		Other	
	Mean	s.d.	Mean	s.d.	Mean	s.d.
Mean time (in seconds)	29.78	16.2	6.89	6.2		
Mean # of fixations	56.44	11.4	14.52	3.9	4.7	2.4
Mean duration of fixation time	18.9	11.4	4.60	3.9	2.0	2.4
Area of first fixation (frequency)	65		54		1	

4   Results

After summarizing participants' use of textual and pictorial zones in the search results page, this section discusses the variables affecting the study results.

4.1   People's Use of Textual and Pictorial Representations

The primary question to be addressed in this study was how people use textual and pictorial representations of video objects. A summary of the results addressing this question is presented in Table 1. It is clear that participants looked at the textual surrogates much longer than the visual surrogates. The mean time that participants spent looking at text, for the study as a whole, averaged more than 22 seconds longer, per search, than time spent looking at pictures—a difference that was statistically significant ($t=14.08$, $p<0.0001$). The differences in mean duration of fixation time over text, pictures or other was found to be statistically significant ($F=170.86$ with 2, 326 df, $p<0.0001$) and Duncan's multiple range test indicated that each mean was different from the other two. Thus, subjects consistently spent much more time decoding the text. The number of fixations appeared to be similarly focused on text, with participants spending 75% of their fixations over text, 18% of their fixations over pictures and less than 6% of their fixations over other sections of the results page. These differences were also statistically significant (F (2, 178)$=181.06$, $p<0.0001$). Interestingly, participants' first fixations were distributed approximately equally between the text (65) and pictures (54).

4.2   Effects of Layout, Tasks and Learning Preference

The effects of the placement of the pictures and the text in the interface was evaluated in two ways: amount of time in each zone and the zone which was examined first. The layout did not affect the total fixation time in each region, nor the number of fixations in each region. The mean time per fixation in the text zone was affected by the layout, with slightly more time spent gazing at text when the text was on the left (.34 seconds versus .31 seconds, $p=0.0018$). The zone examined first also varied with the layout (Fisher's exact test, $p=0.0017$). When the pictures were on the left, participants predominately fixated over text first and when the text was on the left, participants predominately fixated over pictures[2] first.

When looking at differences across search tasks, three results were of interest regarding participants' usage of the textual metadata. The total amount of time spent looking at text was affected by the task ($F=5.19$ with 9, 107 df, $p<.0001$; post hoc tests indicated a gradual change in this variable across the ten search tasks). Regardless of counterbalancing plans, some tasks required more time for completion than others. A similar pattern was detected when examining the amount of time spent in fixations in the text zone ($F=3.74$ with 9, 110df, $p<.0004$). Frequency of fixations in

---

[2] This may simply be due to the fact that participants began each scan on the middle section of the page and as the designs were switched, either text or pictures occupied the middle portion of the page.

the text zone also varied across tasks ($F=4.53$ with 9, 110 df, $p<.0001$). No statistically significant effects of task was found for the time spent in the picture zone, fixation time spent in the picture zone, or number of fixations in the picture zone.

Among these 12 participants, the mean score on the VVQ verbal scale was 5.8 (s.d. = 2.5) and the mean on the visual scale was 8.5 (s.d. = 2.2). When these scores were used to categorize the participants, six were picture-oriented and six were balanced in their preferences; none were text-oriented. Further analysis revealed that the balanced group spent more time looking at text than did the picture-oriented group (Fisher's exact test, $p<.0017$).

5   Discussion

It seems clear from the data that participants looked at and fixated on titles and descriptions far more than on the pictures in the displayed results.

Even more important, it seemed that most people used the text as an anchor from which to make judgments about the search results. In the analyses of scan paths (see sample in figure 2) and interview responses, it was clear that participants felt most comfortable searching for and finding videos with the textual metadata. While the data is consistent with this interpretation, there are some alternative possible explanations. As they searched, participants did spend more actual time and fixations over the text, but this could be attributable to the fact that information encoded in text takes longer to decode than information encoded in a picture [8]. It could also be attributed to the fact that a title and description probably carry more topical information about a video than the three images included in this interface. Were people spending less time looking at and fixating on the pictures because the images offered information that was more quickly accessed or because the images offered less information or different kinds of information? Further study is needed to answer this question, but in this preliminary study, it seems clear that participants were thoroughly proficient at using text as their primary tool for selecting relevant videos.

Even so, the visuals were not ignored completely. Some participants spent upwards of 25-30% of their time looking at and fixating on the pictures. The pattern that began to emerge was one of scanning the text for a possible video candidate and then confirming or rejecting that choice with the pictures. See figure 3 for an example screenshot of the moment a participant found the video that they subsequently chose. Note the fixation numbers begin over the text, with 2-6 falling over the description, and then move to the images, where 7-9 are located, and then back to the text.

It is interesting to note that two participants reported using the images as the main access point for their search, but subsequent analysis of their scan path didn't reveal this to be true. Regardless, participants consistently noted that they liked the pictures and felt that they were necessary to their searches. Even though the visuals weren't utilized as much temporally, they were obviously adding some value to the search process. Our study was not designed to reveal what this added value might be, but some exploratory conclusions can be made.

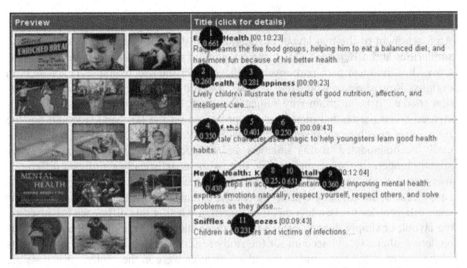

Fig. 2. Example Text Scanning Pattern. (black circles are areas of fixation with number of fixation and time of fixation noted)

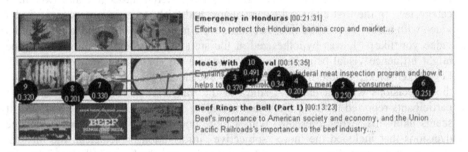

Fig. 3. Example of Text Scanning with Image Confirmation

Pictures were consistently used to confirm video choices that were made with the text. The added visual metadata seemed to make people more comfortable with their choices. One participant said pictures give you an "an actual visual object to look at." This makes sense in a medium (i.e., video) where visual information is one of two main signals (sound being the other). People want to "see" what the video looks like, not just read what it's about. It also makes sense that the visuals were communicating certain amounts and types of information that the text couldn't encode, such as the "feel of the film", what the characters looked like, and the colors used in the film. It was also noted by more than one participant that pictures can give you a quick over-view of the film without having to read the text. To hazard a contrast between the two sources of metadata, text seemed to transmit information regarding what the video was about and the visuals seemed to transmit information regarding what the video was like.

5.1   Discussion of Layout, Tasks and Learning Preference

An assessment of the two layout designs used in this study reveals some interesting similarities and differences. First, the layouts did not radically affect searching patterns. For the most part, participants utilized a personal searching style across both designs. Regardless of where the text was placed it was utilized as the main information source. It is uncertain why subject's average length of fixation was slightly increased when the textual metadata was presented on the left hand side and not the right. It is possible that peoples preference for reading from left to right was more easily accommodated in this situation and therefore they fixated, on average, for slightly longer. It also seems possible that, while a statistically significant difference was found, the actual temporal difference of three one hundredths of a second was simply due to small sample size. As to the finding that participants' first fixations were different for the two layouts, it is uncertain whether this difference is caused by the layout, or simply due to people's tendency to start in the middle of the page. This tendency, alone, would account for the study results, because in one design, text was in the center of the page and in the other, pictures were in the center. It is possible that people weren't being influenced by the layout at all.

In any study that involves search tasks, the ways in which those tasks may have affected performance must be evaluated. The ten different tasks fall into two main categories. In the first eight tasks participants had fairly specific targets (e.g., find a video with nurses), while the final two tasks were much more open ended (e.g., find a video you like). It was hypothesized at the start of the study that the search type might influence visual behavior, but no evidence for such an influence was found. For all ten tasks, people made their initial decisions based on text and confirmed those decisions with pictures. A study of the transcriptions does reveal that most participants reported utilizing the visual metadata more for searches nine and ten. It seems likely that, when presented with a more open choice, people made relevance decisions that included the more "subjective" information presented in the images. Further study regarding the characteristics of search tasks and their effects on searching performance will need to be conducted to verify this preliminary finding.

The statistically-significant effects of individual tasks on performance must also be interpreted. Certainly some tasks took longer than others and we can surmise that those tasks were either harder to accomplish or had some inherent randomness that forced participants to search longer. Why this is true is not easily discerned from the data. Perhaps a larger sample size or a different set of search tasks specifically designed to investigate this issue would produce more interpretable results.

The Verbalizer Visualizer Questionnaire scores revealed an interesting result. The group that had a balanced score, meaning that they had no preference for either visual or verbal learning, spent more time looking at the text than the visual group. The most likely explanation for this result is that the balanced learners had a stronger preference for text than the visual group, and so spent more time with it. It is also possible that balanced learners couldn't decode the information presented in the text as quickly as the visual learners could, but to make this assumption would require more research.

6   Conclusion

This study explored the role of text and image representations of the video objects listed on a search results page. A small number of study participants were asked to react to a specific set of search results pages in relation to ten specific search tasks. Thus, the conclusions from the study should be generalized only with caution.

This research began with an overall question regarding the inclusion of visual metadata in a search results page. Would this help or hinder users as they tried to find videos? Will people use images if they are included with other textual metadata while they search for videos? Based upon the evidence presented in this study, the answer seems to be positive. Participants actively utilize visual metadata and include it in the process of making relevance judgments. Text was certainly utilized to a higher degree, but the images were frequently accessed by participants as well, especially to confirm judgments.

Many claims have been made about the value of non-textual cues in supporting video retrieval. This study demonstrated that although text dominates how people make sense of retrieval sets, images add confirmatory value and are strongly liked. In future work, we will continue to investigate how textual surrogates and visual surrogates interact to benefit video retrieval performance. A second iteration of the above study could investigate further variations in the design of the results page by including only text, only images or by comparing manually selected surrogates with randomly selected surrogates. It would also be worthwhile to investigate the amount and variety of information transfer through images and text as they relate to the source video. This work could be further extended through a study of search tasks and their effects on subject performance. It is anticipated that results from this line of research will support the architecture and design of future digital video retrieval interfaces.

Acknowledgements

This research was supported by grant NSF IIS-0099638 from the National Science Foundation.

References

[1]   Wildemuth, B., Marchionini, G., Wilkens, T., Yang, M., Geisler, G.,
        Fowler, B., Hughes, A., & Mu, X. (2002) Alternative surrogates for video objects in a digital library: users' perspectives on their relative usability. In *Proceedings of the European Conference on Digital Libraries*. Rome, September 16-18, 2002. pp. 493-507.

[2]   Marchionini, G. & Geisler, G. (2002). The Open Video Digital Library.
        dLib Magazine, 8(12).
        http://www.dlib.org/dlib/december02/marchionini/12marchionini.html

[3]   Just, M. & Carpenter A. (1976) Eye Fixations and Cognitive Processes. *Cognitive Psychology, 8*. pp. 441-480.

[4]   Jacob, R. (1990) What You Look at is What you Get: Eye Movement-Based
        Interaction Techniques. *ACM Transaction on Information Systems*, 9(3). pp.
        152-169.
[5]   Salvucci, D. & Goldberg, H. (2000). Identifying Fixations and Saccades in
        Eye-Tracking Protocols. *Proceedings of the Symposium on Eye Tracking Re-
        search and Applications 2000*. 2000, Palm Beach Gardens, Florida, US. pp.
        71-78.
[6]   Velichkovsky, B., Dornhoefer, S., Pannash, S. & Unema, P. (2000) Visual
        Fixations and Level of Attentional Processing. *Proceedings of the Symposium
        on Eye Tracking Research and Applications 2000*. 2000, Palm Beach Gardens,
        Florida, US. pp. 79-85.
[7]   Peiz, J., Canosa, R. & Babcock, J. (2000) Extended Tasks Elicit Complex Eye
        Movement Patterns. *Proceedings of the Symposium on Eye Tracking Research
        and Applications 2000*. 2000, Palm Beach Gardens, Florida, US. pp. 37-43.
[8]   Rayner, K., Rotello, C., Stewart, A., Keir, J., & Duffy, S. (2001) Integrating
        text and pictorial information: eye movements when looking at print adver-
        tisements. *Journal of Experimental Psychology: Applied*, 7(3). pp. 219-226.
[9]   Faraday, P. & Sutcliffe, A. (1998) Making Contact Points between Text and
        Images. *Proceedings of the sixth ACM International Conference on Multime-
        dia*. Bristol, UK. pp. 29-37.
[10]   Hegarty, M. (1992) The Mechanics of Comprehension and Comprehension of
        Mechanics. In *Eye Movements and Visual Cognition: Scene Perception and
        Reading*. ed. Rayner, K. New York: Springer-Verlag. pp. 428-448.
[11]   Hegarty, M. (1992) Mental Animation: Inferring Motion from Static displays
        of Mechanical Systems. *Journal of Experimental Psychology: Learning,
        Memory and Cognition*, 18. pp. 1084-1102.
[12]   Fox, R., Krugman, D., Fletcher, J. & Fischer, P. (1998) Adolescents' Atten-
        tion to Beer and Cigarette Print Ads and Associated Product Warnings. *Jour-
        nal of Advertising*, 27. pp. 57-68.
[13]   Lohse, G. (1997) Consumer Eye Movement Patterns on Yellow Page Adver-
        tising. *Journal of Advertising*, 26. pp. 61-73.
[14]   Kirby, J., Moore, P., & Schofield, N. (1988) Verbal and Visual Learning
        Styles. *Contemporary Educational Psychology*, 13. pp. 169-184.

A State Transition Analysis
of Image Search Patterns on the Web

Abby A. Goodrum[1], Matthew M. Bejune[1], and Antonio C. Siochi[2]

[1] Syracuse University, School of Information Studies,
Center for Science & Technology
4-110 Syracuse, New York, U.S.A. 13210
aagoodru@syr.edu; mbejune@syr.edu
http://istweb.syr.edu
[2] Christopher Newport University,
Department of Physics, Computer Science & Engineering
Newport News, Virginia, U.S.A. 23606
siochi@pcs.cnu.edu

Abstract. Image seeking behavior is a complex interaction among many factors. One approach to the study of this behavior is to examine and categorize the search moves made by individuals as they transition from one search state to another. Seventy-one image searches conducted by graduate students on the web were analyzed to identify patterns of search state transitions used and the overall frequency of specific state transitions. Over a thousand state transitions were identified within eighteen state categories. The categories included search tool and collection selection, queries, context moves, and relevance judgments. Maximal Repeating Pattern Analysis (MRP) was used to examine patterns of transition from one search state to another. The patterns of state transition sequences were conceptualized within a framework of search tactics and search strategies.

1 Introduction

Image seeking behavior is a complex interaction among many factors. One aspect of this behavior, are the search moves, tactics, and strategies that users employ when seeking images on the Web. An extensive body of research examining search moves through Markov analysis of state transitions has focused primarily on users seeking textual materials from structured databases [1], [2], [3]. The current study expands upon this theoretical framework by examining patterns of image search moves on the web. The current study is part of a multi-year research project examining image intermediation, image seeking and image choice behavior [4], [5]. The study reported here examines the moves that users make when seeking images on the Web with selected tasks. The specific focus is identification and categorization of image search state transitions, search tactics, and search strategies. Although transaction log analysis combined with think aloud protocols have been used to explore information

E. M. Bakker et al. (Eds.): CIVR 2003, LNCS 2728, pp. 281–290, 2003.

seeking behavior, the strength of categorizing state transitions and patterns of transitions in this way rather than a strict keystroke or system centric approach is that it enables a finer grained analysis of image seeking behavior than is possible with transaction analysis alone.

1.1   Research Questions

The overall goal guiding this study was to describe a model of image searching on the Web by identifying and categorizing search states and state transitions, and to develop transition matrices to examine image search patterns. Specific research questions driving this study were:

1.   What search patterns are exhibited by users seeking images on the Web?
2.   What do frequently occurring search patterns have in common with one another?
3.   What do common search patterns represent in terms of users' cognitive approach to image seeking?

2   Research Design

The general procedure was to collect search data, identify search states, develop a taxonomy to describe state transitions, develop transition matrices, count occurrences of transitions, identify patterns of recurring transitions, calculate frequency of state transition patterns, and identify common facets of frequently occurring patterns.

2.1   Data Corpus

Subjects for this study were eighteen students in a graduate course on Visual Information Retrieval. Each received three hours of training about general and specialized image search engines and collections on the web. Included in this training were: Google, Altavista, PictureQuest, WebSeek, HotBot, BlobWorld, Library of Congress American Memory, Corbis, and Associated Press. Subjects were given one week to conduct searches for five images to illustrate a lecture on one of six topics. Search topics included humanities, social sciences, sciences and medicine (Table 1). Prior to searching, subjects were asked to write a brief description of their image needs and to describe the kinds of images they hoped to find. Transaction data and think aloud protocol data was generated and for each image sought, the subjects logged their starting point, subsequent moves, queries, decision points for browsing, relevance criteria, and the amount of time spent. Subjects provided printouts of the images selected, and answered a post search questionnaire that elicited information on their overall satisfaction with the experience.

2.2   Unit of Analysis

The primary unit of analysis was the *state transition*, of which over one thousand were found and studied. We define a state transition in this study as a system command or combination of system commands issued in order to accomplish a single goal. For example, a login procedure may require several discrete keystrokes and menu choices, but represents a single state in terms of the user's goals. Although think-aloud protocols were also collected, no attempt was made in this phase of the study to link search state transitions to users' intent or personal interpretation of these transitions. The first type of analysis involved examination of individual commands, which were assigned state codes to represent facets of searching. The second type of analysis examined sequential strings of commands.

Table 1. Summary of Data Corpus, N=18. The number of searches is less than the number of images sought because one user found all five images with a single search. While this does not represent typical search behavior among the subjects in this study, it does represent a goal for many users

Data Item	Value
Number of searchers by topic:	
Dangers of smoking for teens	2
Fragility of our wetlands	1
Putting a man on the moon	4
Impact of global warming	4
Life of Abraham Lincoln	2
History of the blues	5
Number of images sought	90
Number of searches	71*
Total number of state transitions	1, 046
Average number of transitions per search	11.6
Range of transitions	4-64
Average time spent	20 minutes
Number of queries	202
Number of terms (excluding stop words)	545
Average terms per query	2.69
Number search engines/collections	16
Average number search engines	2.5

2.3   Methodology

2.3.1   Coding Search States

Using the data described in the Data Corpus section (Table 1), the individual actions performed by each user were analyzed. This analysis was an iterative process of examining 71 search transcripts. Two researchers coded a small subset of search transcripts together to establish a baseline taxonomy of state transitions. The remaining search transcripts were divided between them for coding, and then the sets were swapped for re-coding. The initial baseline taxonomy was refined iteratively until consensus was reached and then all transcripts were recoded based upon the revised schema. To check for coding reliability and consistency, a third coder was trained on the schema and then asked to code four search transcripts previously coded by the researchers.

Eighteen state codes were used to represent the individual steps taken within the course of a search (Table 2). These codes were further grouped into categories representing facets of the search. These categories include the following:

Collections. We use the term 'Collections' in this context to designate a collection of images and (sometimes) text that is searchable within the collection and where access to those images resides under the control of the collection owner. We distinguish here, primarily, between specific collections such as Corbis, and the 'collection' of retrieved results generated by a general search engine such as Google Image Search.

Search Engines. We acknowledge that search engines/search tools may reside on local websites, but we distinguish our use of the term to mean generic, general-purpose search engines that locate materials on the publicly indexable web (e.g., Google, HotBot, Altavista).

Queries. These are any combination of alpha, numeric, mathematical symbol, or image features input in order to match against system surrogates. Further divided into:

- Original Queries: used to distinguish the opening query in a search
- New Queries: used for any modification of existing query elements, including adding or removing terms, punctuation, image features, or math; substitution or re-ordering query elements.

Surrogates. The set of retrieved items resulting from a query may be presented as either alphanumeric character strings representing websites, or as image thumbnails, sometimes with accompanying text. Multiple pages of surrogates may be retrieved by the system.

Context Moves. Used for moves that provide additional context to retrieved surrogates. Generally characterized as transitions from surrogates to objects; i.e., from website surrogate lists to websites, or from image thumbnails to images. Also used when following links within retrieved websites.

Relevance Judgments. Relevance judgments are made whenever searchers select an image to be included in their presentation. Users may identify relevant images at any point in their search and may also continue to search for other, more relevant images. We take as an indication that an image is relevant whenever searchers have saved an image, printed out an image, or indicated verbally that they have selected an image for later use.

Table 2. Summary of State Codes

Category	Code	Explanation
Original Collection	CO	Used for opening moves beginning in a collection only. Not used when returning to a collection after exploring other collections or search engines.
Change Collection	CC	Used to designate a move from one collection to another even when the collection has been accessed previously in the search.
Collection Login	LOG	Used to designate a series of moves required for access to some collections.

Table 2. continued

Category	Code	Explanation
Original Search jEngine	SO	Used for first, opening moves beginning at a search engine only. Not used when returning to a search engine after exploring other collections or search engines.
Change Search Engine	CS	Used to designate a move from one search engine to another even when the search engine has been accessed previously in the search.
Original Collection	CO	Used for opening moves beginning in a collection only. Not used when returning to a collection after exploring other collections or search engines.
Change Collection	CC	Used to designate a move from one collection to another even when the collection has been accessed previously in the search.
Collection Login	LOG	Used to designate a series of moves required for access to some collections.
Original Search Engine	SO	Used for first, opening moves beginning at a search engine only. Not used when returning to a search engine after exploring other collections or search engines.
Change Search Engine	CS	Used to designate a move from one search engine to another even when the search engine has been accessed previously in the search.
Original Query Text	QOT	Used when the opening query is submitted to a collection or search engine without specific image designation.
Original Query Text-Image	QOT-I	Used when the opening query is submitted to a collection or search engine with specific image designation.
Original Query Image	QOI	Used when the opening query is submitted to a collection or search engine as image features such as color, texture, or shape. Rather than alphanumeric character strings.
New Query Text	QNT	Used when a new query is submitted to a collection or search engine without specific image designation.
New Query Text-Image	QNT-I	Used when a new query is submitted to a collection or search engine with specific image designation.
New Query Image	QNI	Used when a new query is submitted to a collection or search engine in the form of image features such as color, texture, or shape rather than alphanumeric character strings.
Website Surrogates	WS	Used for lists of websites retrieved by the system in response to a query.

Table 2. continued

Category	Code	Explanation
Image Surrogates	IS	Used for groups of images retrieved by the system in response to a query.
Website	W	Used when moving from a website surrogate to a website linked from the surrogate list.
Image	I	Used when moving from image surrogates or from websites to an individual image.
Link From	LFW	Used when moving between a website that was retrieved in response to a query, and websites linked from these sites.
Intermediate Relevance	IR	Used when a user prints out, saves or notes that an image is potentially useful, yet continues searching.
Final Relevance	FR	Used when the search ends and an image or images have been selected, regardless of utility.

2.3.2 Maximal Repeating Patterns

If we assume that moving to any state is dependent on the previous state, patterns of transitions sequences can be modeled as a Markov process. Transition matrices for different sequences of various lengths can be compiled and compared. This method of examining information seeking behavior was first used by Penniman [1] to identify patterns of users' searching in a bibliographic database.

Siochi and Ehrich [6] extended this work by developing a program for identifying maximally repeating patterns in transcripts of user sessions as a means of exploring problems in interface design. They define a repeating pattern as a substring of length at least two that occurs at more than one position in a string of commands. A maximal repeating pattern (MRP) is a repeating pattern that is as long as possible and may also occur as a part of a longer pattern. For example, in the string "abcdfabcdeabx", "abcd", and "ab " are maximal repeating patterns but "abc" is not. "ab" is considered an MRP even though it is a substring of "abcd", since "ab" occurs in two contexts: "abc", and "abx".

In this study, we were interested in maximal repeating patterns of states across all users. Each user's session was modeled as a string of states listed in the order of their occurrence. All such strings were concatenated to form one long string, and the MRP analysis was performed on that string. Consequently, we were able to identify patterns common to several users.

3   Results

On average, the subjects input 2 queries, spent 20 minutes searching per image, and changed their initial queries frequently. Most of this time was spent browsing surrogates and websites and inspecting images for relevance. Image seeking is an intensively visual activity and users spend nearly two thirds of their time browsing and visually inspecting images for relevance.

All subjects began their searches with a query. Eighty-three percent of the initial queries were revised and resubmitted in some way before an image was selected. Subjects utilized sixteen search sites including major search engines and specialized sites such as PictureQuest, AP Archives, and Library of Congress Prints and Photos as beginning points for their searches. Most students used at least 2 different search sites in the course of looking for each image. The most popular search tools were Altavista Image Search, Google and Hotbot. Although subjects were aware of and had training in content-based image searching, none used readily available CBIR tools for their searching.

A total of 1,046 state transitions were identified and categorized according to the coding schema presented in Table 2. Analyses were conducted to address each of the three research questions. The number of queries, terms per search, number of results viewed, time on task, and frequency of each state transition was also calculated. Maximal Repeating Pattern analysis was implemented to identify patterns of state transitions. Data from search logs, verbal protocols, pre-search and post-search surveys were also examined in order to better interpret the results. Table 3 presents the most frequently occurring state transitions with their percentages.

Table 3. Abbreviated ranked frequency of search states. Total number of transitions is 1,046

From State	To State	Frequency
W	WS	138
IS	IS	80
I	FR	77
W	WS	71
IS	I	57
QNT-I	IS	52
QNT	WS	39
QOT-I	IS	37
W	I	37
SO	QOT	35

A number of researchers have noted that users adopt both querying and browsing as information seeking tactics on the web. In this study, non-query transitions were conceptualized as browsing tactics (with the exception of login actions and relevance judgments). For example, a typical browsing sequence in this study was:

Input Text-Image Query - Browse 1st page image surrogates - Browse next page image surrogates - Browse next page image surrogates - Browse next page image surrogates - Inspect an individual image from surrogates - Select image as relevant.

As can be seen in Table 4, sixty-eight percent of state transitions demonstrate this type of browsing activity while only eighteen percent were directly related to querying.

Table 4. Querying and browsing moves

Activity Type	Moves	% of Moves
Querying	QOT, QOT-I, QOI	18 %
	QNT, QNT-I, QNI	
Query initialization	QOT, QOT-I, QOI	8 %
Browsing	WS, IS, W, I, LFW	68%
Browsing Surrogates	WS, IS	34%
Inspecting individual websites or images	W, I, LFW	34%

3.1   MRP Analysis

There were 198 patterns identified having a sequence longer than two transitions. The longest pattern was 18 transitions in length and occurred twice in four positions in the data. The average search pattern was four transitions long. There were 35 different MRPs with length of four, the most frequently occurring MRP of this length appears 27 times (Table 6).

Because of limited space, it is not possible to show all the frequntly occuring state transition patterns. We therefore present the top transition strings based on frequency of occurence.

Table 5. Maximal Repeating Pattern frequency data

Length	Freq.	Total Pos.	Min. Pos.	Avg. Pos.	Max. Pos.
18	2	4	2	2	2
15	2	4	2	2	2
13	1	7	7	7	7
12	2	7	3	3	4
11	1	2	2	2	2
10	3	9	2	3	5
9	2	18	2	9	16
8	6	18	2	3	6
7	13	36	2	2	7
6	13	68	2	5	24
5	24	127	2	5	37
4	35	154	2	4	27
3	50	230	2	4	26
2	44	423	2	9	51

The longest MRPs are both 18 moves long. The strings for these sequences are dominated by multiple patterns of W:WS and WS:W transitions.

The main characteristic of the patterns of transitions was that the longer strings (and lengthier search times) occured when users searched for images using text-only search tools that retrieved lists of website surrogates rather than image surrogates. Another characteristic pattern was the IS:IS pattern. This pattern occured in more than half the users, and it appeared 51 times as a sequence of IS:IS:IS. It is clear that many more pages of image surrogates were inspected than were pages of website surrogate lists. This is not surprising given the visual nature of image seeking and the need to inspect images directly in order to make relevance judgements.

Users examined more pages of image surrogates than pages of website surrogates but they inspected fewer of the individual results from image surrogates pages. This indicates that users are able to assess the relevance of images more easily from small thumbnails than they are from textual descriptions. Moreover, image seekers are motivated to browse a greater number of retreived pages of thumbnails than they are of textual descriptions.

Greater numbers of intermediate and final relevance judgments were made after browsing image surrogates than website surrogates. In general, users do not make relevance judgements without having seen the image first. Even if an image is only a thumbnail surrogate, users prefer it to textual descriptions.

Table 6. Patterns of frequently occurring MRPs

Transition Pattern	Number of Positions	Comments
IS:IS IS:IS IS:IS IS:IS	27	Rapid browsing of image thumbnails.
START SO:QOT QOT:WS WS:W	18	Starting search with a textual query followed by viewing website surrogates and individual websites.
START SO:QOT-I QOT-I:IS IS:I	12	Starting search with a textual query at an image search engine followed by viewing image thumbnails and individual images.
WS:W W:QNT QNT:WS WS:W	11	This represents query reformulation after viewing retreived website.

4 Discussion

Each state transition is embedded within a series of transitions that constitutes a search tactic. Frequently occuring combinations of search tactics form patterns of searching that might be thought of as representing search strategies. A combination of search tactics might be used within a single search strategy. Occasionally we can see users trying different search tactics in an attempt to refine their search strategy based on the retrieved results.

The results here present a limited view of image search behavior and it is anticipated that ongoing analysis of the think-aloud and survey data will provide greater understanding of the cognitive motivations for the searching behavior described in this study.

A primary goal of this research was to systematically explore the image searching behavior of users on the web through a detailed analysis of the patterns of state transitions they made. Results reveal that a number of common tactics are employed across all domains and are not dependent on the type of image sought.

The results also suggest that due to the visual nature of the search strategies, an improvement to thumbnails might be to increase their size and reduce their resolution. This would enable better recognition of image content while not increasing page load times. Optimal image size and resolutions will need to be explored in a future image search study.

Finally, results from this study begin to suggest ways to automatically predict how users will search (and what lnks they may select) based on their search stretegies and opening search tactics. Understanding how users are likely to search will enable us to provide automatically generated web tours and navigation aids.

References

[1]   Penniman, W. D. (1975). A Stochastic Process Analysis of On-line User Behavior,_Proceedings of the American Society for Information Science, 38th Annual Meeting, 1975.

[2]   Chen, H. & Cooper, M. D. (2002). Stochastic modeling of usage patterns in a Web-based information system. Journal of the American Society for Information Science & Technology, 53(7). 536-548.

[3]   Xie, H. (2000) Shifts of interactive intentions and information seeking strategies in interactive information retrieval. Journal of the American Society for Information Science and Technology, 51(9):841-857.

[4]   Goodrum, A. (2003) Visual Resource Reference: Collaboration Between Digital Museums and Digital Libraries. D-Lib Magazine 9(2). http://www.dlib.org/

[5]   Goodrum, A., & Spink, A. (2001) Image searching on the World Wide Web: Analysis of visual information retrieval queries. Information Processing and Management. 37(2), 295-311.

[6]   Siochi, Antonio C. & Ehrich, Roger W. (1991) Computer analysis of user interfaces based on repetition in transcripts of user sessions. ACM Transactions on Information Systems. 9(4) 309-335.

Towards a Comprehensive Survey of the Semantic Gap in Visual Image Retrieval

Peter Enser and Christine Sandom

School of Computing, Mathematical and Information Sciences
University of Brighton, U.K.
pgbe@bton.ac.uk
c.sandom@bton.ac.uk

Abstract. This paper adopts the premise that the 'semantic gap' is an incompletely surveyed feature in the landscape of visual image retrieval, and proposes a framework within which this deficiency might be made good. Simple classifications of types of image and of types of user are proposed. Consideration is then given in outline to how semantic content is realised by each class of user within each class of image. The argument is advanced that this realisation finds expression in perceptual, generic interpretive and specific interpretive content. This analytic framework provides the basis for the specification of a broadly encompassing evaluation study, which will employ the image/user type classification and the expert domain knowledge of selected user groups in the construction of segmented test collections of real queries, images and relevance judgements. From this study should come a better-informed view on the nature of semantic information need, and on the representation and recovery of semantic content across a broad spectrum of image retrieval activity.

1 Introduction

Within the last ten years content-based image retrieval (CBIR) has risen to prominence in the research agenda for computer science. The digitised image offers some enticing processing opportunities derived from quantifiable attributes of colour, texture and the spatial (or, in the case of moving images, spatio-temporal) distribution of shapes. With developing maturity has come a realisation of the limitations of CBIR processes in practice, however. These limitations reflect the fact that the retrieval utility of visual images is generally realised in terms of their inferred semantic content. The context for this inferential reasoning process is to be found in the distinction drawn in semiotics between the denotation, or presented form, of the image and the connotation(s) to which it gives rise [1]. It is clear that personal knowledge and experience, cultural conditioning and collective memory – the shared knowledge of a society – contribute towards that reasoning process. The CBIR community has attached the label 'semantic image retrieval' to the formulation and resolution of infor-

E. M. Bakker et al. (Eds.): CIVR 2003, LNCS 2728, pp. 291-299, 2003.

mation needs which engage that intellectual process. The sharply drawn distinction between that process and the automatic extraction of low level features from denotative pixel structures is characterised as the 'semantic gap'[2].

Given the vast and constantly expanding scale upon which visual resources are made available via the World Wide Web, users, providers and the CBIR research community collectively have much to gain from a narrowing of that semantic gap. This paper adopts the premise that a complete survey of this feature in the landscape of visual image retrieval has yet to be undertaken, and proposes a framework within which this might be undertaken.

The approach taken in this paper is, first, to propose a classification of types of image, followed by an even simpler classification of types of user. Consideration is then given in outline to how semantic content is *realised* by each class of user within each class of image. This framework provides the basis for a proposal to set up a formal study which is intended to generate a more comprehensive evaluation of visual image retrieval paradigms than any reported thus far.

2   A Categorisation of Image Type

2.1   Documentary – General Purpose

Documentary images are interpreted here as faithful representations of reality. They may be captured as a result of a photographic process, or created by some form of human or human-initiated endeavour. In their captured form they represent a momentary entrapment of reality, typical examples being photographs taken above, on or under the land and sea. In their created form they are artworks using any of a variety of materials.

2.2   Documentary – Special Purpose

Images in this category are a faithful representation of a specific part of some larger reality, that part being the subject of specialised analysis and not necessarily visible without special equipment. As in the general purpose case, such images may be captured or created. Typical examples of the former are medical X-rays, ultrasound scans and microscopy images, whilst fingerprints are one example of the created form of such images.

2.3   Creative

Images in this category may be placed on a spectrum of reality representation, from documentary images which have been subject to some degree of amendment or manipulation, through to completely abstract artworks.

2.4   Models

In this category may be found 2- and 3-dimensional images which model aspects of reality such as processes and geographical phenomena. Typical examples are maps, diagrams, charts, plans, architectural and engineering drawings.

2.5   Moving Images

The classification shown in Figure 1 is couched in terms of still images, but may be applied to moving images as well. The animation of photographically or digitally captured sequences of any of the still image types is theoretically possible, although the footage resulting from some of the stills might have little practical significance. For example, TV news footage belongs to the class of general-purpose documentary images, and digital video microscopy is a moving image variant of the special-purpose documentary image. The feature film is the dominant, animated version of the creative image, and animated weather maps which feature in TV broadcasts are one example of the moving image version of the 2-dimensional model.

3   A Categorisation of User Type

For each of the four classes of image a variety of *specialist* users can be identified. For example, among the class of general purpose documentary images, archive photographs of urban scenes may be sought by transport historians and historical geographers. Surgeons, conservators and art historians are among the diverse users of X-ray photographs, an example of special purpose documentary images. Among the various types of artwork which contribute to the class of creative images, games designers will make use of computer-generated images; and astronomers will use (celestial) charts and maps within the class of 2-dimensional images. Other examples of specialist users of particular types of image are shown in Figure 1.

  Generalist users, characterised in Figure 1 as the general public, may seek general purpose documentary images, 2-dimensional models and creative images, expressing visual information needs which we may expect to be different from those of the specialist users. Generalist users would not normally engage with special-purpose documentary images, although passport photographs – a variety of facial recognition image – and foetal scans are exceptions to the general rule.

4   Realisation of the Semantic Content of an Image

The two-way classification of image and user types shown in Figure 1 provides a framework within which the semantic gap in visual image retrieval may be analysed. For each class of image we consider what is meant by semantic content, and further consider how both types of user perceive that semantic content.

4.1   General Purpose Documentary Images

The semantic content of general purpose documentary images is multi-layered. This multi-layering has been described in different ways. The art historian Panofsky, working with creative images, identified 'pre-iconographic', 'iconographic' and 'iconologic' levels of expression [3], which Shatford's generalisation in terms of generic, specific and abstract content, respectively, made amenable to general purpose documentary images [4]. Shatford is more particularly associated with the *of-ness* and *about-ness* of image content, the former derived from Panofsky's *factual* pre-iconography and iconography levels, and the latter from his *expressional* pre-iconography and iconography levels of analysis [4]. The of-ness and about-ness content finds alternative expression in *hard* and *soft* indexing [5], an approach which resonates with the *perceptual* and *interpretive* layers of meaning postulated by Jör-gensen [6]. In her study of human pictorial image perception, participants – asked to identify the attributes present in an image – also recognised *reactive* content. The latter was defined in terms of subjective response to the image (such as uncertainty and pleasure) and is not further considered here. Perceptual attributes were those named as interpretation-free responses to a visual stimulus, and correspond broadly with the generic/pre-iconographic category of Shatford/Panofsky.

Interpretive attributes in the Jörgensen study "are those which require both inter-pretation of perceptual cues and application of a general level of knowledge or infer-ence from that knowledge to name the attribute" [6]. In the case of people, interpre-tive qualities include the nature of the relationship among depicted persons, their mental or emotional state, or their occupation, for example. Such attributes do not conform with Panofsky's analysis since, although they are generic features, they are not interpretation-free. The specific name by which the person was known would also be an interpretive attribute, whereas Shatford/Panofsky distinguish such spe-cific/iconographic content from the generic subject matter featured in an image. Jör-gensen's interpretive attributes also encompass the abstract/iconological category of pictorial content specified by Shatford/Panofsky.

A simple characterisation of the semantics of an image in terms of perceptual and interpretive content is attractive. On the other hand, studies of user need for general purpose documentary images, both still and moving, have revealed a high incidence of requests for specific, named features such as objects, places, events and people [7-12]. There would appear to be some value, therefore, in adapting the Jörgensen model for our present purposes, by recognising semantic content in terms of perceptual, *generic* interpretive and *specific* interpretive attributes.

How a user recognises perceptual and generic interpretive matter in an image is a cognitive phenomenon which is, as yet, incompletely understood [13,14]. Greisdorf & O'Connor, reporting that "the research consensus points to an integrated cortical process involving, at least, perception and cognition", suggest that the visual impres-sion engendered by the sensory stimuli is first cognitively matched to some form of syntactic equivalence. First time viewers, moreover, "appear to determine initially what the image represents to them before making any evaluations of its topicality, meaning and utility in regard to an information need" [13]. It might seem reasonable to suggest that the user recognises perceptual and generic interpretive content by low-level features within the image; shape may be especially significant, complemented by colour and texture, bringing to bear a previously learned linguistic identifier to generate meaning. For example, a paddle steamer may be detected within an image by matching an outline (despite the complexities of occlusion, orientation, perspective, etc.), with memorised profiles associated with the verbal tag 'paddle steamer'.

User type / Image type	Generalist	Specialist
Documentary - general purpose archive photo – urban scene aerial photo contemporary photo - society	general public general public general public	transport historian; historical geographer town planner; military intelligence agent journalist; fashion designer
Documentary – special purpose X-ray photo microscopy image ultrasound scan fingerprint facial identification photo	n/a n/a n/a n/a [general public]	Surgeon; conservator, art historian microbiologist obstetrician police officer immigration officer; police officer
Creative painting trademark; logo tapestry computer-generated graphic.,	general public general public general public general public	art historian; curator trademark lawyer textile designer graphic designer; cartoonist; games software programmer
Model map chart technical drawing diagram	general public general public general public general public	geographer; civil engineer; archeologist astronomer; navigator; genealogist architect; engineer engineer; graphic designer; technical author

Fig. 1. A classification of image types and user types, with example members

One might expect the same to be true for specific interpretive features, which, it is postulated, the user also recognises by feature matching underpinned by a defining linguistic identifier. Thus, we recognise President Bush when we see his image. Furthermore, we continue to recognise him in creative images, even when his features are subject to some degree of denotational degradation under the influence of the cartoonist's pen – an aspect of recognition by components which has been investigated in the psychology literature [15]. Whatever the perceptual processes involved it would seem to be the case that *identification* is dependent upon the prior existence – and knowledge by the user – of a defining linguistic tag. However, we heed Eakins' warning that too many investigators have made unwarranted assumptions about the nature of perceptual similarity [16], and lend support to the call for further research into the psychophysical aspects of human perception [13,14].

As an added complication, the process of identification may involve *context*, recognition of which would seem to invoke high-level cognitive analysis supported by domain and tacit knowledge. Contextual anchorage is an important role played by text annotation within the image metadata [1,5].

When the focus of interest lies with the abstract content of the image – the client wanting images of suffering or happiness, for example - shape may be of limited use, unless we use recognition of features within an image to recall scenes within our memory which invoke the appropriate cognitive response . Colour might be significant, since it can be an effective communicator of mood. We are likely to be dependent, however, on the presence within metadata of an appropriate textual cue which conditions our *interpretation* of the semantic content of an image.

Both generalist and specialist users will realise semantic content of general-purpose documentary images in terms of perceptual and interpretive attributes. Such attributes in the case of the specialist user may involve linguistic identifiers of high specificity drawn from the specialised vocabulary of the subject domain in question.

4.2   Special Purpose Documentary Images

The image might take a variety of forms, but realisation of semantic content is likely, again, to reveal a heavy dependency on an intial detection of primitive features. In some applications – those which employ images captured by scanning technology or microscopy, for example - the spatial distribution of shapes, colours and textures may be particularly significant. For the specialist user, the existence and spatial distribution of such features within the image may lead to inferential reasoning about some external condition for which the image is a passive signal; examples would be the presence of a tumour within an organ of the body, or a structural mass beneath the surface of the land or water.

The user's inferential reasoning may thus establish *significance* and *identification* - semantic properties which, it would seem clear, depend on linguistic identifiers for their realisation. Again, such identifiers may be highly specific and drawn from the specialised vocabulary of a particular subject domain.

4.3   Creative Images

Creative images assume a greater variety of physical forms than is the case for general-purpose documentary images; some indication of this variety may be found in [17]. In many cases the realisation of semantic content does not depart in any significant way from the analysis presented in 4.1 above. However, as the accuracy with which reality is represented in this class of images is progressively relaxed towards totally abstract form, the more significant become the perceptual and generic interpretive attributes. Correspondingly, the more potentially effective becomes the application of CBIR techniques to this class of image, for both generalist and specialist users.

There are specialised types of creative image, the perceptual attributes of which predominate over the interpretive, or in which interpretive attributes are missing. These are context-free images which do not have the foreground/background disambiguation problem which, from the CBIR perspective, bedevils 'real scene' images. In such cases CBIR can be a powerful tool for retrieving images which are similar, on the basis of some chosen metric, to a target image. For the specialist user in particular, significant applications in trademark matching [2,18,19], and experimental work in fabric design pattern matching [2] have been reported.

4.4   Models

A particular characteristic of this class of image is the presence of symbols with domain-specific meanings, shapes and delineated regions. Typically, the spatial distribution of, and relationships between, the components are highly significant. Texture and, especially, colour may also be significant, and embedded text is a frequently encountered additional feature.

In the context of a particular image, these components combine to act as a surrogate of its semantic content. For example, a diagram of a city subway system uses a range of symbols and lines to represent the reality of a particular public transport infrastructure; the diagram 'means' the transport system. The image lends itself to a single, correct - one might say objective – interpretation. For this class of images, as with context-free creative images, it is the perceptual, or denotational content which is significant.

In many cases, retrieval will be a matter of recovering a specific artefact on the basis of its title or other unique identifier. However, for the specialist user in particular, CBIR offers a promising approach to searching digital archives for similar versions of some target image, on the basis of a primitive attribute, most obviously shape [2]. A pecific application in engineering drawings is one such example [20].

5   Retrieval Evaluation Study Proposal

In the preceding sections a framework has been outlined within which a comprehensive survey of the 'semantic gap' might be undertaken. Such a comprehensive survey would seem overdue: the scale on which visual image retrieval activity is conducted is now very significant indeed, and must continue to grow as access to ever larger quantities of image material is liberated.

As yet there has been no study which acknowledges the full plurality of image and user types, as represented in the framework shown in this paper. There have been a limited number of end-user needs studies which have taken a partial view, including the use of general-purpose documentary images by generalist and specialist users [7-9,12,21-24]; also the use of creative images by specialist users [25,26]. Subject requests recorded by generalist and specialist users of general-purpose documentary film and video has also been reported [10,11]. But user needs analysis of special-purpose documentary images and of models awaits even this level of attention.

In order to arrive at a better informed view of the semantic gap and the possibilities for bridging it there would seem to be merit in the specification of a broadly encompassing evaluation study. Central to this study is the construction of segmented test collections of real queries and images, the segments structured in accordance with the image/user type classification outlined above. The assembly of the test collections, together with the accompanying relevance/pertinence judgements, will employ the expert domain knowledge of selected user groups. From this endeavour should come a better appreciation of the incidence of perceptual, generic interpretive and specific interpretive content of image requests across a broad spectrum of image use.

From the same evaluative platform will come an informed view on the representation and recovery of perceptual, generic interpretive and specific interpretive content by means of a consistently-applied indexing strategy, including both textual and non-textual metadata. From such an informed view will emerge, hopefully, any prospect for narrowing the 'semantic gap' in visual image retrieval.

References

[1]   Barthes, R.: The Elements of Semiology. Cape, London, (1967)
[2]   Eakins, John P.; Graham, Margaret E.: Content-based Image Retrieval. A report to the JISC Technology Applications Programme. Institute for Image Data Research, University of Northumbria at Newcastle, Newcastle upon Tyne, (1999). http://www.unn.ac.uk/iidr/. Accessed February 2003
[3]   Panofsky, E.: Studies in Iconology: Humanistic Themes in the Art of the Renaissance. Harper & Rowe, New York, (1962)
[4]   Shatford, S.: Analyzing the Subject of a Picture: A Theoretical Approach. Cataloguing & Classification Quarterly, 5(3) (1986), 39-61
[5]   Krause, M. G.: Intellectual Problems of Indexing Picture Collections. Audiovisual Librarian, 14(2), (1988) 73-81
[6]   Jörgensen, Corinne: Indexing Images: Testing an Image Description Template. Paper given at the ASIS 1996 Annual Conference, October 19-24, 1996. http://www.asis.org/annual-96/ElectronicProceedings/jorgensen.html. Acessed February 2003
[7]   Enser, P.G.B.: Query Analysis in a Visual Information Retrieval Context. Journal of Document and Text Management, 1(1), (1993) 25-52
[8]   Enser, P.G.B.: Pictorial Information Retrieval. (Progress in Documentation). Journal of Documentation, 51(2) (1995) 126-170
[9]   Armitage, L. H.; Enser, P. G. B.: Analysis of User Need in Image Archives. Journal of Information Science, 23(4) (1997), 287-299
[10]   Sandom, C.; Enser, P.: VIRAMI – Visual Information Retrieval for Archival Moving Imagery. In: Bearman, D.; Garzotto, F. (eds.): ichim01 International Cultural Heritage Informatics Meeting: Cultural Heritage and Technologies in the Third Millennium, Politecnico di Milano, Italy, September 3-7 2001, 141-152
[11]   Enser, P. and Sandom, C.: Retrieval of Archival Moving Imagery - CBIR Outside the Frame? In: Lew, Michael S.; Sebe, Nicu,; Eakins, John P. (eds.): Image And Video Retrieval. International Conference, CIVR 2002, London, UK, July 18-19, 2002 Proceedings. Springer, Berlin, (2002) 202-214
[12]   Markkula, M.; Sormunen, E.: End-user Searching Challenges Indexing Practices in the Digital Newspaper Photo Archive. Information Retrieval 1(4), (2000) 259-285
[13]   Greisdorf, Howard; O'Connor, Brian: Modelling What Users See When They Look at Images: A Cognitive Viewpoint. In: Journal of Documentation. Vol 58. No. 1, (2002) 6-29

[14] Rui, Y.; Huang, T.S.; Chang, S.-F.: Image Retrieval: Current Techniques, Promising Directions, and Open Issues. Journal of Visual Communication and Image Representation 10, (1999) 39-62

[15] Biederman, I.: Recognition-by-components: A Theory of Human Image Understanding. Psychological Review 94(2), (1987) 115-147

[16] Eakins, J.P.: Content-Based Image Retrieval – What's Holding It Back? Paper given at the ASCI [Advanced School for Computing and Imaging] 2002 Conference, Lochem, the Netherlands, June 19-21 2002

[17] Graham, Margaret E.: The Description and Indexing of Images. Report of a survey of ARLIS members, 1998/1999. (1999). http://www.unn.ac.uk/iidr/RLIS/rlisrep.htm. Accessed February 2003

[18] Eakins,, J.P.; Graham, M.E.; Boardman, J.M.: Trademark Image Retrieval by Shape Similarity. IEEE Multimedia, 5(2), April-June 1998, 53-63

[19] Wu, J.K. et al.: Content-Based Retrieval for Trademark Registration. Multimedia Tools and Applications 3, (1996) 245-267

[20] Eakins, J. P. Design Criteria for a Shape Retrieval System. Computers in Industry, 21 (1993), 167-184

[21] Conniss, L.R; Ashford, L.R; Graham, M.E.: Information Seeking Behaviour in Image Retrieval. VISOR 1 Final Report. Library and Information Commission Research Report 95. Institute for Image Data Research, University of Northumbria at Newcastle' Newcastle upon Tyne, (2000)

[22] Fidel, Raya: The Image Retrieval Task: Implications for the Design and Evaluation of Image Databases. New Review of Hypermedia and Multimedia. 1997 (3) 181-199

[23] Ornager, Susanne: The Newspaper Image Database: Empirical Supported Analysis of Users' Typology and Word Association Clusters. In Fox, E.A.; Ingwersen, P.; Fidel R.; (eds): SIGIR 95, Proceedings of the 18th International AGM SIGIR Conference on Research and Development in Information Retrieval. Association for Computing Machinery, New York, (1995). 212-218

[24] Markkula, M.; Sormunen, E.: Searching for Photos - Journalists' Practices in Pictorial IR. In: Eakins, J.P.; Harper, D.J.; Jose, J. (eds) The Challenge of Image Retrieval: papers presented at a Wokshop on Image Retrieval, 5 February 1998, University of Northumbria at Newcastle, UK. University of Northumbria at Newcastle, Newcastle upon Tyne, (1998)

[25] Hastings, S.K.: Query Categories in a Study of Intellectual Access to Digitized Art Images. ASIS '95: Proceedings of the 58th ASIS Annual Meeting, Vol.32, (1995), 3-8

[26] Hastings, S.K. Evaluation of Image Retrieval Systems: Role of User Feedback. In: Sandore, B. (ed.) Progress in Visual Information Access and Retrieval. Library Trends 48(2), (1999) 438-452

Audio-Based Event Detection for Sports Video

Mark Baillie and Joemon M. Jose

Department of Computing Science, University of Glasgow
17 Lilybank Gardens, Glasgow, G12 8QQ, UK
{bailliem,jj}@dcs.gla.ac.uk

Abstract. In this paper, we present an audio-based event detection approach shown to be effective when applied to the Sports broadcast data. The main benefit of this approach is the ability to recognise patterns that indicate high levels of crowd response which can be correlated to key events. By applying Hidden Markov Model-based classifiers, where the predefined content classes are parameterised using Mel-Frequency Cepstral Coefficients, we were able to eliminate the need for defining a heuristic set of rules to determine event detection, thus avoiding a two-class approach shown not to be suitable for this problem. Experimentation indicated that this is an effective method for classifying crowd response in Soccer matches, thus providing a basis for automatic indexing and summarisation.

1 Introduction

With the continual improvement of digital video compression standards and the availability of increasingly larger, more efficient storage space, new methods for accessing and searching digital media have become possible. A simple example would be the arrival of digital set top devices such as 'TiVo' [4] and 'Sky+' [16], that allow the consumer to record TV programmes straight to disk. Once stored, users can manually bookmark areas of interest within the video for future reference. Other advancements include Digital TV, where broadcasters have introduced interactive viewing options that present a wider choice of information to users. For example, viewers of Soccer can now choose between multiple camera angles, current game stats, email expert panelists and browse highlights, whilst watching a match. However, in order to generate real time highlights, it is necessary to log each key event as it happens, a largely manual process.

There has been a recent effort to automate the annotation of Sports broadcasts, which include the recognition of pitch markings [1, 3], player tracking [5], slow-motion replay detection [9, 17] and identification of commentator excitement [15]. Automatic indexing is not only beneficial for real time broadcast production but also advantageous to the consumer, who could automatically access indexed video once recorded to disk. However, current real-time production and in-depth off-line logging, required to index key events such as a goal, are on the whole manual techniques. It has been estimated that off-line logging, an in

E. M. Bakker et al. (Eds.): CIVR 2003, LNCS 2728, pp. 300–309, 2003.

depth annotation of every camera shot, can take a team of trained Librarians up to 10 hours to fully index one hour of video [8].

In this paper, we outline an approach to automatically index key events in Soccer broadcasts through the use of audio-based content classes. These content classes encapsulate the various levels of crowd response found during a match. The audio patterns associated with each class are then characterised through Mel-Frequency Cepstral Coefficients (MFCC) and modelled using Hidden Markov Model-based (HMM) classifiers, a technique shown to be effective when applied to the detection of explosions [11], TV genre classification [18] and speech recognition [14]. In Section 2, we will introduce the concept of event detection using audio information and, in Section 3 we evaluate the performance of our system, concluding our work in Section 4.

2   Audio-Based Indexing

Microphones are strategically placed at pitch level to recreate the stadium atmosphere for the armchair supporter[1]. As a result, the soundtrack of a Soccer broadcast is a mixture of speech and vocal crowd reactions, alongside other environmental sounds such as whistles, drums, clapping, etc. This atmosphere is then mixed with the commentary track to provide an enriched depiction of the action unfolding.

For event detection, we adopt a statistical approach to recognise audio-based patterns related to excited crowd reaction. For example, stadium supporters react to different stimuli during a match, such as a goal, an exciting passage of play or even a poor refereeing decision by cheering, shouting, singing, clapping or booing. Hence, an increase in crowd response is an important indicator for the occurrence of a key event, where the recognition of crowd reaction can be achieved through the use of Hidden Markov Model (HMM) based classifiers that identify audio patterns. These audio patterns are parameterised using Mel-Frequency Cepstral Coefficients (MFCC).

2.1   Feature Set

For this study, we selected Mel-Frequency Cepstral Coefficients (MFCC) to extract information and hence parameterise the soundtrack. MFCC coefficients, widely used in the field of speech detection and recognition (for an in-depth introduction refer to [14]), are specifically designed and proven to characterise speech. Also, MFCC have been shown to be robust to noise as well as being useful for discriminating between speech and other sound classes, such as music [2, 13]. Thus, as an initial starting point, MFCC coefficients were considered to be an appropriate selection for this problem, where the Feature Set consisted of 12 uncorrelated MFCC coefficients with the additional Log Energy [14]. Each

---

[1] An armchair supporter is a fan who prefers to view sport from the comfort of their armchair rather than actively attend the match.

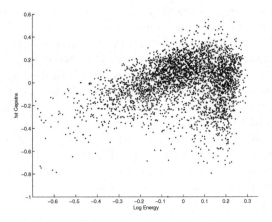

Fig. 1. Plot of the mean observation of Log Energy versus the 1st MFCC coefficient. There are two main clusters, the left containing observation sequences with speech, the right observations with no speech

Soccer broadcast was then split sequentially into one second observations, where the cepstra coefficients were computed every 10ms with a window size of 25ms, normalised to zero mean and unit variance.

2.2   Pattern Classes

An ideal solution to the problem of event detection would be a data set consisting of two content classes. One class made up of all audio clips that contained key events and the other class, the rest. But in reality this is not the case. Thus, in order to identify the relevant pattern classes that correspond to key events, we created a small random sample generated from 4 Soccer Broadcasts, digitally captured using a TV capture card. The audio track was sampled at 44100 Hz, using 16 bits per sample, in 'wav' format. Next, the soundtrack from each game was divided into individual observation sequences, one second in length. The training sample contained 3000 observation sequences, approximately 50 minutes of video. To visualise each observation, the mean measurement was calculated per feature.

Given the representative sample, scatter plots were created for all two dimensional Feature sub-space combinations, Fig. 1 is an example. From inspection of each plot, Fig. 1, it was clear that there were two main populations, those clips containing speech and those without, where each main group was a collection of smaller, more complex sub-classes. These sub-classes include differing levels of crowd sounds as well as the variation within and between the different speakers. Those clips containing high levels of crowd response, correlated to 'key events', were found to be grouped together, where in Fig. 1, these groups were positioned towards the 'top' of both main clusters. The data also contained a high frequency of outliers that through examination were discovered to be a mixture

Table 1. The selected audio-based pattern classes

Class Label	Class Description
S-l	Speech and Low Levels of Crowd Sound
N-l	Low Levels of Crowd Sound
S-m	Speech and Medium Levels of Crowd Sound
N-m	Medium Levels of Crowd Sound
S-h	Crowd Cheering and Speech
N-h	Crowd Cheering

of unusual sounds, not identifiable to any one group. These include signal interference, stadium announcements, music inside the stadium and also complete silence.

From this exploratory investigation, 6 representative pattern classes were selected, Table 1, where three of the classes contained speech and three did not. The first two classes, 'S-l' and 'N-l', represent a 'lull' during the match, one class containing speech and the other class not. During these periods, there was little or no sound produced from the stadium crowd. Classes 'S-m' and 'N-m', represent periods during a match that contain crowd sounds such as singing. During a match it is not unusual for periods of singing from supporters, usually these periods coincide with the start and end of the game, as well as after important events, such as a goal. Singing can also occur during lulls in the game where supporters may vocally encourage their team to improve performance. It is important for event detection to discriminate between crowd singing and those responses correlated to key moments during a game. Hence, the last two classes, 'S-h' and 'N-h', are a representation of crowd cheering. These classes are a mixture of crowd cheering, applause and shouting, normally triggered by a key incident during the game.

2.3   Hidden Markov Model-Based Classifiers

The audio-based pattern classes were modelled using a continuous density Hidden Markov Model (HMM). HMM is an effective tool for modelling time varying processes, widely used in the field of Speech Recognition (refer to [14], for an excellent tutorial on HMM). The basic structure of a HMM is: $\lambda = (A, B, \Pi)$, where A is the state transition matrix, B is the emission probability matrix and Π is the initial state probabilities. A HMM is a set of connected states $S = (s_1, s_2, \ldots s_n)$, where transition from one state to another is dependent only on the previous time point. These states are connected by transition probabilities $a_{ij} = p(s_i|s_j)$, where each state s_i has a probability density function, $b_{ij} = p(x|s_i)$ defining the probability of generating feature values at any given state. Finally, the initial state probabilities define the probability of commencing at any state given the observation sequence.

One difficulty when working with HMMs is model selection. For example, restrictions within A, the state transition probability matrix, can prevent move-

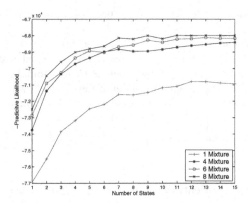

Fig. 2. Plot of predictive likelihood versus number of states

ment from one state to another, thus defining the behaviour of the model. A model that restricts movement from only left to right, is called a 'Bakis' Hidden Markov Model. This type of HMM can be very successful when applied to Automatic Speech Recognition [14], where each state(s) represents a phoneme in a word. Hence, as a sensible starting point, 'Bakis' HMMs were chosen to model each pattern class.

Another crucial issue to decide is the selection of both the optimal model size and number of (Gaussian) mixtures per state, where model size corresponds to the number of states. As the number of states and mixtures per state increase[1], so does the number of parameters to be estimated. To achieve successful classification these parameters must be estimated as accurately as possible. Note, there is a trade off in terms of better model fit associated with larger more enriched models, where precise and consistent parameter estimation is limited by the size and quality of the training data [6]. As the number of parameters increase so does the number of training samples required for accurate estimation.

To tackle this problem, we ran an experiment to identify a suitable number of states and mixtures per state. A number of 'Bakis' HMMs were generated, with states ranging from 1 to 15 and mixtures per state ranging from 1 to 8, using a pre-labelled training collection. 75% of the sample was used to train the models and 25% to generate the new predictive likelihood scores [7], where the predictive likelihood indicated how well a model 'fits' the data sample. The model parameters were then initialised, using the k-means segmentation process, and then re-estimated applying the 'Baum-Welch' Expectation-Maximisation algorithm. Note, because of the limited training data, the covariance matrices were constrained to be diagonal for each individual mixture. For each mixture number, Fig. 2, there was a 'levelling off' in performance at approximately 7 states.

---

[1] The number of computations associated with a HMM grow quadratically when increasing the number of states. That is $O(TN^2)$, where N is the number of states and T is the number of time steps in an observation sequence.

Increasing the number of mixtures per state, also produced a small improvement in performance. From the results, it was decided to select a 7 state HMM with 6 mixtures per state, since the increased number of parameters to be estimated using 8 mixtures outweighed the minimal improvement in model fit.

2.4   Decision Process

Once a sequence of new observations has been classified, we can then identify possible key events within the sequence, where a key event is likely to occur during periods of high crowd response, i.e. classes 'S-h' and 'N-h'.

Classification Given a new observation sequence, we measure the likelihood of it belonging to one of the 6 pattern classes, where the likelihood is determined using 'Viterbi's' decoding algorithm [14]. A new observation sequence is placed in the group that produces the highest model likelihood score. Given that this was an 'open world' problem and that each model would not have been shown all possible eventualities, a filtering process was required. The evidence of outliers during the exploratory analysis, Section 2.2, provided further proof of this requirement, so a threshold was introduced to flag possible outliers whose model likelihood scores exceed an experimentally set threshold. Flagged observation sequences were placed in a seventh 'ambiguous' outlier class.

Event Detection To identify key events, given a classified audio sequence, a further decision process was formed. Since a key event triggers a crowd response which normally lasts longer than 1 second, the length of an observation sequence, an 'event window' was introduced, where a key event was flagged if n sequential observations were classified as either 'S-h' or 'N-h'. Fig. 3 is an illustration of a detected event, where the top graph is 60 concurrent observation sequences grouped into one of the 7 categories. The bottom graph indicates the location of a true event. For this example we assume the 'event window' is set at 10 seconds. Hence, the soundtrack enters the 'S-h' class at 27 seconds and exits at 43 seconds, 16 observations later, thus flagging a key event. A correctly detected event was assumed to be an 'event window' that overlapped the location of a true event.

3   Experimental Results

This section outlines and presents the two experiments carried out to evaluate this approach to event detection. For the first experiment, each HMM-based classifier was first trained and then evaluated using a separate test set. The second experiment presents the results for the evaluation of the event detection process on two new unseen games.

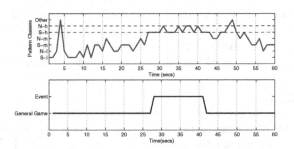

Fig. 3. Example of a detected event

Table 2. Labelled data for each class generated from 4 matches

Class	#1sec Observation Sequences
S-l	4020
S-m	1062
S-h	353
N-l	1832
N-m	545
N-h	213

Table 3. Confusion matrix for the HMM-based classification results

	Input - Actual					
Output Class	S-l	S-m	S-h	N-l	N-m	N-h
Outliers	1.21	4.43	7.12	5.02	4.3	10.76
S-l	**85.43**	13.32	1.11	3.21	0.01	0
S-m	9.5	**75.78**	4.3	0.2	2.94	1.2
S-h	3.5	4.21	**74.1**	0.65	0.24	4.21
N-l	0.33	1.23	0	**79.2**	5.32	5.34
N-M	0.03	0.4	1.22	9.6	**76.54**	9.81
N-H	0	0.63	12.15	2.12	10.65	**68.68**
Total	100%	100%	100%	100%	100%	100%

3.1 Classifier Performance

Each classifier was trained and evaluated on two separate, manually labelled, data samples, generated from 4 soccer broadcasts, see Table 2. Those content classes with high levels of crowd response contained lower numbers of samples in comparison with the other groups, due to the infrequency of key events. So, given these small numbers, 75% of the samples were used for training and 25% for testing and the performance of each classifier is presented in Table 3.1.

The two important classifiers for event detection, 'S-h' and 'N-h', representing high levels of crowd response, produced classification rates of 74% and 69%

Table 4. Event Detection

Class	#Key Events	#Detected	#False
Game1	24	20	8
Game2	16	14	7

respectively. For both classes, several of the observation sequences were misclassified as outliers. This may be an indication of the large intra-class variation within these two pattern classes. We also found an apparent overlap between the two groups 'N-m' and 'N-h', where a large number of observations from each group were falsely classified into the other class. This indicated a possible need for extending the framework into further, well defined sub-classes. Finally one common theme, indicated from the experiment, was that those models with a larger training sample performed better.

3.2 Event Detection Results

To measure the event detection approach, we gathered match reports and detailed game statistics for two new unseen games. The match reports were taken from 'OPTA' [12], a web-site dedicated to producing detailed summaries of soccer matches. Important events were considered to be goals, scoring attempts, cautions or other key incidents highlighted in the match report, forming the ground truth against which our system could be compared. The match reports also indicated approximate time points for each event, which aided this process. Using this information, a window from the start of the event to the end of the crowd response was created, for each true event.

To measure performance, a correctly identified event was determined to be: *"if a flagged 'event window' overlapped a 'true event window' at any time-point"*. If there was some overlap between an actual event and an 'event window', a correct detection was noted. If there was no true event during a flagged 'event window', a false detection was noted. For the experiment the 'event window' was experimentally set at 10 consecutive 1 second audio clips.

Comparing the automatically generated event index for the two games with the truth data from the match report, we found a high success rate, where only six events were not identified (Table 4). However, one of the missed events was a goal that was scored by the 'away' team, who were supported by a small section of the crowd in the stadium. The small support produced little crowd response in the stadium, thus the event was not detected by the system. Among the false detections were noticeable periods of singing from the stadium crowd. For example, after a 'goal', supporters sing for long periods, often triggering false events. Another interesting observation was one false event detection did in fact contain crowd cheering. During this period an amusing event occurred, triggering a large crowd reaction that was not reported in the match summary.

4   Conclusions and Future Work

The audio-based event detection approach outlined in this paper, was shown to be effective when applied to Soccer broadcasts, where the main benefit of the system was its ability to recognise patterns that indicate high levels of crowd response, correlated to key events. By applying HMM-based classifiers to the problem, we were able to eliminate the need for defining a heuristic set of rules to determine event detection thus avoiding a two-class approach, shown not to be suitable. Hence, the performance of the individual HMM-based classifiers was encouraging given the difficult nature of the Soccer soundtrack and the limited size of the training data, where the system overall detected 85% of the key events from a new unseen collection. Further experimentation is planned to train and test the system over a larger, more varied collection as well as compare the approach against other techniques.

The experiments also highlighted other potential improvements to this approach. These include the introduction of further representative classes that would manage the large variability found in a soundtrack, as well as further investigation into the development of model selection and the Feature set. For example, the test collection used in this study contained only male commentators, where a potential problem would be new broadcasts that contain female speech. Male and female voice is known to contain different characteristics, so future development will be required to identify new or modify current content classes to cope with various speakers from either gender.

In regards to model selection, the Bayesian Information Criterion (BIC) [10] is a technique that can be used to estimate the optimal model size, balancing predictive likelihood against model parameter size. Also, investigation and development into the identification of audio features, specifically suited for discriminating between the defined pattern classes, would be advantageous. Current research into audio-based content retrieval, differentiating between classes such as music and speech [2, 13], highlight this need.

On a final note, the event detection algorithm did fail to recognise key events coinciding with little to no crowd response. One possible solution to this problem would be the inclusion of new features possibly from different modalities such as vision or motion. Examples of classification using a combination of different modalities can be found in [11, 18], where a combination of visual and audio features was applied to the problems of explosion detection and video genre classification respectively.

Acknowledgements

Thanks to Prof. Keith van Rijsbergen, Prof. Mark Girolami, Robert Villa, Craig Hutchison, Marcos Theophylactou, Vassilis Plachouras, Sumitha Balasuriya and Tassos Tombros for their helpful advice, support and comments.

References

[1] Y.L. Chang, W. Zeng, I. Kamel, and R. Alonso. Integrated image and speech analysis for content-based video indexing. In *ICMCS*, pages 306–313. IEEE, 1996. 300

[2] D. Keislar E. Wold, T. Blum and J. Wheaton. Content-based classification, search, and retrieval of audio. In *In IEEE Multimedia*, volume 3, pages 27–36. IEEE, 1996. 301, 308

[3] Y. Gong, T.S. Lim, and H.C. Chua. Automatic parsing of tv soccer programs. In *ICMCS*, pages 167–174, Washington DC, May 1995. 300

[4] TiVo Inc. http://www.tivo.com/. Last visited 24th April 2003. 300

[5] S. Intille and A. Bobick. Visual tracking using closed worlds. Technical report, MIT Media Laboratory, 1995. http://web.media.mit.edu/ intille/. 300

[6] A.K. Jain, R.P.W. Duin, and J. Mao. Statistical pattern recognition: A review. *IEEE Transactions on Pattern Analysis and Machine Intelligence*, 22(1):4–37, January 2000. 304

[7] J.P. Cambell Jnr. Speaker recognition: A tutorial. In *Proceedings of the IEEE*, volume 85, pages 1437–1462, September 1997. 304

[8] J. Kittler, K. Messer, W. Christmas, B Levienaise-Obadia, and D. Koubaroulis. Generation of semantic cues for sports video annotation. In *ICIP*, pages 26–29, Thessaloniki, Greece, October 2001. 301

[9] K. Kobla, D. Doermann, and D. DeMenthon. Identification of sports videos using replay, text, and camera motion features. In *Conference on Storage and Retrieval for Media Databases*, volume 3972, pages 332–343. SPIE, January 2000. 300

[10] C. Li and G. Biswas. A bayesian approach to temporal data clustering using hidden markov models. In *ICML*, pages 543–550, Stanford, California, 2000. 308

[11] M.R. Naphade, A. Garg, and T.S. Huang. Duration dependent input output markov models for audio-visual event detection. In *ICME*, Tokyo, Japan, August 2001. IEEE. 301, 308

[12] OPTA. http://www.opta.co.uk/. Last visited 24th April 2003. 307

[13] D. Pye. Content-based methods for the management of digital music. In *ICASSP*, volume IV, pages 2437–2400, 2000. 301, 308

[14] L. Rabiner and B.H. Juang. *Fundamentals of Speech Recognition*. Prentice Hall, Englewood Cliffs, NJ, USA, 1993. 301, 303, 304, 305

[15] Y. Rui, A. Gupta, and A. Acero. Automatically extracting highlights for tv baseball programs. In *ACM Multimedia*, pages 105–115, LA, 2000. 300

[16] Sky+. http://www.sky.com/. Last visited 24th April 2003. 300

[17] P. van Beek, H. Pan, and M.I. Sezan. Detection of slow-motion replay segments in sports video for highlights generation. In *ICASSP*, Utah, May 7-11 2001. 300

[18] Y. Wang, Z. Liu, and J. Huang. Multimedia content analysis using both audio and visual clues. In *IEEE Signal Processing Magazine*, volume 17, pages 12–36. 2000. 301, 308

Spectral Structuring of Home Videos

Jean-Marc Odobez, Daniel Gatica-Perez, and Mael Guillemot

IDIAP, Martigny, Switzerland
{odobez,gatica,guillemo}@idiap.ch

Abstract. Accessing and organizing home videos present technical challenges due to their unrestricted content and lack of storyline. In this paper, we propose a spectral method to group video shots into scenes based on their visual similarity and temporal relations. Spectral methods have been shown to be effective in capturing perceptual organization features. In particular, we investigate the problem of automatic model selection, which is currently an open research issue for spectral methods, and propose measures to assess the validity of a grouping result. The methodology is used to group scenes from a six-hour home video database, and is assessed with respect to a ground-truth generated by multiple people. The results indicate the validity of the proposed approach, both compared to existing techniques as well as the human ground-truth.

1 Introduction

The development of efficient browsing and retrieval techniques for home video is of great importance for video albuming and other multimedia applications [4, 5, 3], but represents a technical challenge due to the unrestricted content and the absence of storyline in consumer videos. These videos are composed of a set of scenes, each composed of few shots, visually consistent, localized in time, and randomly recorded, making them unsuitable for analysis approaches based on storyline models. However, recent studies have shown that people implicitly follow certain rules of attention focusing and recording [5, 3], and that the scene structure of home video can be disclosed from such rules [3].

At the same time, there is an increasing interest in computer vision and machine learning towards spectral clustering methods [11, 12, 14, 6], which aim at partitioning a graph based on the eigenvectors of its pairwise similarity matrix. These methods have provided some of the best known results for image segmentation and data clustering. However, the automatic determination of the number of clusters has not been fully addressed in most of these references.

In this paper, we propose a methodology to discover the cluster structure in home videos using spectral algorithms. Our paper has two contributions. In the first place, we present a novel analysis related to the problem of model selection in spectral clustering for the algorithm of [7], and study some measures to assess the quality of a partition, discussing the balance between the number of clusters and the clustering quality. In particular, we discuss the use of the eigengap, a measure referred to as a potential tool for clustering evaluation [7], but for

E. M. Bakker et al. (Eds.): CIVR 2003, LNCS 2728, pp. 310–320, 2003.
© Springer-Verlag Berlin Heidelberg 2003

which we are not aware of any experimental studies showing its usefulness in practice. In the second place, we show that the application of spectral methods to home video structuring results in a powerful method, despite the use of simple features of visual similarity and temporal relations. The methodology shows good performance with respect to cluster detection and individual shot-cluster assignment, both compared to existing techniques and to people performing the same task, when evaluated on a six-hour home video database for which a third-party ground-truth generated by multiple subjects is available. [1]

The paper is organized as follows. Section 2 describes the spectral clustering algorithm, discussing the model selection issue and the use of various clustering quality measures. Section 3 describes the application of the methodology to structuring of home videos. Section 4 describes the database and the performance measures, and presents results. Section 5 provides some concluding remarks.

2 The Spectral Clustering Algorithm

First, we briefly describe the spectral algorithm (proposed in [7] and inspired by [12, 11]). We then analyze it for both ideal and general cases. Model selection is then discussed, and several measures of assessing clustering quality are presented.

2.1 The Algorithm

Let us define a graph $\mathcal{G}$ by (S, A), where S denotes the set of nodes, and A is the affinity matrix encoding the similarity between any two nodes in the set S. We ensure that $A_{ii} = 0$ for all i in S. The affinity A_{ij} is often defined as :

$$A_{ij} = \exp^{-\frac{d^2(i,j)}{2\sigma^2}} , \tag{1}$$

where $d(i, j)$ denotes a distance measure between two nodes, and σ is a scale parameter. The algorithm consists of the following steps :

1. Define $D(A)$ to be the degree matrix of A (i.e. a diagonal matrix such that $D_{ii} = \sum_j A_{ij}$), and construct $L(A)$ by $L(A) = (D(A))^{-1/2} A (D(A))^{-1/2}$.
2. Find $\{x_1, x_2, \ldots, x_k\}$ the k largest eigenvectors of L (chosen to be mutually orthogonal in the case of repeated eigenvalues), and form the matrix $X = [x_1 x_2 \ldots x_k]$ by stacking the eigenvectors in columns.
3. Form the matrix Y from X by renormalizing each row to have unit length. The row Y_i is to the new feature associated with node i.
4. Cluster the rows Y_i into k clusters via K-means.
5. Assign to each node i the cluster number corresponding to its row.

[1] The authors thanks the Eastman Kodak Company for providing the Home Video database, and N. Triroj (University of Washington) for providing the multiple-subject third-party ground-truth.

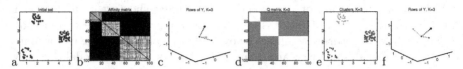

Fig. 1. Clustering example: (a) initial points; (b) affinity matrix; (c) rows of Y (in $\mathbb{R}^3$) when $K=3$ and eigensystem solved with *eig* from matlab; (d) Q matrix; (e) clustering result; (f) rows of Y, but with the eigensystem solved with the *eigs* function

When the value of K corresponds to its true value, the rows of Y should cluster in K orthogonal directions. Thus, the K initial centroids $(Y_i^c)_{i=1,\dots,K}$ in the fourth step of the algorithm can be selected by first finding the row of Y for which the $Ninit$ neighbours form the tightest cluster, and then recursively selecting the row whose inner product to the existing centroids is the smallest according to

$$Y_{i+1}^c = \operatorname*{argmin}_{Y_j}\ \max_{(Y_l^c)_{l=1:i}}\ (Y_l^c.Y_j).$$

2.2   Algorithm Analysis

Figure 1(e) and 4(b) show examples of clustering results that can be obtained with this algorithm. It was shown in [7] that the above algorithm is able to find the true clusters under the condition that K corresponds to the true number of clusters (whenever such a value exists). In this section we extend this result by analyzing the behaviour for the case when K is above or below this ideal number. Two cases are considered: the ideal case, when the true clusters are well separated; and the general case, when noise due to inter-cluster similarity exists.

The Ideal Case To understand the behaviour of the algorithm, we consider an ideal case in which the different clusters have infinite separation. Without loss of generality, if we additionally suppose that $K_{ideal}=3$, the set of all node indexes is given by $S = S_1 \cup S_2 \cup S_3$, where S_i denotes the ith cluster of size n_i. We also assume that the node indexes are ordered according to their cluster. An example obeying these assumptions is illustrated in Fig. 1, where the distance employed to define the affinity between two nodes is the usual euclidian distance between the 2D coordinates, and affinity is computed by Eq. 1.

In this case, A (resp. L) is a diagonal matrix composed of 3 blocks $(A^{(ii)})_{i=1,2,3}$ (resp. $(L^{(ii)})_{i=1,2,3}$) which are the intra-cluster affinity matrices for L. It follows that (i) its eigenvalues and eigenvectors are the union of the eigenvalues and eigenvectors of its blocks $L^{(ii)}$ (the latter appropriately padded with zeros); (ii) its highest eigenvalue is unity; (iii) unity is a repeated eigenvalue of order 3; (iv) the 4th eigenvalue is stricly less than 1 (assuming $A_{jk}^{(ii)} > 0, j \neq k$), and (v) the eigenspace of the unity eigenvalue has dimension 3, and thus, the eigenvectors provided by a particular decomposition algorithm are not unique. X_3

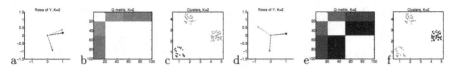

Fig. 2. Same data as in figure 1, with $K=2$: (a,b,c) when the eigensystem is solved with *eig* on matlab ; (d,e,f) when using *eigs*. (a) (d) denote the rows of Y (in $\mathbb{R}^2$); (b) (e) denote the Q matrix; (c)(f) show the clustering result

(where X_K denotes the first K eigenvectors stacked in columns) has the form

$$X_3 = \begin{bmatrix} v_1^{(1)} & 0 & 0 \\ 0 & v_1^{(2)} & 0 \\ 0 & 0 & v_1^{(3)} \end{bmatrix} \times R, \qquad \text{with } R = \begin{bmatrix} \mathbf{r}_1 \\ \mathbf{r}_2 \\ \mathbf{r}_3 \end{bmatrix},$$

where R is a 3×3 rotation matrix composed out of the three row vectors $\mathbf{r}_i$, and $v_l^{(j)}$ denotes the lth eigenvector of the matrix $L^{(jj)}$. Thus, each row of X_3 is of the form $v_{1i}^{(j)} \times \mathbf{r}_j$, where $v_{1i}^{(j)}$ is a scalar (the ith component of $v_1^{(j)}$). Therefore, after renormalizing the rows of X_3 (step 3 of the algorithm), the matrix Y has rows that fulfill $Y_i = \mathbf{r}_j \; \forall i \in S_j$. Fig. 1(c) illustrates this result for the data set of Fig. 1(a). Fig. 1(f) shows the result obtained by changing the matlab function that solves the eigensystem. Note that the three vectors are still orthogonal, but have a different configuration. An alternative formulation defines $Q = Y \times Y^T$ [11]. In the ideal case, we have $Q(i,j) = 1$ for nodes i and j belonging to the same cluster, and $Q(i,j) = 0$ otherwise (see Fig. 1(d)).

Variation in the Number of Clusters in the Ideal Case We can now consider the two cases when $K \neq K_{ideal}$, which have not been previously studied in [7]:
1. For $K < K_{ideal}$, X_K corresponds to the first K columns of $X_{K_{ideal}}$. After normalization, we get a Y matrix whose entries are (in our example, with $K=2$) :

$$Y_j = (r_{i1}, r_{i2})/\|(r_{i1}, r_{i2})\| \dot{=} \mathbf{r}'_i \qquad \forall i \text{ and } \forall j \in S_i.$$

This simply corresponds to projecting and normalizing the initial orthogonal vectors $\mathbf{r}_i$ into a lower dimensional space. Since (as pointed out above) the vectors $\mathbf{r}_i$ can be in any orthogonal configuration, there is no general rule about the configuration of their projections $\mathbf{r}'_i$. As an example, Fig. 2 shows these projections in the case of the data of Fig. 1. Depending on the specific eigensystem solver, the projections and the clustering results can differ.
2. For $K > K_{ideal}$, consider for simplicity that $K = 4$. X_4 now consists of the matrix X_3 with the 4th eigenvector appended as an extra column. As mentioned above, this eigenvector comes from one of the $L^{(ii)}$ matrices. More precisely

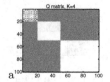

Fig. 3. Same data as in Fig. 1. (a) Q for $K=4$; (b) clustering; (c) clustering for $K=5$

$\lambda_4 = \max_i \lambda_2^{(i)}$. Assume that we choose this 4th eigenvector in the first cluster,

$$X_4 = \begin{bmatrix} v_1^{(1)} \mathbf{r}_1 & v_2^{(1)} \\ v_1^{(2)} \mathbf{r}_2 & 0 \\ v_1^{(3)} \mathbf{r}_3 & 0 \end{bmatrix} .$$

After row normalization, it can be shown that $Q(i,j) = 0, \forall i \in S_k, \forall j \in S_l, k \neq l$. i.e., the true original clusters remain orthogonal to each other [8]. Furthermore, $Q(i,j) = 1, \forall (i,j) \in S_k^2, k = 2$ or 3, indicating that the second and third cluster remain unchanged. Only the first cluster is affected (divided into two parts). The same reasoning applies for higher values of K. Summarizing, if $K > K_{ideal}$, the resulting clustering corresponds to an overclustering of the ideal case (Figs. 3-4).

The General Case In the ideal case, we have seen that the Q matrix should only have 0 and 1 entries when the true K is selected, and that there might be other entry values when $K \neq K_{ideal}$ (esp. $K > K_{ideal}$). Indeed, this can be related to the distortion obtained at the end of the K-means algorithm :

$$MSE = \frac{1}{n} \sum_{i=1}^{K} \sum_{j \in cluster_i} \|Y_j - Y_i^c\| , \tag{2}$$

where Y_i^c represent the centroids at the end of the K-means. In the ideal case, and when $K = K_{ideal}$ the distortion should be 0. Given the correct K value, the authors in [7] use the distortion as a measure to select the clustering result from a set of results obtained by varying the scale parameter σ in the affinity matrix computation (Eq. (1)). However, there is no indication of how this measure would behave for varying values of K. Note in particular that the distortion measure is computed in spaces of different dimension (Y_j lie in $\mathbb{R}^K$), so distortion values may not be easily compared, and that the MSE may be low or not when $K < K_{ideal}$.

2.3 Automatic Model Selection

The selection of the "correct" number of clusters is a difficult task. We have seen in the previous Section that the analysis of the MSE measures for different K is not trivial. For this reason, we considered other criteria stemming from matrix perturbation and spectral graph theories to perform model selection.

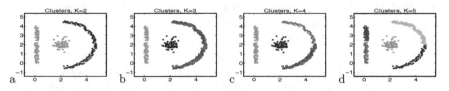

Fig. 4. Another example. Result with (a) K=2, (b) K=3, (c) K=4 (d) K=5

We have adopted the following strategy. The spectral clustering algorithm is employed to provide candidate solutions (one per value of K), and the selection is performed based on the criteria discussed in the following sections.

The Eigengap The eigengap is an important measure in spectral methods [6, 7] (see [1] for basic definitions). The eigengap of a matrix A is defined by $\delta(A) = 1 - \frac{\lambda_2}{\lambda_1}$ where λ_1 and λ_2 are its two largest eigenvalues [6]. In practice, the eigengap is often used to assess the stability of the first eigenvector[2] of a matrix and it can be shown to be related to the *Cheeger constant* [1], a measure of the tightness of clusters. To clarify this relation, let us define the *cut value* of the partitioning $(\mathcal{I}, \bar{\mathcal{I}})$ of a graph characterized by its affinity matrix A by $Cut_A(\mathcal{I}, \bar{\mathcal{I}}) = \sum_{i \in \mathcal{I}} \sum_{j \notin \mathcal{I}} A_{ij}$, the *volume* of the subset $\mathcal{I}$ by $Vol_A(\mathcal{I}) = \sum_{i \in \mathcal{I}} \sum_{j \in \mathcal{I}} A_{ij}$, and the *conductance* ϕ of the partitioning $(\mathcal{I}, \bar{\mathcal{I}})$ by

$$\phi_A(\mathcal{I}) = \frac{Cut_A(\mathcal{I}, \bar{\mathcal{I}})}{\min(Vol_A(\mathcal{I}), Vol_A(\bar{\mathcal{I}}))}.$$

The Cheeger constant h_G is defined as $h_G(A) = \min_{\mathcal{I}} \phi_A(\mathcal{I})$ and can be shown to be bounded by the eigengap [7, 6] : $h_G(A) \geq \frac{1}{2}\delta(A)$. The conductance indicates how well $(\mathcal{I}, \bar{\mathcal{I}})$ partitions the set of nodes into two subsets, and the minimum over $\mathcal{I}$ corresponds to the best partition. Therefore, if there exist a partition for which (i) the weights A_{ij} of the graph edges across the partition are small, and (ii) each of the regions in the partition has enough volume, then the Cheeger constant will be small. Starting from $K = 1$, we would like to select the simplest clustering model (i.e., the smallest K) for which the extracted clusters are tight enough (hard to split into two subsets). This is equivalent to request that the Cheeger constant is large enough for each cluster, or to request that the eigengap is large for all clusters. Our first criterion is

$$\delta_K = \min_{i \in 1...K} \delta(L(A_K^{(ii)})), \qquad (3)$$

where $A_K^{(ii)}$ are the submatrices extracted from A according to the model obtained by the spectral algorithm, and L is defined in Section 2.1. The algorithm selects the smallest K for which the eigengap δ_K exceeds a threshold.

---

[2] Or the first k eigenvectors, in cases where we have a k-repeated, largest eigenvalues.

The Relative Cut The measure defined by Eq. (3) has a drawback, as it only considers intra-cluster information. When part of the data have no clearly defined clusters, the algorithm may over-estimate the number of clusters so that all clusters (possibly reduced to a single element) are tight enough. We thus considered a second criterion that characterizes the overall quality of a clustering. This criterion is defined as the fraction of the total weight of edges not covered by the clusters,

$$\text{rcut}_K = \frac{\sum_{k=1}^{K} \sum_{l=1, l \neq k}^{K} \sum_{i \in S_k} \sum_{j \in S_l} A_{ij}}{\sum_i \sum_j A_{ij}}. \tag{4}$$

The algorithm outputs the largest K for which rcut is below a threshold.

3   Spectral Structuring of Home Videos

Home videos contain series of ordered and temporally adjacent shots that can be organized in groups usually related to distinct scenes. In our approach, shot grouping exploits visual similarity and temporal adjacency, two of the main criteria that allows people to identify clusters in video collections, when nothing else is known about the content (unlike the filmmaker, who knows details of context). Previous formulations in the literature are based on similar concepts [13]. We use spectral clustering as follows.

Home video shots usually contain more than one appearance, due to hand-held camera motion. Consequently, a shot is represented by a small fixed number of key-frames, $N_{kf} = 5$. The $i - th$ key-frame f_i of a video is characterized by a color histogram h_i in the RGB space (uniformly quantized to $8 \times 8 \times 8$ bins).

The pairwise affinity matrix A is directly built from the set of all key-frames in a video by defining

$$A_{ij} = e^{-\left(\frac{d_v^2(f_i, f_j)}{2\sigma_v^2} + \frac{d_t^2(f_i, f_j)}{2\sigma_t^2} \right)}, \tag{5}$$

where A_{ij} is the affinity between key-frames f_i and f_j, d_v and d_t are measures of visual and temporal similarity, and σ_v^2 and σ_t^2 are scale parameters.

Visual similarity is computed by the metric based on Bhattacharyya coefficient, which has proven to be robust to compare color distributions [2],

$$d_v(f_i, f_j) = (1 - \rho_{BT}(h_i, h_j))^{1/2}, \text{ with } \rho_{BT} = \sum_k (h_{ik} h_{jk})^{1/2} \tag{6}$$

Temporal similarity exploits the fact that distant shots along the temporal axis are less likely to belong to the same scene. It is defined by $d_t(f_i, f_j) = \frac{||f_j| - |f_i||}{|v|}$ where $|f_i|$ denote the absolute frame number of f_i in the video, and $|v|$ denotes the entire video clip duration. Note that the range for both d_v and d_t is $[0, 1]$.

We further set the scale parameters σ_v and σ_t in the following way. Building upon a previous study [3], we fixed the σ_v value to 0.25 which represents a good threshold for separating intra and inter-cluster similarities distributions in home videos. Similarly, it was shown in [3] that in average 70% of home video scenes are composed of four or less shots. Thus, the σ_t value was set to the average temporal separation between four shots in a given video.

The spectral method is applied as discussed in Section 2. A cluster number is assigned to each shot using a majority rule on the cluster labels of its key-frames. In the case of a tie, the cluster is randomly selected from the candidates.

4 Experiments

4.1 Data Set and Ground-Truth

The data set consists of 20 MPEG-1 home videos, digitized from VHS tapes provided by seven different people, and with approximate individual duration of 20 minutes. The videos depict vacations, school parties, weddings, and children playing in indoor/outdoor scenarios. A ground-truth (GT) at the shot level was semi-automatically generated, resulting in a total of 430 shots. The number of shots per video varies considerably (between 4 and 62 shots).

There are two typical options to define the GT at the scene level. In the first-party approach, the GT is generated by the video creator [9]. This method incorporates specific context knowledge about the content (e.g., family links, and location relationships). In contrast, a third-party GT is defined by a subject not familiar with the content. In this case, there still exists human context understanding, but limited to what is displayed. This "blind context" makes third-party GTs a fairer benchmark strategy for automatic algorithms [10].

In this paper, we use a third-party GT based on multiple subject judgement that takes into account the fact that different people might generate different results. Scenes for each video were found by twenty subjects using a GUI that displayed a key-frame-based video summary (no real videos were displayed). A very general statement about the clustering task, and no initial solution were provided to the subjects at the beginning of the process. The final GT set consists of about 400 human segmentations.

4.2 Performance Measures

The performance measures that we consider are (i) the number of clusters selected by the algorithm and (ii) the shots in errors (SIE). For the number of clusters, we report the value we obtain and compare it with the numbers provided by people. For shot in errors, let us denote $GT^i = \{GT^i_j, j \in 1, ..., N_i\}$ the set of human GTs for the video V_i, and C^i the solution of an algorithm for the same video. The SIE between C^i and a ground-truth GT^i_j is defined as the number of shots whose cluster label in C^i does not match the label in the GT. For each video, the SIEs between C_i and each GT^i_j are computed. Then, from the ranked SIE values, we keep the minimum, the median and the maximum, denoted SIE^i_{min}, SIE^i_{med} and SIE^i_{max} respectively. The minimum value indicates how far an automatic clustering is from the nearest segmentation provided by a human. The median value can be considered as a fair measure of how well the

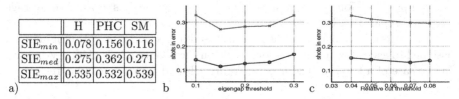

	H	PHC	SM
SIE_{min}	0.078	0.156	0.116
SIE_{med}	0.275	0.362	0.271
SIE_{max}	0.535	0.532	0.539

a)   b   c

Fig. 5. (a) Average of the percentage of shots in error for humans (H), baseline (PHC), and spectral method (SM). (b)-(c) Variation of the average of percentage of shots in error (average of the median in red, of the min in blue) for different criteria as function of their threshold: (b) eigengap; (range: (0.1,0.3)); (c) relative cut (range: (0.04,0.08))

algorithm performs, taking into account the majority of the human GTs and excluding the largest errors. These large errors may come from outliers and are taken into account by SIE^i_{max}, which gives an idea of the spread of the measures. For the overall performance measure, we computed the average SIE measures over all the videos, of the percentage of shots in errors w.r.t. the number of shots in each video. Note that this normalization is necessary because the number of clusters (and shots) varies considerably from one video to another.

4.3   Results

The best result with our method was obtained using the eigengap criterion and a threshold $\delta_K = 0.15$. We compared it with a probabilistic hierarchical clustering method (PHC) described in [3], as well as with human performance. The latter was obtained in the following way : for each video, the minimum, median and maximum shots in error were computed for each human GT against all the others. These values were then averaged over all subjects. These averages are plotted in Fig. 6 for each video. Finally we computed the average over all the videos to get the overall performance.

The Table of Fig. 5(a) summarizes the results. We can first notice from the minimum and maximum values that the spread of performances is high, given the performance measure. Secondly, the spectral method is performing better than PHC, as can be seen from the median and minimum value, and approximately as well as the humans.

Fig. 6 displays the results obtained for each video. First, in Fig. 6(a), we show the number of detected clusters (the red circles) as predicted by the algorithm and compare them to the mean of the number of clusters in the GT. The spread of the cluster numbers in the GT is represented by the blue bar (plus or minus one standard deviation). Note that the videos have been ordered according to their number of shots. The detected cluster numbers are in good accordance with the GT, though slightly underestimated. Fig. 6(b) displays the values of the shot in error measures in comparison to the average of human performance. The circles depict the measures obtained with our method and the crosses denote

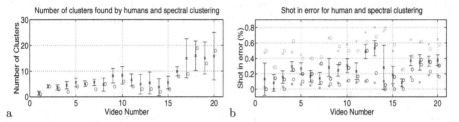

Fig. 6. (a) Determination of number of clusters. (b) Percentage of shot in error. The blue bar indicates the spread of the human performances of the SIE_{med} value

Fig. 7. Home video structuring examples. Only one keyframe per shot is displayed

human performance. The color represents the differents measures (minimum in red, median in blue, and maximum in green). The median performance of our algorithm is better than the average human in eight cases and worse in six cases. Notice that in 25% of the cases, our algorithm provides a segmentation that also exists in the GT.

Two examples of the generated clusters are shown in Fig. 7. Each cluster is displayed as a row of shots, which in turn are represented by one keyframe. Qualitatively, the method provides sensible results.

Fig. 5 shows the obtained results using the two criteria. The selection with the eigengap criterion slightly outperforms the results obtained with the relative cut. Notice that the results are quite consistent over a relatively large range of thresholds, and better than the probabilistic hierarchical clustering algorithm.

Finally, let us mention that, given the distance matrices, the clustering algorithm implemented in matlab takes around 4 seconds per video in average.

5   Conclusion

We have presented an approach for structuring home videos using a spectral method. We investigated the automatic selection of the number of clusters, which is currently an open research issue for spectral methods. We have shown in our experiments that the eigengap measure could be used to estimate this number.

The algorithm was applied to a six-hour home video database, and the results are favorably compared to existing techniques as well as human performance.

References

[1] F. R. K. Chung, *Spectral Graph Theory*, American Mathematical Society, 1997. 315

[2] D. Comaniciu, V. Ramesh, and P. Meer, "Real-Time Tracking of Non-Rigid Objects using Mean Shift," in *Proc. IEEE CVPR.*, Hilton Head Island, S. C., June 2000. 316

[3] D. Gatica-Perez, A. Loui, and M. T. Sun, "Finding Structure in Home Videos by Probabilistic Hierarchical Clustering," *IEEE Trans. on Circuits and Systems for Video Technology*, Vol. 13, No. 5, Jun. 2003. 310, 316, 318

[4] G. Iyengar and A. Lippman, "Content-based browsing and edition of unstructured video," in *Proc. IEEE ICME*, New York City, Aug. 2000. 310

[5] J. R. Kender and B. L. Yeo, "On the Structure and Analysis of Home Videos," in *Proc. ACCV*, Taipei, Jan. 2000. 310

[6] S. Vempala R. Kannan and A. Vetta, "On clusterings - good, bad and spectral," in *Proc. 41st Symposium on the Foundation of Computer Science, FOCS*, 2000. 310, 315

[7] A. Ng, M. I. Jordan, and Y. Weiss, "On spectral clustering: analysis and an algorithm," in *Proc. NIPS*, Vancouver, Dec 2001. 310, 311, 312, 313, 314, 315

[8] J.-M. Odobez, D. Gatica-Perez and M. Guillemot, "On Spectral Methods and Structuring of Home Videos," IDIAP Technical Report, IDIAP-RR-55, Nov. 2002. 314

[9] J. Platt "AutoAlbum: Clustering Digital Photographs using Probablisitic Model Merging," in *Proc. IEEE Workshop on CBAIVL*, Hilton Head Island, S. C.,2000. 317

[10] A. Savakis, S. Etz, and A. Loui, "Evaluation of image appeal in consumer photography," in *Proc. SPIE Conf. on Human Vision and EI*, Jan. 2000. 317

[11] G. L. Scott and H. C. Longuet-Higgins, "Feature grouping by relocalisation of eigenvectors of the proximity matrix," in *Proc. BMVC*, 1990, pp. 103–108. 310, 311, 313

[12] J. Shi and J. Malik, "Normalized cuts and image segmentation," *IEEE Trans. on Pattern Analysis and Machine Intelligence*, vol. 22, no. 8, pp. 888–905, 2000. 310, 311

[13] M. Yeung, B. L. Yeo, and B. Liu, "Segmentation of Video by Clustering and Graph Analysis," *Comp. Vision and Image Underst.*, Vol. 71, No. 1, pp. 94-109, July 1998. 316

[14] Y. Weiss, "Segmentation using eigenvectors: a unifying view," in *Proc. ICCV*, 1999. 310

Home Photo Retrieval: Time Matters

Philippe Mulhem[1] and Joo-Hwee Lim[2]

[1] IPAL-CNRS
[2] Institute for Infocomm Research
21 Heng Mui Keng Terrace, Singapore 119613, Singapore
{mulhem,joohwee}@i2r.a-star.edu.sg

Abstract. Temporal information has been regarded as a key vehicle for sorting and grouping home photos into albums associated with events. While time-based browsing might be adequate for relatively small photo collection, query and retrieval would be very useful to find relevant photos of an event in large collection. In this paper, we propose the use of temporal events for organizing and representing home photos using structured document formalism and hence a new way to retrieve photos of an event using both image content and temporal context. We describe a hierarchical model of temporal events and the algorithm to construct it from a collection of home photos. In particular, we compute metadata of a node from the metadata of its children recursively to facilitate content-based and context-based matching between a query and an event. With semantic content representation extracted using Visual Keywords and Extended Conceptual Graphs, we demonstrate the effectiveness of photo retrieval on 2400 time-stamped heterogeneous home photos with very promising results.

1   Introduction

It had been shown [15,16] that time is the most prominent aspect used by consumers to retrieve their photos: when they want to retrieve photos of one event, they consider *"I roughly know when it is [...]"* (p. 5 of [16]) and they browse their collections until they found what they are looking for. Indeed temporal information has been utilized for sorting and grouping home photos into albums associated with events, which is the most requested feature for photo organization [15].

For instance, MyPhotos [18] proposes effective temporal navigation in photo collections. The Hierarchical Browser described in [7] exploited photo creation time to cluster photos and to generate meaningful summaries. The PhotoTOC [13] and AutoAlbum [12] used adaptive gap threshold to split photos sorted by creation time into albums and a left-right Hidden Markov Model on the color information to further cluster the ordered photos in large albums. These works share a common insight and assumption: the irregular and recursive busty time patterns of home photos taking

E. M. Bakker et al. (Eds.): CIVR 2003, LNCS 2728, pp. 321-330, 2003.
© Springer-Verlag Berlin Heidelberg 2003

correlate well with events [7] and a noticeable time gap correspond to a change in event [13].

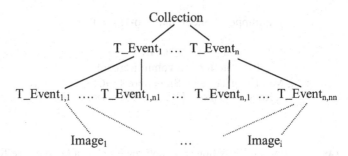

Fig. 1. A typical temporal organization of a home photo collection

While time-based browsing might be adequate for relatively small photo collection (average of 1000 photos in [16]; 1300 or less photos in [13]), query and retrieval would be very useful to find relevant photos of an event in large collection. In this paper, we propose the use of temporal events for organizing and representing home photos using structured document formalism and hence a new way to retrieve photos of an event using both image content and temporal context.

Though time-based photo clusters are good and sensible approximation to photo events, we remind that in some situations, the time gap may not reflect the true semantic boundary of an event. Hence we prefer to use the term "temporal event" to reflect the approximation in this paper. Furthermore, we draw the analogy of a home photo collection to a structured document. Images grouped into temporal events are indeed considered similar in some way to parts in a structured document as shown in Fig. 1. The images at the leaf nodes correspond to passages in a structured document.

For such documents, several approaches try to use the explicit structure to provide clues to retrieve the best document parts that match the queries: [2] for the FERMI Esprit II project defined a logical-based expression of information propagation and query processing. This work was used in [8] to provide a Dempster-Shafer frameword for structured document retrieval. Other approaches use the structure to facilitate the computation of relevance status values, but not for the selection of the level of structure retrieved: the work reported in [19] employed the usual vector space model to index whole documents and document parts and to retrieve document parts, showing that the context of document parts may be used to retrieve relevant chapters of legal documents; [11] use probabilistic belief networks to represent the impact of retrieval of the structure of documents. Our approach is more related to the latter approaches: we study the impact of the temporal structure on image retrieval.

From another point of view, some works have considered different uses of links in, or between, web or hypertext pages. [9] defined a notion of "local neighborhood" of a web page that is used to compute the relevance of a page using the out-going links to provide better results than usual non-contextual searches. [4] shown that the links between web pages are important to find out what are the "best" entries of the entire web sites. [6] used the links of texts nodes connected to image nodes in hypertext documents to index images. [1] uses the context of occurrence of images or video links to classify them. We adopt similar belief that the composition of temporal events may be used as contexts during the query processing of image retrieval.

We organize the rest of the paper as follows. We describe a hierarchical model of temporal events and the algorithm to construct it from a collection of home photos in the next section. The metadata definition of a temporal event based on the metadata of its children as well as content-based and context-based query processing is presented in Section 3. We demonstrate the effectiveness of photo retrieval on 2400 time-stamped heterogeneous home photos with very promising results in Section 4 followed by conclusion.

2   Temporal Events Modeling

A temporal event $T \in \mathbf{T}$, on a collection of image $\mathcal{I}$ is a triplet (*Sub-T, Image, Index*) where *Sub-T* ($\subset \mathbf{T}$) is the set of temporal events that compose T, *Image* ($\subset \mathcal{I}$) is the set of images that compose T, and *Index* is the content representation of T. We ensure that a temporal event T is composed of either images or sub-events but not both i.e. *T.Sub-T XOR T.Image* = $\varnothing$ where a dot notation $A.B$ indicates the access to the element B of the instance A.

An image *Im* is described by a triplet (*Image_Data, Time, Index*), with *Image_Data* being the raw pixel data of the image, *Time* as time and date of image creation, *Index* as the metadata describing the content of the image. We define F_{images} as a mapping from $\mathbf{T}$ to $\mathcal{I}$ that contains the list of all the images (directly or transitively) belonged to a temporal event. Using the F_{images} function, we formalize the fact that a temporal event contains only consecutive images:

$$\forall I_1, I_2 \in F_{images}(T), \neg (\exists I_3 \in \mathrm{I} \setminus F_{images}(T) \ between(I_1.Time, I_2.Time, I_3.Time))$$

where *between* denotes a ternary predicate that is true if the time symbol in the third place is between the other two time symbols.

To build a hierarchy of temporal events, we use an approach inspired from the single-link clustering [5, p.233]. For level of granularity G_k, we compute the matrix storing the image×image temporal differences. Then we use a one-pass single link algorithm to build the temporal events using these temporal distances and a threshold over which the images are not linked. We denote I_{Gk} the set of initial temporal events for the granularity G_k. A nice property of this approach is that for two granularities G_i and G_j with respective thresholds Th_{gi} and Th_{gj}, $Th_{gi} < Th_{gj}$, we ensure that for each initial temporal event T_l of T_{Gi} the images of T_l are strictly included in the images of one and only one initial temporal event T_m of T_{Gj}. This is very similar to that of PhotoTOC [13] and the first step of the clustering in [7]. In implementation, the difference between Gregorian date and time are computed with the use of Julian day numbers. For example, consider a collection I of 6 images with a DDMMYYYY time format, $I = \{Im_1[15081998], Im_2 [16081998], Im_3[19081998], Im_4[20081998], Im_5[27081998], Im_6[28081998]\}$. A first generation of initial temporal events T_{G1} for a threshold of one day is $\{\{Im_1, Im_2\}, \{ Im_3, Im_4\}, \{Im_5, Im_6\}\}$. The generation T_{G5} of a threshold of 5 days is $\{\{Im_1, Im_2, Im_3, Im_4\}, \{Im_5, Im_6\}\}$. In this paper, we decided to limit the temporal definition using temporal features, to be able in the future do study the impact of other ways (like imag content) to define such events.

3   Content Representation and Query Processing

The content representation (or index) of a temporal event is based on the content representation of its composing images. For a temporal event T, we define $T.Index = F_{index}(\{im.time, im.index\} \mid im \in F_{images}(T)\})$ where the function F_{index} computes the index of a temporal event based on the time and indexes of the images that belong to it. In this paper, the index associated with an image I, denoted as $(I.Index_{vk}, I.Index_{cg})$, is composed of both a Visual Keywords representation $Index_{vk}$ and an Extended Conceptual Graph representation $Index_{cg}$ (please refer to [10] for details). We compare in this paper two simple definitions of the function F_{index}:

- The index of a temporal event is that of the image with the highest burst rate in the temporal event suggesting that this photo is important (as mentioned in [16], people take several digital photos to ensure they obtain a good one);
- The index of the temporal event is considered as a simple concatenation of the indexes of the images that belong to the event

3.1   Image Index Based on Visual Keywords

Visual Keywords are local semantic regions derived from statistical learning (e.g. Support Vector Machines). Fig. 2 shows the 26 classes of Visual Keywords defined and learned for the 2400 home photos in our experiments. For the purpose of image indexing, multi-scale view-based recognition against these 26 Visual Keywords are performed on each image and the probabilistic recognition results are reconciled upon multiple resolutions and aggregated according to configurable spatial tessellation (e.g. five coarse areas: left, right, top, bottom, center) as the image index. In essence, an image area is represented as a histogram of Visual Keywords based on the certainties of local recognition. The similarity matching function beween a query Q_{vk} represented by the index of a query image and the index of a image I of the database, $Match_{VK}(Q_{vk}, I.Index_{vk})$, is simply a weighted similarity between the corresponding areas in the query and the image (for example, we can assign higher weight for the center area as consumers tend to place the subject at the center while taking pictures). The similarity between two images areas is a simple histogram city-block distance computed between the visual keywords histograms in which the bins now possess semantic meanings. The choice of visual keywords is specific to a given context, because it's well known that the current state of the art of computer vision and image understanding is far from being able to provide accurate results in any context. So, the Visual Keywords are defined *a priori* and each Visual Keyword specificity is learned using examples, and each photo of the collection is then labelled automatically without any human intervention.

People: Face, Figure, Crowd, Skin

Sky: Clear, Cloudy, Blue

Ground: Floor, Sand, Grass

Water: Pool, Pond, Water

Foliage: Green, Floral, Branch

Mountain: Far, Rocky

Building: Old, City, Far

Interior: Wall, Wooden, China, Fabric, Light

Fig. 2. The 26 Visual Keywords adopted for home photos

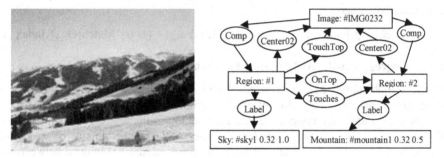

Fig. 3. The conceptual graph of an image

3.2   Image Index Based on Extended Conceptual Graphs

The description of the images using Extended Conceptual Graphs is achieved through the use of a knowledge representation formalism, namely the Conceptual Graphs [17]. Because of space constraints, we only present an example in Fig. 3, where the left part presents a photograph and the right part an excerpt of the conceptual graph that index this image. Such conceptual graph representation is based on the VK labeling process decribed above, but the advantage of using graphs if the possiblity of simulating deduction. Compared to the initial definition of conceptual graphs by Sowa, we use additional elements dedicated to represent the certainty of recognition of elements (for instance, the Mountain concept of Fig. 3 is recognized with a certainty of 0.5), and the importance of the elements (for instance the Sky concept of Fig. 3 has an importance of 0.32). The query processing for the conceptual graphs is related to the function $Match_{CG}(Q_{cg}, I.Index_{cg})$, and based on sub-graph matching (the query Q_{cg} being also a conceptual graph), considering the importance and certainty of recognition of the elements of the image index $I.Index_{cg}$ and the query. The query Q_{cg} may be an image index, as in the experiments conducted in Section 4. The matching value uses the concepts weights as well as relationships weights.

3.3   Selection-Based Temporal Event Index

The first option, in order to generate the index of a temporal event, is to select one image, hopefully the most representative, and to use its index as the index of the temporal event.

To integrate the use of such temporal aspects when finding the most important image of a temporal event, we define the function f_k, from N^+ (going from the time and date of the first image of the event, in seconds, to the time and date of the last image of the event) to N^+ (image numbers going from 1 to y), as an interpolation of the cumulative function indicating for one time point t_x the number of images taken before (or at) t_x in the event. Such a function f_k is generated by using cubic spline interpolation [14]. The temporal representative value of an image p is then computed as the absolute value of the derivative $f'_k = df_k/dt$ for the value t_p.

The index of a temporal event T is then similar to that of an image i.e. ($T.Index_{vk}$, $T.Index_{cg}$). The query processing is computed using a matching function $Match_{TE}$ defined as a linear combination of the $Match_{cg}$ and $Match_{vk}$ of the query and the representative image:

$$Match_{TE}(Q,T.Index) = \alpha*Match(Q_{vk},T.Index_{vk}) + (1-\alpha)*Match(Q_{cg},T.Index_{cg})$$

3.4   Aggregation-Based Temporal Event Index

If one is not convinced that a selected image is always adequate to represent a temporal event effectively for different queries, then as a second approach we represent the index of a temporal event as the union of the indexes of its images, so $T.Index$ is a set of couples ($c.Index_{vk}$, $c.Index_{cg}$), one c per image of T. Query processing is based on the maximum matching (i.e. best match) obtained between the query and the indexes:

$$Match_{TE}(Q,T.Index)= \max_{c \in T.Index} \{\alpha*Match(Q_{vk},c.Index_{vk}) + (1-\alpha)*Match(Q_{cg},c.Index_{cg})\}$$

3.5   Query Processing for Temporal Events

The query processing for a temporal event is analogous to that for text passage retrieval [19] with a query image being a passage and a temporal event as a document part. The retrieval function performed for a query Q and one image I depends on 3 representations: the query representation, the index of I, and the indexes of the temporal events that contain I. As we described earlier, in our case the query Q, the image index, and temporal event index are based on both VK and CG representations.

Using the temporal event indexes during query processing, we intend to capture both the relevance of an image *per se* and the relevance of temporal context. We assign the importance of a temporal event as inversely proportional to its duration for query processing. Hence we compute the relevance status value of an image Im for a query Q as

$$RSV(Q,I) = \alpha*Match_{vk}(Q_{vk}, I.Index_{vk}) + (1-\alpha)*Match_{cg}(Q_{cg},I.Index_{cg}) +$$
$$\sum_{T \in \mathbf{T} \text{ s.t. } I \in F_{images}(T)} \beta(T,I) * Match_{TE}(Q,T.Index)$$

where β is a function that returns the value of importance of a temporal event based on its duration and on the structural distance between the temporal event T and I, assuming that the longer an event is, the lower it representents accurately one image, and that the further the event from the image in the structure representation the lower in impacts the image retrieval.

4   Experiments on Image Retrieval by Content and Context

The experiments were conducted on a set I of 2400 home photos with temporal metadata year, month, day, hour, minute, and second. The temporal events were built as described in Section 2, with a granularity level of 1 hour: photos taken within an one-hour interval are assumed to be related to a short event. Thus in this paper, we only consider one level of temporal events that plays important role as temporal context. The number of temporal events obtained is 278, giving an average of 8 photos per event, with a maximum of 90 images and a minimum of 1 image. The β function is a linear function that only considers 1) temporal events duration within a day (i.e. 86400 seconds), assuming the existence of the function $duration(T)$ that gives the duration (in seconds) of the event T, and 2) the inverse of the distance ($Str\_distance$) between the event and one image in the events structure:

$$\beta(T, I) = \begin{cases} \dfrac{1}{Str\_distance(T, I)} \cdot (1 - \dfrac{duration(T)}{86400}) & \text{if } duration(T) \le 86400 \\ 0 & \text{if } duration(T) > 86400 \end{cases}$$

The experiments were conducted on a set of 26 queries, using query by example, with the VK (c.f. 3.1) and CG (c.f. 3.2) representations, using α equal to 0.9. The assesment of the relevant images for each query has been made by two persons, and we kept the intersection of the two assessments. The queries correspond to different runs of the system to retrieve images corresponding to meals, weddings, parks, watersides and beaches, swimming pool, streets and roadsides photos. The images of the query by examples were selected randomly from the relevant set for each query. We present the recall versus precision[1] curves (Fig. 4), averaged over the 26 queries, obtained with and without the use of the temporal events using our approach (denoted as SYMB) and we compare as a baseline to a color-only approach using a 4x4 grid of HSV color-space local histograms (similar to the PicHunter System [3], denoted as HSV). We study the use of the representative image (c.f. 3.3, denoted as Rep) and the use of the whole set of image indexes (c.f. 3.4, denoted as Max).

In Fig. 4, we see that the use of both representative-based or max-based temporal events increases the quality of the results obtained: +5.6% for Rep SYMB compared to SYMB, +6.9% for Rep HSV, but the most convincing results are +25% for Max SYMB as well as for Max HSV. This clearly shows that the use of contextual information for the retrieval of home photos impacts positively each of the content representations. It also shows that the use of the representative image (Rep) does not

---

[1] Using the trec_eval software from ftp://ftp.cs.cornell.edu/pub/smart/ .

perform as well as the Max, as expected. We also confirm that our use of symbolic representations surpasses the low-level color-based representation scheme. We notice also that the Max HSV scheme (average precision 0.3178) performs almost as good as the basic SYMB scheme (average precision of 0.3253), wich reinforce our idea that the context is important when considering image retrieval.

Table 1 presents average precision values at top 5, 10, 20 and 30 photos for the 26 queries. The values in parentheses indicate the relative increase. This table highlights the importance of the precision improvement when presenting results to the user. For instance, at top 10 photos, the average number of relevant photos is 0.65 for SYMB and 0.8 for Max SYMB (meaning that there is on average 8 relevant photos among the first 10 retrieved), and 0.4 for HSV and 0.65 (on average 6.5 relevant photos in the first 10 retrieved). At top 30 photos, the number of relevant documents is on average 15 for SYMB and 20 for Max Symb, and also 10 for HSV and 15.9 for Max HSV; the precision of Max SYMB at top 30 photos is greater than 2/3, empirical threshold under which we consider such system to be unusable by consumers. We notice once again that the Max HSV using the event infomartion performs as well as the basic SYMB sheme.

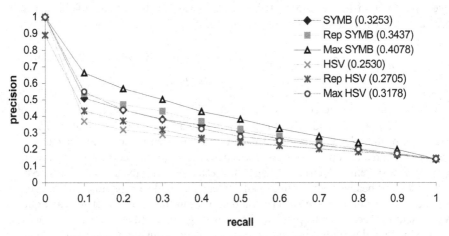

Fig. 4. Recall Precision with and without using the temporal events

Table 1. Average precision values at 5, 10, 20 and 30 images

Avg. Prec.	SYMB	Max SYMB	HSV	Max HSV
@ 5 photos	0.731	0.88 (+20.4%)	0.508	0.72 (+41.8%)
@ 10 photos	0.658	0.80 (+21.6%)	0.400	0.65 (+62.5%)
@ 20 photos	0.552	0.73 (+31.5%)	0.348	0.58 (+67.2%)
@ 30 photos	0.506	0.67 (+32.7%)	0.341	0.53 (+55.2%)

5   Conclusion

In this paper, we have proposed a structured document formalism of temporal events for organizing and representing home photos. We defined how to create the temporal events from a collection of temporally tagged home photos, and we described several ways to create the index corresponding to these temporal events. We formalized and developed a new way to retrieve photos using both image content and temporal context (the temporal events) and demonstrated its effectiveness and practicality for photo retrieval on a collection of 2400 home photos using 26 queries by example.

The results obtained are very promising, and we will consider in future works the retrieval of photos belonged to an entire event. Other future directions will focus on other approaches to find one or more representative image of events, in a way to avoid the use of all the images to represent the index of each temporal event.

References

[1]   S.-F. Chang and J. Smith, Searching for Images and Videos on the World-Wide Web, *Technical Report #459-96-25*, Columbia Univ., Aug. 1996.

[2]   Y. Chiaramella and P. Mulhem and F. Fourel, A Model for Multimedia Information Retrieval, Technical Report 4-96, *FERMI ESPRIT BRA 8134*, 1996.

[3]   Cox, M. Miller, T. Minka, T. Papathomas, and P. N. Yianilos, The Bayesian Image Retrieval System, PicHunter: Theory, Implementation and Psychophysical Experiments, *IEEE Tran. on Image Processing* 9(1): 20-37, 2000.

[4]   N. Craswell, D. Hawking and S. Robertson, Effective site finding using link anchor information, *ACM SIGIR*, New Orleans, 2001.

[5]   R. O. Duda and P. E. Hart, *Pattern Classification and Scene Analysis*, John Wiley & Sons, 1973.

[6]   M. Dunlop, *Multimedia Information Retrieval*, PhD thesis, Department of Computer Science, University of Glasgow, 1991.

[7]   A. Graham, H. Garcia-Molina, A. Paepcke and T. Winograd, Time as an Essence for Photo Browsing Through Personal Digital Libraries, *ACM JCDL*, USA, pp.326-335, 2002.

[8]   M. Lalmas, Dempster-Shafer's Theory of Evidence Applied to Structured Documents Modelling Uncertainty, *ACM SIGIR*, USA, pp.110-118, 1997.

[9]   M. Marchiori, The Quest for Correct Information on the Web: Hyper Search Engines, *6th Intl. World Wide Web Conference*, California, U.S.A., pp.265-276, 1997.

[10]   P. Mulhem and J.H. Lim, Symbolic photo content-based retrieval, *ACM CIKM*, McLean, VA, USA, Nov. 4-9, pp. 94-101, 2002.

[11]   S. H. Myaeng, D.-H. Juang, M.-S. Kim and Z.-C. Zhoo, A Flexible Model for Retrieval of SGML Documents, *ACM SIGIR*, Australia, pp. 138-145, 1998.

[12] J. Platt, AutoAlbum: Clustering Digital Photographs Using Probabilistic Model Merging, *IEEE Workshop on Content-Based Access of Image and Video Libraries 2000*, pp. 96-100, 2000.

[13] J. C. Platt, M. Czerwinski, B. Field, PhotoTOC: Automatic Clustering for Browsing Personal Photographs, Microsoft Research Technical Report MSR-TR-2002-17, (2002).

[14] W. H. Press, B. P. Flannery, S. A. Teukolsky, W. T. Vetterling, Cubic Spline Interpolation, Sub-Chapter 3.3 of Numerical Recipes in C – The Art of Scientific Computing, Second Edition, Cambridge Universoty Press, 1993, pp. 113-117.

[15] K. Rodden, How do people organise their photograpghs? *BCS IRSG 21st Annual Colloquium on Information Retrieval Research*, Glasgow, April 1999.

[16] K. Rodden and K. Wood, How People Manage Their Digital Photos? *ACM CHI*, USA, 2003 (to appear).

[17] J. Sowa. Conceptual Structures: Information Processing in Mind and Machine. Addison-Wesley Publisher, 1984.

[18] Y. Sun, H. Zhang, L. Zhang and M. Li, MyPhotos – A System for Home Management and Processing, *ACM Multimedia*, France, pp. 81-83, 2002.

[19] R. Wilkinson, Effective Retrieval of Structured Documents, *ACM SIGIR* 1994, Ireland, pp.311-327, 1994.

Automatic Annotation of Tennis Action
for Content-Based Retrieval
by Integrated Audio and Visual Information

Hisashi Miyamori

Keihanna Human Info-Communication Research Center
Communications Research Laboratory
2–2–2, Hikari-dai, Seika-cho, Souraku-gun, Kyoto, 619–0289 Japan
miya@crl.go.jp

Abstract. This paper proposes a method of automatically annotating
tennis action through the integrated use of audio and video information.
The proposed method extracts ball-hitting times called "impact times"
using audio information, and evaluates the position relations between
the player and the ball at the impact time to identify the player's basic
actions, such as forehand swing, overhead swing, etc. Simulation results
show that the detection rate for impact time influences the recognition
rate of the player's basic actions. They also reveal that using audio information avoids some event recognition failures that cannot be averted
when using only video information, demonstrating the performance and
the validity of our approach.

1 Introduction

Recently, content-based retrieval and its annotation techniques have become
more and more important, because they enable efficient searching and browsing
of necessary segments from hours of multimedia contents.

Previous approaches to annotation for content-based retrieval have mainly
focused on visual features such as color, shape, texture, and motion[1]-[2]. Although they have an advantage that they can be applied to a wide variety of
generic video, these visual features have a common drawback that they can represent only low-level information.

Several studies have attempted to make specific content retrieval more realistic based on the use of domain knowledge[3]-[6]. These studies have mainly
used information about the position of objects in a scene such as loci, relative
positions, their transitions, etc., and have analyzed it with a specific field in
mind such as soccer, basketball, tennis, etc., in order to relate it to particular
events that corresponded to high-level information.

Since these approaches are based on the use of field-specific knowledge, they
can efficiently represent high-level information if all the necessary objects are
successfully extracted. However, previous studies still have a problem in that
several important time points and positions could not be detected due to tracking
errors or a lack of necessary information in the video.

E. M. Bakker et al. (Eds.): CIVR 2003, LNCS 2728, pp. 331–341, 2003.

Other studies have tried to use audio and video information for effective tracking of specific objects. In [7], active contours were exploited along with audio data from stereo microphones, to effectively identify and track a speaker from multiple participants in a teleconference.

This paper presents a method of accurately identifying human behaviors for content-based retrieval using audio and video information. In our approach, we combine the use of audio information with conventional video methods, to develop an integrated reasoning module that recognizes some events not identifiable by the conventional methods. The proposed method enables robust event recognition that is not strongly affected by a partial lack of information or identification errors.

The rest of the paper is organized as follows. In Section 2, the system overview is presented. In Section 3 and 4, the moments when the players hit the ball, which are called "impact times", are extracted by using, respectively, ball tracking methods and audio information. In Section 5, the basic actions of the players are analyzed using the detected impact times. Experimental results for a real tennis video are presented in Section 6, and the conclusion is given in section 7.

2   System Overview

Figure 1 shows the block diagram of the proposed system. Our test domain is tennis. Our goal is to retrieve, from the whole video of tennis matches, video segments containing the basic actions of a player such as forehand swing, backhand swing, and overhead swing.

A tennis video generally includes various scenes such as close-up shots of each player, judges, etc., but most typical shots are those of the tennis court, which are shot diagonally from above the ground. In this paper, we assume that the input is shots including those of the tennis court, which has been already partitioned, for example, by a certain colour-based selection approach[5].

Annotation is performed by using the following steps (figure 1):

Step 1. Extraction of Court and Net Lines
   Court and net lines c are extracted from the binary image I_B of the original image at time t, by using a court model and Hough transforms[6].

Step 2. Extraction of Player's Position
   Eliminate court and netlines c from I_B. Interpolate the region that was originally considered to overlap the player's region and that was removed by the elimination. Detect the initial player's position as a region larger than a certain area around the court at time $t = 0$. At time $t = t$, determine the player's region p as the region overlapping most of the player's region at $t = t - 1$ (figure 3).

Step 3. Extraction of Ball's Position
   Extract ball region b through ball tracking taking the distance to the player's region p into account (described in section 3).

Step 4. Extraction of Impact Times

Impact times are extracted with two methods. The first is by estimating the time point when the ball bounces back around the player using b, p, c, and the second is by determining the time point through analyzing the audio information in the frequency domain (elaborated in section 3, 4).

Step 5. Identification of Player's Basic Actions

These positions and temporal information become the input to the integrated reasoning module, which evaluates the event occurrence conditions and outputs the indices of the player's basic actions to the database.

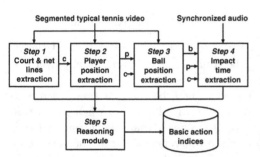

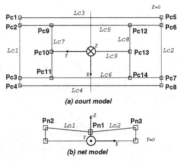

Fig. 1. Block diagram of the system

Fig. 2. Court and net model

Fig. 3. Extraction of court lines and player's position

Fig. 4. Tracking result of ball position

3   Impact Time Extraction by Tracking the Ball

The tracking of the ball is done as follows:

1. Detect all candidate positions of the ball that are outside the player's rectangle, that are smaller than a certain area, and that are within a certain

distance from the player's rectangle (detect mode). Repeat this for several successive frames and keep track of the candidates that move radially away from the player's position center. Repeat this step until it becomes the final single candidate for the ball orbit $b(t)$. Go to step 2.

2. Search the actual ball position $b(t)$ around the predicted ball position $b_{pred}(t)$ at time t (track mode). We have assumed that the ball locus can be approximated on a straight line over a short period. $b_{pred}(t)$ is calculated by adding the detected displacement $v_b(t-1)$ to the ball position $b(t-1)$ at time $t-1$. Select the region $b(t)$ which is smaller than a certain area and nearest to the predicted center, from regions within the search range. If the distance between the ball and a player becomes smaller than a certain threshold, go to step 1, otherwise repeat step 2.

Using these tracking results, impact times are extracted as follows.

1. Let t_1 be the time when the ball is detected for the first time. If the ball position is at the bottom side of the court at time t_1, the target player is set to the bottom player, otherwise it is set to the top player.
2. Incrementing from $t = t_1$, let impact time T be the first time when either of the following conditions is satisfied during the period when the distance between the ball and the player $d_{bp}(t)$ is shorter than the threshold TH_{dist}.
   - $d_{bp}(t+1) - d_{bp}(t) > TH_{diff}$ (The difference of d_{bp} at the current and following frames exceeds the threshold TH_{diff}.)
   - $v_b(t) \cdot v_b(t+1) < 0$ (The inner product of the ball velocity vectors V_b at the current and following frames becomes negative.)
3. Swap the target player for the opposite player. Let t_1 be the time when the ball moves into the target player's court for the first time after the previous impact time T. However, if the new target player is the bottom player, and if the player is located in front of the service line near the net, set $t_1 = T+1$. Go to step 2.

4   Impact Time Extraction by Using Audio Information

Impact points are also extracted by using audio information and template matching in the frequency domain. The following steps are performed.

1. Template Selection
   First, several video scenes including one of the players hitting the ball are selected randomly, and audio data are segmented accordingly so that they include the impact times corresponding to the selected video scenes. Audio data is sampled at 48 kHz with the resolution of 16 bits. In this paper, the template size was set to 2048 due to the following reasons.
   - The sound of each impact time is shorter than the data size of 2048 points (≈ 0.043 seconds).
   - The template size should be 2 to the power of n to enable the use of Fast Fourier transforms.

2. Selection of Frequency Range for Matching

The selected templates are Fast-Fourier-transformed in order to choose the frequency range used for detection. In this paper, preliminary analysis showed that the frequency range between 100Hz-1500Hz included spectra representing the features of impact times, and that the higher frequency range contained many noise components. Thus, the frequency range between 100Hz-1500Hz was selected for impact time detection.

3. Extraction using Fast Fourier Transform

Fast Fourier transform was performed for each of the 2048 samples segmented from the audio data. The starting point in the segmentation was shifted every 128 points ($\approx$ 0.0027 seconds). Template matching was done by obtaining correlation coefficients between the transformed originals and the templates. Impact points were determined by choosing audio segments whose correlation coefficients were larger than the predefined threshold, and by calculating the temporal position of the detected audio segments in video frame unit.

5   Analysis of Player's Basic Actions

The basic actions of a player were analyzed by using an integrated reasoning module with information about the court lines, the player and ball positions, and the extracted impact times. The following indices were used for the player's basic actions: $(obj\_id, t_s, t_e, t_r, act\_class, locus)$, where obj_id denotes player's id, which is an integer value representing each player on the court; t_s and t_e are, respectively, the starting and ending time points of each basic action; t_r describes the key frame of each basic action, such as the time when the player hits the ball; act_class shows the basic action class index, with the values of "stay", "move", "forehand swing", "backhand swing", and "overhead swing" used in this paper; and $locus$ indicates the player's locus on the court model, which was specified by using the perspective projection matrix derived from the detected court lines. The $locus$ consists of several typical points that can be used to approximate the player's position at an arbitrary time between the starting and ending time points of an action.

In this paper, it is particularly important to correctly identify player's basic actions of "forehand swing", "backhand swing", and "overhead swing". These actions are identified by evaluating the relationship between the position of the player and that of the ball at an impact time. In this paper, as shown in figure 5, when the ball was above the distinction line set in the upper position of the circumscribed rectangle for the player at an impact time, the action was identified as an overhead swing. When the ball was in the forehand/backside of the player's gravity center, the action was identified as a forehand/backhand swing. Here, the distinction line was set in the upper position of the player's region determined by a fixed ratio and the vertical size of the player's circumscribed rectangle. Therefore, in order to identify player's basic actions correctly, it is important to detect impact time t_I and ball position P_I at time $t = t_I$ as accurately as possible.

Let us consider the following three methods that can be used to identify the player's basic actions by using impact times.

Method 1. Let t_1 be the impact time obtained from the analysis of the ball tracking results, and $P_I(t_1)$ be the ball position at time $t = t_1$. The basic actions are estimated by using $P_I(t_1)$ and the player's position.

Method 2. Let t_2 be the time added/subtracted compensation value t_{comp} to/from the time t_1. Ball position $P_I(t_2)$ at $t = t_2$ is calculated by extrapolating the ball orbit using the last/next N points successfully detected in the ball tracking process. The basic actions are identified by using $t_I(t_2)$ and the player's position.

Method 3. Let t_a be the impact time obtained from the analysis of the audio information. Ball position $P_I(t_a)$ at $t = t_a$ is computed by extrapolating the ball orbit using the last/next N points successfully detected in the ball tracking process. The basic actions are identified by using $P_I(t_a)$ and the player's position.

Method 1 is a simple method because it directly uses the impact time analysis results of the ball tracking process. However, this method can be affected by the switching between the tracking and detection modes in the ball tracking process. For example, in figure 5(a), t_0 represents the ball position and time when the tracking mode is switched to "detection" in the ball tracking process, and t_1 indicates the ball position and time when the ball is successfully detected for the first time in the detection mode. Here, period $[t_0 + 1, t_1 - 1]$ is the length of time when the ball position cannot be determined due to the occlusion by the player.

When we extract the impact time by using method 1 based on the ball tracking results, the impact time, and the ball position become, respectively, t_1 and $P_I(t_1)$ in figure 5(a). When the basic action is estimated at this point, the result is a mistaken recognition of an overhead swing because the ball is above the distinction line, while the correct result should be the backhand swing.

Method 2 tries to avoid the problem of method 1 by introducing a fixed compensation value, t_{comp}, for the impact time obtained from the ball tracking. In figure 5(a), if the impact time is set to $t_2 = t_1 - t_{comp}$, the ball position $P_I(t_2)$ is calculated by estimating the ball orbit by using the last N points successfully detected during the ball tracking. Thus, method 2 can temporarily prevent the problem of method 1.

Let's look at the example of a smashing action in figure 5(b). $P_I(t_1)$ denotes the impact time and ball position obtained by using method 1. If the action is recognized at this point, method 1 gets the correct result of an overhead swing. However, the impact time and ball position obtained by using method 2 become $P_I(t_2)$ as a result of orbit estimation, and the action recognition gives a wrong result of a forehand swing.

Method 3 is a simple method because it directly uses the results of impact time analysis of audio information. This method enables easier extraction of impact times that cannot be properly estimated by methods 1 or 2 due to occlusion. Figure 5(a) and (b) show the appropriate estimation of ball position $P_I(t_a)$, which gives more accurate recognition results.

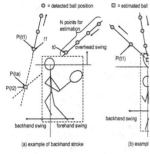

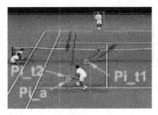

Fig. 5. Different recognition results based on ball and player positions detected at different impact times

Fig. 6. Estimated ball positions at different impact times (1)

Fig. 7. Estimated ball positions at different impact times (2)

Fig. 8. Estimated ball positions at different impact times (3)

Fig. 9. Estimated ball positions at different impact times (4)

Fig. 10. Estimated ball positions at different impact times (5)

6   Results and Discussion

We extracted court lines, the positions of the players and those of the ball from the actual video and audio data of two tennis matches in men's and women's singles, and identified the impact times and basic actions of the players.

Table 1 shows the results of extracting the impact times by using ball-tracking and audio-analysis results. "M1", "M2" and "M3" indicate the methods 1-3. F-measure[8] in the table represents the harmonic mean of precision (P) and recall (R): $F = 2PR/(P + R)$.

In the case of method 1, too many candidate impact times tended to be detected. This is mainly because the results of impact time analysis were affected by changes in the apparent distance in the image between the player and the ball. The observed oversights were often caused because the ball's orbit did not change very sharply in the image.

In case of method 2, detection accuracy was improved to some extent compared to method 1. This is mainly because more correct impact times were detected due to compensation value t_{comp}, as considered in figure 5(a). Theoretically, method 2 was predicted to yield more incorrect results according to

Table 1. Extracted impact times

	Precision	Recall	F
M1	0.428 (693/1619)	0.646 (693/1072)	0.515
M2	0.563 (784/1393)	0.731 (784/1072)	0.636
M3	0.865 (1063/1229)	0.992 (1063/1072)	0.924

Table 2. Recognition results of player's basic actions

	Precision	Recall	F
M1	0.176 (285/1619)	0.266 (285/1072)	0.212
M2	0.477 (664/1393)	0.619 (664/1072)	0.539
M3	0.753 (926/1229)	0.864 (926/1072)	0.805
M4	0.882 (946/1072)	0.882 (946/1072)	0.882

Table 3. Recognition results of player's basic actions (action-wise)

		Precision	Recall	F
overhead swing	M1	0.117 (86/736)	0.266 (86/323)	0.162
	M2	0.351 (148/422)	0.458 (148/323)	0.397
	M3	0.686 (286/417)	0.885 (286/323)	0.773
	M4	0.824 (277/336)	0.858 (277/323)	0.841
forehand swing	M1	0.211 (112/498)	0.324 (112/324)	0.255
	M2	0.466 (223/464)	0.667 (223/324)	0.548
	M3	0.755 (286/379)	0.883 (286/324)	0.814
	M4	0.680 (295/343)	0.910 (295/324)	0.885
backhand swing	M1	0.208 (87/385)	0.188 (87/425)	0.198
	M2	0.550 (293/507)	0.656 (293/425)	0.599
	M3	0.816 (354/433)	0.833 (354/425)	0.825
	M4	0.952 (374/393)	0.880 (374/425)	0.914

figure 5(b). However, in practice, it was confirmed that the cases in figure 5 gave more examples with a relatively shorter duration of occlusion, and that the ball orbit around the impact times was often only above the player's region, as shown in figure 7. Due to these two factors, method 2 provided more accurate results than method 1, as a result. Detection oversights in method 2 were influenced directly by those in method 1 in general.

In contrast, method 3 using audio information gave more accurate results. Table 1 lists nine oversights, which occurred when the sound of the ball being hit did not match the detection pattern used in this paper. This is because these sounds sometimes vary depending on the impact conditions between the ball and racket. Also, there were 166 errors when the sound was:

- the ball hitting the net or an object around the court,
- the ball bouncing before/after serving or during points,
- the ball bouncing by a half volley, forcing the data corresponding to the actual impact time to be judged an error.

As mentioned above, errors occurred more often than oversights. However, these errors were the sounds of the ball hitting a certain object. This means that the template used to detect the sound of a ball being hit in this paper represented the sound character of a ball bouncing well, and that the template matching in the frequency range worked well despite its comparatively simple processing.

Table 2 shows the recognition results of player's basic actions based on the impact times extracted above. Here, method 4 shows the detection results where the player's basic actions were identified in the same way as method 3, given the correct impact times.

In case of method 1, typical errors were mainly a result of mistaking a forehand/backhand swing for an overhead swing (figure 6). Overhead swings when serving were often detected correctly (figure 7), which matches the consideration in figure 5. However, the ball orbits after it was hit sometimes overlapped with the player for a comparatively long time such as after being smashed by the top side player (figure 10). In this case, the errors by mistaking a forehand/backhand swing for an overhead swing were observed. The detection accuracy of method 1 in table 2 is even lower than that in table 1. This is because a forehand/backhand swing was often mistaken for an overhead swing even when the impact times extracted with method 1 gave correct results, as shown in figure 9. Also, oversights mainly occurred because the extraction accuracy of the impact times was low to begin with.

In case of method 2, many examples were confirmed where the ball positions were appropriately calculated as a result of compensating time displacement due to occlusion, by using t_{comp}. Also, it was predicted from the consideration in figure 5 that method 2 would mistakenly recognize an overhead for a forehand/backhand swing. However, in practice, overhead swings were often identified correctly because the duration the ball occluded the player were comparatively short (figure 7). Typical errors occurred when the difference between the actual impact time and that extracted by method 1 was short, making the displacement of impact times compensated for by t_{comp} become large, resulting in the mistaken recognition of a forehand for a backhand swing and vice versa (figure 8), or a forehand/backhand swing for an overhead swing (figure 9). Oversights basically occurred because the extraction accuracy of the impact times was low, as could be seen in method 1.

In case of method 3, detection results were quite favorable, as considered in figure 5. The major reason for this was the high extraction accuracy of impact times. Typical errors occurred when the forehand and backhand swings were misidentified for one another due to the slight displacement in the impact time, when ball positions were mistakenly estimated, or when there were erroneous decisions caused by errors of the extracted impact times themselves. Detection oversights were mainly caused by oversights in extracting impact times.

In addition, player's basic actions were recognized in the same way as they were in method 3, assuming correct impact times were known (method 4). Typical errors occurred due to failure in estimating the ball positions at impact times because of unsuccessful ball tracking. The accuracy of ball tracking needs to be improved in the future. The accuracy of extracting impact times using the audio information in method 3 also needs to be improved based on the causes of errors and oversights that have been recognized in the study.

Table 3 shows action wise recognition results of player's basic actions. On the whole, the results of each action showed the same tendency as in table 2. Also, the causes of errors and oversights were the same as those mentioned above.

In summary, it is confirmed that in the field of tennis, when audio information is used, more accurate results can be obtained compared to those obtained by using only visual information.

This system uses the following information as domain knowledge:

- specification of tennis court
- color clusters corresponding to player's regions
- templates of the sound when the players hit the ball
- rules for identifying basic actions of the players.
- other parameters (TH_{dist}, TH_{diff}, t_{comp}, etc.)

With this information, all the processes are performed automatically.

Furthermore, several parameters including TH_{dist}, TH_{diff}, and t_{comp} were not constant throughout the experiments, but were programmed to automatically adjust their values corresponding to the position of the player in the tennis court. The system was fairly robust against noise, but a valid criterion to select and determine parameters for more robust performance against noise needs to be studied in future work.

As for computational complexity, it takes more than half a day to compute the basic actions of the players from the original input video and audio data of about-an-hour-long tennis match. It is necessary to enhance the total processing speed by frame-skippings, optimization, etc.

For other methods to identify basic actions of a player, gesture recognition techniques using silhouette images of a player could be considered as an alternative. However, such a method generally has the following drawbacks:

- it requires a great deal of training data for reasonable recognition results,
- there are many variations of silhouette appearances according to the orientation of the human posture, the direction of the camera, insufficient resolutions of the silhouette, individual characteristics, etc.

The recognition results tend to depend heavily on these factors.

In contrast, the method used in this study is rather simple because it is based on the relationships between the positions of the player and the ball at an impact time. Using the information about these positions and time points is expected to give more robust results especially against variation by individual characteristics. It is necessary to compare these methods for further validations in future work.

The indices for basic actions of a player can be used to retrieve various general actions, such as "serving" and "dashing to the net". For example, the general action "serving" can be defined as follows: *when both players "stayed" outside the court in the region called "backout" at a same time, and when either player did an "overhead swing" here the next time* (figure 11). Scenes of the general action "serving" can be retrieved by searching for combinations of basic action indices satisfying this definition, from the collection of these indices derived from the proposed method. Figure 12 shows the result of retrieving "serving" from a particular set and game.

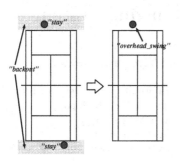

Fig. 11. Definition of "serving"

Fig. 12. Retrieval result for "serving"

7 Conclusion

A method of identifying human behaviors for content-based retrieval that uses both audio and video information was presented. The positions of the players and those of the ball were extracted from a real tennis video, and the impact times were detected with ball tracking and audio analysis. The player's behavior was identified using an integrated reasoning module containing information about the court and net lines, the player positions, the ball positions, and the impact time analysis results. Simulation results showed that the use of audio information enabled identifying forehand/backhand and overhead swings, which cannot be properly detected with conventional methods. In the future, we intend to improve the evaluation procedures and the steps used in the reasoning module, and continue tests using more content data.

References

[1] M.Flickner, et al.: "Query by image and video content: the QBIC system", IEEE Computer Magazine, pp.23-32, 1995. 331
[2] A. Akutsu, Y. Tonomura, H. Hashimoto, Y. Ohba: "Video indexing using motion vectors", In SPIE Proc. VCIP '92, pp.522-530, 1992. 331
[3] Y. Gong, L. T. Sin, C. H. Chuan, H. Zhang, M. Sakauchi: "Automatic parsing of TV soccer programs", Proc. ICMCS, pp.167-174, 1995. 331
[4] D. D. Saur, Y-P. Tan, S. R. Kulkarni, P. J. Ramadge: "Automated analysis and annotation of basketball video", Storage and Retrieval for Image and Video Databases V, SPIE-3022, pp.167-187, 1997.
[5] G. Sudhir, J. C. M. Lee, A. K. Jain: "Automatic classification of tennis video for high-level content-based retrieval", Proc. of IEEE Workshop on Content-based Access of Image and Video Databases, CAIVD'98, 1998. 332
[6] H. Miyamori: "Video Annotation for Content-based Retrieval using Human Behaviour Analysis and Domain Knowledge", FG2000, pp.320-325, 2000. 331, 332
[7] A. Blake et al.: "Integrated Tracking with Vision and Sound", Proc. of the International Conference on Image Analysis and Processing, pp.354-357, 2001. 332
[8] C. J. van Rijsbergen: "Information Retrieval", Buttersworth, 1979. 337

Indexing of Personal Video Captured by a Wearable Imaging System

Yasuhito Sawahata and Kiyoharu Aizawa

University of Tokyo, Dept. of Frontier Informatics and Dept. of Elec. Eng.
7-3-1 Hongo, Bunkyo, Tokyo, 113-8656, Japan
{sawa,aizawa}@hal.t.u-tokyo.ac.jp
http://www.hal.t.u-tokyo.ac.jp

Abstract. Digitization of lengthy personal experiences will be made possible by continuous recording using wearable video cameras. It is conceivable that the amount of video content that results will be extraordinarily large. In order to retrieve and browse the desired scenes, a vast amount of video needs to be organized using context information. In this paper, we develop a "Wearable Imaging System" that is capable of constantly capturing data, not only from a wearable video camera, but also from various sensors, such as a GPS, an acceleration sensor and a gyro sensor. The data from these sensors are analyzed using Hidden Markov Model (HMM) to detect various events for efficient video retrieval and browsing. Two kind of browsers are developed which are a chronological viewer and a location based viewer.

1 Introduction

Digitization of lengthy personal experiences will become possible through continuous recording using wearable video cameras. Because of progress in storage device technology, we will be able to capture and store 70 years of our life. The amount of video content will be extraordinarily large. In order to achieve efficient browsing, video indexing techniques are indispensable, and we focus on the problem of indexing wearable video (wearable video is our abbreviation for video captured by a wearable camera).

It is important to assess the user's behavioral context to facilitate efficient indexing of wearable video, which differs from TV program indexing. In order to extract the user context, it is useful to have not only the camera and microphone, but several different types of sensors attached to a wearable imaging system. In our previous work [6, 7], we summarized wearable videos using low-level video/audio features and brainwaves. Using brainwaves that reflect the user's subjective arousal status, it was possible to extract the user's subjectively-important context.

In this paper, we present our "Wearable Imaging System" which comprises sensors such as a GPS, an acceleration sensor and a gyro sensor. We then describe the extraction of the user's important behavioral context using those sensors.

E. M. Bakker et al. (Eds.): CIVR 2003, LNCS 2728, pp. 342–351, 2003.

A wearable camera was developed in the field of wearable computers [1], where real-time applications such as navigation are the main focus. Previously, skin conductivity was used to turn the camera on and off [2]. Apart from a few previous studies, indexing has rarely been discussed in relation to wearable computer applications [5, 6, 7].

Content-based video indexing has been one of the major issues in the field of image processing, where the main focus has been on broadcasting TV program and cinema movies, where scene changes are well defined and indexing based on objective features has been applied. Indexing wearable video differs from these because it needs to take into account the user's context.

2 Feasibility and Potential of Wearable Imaging

Imagine we could wear a single camera and constantly record what we see. How large a volume of images could we capture over 70 years? (The captured video would first be stored in the wearable device and then occasionally moved to a huge storage.) Video quality would depend on compression. Assuming 16 hours per day is captured for 70 years, the amount of video data is listed below.

quality	rate	data size for 70 years
TV phone quality	64kbps	11 Tbytes
VCR quality	1Mbps	183 Tbytes
Broadcasting quality	4Mbps	736 Tbytes

Let us consider video of TV phone quality, which needs only 11 Tbytes to record 70 years. Even today, we have a lunch box size of 100GB HDD available for less than $150. Therefore, if we have 100 of them, their capacity is almost adequate for 70 years! Improvements in HDD capacity are taking place rapidly. In the not too distant future it will be feasible to hold 70 years of video in a single lunch box-sized HDD.

As for sensing devices, CCD or CMOS cameras are also becoming smaller. A miniature camera on a mobile phone is already on the market. Using such a small camera, we can capture video anytime and anywhere. Progress in wearable computers will reduce the size of imaging devices still further.

Then, we believe that in the not too distant future, it will be possible from the hardware point of view to capture and maintain life-long video within a person's environment. Let us look at potential advantages and disadvantages, listed below.

* Advantages
 - we can catch the best moment that we want to keep forever.
 - we can vividly reproduce and recollect our experiences by video.
 - we can remember what we almost forgot.
 - we can see what we did not see at the time.
 - we can prove that we did not do something.

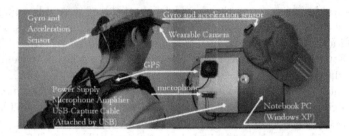

Fig. 1. Wearable Imaging System

* Disadvantages
- we may see what we do not want to remember.
- we may violate the privacy of other people.

3   Development of a Wearable Imaging System

As shown in Fig.1, we have developed a wearable imaging system that simultaneously records data from a wearable camera, a microphone, a GPS, an acceleration
sensor and a gyro sensor. By processing data from the various sensors, the user's
context can be appropriately extracted. The acceleration sensor and the gyro
sensor are attached to the back of the user's head to capture the motion of the
camera.

The platform for the system is a notebook PC. All sensors are attached to
the PC through the Universal Serial Bus (USB), serial port and PCMCIA slots.
All data from the sensors are recorded directly into the notebook PC. Software
is written in Visual C++ and run using Microsoft Windows XP. The software
specification is shown in Fig.2. In particular, visual and audio data are encoded
into MPEG4 and MP3, respectively, using Direct Show.

In order to simplify the system, we modified the sensors so that they could
be powered from the battery of the notebook PC. We also customized the device
drivers to recognize the sensors used in our wearable imaging system.

The wearable imaging system is also capable of taking a brainwave sensor. If
a brainwave signal is available, we can estimate the subjective arousal status of
the user as we did in the previous study [6, 7]. In a case where we use brainwaves,
the system obtains the data from the sensor and extracts the status of α wave
by performing a FFT in real-time. In this paper, we present our study without
the brainwave sensor.

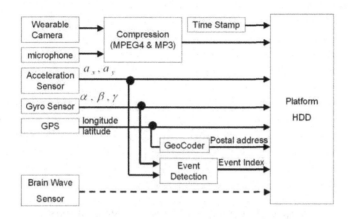

Fig. 2. Software specification

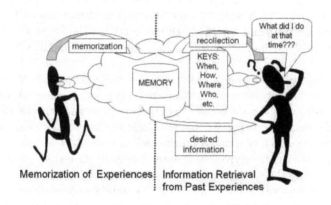

Fig. 3. Human recollection

4 Indexing of Personal Experiences

The use of context as an information retrieval key is based on human recollection [3]. The Wearable Imaging System enables efficient scene retrieval to aid recollection. For example, in order to recall the scenes of the last conversation, the typical keys used in the recollection process are information such as 'where', 'who', 'when', etc. (Fig.3).

Therefore, by using the user's context as indices for wearable video, it is expected to be possible to efficiently browse and retrieve the desired scenes. Use of sensor data, in addition to audio/visual data, will allow good estimation of the user's behavioral context, because the sensor data we use directly indicates the motion and location of the user.

For example, suppose we wish to find conversation scenes as the user's context. Scenes with voice audio signal will be detected by extracting the zero-

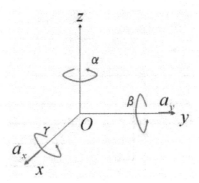

Fig. 4. Output of gyro and acceleration sensor

crossing rate (ZCR), volume, pitch, etc. Moreover, facial detection using visual data will be useful. However, it is not practical to detect scenes by performing these complex algorithms for the entire video. Choosing scenes to which these algorithms are to be applied is essential in maintaining scalability in the indexing process.

   Therefore, we use the sensor data to choose candidate scenes. We assume that people do not move rapidly when they are engaged in a conversation. Whether the person is moving or not is easy to detect by processing the acceleration sensor or GPS data. In addition, when a person is speaking to someone, they will be looking at someone's face without much head movement. Head motion can be detected by processing the gyro sensor data. The candidate scenes can be properly chosen using only the sensor data. Finally, voice detection and face detection will be performed for those scenes judged to be candidates for conversation scenes.

   In the following sections, we will describe the method for event detection using an acceleration sensor and a gyro sensor.

5   Event Detection Using Sensor Data

The motion status of the user, such as "standstill (no movement)", "walking", "running", is what we wish to determine using the sensor data. We make use of a Hidden Markov Model (HMM)[4] to detect these events. We first form feature vectors from the output data of the gyro and acceleration sensor. These are x- and y-direction acceleration a_x and a_y from the acceleration sensor and α, β and γ angles around the z, y and x axes, respectively, from the gyro sensor (Fig.4). Therefore, we define a feature vector as follows:

$$FeatureVector = \begin{bmatrix} a_x & a_y & \Delta\alpha & \beta & \gamma \end{bmatrix}^t \tag{1}$$

$\Delta\alpha$ is the temporal difference of α and $| \alpha_t - \alpha_{t-1} |$, because of the importance of relative rotation around z which corresponds to head rotation. We set the rate to produce these feature vectors at 30 samples per second.

The procedure for the HMM training stage is as follows:

1. Store sample data from sensors and make feature vectors defined by Eq.(1).
2. The K-Means clustering method is applied; the sequences of feature vectors are quantized into sequences of symbols. At this step, C is the number of clusters, then the feature vectors are clustered into C types of symbols. A representative feature vector of the cluster is defined as $\overline{FV}_j (0 \leq j < C)$. They are used to quantize a feature vector into a symbol at step 2 for the new sequence.
3. Select typical sequences and define them as event $E_i (0 \leq i < N)$. N indicates a total number of events and equals the total number of HMMs.
4. Create N HMMs λ_i corresponding to event E_i and train them according to the defined sequences. The initial model parameters of the HMMs are random. HMMs are basic left-right structure. S is the total number of states.

The procedure for the HMM applied to a new sequence is as follows:

1. Read data from sensors and form feature vectors defined by Eq.(1).
2. Calculate the distances between the feature vectors and the representative vectors $\overline{FV}_j$. If the distance between the current feature vector and $\overline{FV}_K$ is the smallest for all $\overline{FV}_j$s, then it is quantized into symbol K.
3. Make sequences of symbols. Symbols are stored in a buffer. If the length of the sequence of the buffer is less than L, then go back to step 1. Note that L is the maximum length of the sequence. If the length of the sequence reaches L, then all the symbols in the buffer are defined as an observation sequence of symbols $\mathbf{O}$.
4. Calculate $P(\mathbf{O} \mid \lambda_i)$ for all HMMs. If $P(\mathbf{O} \mid \lambda_M)$ indicates the highest probability, then event E_M is detected.

In [5], HMM-based event detection of wearable video was investigated, using audio and visual features only. From the results of their experiments, the HMM-based method showed high correlation between actual events and estimated events. However, because only visual/audio features were used as observation sequences for HMMs, their technique is not very robust under environmental changes. In contrast to their work, our system uses the different sensors and it is robust under environmental changes.

6   Experiments of Event Detection

We captured data for approximately an hour on our campus at the University of Tokyo. We used the first half of the data for HMM training and the other half for analysis of the new sequence. We selected sequences from the training sequences and labeled them as "walking", "running", "no movement (standstill)", etc. We trained the HMMs using the sequences corresponding to these labels.

Fig.5 and Fig.6 show transition of $P(\mathbf{O} \mid \lambda_i)$ and manual labeled training data for "no movement" and "running" events. Parameters of HMM-based event detection, such as L, the length of training sequences, S, the number of states,

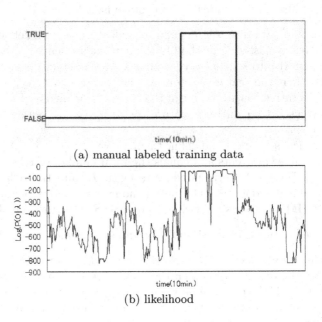

(a) manual labeled training data

(b) likelihood

Fig. 5. Manual labeled training data and transition of $P(\mathbf{O} \mid \lambda=$ "no movement")

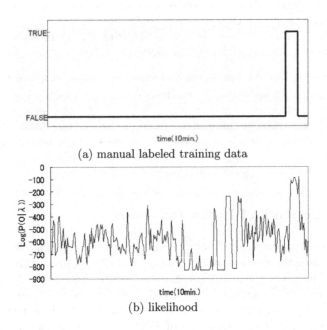

(a) manual labeled training data

(b) likelihood

Fig. 6. Manual labeled training data and transition of $P(\mathbf{O} \mid \lambda=$ "running")

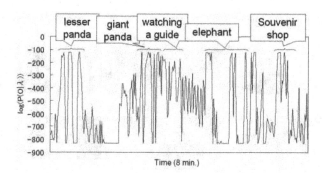

Fig. 7. A result of "no movement (standstill)" event detection performed for Zoo data. The result for 8 minutes from 13:50 until 13:58 is shown. The data almost corresponds to those shown in Fig.8

and C, the number of clusters, were set at 60, 10 and 50, respectively. (If $L = 60$ the length of the sequence is two seconds.) Note that the likelihood value in Fig.5 and Fig.6 are the logarithmic value of $P(\mathbf{O} \mid \lambda_i)$. The results for the HMM are satisfactory for deciding to which event the sequence belongs.

We also used data captured in the Zoo near our campus. In the Zoo, the person frequently moved and stopped. Often he was watching animals while standing still. While moving, he was walking from one cage to another. Therefore, if events where the user did not move are detected, the corresponding scene has a high probability of containing animals seen by the person.

Fig.7 shows the observation probabilities for "no movement" HMM. Words such as "lesser panda", "giant panda", "watching a guide", "elephant" and "souvenir shop" in Fig.7 were written manually by checking the time stamps and the actual video contents. Fig.8 shows the key frames when a "no movement" event occurred. Note that the HMMs we used here were trained by the campus data. Most of the key frames show scenes in front of animal cages, signs, or at the souvenir shop.

7 Viewer of Scenes, Events and Locations

Our system can also record GPS data so that we can then show the location of the scenes and events by following the trace left by the person. Fig.9 is the Location-based viewer.

In our system, in addition to showing the trace, latitude and longitude from GPS are converted into a postal address by referring to external database modules. Latitude and longitude are not readable to an observer. The postal address is very useful for handling large quantities of data, because it has a good hierarchical structure.

The address is added to the "tree view" on the left side of the viewer as shown in Fig.9. When an address is selected from the tree, the map around it is shown.

Fig. 8. Key frame viewer: key frames for "no movement" events are shown in chronological order. In addition to "no movement", events such as "walking", "running", etc. were also detected using HMMs

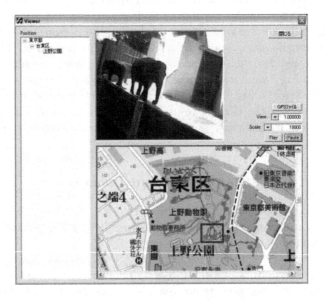

Fig. 9. Location-based viewer. The user movement is traced on the map and detected events are shown as dots along this trace. The location is translated into a postal address and shown on the left hand side in the tree structure

By using latitude and longitude, the path of the user's movement is traced on the map. We can view the desired scenes by choosing the relevant point on the trace. Dots on the trace indicate events that were detected at those locations. The dots in Fig.9 correspond to "no movement (standstill)" events. When the user selects a part of the trace by drawing a rectangle, then the corresponding video is replayed in the video window.

8   Conclusion

In this paper, we have described our wearable imaging system, which obtains video, audio, GPS, gyro and acceleration sensor data. The additional sensors were used to determine events in the user's context, which makes browsing of wearable video easier. HMM-based event detection using sensor data showed good performance. Because of the small dimensional feature vector of the sensor data, it was possible to label a large quantity of video very efficiently.

We are integrating a face detection module. By combining the current event detection and face detection capabilities, the wearable video will have richer descriptions. Audio processing for background scene detection is also being investigated.

References

[1] Mann, S.: 'WearCam' (The Wearable Camera): Personal Imaging System for long-term use in wearable tetherless computer-mediated reality and personal Photo/Videographic Memory Prosthesis, Proceedings of ISWC98, IEEE, pp 124-131, Oct. 1998   343

[2] Healey, J. and Picard, R. W.: A Cybernetic Wearable Camera, Proceedings of ISWC98, IEEE, pp 42-49, Oct. 1998   343

[3] Lamming, M. and Flynn, M.: 'Forget-me-not' Intimate Computing in Support of Human Memory, in Proceedings of FRIEND21, '94 International Symposium on Next Generation Human Interface, Feb., 1994   345

[4] Rabiner, L.: A tutorial on hidden Markov models and selected applications in speech recognition, Proceedings of the IEEE, 77(2):257-286, Feb. 1989   346

[5] Clarkson, B. and Pentland, A.: Unsupervised Clustering of Ambulatory Audio and Video, Proceedings of ICASSP'99, 1999   343, 347

[6] Aizawa, K., Ishijima, K-I. and Shiina, M.: Summarizing Wearable Video, Proceedings of ICIP 2001, IEEE, pp 398-401, Oct. 2001   342, 343, 344

[7] Ng, H. W., Sawahata, Y. and Aizawa, K.: Summarization of wearable videos using support vector machine, Proceedings of IEEE ICME 2002, Aug. 2002   342, 343, 344

Constructive Learning Algorithm-Based RBF Network for Relevance Feedback in Image Retrieval[*]

Fang Qian[1,2], Bo Zhang[1,2], and Fuzong Lin[1,2]

[1] State key laboratory of Intelligent Technology and Systems, Tsinghua University
[2] Department of Computer Science and Technology, Tsinghua University
Beijing, 100084, China
qf@s1000e.cs.tsinghua.edu.cn

Abstract. It has been generally acknowledged that relevance feedback in image retrieval can be considered as a two-class learning and classification process. The classifier used is essential to the performance of relevance feedback. In this paper, a RBF neural network is employed during the relevance feedback process. The architecture of the RBF network is automatically determined by the constructive learning algorithm (CLA). The weights in the output layer of the network are learned by Least-mean-square method. Experiment results on 10,000 heterogeneous images demonstrate the proposed CLA-based RBF network can achieve comparable performance with support vector machines and support vector learning based RBF during the relevance feedback process. Furthermore, a practical advantage of the CLA-based RBF network is that the width of Gaussian kernel does not need to manually set while for SVM it need to be predefined according to experience.

1   Introduction

Relevance feedback has been perceived to be one of the most promising candidates to map from low-level features to high-level concepts in content-based image retrieval. The basic idea of relevance feedback is to leverage user's knowledge to find better mappings. During retrieval process, the user interacts with the system and rates the relevance of the retrieved images, according to his/her subjective judgment. Based on the feedback information, the system dynamically learns the user's intention, and gradually presents better results.

The pioneering work on relevance feedback is to adaptive query and similarity measure [4, 3]. These approaches can be grouped into geometric methods, relying on the Euclidean distance or its variations. Another group of relevance feedback is statistical methods, which can be further subdivided into probability-based approaches

---

[*] The work is supported by National Nature Sciences Foundation of China No. 60135010.

E. M. Bakker et al. (Eds.): CIVR 2003, LNCS 2728, pp. 352-361, 2003.

and classification-based approaches. Probability approaches are based on the MAP (Maximum *A Posterior*) criteria. Cox [1] and Vasconcelos [10] used Bayesian learning to incorporate user's feedback to update the probability distribution of all images in the database. Recently, it has been generally acknowledged that relevance feedback can be considered as a two-class learning and classification process. During the feedback process, a classifier is dynamically trained on the user-labeled positive and negative images, which then divides the database images into two classes, either relevant or irrelevant. Many kinds of classifiers have been used, such as support vector machine [2,13], neural network [12], AdaBoost [8] and so on.

Constructive Learning Algorithm (CLA) neural network is used in relevance feedback process for image retrieval [12]. The idea of CLA is to transform the design of network to a training sample covering problem based on a geometrical interpretation of M-P model [11]. In [12], a set of sphere neighborhoods is used to cover all positive examples in each round of relevance feedback, i.e. a CLA network is formed. In the following retrieval of the same query session, all images are classified and ranked by the CLA network. This approach has been proved to be much better than the weight and query adaptation relevance feedback approach [12]. However, there are still some shortages of the approach that limited its performance. First, the sphere neighborhood, the basic neuron in the network, has a clear bound that brings difficulty to judge the class information of those images not included by any sphere neighborhood. Second, there is no an effective rule to combine all neurons in the output layer.

To address the above problems, we propose the CLA-based RBF network for relevance feedback in this paper. Gaussian basis function is substituted for sphere neighborhood as the basic neuron in network, and all Gaussian functions are combined by weight in the output layer. On the other hand, the constructive learning algorithm is employed to automatically determine the number, the center and width of Gaussian functions. Therefore, the CLA-based RBF can take advantage of both CLA and RBF network. Experiments will demonstrate its good performance in relevance feedback for image retrieval.

The rest of the paper is organized as follows. First, in section 2, constructive learning algorithm is briefly introduced. Then, in section 3, the proposed CLA-based RBF network is presented. Experimental results are reported in section 4. Finally, we conclude the work in section 5.

2   A Constructive Learning Algorithm of Neural Networks

The constructive learning algorithm of neural networks is based on a geometrical representation of McCulloch-Pitts neural model [11].

2.1   A Geometrical Representation of M-P Model

An M-P neuron is an element with n inputs and one output. The general form of its function is

$$y = \text{sgn}(\mathbf{W}^T\mathbf{X} - \psi) \tag{1}$$

where **X** is an input vector, **W** is the weight vector, and ψ denotes the threshold. Function sgn(ν) is defined as

$$sgn(v) = \begin{cases} 1, & v \geq 0 \\ -1, & v < 0 \end{cases} \tag{2}$$

Assume that all input vectors are restricted to an n-dimension sphere surface S^n. (This assumption can always be satisfied through a transformation, see [11] for detail.) Note that $\mathbf{W}^T\mathbf{X}-\psi=0$ can be interpreted as a hyper-plane P, so $\mathbf{W}^T\mathbf{X}-\psi>0$ represents the intersection between S^n and the positive half-space partitioned by the hyperplane P. The intersection is called a "sphere neighborhood" as shown in Fig.1. Thus an M-P neuron corresponds to a sphere neighborhood on S^n. The center of the sphere neighborhood corresponds to the weight vector of the M-P neuron. If input **X** falls into the region, i.e. **X** is covered by the corresponding sphere neighborhood, the output of the M-P neuron y=1, otherwise y = -1.

Based on the above geometrical interpretation, the design of a neural classifier can be transformed to a training sample covering problem. That is, a set of sphere neighborhoods is constructed to cover the training samples belonging to the same class and different classes of samples are covered by different sets of sphere neighborhoods. The CLA network determines an input vector's class by selecting the class whose corresponding set of sphere neighborhoods covers the vector.

2.2   CLA Network for Image Retrieval

Zhang employed the CLA network into the relevance feedback process for image retrieval [12]. Initially, the image retrieval system presents initial retrieval results based on the similarity in the low-level feature space, and then the user labels the top-*n* images as either positive or negative.

Let $\mathbf{I}^+ = \{I_1^+, I_2^+, \cdots, I_{N^+}^+\}$ represent the set of positive examples, and $\mathbf{I}^- = \{I_1^-, I_2^-, \cdots, I_{N^-}^-\}$ represent the set of negative examples. Note that the initial query is treated as a positive image in $\mathbf{I}^+$ by default. The aim is to find a set of coverings $\mathbf{C}^+ = \{(C_k^+, R_k^+), k = 1, \cdots, K\}$ to cover $\mathbf{I}^+$, where C_k^+ and R_k^+ is the center and radius of the k-th covering.

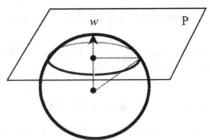

Fig. 1. A Sphere Neighborhood

If $\mathbf{I}^+$ is not empty, a covering can be constructed in the following way. First, select an uncovered image from $\mathbf{I}^+$, identified as I_i^+, and set the center of new covering to I_i^+. Next, calculate the maximal distance between I_i^+ and $\mathbf{I}^+$, and the minimal distance between I_i^+ and $\mathbf{I}^-$, i.e.:

$$d_{max} = \max_j D\left(I_i^+, I_j^+\right),$$

(3)

$$\forall I_j^+ \in \mathbf{I}^+$$

$$d_{min} = \min_j D\left(I_i^+, I_j^-\right),$$

(4)

$$\forall I_j^- \in \mathbf{I}^-$$

Then the radius of covering can be determined as follows:

$$r = \begin{cases} \left(d_{min} + d_{max}\right)/2, & \text{if } d_{min} \geq d_{max} \\ \rho \cdot d_{min}, & \text{otherwise} \end{cases}$$

(5)

where ρ is a constant satisfying $0 < \rho < 1$, usually it can be set to 0.95. Last, positive examples in $\mathbf{I}^+$ that fall in this covering are assigned to the covering.

This process is repeated until all positive examples have been covered. In other words, the set of coverings can well represent all positive samples. In the following retrieval, all images in the database are ranked according to the relationship to these coverings. If an image falls into any one of the coverings, it is considered relevant; otherwise, its distance to the nearest covering is used as ranking score.

3   CLA-Based RBF Network

Although the above algorithm had achieved good performance in image retrieval [12], there are some points that could be improved. First, in CLA network, the basic neuron in networks is the sphere neighborhood which has a clear bound, thus such a problem produces: how to judge which class an input vector belongs to when it is not covered by any sphere neighborhood? In this paper, we use Gaussian functions to replace sphere neighborhoods as the neurons in networks, so that the class of each input vector can be determined by its membership to each Gaussian kernel. Second, an effective rule to combine all neurons in the output layer is needed. We propose the CLA-based RBF network, using the advantage of RBF network to make up the drawback of the CLA network while employing CLA to determine the architecture of RBF network.

3.1   RBF Neural Network

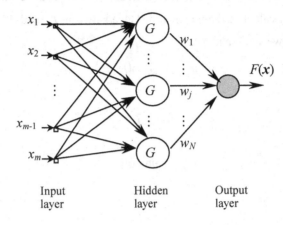

Fig. 2. Architectural graph of a RBF neural network

Figure 2 shows the architecture of a RBF neural network. Without loss of generality, assume there is a node in the output layer. The architecture can be easily generalized to the case with multiple output nodes. The weights between the input layer and the hidden layer are fixed as 1. The hidden layer consists of a group of radial basis functions, usually Gaussian functions. The mapping function between input and output is as follows:

$$F(\mathbf{x}) = \sum_{i=1}^{N} w_i \exp(-\frac{1}{2\sigma_i^2} \|\mathbf{x} - \mathbf{c}_i\|^2) \tag{6}$$

where $\mathbf{x}$ is an input vector, $\mathbf{c}_i$ and σ_i is the center and width of the i-th Gaussian respectively, w_i is the weight of the i-th Gaussian, N is the total number of Gaussian. The training of RBF networks consists of determining the total number of Gaussian basis functions, finding their centers and widths, and calculating the weights of the output nodes. In the following, we use CLA to initialize the architecture. After that, the weights are estimated by least-mean-square method.

3.2   Initialize Architecture by CLA

In [12], only positive examples are covered, the negative samples having not been taken full advantage. In this work, positive and negative examples are covered respectively in constructing the architecture of RBF network. One problem in covering training samples is how to obtain minimum coverings. Less numbers of coverings means simpler network architecture, thus possible stronger generalization ability of the classifier. However, the minimum covering is a NP hard problem [11], we just use a heuristic approach here to reduce the number of coverings. For point i, define its local density as within a local area the proportion of the points that are the same class with i. It can be formulated as

$$P(i) = \begin{cases} n_{Pos}/k, & \text{if } i \text{ is positive} \\ n_{Neg}/k, & \text{if } i \text{ is negative} \end{cases} \tag{7}$$

where k is a positive integer which is predefined, n_{Pos} and n_{Neg} is the number of positive and negative points within the k-nearest neighbor of point i. The defined local density can reflect the role of the point in its own class. So in constructing the network, we follow this sequence: the point with largest local density is covered first.

Step1: Calculate the local density for each positive and negative sample according to Formula (7). k is set to 10 in the experiment;

Step2: Sort the positive and negative samples respectively according to the local densities;

Step3: Cover the positive and negative samples respectively;

Step4: Use the covering results to initialize the RBF network. Let the number of Gaussian equal to the number of coverings, the mean vector and width of each Gaussian be the center and the radius of the corresponding covering respectively.

3.3   Weights Estimation by LMS

Provided the architecture of RBF, the weights of the output layer can be calculated. We assume N basis functions in the hidden layer of the RBF network. Let $\mathbf{w} = [w_1, \cdots w_N]^T$ denote the weight vector to be estimated. Let $\{\mathbf{x}_i | i=1,\ldots,M\}$ be the set of training samples consisting of the top m positive samples and the rest n negative samples, that is $M=m+n$. The desired response vector is denoted as $\mathbf{d} = [\mathbf{1}_{m\times1} \ \mathbf{0}_{n\times1}]^T$. Let $\mathbf{G}$ denote M-by-N matrix $\mathbf{G} = \{g_{ij}\}$ ($i=1,\ldots,M, j=1,\ldots,N$), where the element $g_{ij} = \exp(-\dfrac{\|\mathbf{x}_i - \mathbf{c}_j\|^2}{\sigma_j^2})$ denote the outcome of the j-th basis function with the i-th feature vector $\mathbf{x}_i$ as input. Now the weights estimation can be formulated as

$$\mathbf{Gw} = \mathbf{d} \tag{8}$$

The solution is given explicitly in the form

$$\mathbf{w} = \mathbf{G}^+\mathbf{d} \tag{9}$$

where $\mathbf{G}^+$ denotes the pseudo inverse matrix of $\mathbf{G}$ which can be defined as

$$\mathbf{G}^+ = (\mathbf{G}^T\mathbf{G})^{-1}\mathbf{G}^T \tag{10}$$

After this final step of calculating the output layer weights, all parameters of the RBF network have been determined.

3.4   Related Work

Many learning algorithms of RBF network have been explored. A detail discussion has been presented in [6]. According to its experiment results, the performance of the support vector learning based RBF classifiers (SV-RBF) is superior to most learning algorithms. So we can use SV-RBF as a baseline to verify the effectiveness of the proposed CLA-based RBF.

Here only give a brief introduction to Support vector machines (SVM) and support vector learning based RBF. For details, please refer to [5,6]. SVMs are based on the Structural Risk Minimization (SRM) principle from statistical learning theory [9]. The idea of SVM is to map the input vectors $\mathbf{x}$ into a high-dimensional feature space $\mathbf{H}$ through a kernel function which defines an inner product in $\mathbf{H}$, and then in feature space $\mathbf{H}$ construct a separating hyperplane with the largest distance to the closest training samples. The most common used kernel function is Gaussian kernel function:

$$K(\mathbf{x}_i,\mathbf{x}_j)=\exp(-g\|\mathbf{x}_i-\mathbf{x}_j\|^2) \tag{11}$$

The Gaussian kernel parameter g is predefined for SVM. Then by solving a quadratic programming problem, the separating surface obtained is a linear combination of Gaussian functions located at the support vectors. In this case, the SVM reduces to an RBF network whose parameters (the number and the centers of the basis function, the output layer weights) are automatically determined.

The support vector learning based RBF network is a hybrid system with the number and location of centers determined by SV method and the weights estimated by LMS, so that it can assess the relative influence of the SV center choice and the SV weight optimization, respectively. In SV-RBF, all Gaussians are radially symmetric, all with the same kernel width fixed in advance.

4   Experimental Results

The image database we used consists of 10,000 heterogeneous images from the Corel dataset. The query set includes 200 images randomly chosen from ten categories: beads, bonsai, buses, butterfly, eagle, elephants, flags, forests, sky and tiger. Images from the same category as that of a query are used as the ground truth and as positive examples in relevance feedback in the experiment. In each round of feedback, top 30 images of the retrieval results are checked and labeled as either positive or negative examples. All of the labeled images in each round are accumulatively used, and the system always ranks the labeled positive images at the beginning and the labeled negative images at the end. Five iterations of feedback were tested. The image retrieval performance is evaluated by the measure of precision averaged on the query set. The precision at a scope s is defined as the ratio of the number of the relevant images within top-s to the scope s.

Since we focus on the comparison of classifiers, we just use two simple features with low dimensions for efficiency: color moments [7] and wavelet based texture feature. Color moments consist of 6 dimensions which are he first two moments (mean and standard deviation) extracted from the three color channels (HSV space).

For wavelet-based texture, the original image is decomposed into 10 de-correlated sub-bands through 3-level wavelet transform. In each sub-band, the standard deviation of the wavelet coefficients is extracted, resulting in a 10-dimensional feature vector.

We compare the proposed CLA-based RBF network with other three classifiers: CLA network, SV-RBF and SVM. During each round of relevance feedback, the classifier is trained on the positive and negative images, and then it classifies all images as positive or negative. We compare the retrieval precision (scope=100) at each round of RF of the four classifiers. Figure 3 shows the comparison results. We can see all the four classifiers have improved the retrieval precision as the feedback goes on. Without surprise, SVM achieves the best performance. CLA obviously lags behind the other three methods because of its drawbacks mentioned before. On the other hand, the proposed CLA-based RBF network improved the performance significantly. It combines the advantages of CLA and RBF, achieving a comparable performance with SVM and SV-RBF. The reason why SV-RBF is a little better than CLA-RBF is the SV center choice. The support vectors are those critical points containing discriminating information for a given classification task. Choosing them as the centers of basis function is more possible to result in higher classification accuracy.

However, note that in SVM and SV-RBF, the parameters of Gaussian kernel need to be predefined which is essential to the generalization ability of classifiers. In Gaussian kernel case, if g is set too large, correspondingly, the width of Gaussian kernel is too small, so it tends to over-fitting; if g is set too small, the width of Gaussian kernel is too large, so it will increase the non-separability. However, choosing a suitable kernel parameter is not an easy thing. So far, the most common method is still based on experiments. In the above experiment, the kernel parameter g in Formula (11) is set to 5.0 according to experience.

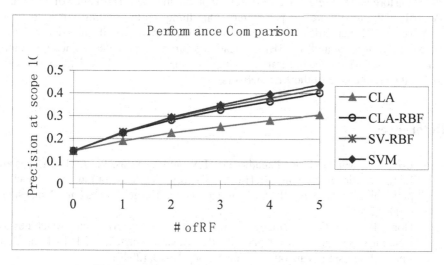

Fig. 3. Performance comparison on different classifiers

Table 1. Performance comparison on different kernel parameters

P100 (%)	SVM	SVRBF	SVM	SVRBF	SVM	SVRBF	CLA -RBF
	(g=0.5)		(g=5.0)		(g=50.0)		
1RF	16.99	15.61	22.53	22.96	21.31	17.47	22.66
2RF	28.77	24.39	29.50	29.24	26.27	22.03	28.30
3RF	34.09	29.92	34.82	34.06	31.42	26.28	32.80

Table 1 compares the retrieval precision (scope=100) under different kernel parameters during top 3 round of relevance feedback. From Table 1, we can observe clearly that when g is set either too small (g=0.5) or too large (g=50.0), the performance of SVM and SV-RBF lags behind the case when g is suitable (g=5.0). On the other hand, the proposed CLA-RBF network does not need to set the parameters of Gaussian kernels, but determine them automatically from the analysis of the training samples. Furthermore, its performance approaches that of SVM and SV-RBF with a suitable kernel parameter.

5   Conclusion

In this paper, we have proposed a relevance feedback method based on RBF neural network for image retrieval. The architecture of RBF network is initialized by Constructive Learning Algorithm. The number of basis function, the center and width of each basis function are all automatically determined by CLA. The weights of the output layer are estimated by LMS method. The proposed CLA-based RBF network combines the advantages of both CLA and RBF. It significantly improved the retrieval performance in relevance feedback, approaching the performance of SVM and SV-RBF with suitable kernel parameters. One thing worth pointing out is that the CLA-based RBF network does not need to set the parameters of Gaussian kernels, comparing with SVM and SV-RBF. Instead, the parameters are determined automatically from the analysis of the training samples. Our future work will focus on optimizing the architecture of the RBF network.

References

[1]   Cox, I. J., Minka, T. P., Papathomas, T.V. and Yianilos, P. N.: The Bayesian Image Retrieval System, PicHunter: Theory, Implementation, and Psychophysical Experiments, IEEE Transactions on Image Processing, Vol. 9(1), (2000) 20-37

[2]   Hong, P., Tian, Q. and Huang, T. S.: Incorporate Support Vector Machines to Content-Based Image Retrieval with Relevance Feedback, IEEE Int'l conf. on Image Processing, Vancouver, Canada, Sep 10-13, (2000)

[3]   Ishikawa, Y. and Subramanya, R.: MindReader: Query databases through multiple examples, Proc. of the 24th VLDB conference, New York, (1998)

[4]   Rui, Y., Huang, T. S., Ortega, M. and Mehrotra, S.: Relevance feedback: A power tool in interactive content-based image retrieval, IEEE Transaction on Circuits and Systems for Video Technology, Special Issue on Segmentation, Description, and Retrieval of Video Content, 8(5), (1998) 644-655

[5]   Schoelkopf, B., Sung, K., Burges, C., Girosi, F., Niyogi, P., Poggio, T. and Vapnik, V.: Comparing Support Vector Machines with Gaussian Kernels to Radial Basis Function Classifiers, IEEE Transcations on Signal Processing, Vol.45:11, (1997) 2758 –2765

[6]   Schwenker F, Kestler HA, Palm G.: Three learning phases for radial-basis-function networks, Neural Networks, 14 (4-5), (2001) 439-458

[7]   Stricker M. and Orengo, M., Similarity of color images. in Proc. SPIE Storage and Retrieval for Image and Video Databases. 1995

[8]   Tieu, K. and Viola, P.: Boosting image retrieval, Proc. IEEE Conf. Computer Vision and Pattern Recognition, Hilto Head Island, SC. (2000)

[9]   Vapnik, V. The nature of statistical learning theory. Springer-Verlag, New York. (1995)

[10]   Vasconcelos, N. and Lippman, A.: A Probabilistic Architecture for Conten-based Image Retrieval, Proc. IEEE Computer Vision and Pattern Recognition Conf., Hilton Head, North Carolina, (2000)

[11]   Zhang, L. and Zhang, B.: A geometrical representation of McCulloch-Pitts neural model and its application, IEEE Transaction on Neural Networks, 10(4), (1999) 925-929

[12]   Zhang, L., Lin, F. Z. and Zhang, B.: A neural network based self-learning algo-rithm of image retrieval, Chinese Journal of Software, 12(10), (2001) 1479-1485

[13]   Zhang, L., Lin, F. Z. and Zhang, B.: Support vector learning for image re-trieval, IEEE International Conference on Image Processing , Thessaloniki, Greece. (2001) 721-724

Spatial-Temporal Semantic Grouping
of Instructional Video Content

Tiecheng Liu and John R. Kender

Department of Computer Science
Columbia University
New York, NY 10027
{tliu,jrk}@cs.columbia.edu

Abstract. This paper presents a new approach for content analysis and semantic summarization of instructional videos of blackboard presentations. We first use low-level image processing techniques to segment frames into board content regions, regions occluded by instructors, and irrelevant areas, then measure the number of chalk pixels in the content areas of each frame. Using the number of chalk pixels as heuristic measurement of video content, we derive a content figure which describes the actual rather than apparent fluctuation of video content. By searching for local maxima in the content figure, and by detecting camera motions and tracking movements of instructors, we can then define and retrieve key frames. Since some video content may not be contained in any one of the key frames due to occlusion by instructors or camera motion, we use an image registration method to make "board content images" that are free of occlusions and not bound by frame boundaries. Extracted key frames and board content images are combined together to summarize and index the video. We further introduce the concept of "semantic teaching unit", which is defined as a more natural semantic temporal-spatial unit of teaching content. We propose a model to detect semantic teaching units, based on the recognition of actions of instructors, and on the measurement of temporal duration and spatial location of board content. We demonstrate experiments on instructional videos which are taken in non-instrumented classrooms, and show examples of the construction of board content images and the detection of semantic teaching units within them.

1   Introduction

We view video understanding as having two levels: a syntactic level and an event level. The syntactic level refers to video understanding based on low-level image structures of videos [2, 5, 3], while the event level refers to an understanding based on video content rather than how the video is captured and edited. Prior work [14, 7] on video summarization and understanding has concentrated on highly structured and commercially edited videos, where the explicit and implicit rules of their construction are a great aid in their analysis and summary. However, syntactic structures have restrictions. Although they may help us in

E. M. Bakker et al. (Eds.): CIVR 2003, LNCS 2728, pp. 362–372, 2003.

understanding videos with a strong narrative structure, the diversity of editing styles still has not been fully explored. Moreover, in unedited instructional or home videos, or in semi-edited videos such as real-time sports videos, pure syntactic approaches seem unlikely to be effective.

In this paper, we present an approach to understanding and summarizing instructional videos of blackboard presentations. These instructional videos are typically produced by a lightly trained staff who do poor camerawork and almost no editing. In these videos, the syntactic structures of shot and scene lose much of their meaning, and camera movement is often a kind of noise rather than purposive information. Additionally, the visual content tends to be highly redundant. Therefore, summarization based on video content is essential.

Previous work [4, 13, 12, 6, 11] on content analysis and event detection of such videos include an approach [8] that captures key hand-written slides based on a heuristic measurement of content, and an approach [10] that segments the content areas of a blackboard within a specially instrumented classroom with a fixed wide-angle camera. In contrast to the latter work, we use videos captured in real classrooms: the board may have multiple panels, there may be changes of lighting conditions, the camera moves under the control of a camera man, and the board background may not have spatial and temporal variations in color due to the accumulation of erased chalk. In contrast to the former work, we propose a method for high level semantic content analysis of blackboard frames, by defining and extracting spatial-temporal "semantic teaching units" based in part on the recognition of significant actions of instructors and the spatial and temporal coherence of blackboard content. The same method can be also applied to videos of whiteboard presentations.

2   Board Content Retrieval

2.1   Model of Board Area

There are many difficulties in processing instructional videos taken from real classrooms: different light conditions as seen by multiple cameras, the movements of cameras and instructors, multiple sliding board panels, and the non-uniform color distribution within panels due to board wear and chalk dust. Straightforward models that assume a uniform background color do not work well. The remaining chalk dust after erasure sometimes could be confused with normal text lines. To overcome these difficulties, we model the color distribution of board background and use that model to segment video content areas.

Considering the color of a board background pixel as a combined effect of board background and the trail of erased chalk characters, we model the color of that pixel as $\{r, g, b\} = \{\bar{r} + k \cdot r^*, \bar{g} + k \cdot g^*, \bar{b} + k \cdot b^*\}$, where $\{\bar{r}, \bar{g}, \bar{b}\}$ represents the color of the board, $\{r^*, g^*, b^*\}$ represents the color of chalk, and k represents how much chalk has been left on that pixel, sometimes unintentionally through accumulated erasures. Since for chalk $r^* \approx g^* \approx b^*$, the model is simplified to $\{r, g, b\} = \{\bar{r} + n, \bar{g} + n, \bar{b} + n\}$. However, each pixel differs in the effects of chalk erasure. Based on empirical data, we model n as a binomial distribution, and estimate the real board color $\{\bar{r}, \bar{g}, \bar{b}\}$ and the parameters of the distribution of n. Since board color $\{\bar{r}, \bar{g}, \bar{b}\}$ depends on lighting conditions, each time a change of camera (a new shot) is detected, we need to re-estimate the board color. Our experiments indicate that the content areas can be detected with required accuracy based on RGB color space.

2.2   Estimation Parameters of Board Model

We first use a block-based process to estimate the parameters of the unchalked board background. We divide the frame into blocks with size 16 by 16. For all blocks that have edge points less than a predefined threshold, we cluster the average color of these blocks and retrieve the main cluster by iteratively discarding outliers. We consider all blocks in the main cluster as board background blocks, among which the blocks with less standard deviation of color are those less affected by chalk dust. For the block with the least color variance in this cluster, it is assumed to be the one least affected by chalk pixels, and the average color $\{\bar{r}, \bar{g}, \bar{b}\}$ of that block is selected as an estimation of board background color. We use all pixels in board background blocks to estimate the average and standard deviation of k, i.e. μ and σ.

2.3   Classification of Blocks of Frames

Based on our board model, we estimate board background color $\{\bar{r}, \bar{g}, \bar{b}\}$ and value of the chalk parameters, μ and σ, in successor frames of the same shot we classify blocks into three categories: board background, board content, and irrelevant. The process is block-based simply to reduce computational complexity, but empirical analyses shows it produces reasonable results.

We apply the following three tests to each block:

1. Block color test. This tests if the average color of a block is similar to that of a board background block. Suppose the average color of the block is $\{R, G, B\}$, we test if the following conditions are satisfied: $|R - \bar{r}| < \mu + 2\sigma$ and $|G - \bar{g}| < \mu + 2\sigma$ and $|B - \bar{b}| < \mu + 2\sigma$.
2. Pixel color test. If the first test is satisfied, the block resembles a board background block, but this does not automatically mean that most of the pixels in the block are board background pixels. We therefore test each pixel $\{r, g, b\}$ in the block. If $|r - \bar{r}| < \mu + 2\sigma$ and $|g - \bar{g}| < \mu + 2\sigma$ and $|b - \bar{b}| < \mu + 2\sigma$, we consider this pixel as a board background pixel. We calculate the portion of board background pixels to all pixels in a block, and test if this portion is larger than a threshold.
3. Edge point test. Lastly, we test if the number of edge points in a block is less than a predefined threshold; board background blocks contain almost no edge points.

If a block passes all three tests, it is a board background block. If it satisfies only the first two, it is a board content block. All other cases are labeled irrelevant blocks.

Fig. 1. Retrieval of the teaching content of the blackboard by segmenting a frame into board region, region occluded by instructor (shown as white areas), and irrelevant region (shown as black areas), the position of insructor is estimated and shown in the figure

2.4   Segmentation of Board Areas

After classifying blocks, we merge blocks into four region types: board background, board content, occlusion by instructor, and irrelevant. Since there may be more than one board panel in a frame, we use a color similarity least squares method [9] to detect the boundaries of panels. The main panel is characterized by having the largest amount of board area. Within the main panel, all board background blocks form the board background region, all board content blocks form the board content region, all irrelevant blocks form the occlusion by instructor region, and all the other blocks form the irrelevant region. We also estimate the position of the instructors by the center of mass of the occlusion by instructors region, and record also its area. As shown in Figure 1, one frame is segmented into different regions. The region of board content is retrieved, and the position of instructor is estimated.

3   Semantic Summarization of Video Content

3.1   Heuristic Measurement of Content

After segmenting a frame into four classes of regions, we detect content chalk pixels from board content area. For each pixel $\{r, g, b\}$, it is a chalk pixel if $r - \bar{r} > \mu + 2\sigma$ and $g - \bar{g} > \mu + 2\sigma$ and $b - \bar{b} > \mu + 2\sigma$. The count of all the chalk pixels in the board content area is a heuristic measurement of content, and it varies as a function of frame number. Local maxima in the function correspond to those frames that contain more content. These maxima and the movements of camera and instructor give cues for extracting the key frames from the video.

3.2   Key Frame Selection

The change of the value of the content function may be caused by camera motion or by camera zoom. It is most reliable within those static video segments with no detected camera changes. In instructional videos, most camera motions are pans, some are zooms, and very few are tilts. We use a fast approximation method to detect camera motion, based on optical flow. Using four border regions along the four edges of a frame, for each pixel in a boarder area, we find the least squares solution to the local smoothness constraint optical flow equation [1], which relates the optic flow vector to the image spatial gradient (obtained by the Soble operator) and the image temporal gradient (obtained by subtracting temporally adjacent frames). We define the motion of a border area as the average motion vector of all pixels in that area.

We declare a frame to be static if there exists one border area with almost no motion. This test is based on the observations that most motions are motions of instructors, and that instructors rarely occupy all the area of a frame. Only when all of the four border areas show large motion vectors do we estimate the motion of camera. This condition significantly reduces the computation time taken for camera motion detection.

Detection of the movements of instructors is based on the results of the blackboard segmentation. We choose the center of the region occluded by instructor as the approximate position of the instructor, and measure its area.

Now, to detect key frames, for each segment of the content function that is without camera movement, we search for the local content maxima. In the case that several frames have the same content value, we choose the frame with minimal instructor occlusion.

3.3   Mosaic of Video Frames

Some video content may not appear in any given frame due to occlusion by instructors, even if the camera doesn't move. We therefore mosaic together board content into board content images, for each static video segment. We use an image registration method to effectively remove the instructor. To further simplify the process, we compare and register content blocks we detected. In each segment of video content without camera motion, we compare mosaiced image with selected key frames: if this mosaic image is not better than one of the already selected key frames which has no instructor either, we discard it.

4   Semantic Teaching Unit

4.1   Definition of Semantic Teaching Unit

We introduce and define the concept of semantic teaching unit, a temporal-spatial unit of writing related to one topic of teaching content. Key frames, and even mosaiced images, are inadequate for this purpose, as they are simple spatial constructs which may contain more than one teaching topic, or only a portion of one. A unit more semantically related to teaching purpose would allow for more useful indexing and summarization.

A semantic teaching unit is characterized as a series of frames (not necessarily contiguous) displaying a certain sequence of instructor actions within the spatial

Fig. 2. One semantic teaching unit: the eight images show the development of the teaching unit. The structure of this unit is $STETWTWT$, a realization of the grammar $ST((W|E)T)^n$

neighborhood of a developing region of written content. The visual content of one semantic teaching unit tends to have content pixels around a compact area in board, and usually lasts for a substantial fraction of the video. Let S represent the action of instructor starting a new topic by writing on board area which is not close to areas of other teaching units, W represent the action of instructor writing one or more lines of content on the same topic, E represent the action of instructor emphasizing teaching content by adding symbols, underlining, or a few words, and T represent the action of the instructor talking, on camera or off. The grammar of a semantic teaching unit is then $ST((W|E)T)^n$. That is, a semantic teaching unit usually starts with instructor initiating a new topic by writing on the board, followed by discussion, and usually followed by actions of writing or emphasis alternating with talking. By recognizing the actions of instructors, and by detecting the spatial location and temporal duration of the written content, we can recognize these larger semantic units that are more related to instructional topics. Figure 2 shows an example of teaching unit and its structure.

4.2   Recognition of Semantic Teaching Units

To recognize semantic teaching units, we first need to classify the instructor's actions into starting, writing, emphasizing, or talking. We recognize these categories by measuring the area occluded by the instructor and by detecting the instructor's face. Since we have already segmented the region occluded by instructor within the board area, we can detect the head region. If there is a large amount of skin tone color there, the instructor is facing audience, otherwise he is facing board. Although audio information may help us determine the video segments of talking, we still need visual information to further differentiate the segment of instructor explainign to audience or talking while writing on blackboard. We classify the actions of instructors as follows:

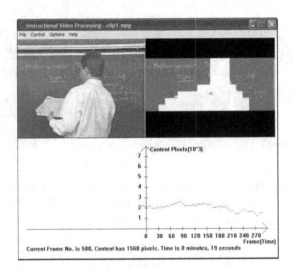

Fig. 3. The research software tool for blackboard content retrieval and summary image extraction. The image in upper left area is the original video frame, the image in upper right area is the processed image, and the figure below dynamically shows the number of content pixels of the current frame

1. If we find no instructor region, or the instructor is facing audience, we classify that video segment as talking.
2. If the instructor faces the board, and after that action, there is no increase in content area, it is also an action of talking.
3. If the instructor faces the board, and after that action there is an increase in the number of content pixels, we have two cases: if the newly added content area is not close to any other content areas, it is an action of starting a new teaching unit; otherwise we further classify that video segment as either writing or emphasizing, depending on the relative increase in content and the relative amount of time spent facing the board.

5 Experimental Results

We develop a software tool for on-line retrieval of video content and extraction of summary images. As shown in Figure 3, the original video frames (in upper left area of the interface) are segmented into different regions and enhanced. The processed image is shown in upper right area of the interface, and the number of chalk pixels are also measured and displayed to show the change of video content. Motions of cameras and instructors are also detected and measured on-line. In a Pentium III 500 MHz computer, we can reach a processing speed of around 7 frames per second.

We applied our algorithm of extracting board summary images on a 17-minute video segment of an instructional video taken in a real non-instrumented

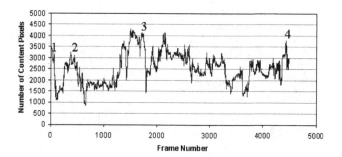

Fig. 4. This figure represents the fluctuation of the number of chalk pixels in a video segment of 4500 frames. It reflects the change of video content. The four marks 1, 2, 3, 4 show approximate positions of extracted summary frames

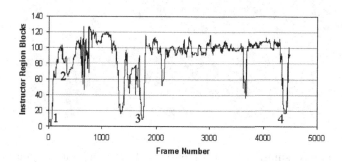

Fig. 5. This figure shows the area occluded by instructor in board area for each frame. The area is measured in terms of blocks. instructional video content of 4500 frames by measuring the number of content chalk pixels in each frame

classroom. We show the result of the first 4500 frames in Figure4, 5, and 7. Figure4 shows the fluctuation of the number of chalk pixels. Figure5 shows the area of occlusion by instructor region, measured in terms of the number of blocks. Four extracted summary images of this segment are shown in Figure7, and their temporal positions in the video segment are indicated in Figure4 and Figure5. A compression ratio of $O(10^3)$ may be achieved in instructional videos by using summary images as a version of compressed video. By matching extracted summary images, we may further reduce the number of summary images.

We also apply our proposed method of semantic teaching unit recognition to a 7-minute video segment (around 13K frames). We successfully recognized three independent teaching units (as shown in Figure6) and recognized the structures of these units. The structure of one of the semantic units is shown in Figure8. Compared with hand-selected teaching topics, these three units represent all instructional topics in that video segment, and the extracted summary images cover all of the instructional video content of that video segment.

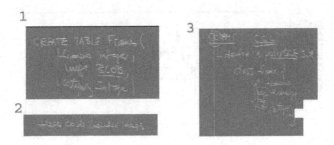

Fig. 6. Summary images of three semantic teaching units recognized from a video segment

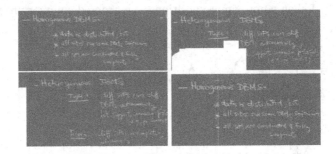

Fig. 7. Semantic summary images extracted from a video segment of 4500 frames. Summary image 1, 3, 4 are content regions of extracted key frames, summary image 2 is a content region of a mosaiced image

6   Conclusion and Future Work

We presented a new approach to summarize and understand instructional videos on semantic level. We demonstrated a low-level image processing technique to segment each frame into content regions, instructor regions, and irrelevant regions. Using the number of chalk pixels as a heuristic measurement of video content, we extracted and mosaiced together board content images. We defined the concept of a semantic teaching unit, a more meaningful temporal-spatial unit for instructional videos, and proposed an approach to recognize such unit on understanding the actions of instructor and the temporal and spatial relations of the board content of the units. Future work includes further study of the definition and interrelation of semantic teaching units, and user studies of their significance in indexing and retrieval.

Fig. 8.   The structure of one recognized semantic teaching unit is *STWTWTWTETET*

References

[1] S. S. Beauchemin and J. L. Barron. The Computation of Optical Flow. In *ACM Computing Surveys*, pages 433–467, 1995. 366

[2] H. S. Chang, S. Sull, and Sang Uk Lee. Efficient Video Indexing Scheme for Content-based Retrieval. In *IEEE Trans. on Circuits and Systems for Video Technology*, pages 1269–1279, Dec. 1999. 362

[3] Tat-Seng Chua and Li-Qun Ruan. A Video Retrieval and Sequencing System. In *ACM Transactions on Information Systems*, pages 373–407, Oct. 1995. 362

[4] Liwei He, Elizabeth Sanocki, Anoop Gupta, and Jonathan Grudin. Auto-summarization of audio-video presentations. In *ACM Conference on Multimedia*, pages 489–498, 1999. 363

[5] F. Idris and S. Panchanathan. Review of Image and Video Indexing Techniques. In *Journal of Visual Communication and Image Representation*, pages 146–166, June 1997. 362

[6] Shanon X. Ju, Michael J. Black, Scott Minneman, and Don Kimber. Summarization of videotaped presentations: Automatic analysis of motion and gesture. In *IEEE Trans. on Circuits and Systems for Video Technology*, pages 686–696, Sept 1998. 363

[7] T. Liu and J. R. Kender. A Hidden Markov Model Approach to the Structure of Documentaries. In *Proceedings of the IEEE International Worksop on Content-based Access of Image and Video Databases*, Jun. 2000. 362

[8] Tiecheng Liu and John R. Kender. Rule-based semantic summarization of instructional videos. In *International Conference on Image Processing*, pages I601–I604, 2002. 363

[9] Tiecheng Liu and Rune Hejelsvold John R. Kender. Analysis and enhancement of videos of electronic slide presentations. In *International Conference on Multimedia and Expo*, 2002. 365

[10] Masaki Onishi, Masao Izumi, and Kunio Fukunaga. Blackboard segmentation using video image of lecture and its applications. In *International Conference on Pattern Recognition*, pages 615–618, 2000. 363

[11] Eric Saund. Bringing the marks on a whiteboard to electronic life. In *CoBuild'99 Second International Workshop on Cooperative Buildings*, 1999. 363

[12] Tanveer Syeda-Mahmood. Indexing for topics in videos using foils. In *IEEE Conference on Computer Vision and Pattern Recognition*, 2000. 363

[13] Tanveer Syeda-Mahmood and S. Srinivasan. Detecting topical events in digital video. In *ACM Conference on Multimedia*, 2000. 363

[14] M. Yeung and B. L. Yeo. Time-Constrained Clustering for Segmentation of Video into Story Units. In *International Conference on Pattern Recognition*, pages 375–380, 1996. 362

A Novel Scheme for Video Similarity Detection

Chu-Hong Hoi, Wei Wang, and Michael R. Lyu

Department of Computer Science and Engineering
The Chinese University of Hong Kong
Shatin, Hong Kong
{chhoi,wwang,lyu}@cse.cuhk.edu.hk

Abstract. In this paper, a new two-phase scheme for video similarity detection is proposed. For each video sequence, we extract two kinds of signatures with different granularities: coarse and fine. Coarse signature is based on the Pyramid Density Histogram (PDH) technique and fine signature is based on the Nearest Feature Trajectory (NFT) technique. In the first phase, most of unrelated video data are filtered out with respect to the similarity measure of the coarse signature. In the second phase, the query video example is compared with the results of the first phase according to the similarity measure of the fine signature. Different from the conventional nearest neighbor comparison, our NFT based similarity measurement method well incorporates the temporal order of video sequences. Experimental results show that our scheme achieves better quality results than the conventional approach.

1 Introduction

With the rapid development of compute networks and Internet, digital videos become more and more easily copied and distributed. How to fast and effectively search similar video copies among huge volume database has attracted more and more focuses recently [1, 2, 3, 4, 5]. Two major applications of video similarity detection are video copyright issue and video retrieval by a given sample [6].

More and more copyright problems have been aroused as digital video data can easily be copied, modified and broadcasted over the Internet. Although digital watermarking provides a possible solution, it may not be suitable in every case. Video similarity detection has been proposed as a good complementary approach of digital watermarking for the copyright issues [3].

Furthermore, content-based video retrieval has been considered an important and challenging task in multimedia domain. Seeking an effective similarity measurement metric is regarded as a significant step in content-based video retrieval [7].

In this paper, we propose a novel scheme for video similarity detection. The rest of this paper is organized as follows. Section 2 discusses challenges of video similarity detection and related work. Section 3 presents our framework for video similarity detection and related contents are briefly discussed. Section 4 proposes

E. M. Bakker et al. (Eds.): CIVR 2003, LNCS 2728, pp. 373–382, 2003.

the coarse similarity measure scheme. Section 5 presents the fine similarity measure scheme. Finally, Section 6 provides our experimental results and Section 7 gives the conclusions and future work.

2   Challenges and Related Work

It is a challenging task to fast and effectively search similar videos from large video databases. Several papers have addressed how to tackle the problem [2, 3, 4, 9]. In general, two major research efforts for content-based video similarity detection are feature representation techniques and similarity measurement methods. Effective feature representation for video content is the first key step toward similarity detection. The second step is to find effective similarity measurement methods for cost-efficient similarity detection. We focus on the research work of the second step in this paper.

Although many efforts have addressed the problem, it is still difficult to solve the problem effectively and efficiently. Naphade et al. provide a video sequence matching scheme based on compacted histogram in [2]. A. Hampapur et al. examine several distance measurement methods and compare their performances in [3]. R. Mohan presents a scheme for video sequence matching based on similarity of temporal activity in [9]. However, most of them are based on the key-frame comparison of video shots to measure the similarity. None of them carefully consider the temporal order of video sequences and the efficiency problem. In [4], S.C. Cheung et al. develop an efficient randomized algorithm to search similar video. Their idea is based on generating a set of frames which are most similar to a set of randomly seeded frames. Although the algorithm is efficient, the idea of random order and frame-based comparison do not exploit the temporal order among video sequences as well.

3   A Two-Phase Similarity Detection Framework

Toward the challenging issue of fast and effective similar video detection from vast video databases, we propose a two-phase similarity detection framework based on different granular signatures, shown in Fig.1. In the preprocessing step, the low level features of the query video example and compared video data are first extracted. Based on the low level features, we generate two kinds of signatures with different granularities for each video sequence. Coarse signatures are generated based on the density histogram of feature points by mapping the original data space to a new pyramid space [10], while fine signatures are obtained by generating simplified feature trajectories of video sequences. In the first phase, most of statistically unrelated video data are fast filtered out by coarse similarity measure based on the Pyramid Density Histogram technique. In the second phase, fine similarity measure is performed by computing the similarity of feature trajectories of the video sequences based on the result set of the first phase. Different from the conventional approach, our fine similarity measurement method based on feature trajectories thoroughly considers the temporal order of video sequences. In the following sections, we discuss these techniques in detail.

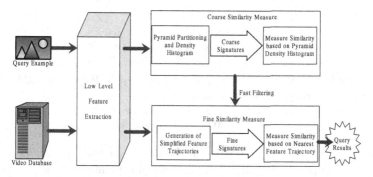

Fig. 1. A two-phase similarity detection framework

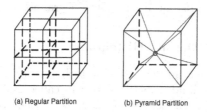

(a) Regular Partition   (b) Pyramid Partition

Fig. 2. Partitioning of the high dimension data space

4 Coarse Similarity Measure

Based on our proposed framework, each frame of a video sequence is considered as a feature point in the original data space after the feature extraction. Thus, a video sequence is formed by a set of feature points in the high dimension data space. For efficient similarity measure, it is impossible to conduct the similarity measurement frame-by-frame of video sequences. Therefore, we propose a Pyramid Density Histogram (PDH) technique to fast filter out the unrelated video sequences.

4.1 Pyramid Partitioning and Density Histogram

Pyramid partitioning technique is first proposed for dimension reduction and indexing problems in [10]. For a d-dimension data space, instead of infeasible regular partitioning of Fig. 2(a), the pyramid partitioning technique splits the data space into $2d$ pyramids with a center point $(0.5, 0.5, ..., 0.5)$ as their top and a $(d-1)$-dimension hyperplane of the data space as their base, shown in Fig. 2(b).

Suppose a video sequence S is formed by M frames corresponding to M feature points with d–dimension. Each feature point v in the video sequence S is denoted as $v = (v_1, v_2, ..., v_d)$, where $0 \leq v_i \leq 1$. Based on the pyramid partitioning technique, for a given feature point v, we assign v to the i-th pyramid by following the condition below

$$i = \begin{cases} j_{max}, & \text{if } (v_{j_{max}} < 0.5) \\ j_{max} + d, & \text{if } (v_{j_{max}} \geq 0.5) \end{cases} \quad (1)$$

where $j_{max} = \{j | (\forall k, 0 \leq (j, k) < d, j \neq k : |0.5 - v_j| \geq |0.5 - v_k|)\}$. The height of point v in the i-th pyramid is defined as [10]

$$h_v = |0.5 - v_{iMODd}|. \quad (2)$$

For each feature point v in the video sequence S, we can locate it in a unique pyramid. By computing the distribution of feature points in each pyramid, we propose the PDH technique to map the video sequence S in the original data space to the new pyramid data space. Two kinds of PDH techniques are engaged: Naïve Pyramid Density Histogram and Fuzzy Pyramid Density Histogram.

4.2   Naïve Pyramid Density Histogram

By applying the basic pyramid partitioning technique to density histogram, we present the original pyramid density histogram called Naïve Pyramid Density Histogram (NPDH). Given a video sequence S, the NPDH vector of S is denoted as $u = (u_1, u_2, ..., u_{2d})$. For each point v in S, the NPDH vector u is iteratively updated as

$$u_i = u_i + h_v \quad (3)$$

where i is defined in Eq.(1) and h_v is defined in Eq.(2). After processing all points in video sequence S, we obtain the NPDH vector as a coarse signature for video sequence S.

4.3   Fuzzy Pyramid Density Histogram

From NPDH, we found that it cannot fully exploit all information in each dimension. Thus, we propose another alternative technique called Fuzzy Pyramid Density Histogram (FPDH). For each point v in a video sequence S, instead being completely allocated to a unique pyramid in NPDH, the point v is assigned to d different pyramids based on the value of each dimension of v. The FPDH vector u is thus calculated as below

$$u_i = u_i + h_v \quad (4)$$

$$i = \begin{cases} j, & \text{if } (v_j < 0.5) \\ j + d, & \text{if } (v_j \geq 0.5) \end{cases} \quad (5)$$

where j=1,2,...,d and h_v is defined in Eq.(2). Performance comparison result of FPDH and NPDH is shown in Section 6.

4.4   Coarse Similarity Measure Based on PDH

Based on the PDH technique, each video sequence is mapped to a $2d$-dimension feature vector as a coarse signature in the pyramid data space. We then conduct the coarse filtering based on the coarse signatures. Suppose u_q is the PDH vector for a query example Q and u_c is the PDH vector for a compared video sample C in a database. Let us denote by ε a threshold for the coarse similarity filtering. Then we conduct the coarse filtering based on the comparison result of the Euclidean distance of two vector u_q and u_c. That means the compared video C is filtered out if the following condition is satisfied

$$||u_q - u_c|| > \varepsilon. \tag{6}$$

Based on the PDH technique, we can perform the coarse filtering very fast and obtain a small subset of original video database. In order to improve the precision rate, we need to make a further fine similarity measurement in the second phase.

5   Fine Similarity Measure

Although there remains a small subset of compared samples in the second phase, it is still infeasible to perform the similarity measure with the frame-by-frame comparison. Considering the temporal order of video sequences, we propose a Nearest Feature Trajectory (NFT) technique for effective similarity measurement. Instead of regarding a video sequence as a set of isolated key-frames in the conventional ways, we consider the video sequence as a series of feature trajectories formed by continuous feature lines. Each feature trajectory reflects a meaningful shot or several shots with gradual transition. Different from the conventional key-frame based comparison, our proposed similarity measure based on the nearest feature trajectories of video sequences can well exploit the temporal order of video sequences and obtain more precise results.

Nearest Feature Line (NFL) technique is first proposed for audio retrieval in [11]. It is also proved to be effective in shot retrieval of video sequence in [12]. In here, we use the similar technique to solve the similarity detection issue. Different from the NFL used in [12], our proposed NFT scheme consider the global similarity measurement of feature trajectories in two video sequences. A feature trajectory in our scheme is formed by a lot of continuous feature lines. Different from the Simple Breakpoint (SBP) algorithm used in [12], we propose a more effective algorithm to generate the simplified feature trajectories.

5.1   Generation of Simplified Feature Trajectories

As we know, each frame in a video sequence is considered as a feature point in the feature space. Two neighboring feature points form a feature line. A lot of feature lines in a shot form a feature trajectory. Thus a video sequence can be represented by a series of feature trajectories called a fine signature. However, it is impractical to regard all frames in the video sequence as the feature trajectory for the efficiency problem. Thus, we propose an efficient algorithm to generate the simplified trajectory.

Given a video sequence, we first detect the hard cut transitions of shots. For each shot, we generate a simplified feature trajectory as follow. Suppose we have a shot S and the number of frames in the shot is N, denoted as $S = \{v(t_1), v(t_2), ..., v(t_N)\}$. And let us denote by S' the simplified feature trajectory and denote by N^ψ the number of frames in S', which is a subset of S. However, it is time-consuming to obtain an global optimum subset S'. Therefore, we propose the following effective algorithm which can achieve a local optimum answer.

Assume that $\{v_k | k = 1, 2, ..., N\}$ represent the frames in a video sequence. Let us denote by $LR(v_k)$ the local similarity measure function of point v_k. Then, we define the following similarity measure function

$$LR(v_k) = |d(v_k, v_{k-1}) + d(v_{k+1}, v_k) - d(v_{k+1}, v_{k-1})| \qquad (7)$$

where $d(v_i, v_j)$ means the distance between point v_i and point v_j. Obviously, v_{k-1}, v_k and v_{k+1} satisfy the triangle-inequality relation. In the special case, if $LR(v_k)$ is equal to 0, then point v_k is on the line of points v_{k-1} and v_{k+1}. That means the variance of trajectory at point v_k can be neglected; otherwise v_k deviates from the line of points v_{k-1} and v_{k+1}. Apparently, the larger the value of $LR(v_k)$ is, the larger the deviation of the trajectory at that point is. After computing the $LR(v_k)$ value of each point, we remove the point whose value of $LR(v_k)$ is the minimum of all points. Repeat the procedure until the number of remaining points in the simplified trajectory is equal to N^ψ.

5.2   Similarity Measure Based on the Nearest Feature Trajectory

Based on the fine signatures discussed above, we proposed an effective algorithm for fine similarity measure of video sequences. Given two video sequences, the dissimilarity measure focuses on measuring the similarity distance of different feature trajectories. In the following part, we focus how to formulate the similarity measure of two feature trajectories.

Let us denote by $S^{(x)}$ the x-th simplified feature trajectory in a compared video sequence S and denote by $T^{(y)}$ the y-th simplified feature trajectory in a query video sequence T. Such two feature trajectories are illustrated in Fig. 3. Let us denote $S^{(x)} = \{s_1, s_2, ..., s_i, ..., s_N\}$ and $T^{(y)} = \{t_1, t_2, ..., t_i, ..., t_M\}$. The similarity of $S^{(x)}$ and $T^{(y)}$ is measured as follows.

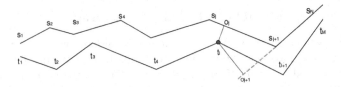

Fig. 3. Feature trajectories of two video sequences

As we know, the simplified feature trajectory $S^{(x)}$ is actually formed by $(N-1)$ ordered line segments $\overline{s_1 s_2}, ..., \overline{s_{N-1} s_N}$, denoted as $l_1^s, l_2^s, ..., l_{N-1}^s$. For each key point t_i in the simplified feature trajectory of the compared video sequence, we consider the distance from t_i to the line segment l_j^s. As shown in Fig. 3, assume that o_j is the foot of the perpendicular line from t_i to l_j^s, then o_j can be written as

$$o_j = s_j + \lambda(s_{j+1} - s_j) \tag{8}$$

where λ is a real number. Since $\overline{t_i o_j} \perp \overline{s_j s_{j+1}}$, we have

$$\overline{t_i o_j} \bullet \overline{s_j s_{j+1}} \equiv 0. \tag{9}$$

Combining Eq.(8) and Eq.(9), we obtain the expression of λ

$$\lambda = \frac{(t_i - s_j) \bullet (s_{j+1} - s_j)}{(s_{j+1} - s_j) \bullet (s_{j+1} - s_j)}, \tag{10}$$

and the distance from t_i to line segment l_j^s is composed by vertex s_j and s_{j+1}

$$d(t_i, \overline{s_j s_{j+1}}) = d(t_i, o_j) = d(t_i, s_j + \lambda * (s_{j+1} - s_j)). \tag{11}$$

However, if point o_j falls out of the range of line segment $\overline{s_j s_{j+1}}$, it is unsuitable to adopt the Eq.(11). Therefore, we define the following equation to process the out of range cases

$$d(t_i, l_j^s) = \begin{cases} d(t_i, \overline{s_j s_{j+1}}), & \text{if } 0 \leq \lambda \leq 1 \\ min(d(t_i, s_j), d(t_i, s_{j+1})), & \text{if } \lambda > 1 \text{ or } \lambda < 0 \end{cases} \tag{12}$$

where $d(t_i, s_j)$ and $d(t_i, s_{j+1})$ are the distances from point t_i to point s_j and to point s_{j+1}, respectively.

Based on the discussion above, we can obtain the similarity distance between two trajectories $S^{(x)}$ and $T^{(y)}$ as follow

$$dist(S^{(x)}, T^{(y)}) = \begin{cases} \frac{1}{N} \sum_{i=1}^{N} min_{j \in [1, M-1]} \, d(s_i, l_j^t), & \text{if } N \leq M \\ \frac{1}{M} \sum_{i=1}^{M} min_{j \in [1, N-1]} \, d(t_i, l_j^s), & \text{if } N > M \end{cases} \tag{13}$$

where N and M are the number of feature points in the feature trajectories $S^{(x)}$ and $T^{(y)}$, respectively. Let us denote by $Dis(S, T)$ the dissimilarity of the video sequence S and T. From Eq.(13), we formulate the final dissimilarity function as follow

$$Dis(S, T) = \frac{1}{X+Y} (\sum_{x=1}^{X} \min_{y \in [1, Y]} dist(S^{(x)}, T^{(y)}) + \sum_{y=1}^{Y} \min_{x \in [1, X]} dist(T^{(y)}, S^{(x)}))$$

where X and Y are the number of feature trajectories in the video sequences S and T, respectively.

6   Experiments and Results

Based on our proposed framework, we implemented a compact system for video similarity detection. In our video database, we collected about 300 video clips with length ranging from 1 minute to 30 minutes. Some of them are downloaded from the Web, and some of them are sampled from the same sources with different coding formats, resolutions, and slight color modifications.

In our experiments, color histogram is extracted as the low level feature for similarity measure. Since we mainly focus on the similarity measurement method with existing features, we adopt the simple and efficient RGB color histogram as the low level feature in our experiments. Based on the extracted 64-dimension color histogram feature, we generate two kinds of signatures with different granularities. Then we conduct the performance evaluation of video similarity measures with these two kinds of signatures.

6.1   Performance Evaluation of Coarse Similarity Measure

In the coarse similarity measurement phase, we compare the performance of two kinds of PDH methods. The performance metrics used in our experiments are *average precision rate* and *average recall rate* [4]. Based on the performance metrics, we compare the performance of two kinds of PDH methods: NPDH and FPDH. The comparison result of precision-recall rate is shown in Fig. 4. We can see that the retrieval performance of FPDH is better than NPDH method. Based on the FPDH, we can obtain average 90% recall with about 50% average precision rate. This means we can filter out most of unrelated data in the coarse phase. However, we also found the average precision rate quickly drops down

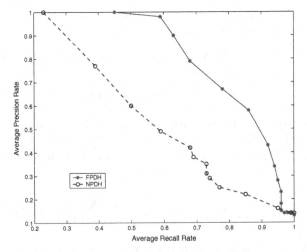

Fig. 4. Precision-recall rate comparison of NPDH and FPDH

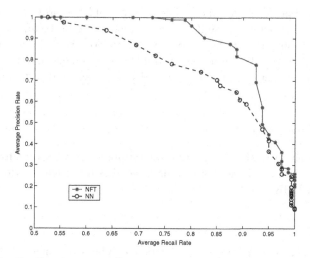

Fig. 5. Precision-recall curves comparison of NFT and NN

when the average recall rate approaches 100%. This indicates that RGB color histogram may not be an effective low level feature and more effective features need to be adopted for us to improve the performance in the future.

6.2 Performance Evaluation of Fine Similarity Measure

In order to evaluate the performance of our fine similarity measure based on the nearest feature trajectory method, we compare the retrieval performance between our NFT method and the conventional nearest neighbor (NN) method. Comparison results of these two methods are shown in Fig. 5. From the results, we can see that our proposed NFT method achieves better performance than the conventional NN method. However, we also found that even based on NFT comparison, we can, at best, achieve the best operating point at 90% precision rate with about 85% recall rate. The reason is that color feature representation is fragile to the color distortion problem. In [3], A. Hampapur et al. provide a lot of distance measure techniques using varied features, such color, shape, texture and motion, etc. We believe our proposed framework can obtain better results by using other features in the future.

7   Conclusions and Future Work

In this paper, we propose an effective two-phase framework to achieve video similarity detection. Different from the conventional way, our similarity measurement scheme is based on different granular similarity measure. In the coarse phase, we suggest the PDH technique. In the fine phase, we formulate the NFT technique. Experimental results show that our scheme is better than the conventional approach.

However, the performance of our scheme can still be improved since the color histogram based scheme is fragile to color distortion problem. In our future work, we will adopt other features to tune our video retrieval performance. We believe that better results can be achieved if we use more effective features in our framework. Also we need to enlarge our video database and test more versatile data in the future.

Acknowledgement

The work described in this paper was fully supported by a grant from the Research Grants Council of the Hong Kong Special Administrative Region, China (Project No. CUHK4360/02E).

References

[1] S.-C. Cheung and A. Zakhor: Estimation of web video multiplicity. In *Proc. SPIEíVInternet Imaging*, vol. 3964, pp. 34-36, 2000. 373
[2] M. Naphade, M. Yeung, and B. L. Yeo: A novel scheme for fast and efficient video sequence matching using compact signatures. In *Proc. SPIE, Storage and Retrieval for Media Databases*, San Jose, CA, Jan 2000. 373, 374
[3] A. Hampapur and R. Bolle: Comparison of distance measures for video copy detection. In *Proc. of International Conference on Multimedia and Expo 2001*, 2001. 373, 374, 381
[4] S. C. Cheung and A. Zakhor: Efficient video similarity measurement and search. In *Proc. of ICIP2000*, vol. 1, pp. 85-89, Canada, Sep 2000. 373, 374, 380
[5] H. S. Chang, S. Sull, and S. U. Lee: Efficient video indexing scheme for content based retrieval. In *IEEE Transactions on Circuits and Systems for Video Technology*, vol. 9, no. 8, pp. 1269-1279, Dec 1999. 373
[6] Y.-P. Tan, S. R. Kulkarni, and P. J. Ramadge: A framework for measuring video similarity and its application to video query by example. In *Proc. of ICIP1999*, vol. 2, pp. 106-110, 1999. 373
[7] Man-Kwan Shan and Suh-Yin Lee: Content-based video retrieval based on similarity of frame sequence. In *Proc. of International Workshop on Multi-Media Database Management Systems*, pp. 90-97, Aug 1998. 373
[8] Yi Wu, Y. Zhuang, and Y. Pan: Content-Based Video Similarity Model. In *Proc. of the 8th ACM Int. Multimedia Conf. on Multimedia*, USA, pp. 465-467, 2000.
[9] R. Mohan: Video sequence matching. In *Proc. of IEEE International Conference on Acoustics, Speech, and Signal Processing*, vol. 6, pp. 3697-3700, May 1998. 374
[10] Stefan Berchtold, Christian Böhm, and Hans-Peter Kriegel: The Pyramid-Technique: Towards Breaking the Curse of Dimensionality. In *Proc. Int. Conf. on Management of Data, ACM SIGMOD*, Seattle, Washington, 1998. 374, 375, 376
[11] S. Z. Li: Content-based Classification and Retrieval of Audio Using the Nearest Feature Line Method. In *IEEE Transactions on Speech and Audio Processing*, 2000. 377
[12] Li Zhao, W. Qi, S. Z. Li, S. Q.Yang, and H. J. Zhang: Key-frame Extraction and Shot Retrieval Using Nearest Feature Line (NFL). In *Int. Workshop on Multimedia Information Retrieval*, in conjunction with *ACM Multimedia Conf.*, Nov 2000. 377

Concept-Based Retrieval of Art Documents

Jose A. Lay[1] and Ling Guan[2]

[1] University of Sydney, Electrical and Information Engineering,
Sydney, NSW 2006, Australia
Jlay@ee.usyd.edu.au

[2] Ryerson University, Electrical and Computer Engineering,
Toronto, Ontario M5B-2K3, Canada
Lguan@ee.ryerson.ca

Abstract. This paper presents our work on the retrieval of art documents for color artistry concepts. First we show that the query-by-example paradigm popularly used in content-based retrieval can support only limited queryability. The paper then proposes a concept-based retrieval engine based on the generative grammar of elecepts methodology. In the latter, the language by which color artistry concepts are communicated in art documents is used to operate the retrieval processes. The concept language is explicated into a lexicon of elecepts and the associated generative grammar. Documents are then indexed with elecept indices, while the generative grammar is used to facilitate the query operation. More extensive color artistry concept queries can then be supported by post-coordination of the elecept indices.

1   Introduction

Leveraging content-based indexing techniques for the retrieval of art documents is both appealing and challenging. It is appealing as the techniques hold potentials to discern rich content information of an art document just as full-text indexing unveils keywords from a text document. It is also challenging, as evident by the fact that into the third decade of the content-based retrieval (CBR) practice, search tools at museums and art galleries across the world remain mostly text-based.

Two representative systems of CBR concerned with art documents are the QBIC at the State Hermitage Museum [1] and PICASSO [2]. QBIC is used at the site to support two types of syntactic search: (1) the dominant color search where a user specifies one or more colors to search for artworks matching the color specifications; (2) the color layout search where a user specifies an arrangement of color areas to search for artworks matching the spatial color structure of the example query. PICASSO, on the other hand, also supports semantic queries on contrast and harmony based on the inter-region color relationships. Typical queries supported by the system are: (1) two regions of certain sizes are sketched and the property of contrasting luminance is

E. M. Bakker et al. (Eds.): CIVR 2003, LNCS 2728, pp. 383-393, 2003.

selected. This example query searches for paintings of contrasting luminance; (2) two regions of certain sizes are sketched, one region is filled with color green and the properties of hue and contrasting warmth are selected. This example query is used to search for paintings showing contrasting warmth where one of the two regions is green in color; (3) three uncolored regions of certain sizes are sketched and the property of harmony is selected. The latest query is used to search for painting matching a ternary accordance such as paintings of blue, orange, and green regions.

We construe that a key issue impeding the wider applicability of CBR on art documents lies with the inflexibility of the Query-by-Example (QBE) paradigm. Intuitively, the retrieval of perceptually similar documents by example queries is useful for finding variants of art documents for which examples are available at hand. Beyond this functionality, the usefulness of QBE appears to be ill-fated, as posing visual example queries is difficult to be operationalized. For instance to pose an example query to *retrieve paintings of primary triadic color scheme which are brilliant but must not contain the complementary pairs of purple* is at best a very tedious operation. Consequently, access to color artistry concepts has remained restricted to intellectually indexed entities operated by the traditional cataloging practice.

This paper presents our work on operationalizing a concept-based retrieval engine for color artistry concepts based on the generative grammar of elecepts (G2E) methodology [9]. We demonstrate that once the language by which color artistry concepts are communicated in art documents is identified; retrieval for color artistry concepts can be operationalized by using the post-coordination indexing scheme where more queries can be supported through post-coordination of the index terms.

2   Color Artistry Concepts

Color artistry deals with the artful skill to communicate thought and to render perceptual experience with colors. In this section, we briefly present the color opponent theory of Ewald Hering [3] and the color harmony schemes of Faber Birren [5].

Color Opponent Theory

In the last decade of the 19th century, Ewald Hering noted that trichromatic human vision based on long-, medium-, and short-wavelength (LMS or RGB) cones commonly referred to as the Young-Helmholtz theory is inadequate for explaining human perceptual experience. Hering observed that yellow is as elementary as red or green and mixtures of red-green and yellow-blue are inconceivable, for there is not a reddish-green or a yellowish-blue. He also noted that the effect of chromatic contrast does not seem to apply to achromatic black and white, which blend to produce a range of gray. Thus he added yellow to the trichromatic RGB to introduce RYGB as perceptual primaries and proposed luminosity as an independent process to form what is currently known as the three color-opponent pairs of light-dark, red-green, and yellow-blue [3]. Hering then went on to devise a color-opponent wheel. On the wheel, perceptual primaries RYGB are arranged as color complements: red opposed to green, and yellow contrasted with blue.

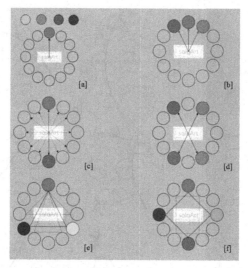

Fig. 1. Color Harmony Schemes. [a] Monochromatic. [b] Analogous. [c] Complementary. [d] X-complementary. [e] Triadic. [f] Quad

Color Harmony Schemes

In Arts, a number of color schemes are known for exhibiting certain effects on their use. These color schemes are often described as principles for attaining color harmony [5]. An illustration of a few color harmony schemes is given in Figure 1.

The monochromatic scheme deals with the harmony of a hue. It is instantiated by applying shades (adding black), tones (adding gray) and tints (adding white) on a single hue. Tones can also be introduced by varying saturation of a color. On the other hand, the analogous scheme is concerned with the harmony of similar hues. It is normally created by mixing no more than three adjoining colors on a 12-color wheel. Typically one of the three colors is used more predominantly than the others. Next the complementary scheme relates to the equilibrium harmony of complementary colors. In the simplest form, it is created by using two colors opposite to each other on the wheel. Alternatively, double- and split- complementary can be used. Two hues adjacent to each other can be coordinated with their respective complements to form a double complementary pairs of an X structure, while the split complementary is created by pairing a hue with either sides of its complement on a color wheel to form a Y structure. Color schemes are also commonly communicated by geometric metaphors. For example, the basic complementary is also known as a dyad, the scheme for the three primary hues is known as primary triadic, etc. Geometric color schemes can be expanded both in terms of structure (e.g. pentad) and dimensionality (from color wheel to color sphere).

The monochromatic color scheme is particularly popular in Arts. The school of Impressionism, for instance, is devoted to the combination of saturated color, tint, and white and avoided the darker tones and black. The eight monochromatic color schemes created through combinations of the tint-tone-shade processes [5] are replicated in Figure 2.

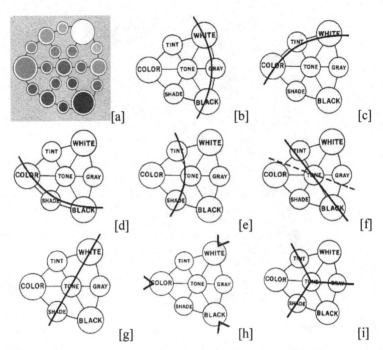

Fig. 2. Monochromatic Schemes. [a] Triangle of a color sphere. [b]-[i] Tint-tone-shade color harmony schemes

3   Generative Grammar of Elecepts

In G2E, an art document is seen as a communication medium whose contents comprise a set of artistry concepts communicated by a *painterly language*. The language comprises a set of *artistry structures* constructed out of a lexicon of finite color artistry elecepts. For the purpose of this work, we can think of *colors* as *words* and the *perceptual elements* of colors as *phonemes*. It follows that an artistry structure has a finite series of colors (respectively perceptual elements) just as a sentence has a finite sequence of words (respectively phonemes). Furthermore, just as not every sequence of words constitutes a sentence, not every composition of colors is a well-formed artistry structure. Based on [6], the set of explicit rules used to generate all and only well-formed artistry structures is called the generative grammar of color artistry. Figure 3 shows the hierarchical abstraction of the generative concept expression. A color artistry concept is seen as a compound concept constructed out of a set of color artistry elecepts coordinated by certain rules of the color artistry generative grammar.

A fundamental process in G2E is thus to derive the elecepts and generative grammar of the color artistry language such that color artistry concept queries can be conceived and expressed in terms of the color artistry elecepts and retrieval can be treated as a process of collocating the set of documents for which the query expression has a *model*. The elecepts are used to index the documents, while the generative grammar is used to facilitate the query operation.

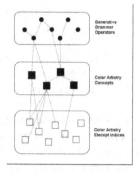

Fig. 3. Coordinating elecepts for color artistry concepts

Table 1. Color artistry relevance-concepts

Color Contrast	Color Scheme	Other
Hue	Monochromatic	Color Names
Light-dark	Analogous	Pale
Cold-warm	Complementary	Vivid
Complementary	Triadic	Tone
Simultaneous	Y-complementary	Colorfulness
Saturation	X-complementary	Dull, etc.
Extension		

In this work, the color artistry concepts (CACs) in [4][5] are used. A summary of the CACs introduced in the works is listed in Table 1.

To derive the elecepts and the generative grammar, a generative concept analysis is carried out. We begin by introducing a concept language *LANG* for the color artistry concepts. Principally, an expression in *LANG* takes the form of a color structure. The expression thus can be interpreted at two abstract levels which we shall call the topological language *LANG1* and the compositional language *LANG2*. The former is concerned with the geometric properties and the spatial relationship of colors, while the latter deals with the perceptual quality and interactivity of colors. Intuitively, CACs are primarily a set of expressions in the compositional language.

Treating CACs as expressions of *LANG-2* confers a rather simple lexicon to the color artistry language. Clearly, CACs can be factored into certain compositions of colors. The elecepts and generative grammar of *LANG2* can then be defined by using a color opponent color model—a color wheel or sphere where contrasting hues are arranged as complements. The lexicon of the elecepts comprises all colors specifiable in that color model, while the generative grammar comprises the various topological relationships needed to represent concepts presented in Table 1.

To offer a formal syntax for *LANG2*, we use $\mathcal{ALCN}$ from the family of Description Logics (DL) introduced in [7]. The basic elements of DL are *concepts* and *roles* which respectively correspond to classes and binary relations. Concepts and roles are constructed from *elecepts* along with some *constructors*. The syntax of the grammar is given by:

$$C, D \rightarrow C_E \mid \neg C \mid C \sqcap D \mid C \sqcup D \mid$$
$$\forall R.C \mid \exists R.C \mid \exists^{\geq n}R.C \mid \exists^{\leq n}R.C$$

where C_E denotes elecepts, C and D are color artistry concepts, R represents grammar roles, $^{\geq n}R$ and $^{\leq n}R$ are respectively the at-least and at-most number restrictions where n ranges over positive integers. The constructors are negation ($\neg$), union ($\sqcup$), and intersection ($\sqcap$).

Meanwhile to represent the topological relationships on a color model, we introduce three operators: adjacent, opposite, and triad. On a color wheel, the adjacents at distance n of h are the pairs (h_1,h_2) such that (h_1,h_2) located on the counter-clock-wise and clock-wise at distance n from h on the color wheel. The opposite of h is h_1 such that $\angle(h,h_1) = 180$ degree. The triad of h is a triple (h,h_1,h_2) such that (h,h_1,h_2) is a equilateral triangle. Lastly the temperature operator maps the hues on the color wheel into two sequence of warmth W_i and C_i based on some interpretation of warmth. While on a color sphere, the hue operators are extended to deal with the dimensions of chroma and lightness. Accordingly three elemental adjacent operations are perceptible for each color on the surface of the sphere: towards other hues along the equator (hue operation); up towards white and down towards black (lightness operation); and inwards towards grey at the centre and continuingly toward its complementary hue (chroma operation).

By using the syntax and the topological relationship operators, we now define some concepts and grammar roles:

color	$\doteq$	hue $\sqcap$ *saturation* $\sqcap$ *lightness*
color-name	$\doteq$	color-constant
warmth	$\doteq$	hue-constant
lightness-name	$\doteq$	lightness-constant
colorfulness-name	$\doteq$	saturation-constant
rAnalogous	$\doteq$	$\exists^{\geq n}adjacent.x$ $\sqcap$ $\exists^{\leq n}adjacent.x$
rMono	$\doteq$	$\exists^{\geq 0}adjacent.x$ $\sqcap$ $\exists^{\leq 0}adjacent.x$
rComplement	$\doteq$	$\exists\, opposite.x$
rTriadic	$\doteq$	$\exists\, triad.x$
rTone(n)	$\doteq$	$\exists^{\geq n}adjacent.sat.$
rTint(n)	$\doteq$	$\exists^{\geq n}adjacent.lightness$
rShade(n)	$\doteq$	$\exists^{\leq n}adjacent.lightness$
rY-complement(n)	$\doteq$	$\exists^{\geq n}adjacent.(complement.x)$ $\sqcap$
		$\exists^{\leq n}adjacent.(complement.x)$
rWarmer(n)	$\doteq$	$\exists^{\geq n}temperature$

Subsequently, arbitrary CACs can be written as expression in *LANG2*, for example:

(1)　　　Purple $\sqcap$ rTriadic.hue

(2)　　　Purplish-red　$\sqcap$　rComplement.hue　$\sqcap$
　　　$\neg$ Analogous.sat

(1) represents the triadic scheme for hue purple; and (2) stands for the hue complement of color purplish-red which must not have analogous saturation.

The query operation thus can be seen as a *satisfiability check*. Given an *interpretation* $\mathcal{I}$ a pair of $(\Delta^{\mathcal{I}}, \bullet^{\mathcal{I}})$ where $\Delta^{\mathcal{I}}$ is the domain of the interpretation and $\bullet^{\mathcal{I}}$ is an interpretation function which assigns to every concept A a set $A^{\mathcal{I}} \subseteq \Delta^{\mathcal{I}}$ and every grammar role R a binary relation $R^{\mathcal{I}} \subseteq \Delta^{\mathcal{I}} \times \Delta^{\mathcal{I}}$. The interpretation function of other compound concepts is defined inductively by the following rules:

$$
\begin{aligned}
\top^{\mathcal{I}} &= C^{\mathcal{I}} \cup \neg C^{\mathcal{I}} = \Delta^{\mathcal{I}} \\
\bot^{\mathcal{I}} &= C^{\mathcal{I}} \cap \neg C^{\mathcal{I}} = \varnothing \\
(\neg C)^{\mathcal{I}} &= \Delta^{\mathcal{I}} \setminus C^{\mathcal{I}} \\
(C \sqcap D)^{\mathcal{I}} &= C^{\mathcal{I}} \cap D^{\mathcal{I}} \\
(C \sqcup D)^{\mathcal{I}} &= C^{\mathcal{I}} \cup D^{\mathcal{I}} \\
(\exists R.C)^{\mathcal{I}} &= \{a \in \Delta^{\mathcal{I}} \mid \exists b.(a,b) \in R^{\mathcal{I}} \wedge b \in C^{\mathcal{I}}\} \\
(\geq^n R)^{\mathcal{I}} &= \{a \in \Delta^{\mathcal{I}} \mid |\{b|(a,b) \in R^{\mathcal{I}}\}| \geq n\} \\
(\leq^n R)^{\mathcal{I}} &= \{a \in \Delta^{\mathcal{I}} \mid |\{b|(a,b) \in R^{\mathcal{I}}\}| \leq n\}
\end{aligned}
$$

Thus a query of concept C is *satisfiable* with respect to the grammar $\mathcal{G}$ ($\mathcal{G} \vDash C$) if there exists a *model* $\mathcal{I}$ of $\mathcal{G}$ such that $C^{\mathcal{I}}$ is a nonempty set. It follows that two concepts C and D are equivalent (or disjoint) with respect to $\mathcal{G}$, if $C^{\mathcal{I}} = D^{\mathcal{I}}$ (or $C^{\mathcal{I}} \cap D^{\mathcal{I}} = \varnothing$) for every model $\mathcal{I}$ of $\mathcal{G}$.

4   Retrieving Color Artistry Concepts

To represent the elecepts, the CIE-LAB color system is used. The choice is judicious, as CIE-LAB is a color-opponent model. The long axis of CIELAB represents lightness (L), while the other two color axes are based on Hering's color opponent pairs of red-green (A: a,-a) and yellow-blue (B: b,-b). However, as CACs are conceived in terms of hue, saturation, and lightness; the LAB coordinates are impractical and will need to be transformed. In this work, the normalized color histograms of lightness (L), chroma/saturation (C), and hue (H) of CIE-LCH are used. The latter is derived by transforming the CIE-LAB cube into polar coordinates:

$$ L = L; \quad C = \sqrt{a^2 + b^2}; \quad H = \arctan(\frac{b}{a}) $$

The lexicon of *LANG-2* thus comprises all colors in the LCH sphere, while its generative grammar is defined by the extended adjacent, opposite, triad, and the temperature operators on the LCH color sphere. However, color is hardly perceived in such a granularity for general artistry use. Thus, a coarser color specification is often desirable. In this work, we define a color cube by introducing a tolerance block. A color cube of a color is obtained by extending the color point with ΔL, ΔC, and ΔH defined by the tolerance block. Meanwhile, natural language color names are supported by mapping of the ISCC-NBS color system [8].

We now demonstrate a naïve retrieval mechanism by using the relational data model. The implementation on the latter is often desirable as a large number of art document collections are maintained as relational database systems. To operate the retrieval as set theoretic operations of relational database, elecepts of hue, chroma, and lightness are treated as relations. The database schema are (hue) = $\{H_1, H_2, ..., H_{360}\}$, (chroma) = $\{C_1, C_2, ..., C_{60}\}$, and (lightness) = $\{L_1, L_2, ..., L_{100}\}$. The lexicon of *LANG-2* is thus the Cartesian products of the domain of the three elemental concept relations: dom{H}x dom{C}x dom{L} where the domains of {L},{C},{H} range over 0 to 100 for each attribute (histogram bin) representing normalized percentage distribution over the elecepts.

As elecepts of an artwork is indexed by the LCH tuples, collocating for a concept query is essentially a two-step process of expanding the *LANG-2* expression into relations of elecepts and a satisfiability check for its model in the database. The expression expansion is carried out by using the generative grammar, while the satisfiability check utilizes the projection, selection, join, difference, and other set theoretic operators in the relational data model. For instance, the concept of lightness may be differentiated as {very-light, light, normal, dark, and very-dark}, by the grammar; these concepts are expanded as a function over the tuple {L}. Each concept is then operationalized by a projection onto the set of attributes in {L}. Suppose the perceptuality over the set of attributes of {L} is evenly distributed, then t[very-light]=<t(L_{81}), t(L_{82}), ..., t(L_{100})> where t[very-light] is the projection of the elecept onto the set of attributes in the relation schema of (lightness). Thus the query **Q1: green · rComplementary.hue** can be operationalized as the selection over:

$$Q1: \quad \mathcal{G} \vDash < green > \; \sqcap \; \mathcal{G} \vDash rComplementary.hue(green)$$
$$\equiv \; \mathcal{Q} \vDash \pi_{green}(hue) \; \cap \; \mathcal{Q} \vDash \pi_{red}(hue)$$

where $\mathcal{G}$ is the generative grammar of the *LANG-2* and $\mathcal{Q}$ is the operational satisfiability qualifier for the concepts in the relational data model. In practice, $\mathcal{Q}$ can be defined based on some heuristic or by adaptive learning. In the simplest form, $\mathcal{Q}$ may just be defined as a threshold function.

Intuitively, other query models are also supported. For example, a system based on inverted elecept indices can be devised. In the latter, each elecept index is treated as a term. Then for each elecept term t_i, a posting (d_j, w_{ji}) is created to point to all documents d_j for which the term t_i has a normalized histogram weight w_{ji}.

	Document, Weight					
$term_1$	d_i, w_{i1}	d_j, w_{j1}	...	...	...	d_m, w_{m1}
$term_2$	d_h, w_{h2}	d_j, w_{j2}	...	...	...	d_n, w_{n2}
...	...	...	...	...	...	...
...	...	...	...	...	...	...
...	...	...	...	...	...	...
$term_N$	d_j, w_{jN}	d_k, w_{kN}	...	...	...	d_p, w_{pN}

In a search operation, the query is again treated as a two-step process. First it is expanded into a relation of elecept terms along with their qualifiers. Then each associated term vector in the inverted elecept indices is evaluated, qualified documents are then retrieved. Relationships such as *triadic* AND *warm* are supported by intersecting the associated document sets. The use of inverted elecept index is operationally advantageous. Its efficiency has been well exemplified by the capacity of online search engines to support billions of web pages.

5   Retrieval Examples

Figure 4 shows several retrieval examples of the SoloArt[1]. The examples were based upon a database comprising 40,000+ images from the Corel Photo Collection. Figure 4[a] shows the retrieval of the simple analogous scheme for the hue green. The search was interpreted as a projection onto the adjacent range of the hue green and then sorted by decreasing cumulative hue containments. The sort operation resembles the similarity ranking of content-based retrieval. Figure 4[b] and Figure 4[c] respectively show the retrieval for analogous color scheme with dominant warmth and the retrieval for highly saturated color of blue or red hues. In *LANG-2*, a structured query can be posed by combining various color artistry concepts with Boolean operators. Structured queries are a major advantage of the G2E methodology. Boolean operators allow complex concepts to be expressed intuitively, while the search can be supported naturally by using relational data model or inverted elecept indices. Meanwhile by using the few operators defined in the generative grammar, artists can instantiate, experiment, and store various color artistry concepts. Figure 4[d] demonstrate the retrieval example in supporting the customization of color artistry concepts where images constituting models for the major triadic harmony scheme are retrieved. The formulation of well-known concepts is a convenience for novice users. However, artists often contemplate with new ideas and may seek to retrieve examples on them. The latter in turn highlights another salient feature of the G2E methodology. Users can make use of the elecepts and the generative grammar to build customized concepts and when appropriate saving them as personal concepts.

6   Conclusions

In this paper, we presented a new treatment for the retrieval of art documents by color artistry concepts. The color artistry language was identified and explicated into a lexicon of elecepts and the associated generative grammar. Documents are then indexed with the elecept indices, while the generative grammar is used to facilitate the query operation. As elecept indices and generative grammar are rendered accessible, more extensive queryability is operationalized without the need to devise a visual example query.

---

[1] A collaborative project supported by the Art Gallery of NSW Australia.

[a] Analogous of green hues

[b] Analogous color scheme with dominant warm

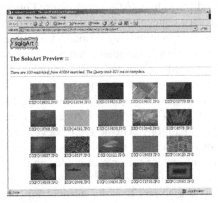

[c] Bright saturated colors of Blue or Red

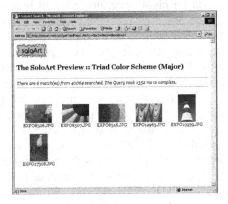

[d] Major triadic harmony scheme of the RYB primaries

Fig. 4. Retrieval examples of the SoloArt

References

[1]   IBM QBIC Online at the State Hermitage Museum: http://www.hermitagemuseum.org/.

[2]   J. M. Corridoni, A. del Bimbo, and P. Pala, *Retrieval in Paintings using Effects induced by Color Features*, IEEE Multimedia, Vol.6, No.3, July-September 1999, pp.38-53.

[3]   E. Hering, *Outlines of a Theory of the Light Sense*, translated by L. Hurvich and D.H. Jameson, Harvard University Press, Cambridge MA, 1964.

[4]   J. Itten, *The Art of Color: the Subjective Experience and Objective Rationale of Color*, translated edition by Ernst van Haagen, Reinhold Publishing, New York, 1961.

[5]   F. Birren, Principles of Color – A review of past traditions and modern theories of color harmony, VN Reinhold, New York, 1969.

[6]   N. Chomsky, *Aspects of the Theory of Syntax*, M.I.T. Press, Cambridge, 1965.

[7]   M. Schmidt-Schauß and G. Smolka, *Attributive Concept Description with Complements*, Artificial Intelligent, 48, 1, 1991, pp. 1-26.

[8]   K.L. Kelly and D.B. Judd, *Color: Universal Language and Dictionary of Names*, National Bureau of Standards, 1976.

[9]   J.A Lay, Concept-based Retrieval of Images and Audiovisual Documents, Ph.D. Thesis, University of Sydney, 2003.

Video Retrieval of Human Interactions Using Model-Based Motion Tracking and Multi-layer Finite State Automata*

Sangho Park[1], Jihun Park[2], and Jake K. Aggarwal[1]

[1] Department of Electrical and Computer Engineering,
The University of Texas at Austin
Austin, TX 78712
{sh.park,aggarwaljk}@mail.utexas.edu
[2] Department of Computer Engineering, Hongik University
Seoul, Korea
jhpark@hongik.ac.kr

Abstract. Recognition of human interactions in a video is useful for video annotation, automated surveillance, and content-based video retrieval. This paper presents a model-based approach to motion tracking and recognition of human interactions using multi-layer finite state automata (FA). The system is used for widely-available, static-background monocular surveillance videos. A three-dimensional human body model is built using a sphere and cylinders and is projected on a two-dimensional image plane to fit the foreground image silhouette. We convert the human motion tracking problem into a parameter optimization problem without the need to compute inverse kinematics. A cost functional is used to estimate the degree of the overlap between the foreground input image silhouette and a projected three-dimensional body model silhouette. Motion data obtained from the tracker is analyzed in terms of feet, torso, and hands by a behavior recognition system. The recognition model represents human behavior as a sequence of states that register the configuration of individual body parts in space and time. In order to overcome the exponential growth of the number of states that usually occurs in single-level FA, we propose a multi-layer FA that abstracts states and events from motion data at multiple levels: low-level FA analyzes body parts only, and high-level FA analyzes the human interaction. Motion tracking results from video sequences are presented. Our recognition framework successfully recognizes various human interactions such as approaching, departing, pushing, pointing, and handshaking.

1 Introduction

Analysis of video data is important due to the rapid increase in the volume of information recorded in the form of video. Most research has focused on

---

* This work was partially supported by grant No. 2000-2-30400-011-1 from the Korea Science and Engineering Foundation.

E. M. Bakker et al. (Eds.): CIVR 2003, LNCS 2728, pp. 394–403, 2003.

shot detection [1], video indexing [2], and video summarization [3] by analysis of meta-data. Detailed recognition of human interaction in a video is desired for content-based video retrieval. Recognizing human interactions is a challenging task because it involves segmentation and tracking of deformable human body parts at low level and recognition of semantics in behavior at high level. There have been two types of approaches to human motion analysis: model-based approaches and view-based approaches [4] depending on the availability of an explicitly defined *a priori* model.

This paper presents a model-based approach to motion tracking and recognition of human interaction in widely-available, static-background monocular video sequences. We assume the following constraints: the use of a monocular video camera with fixed parameters and a stationary background, that the projection plane is perpendicular to the camera viewing direction, and that people move parallel to the projection plane within tolerance. We represent human interactions as sequences of states that register the configuration of individual body parts in space and time. In order to overcome the exponential growth of the number of states that usually occurs in single-level finite state automata (FA), we propose a multi-layer FA that abstracts states and events from motion data at multiple levels: low-level FA analyzes body parts only, and high-level FA analyzes the human interaction.

The rest of the paper is organized as follows: Section 2 summarizes previous work related to model-based human tracking and behavior recognition. Section 3 describes an overview of our system. Section 4 describes the procedure of image background subtraction. Section 5 presents human body modeling and cost functional for fitting, and Section 6 explains how to generate finite states and events for behavior recognition. Experimental results and conclusions follow in Sections 7 and 8 respectively.

2 Previous Work

Model-based human tracking aims at estimating the kinematic parameters of body configuration. *Kinematics* deals only with the motion of a body, its displacement, velocity, and acceleration. All kinematics-based motion tracking methods may be classified into two groups: *inverse kinematics-based* and *forward kinematics-based* methods. The inverse method [5, 6] computes joint angles given the end-tip parameters (i.e., the parameters of end points of the body parts), whereas the forward method [7] computes the end-tip parameters given the joint angles.

Morris et al.[5] presented an early model-based work for deriving differential inverse kinematics equations for image overlap. In [5], they used a 2D (two-dimensional) scaled prismatic model for figure fitting, and reduced the singularity problem by working in the projection plane (2D). But the appearance of the singularity is inevitable because this method is based on differential inverse kinematics. Huang, et al., [6] extended the inverse kinematics work presented in [5] to solve motion parameters of the articulated body in a statistical framework using the expectation-maximization (EM) algorithm. Sidenbladh et al.[7] converted the human motion tracking problem into a probabilistic inference problem aimed at estimating posterior probability of body model parameters given the input image.

The motion data obtained from the human tracker is used for human behavior recognition. We may classify human interaction recognition into two groups: gross-level and detailed-level. Gross-level behavior is relevant to wide-view video data where each person is represented as a small moving blob. Examples include interactions between people such as *approaching, departing,* and *meeting* [8, 9]. Detailed-level behavior involves movement of individual body parts such as head, torso, hand, and leg, ect. Examples include interactions such as *hand-shaking, pointing, pushing,* and *kicking.* [10, 11]. Both levels of recognition are desired for surveillance applications, but most research has focused on the gross-level recognition tasks.

We may classify human motion analysis methods according to the recognition algorithms used: the algorithms are either stochastic, such as hidden Markov models (HMM), or deterministic, such as finite state automata (FA). In general, stochastic methods are useful to handle uncertainty due to image noise, imperfect segmentation / tracking, etc., at low level processes in view-based approaches. If the uncertainty can be effectively resolved by model-based methods at low level, then we can use deterministic methods for interaction recognition. In this case, the reliable fitting of the model body to image data is important.

Many approaches have been proposed for behavior recognition using various methods including hidden Markov models, finite state automata, context-free grammar, etc. Oliver et al.[8] presented a coupled hidden Markov model (CHMM) for gross-level human interactions between two persons such as 'approach', 'meet', 'walk together', and 'change direction'. Hongeng et al.[9] proposed probabilistic finite state automata(FA) for gross-level human interactions. Their system utilized user-defined hierarchical multiple scenarios of human interaction. Hong et al.[11] proposed a deterministic FA for detailed-level recognition of human gestures such as 'hand-waving', 'drawing a circle', and 'drawing a figure 8'. Their system was used for computer games based on a human computer interface. Park et al.[10] proposed a string-matching method using a nearest neighbor classifier for detailed-level recognition of two-person interactions such as 'hand-shaking', 'pointing', and 'standing hand-in-hand'. Wada et al. [12] used nondeterministic finite state automata (NFA) using *state product space*. They preferred NFA to HMM because NFA provides transparent information about state transitions whereas HMM's state transition is *hidden* to the user.

3 Overview of Our System

Our system is motivated by model-based human motion tracking and recognition of human interactions in a surveillance video. We use a 3D (three-dimensional) human body model with 11 degrees of freedom (DOF) using a sphere and cylinders (See figure 1(a).) In order to apply the model-based human tracker, we remove the background of the input image using a background subtraction method similar to [13]. A 3D human body model projected to the 2D projection plane is used to fit the foreground image silhouette.

We convert the human motion tracking problem into a parameter optimization problem. A cost functional for optimization is used to estimate the degree of overlap between the foreground input image silhouette and the projected 3D body model silhouette. The degree of overlap is computed using computational geometry by converting a set of pixels from the image domain to a polygon in the real projection plane domain.

The kinematic parameters of the fitted model body are concatenated along the sequence and give the motion parameters, and the motion data is analyzed by a recognition system. We propose a *multilevel* deterministic finite state automata (DFA) as the recognition model. The multilevel DFA is composed of basic-level DFA's to abstract numerical motion data and analyze the motion data with respect to feet, torso, and hands. The low-level DFAs independently represent the individual body-part poses as discrete states and the body part motion as a transition between the states. The high-level DFAs concatenate the outputs of the low-level DFAs along the sequence, and analyze the patterns for the recognition of body gestures and interactions between two persons.

4   Background Subtraction

Our video data involves the use of a monocular video camera with fixed parameters and a stationary background. We transform the color video from RGB color space to HSV (hue, saturation, value) color space to make the intensity or brightness explicit and independent of the chromaticity: $Z \in \{H, S, V\}$. We build the background model in terms of a Gaussian distribution with the mean $\mu_Z(x, y)$ and standard deviation $\sigma_Z(x, y)$ of each color channel, Z, at every pixel location (x, y). The Gaussian parameters μ_Z and σ_Z are estimated using k_b background frames ($k_b = 20$) that do not contain humans.

The foreground image region is segmented by background subtraction performed in each frame [13]. Foreground segregation is performed for every pixel $v = [v_H, v_S, v_V]^T$ as follows: at each image pixel (x, y) of a given input frame, the change in pixel intensity is evaluated by computing the Mahalanobis distance $\delta_Z(x, y)$ from the Gaussian background model for each color channel Z.

$$\delta_Z(x, y) = \frac{|v_Z(x, y) - \mu_Z(x, y)|}{\sigma_Z(x, y)} \tag{1}$$

The foreground image $F(x, y)$ is obtained by choosing the maximum of the three distance measures, δ_H, δ_S, and δ_V for the H, S, V channels;

$$F(x, y) = max[\delta_H(x, y), \delta_S(x, y), \delta_V(x, y)] \tag{2}$$

A binary foreground mask image is obtained by thresholding F. At this stage, morphological operations are performed as a post-processing step to remove small regions of noise pixels.

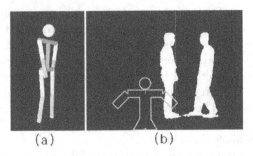

(a)   (b)

Fig. 1. 3D body model (a), and the initial stage for fitting the model to image (b)

5   Human Body Modeling and Cost Functional

5.1   Human Body Modeling

As shown in fig. 1(a), the body is modeled as a configuration of nine cylinders and one sphere according to anthropometric data. The body model is projected onto a 2D real projection plane. The sphere represents the head, while the rest of model body is modeled using cylinders of various radii and lengths. Our body model is similar to that used in [7]. Currently, we use only nine 1-DOF (degree-of-freedom) joints plus body displacement, and a vertical rotation to compensate for the camera view. These are our control variables for the cost functional. Body parts are linked together by kinematic constraints in a hierarchical manner. This may be considered to be a tree structure with the base at the pelvis (i.e., the bottom of the cylinder representing the torso) of the model body. We have overcome the body occlusion problem using computational geometry, by computing the union of the projected model body parts and then computing the intersection with overlapping input image silhouettes. Fig. 1(b) shows the initial step of optimization.

5.2   Forward Kinematics-Based Cost Functional

Given a set of joint angles and body displacement values, the forward kinematics function, $h(\cdot)$, where $\cdot$ is a generic variable(s), computes the boundary points of individual body segments. The P matrix projects the computed boundary points on a 2D projection plane, which will be compared to a foreground image silhouette. $g(\cdot)$ converts projected points to a polygon(s). The input image is preprocessed using the background subtraction function, $f(\cdot)$. The projection plane is represented in real numbers. $r(\cdot)$ converts the input image silhouette to a polygon(s) in the real number domain. The representation in the real number domain makes the derivative-based parameter optimization possible.

$$c(I,\bar{\theta}) = -w_1 \times [a(r(f(I)) \cap (\cup_l g(P \cdot h_l(\bar{\theta},t))))]$$
$$+ w_2 \times \sum_{xy}(w_d(x,y) \times a(d(x,y) \cap (\cup_l g(P \cdot h_l(\bar{\theta},t))))) \qquad (3)$$

Let us explain the notation used in equation (3) in more detail.

$c(I, \bar{\theta})$ is a cost functional for parameter optimization, which depends on a raw input image I and model DOF variables $\bar{\theta}$.

$\bar{\theta}$ is a joint DOF vector, represented in a column matrix. $\bar{\theta}$ is a function of time when a complete sequence is considered.

P is an orthographic camera projection matrix, projecting a 3D body model to the 2D plane.

$h_l(\cdot)$ is a nonlinear forward kinematics function of an l-th body part in terms of joint DOF.

$g(\cdot)$ is a function with the argument 2D input points and converts them to a polygon.

$r(\cdot)$ is a real function with the argument an input imag and converts its foreground (non-zero value) part to a set of polygons, possibly with holes.

$f(\cdot)$ represents a preprocessed foreground image, given a raw image.

I is a raw input image.

$I(x, y)$ denotes a grey level pixel value at image location (x, y).

$d(x, y)$ is a square polygon of area size 1, representing a pixel located at the (x, y)-th position in the distance map [14].

t represents time related with frames.

$w_d(x, y)$ is a distance map value at position (x, y), and has a scalar value.

$\cap$ is an operation that takes two polygons and returns their intersection.

$\cup$ is an operation that takes two polygons and returns their union.

$a(\cdot)$ is a function that gives the area of a polygon.

w_i , $i = 1, 2$ are weighting factors.

Because the vector of joint DOF variables, $\bar{\theta}$, is the input to the optimization process, this computation is purely forward kinematics-based and thus presents no singularity problems. We may limit the range of joint variation for individual model-body parts. If there is an occlusion between two persons, our method relies on a distance map [14] for each person to be tracked correctly.

5.3   Computational Geometry for the Cost Functional

An image silhouette is one that is converted from the 2D integer pixel domain to a real domain such that the resulting image silhouette becomes a jagged-edge polygon with only horizontal and vertical edges. The resulting polygons may have holes in them. We compute polygon intersection between the input image silhouette and the model silhouette. Pixel-based computational geometry is needed to compute the distance map [14] that is used to fit the model to foreground image regions. Our computation is a modified version of Weiler-Atherton's polygon union/intersection computation[15]. We found the best fitting configuration using the GRG2[16] optimization package with the cost functional in equation (3). Figure 2 shows possible cases where either a model head or polygon-shaped body overlaps with a pixel. In figure 2, the circle represents a projected head outline and an oblique polygon represents a body part, while a square represents a pixel. The union of these irregular-shaped objects results in a projected model body silhouette. After obtaining the union, a triangulation process is used to compute the area of the union of polygon-shaped object. It may be noted that

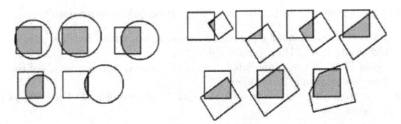

Fig. 2. Five possible cases of a pixel(square) partially occluded by a model head, and seven possible cases of a pixel(square) partially occluded by a polygon body

there are arcs involved in the computation. Our cost functional does not allow ridges, an area of a function with zero gradient. As a consequence, we cannot work on a purely pixel-based integer cost functional. Therefore, we compute the area of overlap between pixels and the projected body model in the sub-pixel accuracy in order to eliminate ridges in our cost functional. Even a small change in the 3D body model is reflected in the cost functional.

6   Multi-layer Deterministic Finite State Automata (DFA) for Behavior Recognition

We employ a *sequence analyzer* and an *event detector* that are similar to those of [12]. The sequence analyzer is a DFA, while the event detector allows state transition. Our finite state automata consists of a finite set of states(Q), an initial state(q^0), a finite set of events($\sum$), a state transition function(δ), and a finite set of final states(F). The sequence analyzer is represented by $(Q, q^0, \sum, \delta, F)$. Each intermediate state q^i in the sequence $(q^0, q^1, \cdots, q^n)$ corresponds to a frame. The event detector analyzes motion data obtained from a parameter optimization sequence and detects events. We designed separate sequence analyzers (DFAs) for each body part: hands, body center (torso), and feet. We consider all possible states for feet, hands and torso, independent of the rest of the body. These DFAs abstract motion data from each body part. We employ a higher-level DFAs to handle motion recognition given low-level motion abstraction. For a single person, we employ three low-level sequence analyzers. Since there can be more than one person present in a scene, our low level sequence analyzer is of the form $(^p_m Q, ^p_m q^0, ^p_m \sum, ^p_m \delta, ^p_m F)$, where $p \in \{1, 2, 3\}$ is an index for body parts, and m is an index for each person in the scene. $^1_2 q^i \in ^1_2 Q$ means $^1_2 q^i$ is a state of sequence index number i, of a *second* person in the scene, of body part index *one*.

The use of multi-layer DFAs reduces the large number of states to be handled in interaction recognition. Assuming that there are two persons in a scene to generate motion states of the model body, each person has 27 (3^3) possible states (three states for each of three body parts.) If two persons are involved in an interaction, the DFA will classify 729 (27^2) states. Generally, we need

Fig. 3. The subject with the model figure superimposed, shown over a walking motion

$|^1_1Q| \times |^2_1Q| \times |^3_1Q| \times |^1_2Q| \times |^2_2Q| \times |^3_2Q|$ states for an interaction of two persons, where $|Q|$ is the number of states in Q. This exponential growth quickly becomes intractable. Rather than generating 729 states and designing state transitions, we design three states to recognize each motion of a body part, totaling nine states for a single person. Then we consider a tuple of states, $(^1_mq^i, ^2_mq^i, ^3_mq^i)$, a token made of low-level state transitions, to recognize the motion of a person with an index number m. To recognize an interactive motion between two persons, we use a tuple of states, $(^1_1q^i, ^2_1q^i, ^3_1q^i, ^1_2q^i, ^2_2q^i, ^3_2q^i)$. Therefore, we design a higher-level DFA to recognize behavior based on lower-level sequence analyzers, plus nine lower-level states to abstract motion data rather than 729 state and state transition designs. The high-level DFA also refers to the data related to the low-level state transition. Figure 3 shows an example. For the departing/approaching motion, abstract motion data allows us to recognize that two persons are walking, but we cannot tell whether they are departing/approaching without referring to the distance between the two persons. (Refer figure 3.)

The high-level DFAs analyze the interaction in a cause and effect framework. Figure 4 shows an example of 'pushing' interaction, in which the right person approaches and pushes the left person (cause), and the left person moves backward as a result of being pushed (effect). Our observation shows that meaningful interactions are characterized by a sequence of specific states belonging to relatively small number of states. Therefore, our high-level DFAs focus on a subset of all possible states instead of analyzing all 729 states. In the 'pushing' interaction, we define a minimum of four states to recognize the pushing motion: two states representing the contact states by the left/right pushing person, respectively, and the other two states representing the moving backwards of the right/left pushed person, respectively.

7 Experimental Results

We have analyzed several different 2D-based human motions; walking (i.e., approaching, departing), pushing, kicking, pointing, and hand-shaking. The example shown in figure 5 involves two persons in hand-shaking interaction. The body model properly fitted to image sequence shows the effectiveness of our geometry union process. The model body cannot distinguish between the left/right side of the body to be tracked. This limitation is the result of using monocular video

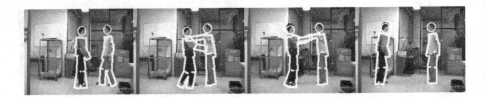

Fig. 4. The subject with the model figure superimposed, shown over a pushing motion

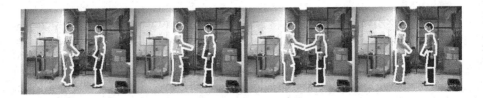

Fig. 5. The subject with the model figure superimposed, shown over a hand-shaking motion

input, which provides very limited input information. Our method finds one locally optimum solution from a search space. The motion tracking is excellent, as shown in figures 3, 4, and 5. After motion tracking, we get two sets of motion data in terms of frames, one for each person appearing in the scene. The multilevel DFA processes the motion data to recognize human interactions; the low-level DFA analyzes the motion of individual body parts to generate states, and the high-level DFA analyzes the sequence of the state changes to generate the recognition results of the interaction. Recognition of interaction is achieved when the multilevel DFA stops in a final accepting state. Computation time depends on the degree of accuracy that is sought and the size of the input image.

8 Conclusion

In this paper, we have presented a model-based approach to human motion tracking and a multilevel DFA-based approach to behavior recognition. The model based-method uses a 3D human body model and parameter optimization techniques to track the moving humans. Our forward kinematics-based system overcomes the problem of singularity in inverse kinematics-based systems. We have presented a solution to the model body part occlusion problem using computational geometry. The motion data of the body model enables us to apply our DFAs to the problem of recognizing human interaction. We used a multilevel DFA to overcome the exponential growth of the number of states in usual single-level DFA. The results of motion tracking from video sequences are excellent for a number of activities, and our recognition framework successfully recognizes various human interactions between two persons.

References

[1] Kim, K., Choi, J., Kim, N., Kim, P.: Extracting semantic information from basketball video based on audio-visual features. Lecture Notes in Computer Science **2383** (2002) 268–277   395

[2] Chang, Y., Zeng, W., Camel, I., Aonso, R.: Integrated image and speech analysis for content-based video indexing. In: IEEE proc. Int'l Conference on Multimedia Computing and Systems. (1996) 306–313   395

[3] Denman, H., Rea, N., Kokaram, A.: Content based analysis for video from snooker broadcasts. In: Int'l Conference on Image and Video Retrieval, Lecture Notes in Computer Science. Volume 2383., Springer (2002) 186–193   395

[4] Aggarwal, J., Cai, Q.: Human motion analysis: a review. Computer Vision and Image Understanding **73(3)** (1999) 295–304   395

[5] Morris, D., Rehg, J.: Singularity analysis for articulated object tracking. In: Computer Vision and Pattern Recognition, Santa Barbara, California (1998) 289–296   395

[6] Huang, Y., Huang, T. S.: Model-based human body tracking. In: International Conference on Pattern Recognition. Volume 1., Quebec city, Canada (2002) 552–555   395

[7] Sidenbladh, H., Black, M. J., Fleet, D. J.: Stochastic tracking of 3d human figures using 2d image motion. In: ECCV (2). (2000) 702–718   395, 396, 398

[8] Oliver, N. M., Rosario, B., Pentland, A. P.: A Bayesian Computer Vision System for Modeling Human Interactions. IEEE Trans. Pattern Analysis and Machine Intelligence **22** (2000) 831–843   396

[9] Hongeng, S., Bremond, F., Nevatia, R.: Representation and optimal recognition of human activities. In: IEEE Conf. on Computer Vision and Pattern Recognition. Volume 1. (2000) 818–825   396

[10] Park, S., Aggarwal, J.: Recognition of human interaction using multiple features in grayscale images. In: Int'l Conference on Pattern Recognition. Volume 1., Barcelona, Spain (2000) 51–54   396

[11] Hong, P., Turk, M., Huang, T. S.: Gesture modeling and recognition using finite state machines. In: IEEE Conf. on Face and Gesture Recognition. (2000)   396

[12] Wada, T., Matsuyama, T.: Multiobject behavior recognition by event driven selective attention method. IEEE transaction on Pattern Analysis and Machine Intelligence **22** (2000) 873–887   396, 400

[13] Park, S., Aggarwal, J.: Segmentation and tracking of interacting human body parts under occlusion and shadowing. In: IEEE Workshop on Motion and Video Computing, Orlando, FL (2002) 105–111   397

[14] Gavrila, D. M., Philomin, V.: Real-time object detection using distance transforms. In: Proc. IEEE International Conference on Intelligent Vehicles, Stuttgart, Germany (1998) 274–279   399

[15] Hill, F.: Computer Graphics. Macmillan (1990)   399

[16] Lasdon, L., Waren, A.: GRG2 User's Guide. (1989)   399

Fast Video Retrieval under Sparse Training Data

Yan Liu and John R. Kender

450 Computer Science Building, 1214 Amsterdam Avenue, New York, NY,
10027, USA
{liuyan,jrk}@cs.columbia.edu

Abstract. Feature selection for video retrieval applications is impractical with existing techniques, because of their high time complexity and their failure on the relatively sparse training data that is available given video data size. In this paper we present a novel heuristic method for selecting image features for video, called the Complement Sort-Merge Tree (CSMT). It combines the virtues of a wrapper model approach for better accuracy with those of a filter method approach for incrementally deriving the appropriate features quickly. A novel combination of Fastmap for dimensionality reduction and Mahalanobis distance for likelihood determination is used as the induction algorithm. The time cost of CSMT is linear in the number of features and in the size of the training set, which is very reasonable. We apply CSMT to the domain of fast video retrieval of extended (75 minutes) instructional videos, and demonstrate its high accuracy in classifying frames.

1   Introduction

The rapid growth and wide application of digital video has led to a significant need for efficient video data set management. The problem of efficient retrieval and manipulation of semantically labelled video segments is an important issue.

One typical approach is to use existing image retrieval algorithms, starting from a good segmentation of the video into shots and then selecting certain images of the shots as key-frames [1]. But as Lew et al mentioned in [3], the gap between the high level query from the human and the low-level features persists because of a lack of a good understanding of the "meanings" of the video, of the "meaning" of a query, and of the way a result can incorporate the user's knowledge, personal preferences, and emotional tone. Machine learning methods such as classification [4] and boosting [5] are introduced to help retrieve matching video sequences semantically, and some methods use audio information analysis and text extraction and recognition as well. But there appears to be little work that supports efficient feature selection for video retrieval, due to the huge volume of data.

Researchers therefore work on speeding up their algorithms; one way is by seeking efficient ways of reducing the dimensionality of the data prior to classification and retrieval. Vailaya et al [6] and Smeulders et al [7] discuss this problem from the view

E. M. Bakker et al. (Eds.): CIVR 2003, LNCS 2728, pp. 404-413, 2003.

of image processing and computer vision. They assume that some features, such as color histograms or texture energies, are more sensitive than others, based on the researchers' intuition. They provide theoretical analyses and empirical validations for their choices, but this approach is difficult to extend to other domains where the relationships between features and categories are unclear and changeable.

The heart of this paper is a novel feature selection algorithm, which focuses on selecting representative features in the massive and complex dataset automatically; no manual definition or construction of features is required [8]. This form of learning has received significant attention in the AI literature recently and has been applied to moderately large data sets in applications like text categorization [8] and genomic microarray [9] analysis. Another emphasis of this paper is that our novel selection algorithm also addresses the problem of sparse and noisy training data. The training sets available for the learning of semantic labels is a very small fraction of the total in video retrieval. Classification using sparse training data is a classical problem of machine learning and few papers [9] support feature selection under these circumstances.

This paper is organized as follows. Section 2 introduces some related work in feature selection. Section 3 proposes the feature selection algorithm, CSMT, and provides a framework for video retrieval using this algorithm. Section 4 presents empirical validation of the accuracy of algorithm when applied to the particular genre of instructional videos, and validates the algorithm in a generic data. We close the paper with discussion and planned future work in section 5.

2   Related Work of Feature Selection

There appears to be two major approaches to the feature selection problem. The first emphasizes the discovery of any relevant relationship between the features and the concept, whereas the second explicitly seeks a feature subset that minimizes prediction error of the concept. The first is referred to as a filter method, and the second approach is referred to as a wrapper method. In general, wrapper methods attempt to optimize directly the classifier performance so that they can perform better than filter algorithms, but they require more computation time. Seen in this context, this paper proposes a wrapper feature selection method with time cost considerably less than that of filter methods. For an alternative viewpoint, see [13].

Feature selection methods are typically designed and evaluated with respect to the accuracy and cost of their three components: their search algorithm, their statistical relationship method (in the case of filter methods) or their induction algorithm (in the case of wrapper methods), and their evaluation metric (which is simply prediction error in the case of wrapper methods). The dominating cost of any method, however, is that of the search algorithm, since feature selection is fundamentally a question of choosing one specific subset of features from the power set of features. So far, three general kinds of heuristic search algorithms have been used: forward selection, backward elimination, and genetic algorithms.

Sparse training data is a hard problem in machine learning. As Xing et al mentioned in [9], the number of replicates in some experiments is often severely limited; he gives a real world problem in which only 38 observation vectors exist, each one encoding the expression levels of 7130 features. Feature selection when there are so few observations on so many features is very different from the more general cases typical in the learning literature; it even renders some powerful algorithms ineffective. This is easy to see in Xing's case: since there are only 38 observations, no matter what feature set has been chosen the prediction error is severely quantized to one of 39 levels. With 7130 features, on average we could expect about 183 features to produce each of these error levels; either a forward or backward wrapper method will be forced to choose randomly over this large set at each iteration. If ultimately we wish only a small set of about. 50 features to avoid overleaning as in [9], too much randomness is introduced by these methods. Moreover, randomness accumulates, with the chose of each feature heavily influencing the choice of its successors.

The alternatives to wrapper methods are filter methods, which select feature subset independently of the actual induction algorithm. Koller and Sahami in [2] employ a cross-entropy measure, designed to find Markov blankets of features using a backward greedy algorithm. In theory going backward from the full set of features may capture interesting features more easily [12], especially under sparse training data. However, in Xing's case this means that if we want a target feature space with 50 features, we have to remove 7080. To avoid this expensive time cost, Xing proposes to sort the 7130 features based on their individual information gain in classification (a wrapper method), but then abandons the wrapper approach, and uses only the best N features in a series of filter methods. Additionally, he selects N=360 manually. It is not clear how well such a technique generalizes or how effective it is, given its mixture of models.

3   Feature Selection for Video Retrieval

This section presents a method of efficient semantic video retrieval, based on automatically learned feature selection. This novel feature selection algorithm, called CSMT combines the strengths of both filter and wrapper models, and exploits several properties unique to video data.

3.1   Complement Sort-Merge Tree

Our overall approach is to use an outer wrapper model for high accuracy, and an inner filter method for resolving the problem of random selection when the training set is relatively small and errors are quantized (as they inevitably are for video data).

This Complement Sort-Merge Tree (CSMT) algorithm combines the features of forward selection, backward elimination, and genetic algorithms. To avoid irrevocable adding or subtracting, it always operates on some representation of the original feature space, so that at each step every feature has an opportunity to impact the selection. To avoid heuristic randomness, at each step a complement test is used to govern subset formation. The tree structure of the CSMT leads to low time cost. Further, the recursive nature of the method enables the straightforward creation of a hierarchical family of feature subsets with little additional work. The entire CSMT of progressively more accurate feature subsets can be stored in space O(N), to be accessed when needed at a later time.

The CSMT algorithm can be divided into two parts: the creation of the full tree of feature subsets, and subsequent manipulation of the tree (if necessary) to create a feature subset of desired cardinality or accuracy. Each part uses a different heuristic greedy method.

Table 1 shows the CSMT basic algorithm. Initially, there are N singleton feature subsets. Using a wrapper method, their performance is evaluated on training data, and they are sorted in order of performance. Features are then paired into N/2 subsets of cardinality 2, by merging them according to the complement requirement. After another round of training, sorting, and pair-wise merging according to complement requirement, a third level of N/4 subsets of cardinality 4 are formed. The process continues until it attains a level or condition prespecified by the user, or until the entire tree is constructed.

Table 1. Complement Sort-Merge Tree

Initialize level = 0
    Create N singleton feature subsets.
While level < $\log_2 N$
    Induce on every feature subset.
    Sort subsets based on their classification accuracy.
    Choose pairs of feature subsets based on the complement requirement.
    Merge to new feature subsets.

Table 2. Algorithm to select exactly r features from the tree of feature subsets

Select the leftmost branch of size $2^{\lceil \log_2 r \rceil}$.
Initialize cutout = $2^{\lceil \log_2 r \rceil} - r$.
While cutout >0
    Let branch-size = $2^{\lfloor \log_2 cutout \rfloor}$.
    For all remaining branches of this size, evaluate the induction result of
        removing those branches individually.
    Remove the branch with best result.
    Let cutout = cutout – branch-size.

Figure 1 illustrates the algorithm with an initial set of features with cardinality N = 256. Table 2 shows the related algorithm that further manipulates the full CSMT tree if it is necessary to select exactly r features (r not a power of 2) from the hierarchy of feature subsets. It is not hard to show that the time cost of the search algorithm of CSMT is linear in the number of nodes in the Sort-Merge tree, i.e., $T \sim O(N*T_m)$, where T_m is the induction time complexity using m training data.

Figure 2 illustrates the complement test, which uses a filter method to inform the otherwise random selection of feature subsets. It employs a heuristic approximation to a markov blanket that attempts to maximize classification performance on the m training samples. An m-length performance vector records for each feature subset correct classifications with a 1 and failures with a 0. Any feature subset seeking a complementary feature subset will examine all unpaired feature subsets sharing identical error rates with it. It then selects from these that feature subset which maximizes the number of 1s in the OR of their two performance vectors. These complementary feature subsets are then merged. This step of the CSMT method is a greedy algorithm, but one that is more informed than random choice.

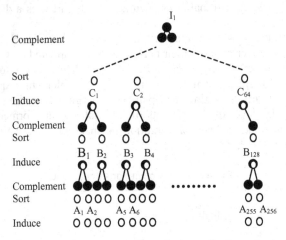

Fig. 1. CSMT for N=256. Leaves correspond to singleton feature subsets. White nodes are unsorted feature subsets and gray nodes are the white nodes rank-ordered by performance. Black nodes are the pairwise mergers of gray nodes, with pairs formed under the complement requirement

3.2   Induction Algorithm for Feature Selection

The performance of a wrapper feature selection algorithm not only depends on the search method, but also on the induction algorithm. For our induction method during the course of the learning we use a novel, low-cost, and scalable combination of Fastmap for dimensionality reduction with Mahalanobis maximum likelihood for classification. We refer readers to the literature for a detailed explanation of these two component methods, but summarize their significance here.

The fastmap method proposed in [10] approximates Principal Component Analysis (PCA), with only linear cost in the number of reduced dimensions sought, c, and in the number of features, N. The method heuristically replaces the computation of the PCA eigenvector of greatest eigenvalue, which represents the direction in the full feature space that has maximum variation, with a (linear) search for the two data elements that are maximally separated in the space. The vector between these two elements is taken as a substitute for the eigenvector of greatest eigenvalue, and the full space is then projected onto the subspace orthogonal to this substitute vector for the first eigen dimension. The process then repeats for a desired and usually small number of times. By the use of clever bookkeeping techniques, each additional new dimension and projection takes time approximately linear in the number of features.

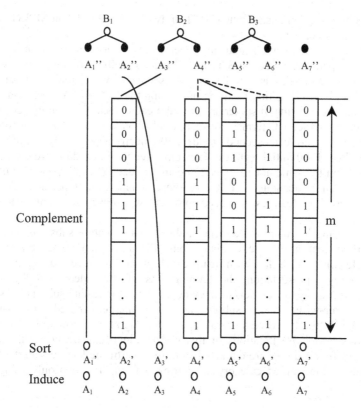

Fig. 2. The complement requirement, illustrated for the A level of Figure 1. The sorted singletons A_1' and A_3' have already been paired to form pair B_1. To find the best complementary feature subset for A_2', examine all sorted subsets $(A_4',\ A_5',\ A_6')$ with the same error rate on the m training samples. The bitwise OR of performance vectors of A_2' and A_5' maximizes performance coverage; A_5' complements A_2' for B_2

In brief, as defined in statistical texts Duda et al. [11], or in the documentation of Matlab, the Mahalanobis distance computes the likelihood that a point belongs to a distribution that is modeled as a multidimensional Gaussian with arbitrary covariance. During training, each image frame in a training set for a video category is first mapped to a point in the space of reduced dimension c. Then the distribution of these mapped points is approximated by a c-dimensional Gaussian with a non-diagonal covariance matrix. Multiple categories and training sets are represented each with their own Gaussian distribution. The classification of a test image frame is obtained by mapping it, too, into the reduced c-dimensional space, and then calculating the most likely distribution to which it belongs. The time cost is also linear with the number of features N.

3.3   Framework of Video Retrieval Using CSMT

The linear time cost and the increased accuracy of the complement requirement allow an efficient and effective implementation of video retrieval under sparse training data.

In this section, we demonstrate the CSMT on two retrieval tasks on MPEG1-encoded instructional videos.

First, in our application and in general, the video may be down-sampled temporally, spatially, and/or spectrally. We temporally subsample by using only every other I frame (that is, one I frame per second). We spatially subsample by a factor of 16 in each direction by using only using the DC terms of each macro-block of the I frame (consisting of six terms, one from each block: four luminance DC terms and two chrominance DC terms); this subsampling is very popular in video retrieval [1]. This gives us, for each second of video, 300 macroblocks (15 by 20) of 6 bytes (4 plus 2) of data: 1800 initial features. For convenience of decoding, we consider the 6 DC terms from the same macro-block to be an un-decomposable vector, so our initial data consists more accurately of 300 six-dimensional features per second of video. Each of these 300 features is placed into its own subset to initialize the CSMT algorithm.

Second, using Fastmap, the dimensionality of each feature subset is reduced to a pre-specified small number, c, of dimensions. (This makes more sense after the first several steps.) Third, for each feature subset at this level, using the reduced dimensionality representation, the training sets of the video train the induction algorithm to classify the test sets of the video. Fourth, the feature subsets are sorted by accuracy. Pair-wise feature subsets are then merged, based on complement requirement. Fifth, the process repeats again, starting at the Fastmap step. It is clear that at most O(log N) iterations of this CSMT algorithm are necessary. Sixth, if needed, exactly r features are extracted from the tree of the feature subsets. Seventh, the frames of the learned category are retrieved from the video only using these r features.

4   Experiment

The extended instructional video mentioned above is of 75 minutes duration, which has approximately 4500 frames of data, with 300 six-dimensional features for each frame. Existing feature selection methods, which typically have been reported to run for several days on features sets of cardinality at least one decimal order of magnitude smaller, are intractable on video data; see Koller and Sahami [2]. Therefore, we compared the retrieval accuracy of our novel method against an imperfect but feasible method, random feature selection; see the work of Xing et al who were similarly forced into such benchmarks [9]. These experiments use the same data and same classifiers; the only difference is how the feature subset was chosen.

In the first experiment, we attempt to retrieve about 200 "announcement" frames from the 4500 frames, without any prior temporal segmentation or other pre-processing. "announcement" frames look like Figure 3 (a); other video frames look like Figure 4 (b). Although it should not be difficult to find a very small set of features to make these distinctions, we want to do so rapidly and accurately. Only 80 training frames are provided (40 "announcement" and 40 others), and as shown in Figure 4, they include considerable noise.

(a)   (b)

Fig. 3. Task: Retrieve "announcements"(a) from an entire video with competing image types (b)

Normal data   Noise data

Fig. 4. Training data also includes noise

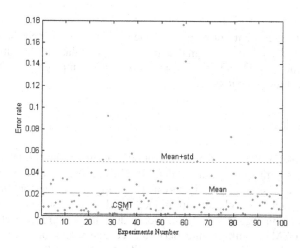

Fig. 5. Error rate of CSMT vs. random for retrieval of "announcements" with features r = 4 and Fastmap dimension c = 2

Figure 5 compares the retrieval results using only 4 features, when Fastmap dimension c is equal to 2. Points show the error rate of 100 experiments that select the features randomly. As expected, the rate of error is highly variable, with the standard deviation being larger than the mean. The error rate using features selected by CSMT, as a solid line, is clearly better. None of the results of random feature selection is better than CSMT. Figure 6 (a) compares the performance of different Fastmap dimensions from 1 to 10 using the same number of features. Figure 6 (b) fixes the Fastmap dimension c=4 and compares the classification error rate of different numbers. The performance of CSMT is much better than that of random selection in all cases.

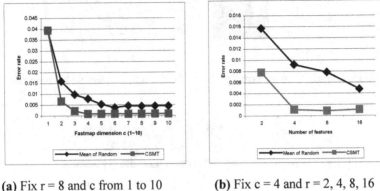

(a) Fix r = 8 and c from 1 to 10   **(b)** Fix c = 4 and r = 2, 4, 8, 16

Fig. 6. Error rate of CSMT vs. random for retrieval of "announcements", with r features and c Fastmap dimensions

In the second experiment not related to video retrieval, we tested the generality of the CSMT method on Xing's original data. Using his data, his definitions, and his evaluation method, CSMT obtains the same error rate compared with his 5.9%. but with much lower time complexity.

5   Conclusion

We have presented a low-cost feature selection algorithm CSMT that is well-suited for large data sets with sparse training data. It relies on the three algorithms working together in linear time of the features: Fastmap for dimensionality reduction, Mahalanobis distance for classification likelihood, and a sort-complement-merge sequence for combining relevant and non-redundant feature subsets into more accurate ones. CSMT combines the performance guarantees of a wrapper method with the speed and logical organization of a filter method. It therefore leads to new feasible approaches for rapid video retrieval. We have demonstrated some of its results on an extended video. We intend to investigate its utility both across a library of videos of this kind, and also on other genres such as situation comedies which share a similar categorization structure.

References

[1]   Irena Koprinska and Sergio Carrato,.: Temporal video segmentation: A survey. Signal processing: Image communication 16, (2001) 477-500.

[2]   Koller, D. & Sahami,M.: Toward optimal feature selection. Proceedings of the Thirteenth International Conference on Machine Learning (1996).

[3]   Michael S. Lew, Nicu Sebe, John P. Eakins.: Challenges of Image and Video Retrieval, International Conference on Image and Video Retrieval. Lecture Notes in Computer Science, vol. 2383, Springer (2002) 1-6.

[4]   Wensheng Zhou, Asha Vellakial and C.-C. Jay Kuo.: Rule-based video classification system for basketball video indexing. ACM Multimedia (2000).

[5]   Pickering, M., Ruger, S., Sinclair, D.: Video Retrieval by Feature Learning in Key Frames. International Conference on Image and Video Retrieval. Lecture Notes in Computer Science, vol. 2383, Springer (2002) 316-324.

[6]   A. Vailaya, M. Figueiredo, A. K. Jain, and H.-J. Zhang.: Image Classification for Contnet-Based Indexing. IEEE Transactions on Image Processing, vol. 10, no. 1, January, (2001) 117-130.

[7]   A. W. M. Smeulders, M. Worring, S. Santini, A. Gupta and R. Jain.: Content-based image retrieval: the end of the early years. IEEE trans. PAMI, 22 – 12 (2000) 1349 -- 1380.

[8]   Yiming Yang and Jan O. Pedersen: A comparative study on feature selection in text categorization. Proceedings of the Fourteenth International Conference on Machine Learning (1997) 412-420.

[9]   Eric P. Xing, Michael I. Jordan, Richard M. Karp: Feature selection for high-dimensional genomic microarray data. Proceedings of the Eighteenth International Conference on Machine Learning (2001).

[10] Christons Faloutsos and king-Ip (David) Lin: FastMap: a fast algorithm for indexing, data-mining and visualization of traditional and multimedia datasets. Proceedings of ACM SIGMOD (1995) 163-174.

[11] Richard O. Duda, Peter E. Hart and David G. Stork: Pattern classification, Wiley, New York (2000).

[12] R. Kohavi and G. H. John: Wrappers for feature subset selection. Artificial Intelligence, special issue on relevance (1997) 273-324.

[13] Douglas Zongker and Anil K. Jain: Algorithms for Feature Selection: An Evaluation. In Proceedings of the 13th International Conference on Pattern Recognition, 1996.

Robust Content-Based Video Copy Identification in a Large Reference Database

Alexis Joly[1], Carl Frélicot[2], and Olivier Buisson[1]

[1] Département Recherche et Études, Institut National de l'Audiovisuel,
94366 Bry/Marne cedex, France
{ajoly,obuisson}@ina.fr
[2] Laboratoire d'Informatique–Image–Interaction, Université de La Rochelle,
17042 La Rochelle Cedex 1, France
carl.frelicot@univ-lr.fr

Abstract. This paper proposes a novel scheme for video content-based copy identification dedicated to TV broadcast with a reference video database exceeding 1000 hours of video. It enables the monitoring of a TV channel in soft real-time with a good tolerance to strong transformations that one can meet in any TV post-production process like: clipping, cropping, shifting, resizing, objects encrusting or color variations. Contrary to most of the existing schemes, the recognition is not based on global features but on local features extracted around interest points. This allows the selection and the localization of fully discriminant local patterns which can be compared according to a distance measure. Retrieval is performed using an efficient approximate Nearest Neighbors search and a final decision based on several matches cumulated in time.

1 Introduction

Recently, *Content-Based Copy Detection* (CBCD) schemes appeared as an alternative to the watermarking approach for persistent identification of images at first, and of video clips afterwards. As opposed to watermarking, which relies on inserting a distinct and invisible pattern into the video stream, the CBCD approach only uses a content-based comparison between the original video stream and the controlled one. For storage and computational considerations, it generally consists in extracting as few features as possible from the video stream and matching them with a database. Since the features must be discriminant enough to identify a video (or an image), the concept of video (or image) *fingerprinting* has been introduced by analogy to human fingerprinting [1].

CBCD presents two major advantages. First, a video clip which has already been distributed can be recognized. Secondly, content-based features are intrinsically more robust than inserted ones because they contain information that cannot be suppressed without considerably corrupting the perceptual content itself. Let us describe the two issues that make video fingerprinting complex:

1. **Tolerance to Attacks.** A copy is never a perfect duplicate of the original video clip. Any identification process must tolerate some transformations that

E. M. Bakker et al. (Eds.): CIVR 2003, LNCS 2728, pp. 414–424, 2003.

can be applied to the original video stream. These transformations, we call "attacks", can be strong. For instance, an image divided in 20x20 blocks and differently reordered is still a copy. The set of attacks constitutes as a matter of fact what the terms "copy" and "identification" cover.

2. **Size of the Reference Video Database.** Fingerprints are generally designed to be as invariant as possible to the set of attacks. However, attacks modify the controlled video and make the fingerprint different to the original one. Consequently, the mismatch risk increases with the number of referenced fingerprints. The closest fingerprint search is also a difficult task in terms of storage and time complexity when large databases are involved.

Most of the existing schemes described in the literature focus more specifically on web video, movie clip and TV commercial detection. Although this problem is similar to the general TV programs copy detection one, it differs on the number of attacks, their intensity and the size of the database. A copied video stream can be displayed in a window of the screen, cropped, resized, partially concealed or can contain additional information (textual data or logos). Temporal re-editing, compression-decompression artifacts, broadcast and digitizer artifacts and histogram modifications (gamma changes, contrast changes, color variations) are attacks that are more commonly studied. Lienhart et al. [2] only take care of broadcast and digitizer artifacts by a color coherence vector to characterize keyframes from the clip. Sanchez et al. tackles color variations using the principal components of the key-frames color histograms [3]. Hampapur et al. completed this work by use of edge features on a fixed grid [4] which is not adapted to geometric attacks described above. These three approaches are dedicated to the detection of at most 224 TV commercials representing less than 3 hours of video. The fingerprint based on the shot boundaries position in time proposed by Indyk et al. [5] is robust to many attacks, except to re-editing handlings which are unfortunately very frequent in the TV distribution process. Recently, Hampapur et al. developed a frame sequence matching algorithm and compare its robustness to resolution changes in MPEG1 encoding [6]. They showed that an ordinal fingerprint outperforms a motion-based or a color based fingerprint, but the reference was only one 2 hours and 12 minutes long movie. In [1], Kalker et al. give simultaneously a feature extraction scheme and a strategy adapted to large databases. Components of a feature vector, based on low resolution spatial and temporal derivatives, are quantized to one single bit. The resulting binary fingerprint is close to the well-known hash function concept in cryptography. This binary structure allows the use of a particular database strategy close to the inverted file techniques. However, the quality of the retrieval has not been evaluated on a real database and the fingerprint is very sensitive to global geometric operations like scaling and shifting. When the attacks are very strong, the copy detection problem is close to the well-known *Content-Based Similarity Search* (CBSS) one. Although fingerprinting is an invariance problem and content-based similarity search is a generalization one, they can both benefit from the same features that are extracted from the video stream. Furthermore, both share the search in large multidimensional databases problem. A very complete state-of-the-art of the widely studied multidimensional similarity search problem is given in [7]. Most studies have focused on multidimensional access methods consisting either in partitioning the data space, or in clustering data or in ordering data with a space filling curve [8]. Their performance is known to significantly degrade as the space dimension increases [9]. Recently, more efficient approaches have been proposed, e.g. the VA File [10] or the Pyramid Tree [11]. They allow time gain with respect to a sequential search in the very high dimensional case. Nevertheless, they become close to linear with the size of the database [12]. In our application, the dimension is not so high whereas the database size could grow indefinitely.

The remaining part of this paper is structured as follows. Section 2 is dedicated to the new fingerprinting scheme we propose; both the strategy and the different steps are described. Illustrative examples are given in Section 3. Finally, we draw some conclusions and perspectives in Section 4.

2   The New Fingerprinting Scheme

2.1   Strategy

In order to be robust to attacks and efficient with respect to a large database, we propose the global scheme shown in Figure 1, based on image local descriptors as suggested in [12] and [13]. The fingerprints extraction includes a key-frame detection, an interest point detection in these key-frames, and the computation of local differential descriptors around each interest point. In the indexing case, fingerprints are simply inserted in the database and identified with a time-code. In the monitoring case, the nearest neighbors of each fingerprint are searched in the database. These results are stored in a buffer for a fixed number of key-frames and a global decision using the entire buffer is made for each key-frame.

Interest points are ideal for matching applications because of their local uniqueness and their high information content [14], [15]. Actually, a local region of interest used to compute a fingerprint can be detected wherever it is in the image. This makes the fingerprint as distinct as possible and robust to strong geometric attacks like shifting, cropping or encrusting. Fingerprints that disappear only correspond to concealed or out the stream information. The key-frame detection has the similar advantages in the one-dimensional temporal space and allows the detection of a temporal reference mark even after re-editing manipulations. The choice of the local descriptor used to compute the local fingerprint depends on the considered attacks.

Storage and computational considerations also lead the choice. The comparison between a reference feature and a candidate feature must be a fast operation. This prohibits the use of tangent distances, phase correlation or time-consuming distances. Since the fingerprint components are 1 byte long, the computation of L2-norm based distances is fast enough. The compression factor must be optimized with respect to the size of the database. Indexing key-frames and interest points instead of all frames and pixels allows us to reduce the spatial and temporal redundancy. The smaller the dimension of the fingerprint is, the easier

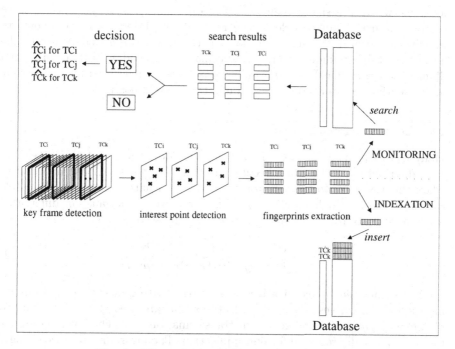

Fig. 1. Fingerprints indexing and monitoring

the search process is (see the "curse of dimensionality" phenomenon detailed in [9]). Interest points allows the use of several small local fingerprints instead of a single high-dimensional fingerprint extracted from an entire frame (or a frame sequence).

2.2   Key Frames Detection

The key-frame detection is based on the mean of the frames difference, also called "intensity of motion", defined by:

$$a(t) = \frac{\sum_{x=1}^{X} \sum_{y=1}^{Y} |I(x, y, t+1) - I(x, y, t)|}{X \, Y} \tag{1}$$

where X and Y are the image dimensions. This feature has already been used to describe the motion characteristics or to detect hard-cut [16]. After applying a gaussian filter, we use the position of the extrema of $a(t)$ to select the key-frames.

2.3   Interest Points Detector

The Harris detector [17] was originally proposed to detect L-junctions or T-junctions. The basic idea was to use the autocorrelation function to determine locations where the signal changes in two directions. As suggested in [13], we compute it using gaussian derivative filters. This stable version is known to be efficient according to two criteria [14]: the *repeatability* that measures the geometric stability under several transformations (including scale changes and illumination variations) and the *information content* measured by the entropy of differential operators computed around the interest points.

2.4   Local Fingerprint

Many features can be used to characterize the local content of an image, e.g.: color distribution, motion and texture features. Nevertheless, it is important to adapt the descriptor to the detector. Since the information content of the stable Harris detector is high for differential features, we use a gaussian differential decomposition of the graylevel 2D signal until the second order:

$$f = \left(\frac{\partial I}{\partial x}, \frac{\partial I}{\partial y}, \frac{\partial I}{\partial x \partial y}, \frac{\partial^2 I}{\partial x^2}, \frac{\partial^2 I}{\partial y^2} \right) \tag{2}$$

As f components are derivatives, f is invariant to a graylevel offset. Combining these 5 derivatives can result in features that are theoretically invariant to illumination variations and geometric transformations [13]. The invariance to rotation is not really required for our application. The invariance to scale changes is possible through specific ratios of derivatives but is very unstable in practice. Since any ratio between two derivatives is invariant to contrast variations ($I'(x,y) = a.I(x,y)$), we chose to use the normalized feature vector $f/\|f\|$. In order to include some temporal information, this feature vector was computed at three other instants around the current key-frame but not at the same position to avoid redundancy in the frequent case of still scenes. The direction of this spatial shift was different for each temporal shift. Finally, a $5 \times (1+3) = 20$-dimensional fingerprint F was obtained.

2.5   Search in the Reference Database

Two kinds of queries are commonly used for similarity search in a multidimensional space : *range* queries that consist in finding all the points within a specified distance to the query and *k-nearest neighbors* queries that result in finding the k best matches. In our application, the original fingerprint should be referenced, so the former approach is appropriate. The time-complexity of the search depends on the query extent. This extent is generally smaller in a CBCD scheme than in a CBSS one and multidimensional access methods are very efficient.

We modified the method proposed in [18] so that it can be entirely executed in main memory because requests on disk are nowadays unacceptable for real time video applications as pointed out in [12]. It is based on the Hilbert's space-filling curve which principle is that two points that are close on the curve remain close in the original N-dimensional space. The database can be physically ordered by the Hilbert's curve and a simple dichotomic search method is used to find the closest Hilbert's derived key in the database. When a range query overlaps strong discontinuities of the Hilbert's curve, it is divided in several subqueries which are not adjacent on the curve. A local sequential scan is then performed for each subquery.

2.6 Decision

A monitored video clip S can be viewed as a series of k_S key frames characterized by their time code : $S = \{t_s(1), t_s(2)...t_s(k_S)\}$. If S was perfectly matching a referenced clip R also characterized by k_R key frames, then $k_S = k_R$ and $\forall k \in [1, k_S]$, $(t_s(k) - t_R(k))$ would be a constant value, say b_S, that identifies the video in the database. Due to attacks, perfect matching does not occur.

A number p_k of interest points $P_{k,i}$ are computed for each key frame k of S. For each $P_{k,i}$, the search algorithm returns $r_{k,i}$ results corresponding to fingerprints in the range query. Each result is a referenced time code $t_{k,i,r}$ ($k \in [1, k_S]$, $i \in [1, p_k]$, $r \in [1, r_{k,i}]$). So there are as many $b_{k,i,r} = (t_s(k) - t_{k,i,r})$ as $t_{k,i,r}$ that can be used to estimate b_S. We used the robust M-estimate $\widehat{b}_S$ defined as the minimum of a global error function:

$$\widehat{b}_S = argmin_b \sum_k \sum_i \sum_r \rho(b - b_{k,i,r}) \tag{3}$$

The difference with the classical least-squares approach is that the contribution of each residual is weighted with a factor $w(\epsilon) = \frac{d\rho(\epsilon)/d\epsilon}{\epsilon}$. Therefore the influence of outliers is reduced and the estimate is more robust. In our application, an outlier may correspond to a false result in the query region or a query result associated with a fingerprint extracted from an encrusted object in the image. In the following, we used the Tukey's biweight function $w(\epsilon)$ [19].

Let $g(b)$ be the triple sum in (3). Comparing $g(\widehat{b}_S)$ to a specified threshold allows us to take the final decision : S is a copy if $g(\widehat{b}_S) < t$. During the monitoring process, a sequence S is defined, each time a key frame d is detected, by the series composed of the $\frac{k_S-1}{2}$ key frames before and after d, where k_S is an odd user-defined number.

3 Experiments and Results

3.1 Computational Performance

Experiments were computed on a Pentium IV (CPU 1,8 GHz, cache size 256Kb, RAM 1Gb). The frames resolution was fixed to 352×288. The number of key frames k_S was set to 11, the number of interest points per key frame was taken up to the $p_k^{max} = 20$, provided their Harris measure is greater than a specified threshold. The number of results in the range query was taken up to $r_{k,i}^{max} = 5$. The size of a fingerprint F was 20 bytes. The total delivery was about 2.34 Mb/hour of video or 117×10^3 fingerprints/hour of video. The following results, measured with the "time" linux command, shows the real time ability of the proposed approach:

- fingerprint computation delivery: $d_F = 110$ ms/sec of video
- average request time for one fingerprint in a 235 hours database (585 Mb): $\bar{t}_{req} = 2.6$ ms
- loading time for 235 hours fingerprint database: $t_{load} = 16$ s
- total time for the monitoring system with a 1040 hours database (processed as five independent databases of various size between 170 and 235 hours): $d_{total} = 9.21$ hours/16 hours of video

3.2   Retrieval Performance

The fingerprint database used for these experiments included 121,251,329 fingerprints (2.45 Gb) representing 1040 hours of TV video archives stored in MPEG1 format. They include colour and black & white extracts from various programs: commercials, news, sport, shows.

Estimating false alarm probabilities on such a large database is a quite tiresome task. We decided to evaluate false alarm rates independently of the experiments by monitoring 16 hours of a foreign TV channel we assumed to be unable to broadcast a copy of our database. For every 10 seconds long segments, we kept the best match of the different key frames. The false alarm rate $P_{fa}(th)$ was then defined, for a given threshold th, as the percentage of detected segments.

1. Experimental Attacks
- spatial gaussian noise addition with different standard deviation values,
- gamma variations $I'(x,y) = (\frac{I(x,y)}{255})^\gamma \times 255$,
- spatial resizing, preserving the fixed resolution by means of a bilinear interpolation (in the zoom out case, the resized image was encrusted at the center of a 352x288 uniform image ; in the zoom in case, only the 352x288 central window was kept),
- vertical shift (with a gray band at the top).

100 clips of 10 seconds were randomly extracted from the 1040 hours database and sequentially reedited. The resulting stream was attacked and monitored. We kept the best match of each clip. The good detection rate P_d was defined as the percentage of detected clips and the good identification rate P_p as the percentage of clips that have been correctly identified for a given temporal precision δT. As an illustration, Figure 2 shows the *Receiver Operational Characteristics* (ROC) curves obtained, under one attack (gaussian noise addition, $\sigma = 15$), for different database sizes. Note that the curves were smoothed with Bezier functions. The three databases were random parts of the original one. As expected, the larger the database, the lower the detection performance. For the largest database, P_d reaches 0.98 for $P_{fa} = 0.0005$.

Figure 3 represents the good identification rate P_p obtained for various attacks and for a fixed $P_{fa} = 10^{-3}$. δT was fixed to 24 frames in order to tolerate a large imprecision in long still scenes. However, the effective average temporal precision is $\overline{\delta T} = 0.18$ frame which is highly precise. It is worth noting that in such a large TV database, all the content is not perfectly controlled. Some

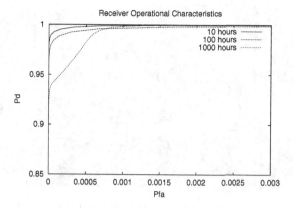

Fig. 2. ROC curves for different database sizes - gaussian noise addition

randomly extracted clips can be test cards or other fixed uniform videos and a 100% good identification rate is difficult to obtain. Excellent robustness to gamma variations as well as to strong gaussian noise addition were observed. The robustness to shifting is also very good and allows the disappearance of 25 % of the image with still a 90 % good identification rate P_p. One can observe a good tolerance to small resizing between 0.8 and 1.2, which is the most frequent range.

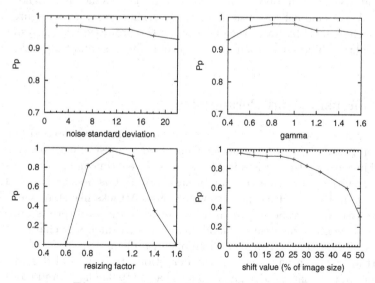

Fig. 3. Precision rate for various attacks

Fig. 4. Real broadcast examples: copies (up) and referenced videos (bottom)

2. Real Attacks

Real broadcast experiments were performed with the same threshold th such as $P_{fa} = 10^{-3}$. A ground truth was manually designed by means of a 2.5 hours long TV program including 23 scenes of various length ($min = 6$ $sec.$, $max = 350$ $sec.$, $average = 59$ $sec.$) copied from the original 1040 hours database. These copies were attacked by: small resizing, a frame encrusting around images, digitizer and broadcast artifacts and several color variations (we noticed overload regions for instance). The program was stored on a VHS tape, which constitutes an additional attack. After monitoring, all the 23 video clips included at least one good match (with a precision $\delta T = 24$ frames). This means that no copy was missed. A TV channel was also monitored during several days. Figure 4 shows four matches that illustrates the efficiency of the proposed CBCD system (from left to right: a shift case, a zoom in case, a zoom out case and a strong encrusting case).

4   Conclusion and Perspectives

In this paper, we proposed a new strategy for robust content-based video identification based on local fingerprints. Compared to most of existing systems described in the literature, it is suitable for the soft real time monitoring of strongly attacked video clips with a very larger database. Robustness to attacks that are often met in TV broadcast process was shown. Attacks like shift operations or data concealing have been seldom investigated. Local fingerprints appeared to be very efficient in such cases. Good robustness to small size changes was also observed, but strong resizing is still an open problem.

Further research will focus on the definition of other local descriptors and strategies in the context of huge video databases (10 000 hours and more) stored on disk. We also believe that a criterion is needed to compare several fingerprint designs for a given set of attacks.

Acknowledgements

The authors would like to thank Louis Laborelli and Nicolas Rasamimanana for their helpful suggestions.

References

[1] Oostveen, J., Kalker, T., Haitsma, J.: Feature extraction and a database strategy for video fingerprinting. Int. Conference on Visual Information and Information Systems (2002) 117–128   414, 415

[2] Lienhart, R., Kuhmunch, C., Effelsberg, W.: On the detection and recognition of television commercials. Int. Conference on Multimedia Computing and Systems (1997) 509–516   415

[3] Sanchez, J. M., Binefa, X., Vitria, J., Radeva, P.: Local color analysis for scene break detection applied to TV commercials recognition. Int. Conference on Visual Information and Information Systems (1999) 237–244   415

[4] Hampapur, A., Bolle, R.: Feature based indexing for media tracking. Int. Conference on Multimedia Computing and Expo. 3 (2000) 1709-1712   415

[5] Indyk, P., Iyengar, G., Shivakumar, N.: Finding pirated video sequences on the Internet. Technical Report, Stanford University (1999)   415

[6] Hampapur, A., Bolle, R., Hyun, I.: Comparison of sequence matching techniques for video copy detection. SPIE Conference on Storage and Retrieval for Media Databases (2002)   415

[7] Veltkamp, R., Burkhardt, H., Kriegel, H. P.: State-of-the-art in content-based image and video retrieval. Kluwer Academic Publishers (2001)   416

[8] Gaede, V., Günther, O.: Multidimensional access methods: ACM Computing Surveys 1(3) (1998) 170–231   416

[9] Weber, R., Schek, H. J., Blott, S.: A quantitative analysis and performance study for similarity-search methods in high-dimensional spaces. 24th Int. Conference on Very Large Data Bases (1998) 194–205   416, 417

[10] Weber, R., Blott, S.: An approximation based data structure for similarity search. Technical Report 24, ESPRIT project HERMES no. 9141 (1997)   416

[11] Berchtold, S., Bohm, C., Kriegel, H. P.: The pyramid-tree: breaking the curse of dimensionality. ACM SIGMOD Int. Conference on Management of Data (1998) 142–153   416

[12] Amsaleg, L., Gros, P., Berrani, S-A.: A robust technique to recognize objects in images, and the DB problems it raises. Multimedia Information Systems (2001) 1–10   416, 418

[13] Schmid, C., Mohr, R.: Local grayvalue invariants for image retrieval. IEEE Transactions on Pattern Analysis and Machine Intelligence 19 (1997) 530–535   416, 418

[14] Schmid, C., Mohr, R., Bauckhage, C.: Comparing and evaluating interest points. Int. Conference on Computer Vision (1998) 230–235   416, 418

[15] Sebe, N., Lew, M. S.: Comparing salient point detectors. Pattern Recognition Letters 24(1-3) (2003) 89–96   416

[16] Eickeler, S., Müller, S.: Content-based video indexing of TV broadcast news using Hidden Markov Models. IEEE Int. Conference on Acoustics, Speech, and Signal Processing (1999) 2997–3000   417

[17] Harris, C., Stephens, M.: A combined corner and edge detector. 4th Alvey Vision Conference (1988) 147–151 417

[18] Lawder, J. K., King, P. J. H.: Querying multi-dimensional data indexed using the Hilbert space-filling curve. SIGMOD Record **30** (2001) 19–24 418

[19] Beaton, A. E., Tukey, J. W.: The fitting of power series, meaning polynomials, illustrated on band-spectroscopic data. Technometrics **16** (1974) 147–185 419

ANSES: Summarisation of News Video

Marcus J. Pickering, Lawrence Wong, and Stefan M. Rüger

Department of Computing, South Kensington Campus, Imperial College London
SW7 2AZ, UK
m.pickering@imperial.ac.uk

Abstract. We describe the Automatic News Summarisation and Extraction System (ANSES), which captures television news each day with the accompanying subtitles and identifies and extracts news stories from the video. Lexical chain analysis is used to provide a summary of each story and important entities are highlighted in the text.

1 Introduction

The need for effective information retrieval systems to manage the vast quantities of digitally stored information is widely recognised, and there have been many increasingly successful attempts at meeting this need. However, as the amount of information available increases, so in many cases does the number of documents relevant to a query. This means that even when a system returns only documents that are technically relevant to a query, the user may still have a vast amount of work to do to sift through all returned documents and decide which are actually useful.

Users with an information need will often find their query satisfied not by a single returned document, but by gathering information from several sources through a process of browsing. The temporal nature of video makes browsing and query refinement difficult, and most users have not progressed beyond the traditional fast forward and rewind method for searching within a video [14]. Despite increases in available bandwidth, the downloading of video material is a time-consuming process, and some form of summary is required in order to provide the user with the means to make rapid and informed decisions about the relevance of returned results.

The Automatic News Summarisation and Extraction System (ANSES) builds on previous work carried out at Imperial College London [20] and aims to provide content-based access to broadcast news through extraction of key frames and summary of text derived from the teletext subtitles transmitted alongside the broadcast. What sets ANSES apart from other video summarisers is its novel method of news story boundary detection, recognition of named entities and the use of text summarisation with lexical chains to guide the user after relevant videos are identified. In Section 2 we outline some of the work already carried out in the area of video summarisation and in Section 3 ANSES is described in detail. In Section 4 we describe how this work is currently being developed to integrate features for content-based summary of the graphical content.

E. M. Bakker et al. (Eds.): CIVR 2003, LNCS 2728, pp. 425–434, 2003.

2   Related Work

Most existing research in the area of video summarisation is focused on reducing the amount of video, with the aim of providing the user only with the most essential or relevant content. Of course, this is a subjective process, and user input is normally required in order to set parameters determining how much information is actually returned.

One of the simplest methods for representing video concisely is to segment the material into *shots* (a shot is defined as a sequence of frames generated during a continuous operation and representing a continuous action in time and space [16]) and to select a *key frame* to represent the shot. A simple method is to use the nth frame (the first frame, for example) of each shot as the representative frame. If accurate shot change detection has been employed then in many cases the first frame will provide an accurate representation of the shot. However, in some cases it will not be sufficient. Consider a zoom: Often a camera operator will zoom in on the object of interest from a great distance and it may be many frames before the object is distinguishable, yet if only the first frame of the shot is used, the object of interest may be missed from the indexing process altogether. Also there is no clue as to the *action* of a shot. This has led researchers to examine more sophisticated techniques for key frame selection.

Zhang [26] states that the challenge in key frame extraction is that it is automatic and content-based and represents the dynamic content of the video while removing redundancy, and has proposed a method whereby several key frames are extracted for each shot. Three criteria are defined for selecting key frames – shot based, colour feature based, and motion based. The shot based criterion states that at least one key frame will be selected for a shot, and this is always the first frame. Whether there is a need for other key frames for a shot is determined by the other two criteria. The colour-feature based criterion states that frames in a shot are processed sequentially and compared to the last chosen key frame. If a significant content change has occurred between the current frame and the previous key frame then the current frame is selected as a new key frame. The motion-based criterion is motivated by the fact that significant motion in a shot is likely to represent important content change, since camera movement explicitly expresses the camera operator's intention in focusing on a particular object. Key frames are added according to types of motion that are classified as 'panning-like' or 'zooming-like'. Mahindroo et al. [15] employ object segmentation and tracking and select key frames based on critical events, such as appearance and disappearance of objects. Huet et al. [12] consider groups of videos of a common type (news, soap operas etc) and look for shots that are specific to a particular episode, aiming to remove redundant shots. The summary then consists of one key frame for each shot that is considered significant. The work of DeMenthon et al. [10] also focuses on finding important key frames, with the assumption that predictable frames are less important than unpredictable ones, for which clues often come from camera techniques employed.

Other researchers have designed systems which manufacture a key frame to try to capture the essence of a shot. Flickner et al. [11] proposed a method in which the whole shot is represented in a single frame. For each shot, a representative frame ('r-frame') is generated. For static shots, this will just be a single frame from the shot, but for shots involving motion, a 'synthesised r-frame' is generated by mosaicking all of the frames in a given shot to give a depiction of the background captured in the shot. Foreground objects are then superimposed on the shot.

Arman et al. [6] also propose a representative frame ('Rframe'). The body of the frame contains a shot from the video sequence (they choose the tenth frame), as well as four motion tracking regions and shot length indicators. The motion tracking regions trace the motion of boundary pixels through time – acting as guides to camera or global motion. The time indicators provide an 'at a glance' view of shot length.

More recent research in video summarisation has attempted to exploit the dynamic content of video, and rather than simply showing a static representation of the video, the aim is to discover relevant sections of the video and to play them to the user, so that the preview is a shortened version of the original. Ng and Lyu's method [18] simply involves playing a few seconds of each shot, while others opt to discover the important shots, and play them in their entirety. Oh and Hua [19] propose a system in which the user marks out a number of important scenes in the video and these are used as keys to search for other similar scenes based on visual content. Li et al. [14] have designed an advanced browser which gives the user the option to view summaries created using compressed video generated by removing audio pauses (and the corresponding video frames) and a time compression technique which increases the playback speed while maintaining the pitch of the audio. Their interface also allows for navigating through the video according to the shot boundaries.

The Informedia project at Carnegie Mellon University makes use of text streams from subtitles and automatic speech recognition transcripts to provide extra information about the video [8]. In news broadcasts, the audio stream (and therefore the subtitles and speech transcripts) are a rich source of information, as most of the important content is spoken. The combination of pictures and captions has been shown to aid recall and comprehension [13], as well as navigation [9], of video material and Informedia exploits this advantage by assembling 'collages' of images, text and other information (maps, for example) sourced via references from the text.

Our system, ANSES, also works mainly to summarise the textual information taken from the subtitles, alongside the video key frame, and as well as giving the user a readable summary, important entities are extracted and highlighted. Text summarisation and named entity display vastly reduce the time taken to digest potentially huge results sets.

3 ANSES

ANSES aims to present news video in such a way that relevant stories can be retrieved and browsed easily. Video and subtitles (closed-captions) are captured for the BBC news each night and the video is split into its constituent shots. The text is summarised, and information extracted from it is used in the merging of shots to form stories. Retrieval takes place through a web-based interface. The main stages in the process are detailed in the following sections.

3.1   Shot Boundary Detection

Shot boundary detection is an important step in discovering the structure of a video, and the resulting shots are widely recognised as the fundamental units of retrieval for video. In order to form complete news stories, ANSES works on the assumption that story boundaries always coincide with these shot boundaries and glues these basic units back together on the basis of the content of the corresponding text segments (see Section 3.4). This merging process can only be effective if accurate shot boundary detection is in place, so that a shot does not mistakenly bridge a story boundary.

Our shot boundary detection method [21] is based on the video component of a scene boundary detection method proposed by Pye et al. [23]. Colour histograms are used to characterise frames, and difference measures for these histograms are examined across time periods up to 16 frames either side of the current frame in order to determine if a shot boundary is occurring at that point. Following extensive empirical analysis, a number of rules were added to Pye's algorithm, defining the characteristics of peaks in the distance measures to detect and distinguish cuts and gradual transitions and to reject transients, such as those caused by camera flashes in news reports.

3.2   Generating Text Segments

Some processing of the captured subtitle text was necessary to render it in a format suitable for entity detection and summary generation. As well as imperfections caused by interference in the broadcast, a number of problems were also caused by the way that live subtitles are transmitted, with many duplicate phrases and lines (which appear seamlessly when displayed on a TV screen). In live news broadcasts, the subtitles often lag several seconds behind the video and audio, and further work needs to be carried out in future to properly re-align the subtitles. This has previously been done by aligning the subtitles with the output of a speech recogniser [25].

3.3   Key Entity Detection

In order to get a sense of the topic of each video shot, it is necessary to identify important keywords in the text and for this purpose we use the General Architecture for Text Engineering (GATE) [1]. Key entities are extracted from the subtitles and tagged with their parts of speech (noun, verb, pronoun etc). This then facilitates the process of merging of video shots according to their content, described in the next subsection.

Table 1. Empirically determined word-type weightings

Word type	Score
Organisation	60
Person	60
First Person	40
Location	40
Date	30
Noun	10
Other words	5

3.4 Segment Merging

In contrast to the mainly text-based methods deployed in the topic detection and tracking research field [5], we work under the assumption that story boundaries always coincide with video shot boundaries, and that providing the shot boundary detector has not missed the boundary, the problem of story segmentation is simply one of merging shots. The following function returning a score for the similarity of two text segments was used:

$$\text{Similarity} = \sum_m \frac{w(m)}{d(m)},$$

where $w(m)$ is the weight of word in match m according to its type and $d(m)$ is the number of subtitle lines between the two words in the match. Words, when matched, will generate a different score according to their type, as shown in Table 1. A word may have more than one type and scores are accumulated accordingly – for example 'Beijing' is both a location and a noun, and would score $40 + 10 = 50$. The 'Other words' category includes all non-stopped words that do not fit another category.

Each text segment is compared to each of its 5 neighbours on either side. When the similarity of two segments is greater than an empirically defined threshold, the two segments are merged with each other, and with any other segments that lie temporally between them. The corresponding video shots are also then merged.

3.5 Text Summarisation Using Lexical Chains

Each new segment should now contain a complete news story, and we wish to provide an accurate summary of the news story, so that the user can glean the important content without reading it in its entirety. We implement summarisation by the use of lexical chains [17]. The algorithm we have devised is inspired by Barzilay and Elhadad [7]. In general there are three stages for constructing lexical chains:

1. Selecting a set of candidate words.
2. Finding an appropriate chain for each candidate word, depending on a *relatedness* criterion among members of the chain.
3. Placing words. If an appropriate chain is found, the word is inserted in the chain, which is updated accordingly. If no appropriate chain is found, a new one is created, consisting only of this candidate word.

The *relatedness* of two candidate words is determined by the distance between their occurrences and the shape of the path connecting them in the WordNet thesaurus [4]. There are three types of relations: *extra strong* – between a word and its repetition, *strong* – between two words connected by a WordNet synonymy or hyponymy relation, and *medium strong* – where the link between synsets of the words is longer than one. When deciding in which chain a candidate word should be inserted, extra strong relations are preferred to strong relations, and both are preferred to medium strong relations. For each chain, a *chain score* is defined as the sum of the scores generated by each link in the chain. The score for a link is generated according to its type.

In our implementation, all nouns in the story are selected as candidate words. Nouns are detected using GATE's Part of Speech tagger. Each time a new noun is considered, we look up all the meanings of that noun. A different set of chains (an interpretation) must be considered for each meaning of each noun. On average, a noun has 8 different meanings, so for a typical story containing 30 nouns, there are $8^{30} = 1.238 \times 10^{27}$ interpretations. This represents a huge search space and necessitates some pruning. After every noun is added, the list of interpretations is sorted in descending order of the interpretation scores, where the interpretation score is the sum of the chain scores for that interpretation. The top 20 interpretations are then kept, the rest discarded.

Once we have considered all nouns in the story, we choose the interpretation with the highest score to represent the story. From this interpretation, we select the 3 strongest (highest scoring) chains, and from each of these chains we choose the word with the highest occurrence as a representative word. For every sentence that this word appears in a score is calculated using the following function:

$$\text{sentence score} = \sum_i n \cdot w(i),$$

where n is the number of occurrences of key entity i in the sentence and $w(i)$ is the weight associated with the type of word i (shown in Table 1). The two highest scoring sentences are used to represent the chain.

3.6   Retrieval

The retrieval interface is web based, and is shown in Figure 1. The Managing Gigabytes search system [2] indexes the full text of the news stories, and provides a ranked list of news stories in response to a keyword search.

The text summary is returned alongside a key frame for each news story. The key frame is currently the first frame of the story, though this is often

Fig. 1. ANSES retrieval interface

inadequate for news material where the first frame is usually an anchor person, and needs consideration in future development of the system. Alongside the text summary, the key entities are listed and colour coded according to their type – organisations, people, locations and dates. The colour scheme and fixed display location next to the summary help the user to quickly answer the critical 'who', 'when' and 'where' questions of news reports.

The video and associated text are stored in the database in the SMIL format [3] and the interface offers a button for each clip to be played back with its corresponding subtitles using the RealPlayer, which is available free for most platforms. Browsing is facilitated by functionality for seeking backwards and forwards through the key frames starting from any clip returned by a query.

4   Future Work

Video contains much more information than is communicated by the audio component, and we intend to extend the summarisation work to include features drawn from the graphical content of the video. We have already shown in other work [22] that the extraction of simple feature vectors based on primitive characteristics of key frames, such as colour and texture, can be useful for retrieval, and the combination of such features with the textual information described here should prove effective. This would also be combined with other work in which *regions* of an image are labelled with one of a number of visual classes, such as grass, sky, skin and wood.

Vasconcelos and Lippmann [24] have shown that combining a number of visual clues in a Bayesian network allowed them to make inferences about the genre of a film, and to isolate regions of interest within the film. Our future work involves extending this idea to the labelling of scenes with more generic concepts, using models derived from visual and textual features. This will be developed within the context of a video summarisation framework which could later be extended to add other features such as face recognition.

5 Conclusions

We have presented a fully automatic television news summarisation system, novel in its approach to news story segmentation and provision of summary material to aid the user in the retrieval process. This in itself greatly facilitates video news browsing, summarising and searching, and has the potential for being seamlessly integrated with existing research in the area of key frame analysis to provide a video summarisation system with some semantic analysis of video content. Our approach complements most existing video summarisation research which focuses on reducing the video content to clips and key frames.

Acknowledgements

This work was partially supported by the EPSRC, UK, and the ARC, Australia.

References

[1] General Architecture for Text Engineering. http://gate.ac.uk. 428

[2] Managing Gigabytes search engine. http://www.cs.mu.oz.au/mg/. 430

[3] Synchronized Multimedia Integration Language (SMIL) 1.0 specification. http://www.w3.org/TR/REC-smil/. 431

[4] WordNet, online lexical database. http://www.cogsci.princeton.edu/~wn/. 430

[5] J. Allan, J. G. Carbonell, G. Doddington, J. Yamron, and Y. Yang. Topic detection and tracking pilot study final report. In *Proceedings of the Broadcast News Transcription and Understanding Workshop (Sponsored by DARPA)*, Feb. 1998. 429

[6] F. Arman, R. Depommier, A. Hsu, and M.-Y. Chiu. Content-based browsing of video sequences. In *Proceedings of ACM International Conference on Multimedia*, Oct. 1994. 427

[7] R. Barzilay and M. Elhadad. Using lexical chains for text summarization. In *Proceedings of the Intelligent Scalable Text Summarization Workshop (ISTS'97)*, *ACL, Madrid, Spain.*, 1997. 429

[8] M. G. Christel, A. G. Hauptmann, H. D. Wactlar, and T. D. Ng. Collages as dynamic summaries for news video. In *Proceedings of ACM Multimedia 2002, Juan-les-Pins, France*, Dec. 2002. 427

[9] M. G. Christel and A. S. Warmack. The effect of text in storyboards for video navigation. In *Proceedings of IEEE International Conference on Acoustics, Speech, and Signal Processing (ICASSP), Salt Lake City, UT*, May 2001. 427

[10] D. DeMenthon, L. J. Latecki, A. Rosenfeld, and M. V. Stückelberg. Relevance ranking of video data using hidden markov model distances and polygon simplification. Technical Report LAMP-TR-067, University of Maryland, 2001. 426

[11] M. Flickner, H. Sawhney, W. Niblack, J. Ashley, Q. Huang, B. Dom, M. Gorkahni, J. Hafner, D. Lee, D. Petkovic, D. Steele, and P. Yanker. Query by image and video content: The QBIC system. *IEEE Computer*, 28:23–32, Sept. 1995. 426

[12] B. Huet, I. Yahiaoui, and B. Merialdo. Multi-episodes video summaries. In *International Conference on Media Futures, Florence, Italy*, May 2001. 426

[13] A. Large, J. Beheshti, A. Breuleux, and A. Renaud. Multimedia and comprehension: The relationship among text, animation and captions. *Journal of the American Society for Information Science*, 46(5):340–347, 1995. 427

[14] F. C. Li, A. Gupta, E. Sanocki, L.-W. He, and Y. Rui. Browsing digital video. In *Proceedings of the SIGCHI conference on Human factors in computing systems, The Hague, The Netherlands*, Apr. 2000. 425, 427

[15] A. Mahindroo, B. Bose, S. Chaudhury, and G. Harit. Enhanced video representation using objects. In *Indian Conference on Computer Vision, Graphics and Image Processing, Space Applications Centre (ISRO), Almedabad, India*, Dec. 2002. 426

[16] M. K. Mandal, F. Idris, and S. Panchanathan. A critical evaluation of image and video indexing techniques in the compressed domain. *Image and Vision Computing*, 17(7):513–529, 1999. 426

[17] J. Morris and G. Hirst. Lexical cohesion computed by thesaural relations as an indicator of the structure of text. *Computational Linguistics*, 17(1):21–43, 1991. 429

[18] C. W. Ng and M. R. Lyu. ADVISE: Advanced Digital Video Information Segmentation Engine. In *Proceedings of the 11th International World Wide Web Conference, Honolulu, Hawaii, USA.*, May 2002. 427

[19] J. Oh and K. A. Hua. An efficient technique for summarizing videos using visual contents. In *Proceedings of the IEEE International Conference on Multimedia and Expo. New York, USA*, July 2000. 427

[20] M. J. Pickering. Video archiving and retrieval. http://km.doc.ic.ac.uk/video-se/, 2000. 425

[21] M. J. Pickering, D. Heesch, R. O'Callaghan, S. Rüger, and D. Bull. Video retrieval using global features in keyframes. In E. M. Voorhees and D. Harman, editors, *Proceedings of the Eleventh Text REtrieval Conference (TREC-11)*, 2003. 428

[22] M. J. Pickering, S. M. Rüger, and D. Sinclair. Video retrieval by feature learning in key frames. In *Proceedings of International Conference on Image and Video Retrieval (CIVR)*, July 2002. 432

[23] D. Pye, N. J. Hollinghurst, T. J. Mills, and K. R. Wood. Audio-visual segmentation for content-based retrieval. In *5th International Conference on Spoken Language Processing, Sydney, Australia*, Dec. 1998. 428

[24] N. Vasconcelos and A. Lippman. Bayesian modeling of video editing and structure: Semantic features for video summarization and browsing. In *Proceedings of International Conference on Image Processing, Chicago.*, 1998. 432

[25] M. J. Witbrock and A. G. Hauptmann. Speech recognition for a digital video library. *Journal of the American Society of Information Science*, 49(7):619–632, 1998. 428

[26] H. J. Zhang, J. Wu, D. Zhong, and S. W. Smoliar. An integrated system for content-based video retrieval and browsing. *Pattern Recognition*, 30(4):643–658, 1997. 426

Spatio-Temporal Decomposition of Sport Events for Video Indexing

Lluis Barceló, Xavier Orriols, and Xavier Binefa *.

Unitat de Processament d'Imatges i Intel.ligència Artificial and Dept. d'Informàtica
Edifici Q, Universitat Autònoma de Barcelona
08193, Bellaterra, Barcelona, Spain
{botey,xevi,xavierb}@cvc.uab.es

Abstract. In this paper we present a robust technique for summarizing sport video sequences. Unlike dense optical flow and parametric methods, we develop a semi-automatic application that uses geometrical information, such as *straight* lines, extracted from sequences of images. This information is used to compute the *homographies* between consecutive frames. This estimation yields a manner of synthesizing a high resolution image of the background plus the field-centered trajectories of the moving objects onto it.

1 Introduction

The large amount of video data needs efficient schemes for browsing, searching and retrieving multimedia content. Traditional schemes allow the user to annotate video sequences through textual information and time codes corresponding to cut detections. More sophisticated techniques include general purpose object recognition (faces, anchors, captioning) in order to facilitate the organization of the video spatio-temporal structure. However, general purpose techniques tend to fail in terms of accuracy and, even more important, in terms of usefulness for the specific user demands. Actually, the use and production of multimedia information is extended to an increasing number of different areas which makes more difficult embracing completely different purposes with general tools.

In this paper, we focus on sport sequences. There are many reasons to consider sport videos as an specific framework, since many uses can be derived from. For instance, the method we propose can assist match commentators, coaches and players when trying to study the movements of an adversary player in order to define and prepare a proper strategy. Analyzing the players movement on the field helps to find higher level structures such as similar games, styles, etc. In this specific case, a more complex and problem oriented technique has to be applied in order to obtain a proper indexing. Nonetheless, it is important to point out that this particular application can be easily integrated in the MPEG-7 [7] framework through *description schemes* [8], since they allow to specify the syntax and semantics of a representation entity for a feature of Audio Visual

---

* Work supported by CICYT grant TEL99-1206-C02-02

E. M. Bakker et al. (Eds.): CIVR 2003, LNCS 2728, pp. 435–445, 2003.

data. There, the temporal organization of a sequence as well as the spatial organization of images are described. In our case, two different types of features are introduced: on one hand, the background image mosaic defining a specific spatial situation on the match field, and on the other, the trajectories which add a dynamic component to the meta-data descriptors. Summarizing a specific play through the decomposition of space and time helps us to perform a wide range of different posterior tasks. The background image itself mainly determines the type of sport we are indexing. For instance, consider the category of tennis fields, which have a set of specific features in common that make them different from a soccer field, or a swimming pool. Color, texture and some straight lines in some particular directions contribute to the categorization of different sports.

At a more specific level, we have to take into account the contribution of the time structure. The study of trajectories embedded in a certain field framework opens the possibility of analyzing the players behavior as well as it yields a higher level of semantic description for posterior more complex types of searches.

In this paper we present a method to summarize tennis sequences. This kind of sequences are generally very difficult of register because contain moving objects (the players) and constant regions without texture or with poor texture (low gradient). For this reason, we implement a method that uses the features always present in these kinds of sequences: the straight lines painted in the field of the match. Therefore, we use these features to find the correct registration in order to construct a final mosaic [9] with the summarization of the trajectories of the players. We want to find the *homography* that relates pairs of consecutive images, because the scene is planar (all match fields are) and then the transformation that pass from one to other is a projective transformation (an homography). It is important to say that there are many classical method like robust dense optical flow [2] and parametric methods [1] but with the presence of constant regions they do not work very fine.

The rest of the paper is organized as follows: in section 2 we describe the methodology that we develop and in section 3 we show results and applications of our method. Finally in section 4 we present the conclusions.

2   The Method

We develop a method to obtain mosaic images that summarizes the movements of the players on the field. With this aim, we construct a semi-automatic method that have two main steps:

- An *Initial Feature Extraction*. This is the only step where the user have to enter information, and
- A *Homography Estimation* step. In this step we use the information from the previous step in order to compute the correct homographies.

Next, we explain in depth the steps that we use to obtain the summarization of the sequences.

Fig. 1. A frame of the tennis sequence with the four *control lines* (blue lines) that we use to register the images

2.1 Initial Feature Extraction

The initial features in our case are only four lines that are entered by the user. These four lines are named as *control lines* and must to have the configuration shown in figure 1. Therefore, we have four straight lines $R = [r_1, r_2, r_3, r_4]$ and we want to use these straight lines to compute the homography that relates the transformations between the frame I_i and the frame I_{i+1}. To do that, first we compute a vector of features for each straight line:

$$F = [f_1, f_2, f_3, f_4] \tag{1}$$

where F are all the sets of features and f_i is the set of features for the straight line r_i. We use as features, points of each line. Now, we have the initial data that we will use to find the projective transformation between consecutive frames.

2.2 Homography Estimation

Once we have the set of features of the frame I_i, F, we want to find the respective features in the next frame F'. Therefore, we apply a *Pyramidal Lucas-Kanade Feature Tracker* [3] to find this set of features.

It is known that, the features in the first image represents a straight line and projective transformations keep the straight lines [6]: therefore features on the second image I_{i+1} will also represent a straight line. Consequently, we have to extract the four straight lines that best approximate the set of features F'.

With this purpose, we use the properties of *Singular Value Decomposition* (SVD) [5]: we have a set of features f_i' that are bidimensional ($[N \times 2]$, where N is the number of features respective to the straight line i) and we want to find the straight line that pass through them. Therefore if we use the obtained eigenvectors using the SVD we can extract the direction of that line (the direction of

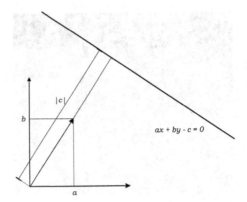

Fig. 2. Schematic representation of the straight line $ax + by - c = 0$, where we can see the interpretation of the *line normal* $n = (a, b)^T$

the line is the eigenvector that have the biggest eigenvalue). In other words, we compute the SVD of $Q = D^T D$ where:

$$D_{|N \times 2|} = f_i' - \mathbf{1}\mu_i \tag{2}$$

and

$$Q_{|2 \times 2|} = U \Sigma V^T \tag{3}$$

where μ_i is the mean of the set of features f_i (or the centroid of the features), $\mathbf{1}$ is a $N \times 1$ matrix of ones, and we find the eigenvectors $V = [v_1 v_2]$, where v_1 is the eigenvector with the largest eigenvalue. Then let

$$ax + by - c = 0 \tag{4}$$

be the equation of the line that we want to find. We can assume without loss of generality that:

$$||n|| = a^2 + b^2 = 1 \tag{5}$$

where the unit vector $n = (a, b)^T$, orthogonal to the line, is called the *line normal*. We also know that the distance from the line to origin is c, like it is shown in figure 2. Then the *line normal* is the second column of the matrix $V_{|2 \times 2|}$, v_2:

$$n = (a, b)^T = v_2 \tag{6}$$

and the third coefficient of the line is the projection of the centroid of the features μ_i over n:

$$c = \mu_i^T n \tag{7}$$

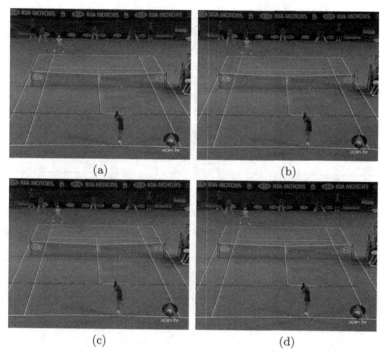

(a)   (b)

(c)   (d)

Fig. 3. Four iterations of the outlayers detection. a) First iteration. b) Second iteration. c) Third iteration. d) Fourth Iteration. Red points are the outlayers of each iteration

and the smallest singular value of Q, λ_2, measures the residual fitting error. Therefore we can easily find the equation of the line that best approximates our features [4]. Consequently, using this method we could extract the four respective straight lines $[r'_1, r'_2, r'_3, r'_4]$ only assuming that the features are being calculated without any error.

However, this fact is almost impossible if we are dealing with sequences that contain moving objects, because the presence of them influences the estimation of the features in the second frame. Therefore, we want to avoid these bad features (*outlayers*) and to solve this problem we use another time the SVD. We know that the error that we do when we approximate the data set F' with a straight line is:

$$\mathcal{E}^i = [\mathcal{E}^i_1, \ldots, \mathcal{E}^i_N] \tag{8}$$

where

$$\mathcal{E}^i_j = |(\boldsymbol{x}_j - \boldsymbol{\mu}_i)^T \boldsymbol{n}|^2 \tag{9}$$

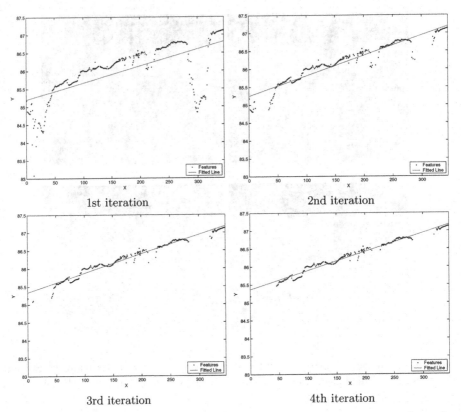

1st iteration   2nd iteration

3rd iteration   4th iteration

Fig. 4. Four iterations of the outlayers detection. In this case we show the features that we use (the blue points) and the fitted line (red line). The four figures shown the four iterations of the outlayer detection step. It is easy to see that we approximate better the features when we discard the outlayers

where $\mathcal{E}_j^i$ is the error of the point $\boldsymbol{x}_j$. Then the outlayers of the feature set f_i will be that ones that have a large error. Therefore, we extract these features (*outlayers*) that are greater than the next threshold:

$$thr^i = \mu_{\mathcal{E}^i} + (j-1)\sigma_{\mathcal{E}^i} \qquad (10)$$

where $\mu_{\mathcal{E}^i}$ is the mean and $\sigma_{\mathcal{E}^i}$ the standard deviation of the vector error $\mathcal{E}^i$, and j is the iteration number, because we repeat the process four times or until the residual fitting error λ_2 is smaller than a certain threshold, in order to avoid to discard all the features. In figure 3 we can see the result of the four iterations to detect the outlayers. In figure 4 and figure 5 we show the evolution of the fitting process and the error of approximation for the four iteration steps respectively.

Once we obtain the respective four lines in the frame I_{i+1} we know that a line r is tranformed into r' using a projective transformation (homography) [6] in the following way:

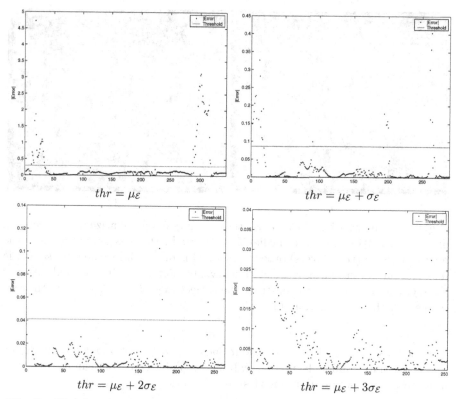

Fig. 5. The four iterations of the outlayer step. We show the evolution of the error and the threshold that we use to discard the outlayers in each case, that corresponds to the features and lines of figure 4. We can see that the error decreases in each iteration and the features that we discard in each case

$$r' = (H^{-1})^T \cdot r \qquad (11)$$

where $r = (a/b, b/c, 1)^T = (t, u, 1)^T$ and H is the homography represented by a non-singular 3×3 matrix. Switching left with right we have:

$$r = H^T \cdot r' \qquad (12)$$

Then each line correspondence in the plane provides two equations in the 8 unknown entries of H ($H_{33} = 1$):

$$t(H_{13}t' + H_{23}u' + 1) = H_{11}t' + H_{21}u' + H_{31} \qquad (13)$$
$$u(H_{13}t' + H_{23}u' + 1) = H_{12}t' + H_{22}u' + H_{32}$$

(a)	(b)

Fig. 6. Summarization of the tennis sequence. a) We summarize the trajectories of the two players onto the median mosaic. b) In this case, we superpose the moving objects (the players) onto the field. This mosaic image denotes semantic information about the movements and events that occur in the field. We use the segmentation masks to construct the trajectories of the players and then we merge it with the background mosaic

It is then necessary to find at least four line correspondences to define the transformation matrix uniquely, up to a scale factor. These equations can be rearranged in matrix form, obtaining the next system equation:

$$
\begin{pmatrix} t'_i & 0 & -t_i t'_i & u'_i & 0 & -t_i u'_i & 1 & 0 \\ 0 & t'_i & -u_i t'_i & 0 & u'_i & -u_i u'_i & 0 & 1 \\ \vdots & \vdots & \vdots & \vdots & \vdots & \vdots & \vdots & \vdots \end{pmatrix}
\begin{pmatrix} H_{11} \\ H_{12} \\ H_{13} \\ H_{21} \\ H_{22} \\ H_{23} \\ H_{31} \\ H_{34} \end{pmatrix}
=
\begin{pmatrix} t_i \\ u_i \\ \vdots \end{pmatrix}
\qquad (14)
$$

And finally, if we solve the above system equation using a least-squares method we find the homography that relates the transformation between the frames I_i and I_{i+1}. Once we have the homography and before continuinig analyzing the next frame, we recalculate the lines in the frame I_{i+1} using the homography previously calculated in order to avoid errors. Then we continue with the frames I_{i+1} and I_{i+2} using the above method until we have process the whole sequence.

3   Experimental Results

Using the previous method we can register sequences that contain moving objects and constant regions. We can obtain the mosaic from the images through the

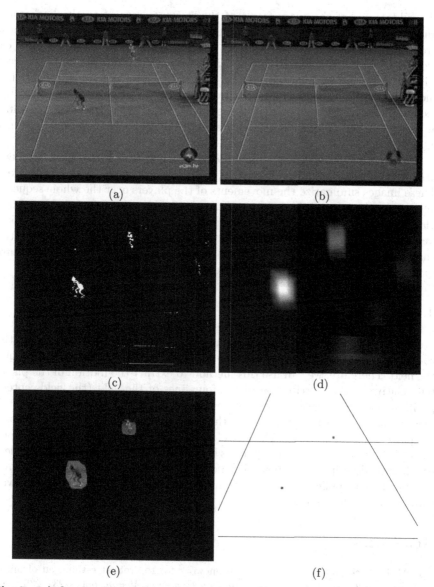

Fig. 7. a) One image of the tennis sequence. b) Image mosaic obtained using median operator. c) Result of subtraction of a) and b). d) Result of applying a convolution to c) using a rectangular kernel. e) Final segmentation masks with the segmented object. f) Schematic representation of the moving objects over the field (the four white lines) limit the field of the match

registration parameters, which will be the background image of the sequence like can be seen in figure 7b. One can easily extract the moving objects using the subtraction of the every frame of the sequence respect to the background image. We obtain using the above method an image like in figure 7c and post-processing this image we can segment the moving objects. In figure 7 we can see the whole process. Finally, we use the information about the moving objects (the players) and the transformation between frames and the localization of the lines of field to extract the position of each player in every frame of the sequence relative to the position of the lines. With this information, we obtain an schematic representation of each frame of the sequence as it can be seen in figure 7g.

Finally, we construct the trajectories of the player over the whole sequence using the information of the position of each player, as it can be seen in figure 6 . These images summarize the movements of the players over the whole sequence, only using one image. Moreover, we have the field-centered trajectories of each player relative to the field match and not to the axes of the mosaic image, like if we use classical algorithms to register the sequence. It is important to say that analyzing the players movement on the field helps to find higher level structures such as similar games, styles, ... in order to perform advance searches.

4   Conclusions

We have develop a robust semi-automatic method to summarize sequences that contain moving objects and constant regions, using the straight lines present in the field. Therefore, we can use this method to extract the motion of the players but relative to the distribution of the four lines of the field (the field-centered positions of the players). Thus, we can use this information to construct the mosaic image with the trajectories of the players, that summarizes the motion of the players in field of the match. Therefore, the study of theses trajectories opens the possibility of analyzing the players behavior as well as it yields a higher level of semantic description for posterior more complex types of searches. Moreover, this particular application can be easily integrated in the MPEG-7 framework through description schemes.

References

[1] M. J. Black and P. Anandan. A framework for the robust estimation of optical flow. In *Fourth International Conf. on Computer Vision*, pages 231–236, 1993. 436

[2] M. J. Black and P. Anandan. The robust estimation of multiple motions: Parametric and piecewise-smooth flow fields. *Computer Vision and Image Understanding: CVIU*, 63(1):75–104, 1996. 436

[3] J.-Y. Bouguet. Pyramidal implementation of the lucas kanade feature tracker description of the algorithm. *Microprocessor Research Labs*, 2000. 437

[4] D. A. Forsyth and J. Ponce. *Computer Vision: A Modern Approach*. Prentice Hall, 2002. 439

[5] G. H. Golub and C. F. V. Loan. *Matrix Computations*. The John Hopkins University Press, third edition, 1996. 437

[6] R. Hartley and A. Zisserman. *Multiple View Geometry in Computer Vision.* Cambridge University Press, 2000. 437, 440

[7] MPEG Requirements Group. MPEG-7 context, objectives and technical roadmap, doc. ISO/IEC/JTC1/SC29/WG11 N2729, Seoul meeting, March 1999. 435

[8] P. Salembier, R. Qian, N. O'Connor, P. Correia, I. Sezan, and P. van Beek. Description schemes for video programs, users and devices. *Signal Processing: Image Communication.*, 16:211–234, 2000. 435

[9] H. Shum and R. Szeliski. Panoramic image mosaics. *Microsoft Research Technical Report MSR-TR-97-23*, 1997. 436

Audio-Assisted Scene Segmentation for Story Browsing*

Yu Cao[1], Wallapak Tavanapong[1], Kihwan Kim[1], and JungHwan Oh[2]

[1] Department of Computer Science, Iowa State University
Ames, IA 50011-1040, USA
{yucao,tavanapo,khkim}@cs.iastate.edu
[2] Department of Computer Science and Engineering, University of Texas at Arlington
Arlington, TX 76019-0015, USA
oh@cse.uta.edu

Abstract. Content-based video retrieval requires an effective scene segmentation technique to divide a long video file into meaningful high-level aggregates of shots called *scenes*. Each scene is part of a story. Browsing these scenes unfolds the entire story of a film. In this paper, we first investigate recent scene segmentation techniques that belong to the visual-audio alignment approach. This approach segments a video stream into visual scenes and an audio stream into audio scenes separately and later aligns these boundaries to create the final scene boundaries. In contrast, we propose a novel audio-assisted scene segmentation technique that utilizes audio information to remove false boundaries generated from segmentation by visual information alone. The crux of our technique is the new dissimilarity measure based on analysis of statistical properties of audio features and a concept in information theory. The experimental results on two full-length films with a wide range of camera motion and a complex composition of shots demonstrate the effectiveness of our technique compared with that of the visual-audio alignment techniques.

1 Introduction

Recent years have seen the proliferation of digital videos in many important applications such as distance learning, digital libraries, and electronic commerce. Searching for a desired video segment from a large video database becomes increasingly more difficult as more digital videos are easily created. Content-based video browsing and retrieval is a promising paradigm that lets users browse and retrieve desired video segments quickly. This paradigm requires effective automatic *video segmentation* techniques. Video segmentation divides a video file into *shots* defined as a contiguous sequence of video frames recorded from a single camera operation. High-level aggregates of relevant shots termed *scenes* are then generated for browsing and retrieval. Scenes are important as (i) users are more likely to recall important events rather than a particular shot or frame [1]; and

---

* This work is partially supported by the National Science Foundation under Grant No. CCR 0092914.

E. M. Bakker et al. (Eds.): CIVR 2003, LNCS 2728, pp. 446–455, 2003.

(ii) the number of shots may be too large for effective browsing (e.g., about 600-1500 shots for a typical film).

In this paper, we investigate audio-assisted scene segmentation techniques for a narrative film that tells a story [2]. In these films, viewers understand a complex story through the identification of important events and the association of these events by cause and effect, time, and locale. Most movies are narrative. The majority of audio-assisted scene segmentation techniques utilize audio information as follows. Audio and visual streams in a media file are first separated. The visual stream is segmented into *visual scenes* using only visual features whereas the audio stream is divided into *audio scenes* using only audio features. Finally, both visual and audio scene boundaries are aligned to create the final scene boundaries. Hence, we categorize these techniques into the *visual-audio alignment (VAA) approach*. In this paper, we investigate a different approach. That is, scene boundaries are first detected using only visual features. Audio analysis is then applied to remove false scene boundaries that do not correspond to the scene boundaries determined by humans. This new audio assisted scene segmentation technique is called *Segmentation using Divergence Distance (SDD)*. The crux of SDD is the new dissimilarity measure based on analysis of statistical properties of audio features and the concept of "divergence" in information theory. Our experimental results on two full-length films show that SDD offers better segmentation accuracy than two VAA techniques.

The reminder of the paper is organized as follows. In Section 2, we summarize the use of audio information by two recent VAA techniques. We present SDD and the results of the performance evaluation in Sections 3 and 4, respectively. Lastly, we provide our conclusion in Section 5.

2   Visual-Audio Alignment Scene Segmentation

Since our focus is on the use of audio information, we only summarize how audio information is utilized by two recent VAA techniques [3,4]. Interested readers in segmentation using visual properties are referred to the original papers. We refer to the use of audio in reference [3] as *Audio Memory Model (AMM)* and in reference [4] as *Segmentation by Classification (SC)*.

2.1   Audio Memory Model

The audio memory model is used to segment a media file into "computable scenes", each defined as "a chunk of audio-visual data that exhibits long-term consistency with regard to three properties: (a) chromaticity (b) lighting and (c) ambient sound". One or more computable scenes forms an actual scene perceived by humans. Ten different audio features are utilized as follows.

AMM uses the buffer window of size T_m seconds and the analysis window of size T_{as} seconds. For each feature, these windows are slid over the feature values. For each position of the analysis window starting from the end of the buffer window, the envelope fit for the feature values in the analysis window is

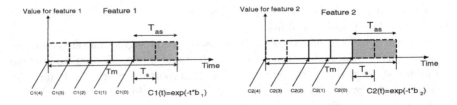

Fig. 1. Audio Memory Model

computed using a curve fitting function. Each position of the analysis window is T_s seconds apart. As an illustrating example, Fig. 1 shows five envelopes for the entire buffer window. Next, the correlation among the first envelope and each of the rest of the envelopes in the buffer window is computed. The same example shows five correlation values in the buffer window of feature 1 ($C1(t), t \in [0 \ldots 4]$) and five correlation values in the buffer window of feature 2 ($C2(t), t \in [0 \ldots 4]$). The change in the correlation values is modeled using an exponential decay function to obtain a decaying parameter b_i for each feature i. For each position of the analysis window, the aggregate decay value of the decaying parameters of all features are used to determine audio scene breaks. An audio scene break is detected by shifting another window of size T_w seconds across the buffer window to the right, starting from the beginning of the buffer window. Each position of the window is T_s apart. If the local minimum of the aggregate decay values in the window is at the center of the window, an audio scene break is detected.

Visual scene and audio scene boundaries are aligned as follows. For visual scene and audio scene boundaries that occur within an ambiguity window of each other, only the visual scene boundary is treated as the actual scene boundary. Otherwise, both boundaries are treated as actual scene boundaries.

2.2   Segmentation by Classification

In this technique, an audio scene boundary is detected when a change in speakers or a change in types of audio segments (e.g., speech type to music type, music type to silence type, etc.) occurs. To detect audio scene boundaries, the audio stream is divided into a number of one second non-overlapping audio segments. A K-Nearest Neighbor (KNN) audio classifier based on zero crossing rate, short time energy, and spectrum flux is used to determine whether each of the audio segments is a speech or a non-speech segment. To ensure good classification accuracy, the segment considered as a speech segment is reexamined by computing the distance between the Linear Spectral Pair (LSP) of the segment and each LSP of four pre-determined speech codebooks. The smallest distance is compared with a threshold to decide whether the segment is indeed a speech segment. A change in the speakers of speech is detected if the distance between the LSP covariance matrices of two consecutive speech segments is a local peak and exceeds a threshold.

Each of the audio segments indicated as a "non-speech" segment is further analyzed to identify its types: silence, music, or environmental sound, according to a set of rules. Only audio boundaries that are exactly aligned with shot boundaries are considered for the alignment with the visual scene boundaries. The actual scene boundary is where the exact alignment between a visual scene boundary and an audio scene boundary occurs.

3   Audio-Assisted Scene Segmentation Scheme

We propose an audio-assisted scene segmentation scheme called *Segmentation using Divergence Distance (SDD)*. Unlike existing techniques that align visual scene boundaries and audio scene boundaries to locate the actual scene boundaries, our scheme is based on the assumption that most scene boundaries are determined by visual properties. This assumption is obtained from film literature [2] that audio is secondary to visual information in maintaining viewers' thought in presence of shot breaks[1]. Hence, we utilize audio information only to remove false visual scene boundaries. The remaining visual boundaries after the removal of false boundaries are the final scene boundaries. We utilize ShotWeave for visual scene segmentation since it has been shown to perform well for narrative films [5]. Since our focus is the use of audio in this paper, we do not present ShotWeave here. The important elements of SDD are (i) the accurate identification of false scene boundaries, (ii) feature selection and analysis of statistical properties of audio features, (iii) the divergence dissimilarity measure between shots, and (iv) the shot clustering algorithm. We assume that shot boundaries and visual scene boundaries are known in the following discussion.

3.1   Identification of False Scene Boundaries

We observe that a detected visual scene that has a very short scene length is highly likely to be a false scene. By observation from the results of ShotWeave, the false scene often has a single shot acting as an establishment of the next scene or a re-establishment of the previous scene. The establishment is used to indicate where the scene takes place or who participates in the scene. The re-establishment appears at the end of a scene to confirm the location or the characters of the scene. Shots in the establishment and re-establishment are typically visually different from the other shots in the same scene. Shots in a scene representing a journey are often visually different from each other. Given scenes detected by ShotWeave, we compute the average scene length (in terms of the number of frames) of the scenes with more than one shot. The single shot scene with its length shorter than the average scene length is marked as a possible false scene. If a different segmentation technique for visual scenes is used instead of ShotWeave, different methods for detecting false scenes can be employed instead.

---

[1] *"..., and so in ordinary life sound is often simply a background for our visual attention. ... We are strongly inclined to think of sound as simply an accompaniment to the real basis of cinema, the moving images"* [2], Page 315.

3.2 Distribution of Audio Features

We often hear several concurrent sounds such as speech, environmental sound, or music altogether in a film. Since *short-time energy, zero-crossing rate, spectrum flux,* and *linear spectral pairs* were shown effective for discriminating different types of audio signals [6,7,8], we use these features and investigate the distribution of the audio features in a shot to design an appropriate measure for dissimilarity of audio information of different shots.

Normalized Short-Time Energy (NSTE) is adapted from Short-Time Energy (STE)—a widely used audio feature for silence detection and discrimination of speech and music signals. *Zero-Crossing Rate (ZCR)* is a very useful feature to characterize speech signals. ZCR is defined as the number of times the audio waveform crosses the zero axis within a time unit. *Spectrum Flux (SF)* can be seen as the average variation of spectrum between two adjacent audio frames in an analysis window. *Linear Spectral Pairs (LSP)* is based on Linear Predictive (LP) model. Due to limited space, the readers interested in the exact calculation of ZCR, SF, and LSP are referred to [7,8].

Each audio frame is represented by a feature vector. Since shots typically have a different number of audio frames, we represent shot i using a $m_i \times k$ matrix where m_i is the number of audio frames in shot i, and k is the number of features in the feature vector. For each video, we have as many matrices as the number of shots in a video. To propose the effective dissimilarity measure of the audio features of any two shots, we analyze the distribution of each of the audio features using S-PLUS statistical software.

Fig. 2 depicts the density plot and the normal Q-Q plot for ZCR and SF values extracted from one sample shot that contains 338 frames. The x-axis of the density plots represents the values of the features, and the y-axis represents the number of the audio frames. The normal Q-Q plot graphically compares the distribution of the given feature values to the normal distribution (represented

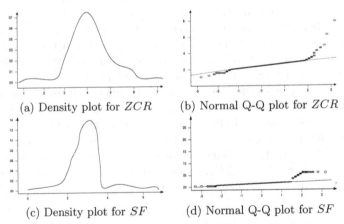

(a) Density plot for *ZCR*   (b) Normal Q-Q plot for *ZCR*

(c) Density plot for *SF*   (d) Normal Q-Q plot for *SF*

Fig. 2. Density plots and normal Q-Q Plots for *ZCR* and *SF*

by a straight line). Since most of our points fall on the straight line, this is a good indicator that our feature values are normally distributed. The other features have a similar distribution. For the vector feature such as LSP, we treat each value in the feature vector independently.

3.3   Weighted K-L Divergence Dissimilarity Measure

The above results allow us to use a k-variate normal distribution to approximate the distribution of k features for each shot. That is, for shot i, we have a corresponding k-variate normal distribution $N(\mu_i, \Sigma_i)$ where $\mu_i = (\mu_{i1}, \mu_{i2}, \dots, \mu_{ik})$ is the vector of the mean values for all the k features, and $\Sigma_i = [\sigma_{rs}]$ is the co-variance matrix of shot i , where σ_{rs} $r, s = 1, 2, \dots, k$ is the correlation between features r and s.

Instead of finding the exact mean and covariance for the audio features of each shot, we use a recursive computation method to estimate the mean and covariance [7] since a shot typically has a large number of audio frames. Let n be the frame index starting from 1 to the number of audio frames in this shot, and y_n is the feature vector of frame n. For each shot, we recursively compute the estimate of the mean vector $(\widehat{\mu}_{n+1})$ and the estimate of the covariance matrix $(\widehat{\Sigma}_{n+1})$ taking the first n audio frames into account as follows.

$$\widehat{\mu}_{n+1} = \widehat{\mu}_n + \frac{1}{n+1}(y_{n+1} - \widehat{\mu}_n)$$

$$\widehat{\Sigma}_{n+1} = \frac{n-1}{n}\widehat{\Sigma}_n + \frac{1}{n+1}(y_{n+1} - \widehat{\mu}_n)(y_{n+1} - \widehat{\mu}_n)^T$$

Given the k-variate normal distribution, we apply the "divergence" concept in information theory for our dissimilarity (distance) measure. To compute the distance between two shots, say shot i and shot j represented by $p_i(x) \sim N(\mu_i, \Sigma_i)$ and $p_j(x) \sim N(\mu_j, \Sigma_j)$, respectively. The *average discrimination information* for shot i against shot j over all observations, also known as *Kullback-Leibler Number* [9], is

$$I(i,j) = \int_x p_i(x) \ln \frac{p_i(x)}{p_j(x)} dx.$$

Similarly, the average discrimination information for shot j against shot i over all observations is

$$I(j,i) = \int_x p_j(x) \ln \frac{p_j(x)}{p_i(x)} dx.$$

Divergence (D_{ij}) is defined as the total average information for discriminating shot i from shot j. Based on Tou's derivation [10], the divergence of the two normally distributed shots is

$$D_{ij} = I(i,j) + I(j,i).$$
$$= \frac{1}{2}tr\Big((\Sigma_i - \Sigma_j)(\Sigma_j^{-1} - \Sigma_i^{-1})\Big) + \frac{1}{2}tr\Big((\Sigma_i^{-1} + \Sigma_j^{-1})\delta\delta^T\Big),$$

where $\delta = \mu_i - \mu_j$.

To combine a shot with its neighboring scene, the frame distance between shots must also be considered in addition to the dissimilarity in the audio properties. Hence, we propose a *weighted K-L Divergence Distance* to reflect this idea. Suppose that scene i is composed of one shot s_{i1} and scene j is the neighboring scene with K shots: $s_{j1}, s_{j2}, \ldots, s_{jK}$. Let $d_{i1,jk}$ be the K-L number between shot s_{i1} and shot s_{jk} ($1 \leq k \leq K$). $L_{i1,jk}$ denotes the number of frames from the center of shot s_{i1} to the center of shot s_{jk}. The weighted K-L divergence between shot i and scene j is as follows.

$$Dis(i,j) = \sum_{k=1}^{K} \frac{(TL(i,j) - L_{i1,jk})}{TL(i,j)} d_{i1,jk}, \text{ where } TL(i,j) = \sum_{k=1}^{K} L_{i1,jk}.$$

3.4   Clustering Algorithm

Our clustering algorithm consists of two passes. Initially, a merge variable is associated with each of the scenes detected by ShotWeave and is initialized to zero. Note that the scene number starts from one. In the first pass, the algorithm identifies the false scenes and sets the merge variable of the false scenes to the scene number of the neighboring scene to merge the false scene into. Each scene is checked whether it is a possible false scene using the method discussed in Section 3.1. For the scene marked as the possible false scene, the weighted K-L divergence between the scene and its immediate preceding scene is computed. If the divergence distance is less than a pre-defined threshold, the merge variable of the possible false scene is set to the scene number of the preceding scene. This is to indicate that this false scene is to be removed by combining it with the preceding scene. Otherwise, the possible false scene is determined whether it can be combined with its immediate succeeding scene in a similar manner. This process is repeated until all scenes have been considered. In the second pass, each scene with the positive merge variable is combined with the scene identified by the merge variable. Hence, the remaining scenes after this step are the final scenes.

4   Performance Study

We evaluate our SDD using the modified SC (MSC) and the modified AMM (MAMM) as the reference techniques. We also determine the effectiveness of our technique when using the weighted Euclidean distance instead of the weighted divergence distance. We call this technique SED. In all the techniques, we only use features that can be derived from STE, ZCR, SF, and LSP. Our objective is to investigate how best to utilize audio information given the same set of features since effectiveness of scene segmentation depends on the distance function and the use of the features besides the feature set itself. ShotWeave is used to segment the test videos into visual scenes. Note that our results should not be taken as the comparative performance evaluation with the original work of SC and AMM since different scene definition, features, and techniques to generate visual scenes are used.

The following performance metrics are used. *Recall* indicates the ability of a scene segmentation technique to uncover most scenes judged by humans. *Precision* is the ratio of the number of the correctly detected scenes to the total number of the detected scenes. High recall and precision are desirable. *Utility* is the weighted sum of recall and precision. We use it to measure the overall accuracy, taking both recall and precision into account. Different weights of recall and precision can be set, depending on which measure is more important to the user. In general, techniques offering high utility are more effective. In this study, an equal weight of one is assigned to recall and precision. Finally, we introduce *Scene Boundary Deviation (SBD)* defined as the average distance (in terms of shots) of the false boundaries to the closest correct scene boundaries. Low SBD value indicates that the false boundaries are not far away from the actual scene boundaries.

Experiments were performed on two test videos: Home Alone and Far and Away. Each video lasts longer than 100 minutes. Scenes were segmented manually as follows. First, shot boundaries were manually determined. These shots were manually grouped into scenes according to the strict scene definition [5] based on continuity editing techniques used in film-literature [2]. The strict definition is more objective, but gives scenes that are familiar by most viewers. Home Alone and Far and Away have 62 and 58 scenes, respectively.

In the following, we first determine the best values for important parameters for each technique by running the techniques with varying parameter values on Far and Away video. The best parameter values enable the technique to offer high utility. Then, we compare the performance of all the techniques, each using their best parameter values to ensure the fairness of our performance comparison.

4.1   Determining Important Parameter Values

We determined the important threshold values for LSP, STE, Noise Frame Ratio, and SF used in MSC. The three important parameters for MAMM are the buffer window size (T_m), the analysis window (T_{as}), and the duration by which the analysis window is shifted (T_s). Table 1 shows the results when T_m and T_{as} were fixed at 28 and 14, respectively, and T_s was varied. The selected values for T_m and T_{as} are the best values on Far and Away video. The parameter T_s determines the number of correlation values. The higher the T_s is , the more the correlation values are. We chose 1 second for T_s because this value gives the highest utility.

The most important parameter for SDD is the divergence threshold. The threshold value of 23 was chosen since it gives the highest utility (see Table 2).

4.2   Performance Comparison

Table 3 shows the performance of all the techniques using their best parameter values. We observe that SDD offers the highest utility whereas MSC offers the least utility. SDD always produces the highest recall. SDD is less dependent on video content than the other techniques since a little performance difference among the two videos is observed for SDD. This is desirable since we do not

Table 1. MAMM performance with different thresholds

T_s	Recall	Precision	Utility
0.5	0.517	0.118	0.635
1	**0.500**	**0.139**	**0.639**
1.5	0.345	0.142	0.487
2	0.31	0.11	0.44
3	0.14	0.15	0.29

Table 2. SDD performance with different thresholds

Threshold	Recall	Precision	Utility
15	0.310	0.131	0.441
20	0.379	0.147	0.526
23	**0.586**	**0.202**	**0.788**
30	0.603	0.099	0.712

need to determine new threshold values for each video. The weighted divergence distance offers better overall accuracy than the weighted Euclidean distance. Performance improvement of precision of SDD over ShotWeave [5] is not quite exciting (about 6%) with the small reduction in recall (about 0.05%). However, Table 4 shows that the SBD value of SDD is the smallest and is less than half of that of ShotWeave. This means the false boundaries produced by SDD is the closest to the actual scene boundaries. Some of these false boundaries may not be significant to the viewers.

5   Conclusions

We have presented a new audio-assisted scene segmentation technique developed based on statistical analysis of audio features and the concept of divergence in information theory. Our experimental results on two full-length films provide the following conclusions. First, utilizing audio information to remove false scenes provides improvement in segmentation accuracy over alignment of visual and audio scenes. The weighted K-L divergence distance is shown to be more effective

Table 3. Performance Comparison: recall, precision and utility

Technique	Home Alone			Far and Away		
	Recall	Precision	Utility	Recall	Precision	Utility
MSC	0.234	0.128	0.362	0.414	0.218	0.632
MAMM	0.403	0.143	0.546	0.50	0.139	0.639
SDD	**0.50**	**0.223**	**0.723**	**0.586**	**0.202**	**0.788**
SED	0.419	0.228	0.647	0.483	0.193	0.676

Table 4. Performance Comparison: Scene Boundary Deviation

Film Title	ShotWeave	MSC	MAMM	**SDD**	SED
Home Alone	30.79	24.31	21.69	**14.23**	16.48
Far and Away	38.76	27.67	25.09	**20.67**	22.36

than weighted Euclidean distance. Future work includes the use of more audio features to further improve the segmentation accuracy.

References

1. Hanjalic, A., Lagendijk, R. L., Biemond, J.: Automated high-level movie segmentation for advanced video-retrieval systems. IEEE Transactions on Circuits and Systems for Video Technology 9 (1999) 580–588 446
2. Bordwell, D., Thompson, K.: Film Art: An Introduction (5 ed.). McGraw-Hill Companies, Inc. (1997) 447, 449, 453
3. Sundaram, H., Chang, S. F.: Determining computable scenes in films and their structures using audio-visual memory models. In: Proc. of ACM Multimedia, LA, CA, USA (2000) 95–104 447
4. Jiang, H., Lin, T., Zhang, H. J.: Video segmentation with the assistance of audio content analysis. In: Proc. of ICME 2000. (2000) 1507–1510 vol.3 447
5. Tavanapong, W., Zhou, J.: Shot clustering techniques for story browsing. To appear in IEEE Transactions on Multimedia (http://www-midea.cs.iastate.edu) (2003) 449, 453, 454
6. Scheirer, E., Slaney, M.: Construction and evaluation of a robust multifeature speech/music discriminator. In: Proc. of the IEEE Int'l Conf. on Acoustics, Speech, and Signal Processing. Volume 2., IEEE (1997) 1331–1334 450
7. Campbell, J. P.: Speaker recognition: A tutorial. In: Proc. of IEEE. Volume 85. (1997) 1437–1461 450, 451
8. Lu, L., Jiang, H., Zhang, H.: A robust audio classification and segmentation method. In: Proc. of ACM Multimedia, Ottawa, Ontario, Canada (2001) 203–211 450
9. Kullback, S.: Information Theory and Statistics. Dover Publications, New York, NY (1997) 451
10. J.Tou, Gonzalez, R.: Pattern recongnition principles. Applied Mathemetics and Computation (1974) 451

Performance Comparison of Different Similarity Models for CBIR with Relevance Feedback

Daniel Heesch, Alexei Yavlinsky, and Stefan Rüger

Department of Computing, South Kensington Campus, Imperial College London
London SW7 2AZ, England
{dh500,agy02,s.rueger}@imperial.ac.uk

Abstract. This paper reports on experimental results obtained from a comparative study of retrieval performance in content-based image retrieval. Two different learning techniques, k-Nearest Neighbours and support vector machines, both of which can be used to define the similarity between two images, are compared against the vector space model. For each technique, we determine both absolute retrieval performance as well as the relative increase in performance that can be achieved through relevance feedback.

1 Introduction

Content-based information retrieval remains a formidable challenge. The fundamental problem appears to be linked to our gaping ignorance regarding content-representation in the human brain, and a major breakthrough may thus have to wait for a corresponding breakthrough in the neurosciences. There undoubtedly exist taxing technological challenges arising from time and storage considerations. With grid computing and nano-technology advancing rapidly, however, these challenges are likely to be met in the foreseeable future. The problem of the semantic gap between primitive features on the one hand and image meaning on the other hand, however, is likely to persist for some time. One promising attempt to at least alleviate the problem has been relevance feedback. It has long been used profitably in traditional information retrieval [13] and is beginning to establish itself as a core paradigm in content-based information retrieval. In the context of image retrieval, relevance feedback requires the user to label retrieved images according to their relevance. A commonly employed techniques to achieve supervised learning through relevance feedback involves updating weights of a parametrized similarity function over several iterations of user-system interaction (see for example [12, 4]). This paper is concerned with the question of how retrieval performance and the effectiveness of relevance feedback is affected by the choice of the similarity model that underlies the ranking of retrieved images. The first similarity model is associated with support vector machines (SVM). This learning technique constitutes the fruit of a number of relatively recent advances in the theory of statistical learning [15]. Owing to their remarkable generalization performance, they have in many areas replaced neural

E. M. Bakker et al. (Eds.): CIVR 2003, LNCS 2728, pp. 456–466, 2003.

networks for prediction and classification problems alike. In CBIR, SVMs have recently been employed in [5] where they are used to determine feature weights following relevance feedback. Theoretical progress in support estimation [14] has recently provided the basis for the application of one-class SVMs to CBIR. In [1], for example, linear and non-linear kernels are used to capture single and multi-modal distributions of relevant images by finding closest-fitting spheres around positive examples.

The second learning technique is based on k-Nearest Neighbours (k-NN), a technique that has been widely used in non-parametric density estimation and classification [3]. A recent application to CBIR is found in the context of key-frame based video retrieval [11].

The paper is structured as follows. Section 2 briefly introduces the image features used. An exposition of the learning techniques and how they can be employed for similarity computation is given in section 3. Section 4 provides a brief description of the relevance feedback technique implemented and section 5 details the experimental set-up. Results will be presented in section 6 and the paper will end with conclusions in section 7.

2   Image Features

Our study concentrates on the use of colour features for capturing image content. While any two such features will necessarily be correlated, we sought to reduce the representational overlap by defining features in different colour spaces and by giving different spatial emphasis as detailed below.

2.1   HSV Colour Histogram

We use a uniform quantization of the HSV colour space using 8 bins for each dimension. Two different features are defined. One feature is a global histogram with no preservation of spatial information, while the other feature consists of an array of five local histograms with the first four forming a partition of the image and the fifth covering the central 25%. This second feature achieves some preservation of local colour information. Moreover, by associating a high weight with the central area it lends itself well for capturing content of images where a centrally located object of interest is enveloped by irrelevant background. The size of the vector for the latter feature is thus $8^3 \times 5 = 2560$.

2.2   HMMD Colour Histogram

The HMMD (Hue, Min, Max, Diff) colour space, which is part of the MPEG-7 standard, derives from the HSV and RGB spaces. The Hue component is the same as in the HSV space, and Max and Min denote the maximum and minimum among the R, G, and B values, respectively. The Diff component is defined as the difference between Max and Min. Three components suffice to uniquely locate a point in the colour space and thus the space is effectively three-dimensional.

Following the MPEG-7 specification, we quantize the HMMD non-uniformly into 184 bins (for details about this quantization see [6]) with the three dimensions being Hue, Sum and Diff (Sum being defined as (Max+Min)/2). Two features are defined with respect to the HMMD colour space, a standard global histogram and the colour structure descriptor as detailed below.

2.3 Colour Structure Descriptor

This feature lends itself well for capturing local colour structure in an image. A 8×8 sliding window is moved over the image. Each of the 184 bins of the HMMD histogram contains the number of window positions for which there is at least one pixel in the area covered by the window with a colour that falls into the bin under consideration. This feature is capable of discriminating between images that have the same global colour distribution but different local colour structures. Although the number of samples in the 8×8 structuring window is kept constant (64), the spatial extent of the window differs depending on the size of the image. Thus, for larger images appropriate sub-sampling is employed to keep the total number of samples per image roughly constant (see [6] for details). The bin values are normalized by dividing by the number of locations of the structuring window and fall in the range $[0, 1]$.

3 Similarity Models

3.1 Support Vector Machines

The idea behind support vector machines (SVMs) is to map n-dimensional vectors $\mathbf{x}$ of the input space non-linearly into high-dimensional vectors of the feature space and to then construct an optimal hyperplane in that feature space. Training a support vector machine, i.e. determining the optimal hyperplane, requires the solution of a quadratic optimization problem of the following form [15]:

$$\text{minimize} \quad W(\alpha) = -\sum_{i=1}^{l} \alpha_i + \frac{1}{2} \sum_{i=1}^{l} \sum_{j=1}^{l} y_i y_j \alpha_i \alpha_j k(\mathbf{x}_i, \mathbf{x}_j) \quad (1)$$

$$\text{subject to} \quad \sum_{i=1}^{l} y_i \alpha_i = 0$$
$$\forall i : 0 \leq \alpha_i \leq C$$

where the number of training examples is denoted by l and α is a vector of l variables where each component α_i corresponds to a training example $(\mathbf{x_i}, \mathbf{y_i})$. Here y_i denotes whether an image is relevant or not and $\mathbf{x}$ is a vector consisting of the bin frequencies of a colour histogram. The size of the optimization problem depends on the number of training examples l. An implementation with good performance characteristics is SVM^{light} (available at http://www-ai.cs.uni-dortmund.de/svm_light) which breaks up the quadratic programming (QP) problem into smallest possible QP sub-problems and solves these analytically.

For our study, SVM^{light} is provided with sets of positive examples (the query images) and negative examples (randomly selected images that are not in the same category as the query) and then finds the optimal hyperplane separating positive from negative examples. Each new image is then assigned a score $s \in \mathbb{R}$, where $|s|$ measures the distance of the image from the hyperplane. A positive score indicates that the image is likely to be relevant. We here make the somewhat stronger assumption that the higher the score, the more relevant the image is likely to be. This relationship is also tacitly assumed in [5]. To turn the s score into a bounded dissimilarity value d, we compute for each image i to be ranked

$$d(i) = 1 - \frac{s_i - \min_j s_j}{\max_j s_j - \min_j s_j}. \tag{2}$$

3.2   k-Nearest Neighbour

We use a variant of the distance-weighted k-NN approach [8]. For each image i to be ranked we identify those images from the two sets of positive (P) and negative (N) images that are among the k nearest neighbours of i (nearness being defined by the l_1-norm). Using these neighbours, we determine the dissimilarity

$$d(i) = \frac{\sum_{n \in N} \text{dist}^{-1}(i, n)}{\sum_{p \in P} \text{dist}^{-1}(i, p)}. \tag{3}$$

In practice a small term is added to the distances so as to avoid division by zero. For all experiments, k is set to 5 and the number of positive and negative examples to 4 and 10, respectively.

3.3   Vector Space Model

All colour features are histograms which have been normalized such that all bins sum up to 1. A similarity metric for histogram features which has given good results in the past is the l_1-norm, $\sum_{j=0}^{N-1} |h_1(j) - h_2(j)|$, where the sum is over all bins. This value is divided by 2 to give an upper bound of 1. Since a query consists of multiple images, the overall distance between an image and a query Q is obtained by averaging the distance over all query images. Hence, the dissimilarity of a query to image i is

$$d(i) = \frac{1}{2|Q|} \sum_{q \in Q} \sum_{j=0}^{N-1} |h_i(j) - h_q(j)|. \tag{4}$$

Since the l_1-norm is defined in vector space, we will henceforth refer to this model as the vector space model (VSM).

3.4   Combination of Image Features

For each colour feature j we determine the distance $d_j(i)$ between the query to each of the images to be ranked according to one of the three similarity models described above. These feature-specific distances are then combined in a weighted sum $D(i) = \sum_j w_j d_j$, where $0 \leq w_j \leq 1$ and $\sum_j w_j = 1$. $D(i)$ is our estimate of the overall dissimilarity between a query and the ith image. The weights w_j provide the plasticity to be exploited by relevance feedback.

4   Relevance Feedback

Thumbnails of retrieved images are displayed such that their respective distance from the centre of the screen is proportional to their dissimilarity to the query Q as computed by the system, $D_s(i)$ (for the GUI see [4]). By moving images further away or closer towards the center, the user provides a real-valued vector of distances, $D_u(i)$, which, in general, differ from the distances computed by the system. To update the feature weights, we minimize the sum of squared errors (SSE) between the user distances and the system-computed distances, i.e.

$$\text{SSE}(w) = \sum_{i=1}^{N} [D_s(i) - D_u(i)]^2 = \sum_{i=1}^{N} \left[\sum_j w_j d_j(i) - D_u(i) \right]^2 \qquad (5)$$

subject to the constraint of convexity ($\sum_j w_j = 1$). Using one Lagrangian multiplier, this problem can readily be solved analytically. We have previously studied the effectiveness of different feedback scenarios and identified positive feedback as being superior to both mixed and negative feedback [4]. In the present study, we shall therefore confine our analysis to the case of positive feedback.

5   Experimental Set-Up

5.1   Selection of the Image Corpus

It is known that the choice of a test collection can heavily influence the perceived performance of a system [9]. We hence sought to use a corpus with a wide range of images and one that could easily be reproduced by other groups. It is desirable for evaluation purposes to work with a set of images for which a ground truth is available. We opted for images obtained from the Corel Gallery 380.000 package, which contains some 30.000 photographs, sorted into 450 categories.

The image collection was created with the aim of being able to assess the performance on realistic search tasks. Some Corel categories were of a very similar kind and were therefore merged. Other categories were of a very abstract nature (e.g. "Lifestyles") and were removed from the corpus. From the resulting collection, 50 categories were randomly chosen. A training set and a test set were then generated by randomly choosing for each set 20 images from each of the 50 categories leaving us with two mutually exclusive sets of 1000 images each.

5.2   Evaluation

For the present study we employ the two measures *recall* and *precision* to measure retrieval performance for *category searches* [7, 2]. Image queries are formed as follows: for each training image, three other images are randomly selected from the remaining set of images of that category. Each query thus consists of four images. For the k-NN and SVM model, ten negative examples are randomly chosen from the training set subject to the condition that they do not belong to the same category as the query images. Retrieval is performed from the test set and performance measured in terms of *mean average precision* which can be thought of being the area enclosed by the precision-against-recall graph and the recall axis (details in [16]).

As the Corel categorization provides us with a ground truth for each image, it is possible to automate the relevance feedback process. Among the 40 top ranked images as many at most three relevant images are randomly selected and their entries in the distance vector $d_u(i)$ set to 0. The weights are then updated as described in section 4. We allow for five such iterations of relevance feedback and evaluate performance for each iteration.

6   Results

6.1   Time Performance

All three learning methods scale linearly with the number of images n to be ranked. The performance results for different values of n, obtained with a Pentium IV 1.8GHz processor, are depicted in Figure 1. The least computationally demanding model is VSM. With the l_1-norm as the similarity metric, computation of the distance between an image and a query of size q requires but $2qm$ additions (qm additions and the same number of subtractions), where m is the length of the feature vector $\mathbf{x}$.

In the case of support vector machines, training needs to be done only once per query since relevance feedback does not affect the position of the hyperplane. With the size of each colour feature vector ranging between 184 and 2560, and only 14 training examples (4 positive examples constituting the query and 10 negative examples), the time required for training the SVM is negligible. Once trained, computing the distance from the hyperplane for each of the n images requires the evaluation of

$$f(\mathbf{x}) = \sum_{i=1}^{l_s} \alpha_i y_i k(\mathbf{x}_i, \mathbf{x}) + b \qquad (6)$$

where l_s is the number of support vectors. Since the number of training examples place an upper bound on the number of support vectors, this function evaluation is also done swiftly. The slightly worse performance of the SVM compared to VSM results from the need to evaluate the polynomial kernel function k.

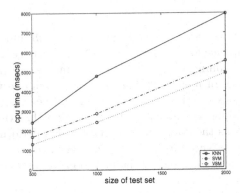

Fig. 1. All three similarity models scale linearly with the number of queries in the test collection. The computationally most expensive method is k-NN

k-NN is computationally more expensive than both SVM and VSM. This is a consequence of the fact that for each image to be ranked, its k-nearest neighbours from among the training examples need to be determined. Given t training examples (here $t = 14$), this requires $2tqm$ additions to be carried out.

6.2   Absolute Retrieval Performance and Gain through Relevance Feedback

Figure 2 depicts the precision-against-recall graphs for the three similarity models. Each graph is obtained by averaging over all 1000 queries. The upper graph in each plot represents the maximum performance that can be achieved in our retrieval model. It is obtained by determining for each individual query the feature weights that maximize mean average precision. These query-specific optima are found in turn by raster scanning the parameter space. The bottom graph represents performance prior to relevance feedback with each of the four features being given equal weight. The graph running nearly halfway between the upper bound and the baseline represents the result of five iterations of relevance feedback. The results are summarized in Table 1. We note a close similarity in performance between the three models k-NN, VSM and SVM in terms of both

Table 1. Mean average precision values for the three similarity models ($\pm$ 1 stdev)

	before RF	after five iterations	upper bound
VSM	0.15 ± 0.17	0.18 ± 0.18	0.23 ± 0.19
k-NN	0.14 ± 0.16	0.17 ± 0.18	0.21 ± 0.19
SVM	0.13 ± 0.15	0.15 ± 0.17	0.19 ± 0.18

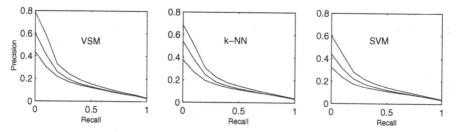

Fig. 2. Precision-against-recall graphs for the three similarity models. See text for details

absolute performance and their responsiveness to relevance feedback. The simple VSM offers a performance that is slightly superior to both k-NN and SVM.

In all three models, relevance feedback has a noticeable effect on performance, but it falls short of tuning the weights for maximum performance. In fact, when looking at the weights after five iterations, we have found that in many cases they were not closer to the optimal weights than the starting weights had been and may thus represent local optima.

Figure 3 displays the relative gain through relevance feedback for all three models. It is evident that the models exhibit a difference in terms of their convergence behaviour under relevance feedback. While in the vector space model, performance increases after the first iteration and remains stable for all subsequent iterations, both k-NN and SVM display a steady increase over the first five iterations. It is known from previous studies (e.g. [10, 4]) that negative feedback tends to keep the system in a more flexible state than does positive feedback and results in a more gradual convergence as it is observed here. Although we explicitly restrict feedback to relevant images, both k-NN and SVM do rely on the presence of negative examples, while VSM does not. The conclusion that it is therefore the set of negative examples that moderates the effect of relevance feedback in k-NN and SVM is tempting. It is worth noting, however, that the negative examples are utilized once at the beginning of the query session for k-NN distance computation and hyperplane construction, and do not affect the computation of new weights during subsequent iterations. Their primary role is thus very different from the role of negative examples fed back by the user in [10] and [4], and further tests need to be carried out to substantiate such a claim.

Although performances for the three models are very similar when averaged over all queries, the models exhibit notable differences for individual queries. In Figure 4, we have taken three colour features and plotted the resulting mean average precision values for all weight combinations. Each row corresponds to a different query. For the upper query image all three similarity models produce similar performance surfaces with roughly coincident optima. For the lower query image the performance surface obtained for the VSM differs markedly from that of the other two models, suggesting that features that works well for one similarity model may not work quite so well for another model.

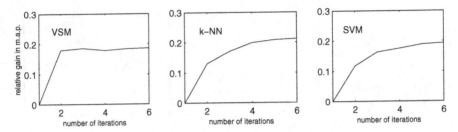

Fig. 3. Gains through relevance feedback for the three similarity models. The gradual increase for k-NN and SVM probably results from the effect of negative examples

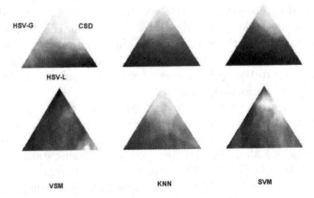

Fig. 4. Parameter simplices for three features and two butterfly queries (each row corresponding to a different query). Performance increases with decreasing gray-level. HSV-L: local HSV; HSV-G: globel HSV; CSD: colour structure descriptor

7   Conclusions

We have compared a number of performance aspects of two rather different techniques for computing similarities between images against a simple vector space model approach. The overall result from this study is that the more sophisticated learning techniques do not prove superior to the vector space model, while being computationally slightly more expensive. Both SVM and k-NN are known to work well with large sets of training examples so that one may not be able to fully exploit their potential in an interactive retrieval context where training is online involving but a small number of training examples.

All three models support an increase in performance through relevance feedback. We found that convergence for k-NN and SVM is more gradual and attributed this difference to the importance of negative examples in those models. Further investigations into the role of negative examples for a model's response to feedback are needed. In this context, the evaluation of one-class SVMs appears to be of particular interest as it relies solely on positive examples.

We have illustrated how the optimal feature combinations differ not only between queries but also between similarity models. If the set of top ranked images is sufficiently different for each model using its optimal feature combination, combining models may help increase performance yet further.

Although the four features we considered are sufficiently different to allow performance gains through relevance feedback, they are all colour representations and thus capture but a fraction of the available image information. The addition of structure and texture features will undoubtedly help clarify some of the open issues this study has raised.

Acknowledgements

This work was partially supported by the EPSRC, UK, and the ARC, Australia.

References

[1] Y Chen, X Zhou, and T S Huang. One-class SVM for learning in image retrieval. In *Proc IEEE Image processing 2001*, 2001. 457

[2] I J Cox, M L Miller, T P Minka, T V Papathomas, and P N Yianilos. The Bayesian image retrieval system, pichunter. *IEEE Transactions on Image Processing*, 9(1):20–38, 2000. 461

[3] B V Dasarathy, editor. *Nearest Neigbour (NN) Norms: NN Pattern Classification Techniques*. IEEE Computer Society Press, 1991. 457

[4] D Heesch and S Rüger. Performance boosting with three mouse clicks — relevance feedback for CBIR. In *Proceedings of the European Colloquium on IR Research 2003*. LNCS, Springer, 2003. 456, 460, 463

[5] T S Huang. Incorporating support vector machines in content-based image retrieval with relevance feedback. In *Proc IEEE Image processing 2000*, 2000. 457, 459

[6] B S Manjunath and J-R Ohm. Color and texture descriptors. *IEEE Transactions on circuits and systems for video technology*, 11:703–715, 2001. 458

[7] C Meilhac and C Nastar. Relevance feedback and category search in image databases. In *Proc. IEEE Int. Conf. Multimedia Comp. and Syst.*, pages 512–517, 1999. 461

[8] T M Mitchell. *Machine Learning*. McGraw Hill, 1997. 459

[9] H Müller, S Marchand-Maillet, and T Pun. The truth about Corel - evaluation in image retrieval. In *Proceedings of CIVR*, pages 38–49, 2002. 460

[10] H Müller, W Müller, D M Squire, M.S Marchand-Maillet, and T Pun. Strategies for positive and negative relevance feedback in image retrieval. In *Proceedings of the 15th International Conference on Pattern Recognition (ICPR 2000), IEEE, Barcelona, Spain*, 2000. 463

[11] M Pickering and S Rüger. Evaluation of key-frame based retrieval techniques for video. *submitted to Elsevier Science and accepted for publication*, 2003. 457

[12] Y Rui and T S Huang. A novel relevance feedback technique in image retrieval. In *ACM Multimedia (2)*, pages 67–70, 1999. 456

[13] G Salton and M J Gill. *Introduction to Modern Information Retrieval*. McGraw-Hill Book Co., 1983. 456

[14] B Schölkopf, J C Platt, J T Shawe, A J Smola, and R C Williamson. Estimation the support of a high-dimensional distribution. *Technical Report MSR-TR-99-87, Microsoft Research*, 1999. 457

[15] V N Vapnik. *The Nature of Statistical Learning Theory*. Springer Verlag, 1995. 456, 458

[16] E M Voorhees and D Harman. Overview of the eigth Text REtrieval Conference (TREC-8). In *Proc. TREC*, pages 1–33 and A.17 – A.18, 1999. 461

EBS k-d Tree: An Entropy Balanced Statistical k-d Tree for Image Databases with Ground-Truth Labels

Grant J. Scott and Chi-Ren Shyu

Department of Computer Engineering and Computer Science
University of Missouri-Columbia
Columbia, MO 65211-2060, USA

Abstract. In this paper we present a new image database indexing structure - Entropy Balanced Statistical (EBS) k-d Tree. This indexing mechanism utilizes the statistical properties and ground-truth labeling of image data for efficient and accurate searches. It is particularly valuable in the domains of medical and biological image database retrieval, where ground-truth labeling are available and archived with the images. The EBS k-d tree is an extension to the statistical k-d tree that attempts to optimize a multi-dimensional decision tree based on the fundamental principles from which it is constructed. Our approach is to develop and validate the notion of an entropy balanced statistical based decision tree. It is shown that by making balanced split decisions in the growth processing of the tree, that the average search depth is improved and the worst case search depth is usually dramatically improved. Furthermore, a method for linking the tree leaves into a non-linear structure was developed to increase the n-nearest neighbor similarity search accuracy. We have applied this to a large-scale medical diagnostic image database and have shown increases in search speed and accuracy over an ordinary distance-based search and the original statistical k-d tree index.

Keywords: Statistical k-d Tree, entropy, multi-dimensional index, image database, content-based image retrieval (CBIR)

1 Introduction

In the past decade, a large number of approaches to CBIR have been proposed and implemented in research prototypes and commercial products. Many great contributions have been made by researchers in the areas of computer vision, image processing, pattern recognition, and database. An in-depth summary and survey of CBIR systems is provided by Smeulders *et al.* [17]. Among those systems surveyed, feature selection (dimensionality reduction) and database indexing are two major approaches to increase retrieval precision and to speed up the database search. To achieve these goals, there has developed an ever increasing need for multi-dimensional indexing structures that are both fast and accurate. One such multidimensional indexing structure is the k-d tree [3]. A k-d

E. M. Bakker et al. (Eds.): CIVR 2003, LNCS 2728, pp. 467–477, 2003.

tree is a multidimensional search tree which uses a set of k keys to partition k dimensional space. The premise of the k-d tree is that there exist of set of k keys, $K_1, K_2, ..., K_k$, upon which a data set of records can be partitioned. The key that determines the navigation decision is dictated by the depth level the search is currently at in the tree.

Prominent systems that deal with natural images [1] include, but not limited to, IBM's QBIC [5] and ImageRover [14]. Both apply principal component analysis (PCA) to reduce dimensionality, then utilize R^*-tree and k-d tree. respectively. CBIR systems designed for ground-truth labeled images include, but not limited to, CANDID [8] and Yale University's cardiac MRI [12] systems. One of the major differences between the CBIR systems for the general case and those designed specifically for the medical domains is that the images for the medical case have specific diagnoses associated with them, these ground-truth diagnoses being supplied by a physician when the images are archived. The diagnoses serve as class labels during the training phase and are also subsequently used during system evaluation. The rich knowledge archived with the images should be used for both feature selection, as well as for database indexing.

Variants of k-d tree related to CBIR include, but not limited to, the *adaptive* k-d tree [13] and the *statistical* k-d tree [15]. Through inspection of the previous algorithms and underlying statistics, it can be seen that instead of an optimized decision tree, an inefficient decision tree may be built. When unbalanced trees are built, they can lead to inefficient retrievals. Furthermore, when a search locates a targeting leaf node that contains an insufficient number of images for retrieval, the inclusion of neighboring nodes is needed. However, nodes linked to the targeting node are not necessary closest to the query point. We have developed possible solutions to these shortcomings, and are presented in the paper as follows. Section 2 provides an overview of the statistical theories and equations used in the tree development. Section 3 covers the motivation and methods for optimizing the statistical k-d tree. Section 4 describes the implementation and benefits of linking the leaves with priority queues. We report our experimental results in Section 5. And finally, we conclude this paper in Section 6 with summary and future work.

2   The Statistics of a Decision Tree

The statistical k-d tree partitions some hyper-cube in a k-dimensional space into various sub-spaces, each containing a sub-set of the original data population. The original k-dimensional space is represented by the entire collection of training samples, and can be partitioned as a set of disjoint classes, represented as $A_1, A_2, ..., A_k$. An obstacle to overcome is the fact that rarely are these classes linearly separable from each other in the context of CBIR. However, by using the statistical properties of the training data, a more efficient and accurate k-d tree can be developed.

---

[1] We roughly categorize images into two classes: "natural" and "ground-truth labeled."

There are two primary statistical concepts from which this tree has evolved, Bayes' Theorem and Shannon's Information Theory. Bayes' Theorem provides a method to determine the probability of some event A_j given an event B that has $P(B) \neq 0$ [10]. Bayes allows us to calculate the probability that some set of features are a member of each class in the hyperspace. From the *Total Probability Theorem*

$$P(B) = \sum_{j=1}^{k} P(B|A_j)P(A_j),\tag{1}$$

and given,

$$P(B|A) = \frac{P(B,A)}{P(A)},\tag{2}$$

Bayes rule can be derived as

$$P(A_j|B) = \frac{P(B|A_j)P(A_j)}{P(B)},\tag{3}$$

where $P(B)$ is the probability density function (*pdf*), see [19] or [10] for an detailed derivation.

In our statistical k-d tree the leaves contain all the data points. As such, given a feature vector the probability of that feature vector being in leaf, j, can be expressed,

$$P(Leaf_j) = \sum_{i=1}^{k} P(Leaf_j, Class_i).\tag{4}$$

Given the joint probability of $Leaf_j$ and $Class_i$ as

$$P(Leaf_j, Class_i) = P(Leaf_j|Class_i)P(Class_i),\tag{5}$$

the probability $P(Leaf_j)$ is just dependent on finding $P(Leaf_j|Class_i)$.

So the task becomes calculating this probability. There are two primary approaches that can derive this probability, using the statistical properties of the distribution of data, or calculating direct probabilities from the data. In general, a good method is to utilize the statistical mean, variance and a *pdf* of a specific distribution. In contrast, if the statistical distribution of the data does not fit in a specific distribution model, the direct probabilities should be calculated. Direct probability calculation, while simpler, can lead to over-fitting the data and a loss of generalization in the tree. For this experiment a normal distribution *pdf* was used for all test cases. Therefore,

$$P(Leaf_j|Class_i) = \prod_{m=1}^{k} \int_{\max(a_T^m, C_{i,L}^m)}^{\min(a_T^m, C_{i,R}^m)} f_i^m(a_m)da_m,\tag{6}$$

where a_T^m is the threshold that bounds a leaf for feature m [15], was pulled from published normal distribution integral values stored in a "look-up-table". In equation (6), the $C_{i,L}^m$ and the $C_{i,R}^m$ represent the bounds of the entire $Class_i$.

From Shannon's Information Theory we know that statistical *entropy* is a measure of the uncertainty of an event [19]. Entropy is defined as

$$H = -\int_x p(x) \ln p(x) dx,\qquad(7)$$

and from [15] we have the entropy of a leaf in the statistical k-d tree as

$$H(Leaf) = -\sum_{i=1}^{L} P(Class_i|Leaf) \log P(Class_i|Leaf).\qquad(8)$$

As the entropy is a measure of the uncertainty, or randomness, of the leaf, we must seek to minimize this uncertainty. This will allow confidence in the contents of the sub-space bounded by the search path through the tree. Shyu et al. offers the idea that a node of the statistical k-d tree should split into two children if their weighted entropy sum is less than the original leaf. The weighted sum of the children can be calculated as

$$H_{children} = \sum_{j=1}^{2} P(Leaf_j)H(Leaf_j)\qquad(9)$$

[15]. From equation (9) we can identify a single child's weight sum component as

$$H_{\sigma^j} = P(Leaf_j)H(Leaf_j).\qquad(10)$$

From equation (10) the desired attribute a^* and threshold t^* that best balances the split between the children is

$$(a^*, t^*) = \operatorname{argmin}_{(a,t)}\left(|H_{\sigma^{right}} - H_{\sigma^{left}}|\right).\qquad(11)$$

In our new approach with the EBS k-d tree, each split decision is chosen on feature a^* at threshold t^* such that equation (11) is optimized for that node.

3   Optimizing the Entropy of a Statistical k-d Tree

The original method of building the statistical k-d tree was to seek the split with maximum entropy reduction for each node by comparing the parent entropy to possible child node pairs. The effect that can be observed is a series of inefficient decisions that simply shave a few data points out of a sub-space at a time, resulting in deep branches in the tree. The true optimal solution would compare $n!$ builds of the tree, with n as the number of data points. Obviously, with thousands or millions of data points, the computationally exhaustive method is intractable[9]. Our strategy of making the decision of which feature and threshold to use is to take the best decision threshold that evenly splits entropy between two children, as defined in equations (9), (10) and (11). This decision must still be bound by the original constraint of reducing the total entropy from parent to children. This helps to limit the depth and create a more balanced tree, in the sense of the entropy decisions. The result is a tree that is more balanced in terms of the entropy upon which the statistical k-d tree is built. If this results in both a shorter maximum leaf depth and average leaf depth, then the tree has been improved by decreasing both the worst-case and average search times.

Our algorithm for building an entropy balanced search tree closely follows standard decision tree top-down induction[9]: read and calculate a priori probabilities of data, load data into a tree root node, call a recursive node splitting algorithm until the tree is complete, then save tree to disk. The recursive splitting of the tree nodes is the key to growing the balanced tree, provided by the entropy balanced split algorithm (see ENTROPY BALANCED SPLIT ALGORITHM).

ENTROPY BALANCED SPLIT ALGORITHM

1. IF node contains a single class, return (RECURSION STOP);
2. Calculate $ParentEntropy$;
3. Set $minVariance$ to some arbitrary large number;
4. FOR each $feature$, $f_1, f_2, ..., f_k$;
5.   FOR each $decisionThresh$ from $min+increment$ to $max-increment$;
6.   Calculate Eq. 10 for $left$ and $right$;
7.   Calculate $|H_{\sigma^{right}} - H_{\sigma^{left}}|$;
8. Split Node using two children $left$ and $right$ with minimum value from step 7 and satisfies the constraint, $H_{Children} <= H(leaf) - \delta$;
9. If a suitable split was found, call Split Algorithm on $left$ and $right$ child.

The above algorithm effectively performs the top down induction of an EBS k-d tree. Steps 4 through 7 perform the search through the current node's hyper space to find the solution to equation (11). There are two points at which recursion terminates, when a node is created with a single class and when the improvement from parent to children does not improve by at least δ. Here, δ is the improvement threshold required for a split.

4 Priority Queues for Leaf Traversal

Though statistical k-d tree improves upon the traditional k-d tree accuracy, accuracy deficiencies still exist as a result of the leaf linking method. The accuracy problem results when a search leads to an un-populated area of the feature space, or outside of the feature space all together. Searches for n-$nearest$ $neighbors$ traverse the tree to the leaf, then scan in both directions along the linked list of leaves creating the sorted result set. As illustrated in Figure 1(b), neighbors in the linked list are not always neighbors in k-dimensional space, depicted in Figure 1(a). A search into leaf $L5$ will go onto search leaves $L4$ and $L6$ and

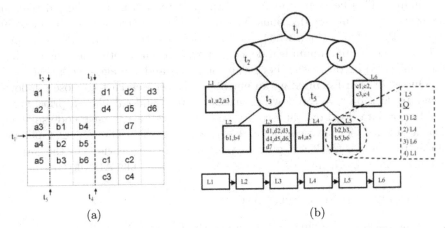

Fig. 1. 2-D Space and Partitioning; (a) the data population in 2-D space and decision thresholds for node splitting; (b) the resulting tree from the thresholds, depth first ordered linked leaves, and an example node priority queue

possibly return a result set before it reaches node *L2*, its adjacent neighbor in k-dimensional space.

As a remedy to this linear scanning condition, a new method for traversing from leaf to leaf while building a sorted similarity result set was developed. To implement this idea, a priority queue was built into each leaf node at build time. The priority queue of a node can be various sizes[2], we chose size of 2 x (dimensionality). This allows the leaf to reference in multiple directions, where appropriate, and provide adequate queue length. Figure 1(b) shows a possible priority queue of *Leaf5* using a queue size of four. The method used for filling the priority queues was the calculation of prototypes, or centroids, for all leaf nodes; then each leaf ranks and stores the similarity of other leaves. This similarity is calculated as $S = d(p_c, p_n)$, where p_c and p_n are the prototype of the current and neighboring node respectively and d is the distance measure most applicable to the data. This results in nodes that are close in the k-dimensional hyperspace being linked together.

If all data is overlapping, the resulting priority queues would form a network, or graph structure, that traverses the entire leaf population. However, when significant gaps exist in the data population's feature space, the resulting leaf traversing structure can form two or more disjoint priority queue networks. This is not interpreted as a shortcoming due to the fact that a similarity search most likely should not return results that would have to cross such a gap in the feature space. Our n-nearest neighbor search first traverses the EBS k-d tree to the leaf node. In this node all data points are added in sorted order to the search result

---

[2] The actual implementation bounds the minimum and maximum queue size. These bounds would be variable based on various parameters of the system (i.e. database size, dimensionality of data, etc.).

set. If the result set is not of the desired size, the search moves into the current node's priority queue, Q_0. To execute a search through Q_0, each listed node has its data points added to the sorted result set. If the desired result set size is not met, the search moves into the priority queues of the nodes in Q_0. This is repeated deeper into the queue network until the desired number of results is found, or all connected leaves are visited.

5   Experimental Results

We have applied our new EBS k-d tree to three sets of high-dimensional data. The first set contains 1826 HRCT images of lungs collected from the routine clinical processes at the University of Missouri Hospital and diagnosed/labeled by radiologists. By applying feature extraction algorithms to capture the presence of visual categories used by the physicians[3], each image is represented by a 40 dimensional vector. Each vector is labeled according to one of 23 possible disease diagnosis, or classes. The second data set is obtained from the first set using sequential forward selection [11] and reduced to 13 dimensions. The third set of data contains 10,000 15-D synthesized data points comprising two 5,000 point classes, where each feature of each class fits a Gaussian distribution model.

There are two experiments conducted for each data set, efficiency and accuracy. Efficiency is measured using leaf density, average and maximum search depth. We have defined efficiency to be

$$Efficiency = \beta\left(\frac{\lceil \log_\tau(N/\varrho)\rceil}{d_{avg}}\right) + \alpha\left(\frac{\lceil \log_\tau(N/\varrho)\rceil}{d_{max}}\right); \qquad (12)$$

where τ is the number of children for each internal tree node, N is the size of the entire data population, and d_{avg} and d_{max} are the average and worst-case search depths, respectively. ϱ is the average data points per leaf, or density, and α and β are the weighting components assigned to each quotient and constrained to $\alpha + \beta = 1$.[4]

To measure retrieval precisions, we apply an *average precision at seen relevant image approach* [2], a different approach from the traditional ones [18]. Let $t = \{I_1, I_2, I_3, ..., I_{n_t}\}$ be the set of images retrieved and displayed to the users and $r \subseteq t$ be the set of relevant images [5] from t. $s(r, i)$ returns the rank of the $i - th$ element in r. The precision is then computed by the following equation:

$$Precision = \frac{\sum_{i=1}^{n_r} i/s(r, i)}{min(n_r, n_t)}. \qquad (13)$$

This precision measurement favors the retrieval results that retrieve relevant images quickly.

---

[3] A detailed description of the HRCT images and the feature extraction methods can be found in [16].

[4] For our experiments we set $\alpha = \beta = 0.5$, giving them equal influence on the efficiency measure.

[5] A database image is relevant if the image has the same diagnosis as the query image.

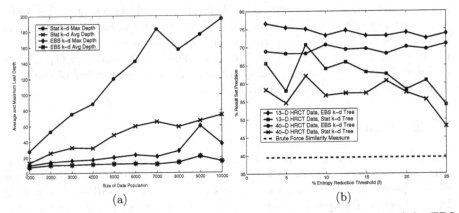

Fig. 2. Depth and Precision: (a) shows the superior search depths of the EBS k-d tree when compared to a normal statistical k-d tree, using a 15-D data population increasing from 1000 to 10,000; (b) a comparison of the precision of both a EBS k-d and normal statistical k-d tree, across varying entropy reduction thresholds

5.1 Shorter Search Depths

As stated previously, the primary goal of increasing search tree efficiency was achieved by reducing the depth by increasing balance. Two trees were built for each data set using identical code, except for the decision basis of node splitting and the manner of leaf linking. All trees used a stored Look-Up-Table (LUT) value for the distribution's statistical integration value, as defined in equation (6). The data set, that most accentuates the depth improvements possible by EBS k-d tree, was composed of two Gaussian clouds in 15 dimensional feature space of 5,000 points each. The worst case search time[6] of the unbalanced tree is 196, while the worst case for balanced tree is only 37 - an 81.1% improvement. Search time improvements based on the average leaf depth are also substantial; 73.67 for the unbalanced and 14.93 for the balanced - or 79.7% search time reduction. Figure 2(a) demonstrates the superior ability of the EBS approach to maintain search depths as population size increases. The 13-D HRCT data showed a reduction from 12.3 to 10.7 in average search depth, and 31 to 15 in maximum search depth.

5.2 Increased N-nearest Neighbor Precision

By utilizing priority queues as a leaf linking structure, we were able to improve the precision, as defined in equation (13). In our test of the 13-D HRCT data, the EBS k-d tree provided an average precision improvement of 19% over the unbalanced statistical k-d tree through the entropy split thresholds tested. Figure 2(b) provides a comparison of the precisions as the splitting threshold, ϱ

---

[6] Time, in this case, is measured in depth, or comparisons needed to navigate to leaf.

from Section 3, is changed from 2.5% to 25%. Also provided is the HRCT data without dimensionality reduction, and the precision of the brute force distance similarity measure. The data was tested by randomly removing 10% of the vectors from each class and building a tree with the remaining 90%, then executing a 20-nearest neighbor search with each of the test vectors. When the precision improvement is coupled with the 51.6% improvement in worst case search depth, the entropy balanced index provides a sufficient improvement over the unbalanced tree for the 13-D HRCT data. Once a search reaches the partitioned data space, the same similarity measure used for brute force searches is employed.

6   Summary and Future Work

It has been shown that building a Entropy Balanced Statistical k-d tree is superior to a standard statistical k-d tree and plain distance comparison methods. By improving the node splitting criteria, the resulting decision tree more efficiently partitions the data in feature space. The approach has been tested with a range of data including purely Gaussian distributed data clusters and data generated from feature extraction algorithms applied to real diagnostic medical images. The primary goal of our building the EBS k-d trees was decreasing the search depth of the tree and achieving an increase in the n-nearest neighbor search accuracy. Scanning of the trees continuously showed improvement in both worst case leaf depth and average leaf depth. This directly translates into lower cost searches into the tree.

The linear linking of the leaves into a depth-first ordered list was found to be a major hinderance to accuracy. This confines the multi-dimensional data to a bi-directional linear search, once the leaves are reached. The reduction from k-dimensions to a linear list is the cause of inaccuracy in many similarity searches. By implementing a ranked non-linear structure to link the leaves, accuracy has improved.

A possible modification to the internal node structure that allows thresholds across multiple attributes in a single decision node might further improve balance and search times. The impact of insertions and deletions was not considered in these experiments. Given the method and time it takes to build the search structure, data points would just be inserted into, or deleted from, the leaf node. This insertion/deletion could then be made to the collection data set used to build the tree. By rebuilding the tree on a periodic basis, these insertions and deletions will not affect the overall accuracy or performance. From our analysis the EBS k-d tree can be applied to image databases with ground-truth labels, especially in the medical and biological imaging domain. In future work, experiments will apply the EBS k-d Tree to collections of unlabeled images by applying clustering algorithms and utilizing cluster labels.

References

[1] S. Arya, D. M. Mount, N. S. Netanyahu, R. Silverman, and A. Y. Wu, An optimal algorithm for approximate nearest neighbor searching in fixed dimensions, *Proc. ACM-SIAM Symp. on Discrete Alg.*, 1994: 573-582.

[2] R. Baeza-Yates and B. Ribeiro-Neto, *Modern Information Retrieval*, 1st Edition, 1999, ACM Press/ Addison Wesley. 473

[3] J. L. Bentley, Multidimensional binary search trees in database applications, in *IEEE Trans. on Software Engineering*, Vol. SE-5, No. 4, July 1979. 467

[4] D. Comer, The ubiquitous B-Tree," in *Computing Surveys*, Vol. 11, No. 2, June 1979.

[5] M. Flickner, H. Sawhney, W. Niblack, J. Ashley, Q. Huang, B. Dom, M. Gorkani, J. Hafner, D. Lee, D. Petkovic, D. Steele, and P. Yanker, Query by image and video content: The QBIC system, *IEEE Computer*, September 1995: 23-32. 468

[6] K. Fukunaga, *Introduction to Statistical Pattern Recognition*, Academic Press, 1990.

[7] R. A. Johnson and D. W. Wichern, *Applied Multivariate Statistical Analysis*, Fourth Edition, Prentice Hall, 1998.

[8] P. M. Kelly, T. M. Cannon, and D. R. Hush, Query by image example: the CAN-DID approach, in *SPIE Vol. 2420 Storage and Retrieval for Image and Video Databases III*, San Jose, CA, 1995: 238-248. 468

[9] L. Grewe and A. C. Kak, Interactive learning of a multi-attribute hash table classifier for fast object recognition, *Computer Vision and Image Understanding*, Vol. 61, No. 3, 1995: 387-416. 470, 471

[10] J. S. Milton and J. C. Arnold, *Introduction to Probability and Statistics: Principles and Applications for Engineering and Computing Sciences*, 3rd Edition, Irwin McGraw-Hill, 1995. 469

[11] P. Pudil, J. Novovicova and J. Kittler, Floating search methods in feature selection, *Pattern Recognition Letters*, 15, 1994: 1119-1125. 473

[12] G. P. Robinson, H. D. Tagare, J. S. Duncan, and C. C. Jaffe, Medical image collection indexing: Shape-based retrieval using KD-Tree, *Computerized Medical Imaging and Graphics*, Vol. 20, No. 4, 1996: 209-217. 468

[13] H. Samet, The quadtree and related hierarchical data structure, in *ACM Computing Survey*, Vol. 16, No. 2, 1984, 187-260. 468

[14] S. Sclaroff, L. Taycher, and M. La Cascia, ImageRover: A content-based image browser for the world wide web, *Proc. IEEE Workshop on Content-based Access of Image and Video Libraies*, June 1997: 2-9. 468

[15] C. R. Shyu, C. E. Brodley, A. C. Kak, A. Kosaka, A. M. Aisen and L. S. Broderick, ASSERT: a physician-in-the-loop content-based retrieval system for HRCT image databases, in *Computer Vision and Image Understanding*, Vol. 75, Nos. 1/2, July/August, 1999: 111-132. 468, 469, 470

[16] C. R. Shyu, C. Pavlopoulou, A. C. Kak, C. E. Brodely, and L. S. Broderick, Using human perceptual categories for content-based retrieval from a medical image database, *Computer Vision and Image Understanding*, Vol. 88, Issue 3, 2002: 119-151. 473

[17] A. W. M. Smeulders, M. Worring, S. Santini, A. Gupta, and R. Jain, Content-based image retrieval at the end of the early years, *IEEE Trans. on Pattern and Machine Intelligence*, Vol. 22, No. 12, December 2000: 1349-1380. 467

[18] J. R. Smith, Image Retrieval Evaluation, *Proc. IEEE Workshop of Content-Based Access of Image and Video Databases*, Santa Barbara, CA, June 1998: 112-113. 473

[19] S. Theodoridis and K. Koutroumbas, *Pattern Recognition*, Academic Press, 1999. 469, 470

Fast Search in Large-Scale Image Database Using Vector Quantization

Hangjun Ye and Guangyou Xu

Department of Computer Science and Technology, Tsinghua University
100084 Beijing, China
yehangjun98@mails.tsinghua.edu.cn
xgy-dcs@mail.tsinghua.edu.cn

Abstract. Practical content-based image retrieval systems require efficient indexing schemes for fast searches. Researchers have proposed many methods using space and data partitioning for exact similarity searches. However, traditional indexing methods perform poorly and will degrade to simple sequential scans at high dimensionality - that is so-called "curse of dimensionality". Recently, several filtering approaches based on vector approximation (VA) were proposed and showed promising performance. In fact, existing VA-based methods assume independent distribution of dataset and utilize scalar quantizer to partition each dimension of data space. In real databases, however, images are from different categories and often clustered. In this paper, a novel indexing method using vector quantization is proposed. This approach introduces a vector quantizer to partition data space. It assumes a Gaussian mixture distribution and estimates this distribution through Expectation-Maximization (EM) method. Experiments on a large database of 275,465 images demonstrated a remarkable improvement of retrieval efficiency.

1 Introduction

Content-based image retrieval (CBIR) has been an important research area in computer vision for over decade [1]. CBIR systems usually represent each image as a high-dimensional feature vector and use distance metric to measure similarity between each pair of feature vectors. The most common retrieval process is performed by similarity query, which accesses the database via similarity measures to find the most similar images to the given query image. Similarity search in image databases is typically implemented by find the k closest feature vectors to the feature vector of query image, which is called the k nearest neighbor (NN) search problem.

The k-NN search problem can be solved by a simple sequential scan over the entire database. Feature vectors are ranked by the ascending order of the distance to the query vector, and the first k vectors are the k-NNs. It will be feasible if there are only thousands of images. However, when the size of the dataset grows and the dimen-

E. M. Bakker et al. (Eds.): CIVR 2003, LNCS 2728, pp. 477-487, 2003.

sionality of feature space is high, the sequential scan will be computationally unbearable. For interactive image retrieval system with relevance feedback [2], the user need get intermediate results after each round of feedback, and so the response time for each round of similarity query will be critical for a successful system. Consequently, a multidimensional index structure is required for a practical CBIR system.

The multidimensional index structure has been an active research issue in database and multimedia for many years. Researchers have proposed many methods based on space and data partitioning for k-NN searches, such as gridfile [3], K-D-B-tree [4], R^*-tree [5], SR-tree [6], etc. These traditional approaches achieved good performance for low dimensionality (e.g. less than ten). Recent studies [7][8], however, showed that the traditional approaches would not do better than brute-force sequential scans over entire dataset when the dimensionality of feature vectors was high enough (e.g. over several tens) - that is so-called "curse of dimensionality".

In this paper, a novel VQ-based indexing scheme for retrieval in large-scale image databases is proposed to aim at the "curse of dimensionality". This approach introduces a vector quantizer instead of simple scalar quantization. It assumes that images in a database are generated from a mixture of Gaussians and utilizes EM method to estimate the distribution of dataset. In theory, any distribution can be represented as a mixture of Gaussians [9], and so this approach deals with real-world datasets from arbitrary distribution reasonably well. This paper is organized as follow. Section 2 reviews the related work. In section 3 the proposed approach is described in detail. Experimental results are shown and compared to existing methods in Section 4. Final discussions and conclusions are given in Section 5.

2   VA-Based Approaches

Many approaches have been proposed for the k-NN search problem. But traditional multidimensional index structures face the same difficulty - "curse of dimensionality", which cause these approaches are outperform by simple sequential scans at high dimensionality. Recently, some new kinds of methods have been employed to aim at the curse of dimensionality. Among these methods, the filtering approach based on vector approximation (VA) is the only one that does better than brute-force sequential scans for exact similarity searches. All other approaches are targeted at the approximate similarity searches.

The VA-file approach proposed by Weber *et al.* [7] is the first filtering method based on vector approximation. This approach divides the data space into 2^b rectangle cells, where b is the number of bits specified by user for the approximation of feature vectors. Each dimension of data space is allocated b_i bits and divided into 2^{bi} equal populated slices, where $\sum_{i=1}^{d} b_i = b$, and d donates the dimensionality of the data space. Instead of hierarchically organizing these cells like in gridfiles or R-trees, the VA-File allocates a unique bit-string of length b for each cell, and approximates data points that fall into a cell by that bit-string. The VA-File itself is simply an array of these compact, geometric approximations. The k-NN searches are performed by scanning the entire approximation file firstly, and by excluding the vast majority of vectors from the search based only on these approximations (filtering step). Fig. 1 (left) shows an example of VA-file partition for a 2-d dataset.

The k-NN searches in a VA-file have two major phases. The first phase is the filtering step. Firstly, the entire approximation file is scanned sequentially and lower and upper bounds on the distance of each vector to the query vector are computed. If an approximation is encountered such that its lower bound exceeds the kth smallest upper bound found so far, the corresponding object can be eliminated since at least k better candidates exist. The second phase is accessing real feature vectors. After the filtering step, only a small fraction of candidates remain. These candidates are then visited in the ascending order of the lower bound on the distance to the query vector, and then the exact distances to the query vector are computed. In fact, not all candidates must be accessed. If a lower bound is encountered that exceeds the kth nearest distance seen so far, the whole query process is completed and the exact k-NNs are found.

The performance of the VA-file approach mainly depends on the filtering efficiency and the filtering efficiency relies on the precision of the lower and upper bounds determined in the first phase. Higher precision of bounds results in more filtering and therefore faster queries. In particular, the precision of the lower bound directly affects the number of vectors visited in the second phase. Therefore, tighter lower bounds can reduce the random disk accesses, which dominate the query time. Several approaches [10][11][12], which are extended from the original VA-file approach, have been proposed to aim at tighter bounds.

The VA-file approach assumes independent and uniform distribution and partitions each dimension independently. Hence the VA-file approach performs well especially for the data with independent and uniform distribution but the performance will degrade if the data is not independently and uniformly distributed.

Ferhatosmanoglu et al. [10] proposed the VA$^+$-file approach to handle non-uniform datasets. The VA$^+$-file approach decorrelates dimensions by the Karhunen Loeve Transform (KLT) firstly, and then non-uniformly allocates bits for each dimension according to its energy. While keeping the total bits allocated for all dimensions unchanged, the dimensions with larger standard deviation (energy) get more bits. The VA$^+$-file approach approximates the data more accurately and achieves promising results. Fig. 1 (middle) shows an example of VA$^+$-file partition for the same 2-d dataset. It's well known that the KLT reduces only the linear dependency among dimensions, such as for joint Gaussian distributions. For more general distribution, the dependency is non-linear and therefore KLT on whole dataset is not a proper approach. In fact, the VA$^+$-file approach also assumes independent distribution of data and partitions each dimension independently, except that the assumption and partition are performed in the transformed domain.

Wu et al. [11] proposed a new approach for non-uniform distribution. The main idea of the method is to model the marginal distributions of the data using a mixture of Gaussians and to use the estimated parameters of the model to partition the data space. By adapting the construction of approximations to data's marginal distributions, the proposed method overcomes the sensitivity of index performance to data's distribution, thus resulting in a significant improvement compared with the original VA-file approach. The Gaussian mixture model (GMM) can represent marginal distributions of data accurately. However, representing joint data distribution by marginal distributions assumes that the dataset is independently distributed too, and thus this approach cannot gain from dependency of dimensions.

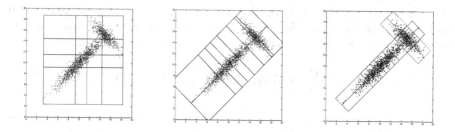

Fig. 1. Partition of a 2-d dataset in VA-file approach (left), VA$^+$-file approach (middle) and VQ-based approach (right)

3   VQ-Based Indexing Scheme

The major drawback in existing VA-based approaches is the simple model of data distribution and thus the simple partition of data space. These approaches represent joint data distribution by marginal distributions and partition data space by scalar quantization.

The VA-file approach assumes independent and uniform distribution and partitions each dimension independently. The assumption of independent distribution results in representing joint data distribution by marginal distributions and each partitioning can be considered as a scalar quantizer carried on each dimension independently. The scalar quantization is suitable for only independent distribution and will get rather large quantization distortion for dependent distribution. In term of quantization distortion, vector quantization always outperforms scalar quantization and will gain from dependency of dimensions [13][14]. For VA-based indexing approaches, less quantization distortion means tighter bounds and therefore better performance.

The VA$^+$-file approach achieves significant improvements over the original VA-file approach for its reasonable assumption of the dependence of data dimensions. It employs KLT to reduce the correlation among dimensions and independently partitions each dimension in the transformed domain by scalar quantization. KLT is successful in decorrelating dimensions of data but considers the entire dataset from a single component or cluster. In fact, KLT assumes the single Gaussian distribution and cannot reveal the intrinsic correlation of dimensions when the data are from multiple clusters. In real-world databases, however, images are from different categories and often clustered. KLT on entire dataset will play improper hypothesis on real-world image databases and lead to imprecise approximation of image data.

The approach proposed by Wu *et al.* can represent marginal distributions of data accurately. However, this method also assumes that the dataset is independently distributed and employs scalar quantization to partition data space. Representing joint data distribution by marginal distributions and scalar quantization cannot gain from dependency of dimensions.

In this paper, a more reasonable assumption is adopted that the dataset is generated from a mixture model with multiple Gaussians. The Gaussian mixture model (GMM) is employed to estimate the joint data distribution instead of marginal distribution. After the parameters of data distribution are estimated, a vector quantization (VQ) method is introduced to partition the data space, which can achieve more accurate vector approximation and less quantization distortion. The *pdf* of data is:

$$f(\mathbf{x}) = \sum_{i=1}^{K} p_i G(\mathbf{x}|\boldsymbol{\mu}_i, \boldsymbol{\Sigma}_i), \sum_{i=1}^{K} p_i = 1, p_i \geq 0 .$$ (1)

where K is the total number of Gaussians, p_i is the prior probability of the ith Gaussian C_i, and $G(\mathbf{x}|\boldsymbol{\mu}_i, \boldsymbol{\Sigma}_i)$ is the Gaussian *pdf* of C_i with mean vector $\boldsymbol{\mu}_i$ and covariance matrix $\boldsymbol{\Sigma}_i$.

There are several desirable properties of the Gaussian mixture model suitable for k-NN searches in real-world datasets:

1. Expressive power: theoretically any distribution can be represented as a mixture of Gaussians [5].
2. Efficient solutions: existing approaches can estimate the Gaussian mixture model efficiently, such as K-Means [15] or EM [16].
3. Suitability to clustering: each Gaussian can be considered as a single cluster.
4. Suitability to indexing: the original approaches can be adopted on each single Gaussian.

The total number of Gaussians K is specified by users, and then the weight (prior probability) p_i, the mean vector $\boldsymbol{\mu}_i$, and the covariance matrix $\boldsymbol{\Sigma}_i$ of each Gaussian need be determined to approximate the data distribution. Like the Maximum-Likelihood (ML) estimation, the Expectation-Maximization (EM) algorithm is a general method for parameter estimation, which is suitable for that some data are unobserved. For a Gaussian mixture model, each vector $\mathbf{x}$ belongs to one cluster softly, that means, with a probability. These probabilistic memberships are hidden data and cannot be observed directly. They are determined by the parameters of Gaussians:

$$f_i(\mathbf{x}) = f(C_i|\mathbf{x}) = p_i G(\mathbf{x}|\boldsymbol{\mu}_i, \boldsymbol{\Sigma}_i) \Big/ \sum_{h=1}^{K} p_h G(\mathbf{x}|\boldsymbol{\mu}_h, \boldsymbol{\Sigma}_h) .$$ (2)

where $f_i(\mathbf{x})$ is the probabilistic membership that vector $\mathbf{x}$ belongs to C_i.

Let $\boldsymbol{\Theta} = \{(p_i, \boldsymbol{\mu}_i, \boldsymbol{\Sigma}_i), i = 1, ..., K\}$ be the set of Gaussian mixture model parameters and the log-likelihood function of data in the dataset D is:

$$L(\Theta) = \sum_{x \in D} \log \left(\sum_{i=1}^{K} p_i G(x | \mu_i, \Sigma_i) \right) . \tag{3}$$

EM algorithm first initializes the estimation of parameters Θ by some approaches, such as K-Means, and then updates the estimation iteratively by a two-step procedure:

E-step: for each vector $x \in D$, compute the probabilistic membership that x belongs to Gaussian C_i:

$$f_i^j(x) = p_i^j G(x | \mu_i^j, \Sigma_i^j) \Big/ \sum_{h=1}^{K} p_h^j G(x | \mu_h^j, \Sigma_h^j) . \tag{4}$$

M-step: update mixture model parameters:

$$p_i^{j+1} = \sum_{x \in D} f_i^j(x) \Big/ |D|, \mu_i^{j+1} = \sum_{x \in D} f_i^j(x) \cdot x \Big/ \sum_{x \in D} f_i^j(x)$$

$$\Sigma_i^{j+1} = \sum_{x \in D} f_i^j(x)(x - \mu_i^{j+1})(x - \mu_i^{j+1})^T \Big/ \sum_{x \in D} f_i^j(x) \tag{5}$$

where the superscript j indicates the j-th iteration. The iterative algorithm stops when the change of log-likelihood $L(\Theta)$ is small enough.

The Gaussian mixture model estimated via EM algorithm is used for constructing the index of dataset. Firstly, an optimal decision rule is presented to classify vectors into appropriate cluster:

$$g_i(x) = \log p_i - \left(\log |\Sigma_i| + (x - \mu_i)^T \Sigma_i^{-1} (x - \mu_i) \right) \Big/ 2 . \tag{6}$$

The vector x is assigned to the cluster C_h which maximizes Equation (6). In fact, it's the Bayes decision rule for minimum error.

As discussed before, KLT is successful for data generated from a single Gaussian and so it's employed to decorrelate each Gaussian cluster. The total VQ-based indexing algorithm is described as follow:

1. Use EM algorithm to determine a best-fit Gaussian mixture model for the image database.
2. Classify each vector into a Gaussian cluster via the Bayes decision rule for minimum error.
3. Decorrelate each Gaussian cluster by KLT.
4. Allocate bits for each dimension non-uniformly according to its standard deviation. The allocation is done for all clusters respectively.
5. Quantize dimensions for all clusters respectively and generate approximations for each vector.

Fig. 1 (right) shows an example of partition after EM clustering for the same 2-d dataset. There are 2 clusters in this example totally. The k-NN search in VQ-based index is similar to search in regular VA-file, except that the query vector is transformed into KLT domain for each cluster firstly.

Table 1. Quantization distortion of Euclidean error metric

	Quantization distortion		
	1 bit/dim	2 bit/dim	3 bit/dim
VA	4.613	3.195	2.149
VA+	2.035	1.287	0.7156
VQ-5	1.432	0.8317	0.4480
VQ-10	1.291	0.7361	0.3933

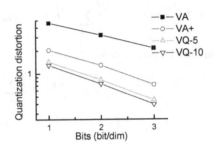

Fig. 2. Quantization distortion of Euclidean error metric

4   Experiment

The dataset is an aerial photo database [17] of 275,465 images and the Gabor texture [18] of 60 dimensions is used. Therefore the dataset is a set of 275,465 vectors with 60 dimensions. This large dataset is a challenge to all multidimensional indexing methods and is widely adopted by other approaches for performance evaluation.

The VA-file (VA), VA$^+$-file (VA+), and VQ-based approaches are implemented for 1, 2, and 3 bits per dimension. Note that it's an average value for each dimension and the allocation is non-uniform in VA$^+$-file approach and VQ-based approach. For VQ-based approach, user need specify the number of Gaussians K. Tests are performed for 5 clusters (K =5, VQ-5) and 10 clusters (K =10, VQ-10) respectively. 1000 vectors are randomly selected from the same dataset as the query vector for k-NN search and the average performance is reported.

Firstly, the quantization distortion is evaluated for each method. The quantization distortion is defined as:

$$QD = \frac{1}{|D|}\sum_{x \in D}\text{dist}(x, Q(x)) = \frac{1}{|D|}\sum_{x \in D}\|x - Q(x)\| .$$

where $Q(x)$ is the quantizer function and its output is the centroid of the cell that vector x falls in. Table 1 and Fig. 2 show the comparison of quantization distortion for the three methods. Obviously, the proposed VQ-based approach achieves a significant reduction of quantization distortion.

The filtering efficiencies of two phases are evaluated, which are the number of remaining candidates after the first phase and the number of vectors accessed in the second phase respectively. The filtering efficiencies of 10-NN, 50-NN, and 250-NN are evaluated and only the result for 250-NN is reported. The results for 10-NN and 50-NN are similar to result of 250-NN. Table 2 and Fig. 3 show the comparison of the three methods for 250-NN searches in the aerial photo database.

It's apparent that the proposed VQ-based approach reduces the remaining candidates after filtering significantly. The filtering efficiencies in the second phase are directly proportional to the number of random disk accesses during the search, which dominate the query time. Despite bad performance in the first phase, the VA$^+$-file approach achieves a notable improvement compared with VA-file approach after two-step filtering - an increase of about twice to 7 times. The VQ-based approach outperforms other VA-based methods under variant conditions and improves the filtering efficiency by about twice to 6 times compared with VA$^+$-file approach after two-step filtering. In fact, the VQ-based approach under just 1 bit/dimension outperforms the VA$^+$-file approach under 2 bits/dimension, and the latter outperforms the VA-file approach under 3 bits/dimension. Hence the proposed VQ-based indexing scheme can archive the same performance only by half-size index structure of VA$^+$-file approach and one-third of VA-file approach.

Table 2. Filtering efficiency for 250-NN searches (in percentage)

	First phase			Second phase		
	1 bit/dim	2 bit/dim	3 bit/dim	1 bit/dim	2 bit/dim	3 bit/dim
VA	98.96	66.19	24.65	39.21	13.29	3.391
VA+	99.99	97.14	47.93	7.561	3.017	1.085
VQ-5	44.84	17.90	2.980	3.241	1.013	0.3897
VQ-10	37.19	11.92	2.001	2.822	0.8616	0.3323

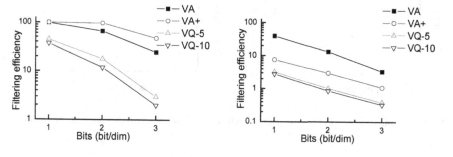

Fig. 3. Filtering efficiency of first phase (left) and second phase (right) for 250-NN searches (in percentage)

The overall search performances are also evaluated, which are the I/O time of accessing vectors in the second phase of k-NN searches and the total time of overall k-NN searches respectively. An ordinary PC workstation is used to perform 250-NN searches and the average performance is reported. The sequential scan (SS) method is also implemented for comparison. Table 3 and Fig. 4 show the comparison of the four methods for 250-NN searches in the aerial photo database. The proposed VQ-based approach achieves a significant reduction of I/O time of accessing vectors and overall search time. The VQ-based approach under 1 bit/dimension have the same overall search time as the VA$^+$-file approach under 3 bits/dimension.

The VQ-based approach performs slightly better for 10 clusters than for 5 clusters. Better performance can be expected for more clusters. Why not choose a large number of clusters? Firstly, the parameter estimation of too many clusters is difficult and often inaccurate. Secondly, quantizer of each cluster needs its own copy of codebook. The overhead of codebooks for few clusters can be neglected compared with the size of approximation vectors. But for a large number of clusters, the codebook overhead must be taken into account and maybe degrades the performance.

Table 3. I/O time of accessing vectors and overall search time for 250-NN searches (in seconds)

	I/O time of accessing vectors			Overall search time		
	1 bit/dim	2 bit/dim	3 bit/dim	1 bit/dim	2 bit/dim	3 bit/dim
SS	15.10	15.10	15.10	15.56	15.56	15.56
VA	24.70	8.787	2.328	26.53	11.05	5.148
VA+	6.595	2.931	1.167	8.415	5.202	3.988
VQ-5	2.532	0.81	0.267	4.313	3.038	3.006
VQ-10	2.178	0.648	0.213	3.940	2.844	2.916

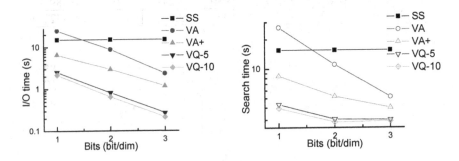

Fig. 4. I/O time of accessing vectors and overall search time for 250-NN searches (in seconds)

5   Conclusions

In this paper, a novel VQ-based indexing scheme is presented to deal with retrieval in real-world image databases. Existing VA-based methods, such as VA-file, VA$^+$-file, assume that images in a database are from a single cluster and utilize scalar quantization to partition feature spaces. The too simple distribution model and quantization method results in inaccurate estimation of data distribution and large quantization distortion and therefore not good similarity search efficiency. The proposed approach introduces a vector quantizer instead of scalar quantizer to partition data space. It assumes that the database is generated from a mixture model with multiple Gaussians and adopts EM algorithm to estimate the mixture model parameters of joint distribution. After vectors are classified into appropriate cluster, an optimal quantizer is trained for each cluster respectively. The proposed indexing scheme is validated for real datasets theoretically. Experimental results show a significant improvement in k-NN search efficiency from existing VA-based methods.

In conclusion, the VQ-based approach is an efficient indexing technique for exact k-NN search in high-dimensional feature spaces. The experiments show a deterministic relation between quantization distortion and indexing efficiency and indicate that less quantization distortion can improve performance of indexing schemes. Our future research will focus on globally optimized vector quantizer and integrating VQ-based indexing scheme with relevance feedback technique for practical CBIR systems.

Acknowledgement

This research was supported by NSF of China under grant no. 60273005.

References

[1]   Y. Rui, T. Huang, S. Chang: Image Retrieval: Current Techniques, Promising Directions and Open Issues. J. of Visual Communication and Image Representation, vol. 10, (1999) 1-23

[2]   Y. Rui, T. S. Huang, M. Ortega, et al.: Relevance feedback: A power tool for interactive content-based image retrieval. IEEE Trans. on CSVT, no. 5, (1998) 644-655

[3]   J. Nievergelt, H. Hinterberger, K. Sevcik: The gridfile: An adaptable symmetric multikey file structure. ACM Transactions on Database Systems, vol. 9, no. 1, (1984) 38-71

[4]   J. Robinson: The k-d-b-tree: A search structure for large multidimensional dynamic indexes. Proc. of the ACM SIGMOD ICMD (1981) 10-18

[5]   N. Beckmann, H. P. Kriegel, R. Schneider, et al.: The R*-tree: An efficient and robust access method for points and rectangles. Proc. ACM SIGMOD ICMD (1990) 322-331

[6] N. Katayama, S. Satoh: The SR-tree: An index structure for high-dimensional nearest neighbor queries. Proc. ACM SIGMOD Int. Conf. Management of Data (1997) 369-380

[7] R. Weber, H. Schek, S. Blott: A quantitative analysis and performance study for simi-larity-search methods in high-dimensional spaces. Proc. ACM VLDB (1998)

[8] K. Beyer, J. Goldstein, R. Ramakrishnan: When Is 'Nearest Neighbor' Meaning-ful?. Proc. of the 7th International Conference on Database Theory, Jerusalem (1999) 217-235

[9] D. W. Scott, Density Estimation, Wiley, New York (1992)

[10] H. Ferhatosmanoglu, E. Tuncel, D. Agrawal: Vector Approximation based Indexing for Non-uniform High Dimensional Data Sets. ACM CKIM, McLean, (2000)

[11] P. Wu, B. Manjunath, S. Chandrasekaran: An adaptive index structure for high-dimensional similarity search. Proc. PCM, Beijing, China, (2001) 71-77

[12] G.-H. Cha, X. Zhu, D. Petkovic, et al: An efficient indexing method for nearest neighbor searches in high-dimensional image databases. IEEE Trans. Multime-dia, vol. 4, no. 1, (2002) 76-87

[13] A. Gersho, R. M. Gray: Vector Quantization and Signal Compression. Kluwer Academic (1992)

[14] T. D. Lookabaugh, R. M. Gray: High-resolution Theory and the Vector Quan-tizer Advantage. IEEE Trans. On Information Theory, no. 35, (1989) 1020-1033

[15] E. Forgy: Cluster analysis of multivariate data: Efficiency vs. interpretability of classifica-tions. Biometrics, vol. 21, no. 768, (1965)

[16] A. P. Dempster, N. M. Laird, D. B. Rubin: Maximum likelihood from incom-plete data via the EM algorithm. J. of the Royal Statistical Society B, vol. 39, no. 1, (1977) 1-38

[17] B. S. Manjunath, Aerial photo image database, http://vision.ece.ucsb.edu/datasets/

[18] B. S. Manjunath, W. Y. Ma: Texture features for browsing and retrieval of image data. IEEE PAMI, vol. 18, no. 8, (1996) 837-842

Speaker Localisation Using Audio-Visual Synchrony: An Empirical Study

Harriet J. Nock, Giridharan Iyengar, and Chalapathy Neti

IBM TJ Watson Research Center
PO Box 218, Yorktown Heights, NY 10598. USA

Abstract. This paper reviews definitions of audio-visual synchrony and examines their empirical behaviour on test sets up to 200 times larger than used by other authors. The results give new insights into the practical utility of existing synchrony definitions and justify application of audio-visual synchrony techniques to the problem of active speaker localisation in broadcast video. Performance is evaluated using a test set of twelve clips of alternating speakers from the multiple speaker CUAVE corpus. Accuracy of 76% is obtained for the task of identifying the active member of a speaker pair at different points in time, comparable to performance given by two purely video image-based schemes. Accuracy of 65% is obtained on the more challenging task of locating a point within a 100×100 pixel square centered on the active speaker's mouth without no prior face detection; the performance upper bound if perfect face detection were available is 69%. This result is significantly better than two purely video image-based schemes.

1 Introduction

Several recent papers discuss the idea of "audio-visual synchrony", which considers the strength of relationship between audio signals and video image sequences. For example, a soundtrack containing drumbeats and an image sequence showing the person beating that drum would be strongly related or strongly "synchronous". Similarly, if one (or both) faces in Figure 1 are saying the words heard in the speech soundtrack, then the audio and video signals are "synchronous". Conversely, if the soundtrack for Figure 1 has a voiceover unrelated to images on screen then the audio and video signals are not "synchronous".

Many definitions of audio-visual synchrony are possible. Those proposed thus far fall somewhere between two extremes. At one extreme are *generic* definitions of synchrony using weak models: these assign good scores to any audio and video signals displaying consistency without regard to the type of audio and video signal under consideration. Examples include [9], which defines synchrony as the Gaussian-based mutual information between audio energy and pixel intensities. At the other extreme are definitions of synchrony that are *specific* to particular types of signal; most existing work of this type considers evaluating consistency between facial movements and speech. Examples include [14], which suggests the speech signal could be used to synthesise a talking head and differences

E. M. Bakker et al. (Eds.): CIVR 2003, LNCS 2728, pp. 488–499, 2003.

Fig. 1. Keyframe from TREC Video Track 2002 Corpus

between synthesised and actual faces compared. The other measures proposed fall somewhere between these two extremes. Suggestions include [14], which uses Canonical Correlation Analysis on a set of training data to find the linear projection of audio and automatically-detected video face data onto a single axis that maximises the (linear) correlation between the projected variables; synchrony of new data is evaluated by calculating the (linear) correlation between the new audio and video in this space. The paper by [6] uses a pre-trained time-delay neural network classifier to predict whether audio and video features at a particular frame correspond to a person talking.

In practice, the appropriate definition of audio-visual synchrony may vary with the intended application. Our research is currently focussing on synchrony measures useful for deciding whether facial movements are related to speech signals, since a good measure for evaluating consistency of face-speech relationships would have many potential applications. An important part of this research is to consider whether these audio-visual synchrony measures scale to larger and more challenging test sets than those used by other authors. In addition to evaluating these measures using relatively large artificial test sets, this paper considers the use of synchrony measures for speaker localisation in eg. broadcast video. A robust solution to this problem would benefit multimedia retrieval applications in two ways[1]. Firstly, a more robust method for speaker localisation in broadcast video would allow wider application of IBM's audio-visual speech recognition systems (eg. [4]), which are more robust than audio-only speech recognition in noisy environments. This should improve transcription accuracy in traditionally challenging non-studio environments, improving speech-based-indexing performance in those video segments. Secondly, systems for automatic semantic concept annotation in video (eg. [1]) could exploit speaker localisation information for distinguishing monologues, dialogues and voiceovers. To illustrate, consider Figure 1 for which (a) absence of synchrony implies a voiceover shot, (b) high synchrony localised to the right face implies a monologue and (c) an alternating pattern of high synchrony implies a dialogue. Similar ideas were used in our TREC Video Track 2002 automatic monologue annotator [10].

---

[1] Potential applications outside the digital library arena include face and voice-based biometrics, systems for marking speaker-level metadata such as speaker turns in video, systems for assessing dubbing quality and systems for animating lip movements in cartoon characters.

The paper is structured as follows. Section 2 reviews selected measures of audio-visual synchrony and investigates their behaviour on artificial test sets. Motivated by these findings, Section 3 describes our synchrony-based approach to active speaker localisation in broadcast video and presents empirical results on the CUAVE corpus. The paper ends with conclusions and future work.

2   Preliminary Studies

This section reviews the generic and specific speech and face consistency measures defined in [11] and discusses their empirical behaviour on artificial test sets.

2.1   Definitions of Audio-Visual Synchrony

Assume we are given a test video clip with a speech soundtrack and a moving face in the video. Let $a_t \in \mathcal{R}^n$ be a feature vector describing the acoustic signal at time t eg. a vector of mel-frequency cepstral coefficients. Let $v_t \in \mathcal{R}^m$ be a feature vector describing the image at time t eg. a vector of discrete cosine transform coefficients of the face region in the frame at t. Let $\mathcal{S}_1^T = ((a_1, v_1), \ldots, (a_T, v_T))$ represent the joint sequence of audio and video feature vectors. Our goal is to define a measure of synchrony between sequences $\mathcal{A}_1^T = a_1, \ldots, a_T$ and $\mathcal{V}_1^T = v_1, \ldots, v_T$ derived from a test clip.

Generic Measures. Let us ignore the information that $\mathcal{A}_1^T$ and $\mathcal{V}_1^T$ correspond to audio containing speech and images containing a face. Consider each vector in $\mathcal{S}_1^T$ to be an independent sample from some joint distribution $p(A, V)$, rather than explicitly modelling temporal dependence in the individual sequences. As suggested in [9], one measure of audio-visual synchrony is the mutual information $\mathcal{I}(A; V)$ between random variables A and V^2. Since the $p(A), p(V), p(A, V)$ forms are unknown in practice, assumptions must be made. Our earlier work investigated two simple assumptions, both allowing straightforward evaluation of mutual information [11]: discrete distributions and, as in [9], continuous multivariate Gaussian distributions. We note here only that assumption of discrete distributions requires a preparation phase which constructs codebooks to quantize a_t, v_t and (a_t, v_t) prior to discrete distribution estimation at test time; in constrast, assumption of multivariate Gaussian distributions allows parameter estimation at test time without prior preparation. We term these implementations *Discrete Mutual Information ("Discrete MI")* and *Gaussian Mutual Information ("Gaussian MI")*.

---

2 Mutual Information (see [5]) is a measure of dependence between random variables or, phrased differently, the amount of information one random variable tells us about another one. To illustrate for the discrete case, let A and V be discrete random variables with joint distribution $p(A, V)$ and marginal distributions $p(A)$ and $p(V)$. Then $\mathcal{I}(A; V) = \sum_{a \in A} \sum_{v \in V} p(a, v) \log \frac{p(a,v)}{p(a)p(v)}$, which is also the Kullback-Leibler distance (ie. relative entropy) between the joint and product distributions.

Face-and-Speech Specific Measures. Require now that $\mathcal{A}_1^T$ and $\mathcal{V}_1^T$ correspond to speech audio and images containing faces. Assume we know the word sequence $\mathcal{W}$ spoken in audio $\mathcal{A}_1^T$. We define likelihood $p(\mathcal{S}_1^T|\mathcal{W})$ as a measure of synchrony. In practice $\mathcal{W}$ may be unknown; audio-only speech recognition gives a reasonable approximation. Similarly, the form of $p(\mathcal{S}_1^T|\mathcal{W})$ is unknown in practice; one implementation uses Hidden Markov Models (HMMs) trained on joint sequences of audio- and visual- data, such as HMMs for audio-visual speech recognition (eg. [4]). We term this implementation *Audio-Visual Likelihood ("AV-LL")*.

2.2 Empirical Behaviour of Audio-Visual Synchrony

This section discusses empirical findings about the definitions of audio-visual synchrony discussed above. Our experiments use artificial test sets constructed from the IBM ViaVoice^{TM} audio-visual database [13], comprising full-face frontal video and audio of multiple speakers reading prompts from a large vocabulary in a continuous speech fashion. These experiments therefore assume prior existence of (good) face and speech detection and focus upon the success of different measures in assessing synchrony between facial movements and speech.

Audio features a_t are extracted as follows. 24 Mel-frequency cepstral coefficients (MFCCs) are extracted from the audio signal at a 100Hz rate. These features are used directly in the Discrete and Gaussian MI schemes; before presentation to the audio-visual HMMs, at every t, 9 consecutive MFCC vectors are concatenated, projected to a lower dimensional space using linear discriminant analysis (LDA) and rotated by a maximum likelihood linear transform (MLLT, [8]) to give a 60-dimensional vector.

Video features v_t are extracted as follows. Operating at a 60Hz sampling rate, a normalised mouth region-of-interest (ROI) is extracted from each frame and then compressed using a discrete cosine transform transform (DCT). The 24 highest energy DCT coefficients are retained and linearly interpolated to give a 100Hz frame rate, matching the audio processing. These features are used directly in Discrete and Gaussian MI schemes; before presentation to the audio-visual HMMs, at every t, 15 consecutive frames are concatenated and LDA and MLLT transforms applied to give a 41-dimensional vector.

Experiment 1: Choose Synchronised Speaker from a Small Set. Previous work used an artificial test set, intended to simulate video-conferencing or CSPAN panel discussion scenarios in which we want to identify the talking face among several in a shot. A total of 1016 "true" speech and face combinations of four seconds in length were extracted from the database; for each of these "true" cases, one, two or three "confuser" examples were formed by pairing the "true" audio with four seconds of video from randomly chosen speaker(s). Table 1 briefly reviews the results, which show that Gaussian MI significantly outperforms the other two definitions of synchrony for this task; reasons are discussed in [11]. We conclude that where good face and speech detection is available, Gaussian

MI will solve at least two practical problems in video analysis. Firstly, it solves the speaker localisation problem that arises when we have already identified one or more faces on screen but need to identify the talking face. Secondly, it gives information for classifying video shots already known to contain talking face(s) into monologues or dialogues via the pattern of activity amongst those faces.

Experiment 2: Classifying Speakers as Synchronous or Non-synchronous. A second experiment examined whether Gaussian MI - the most successful synchrony measure in **Experiment 1** - is useful for absolute classification tasks such as distinguishing between voiceovers and monologues. An artificial test set of 1016 four second examples was constructed, in which 254 examples contain synchronised faces and speech and 762 do not. Despite the earlier success of this measure in correctly ranking synchronised speakers, the absolute classification performance was very poor. The result is explained by Figure 2, which shows the distribution of synchrony scores for the synchronous and non-synchronous test clips. The classes are highly overlapping based on this measure and no good decision boundary can be defined. We conclude Gaussian MI alone is not adequate for video annotation applications such as distinguishing voiceover shots from monologue shots.

3   Using Synchrony for Speaker Localisation

This section studies Gaussian MI further by applying it to speaker localisation on a real test set.

3.1   Corpus

Experiments use the CUAVE corpus [12], a speaker-independent, multiple speaker corpus of connected and continuous digit strings designed to support research into audio-visual speech recognition in adverse conditions. The first ten clips from the **groups** partition form a validation set (where required) and the second twelve clips form a held-out test set. Each clip involves two speakers, arranged as in Figure 3; clips begin with the speakers taking turns in reading digit strings and end with both speakers simultaneously reading different digit sequences. We defer the challenge of determining whether one or two people are speaking at once until future work and consider only the parts of each clip in

Table 1. Synchronised Speaker Detection % Accuracy

Number of Confusers	Discrete MI	Gaussian MI	AV-LL
1	70	91	72
2	53	85	53
3	47	82	45

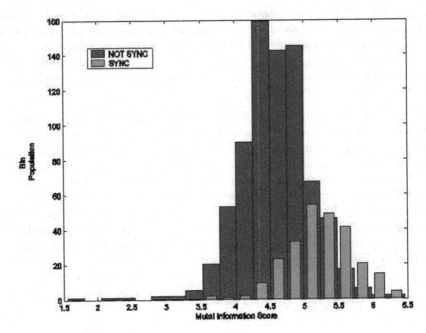

Fig. 2. Per-class histograms of Gaussian MI Scores

Fig. 3. Example two-person clip from CUAVE

which a single person speaks at any one time. CUAVE has properties making it distinctly non-trivial for localisation work: for example, the left speaker in Figure 3 often mouths parts of the text which is being uttered by the right speaker. In addition, the single speaker portion of each clip is on average 20-25 seconds long. Thus this dataset is larger and more varied than used by other authors: the largest comparable test set of which we are aware comprises eight 2-2.5 second utterances of "How's the weather in Taipei?" from different speakers [7].

3.2 Pixel-Wise Gaussian Mutual Information

In these experiments, we will (by nature of the dataset) always have perfect a-priori speech detection. However, in contrast to the artificial dataset experiments earlier, we will not always assume a-priori face detection. This tests the hypothesis that face detection may not be an essential prerequisite for successful

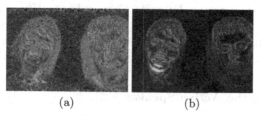

(a)   (b)

Fig. 4. Mutual Information Images: (a) Pixel Intensities (b) Pixel Intensity Changes

speaker localisation. However, we will always present comparative results for the case where we have *perfect* a-priori face detection to see whether performance improves. Our basic approach will be to calculate Gaussian MI between individual pixels and the audio. Specifically, we replace v_t in the earlier discussion by v_{txy}, a value related to pixel x, y in the frame at time t, and assume Gaussian forms for $p(A)$, $p(V)$ and $p(A, V)$ where V now generates a pixel value v_{txy}. Thus, we will now obtain a mutual information value $\mathcal{I}(A; V)$ for each pixel. The full set of per-pixel mutual information values estimated for a test clip can be thought of as a *Mutual Information Image*: Figure 4 shows examples, where lighter pixels indicate higher mutual information values. We localise the speaker by searching the Mutual Information Image for compact regions having high mutual information with the audio[3]. This pixel-wise Gaussian MI implementation is similar to [9], but differs in choice of a_t and v_{txy} as is now described.

Preliminary experiments showed results improve when choosing a_t to be a mel-frequency cepstral coefficient vector rather than audio energy. Results also improve by choosing v_{txy} to be related to grey-scale pixel intensity *changes* rather than the grey-scale pixel intensity, as illustrated by Figure 4. Image (a) is a Mutual Information Image calculated when v_{txy} is the grey scale pixel intensity. High mutual information occurs around both heads rather than being isolated around the speaker's mouth; this trend is seen in most CUAVE Mutual Information Images when v_{txy} is pixel intensity. The paper by [2] suggests this problem is reduced by defining v_{txy} to be related to pixel intensity *changes* and our experimental results confirm this finding. Specifically, [2] defines v_{txy} to be the *pixel intensity change* value $F^{IC}(x, y, t)$ defined as

$$F^{IC}(x, y, t) = \sum_{l,m=-1}^{1} F(x + l, y + m, t + 1) - F(x + l, y + m, t - 1)$$

where $F(x, y, t)$ is the original image pixel (x, y) value in the frame at time t. We refer to the image at a fixed time t whose (x, y) pixel values correspond

---

[3] We find computation of a full mutual information image of dimensionality matching the original image(s) is not essential in practice; a naive subsampling of the original image by factors of 10 or more prior to forming the Mutual Information Images does not significantly degrade results for either of the tasks discussed later in this section.

to $F^{IC}(x, y, t)$ values as the *Intensity Change Image* F_t^{IC}. Figure 4 (b) shows the Mutual Information Image analogous to (a) but calculated using $v_{txy} = F^{IC}(x, y, t)$; mutual information is now highest around speaker's mouth and jawline, as we would like.

3.3 Detecting the Active Speaker

Our first experiment considers whether Pixel-wise Gaussian MI can be used to detect the active speaker (ie. left or right) at one second intervals throughout the test clips. Chance performance is 50%. To solve this problem, a window of two seconds length is used and a Mutual Information Image calculated; the estimate of active speaker is obtained by considering total mutual information in the left of the image relative to the total in the right half. The higher of these values is assumed to indicate the active speaker. The window is then shifted by one second and the same procedure repeated. (Preliminary experiments investigated the effects of different window lengths and window shifts upon performance but no significant variation was noted.) Estimates are scored at one second intervals through each clip, a total of 252 test points. Table 2(a) shows results for two cases: where v_{txy} is the pixel intensity and where v_{txy} is the pixel intensity change. Performance for both schemes is significantly above chance; the higher active speaker detection for the latter case is not unexpected given the discussion in the previous subsection and experiments in the remainder of the paper use only pixel intensity changes. Further analysis shows one third of errors in the "pixel intensity change" case occur close to speaker turn points eg. when the left speaker stops speaking and the right speaker starts. This is not surprising: estimates at those points use pixel-wise mutual information estimated across a window spanning some data from an "active" left speaker and some from an "active" right speaker. One possible solution is to detect speaker turn points using an audio-based technique (eg. [3]) and adjust estimates in these regions. As baselines, we compare against two simple video-only techniques which make an estimate of the active speaker at time t based on the Intensity Change Image F_t^{IC}. In the first scheme (*Intensity Change Image Sums*), we simply compare the total pixel intensity changes on the left and right halves of image F_t^{IC}; this gives performance 77%. In the second scheme (*Intensity Change Image X-Projection Peak*), we sum the intensity changes in each column of F_t^{IC} and use the column with the maximum sum to identify the active speaker; this gives a performance of 81%. We conclude that for the simple task of determining the active speaker, the video-only X-Projection Peak technique is adequate and there is little benefit from using the more computationally expensive (and non-causal) Pixel-wise Gaussian MI. However, there are many assumptions made in this experiment, including a known number of speakers in known regions on screen and a lack of background motion; it is not clear that video-only performance would be maintained when these conditions do not hold, whereas informal experiments on other data sets indicate that Pixel-wise Gaussian MI maintains good performance in such situations. For more challenging tasks, such as active

Table 2. Results (% Accuracy)

CLIP	Pixel Intensity	Intensity Change
	v_{txy}	v_{txy}
G11	50	63
G12	32	64
G13	44	50
G14	82	91
G15	50	75
G16	52	85
G17	47	94
G18	55	64
G19	53	47
G20	78	93
G21	67	83
G22	64	95
ALL	57	76

(a) Active Speaker Detection

CLIP	$T = 100$	$T = 200$
G11	44	69
G12	46	68
G13	19	25
G14	86	91
G15	65	70
G16	57	57
G17	94	94
G18	65	71
G19	41	41
G20	89	93
G21	75	79
G22	74	79
ALL	65	71

(b) Active Speaker Mouth Localisation

speaker mouth localisation in the next section, Pixel-wise Gaussian MI gives clear benefit.

None of these results use a-priori face detection. We repeat Pixel-wise Gaussian MI and Intensity Change Image Sums experiments, this time assuming perfect head detection. This time the techniques compare average (rather than total) mutual information or intensity change within the head regions. Results change by less than 1.5% for each technique. We conclude a-priori face detection is useful but not essential for speaker localisation on data such as CUAVE which does not have high background motion.

3.4   Detecting Active Speaker's Mouth

A second set of experiments investigated a more challenging task: to locate the mouth region of the active speaker during the test clips. We begin by computing Mutual Information Images at each test point as above; then, we locate the active speaker's mouth within each Mutual Information Image by searching for the $M \times N$ region with the highest concentration of mutual information values within some fraction f of the maximum mutual information value in the full Mutual Information Image[4]. Parameters M, N, f are tuned using the validation set. Figure 5 shows two images from a demo illustrating results on held-out data: for each image, the top half shows the original video, the bottom is the Mutual Information Image, the wide but narrow (red) rectangle is placed under the true speaker and the small (white) square indicates the best $M \times N$ region found

---

[4] Smoothing of mouth estimates between frames is not used in these experiments, since our test points are separated in time, but is an obvious direction for future work.

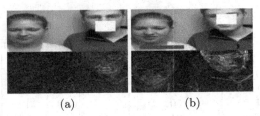

(a)   (b)

Fig. 5. Speaker Localisation Examples: (a) Successful (b) Unsuccessful

by the algorithm. As we would hope, the optimal M,N previously found on the validation set correspond to a region about the size of a speaker's mouth. To quantify results, an estimate of the mouth region centre is defined as "correct" if it falls within a $T \times T$ pixel square centred on the "true" mouth centre, for T of 100 and 200. Figure 6 illustrates "correct" regions for each T using white squares in the upper images. Estimates are scored at one second intervals throughout each clip, a total of 252 test points. Table 2(b) shows results.

As baselines, we again compare against two video-only techniques which make an estimate of the active speaker's mouth at time t based on the Intensity Change Image F_t^{IC}. In the first scheme (*High Intensity Change Region*), we locate the active speaker's mouth at time t by searching the intensity change image F_t^{IC} for the $M \times N$ region with the highest concentration of intensity change values within some fraction f of the maximum; this gives performance 50% at $T = 100$ and 52% at $T = 200$. In the second scheme (*Intensity Change Image X- and Y- Projection Peaks*), we sum the intensity changes in each row and column of F_t^{IC} and use the row and column with maximum sums to locate the mouth; this gives a performance of 49% at $T = 100$ and 51% at $T = 200$. For this task, we conclude that Pixel-wise Gaussian MI performs significantly better. This result is plausible: the X- and Y- Projection scheme has less information available than the High Intensity Change Region scheme and the High Intensity Change Region scheme has less information available than Pixel-wise Gaussian MI, which uses a longer temporal window and incorporates audio information.

None of these results use a-priori face detection. We repeat the Pixel-wise Gaussian MI and High Intensity Change Region experiments, now assuming existence of perfect head detection. We constrain the techniques to search only within the head region. At $T = 100$, High Intensity Change Region improves to 54% (a gain of 2%) and Pixel-wise Gaussian MI improves to 69% (a gain of 4%). We conclude that for best speaker localisation performance, good a-priori face and speech detection is essential. However, it is interesting that Pixel-wise Gaussian MI alone gives reasonable speaker localisation performance on data such as CUAVE which has no background motion.

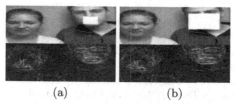
(a)   (b)

Fig. 6. Speaker Localisation Correctness Regions: (a) $T=100$ (b) $T=200$

4   Conclusions

This paper presented an empirical study of audio-visual synchrony measures and their application to speaker localisation in video. The artificial dataset experiments support two conclusions. Firstly, Gaussian MI outperforms the other synchrony measures proposed and potentially solves specific practical problems in video analysis, such as identifying the active speaker from a set of faces on screen or distinguishing monologues from dialogues when it is known one of the two occurs in the shot. Secondly, Gaussian MI is not suitable for making absolute decisions about degree of synchrony, such as distinguishing voiceovers from monologues. Experiments on CUAVE support two further conclusions. Pixelwise Gaussian MI gives performance close to two video-only techniques on the task of active speaker localisation; later informal experiments suggest it scales better to other tasks. For active speaker mouth localisation, the additional visual context and audio information available to Pixel-wise Gaussian MI leads to performance significantly better than two video-only techniques. Future work will follow three directions: to identify new definitions of synchrony suitable for distinguishing monologues from dialogues, to develop methods for robustness to background video motion and to consider efficiency issues (such as whether a similar approach could be implemented in the MPEG compressed domain).

Acknowledgements

We thank Gerasimos Potamianos and Miroslav Novak for technical assistance and the anonymous reviewers for their comments.

References

[1] W. Adams, G. Iyengar, C.-Y. Lin, M. R. Naphade, C. Neti, H. J. Nock, and J. R. Smith. Semantic Indexing of Multimedia Content Using Visual, Audio and Text Cues. *Eurasip Journal on Applied Signal Processing*, 2:170–185, 2003. 489

[2] T. Butz and J.-P. Thiran. Feature Space Mutual Information In Speech-Video Sequences. In *Proc. ICME*, Lausanne, Switzerland, 2002. 494

[3] S. Chen and P. Gopalakrishnan. Speaker, Environment and Channel Change Detection and Clustering via the Bayesian Information Criterion. In *Proc. DARPA Broadcast News Transcription & Understanding Workshop*, VA, USA, 1998. 495

[4] J. Connell, N. Haas, E. Marcheret, C. Neti, G. Potamianos, and S. Velipasalar. A Real-Time Prototype for Small-Vocabulary Audio-Visual ASR. In *ICME (Submitted)*, 2003. 489, 491

[5] T. M. Cover and J. A. Thomas. *Elements of Information Theory*. Wiley-Interscience, 1991. 490

[6] R. Cutler and L. Davis. Look Who's Talking: Speaker Detection using Video and Audio Correlation. In *Proc. ICME*, NY, USA, 2000. 489

[7] J. W. Fisher III and T. Darrell. Informative Subspaces for Audiovisual Processing: High-Level Function from Low-Level Fusion. In *Proc. ICASSP*, 2002. 493

[8] R. Gopinath. Maximum Likelihood Modeling with Gaussian Distributions for Classification. In *Proc. ICASSP*, volume 2, pages 661–664, WA, USA, 1998. 491

[9] J. Hershey and J. Movellan. Using Audio-Visual Synchrony to Locate Sounds. In *Proc. NIPS*, 1999. 488, 490, 494

[10] G. Iyengar, H. Nock, and C. Neti. Audio-Visual Synchrony for Detection of Monologues in Video Archives. In *Proc. ICASSP*, Hong Kong, 2003. 489

[11] H. Nock, G. Iyengar, and C. Neti. Assessing Face and Speech Consistency for Monologue Detection in Video. In *Proc. ACM Multimedia*, Juan-les-Pins, France, 2002. 490, 491

[12] E. Patterson, S. Gurbuz, Z. Tufekci, and J. Gowdy. Moving Talker, Speaker-Independent Feature Study and Baseline Results Using the CUAVE Multimodal Speech Corpus. *Eurasip Journal on Applied Signal Processing*, 11:1189–1201, 2002. 492

[13] G. Potamianos, J. Luettin, and C. Neti. Hierarchical Discriminant Features for Audio-Visual LVCSR. In *Proc. ICASSP*, pages 165–168, 2001. 491

[14] M. Slaney and M. Covell. FaceSync: a linear operator for measuring synchronization of video facial images and audio tracks. In *Proc. NIPS*, 2001. 488, 489

An Efficiency Comparison of Two Content-Based Image Retrieval Systems, GIFT and PicSOM

Mika Rummukainen, Jorma Laaksonen, and Markus Koskela

Laboratory of Computer and Information Science, Helsinki University of Technology,
P.O.BOX 5400, 02015 HUT, Finland
{mika.rummukainen,jorma.laaksonen,markus.koskela}@hut.fi

Abstract. Content-based image retrieval (CBIR) addresses the problem of assisting a user to retrieve images from unannotated databases, based on features that can be automatically derived from the images. Today, there exists several CBIR systems based on different methods. Only few attemps to benchmark these have been made, although the usefulness of benchmarking is undeniable in the development of different algorithms. In this paper we publish our benchmarking results of two CBIR systems with different implementation methods. The CBIR systems in question are GIFT (University of Geneva) and PicSOM (Helsinki University of Technology). The results clearly show that our PicSOM system, which we earlier have not been able to benchmark against other CBIR systems, comes off well in the comparison. Also, the results indicate that tests based on a single ground truth class are not enough for fair system comparisons.

1   Introduction

There has been a growing need for efficient image search engines in the WWW and other domains during the past few years. A number of content-based image retrieval (CBIR) systems have emerged but their performance has developed much slower than the performance of text search engines, such as Google or Altavista.

The human character is competitive by nature and thus a competition is a good way to quickly improve the quality of existing systems. The Benchathlon project (*http://www.benchathlon.net*) and IAPR's Technical Committee 12 (*http://sci.vu.edu.au/~clement/TC-12/benchmark.htm*) both aim to hold an open competition for CBIR researchers where everyone can attend. In the Benchathlon project it has been planned to use the MRML communication language [1] (*http://www.mrml.net*) developed by the Computer Vision Group of the University of Geneva. The purpose of MRML is to divide a CBIR system into separate client and server parts and to create a standard method for communicating with different CBIR servers.

The PicSOM CBIR system [2], developed in the Laboratory of Computer and Information Science of the Helsinki University of Technology, can now communicate using MRML [3]. The PicSOM system also includes a benchmarking tool,

E. M. Bakker et al. (Eds.): CIVR 2003, LNCS 2728, pp. 500–510, 2003.

which can be used for testing other MRML-based CBIR systems as well. Since the only publicly available MRML-based CBIR system was GIFT [4], we were able to run benchmarks between two systems. The results of our experiments are shown in this paper.

2 PicSOM

The PicSOM CBIR system is a framework for research on methods for content-based image retrieval (see [2] for a recent review; the PicSOM home page is at *http://www.cis.hut.fi/picsom*). The system is based on using several parallel Self-Organizing Maps (SOMs) [5] trained with separate statistical feature data. The SOM is an artificial neural network algorithm which defines an elastic, topology-preserving grid of points fitted to the high-dimensional input space. It attempts to represent all the available observations with an optimal accuracy by using a restricted set of models.

As a result of using multiple SOMs, the PicSOM system inherently uses multiple features for image retrieval and generally benefits from using all available features as it automatically neglects those working poorly. Features are usually comprised of statistical low-level visual data such as the MPEG-7 [6] content descriptors used in this work.

To reduce the complexity of training large SOMs, a special form of the algorithm, the Tree Structured Self-Organizing Map (TS-SOM) [7] is used. After training the SOMs with the TS-SOM algorithm, the map units are connected with the images of the database. This is done by locating the best-matching map unit (BMU) for each image. Furthermore, among the images sharing a common BMU, the best-matching one is used as a visual label for that unit.

2.1 Relevance Feedback with Self-Organizing Maps

The relevance feedback mechanism of PicSOM, implemented by using several parallel SOMs, is a crucial element of the retrieval engine [8]. The basic assumption is that images which are similar according to a specific visual feature are located near each other on the corresponding SOM surface. Therefore, we are motivated to spread the relevance information given by the user also to the neighboring map units of the user-rated images. This is done as follows. All relevant images are first given equal positive weight inversely proportional to the number of relevant images. Likewise, nonrelevant images receive negative weights that are inversely proportional to their total number. The overall sum of these relevance values is thus zero. For each SOM, the values are then mapped from the images to the corresponding BMUs where they are summed.

The resulting sparse value fields on the SOM surfaces are low-pass filtered to produce qualification values for each SOM unit and its associated images. The low-pass filtering of the sparse value fields can be performed by convolving the field with a tapered window function. The exact shape of the window function is not significant, e.g. triangular or Gaussian windows can be used, but the length

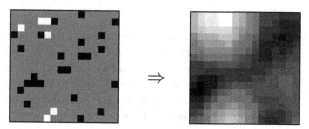

Fig. 1. An example of how a SOM surface is convolved with a low-pass filter. On the left, images selected and rejected by the user are shown with white and black marks, respectively. On the right, the convolution result, where relevance information is spread around the centers

of the window is important for both retrieval performance and computational complexity [9]. Figure 1 illustrates how the positive and negative responses, displayed with white and black map units, respectively, are first mapped on a SOM surface and how the responses are expanded in the convolution. The total qualification value for each image is finally obtained by summing the corresponding responses on all used SOMs. Content descriptors that fail to coincide with the user's conceptions mix positive and negative user responses in nearby map units. Therefore, they produce lower qualification values than those descriptors that match the user's expectations and impression of image similarity. As a consequence, the different content descriptors and the SOMs formed from them do not need explicit weighting as the system automatically takes care of weighting their opinions.

3   GNU Image Finding Tool – GIFT

GIFT or GNU Image Finding Tool [4] is a free CBIR system released under GNU license. It was developed by the Computer Vision Group of University of Geneva (*http://vision.unige.ch*) and it is the first content-based image retrieval system that uses the MRML language [1] for its communications. The first version of GIFT was released in 1999 and was known as Viper [10]. GIFT is, however, still under development, and the latest released version is 0.1.9.

The purpose of the MRML language (*http://www.mrml.net*) is to separate the client part from the server part of the CBIR system and to create a standard method for communicating with different CBIR servers [11]. Thus, MRML sets the basis for easy benchmarking of CBIR systems. MRML is based on the XML language and it was developed by the authors of the GIFT system.

GIFT uses QBPE (Query by Pictorial Example) with user-relevance feedback. An MRML-based client is needed for connecting to GIFT and such a client is for example Charmer [12] (previously SnakeCharmer) also released under GNU license.

3.1   GIFT Features

GIFT utilizes techniques common from textual information retrieval and uses a very large collection of binary-valued features. The number of features can be more than 80 000 and they are both local and global, simple color and texture features [10]. All the features are considered either present or not present in each of the images and each image typically has around thousand present features [11]. GIFT thus has a variable-length list of discrete features for every image.

3.2   Inverted File

The GIFT system includes a tool which is used for indexing new image collections. GIFT uses an inverted-file technique for its database indexing system. In the inverted-file database all existing features are listed [10, 4]. For each feature there is a list of all the images that contain this feature and the frequency of its occurrence in the collection. This inverted-file database system has been used and developed in text retrieval systems so the images can be accessed very efficiently [13].

3.3   GIFT Algorithms

GIFT offers two built-in algorithms: Separate Normalization and Classical Inverse Document Frequency (CIDF). Both of them have been used in a black-box fashion in our experiments. The CIDF algorithm uses the following methods for weighting features:

$$feature\ relevance_j = \frac{1}{N} \sum_{i=1}^{N} (tf_{ij} R_i) \log^2(\frac{1}{cf_i}) \tag{1}$$

$$image\ score_{kq} = \sum_j tf_{kj}\ feature\ relevance_j\ , \tag{2}$$

where tf_{ij} is the term frequency of a feature in either a query or a result image, cf_i the collection frequency of a feature, q is a query with $i = 1, 2, .., N$ input images, k a result image, j the index of a feature and R the user-relevance of a query image between [-1,1] [11].

3.4   Noted Problems with GIFT

When we tried to perform the tests with GIFT we encountered a few problems. First was due to the high number of images (59 995) in our Corel test database, which somehow affected GIFT in such a way that GIFT was not able to create its final inverted-file database in a Pentium-based Linux system. First we assumed the problem occured because of the 2 GB memory limitation of the 32-bit system, but afterwards it seems that this was not the case. However, we had to port GIFT to Compaq GS160 Tru64 UNIX AlphaServer (equipped with 16 Alpha 1001 MHz CPUs and 16 GB of system memory) to complete the database indexing.

The other problems were the relatively low speed of GIFT both in the indexing and especially in the testing phases. The feature extraction for all the images in the database took about three days (70 hours) to complete. Thus, the time needed for the feature extraction of a single image was approximately 4 seconds. After the feature extraction had completed, the indexing phase including the creation of the inverted-file database took approximately 2 days (40 hours).

In the performed experiments the largest ground-truth class held 1115 images, and the most of the classes contained between 500 and 800 images. In the performance evaluation of GIFT, it managed to go through only approximately 20–25 queries per day, which made the running time for the most of the experiments 20–30 days and for the largest class more than 40 days. This is a really long time compared to the time required by PicSOM, which managed even the largest class within five hours.

3.5   PicSOM and GIFT Differences

Between the implementations of PicSOM and GIFT there are several differences. The most important difference is found in the handling of the user-relevant images inside a single query. After the user has selected relevant images and asks for a new set of similar images, GIFT returns also already selected images and even those that have been marked as nonrelevant. Instead, PicSOM keeps a list of shown images and never returns these back to the user in the same query.

One might question the purpose of GIFT performing in such a way, since the prerequisite for reasonable results from performance measurements is that no same image is returned twice. Therefore, in the performed tests we had to change the number of new images asked from GIFT to the number of seen images plus the size of the query window so that GIFT certainly would return enough new images.

In GIFT, the total size of feature-files, 4.1 GB, and also the resulting size of the database, 780 MB, are both quite large compared to the 2.5GB size of the image database itself. With the URL to feature conversion file these take a total of 5 GB of system space which is twice the size of the original database. For PicSOM to store all features and indices it takes only about 1.1 GB in total.

4   Experiment Settings

We used a database of 59 995 images from the Corel Gallery 1 000 000 product. The size of each image is either 384×256 or 256×384 pixels. The images have been grouped by Corel in thematic groups and also keywords are available. However, we have found these image groups rather inconsistent with the keywords. Therefore, we have created six manually-picked ground truth image sets with tighter membership criteria for experimenting with the PicSOM system [2, 14]. All the image sets were gathered by a single subject. The used sets and membership criteria were:

- **Faces,** 1115 images (*a priori* probability 1.85%), where the main target of the image is a human head which has both eyes visible and the head has to fill at least 1/9 of the image area.
- **Cars,** 864 images (1.44%), where the main target of the image is a car, and at least one side of the car has to be completely shown in the image and its body to fill at least 1/9 of the image area.
- **Sunsets,** 663 images (1.11%), where the image contains a sunset with the sun clearly visible in the image.
- **Horses,** 486 images (0.81%), where the main target of the image is one or more horses, shown completely in the image.
- **Planes,** 292 images (0.49%), where all airplane images have been accepted.
- **Traffic Signs,** 123 images (0.21%), where the main target of the image is one or more official traffic signs, so commercial and other signs were rejected.

In PicSOM, we used a subset of MPEG-7 [6] descriptors as visual features. The used descriptors were *Scalable Color* (256), *Dominant Color* (6), *Color Structure* (256), *Color Layout* (12), *Edge Histogram* (80), *Homogeneous Texture* (62), and *Region Shape* (35). The dimensionalities of the descriptors are listed in parentheses. The MPEG-7 standard defines not only the descriptors but also special metrics that can be used with the descriptors when calculating the similarity between images. However, we use Euclidean metrics in comparing the descriptors because the training of the SOMs is based on minimizing a square-form error criterium. Only in the case of *Dominant Color* descriptor this has necessitated a slight modification in the use of the descriptor. MPEG-7's *Dominant Color* descriptor is variable-sized, i.e., the length of the descriptor varies depending on the count of dominant colors found. Because this could not be fit in the PicSOM system, we used only two most dominant colors or duplicated the most dominant color if only one was found.

For each feature, we trained a four-level TS-SOM with level sizes 4×4, 16×16, 64×64, and 256×256 units. The size of the bottommost TS-SOM level is selected so that it roughly equals the size of the database. In the training of the lower SOM levels, the search for the BMU has been restricted to the 10×10-sized neuron area below the BMU on the above level. Every image has been used 100 times for training each of the TS-SOM levels. Because the queries in the used experiment setting are always started with an image that belongs to the studied image class, the retrieval can be initiated in the neighborhoods of the reference image on the bottommost SOM levels ($256\times256=65536$ map units) as they provide the most detailed resolution. After the training phase, the upper TS-SOM hierarchy is thus neglected. In spreading the responses of the sparse value fields, triangular windows of 8 map units in length were used.

In GIFT the algorithms used were both Separate Normalization and Classical Inverse Document Frequency (CIDF). Both algorithms were used with their default configurations, and the usage of GIFT was performed in a black-box style.

If the size of the database, N, is large enough, we can assume that there is an upper limit N_T of images ($N_T \ll N$) the user is willing to browse during a single retrieval session. In our test setting, each image in the studied class is given to the system one at a time as the initial reference image for category search. The system should then return images belonging to the same class, resulting in a leave-one-out type testing of the class. The system was set to return 20 images at each round, and with 20 rounds per query the total number of seen images was $N_T = 400$ images, i.e. 0.67% of the database size.

We chose to show the evolution of *precision* $\mathcal{P}(n)$ as a function of *recall* $\mathcal{R}(n)$ during the image retrieval process [15]. Precision and recall are intuitive performance measures that suite also for the case of non-exhaustive browsing. First, the initial values of $\mathcal{P}(n)$ display the initial accuracy of the system. Then, the intermediate values show how the relevance feedback mechanism is able to adapt to the class, and the final value $\mathcal{R}(N_T)$ – as well as $\mathcal{P}(N_T)$ – reflects the total number of relevant images found that far. With an effective relevance feedback mechanism, it is expected that $\mathcal{P}(n)$ first increases and then turns to decrease when a notable fraction of relevant images have already been shown.

In our experiments, we have normalized the precision value by dividing it with the *a priori* probability ρ_C of the class and call it therefore *relative precision* [2]. This makes the comparison of the recall–precision curves of different image classes somewhat commensurable and more convenient because relative precision values relate to the relative advantage the CBIR system produces over random browsing.

5   Results

Figure 2 displays the results of our experiments. Each of the six subfigures shows the recall–relative precision curves for one particular image class. Every subfigure contains three curves: the PicSOM algorithm, GIFT with the CIDF algorithm, and GIFT with the Separate Normalization algorithm.

The curves show that in three classes (faces, traffic signs, sunsets) PicSOM outperforms both GIFT algorithms clearly. In the faces class the recall values of the GIFT algorithms end at surprisingly low level. In the initial phase of the sunsets class the Separate Normalization algorithm is first better than PicSOM which then adapts better to the class and exceeds GIFT in precision.

In the remaining three classes (cars, planes, horses) GIFT performs better than PicSOM. Only in the last phase (after adaptation) of the planes class PicSOM catches up the Separate Normalization algorithm.

Between the two GIFT algorithms there is no clear winner, either. While the CIDF algorithm manages better in the traffic signs, planes and sunsets classes, the Separate Normalization algorithm is better in the other (cars, horses, faces) classes. In general, one might state that in most of the cases the precision of the CIDF algorithm improves during the iterative query, whereas the precision of the Separate Normalization algorithm either remains the same or begins to decline sooner.

Of the evaluated three algorithms, PicSOM outranks the others in three classes, Separate Normalization in two classes and CIDF in one class. Thus, in

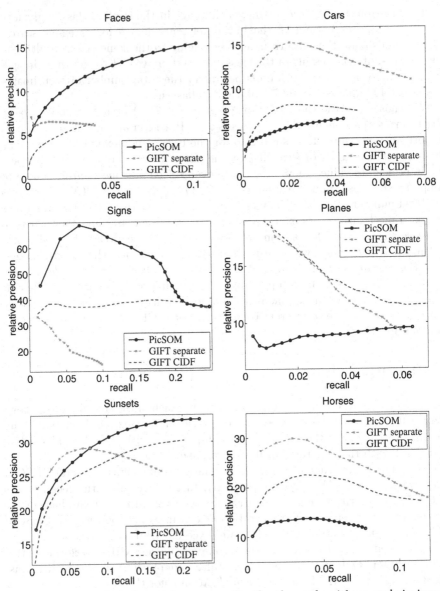

Fig. 2. Recall–relative precision curves for the three algorithms and six image classes

the light of these results, there is no clear winner between the three compared algorithms, but we can at least tentatively say that the performance of PicSOM is on the same level as that of GIFT's.

The image classes can also be analyzed by the performance of the best-performing algorithm. In the faces and sunsets classes the precision of retrieval is increasing all the time, whereas in the other classes it decreases. In the traffic signs and cars classes the decrease of precision starts only after some query rounds, while in the horses and planes classes the decrease starts immediately.

6   Conclusions and Future Plans

In this paper, we have presented a comparison of three content-based image retrieval techniques from two independent CBIR systems. Based on our results from experiments with six manually-selected image classes, we find both PicSOM and GIFT very competitive CBIR systems. Although PicSOM outperforms both of the two GIFT algorithms in three out of the six classes, there is still work to do to improve the efficiency of PicSOM in the other three classes. The public availability of the GIFT system has thus made it possible for us to run this kind of a benchmark and to find out the weaknesses of our own system.

The results of our experiments also show how important it is to include enough variety for comparisons in benchmarking. If the comparison results had been based on a single class only, they would not have revealed all the information we now have. We even could have declared any one of the algorithms as a clear winner with a purposeful selection of the image class. However, since our results are, in fact, based on a single type of comparison only, we do not claim to have thoroughly benchmarked the two CBIR systems. Instead, we note that for a good benchmark, several different types of tests are needed, which all should measure the efficiencies of the systems from different perspectives.

Actually, we would have wanted to run the experiments with 50 rounds per query so that instead of $N_T = 400$ the total number of seen images would have been $N_T = 1000$ as in earlier experiments with PicSOM. However, running GIFT turned out be so time consuming that we had to settle for a lower number of rounds per query. In spite of that, the results distinguish the algorithms adequately and a larger number of rounds per query could only have given more distinctive results in the cases where the performances of two algorithms were close to each other.

We have recently been experimenting with a new modification of the PicSOM algorithm. This novel development incorporates the use of automatically segmented images in the system. Our very preliminary results have shown that the precision of the system can be considerably increased by this method, especially in the cases where the original PicSOM method is performing poorly. It will be very exciting to run a comparison between this approach and the two GIFT algorithms.

Acknowledgment

This work was supported by the Academy of Finland in the projects *Neural methods in information retrieval based on automatic content analysis and relevance feedback* and *New information processing principles*, the latter being part of the Finnish Centre of Excellence Programme.

References

[1] Müller, W., Pecenovic, Z., Müller, H., Marchand-Maillet, S., Pun, T., Squire, D. M., Vries, A. P. D., Giess, C.: MRML: An extensible communication protocol for interoperability and benchmarking of multimedia information retrieval systems. In: Proceedings of SPIE Photonics East – Voice, Video, and Data Communications, Boston, MA, USA (2000) 500, 502

[2] Laaksonen, J., Koskela, M., Oja, E.: PicSOM—Self-organizing image retrieval with MPEG-7 content descriptions. IEEE Transactions on Neural Networks, Special Issue on Intelligent Multimedia Processing 13 (2002) 841–853 500, 501, 504, 506

[3] Rummukainen, M.: Implementing multimedia retrieval markup language for image retrieval systems' comparison. Master's thesis, Helsinki University of Technology, Otaniemi, Espoo, Finland (2003) 500

[4] Müller, H., David McG. Squire, W. M., Pun., T.: Efficient access methods for content-based image retrieval with inverted files. In: Proceedings of Multimedia Storage and Archiving Systems IV (VV02), Boston, MA, USA (1999) 501, 502, 503

[5] Kohonen, T.: Self-Organizing Maps. Third edn. Volume 30 of Springer Series in Information Sciences. Springer-Verlag (2001) 501

[6] MPEG: MPEG-7 overview (version 8.0) (2002) ISO/IEC JTC1/SC29/WG11. 501, 505

[7] Koikkalainen, P., Oja, E.: Self-organizing hierarchical feature maps. In: Proceedings of International Joint Conference on Neural Networks. Volume II., San Diego, CA (1990) 279–284 501

[8] Laaksonen, J., Koskela, M., Laakso, S., Oja, E.: Self-organizing maps as a relevance feedback technique in content-based image retrieval. Pattern Analysis & Applications 4 (2001) 140–152 501

[9] Koskela, M., Laaksonen, J., Oja, E.: Implementing relevance feedback as convolutions of local neighborhoods on self-organizing maps. In: Proceedings of International Conference on Artificial Neural Networks, Madrid, Spain (2002) 981–986 502

[10] Squire, D. M., Müller, W., Müller, H., Pun, T.: Content-based query of image databases, inspirations from text retrieval: inverted files, frequency-based weights and relevance feedback. Technical Report 98.04, Computer Vision Group, Computing Centre, University of Geneva, rue Gnral Dufour, 24, CH-1211 Genve, Switzerland (1998) 502, 503

[11] Müller, H., Müller, W., Squire, D. M., Pecenovic, Z., Marchand-Maillet, S., Pun, T.: An open framework for distributed multimedia retrieval. Technical Report 00.03, Computer Vision Group, Computing Group, University of Geneva, rue Gnral Dufour, 24, CH-1211 Genve, Switzerland (2000) 502, 503

[12] Pecenovic, Z.: (Charmer CBIR client, http://viper.unige.ch/demo/demo.html) Visited 27.03.03. 502

[13] Squire, D., Müller, W., Müller, H., Pun, T.: Content-based query of image databases: inspirations from text retrieval. Pattern Recognition Letters 21 (2000) 1193–1198 503

[14] Koskela, M., Laaksonen, J., Oja, E.: MPEG-7 descriptors in content-based image retrieval with PicSOM system. In: Proceedings of 5th International Conference on Visual Information System, HsinChu, Taiwan (2002) 247–258 504

510   Mika Rummukainen et al.

[15] Müller, H., Müller, W., Squire, D. M., Marchand-Maillet, S., Pun, T.: Performance evaluation in content-based image retrieval: overview and proposals. Pattern Recognition Letters **22** (2001) 593–601 506

Author Index